Proceedings

The 17th Annual International Symposium on
COMPUTER ARCHITECTURE

WITHDRAWN

D1713135

The 17th Annual
International Symposium on
COMPUTER
ARCHITECTURE

Proceedings

The 17th Annual International Symposium on
COMPUTER ARCHITECTURE

May 28-31, 1990   Seattle, Washington

IEEE Computer Society Press
Los Alamitos, California

Washington   ●   Brussles   ●   Tokyo

The papers in this book comprise the proceedings of the meeting mentioned on the cover and title page. They reflect the authors' opinions and are published as presented and without change, in the interests of timely dissemination. Their inclusion in this publication does not necessarily constitute endorsement by the editors, the IEEE Computer Society Press, or The Institute of Electrical and Electronics Engineers, Inc.

Published by IEEE Computer Society Press
10662 Los Vaqueros Circle
P.O. Box 3014
Los Alamitos, CA 90720-1264

Copyright ©1990 by The Institute of Electrical and Electronics Engineers, Inc.

Cover designed by Jack I. Ballestero

Printed in the United States of America

Copyright and Reprint Permissions: Abstracting is permitted with credit to the source. Libraries are permitted to photocopy beyond the limits of U.S. copyright law for private use of patrons those articles in this volume that carry a code at the bottom of the first page, provided the per-copy fee indicated in the code is paid through the Copyright Clearance Center, 29 Congress Street, Salem, MA 01970. Instructors are permitted to photocopy isolated articles for noncommercial classroom use without fee. For other copying, reprint or republication permission, write to Director, Publishing Services, IEEE, 345 East 47th Street, New York, NY 10017. All rights reserved.

IEEE Computer Society Order Number 2047
Library of Congress Number 85-642899
IEEE Catalog Number 90CH2887-8
ISBN 0-8186-2047-1 (paper)
ISBN 0-8186-6047-3 (microfiche)
ISBN 0-8186-9047-X (case)
ACM Order Number 415900
ISBN 0-89791-366-3

Additional copies can be ordered from:

IEEE Computer Society Press Customer Service Center 10662 Los Vaqueros Circle P.O. Box 3014 Los Alamitos, CA 90720-1264	IEEE Computer Society 13, Avenue de l'Aquilon B-1200 Brussels BELGIUM	IEEE Computer Society Ooshima Building 2-19-1 Minami-Aoyama, Minato-Ku Tokyo 107, JAPAN	IEEE Service Center 445 Hoes Lane P.O. Box 1331 Piscataway, NJ 08855-1331	ACM Order Department P.O. Box 64145 Baltimore, MD 21264

THE INSTITUTE OF ELECTRICAL AND ELECTRONICS ENGINEERS, INC.

General Co-Chairs' Message

It is a pleasure to welcome you to Seattle for the 17th Annual International Symposium on Computer Architecture. We hope that you will enjoy not only the technical program but also the beauty of our city and its surroundings. The evenings at the Aquarium and the Harbor Cruise and Salmon Bake should convince you that Seattle is indeed one of the most livable cities in the U.S.

The highlights of the technical program are the 34 papers selected from the 240 submitted papers, the keynote address by Burton Smith, the Eckert-Mauchly Award ceremony (at the luncheon banquet on Wednesday), and two panels: "Big Science Versus Little Science: Do You Have to Build It?", organized by Mark Hill from the University of Wisconsin, and "Better Than One Operation Per Clock: Vectors, VLIW, and Superscalar", organized by Ed Davidson from the University of Michigan.

The Program Chairman, Jim Goodman, did a terrific job in selecting an international program committee with representatives from academia, industry, and government (a list of the program committee members is included in these proceedings). In turn, the program committee worked hard to review and select the best papers among a large number of very high quality papers. We would like to thank Jim and his committee for their outstanding efforts.

In order to be successful, a world-reknown conference like ISCA needs a strong technical program and a team of dedicated individuals to organize the symposium. This 17th ISCA owes a lot to Hank Levy who served as a jack-of-all-trades: local arranger, treasurer, poster discoverer, T-shirt designer, and even program committee member. His contributions were invaluable. Vicky Palm took care of the registration and all inquiries in a more civilized way than any computer architect could have mustered. Ticky Thakkar was in charge of publicity for these Proceedings. Through his efforts, everything happened on time. Mark Franklin was responsible for the student travel grants. Last, but not least, Guri Sohi organized a day of excellent tutorials. To all our most sincere thanks.

As has become the tradition for many years, the Symposium is co-sponsored by ACM's SIGARCH (Special Interest Group on Computer Architecture) and TCCA (Technical Committee on Computer Architecture) of the IEEE Computer Society. These two groups will hold a joint business meeting on Tuesday afternoon, May 29. Our thanks to Doug DeGroot for his encouragement to hold the 17th ISCA in Seattle.

We hope that you will enjoy this 17th edition of the premier conference in the field.

Jean-Loup Baer
Larry Snyder
General Co-Chairs

Program Chair's Message

Now comes one of the most pleasant tasks of the Program Chair, that of acknowledging the many people who collaborated to make it all happen. The 22 members of the Program Committee all put in major efforts to put together more than 700 reviews in less than two months. And 20 even braved the warm Wisconsin weather to attend the committee meetings on the 2nd of February. Among the 242 submissions, the committee was extremely selective, accepting only 34 papers for the final program, for the lowest acceptance rate ever (14%) for this Symposium. It was certainly no embarrassment to have a paper rejected !

I would like to thank especially Mark Hill and Guri Sohi, who often paid the price for my poor planning. Phil Woest and Bill Carlson helped out with numerous reviews with extremely short notice, as did Jim Smith. I'd also like to thank Wen-Hann Wang for his help and John Hennesy for his support. Jean-Loup provided the guidance for all the things that seem so obvious now, but didn't at the time. He and Larry Snyder also took charge of the review process for the 14 papers submitted by Program Committee members. Finally, I'd like to thank Dale Malm for all the support, both secretarial and moral, especially during the frantic periods.

James Goodman
Program Chair

Organizing Committee for the 17th Annual International Symposium on Computer Architecture

Program Chair

James Goodman, University of Wisconsin

General Co-Chairs

Jean-Loup Baer and Larry Snyder, University of Washington

Symposium Committee

Hank Levy, University of Washington
Shreekant Thakkar, Sequent Computer Systems
Guri Sohi, University of Wisconsin
Mark A. Franklin, Washington University
Vicky Palm, University of Washington

Program Committee

Alan Berenbaum, AT&T Bell Laboratories
Bill Brantley, IBM
Doug Clark, Digital Equipment Corporation
Al Despain, University of Southern California
Susan Eggers, University of Washington
Ed Feustel, Prime Computers
James Goodman, University of Wisconsin
John Gurd, University of Manchester
John Hennessy, Stanford University
Bob Jump, Los Alamos National Laboratory
Bob Keller, UC Davis
Hank Levy, University of Washington
Yale Patt, University of Michigan
Dave Patterson, UC Berkeley
Keshav Pingali, Cornell University
Andy Pleszkun, University of Colorado
Dan Siewiorek, Carnegie-Mellon University
Jim Smith, Cray Research
Guri Sohi, University of Wisconsin
John Van Zandt, Intel Scientific Computers
Uri Weiser, Intel Israel

Panel Organizers

Ed Davidson, University of Michigan
Mark Hill, University of Wisconsin

ISCA90 List of Referees

Abraham, S.A.
Adve, S.V.
Adve, V.S.
Agrawal, D.P.
Agrawal, R.
Allemang, M.D.
Allison, D.
Anderson, T.
Archibald, J.
Argade, P.V.
Averbuch, A.
Baer, J.-L.
Barker, R.
Baylor, S.J.
Beck, M.
Beckman, C.
Beckwith, B.
Bennett, J.
Berenbaum, A.
Bershad, B.
Bhuyan, L.
Bic, L.
Bilardi, G.
Birningham, W.
Boehm, W.
Bojancyzk, A.
Boriello, G.
Brackenbury, L.E.M.
Brantley, W.
Brookes, S.D.
Browne, J.C.
Carlson, W.W.
Carmon, I.
Case, B.W.
Clark, D.
Close, P.
Cooper, R.
Culler, D.
Dally, W.
Das, C.R.
Davis, H.
DeGroot, D.
De Leone, R.
DeRosa, J.
Dennis, J.
Dermer, G.E.
Despain, A.M.
Dias, D.M.
Dickman, M.
Dubois, M.
Duchamp, D.
Ebcioglu, K.
Edward, D.
Edward, R.

Eggers, S.
Emer, J.
Emma, P.
Faanes, G.J.
Farrens, M.
Feustel, E.
Feynman, C.
Fleming, P.J.
Franklin, M.A.
Franzo, R.
Fujimoto, R.
Fyler, G.
Gajski, D.
Gandlot, J.-L.
Gee, J.
Gharachorloo, K.
Gifford, P.
Gjessing, S.
Golbert, A.
Goldschmidt, S.
Gopinath, K.
Gottlieb, A.
Gross, T.
Gupta, A.
Gurd, J.
Harper, D.
Hayes, J.P.
Hedayat, G.
Hendren, L.
Hennessy, J.L.
Hill, M.D.
Hillis, D.
Hiraki, K.
Hochschild, P.
Holland, M.
Holmer, B.
Hopkins, T.
Hsu, P.Y.-T.
Hsu, W.-C.
Huttenlocher, D.
Hwu, W.-M.
Iannucci, R.A.
Ibbett, R.
Intrater, G.
Ioannidis, Y.
Irwin, M.J.
James, D.V.
Jenevin, R.
Jensen, D.
Jhingran, A.
Joersz, R.
Jones, W.
Jordan, H.
Jouppi, N.

Jump, J.R.
Kaminski, T.
Keller, R.
Kessler, R.
Kieburtz, R.
King, S.
Kirkham, C.
Klass, F.
Klinger, S.D.
Knight, T.
Koldinger, E.
Koren, I.
Kumar, M.
Kuszmaul, B.C.
Lam, M.
Langdon, G.
Langendorf, E.
Laudon, J.
Lazowska, E.
Lee, C.
Lee, T.C.
Lenski, D.
Levy, H.M.
Li, K.
Lillevik, S.
Lin, E.
Lipovski, J.
Liu, J.C.
Locanthi, B.
Luk, F.
Luke, S.
Malek, M.
Martonosi, M.
Marzullo, K.
Matloff, N.
McFarling, S.
McLellan, R.
Miller, B.
Mohar, S.
Mudge, T.
Nation, W.G.
Nguyen, T.
Nicolau, A.
Niemi, R.
Nikhil, R.
Nordby, K.L.
Nuth, P.
O'Farrell, B.
Oberlin, S.M.
Owicki, S.
Padua, D.
Parker, J.
Patel, J.H.
Patt, Y.

Patterson, D.A.
Pfister, G.
Pieper, K.
Pierce, P.
Pingali, K.
Pinter, R.
Pleszkun, A.R.
Polychronopolous, C.
Przybylski, S.
Ramanujan, R.
Reich, M.
Rogers, A.
Rothberg, E.
Van Roy, P.
Ruzzo, L.
Saghi, G.
Saltz, J.
Saluja, K.
Sano, B.
Sauer, J.
Scheurich, C.
Schwarm, S.
Scott, D.
Scott, S.
Segre, A.
Shapiro, L.G.
Short, R.

Siegel, H.J.
Siewiorek, D.P.
Singhal, A.
Sites, R.
Sloan, K.
Smith, A.J.
Smith, B.
Smith, J.M.
Smith, M.
Snelling, J.D.
Snir, M.
Snyder, L.
Sohi, G.S.
Sprachman, B.
Steenkiste, P.
Stewart, L.
Stone, H.
Su, H.-M.
Subramanian, D.
Szymanski, T.
Szymanski, T.G.
Taylor, G.
Thakkar, S.S.
Thazhuthaveetil, M.
Thompson, J.G.
Tick, E.
Tokuda, H.

Topham, N.
Torrellas, J.
Tzeng, N.-F.
Van Zandt, J.
Veidenbaum, A.
Venkateswaran, R.
Vernon, M.K.
Walker, D.M.
Wang, W.-H.
Watson, I.
Wilson, A.
Wilson, J.E.
Weiser, U.
Woch, T.
Woest, P.J.
Wolman, B.
Wolmar, B.
Yaari, Y.
Yair, E.
Yarkoni, E.
Yoeli, M.
Zahorjan, J.
Zimmerman, A.
Zippel, R.
Zurawski, J.

Table of Contents

Session 1A: Multiprocessor Synchronization and Sequential Consistency

Session 1B: Multiprocessor Network Issues

Session 2A: Special-Purpose Architectures

Session 2B: Shared-Memory Multiprocessors

Panel Session *I*

Session 3A: Cache Memory

Session 3B: Instruction Sets

Session 4A: Processor Implementations

Session 4B: Applications

Session 5A: Memory Traces and Simulation

Session 5B: Prolog/Potpourri

Session 6A: I/O

Session 6B: High-End Design

Panel Session *II*

Session 1A: Multiprocessor Synchronization and Sequential Consistency

Weak Ordering - A New Definition[†]

Sarita V. Adve
Mark D. Hill

Computer Sciences Department
University of Wisconsin
Madison, Wisconsin 53706

ABSTRACT

A memory model for a shared memory, multiprocessor commonly and often implicitly assumed by programmers is that of *sequential consistency*. This model guarantees that all memory accesses will appear to execute atomically and in program order. An alternative model, *weak ordering*, offers greater performance potential. Weak ordering was first defined by Dubois, Scheurich and Briggs in terms of a set of rules for hardware that have to be made visible to software.

The central hypothesis of this work is that programmers prefer to reason about sequentially consistent memory, rather than having to think about weaker memory, or even write buffers. Following this hypothesis, we re-define weak ordering as a contract between software and hardware. By this contract, software agrees to some formally specified constraints, and hardware agrees to appear sequentially consistent to at least the software that obeys those constraints. We illustrate the power of the new definition with a set of software constraints that forbid data races and an implementation for cache-coherent systems that is not allowed by the old definition.

Key words: shared-memory multiprocessor, sequential consistency, weak ordering.

1. Introduction

This paper is concerned with the programmer's model of memory for a shared memory, MIMD multiprocessor, and its implications on hardware design and performance. A memory model commonly (and often

implicitly) assumed by programmers is that of *sequential consistency*, formally defined by Lamport [Lam79] as follows:

> [Hardware is sequentially consistent if] the result of any execution is the same as if the operations of all the processors were executed in some sequential order, and the operations of each individual processor appear in this sequence in the order specified by its program.

Application of the definition requires a specific interpretation of the terms *operations* and *result*. We assume that *operations* refer to memory operations or accesses (e.g., reads and writes) and *result* refers to the union of the values returned by all the read operations in the execution and the final state of memory. With these assumptions, the above definition translates into the following two conditions: (1) all memory accesses appear to execute atomically in some total order, and (2) all memory accesses of each processor appear to execute in an order specified by its program (program order).

Uniprocessor systems offer the model of sequential consistency almost naturally and without much compromise in performance. In multiprocessor systems on the other hand, the conditions for ensuring sequential consistency are not usually as obvious, and almost always involve serious performance trade-offs. For four configurations of shared memory systems (bus-based systems and systems with general interconnection networks, both with and without caches), Figure 1 shows that as potential for parallelism is increased, sequential consistency imposes greater constraints on hardware, thereby limiting performance. The use of many performance enhancing features of uniprocessors, such as write buffers, instruction execution overlap, out-of-order memory accesses and lockup-free caches [Kro81] is heavily restricted.

The problem of maintaining sequential consistency manifests itself when two or more processors interact through memory operations on common vari-

---

[†] The material presented here is based on research supported in part by the National Science Foundation's Presidential Young Investigator and Computer and Computation Research Programs under grants MIPS-8957278 and CCR-8902536, A. T. & T. Bell Laboratories, Digital Equipment Corporation, Texas Instruments, Cray Research and the graduate school at the University of Wisconsin-Madison.

Initially X = Y = 0

P_1	P_2
X = 1	Y = 1
if (Y == 0) kill P_2	if (X == 0) kill P_1

Result - P_1 and P_2 are both killed

Figure 1. A violation of sequential consistency.

Sequential consistency is violated since there does not exist a total order of memory accesses that is consistent with program order, and kills both P_1 and P_2. Note that there are no data dependencies among the instructions of either processor. Thus simple interlock logic does not preclude the second instruction from being issued before the first in either processor.

Shared-bus systems without caches - The execution is possible if the accesses of a processor are issued out of order, or if reads are allowed to pass writes in write buffers.

Systems with general interconnection networks without caches - The execution is possible even if accesses of a processor are issued in program order, but reach memory modules in a different order [Lam79].

Shared-bus systems with caches - Even with a cache coherence protocol [ArB86], the execution is possible if the accesses of a processor are issued out-of-order, or if reads are allowed to pass writes in write buffers.

Systems with general interconnection networks and caches - The execution is possible even if accesses of a processor are issued and reach memory modules in program order, but do not *complete* in program order. Such a situation can arise if both processors initially have X and Y in their caches, and a processor issues its read before its write is propagated to the cache of the other processor.

ables. In many cases, these interactions can be partitioned into operations that are used to order events, called *synchronization*, and the other more frequent operations that read and write data. If synchronization operations are made recognizable to the hardware, and actions to ensure sequential consistency could be restricted to such operations, then higher overall performance might be achieved by completing normal reads and writes faster. These considerations motivate an alternative programmer's model that relies on synchronization that is visible to the hardware to order memory accesses. Dubois, Scheurich and Briggs have defined such systems in terms of conditions on hardware and have named them *weakly ordered* [DSB86,DSB88, Sch89].

We believe that weak ordering facilitates high performance implementations, but that programmers prefer to reason about sequentially consistent memory rather than weaker memory systems or even write buffers. Hence, a description of memory should not require the specification of the performance enhancing features of the underlying hardware. Rather, such features should be camouflaged by defining the memory model in terms of constraints on software which, if obeyed, make the weaker system appear sequentially consistent.

After surveying related work in Section 2, we give a new definition of weak ordering in Section 3. We illustrate the advantages of this definition with an example set of software constraints in Section 4 and an example implementation in Section 5. Finally, in Section 6, we use these example constraints and example implementation to analyze our framework and compare it with that given by Dubois, et al. For the convenience of the reader, the key definitions used throughout the paper are repeated in Appendix C.

2. Related Work

This section briefly describes relevant previous work on sequential consistency (Section 2.1) and weak ordering (Section 2.2). A more detailed survey of the subject appears in [AdH89].

2.1. Sequential Consistency

Sequential consistency was first defined by Lamport [Lam79], and discussed for shared memory systems with general interconnection networks, but no caches. For single bus cache-based systems, a number of cache-coherence protocols have been proposed in the literature [ArB86]. Most ensure sequential consistency. In particular, Rudolph and Segall have developed two protocols, which they formally prove guarantee sequential consistency [RuS84]. The RP3 [BMW85,PBG85] is a cache-based system, where processor memory communication is via an Omega network, but the management of cache coherence for shared writable variables is entrusted to the software. Sequential consistency is ensured by requiring a process to wait for an acknowledgement from memory for its previous miss on a shared variable before it can issue another access to such a variable. In addition, the RP3 also provides an option by which a process is required to wait for acknowledgements on its outstanding requests only on a *fence* instruction. As will be apparent later, this option functions as a weakly ordered system.

Dubois, Scheurich and Briggs have analyzed the problem of ensuring sequential consistency in systems that allow caching of shared variables, without imposing any constraints on the interconnection network [DSB86, DSB88, ScD87, Sch89]. A sufficient condition for sequential consistency for cache-based systems has been stated [ScD87, Sch89]. The condition is satisfied if all processors issue their accesses in program order, and no access is issued by a processor until its previous accesses have been *globally performed*. A write is globally performed when its modification has been propagated to all processors. A read is globally performed when the value it returns is bound and the write that wrote this value is globally performed.

The notion of *strong ordering* as an equivalent of sequential consistency was defined in [DSB86]. However, there do exist programs that can distinguish between strong ordering and sequential consistency [AdH89] and hence, strong ordering is not strictly equivalent to sequential consistency. Strong ordering has been discarded in [Sch89] in favor of a similar model, viz., concurrent consistency. A concurrently consistent system is defined to behave like a sequentially consistent system for most practical purposes.

Collier has developed a general framework to characterize architectures as sets of rules, where each rule is a restriction on the order of execution of certain memory operations. [Col84, Col90]. He has proved that for most practical purposes, a system where all processors observe all write operations in the same order (called write synchronization), is indistinguishable from a system where all writes are executed atomically.

Shasha and Snir have proposed a software algorithm to ensure sequential consistency [ShS88]. Their scheme statically identifies a minimal set of pairs of accesses within a process, such that delaying the issue of one of the elements in each pair until the other is globally performed guarantees sequential consistency. However, the algorithm depends on detecting conflicting data accesses at compile time and so its success depends on data dependence analysis techniques, which may be quite pessimistic.

The conditions for sequential consistency of memory accesses are analogous to the serialization condition for transactions in concurrent database systems [BeG81, Pap86]. However, database systems seek to serialize the effects of entire transactions, which may be a series of reads and writes while we are concerned with the atomicity of individual reads and writes. While the concept of a transaction may be extended to our case as well and the database algorithms applied, practical reasons limit the feasibility of this application. In particular, since database transactions may involve multiple disk accesses, and hence take much longer than simple memory accesses, database systems can afford to incur a much larger overhead for concurrency control.

2.2. Weak Ordering

Weakly ordered systems depend on explicit, hardware recognizable synchronization operations to order the effects of events initiated by different processors in a system. Dubois, Scheurich and Briggs first defined weak ordering in [DSB86] as follows:

> **Definition 1:** In a multiprocessor system, storage accesses are weakly ordered if (1) accesses to global synchronizing variables are strongly ordered, (2) no access to a synchronizing variable is issued by a processor before all previous global data accesses have been globally performed, and if (3) no access to global data is issued by a processor before a previous access to a synchronizing variable has been globally performed.

It was recognized later in [ScD88, Sch89] that the above three conditions are not necessary to meet the intuitive goals of weak ordering. In Section 3, we give a new definition that we believe formally specifies this intuition.

Bisiani, Nowatzyk and Ravishankar have proposed an algorithm [BNR89] for the implementation of weak ordering on distributed memory systems. Weak ordering is achieved by using timestamps to ensure that a synchronization operation completes only after *all* accesses previously issued by *all* processors in the system are complete. The authors mention that for synchronization operations that require a value to be returned, it is possible to send a tentative value before the operation completes, if a processor can undo subsequent operations that may depend on it, after receiving the actual value. In [AdH89], we discuss how this violates condition 3 of Definition 1, but does not violate the new definition of weak ordering below.

3. Weak Ordering - A New Definition.

We view weak ordering as an interface (or contract) between software and hardware. Three desirable properties for this interface are: (1) it should be formally specified so that separate proofs can be done to ascertain whether software and hardware are correct (i.e., they obey their respective sides of the contract), (2) the programmer's model of hardware should be simple to avoid adding complexity to the already difficult task of parallel programming, and (3) the hardware designer's model of software should facilitate high-performance, parallel implementations.

Let a *synchronization model* be a set of constraints on memory accesses that specify how and when synchronization needs to be done.

Our new definition of weak ordering is as follows.

Definition 2: Hardware is weakly ordered with respect to a synchronization model if and only if it appears sequentially consistent to all software that obey the synchronization model.

This definition of weak ordering addresses the above mentioned properties as follows. (1) It is formally specified. (2) The programmer's model of hardware is kept simple by expressing it in terms of sequential consistency, the most frequently assumed software model of shared memory. Programmers can view hardware as sequentially consistent if they obey the synchronization model. (3) High-performance hardware implementations are facilitated in two ways. First, hardware designers retain maximum flexibility, because requirements are placed on how the hardware should appear, but not on how this appearance should be created. Second, the framework of this definition allows new (and better) synchronization models to be defined as software paradigms and hardware implementation techniques evolve.

However, there are some disadvantages of defining a weakly ordered system in this manner. First, there are useful parallel programmer's models that are not easily expressed in terms of sequential consistency. One such model is used by the designers of asynchronous algorithms [DeM88]. (We expect, however, it will be straightforward to *implement* weakly ordered hardware to obtain reasonable results for asynchronous algorithms.)

Second, for any potential performance benefit over a sequentially consistent system, the synchronization model of a weakly ordered system will usually constrain software to synchronize using operations visible to the hardware. For some algorithms, it may be hard to recognize which operations do synchronization. Furthermore, depending on the implementation, synchronization operations could be much slower than data accesses. We believe, however, that slow synchronization operations coupled with fast reads and writes will yield better performance than the alternative, where hardware must assume all accesses could be used for synchronization (as in [Lam86]).

Third, programmers may wish to debug programs on a weakly ordered system that do not (yet) fully obey the synchronization model. The above definition allows hardware to return random values when the synchronization model is violated. We expect real hardware, however, to be much more well-behaved. Nevertheless, hardware designers may wish to tell programmers exactly what their hardware may do when the synchronization model is violated, or build hardware that offers an additional option of being sequentially consistent for all software, albeit at reduced speed.

Alternatively, programmers may wish that a synchronization model be specified so that it is possible and practical to verify whether a program, or at least an execution of a program, meets the conditions of the model. Achieving this goal may add further constraints to software and hardware.

To demonstrate the utility of our definition, we next give an example synchronization model. In Section 5, we discuss an implementation of a system that is weakly ordered with respect to this synchronization model, but is not allowed by Definition 1.

4. A Synchronization Model: Data-Race-Free-0

In this section, we define a synchronization model that is a simple characterization of programs that forbid data races. We call this model *Data-Race-Free-0* (DRF0) and use it only as an example to illustrate an application of our definition. In Section 6, we indicate how DRF0 may be refined to yield other data-race-free models that impose fewer constraints, are as realistic and reasonable as DRF0, but lead to better implementations. In defining DRF0, we have avoided making any assumptions regarding the particular methods used for synchronization or parallelization. The knowledge of any restrictions on these methods (for example, sharing only through monitors, or parallelism only through do-all loops) can lead to simpler specifications of data-race-free synchronization models.

Intuitively, a synchronization model specifies the operations or primitives that may be used for synchronization, and indicates when there is "enough" synchronization in a program. The only restrictions imposed by DRF0 on synchronization operations are: (1) the operation should be recognizable by hardware, and (2) the operation should access only one memory location. Thus, a synchronization operation could be a special instruction such as a TestAndSet that accesses only a single memory location, or it could be a normal memory access but to some special location known to the hardware. However, an operation that swaps the values of two memory locations cannot be used as a synchronization primitive for DRF0.

To formally specify the second feature of DRF0, viz., an indication of when there is "enough" synchronization in a program, we first define a set of *happens-before* relations for a program. Our definition is closely related to the "happened-before" relation defined by Lamport [Lam78] for message passing systems, and the "approximate temporal order" used by Netzer and Miller [NeM89] for detecting races in shared memory parallel programs that use semaphores.

A happens-before relation for a program is a partial order defined for an *execution* of the program on an abstract, idealized architecture where all memory accesses are executed atomically and in program order. For such an execution, two operations initiated by different processors are ordered by happens-before only if there exist intervening synchronization operations between them. To define happens-before formally, we first define two other relations, program order or $\xrightarrow{po}$, and synchronization order or $\xrightarrow{so}$. Let op_1 and op_2 be any two memory operations occurring in an execution. Then,

$op_1 \xrightarrow{po} op_2$ *iff* op_1 occurs before op_2 in program order for some process.

$op_1 \xrightarrow{so} op_2$ *iff* op_1 and op_2 are synchronization operations accessing the same location and op_1 completes before op_2 in the execution.

A *happens-before* relation or $\xrightarrow{hb}$ is defined for an execution on the idealized architecture, as the irreflexive transitive closure of $\xrightarrow{po}$ and $\xrightarrow{so}$, i.e., $\xrightarrow{hb}$ = ($\xrightarrow{po} \cup \xrightarrow{so}$)$^+$.

For example, consider the following chain of operations in an execution on the idealized architecture.

$$op(P_1,x) \xrightarrow{po} S(P_1,s) \xrightarrow{so} S(P_2,s) \xrightarrow{po}$$
$$S(P_2,t) \xrightarrow{so} S(P_3,t) \xrightarrow{po} op(P_3,x)$$

$op(P_i,x)$ is a read or a write operation initiated by processor P_i on location x. Similarly, $S(P_j,s)$ is a synchronization operation initiated by processor P_j on location s. The definition of happens-before then implies that $op(P_1,x) \xrightarrow{hb} op(P_3,x)$.

From the above definition, it follows that $\xrightarrow{hb}$ defines a partial order on the accesses of one execution of a program on the idealized architecture. Since, in general, there can be many different such executions of a program (due to the many possible $\xrightarrow{so}$ relations), there may be more than one happens-before relation defined for a program.

To account for the initial state of memory, we assume that before the actual execution of a program, one of the processors executes a (hypothetical) initializing write to every memory location followed by a (hypothetical) synchronization operation to a special location. This is followed by a (hypothetical) synchronization operation to the same location by each of the other processors. The actual execution of the program is assumed to begin after all the synchronization operations are complete. Similarly, to account for the final state of memory, we assume a set of final reads and synchronization operations analogous to the initializing operations for the initial state. Henceforth, an idealized exe-

cution will implicitly refer to an execution on the idealized architecture augmented for the initial and final state of memory as above, and a happens-before relation will be assumed to be defined for such an augmented execution.

The happens-before relation can now be used to indicate when there is "enough" synchronization in a program for the synchronization model DRF0. The complete formal definition of DRF0 follows.

Definition 3: A program obeys the synchronization model Data-Race-Free-0 (DRF0), if and only if

(1) all synchronization operations are recognizable by the hardware and each accesses exactly one memory location, and

(2) for any execution on the idealized system (where all memory accesses are executed atomically and in program order), all conflicting accesses are ordered by the happens-before relation corresponding to the execution.

Two accesses are said to *conflict* if they access the same location and they are not both reads. Figures 2a and 2b show executions that respectively obey and violate DRF0.

DRF0 is a formalization that prohibits data races in a program. We believe that this allows for faster hardware than an unconstrained synchronization model, without reducing software flexibility much, since a large majority of programs are already written using explicit synchronization operations and attempt to avoid data races. In addition, although DRF0 specifies synchronization operations in terms of primitives at the level of the hardware, a programmer is free to build and use higher level, more complex synchronization operations. As long as the higher level operations use the primitives appropriately, a program that obeys DRF0 at the higher level will also do so at the level of the hardware primitives. Furthermore, current work is being done on determining when programs are data-race-free, and in locating the races when they are not [NeM89].

5. An Implementation for Weak Ordering w.r.t. DRF0

In the last section, we gave an example synchronization model to illustrate the use of the new definition of weak ordering. This section demonstrates the flexibility afforded to the hardware designer due to the formalization of the synchronization model and the absence of any hardware prescriptions in Definition 2. We give a set of sufficient conditions for implementing weak ordering with respect to DRF0 that allow a viola-

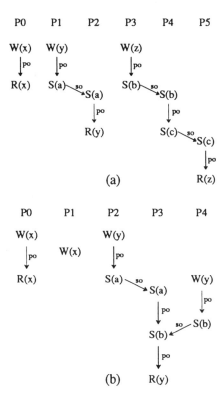

Figure 2. An example and counter-example of DRF0.

Two executions on the idealized architecture are represented. The Pi's denote processors. R(x), W(x) and S(x) respectively denote data read, data write and synchronization operations on the variable x. Time flows downward. An access by processor Pi appears vertically below Pi, in a position reflecting the time at which it was completed. (a) - The execution shown obeys DRF0 since all conflicting accesses are ordered by happens-before. (b) - The execution does not obey DRF0 since the accesses of P0 conflict with the write of P1 but are not ordered with respect to it by happens-before. Similarly, the writes by P2 and P4 conflict, but are unordered.

---

tion of Definition 1 (Section 5.1). To illustrate an application of these conditions, we describe for a fairly general cache-coherent system (Section 5.2), an example implementation that does not obey the second or the third conditions of Definition 1 (Section 5.3).

5.1. Sufficient Conditions

An implementation based on Definition 1 requires a processor to stall on a synchronization operation until all its previous accesses are globally performed. This serves to ensure that any other processor subsequently synchronizing on the same location will observe the effects of all these accesses. We propose to stall only the processor that issues the *subsequent* synchronization operation until the accesses by the *previous* processor are globally performed. Thus, the first processor is not required to stall and can overlap the completion of its pending accesses with those issued after the synchronization operation. Below, we give a set of sufficient conditions for an implementation based on this notion.

For brevity, we will adopt the following conventions in formalizing our sufficient conditions. Unless mentioned otherwise, *reads* will include data (or ordinary) read operations, read-only synchronization operations, and the read component of synchronization operations that both read and write memory. Similarly, *writes* will include data writes, write-only synchronization operations, and the write component of read-write synchronization operations.

A *commit point* is defined for every operation as follows. A read commits when its return value is dispatched back towards the requesting processor. A write commits when its value could be dispatched for some read. A read-write synchronization operation commits when its read and write components commit. Similarly, a read-write synchronization operation is globally performed when its read and write components are globally performed. We will say that an access is *generated* when it "first comes into existence".

Hardware is weakly ordered with respect to DRF0 if it meets the following requirements.

1. Intra-processor dependencies are preserved.

2. All writes to the *same* location can be totally ordered based on their commit times, and this is the order in which they are observed by all processors.

3. All synchronization operations to the *same* location can be totally ordered based on their commit times, and this is also the order in which they are globally performed. Further, if S_1 and S_2 are synchronization operations and S_1 is committed and globally performed before S_2, then all components of S_1 are committed and globally performed before any in S_2.

4. A new access is not generated by a processor until all its previous synchronization operations (in program order) are committed.

5. Once a synchronization operation S by processor P_i is committed, no other synchronization operations on the *same* location by another processor can commit until after all reads of P_i before S (in program order) are committed and all writes of P_i before S are globally performed.

To prove the correctness of the above conditions, we first prove in Appendix A, a lemma stating a (simpler) *necessary* and *sufficient* condition for weak ordering with respect to DRF0. We then show in Appendix B that the above conditions satisfy the condition of Lemma 1.

The conditions given do not explicitly allow process migration. Re-scheduling of a process on another processor is possible if it can be ensured that before a context switch, all previous reads of the process have returned their values and all previous writes have been globally performed.

5.2. An Implementation Model

This section discusses assumptions for an example underlying system on which an implementation based directly on the conditions of Section 5.1 will be discussed. Consider a system where every processor has an independent cache and processors are connected to memory through a general interconnection network. In particular, no restrictions are placed on the kind of data a cache may contain, nor are any assumptions made regarding the atomicity of any transactions on the interconnection network. A straightforward directory-based, writeback cache coherence protocol, similar to those discussed in [ASH88], is assumed. In particular, for a write miss on a line that is present in *valid* (or *shared*) state in more than one cache, the protocol requires the directory to send messages to invalidate these copies of the line. Our protocol allows the line requested by the write to be forwarded to the requesting processor in parallel with the sending of these invalidations. On receipt of an invalidation, a cache is required to return an acknowledgement (ack) message to the directory (or memory). When the directory (or memory) receives all the acks pertaining to a particular write, it is required to send its ack to the processor cache that issued the write.

We assume that the value of a write issued by processor P_i cannot be dispatched as a return value for a read until the write modifies the copy of the accessed line in P_i's cache. Thus, a write commits only when it modifies the copy of the line in its local cache. However, other copies of the line may not be invalidated.

Within a processor, all dependencies will be assumed to be maintained. Read and write components of a read-write synchronization operation will be assumed to execute atomically with respect to other synchronization operations on the *same* location. All synchronization operations will be treated as write operations by the cache coherence protocol.

5.3. An Implementation

We now outline an example implementation based on the conditions of Section 5.1 for the cache-based system discussed in Section 5.2.

The first condition of Section 5.1 is directly implemented in our model system. Conditions 2 and 3 are ensured by the cache coherence protocol and by the fact that all synchronization operations are treated as writes, and the components of a synchronization operation are executed atomically with respect to other synchronization operations on the *same* location. For condition 4, all operations are generated in program order. In addition, after a synchronization operation, no new accesses are generated until the line accessed is procured by the processor in *exclusive* (or *dirty*) state, and the operation performed on this copy of the line. To meet condition 5, a counter (similar to one used in RP3) that is initialized to zero is associated with every processor, and an extra bit called the *reserve* bit is associated with every cache line. The condition is satisfied as follows.

On a cache miss, the corresponding processor counter is incremented. The counter is decremented on the receipt of a line in response to a read request, or to a write request for a line that was originally in exclusive state in some processor cache. The counter is also decremented when an ack from memory is received indicating that a previous write to a *valid* or *shared* line has been observed by all processors. Thus a positive value on a counter indicates the number of outstanding accesses of the corresponding processor. When a processor generates a synchronization operation, it cannot proceed until it procures the line with the synchronization variable in its cache. If at this time, its counter has a positive value, i.e., there are outstanding accesses, the reserve bit of the cache line with the synchronization variable is set. All reserve bits are reset when the counter reads zero, i.e., when all previous reads have returned their values, and all previous writes have been globally performed[1]. When a processor P_i proceeds after a synchronization operation, it has the exclusive copy of the line with the synchronization variable in its cache. Hence, unless P_i writes back the line, the next request for it will be routed to P_i. When a synchronization request is routed to a processor, it is serviced only if the reserve bit of the requested line is reset, otherwise the request is stalled until the counter reads zero[2]. Condition 5 can be met if it is ensured that a line with its reserve bit set, is never flushed out of a processor cache. A processor that requires such a flush is made to stall until its counter reads zero. However, we believe that such a case will occur fairly rarely and will not be detri-

---

1. This does not require an associative clear. It can be implemented by maintaining a small, fixed table of reserved blocks.

2. This might be accomplished by maintaining a queue of stalled requests to be serviced when the counter reads zero, or a negative ack may be sent to the processor that sent the request, asking it to try again.

mental to performance. Thus for the most part, processors will need to block only to commit synchronization operations[3].

While previous accesses of a processor are pending after a synchronization operation, further accesses to memory will also increment the counter. This implies that a subsequent synchronization operation awaiting completion of the accesses pending before the previous synchronization operation, has to wait for the new accesses as well, before the counter reads zero and it is serviced. This can be avoided by allowing only a limited number of cache misses to be sent to memory while any line is reserved in the cache. This makes sure that the counter will read zero after a bounded number of increments after a synchronization operation is committed. A more dynamic solution involves providing a mechanism to distinguish accesses (and their acks) generated before a particular synchronization operation from those generated after [AdH89].

Though processors can be stalled at various points for unbounded amounts of time, deadlock can never occur. This is because the primary reason a processor blocks is to wait for some set of previously generated data reads to return, or some previously generated data writes and committed synchronization operations to be globally performed. Data read requests always return with their lines. Data writes also all always return with their lines, and their invalidation messages are always acknowledged. Hence, data writes are guaranteed to be globally performed. Similarly, a committed synchronization request only requires its invalidations to be acknowledged before it is globally performed. Since invalidations are always serviced, committed synchronization operations are also always globally performed. Hence a blocked processor will always unblock and termination is guaranteed.

6. Discussion

In this section, we analyze the effectiveness of the new definition for weak ordering (Definition 2) as opposed to the old definition (Definition 1). We perform this analysis by comparing the example hardware implementation (Section 5.3) and the example set of software constraints (DRF0), with the hardware and software allowed by the old definition.

We first claim that the hardware of Definition 1 is weakly ordered by Definition 2 with respect to DRF0. Definition 1 implicitly assumes that intra-processor dependencies are maintained, and that writes to a *given*

location by a *given* processor are observed in the same order by all processors [DSB86]. We assume that condition 1 of Definition 1 requires synchronization operations to be executed in a sequentially consistent manner, and not just strongly ordered. With these additional conditions, our claim can be proved formally in a manner analogous to the proof of Appendix B.

We next determine if the example implementation for the new definition can perform better than an implementation that is also allowed by the old definition. One reason the example implementation may perform better is that with Definition 1 a synchronization operation has global manifestations - before such an operation is issued by a processor, its previous accesses should have been observed by *all* processors in the system. With Definition 2 and DRF0, on the other hand, synchronization operations need only affect the processors that subsequently synchronize on the same location (and additional processors that later synchronize with those processors).

Figure 3 illustrates how the example implementation exploits this difference when two processors, P_0 and P_1, are sharing a data location x, and synchronizing on location s. Assume P_0 writes x, does other work, *Unsets* s, and then does more work. Assume also that after P_0 *Unsets* s, P_1 *TestAndSets* s, does other work and then reads x. Assume further that the write of x takes a long time to be globally performed.

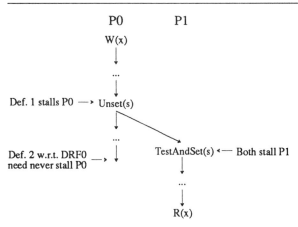

Figure 3. Analysis of the new implementation.

Definition 1 allows P_0 to issue and globally perform data accesses in parallel with the unfinished write of x until it wishes to issue the *Unset* of s. At that time P_0 must stall until the write of x is globally performed. Furthermore, P_1's *TestAndSet* of s cannot succeed until the *Unset* of s, and hence also the write of x, is globally performed.

The example implementation allows P_0 to continue to do other work after it has committed the *Unset* of

_____

3. To allow process migration, a processor is also be required to stall on a context switch until its counter reads zero.

s. P_0's further progress is limited only by implementation restrictions, such as, a cache miss that needs to replace the block holding s. P_1's *TestAndSet* of s, however, will still be blocked until P_0's write is globally performed, and *Unset* of s commits. Thus, P_0 but not P_1 gains an advantage from the example implementation.

One very important case where the example implementation is likely to be slower than one for Definition 1 occurs when software performs repeated testing of a synchronization variable (e.g., the *Test* from a *Test-and-TestAndSet* [RuS84] or spinning on a barrier count). The example implementation serializes all these synchronization operations, treating them as writes. This can lead to a significant performance degradation.

The unnecessary serialization can be avoided by improving on DRF0 to yield a new data-race-free model. In particular, a distinction between synchronization operations that only read (e.g., *Test*), only write (e.g., *Unset*), and both read and write (e.g., *TestAndSet*) can be made. Then DRF0 can be modified so that a processor cannot use a read-only synchronization operation to order its previous accesses with respect to subsequent synchronization operations of other processors. This does not compromise on the generality of the software allowed by DRF0 but will allow optimizations that lead to higher performance. In particular, for the example implementation, the read-only synchronization operations need not be serialized, and are not required to stall other processors until the completion of previous accesses.

Finally, we compare the software for which implementations based on Definition 1 appear sequentially consistent, and the software allowed by DRF0. Although the data-race-free model captures a large number of parallel programs, there exist some programs that use certain restricted kinds of data races for which implementations of Definition 1 appear sequentially consistent. Spinning on a barrier count with a data read is one example. We emphasize however, that this feature is not a drawback of Definition 2, but a limitation of DRF0. To allow such races, a new synchronization model can be defined.

7. Conclusions

Most programmers of shared memory systems implicitly assume the model of sequential consistency for the shared memory. This model precludes the use of most performance enhancing features of uniprocessor architectures. We advocate that for better performance, programmers change their assumptions about hardware and use the model of weak ordering, which was originally defined by Dubois, Scheurich and Briggs in terms of certain conditions on hardware. We believe, howev-

er, that this definition is unnecessarily restrictive on hardware and does not adequately specify the programmer's model.

We have re-defined weak ordering as a contract between software and hardware where hardware promises to appear sequentially consistent at least to the software that obeys a certain set of constraints which we have called the synchronization model. This definition is analogous to that given by Lamport for sequential consistency in that it only specifies how hardware should *appear* to software. The definition facilitates separate analyses and formal proofs of necessary and sufficient conditions for software and hardware to obey their sides of the contract. It allows programmers to continue reasoning about their programs using the sequential model of memory. Finally, it does not inflict any unnecessary directives on the hardware designer.

To illustrate the advantages of our new definition, we have specified an example synchronization model (DRF0) that forbids data races in a program. We have demonstrated that such a formal specification makes possible an implementation not allowed by the old definition, thereby demonstrating the greater generality of our definition. Finally, we have indicated how some constraints on DRF0 may be relaxed to improve the performance of our implementation.

A promising direction for future research is an application of the new definition to further explore alternative implementations of weak ordering with respect to data-race-free models. A quantitative performance analysis comparing implementations for the old and new definitions of weak ordering would provide useful insight.

Another interesting problem is the construction of other synchronization models optimized for particular software paradigms, such as, sharing only through monitors, or parallelism only from do-all loops, or for specific synchronization primitives offered by specific systems, e.g., QOSB [GVW89]. These optimizations may lead to implementations with higher performance.

8. Acknowledgements

We would like to thank Vikram Adve, William Collier, Kourosh Gharachorloo, Garth Gibson, Richard Kessler, Viranjit Madan, Bart Miller, Robert Netzer, and Marvin Solomon for their valuable comments on earlier drafts of this paper. We are particularly grateful to Kourosh Gharachorloo for bringing to our attention an error in an earlier version of the proof in Appendix B and to Michel Dubois for pointing out some of the limitations of DRF0. These had been overlooked by us in [AdH89].

9. References

[AdH89]   S. V. ADVE and M. D. HILL, Weak Ordering - A New Definition And Some Implications, Computer Sciences Technical Report #902, University of Wisconsin, Madison, December 1989.

[ASH88]   A. AGARWAL, R. SIMONI, M. HOROWITZ and J. HENNESSY, An Evaluation of Directory Schemes for Cache Coherence, *15th Annual International Symposium on Computer Architecture*, Honolulu, Hawaii, June 1988, 280-289.

[ArB86]   J. ARCHIBALD and J. BAER, Cache Coherence Protocols: Evaluation Using a Multiprocessor Simulation Model, *ACM Transactions on Computer Systems 4*, 4 (November 1986), 273-298.

[BeG81]   P. A. BERNSTEIN and N. GOODMAN, Concurrency Control in Distributed Systems, *Computing Surveys 13*, 2 (June, 1981), 185-221.

[BNR89]   R. BISIANI, A. NOWATZYK and M. RAVISHANKAR, Coherent Shared Memory on a Distributed Memory Machine, *Proc. International Conference on Parallel Processing*, August 1989, I-133-141.

[BMW85]   W. C. BRANTLEY, K. P. MCAULIFFE and J. WEISS, RP3 Process-Memory Element, *International Conference on Parallel Processing*, August 1985, 772-781.

[Col84]   W. W. COLLIER, Architectures for Systems of Parallel Processes, Technical Report Tech. Rep. 00.3253, IBM Corp., Poughkeepsie, N.Y., 27 January 1984.

[Col90]   W. W. COLLIER, *Reasoning about Parallel Architectures*, Prentice-Hall, Inc., To appear 1990.

[DeM88]   R. DE LEONE and O. L. MANGASARIAN, Asynchronous Parallel Successive Overrelaxation for the Symmetric Linear Complementarity Problem, *Mathematical Programming 42*(1988), 347-361.

[DSB86]   M. DUBOIS, C. SCHEURICH and F. A. BRIGGS, Memory Access Buffering in Multiprocessors, *Proc. Thirteenth Annual International Symposium on Computer Architecture 14*, 2 (June 1986), 434-442.

[DSB88]   M. DUBOIS, C. SCHEURICH and F. A. BRIGGS, Synchronization, Coherence, and Event Ordering in Multiprocessors, *IEEE Computer 21*, 2 (February 1988), 9-21.

[GVW89]   J. R. GOODMAN, M. K. VERNON and P. J. WOEST, Efficient Synchronization Primitives for Large-Scale Cache-Coherent Multiprocessors, *Proc. Third International Conference on Architectural Support for Programming Languages and Operating Systems*, Boston, April 1989, 64-75.

[Kro81]   D. KROFT, Lockup-Free Instruction Fetch/Prefetch Cache Organization, *Proc. Eighth Symposium on Computer Architecture*, May 1981, 81-87.

[Lam78]   L. LAMPORT, Time, Clocks, and the Ordering of Events in a Distributed System, *Communications of the ACM 21*, 7 (July 1978), 558-565.

[Lam79]   L. LAMPORT, How to Make a Multiprocessor Computer That Correctly Executes Multiprocess Programs, *IEEE Trans. on Computers C-28*, 9 (September 1979), 690-691.

[Lam86]   L. LAMPORT, The Mutual Exclusion Problem, Parts I and II , *Journal of the Association of Computing Machinery 33*, 2 (April 1986), 313-348.

[NeM89]   R. NETZER and B. MILLER, Detecting Data Races in Parallel Program Executions, Computer Sciences Technical Report #894, University of Wisconsin, Madison, November 1989.

[Pap86]   C. PAPADIMITRIOU, *The Theory of Database Concurrency Control*, Computer Science Press, Rockville, Maryland 20850, 1986.

[PBG85]   G. F. PFISTER, W. C. BRANTLEY, D. A. GEORGE, S. L. HARVEY, W. J. KLEINFELDER, K. P. MCAULIFFE, E. A. MELTON, V. A. NORTON and J. WEISS, The IBM Research Parallel Processor Prototype (RP3): Introduction and Architecture, *International Conference on Parallel Processing*, August 1985, 764-771.

[RuS84]   L. RUDOLPH and Z. SEGALL, Dynamic Decentralized Cache Schemes for MIMD Parallel Processors, *Proc. Eleventh International Symposium on Computer Architecture*, June 1984, 340-347.

[ScD87]   C. SCHEURICH and M. DUBOIS, Correct Memory Operation of Cache-Based Multiprocessors, *Proc. Fourteenth Annual International Symposium on Computer Architecture*, Pittsburgh, PA, June 1987, 234-243.

[ScD88]   C. SCHEURICH and M. DUBOIS, Concurrent Miss Resolution in Multiprocessor Caches, *Proceedings of the 1988 International Conference on Parallel Processing*, University Park PA, August, 1988, I-118-125.

[Sch89]   C. E. SCHEURICH, Access Ordering and Coherence in Shared Memory Multiprocessors, Ph.D. Thesis, Department of Computer Engineering, Technical Report CENG 89-19, University of Southern California, May 1989.

[ShS88]   D. SHASHA and M. SNIR, Efficient and Correct Execution of Parallel Programs that Share Memory, *ACM Trans. on Programming Languages and Systems 10*, 2 (April 1988), 282-312.

Appendix A[4]: A necessary and sufficient condition for weak ordering w.r.t. DRF0.

Lemma 1: A system is weakly ordered with respect to DRF0 if only if for any execution E of a program that obeys DRF0, there exists a happens-before relation $\xrightarrow{hb}$, defined for the program such that (1) every read in E appears in $\xrightarrow{hb}$, (2) every read in $\xrightarrow{hb}$ appears in E, and (3) a read always returns the value written by the last write[5] on the same variable, ordered before it by $\xrightarrow{hb}$.

Proof of necessity

In proving necessity, we do not consider programs for the executions of which an equivalent serialization of accesses can be found as a result of the nature of the initial values of variables and the immediate operands in the code. Instead, we only concern ourselves with general programs where the immediate operands and the initial values may be looked upon as variables which could be assigned arbitrary values and still result in serializable executions.

The proof proceeds by contradiction. Suppose there exists a system which is weakly ordered with respect to DRF0 but does not obey the above condition. Then for any execution E of a program that obeys DRF0, there must be a total ordering T of all its accesses which produces the same result as E, and which is consistent[6] with the program order of all the processes comprising E.

Since T is consistent with program order, there corresponds an execution E' on the idealized architecture that produces the same result as T. Consider the happens-before relation $\xrightarrow{hb}$ corresponding to E'. In E', the partial ordering of accesses as defined by $\xrightarrow{hb}$ is consistent with the order in which accesses are executed. Since all conflicting accesses are ordered by $\xrightarrow{hb}$, they are all executed in the order determined by $\xrightarrow{hb}$. This implies that a read in E' always returns the value of the write ordered last (this is unique for DRF0) before it

by $\xrightarrow{hb}$. Since the result of an execution depends on the value returned by every read, it follows that for E and E' to have the same result, a read in E must appear in $\xrightarrow{hb}$ and vice versa, and a read in E must return the value of the last write ordered before it by $\xrightarrow{hb}$. This contradicts our initial hypothesis. □

Proof of sufficiency

We now prove that a system that obeys the given condition is weakly ordered w.r.t. DRF0. From the given condition, there exists a happens-before relation $\xrightarrow{hb}$ corresponding to any execution E of a program that obeys DRF0, such that every read in E occurs in $\xrightarrow{hb}$ and vice versa, and a read in E returns the value of the write ordered last before it by this happens-before. Consider the execution E' on the idealized architecture, to which this happens-before corresponds.

The order of execution of accesses in E' is consistent with $\xrightarrow{hb}$. Since all conflicting accesses are ordered by $\xrightarrow{hb}$, it follows that a read in E' always returns the value of the write ordered last before it by $\xrightarrow{hb}$. This implies that the result of E is the same as that of E'. Hence it suffices to show that there exists a total ordering of the accesses in E' that is consistent with program order. This is trivially true since E' is an execution on an architecture where all memory accesses are executed atomically and in program order. □

Appendix B: Proof of sufficiency of the conditions in Section 5.1 for weak ordering w.r.t. DRF0

We prove that the conditions of Section 5.1 are sufficient for weak ordering with respect to DRF0 by showing that a system that obeys these conditions also satisfies the necessary and sufficient condition of Lemma 1 in Appendix A.

Consider a program P that obeys DRF0. Let E be an execution of P on a system that obeys the conditions of Section 5.1. Consider the set of accesses A(t) comprising of all the accesses in E that are committed before or at (wall-clock) time t. Define the relations $\xrightarrow{po(t)}$ and $\xrightarrow{so(t)}$ on the accesses in A(t) as follows: $op_1 \xrightarrow{po(t)} op_2$ if and only if op_1 occurs before op_2 in program order for some processor. $op_1 \xrightarrow{so(t)} op_2$ if and only if op_1 and op_2 are synchronization operations that access the same memory location and op_1 commits before op_2[7]. Define $\xrightarrow{xo(t)}$ as the irreflexive, transitive closure of $\xrightarrow{po(t)}$ and $\xrightarrow{so(t)}$. Intuitively, $\xrightarrow{xo(t)}$ reflects the state of the execution E at time t.

---

4. Throughout Appendices A and B, unless mentioned otherwise, reads and writes include synchronization operations. An execution is assumed to be augmented for the initial and final state of memory, as in Section 4.

5. Strictly speaking, with synchronization operations that read and modify memory, sufficiency is guaranteed only if the read of a synchronization operation occurs before its write. Otherwise, the read should be required to return a *modification* of the last write, where the modification depends on the synchronization operation.

6. Two relations A and B are consistent if and only if $A \cup B$ can be extended to a total ordering [ShS88].

---

7. Condition 3 ensures that $\xrightarrow{so(t)}$ defines a total order for all synchronization operations to the *same* location in A(t).

Let the entire execution complete at some time T. We will show that $\xrightarrow{\text{xo(T)}}$ is a happens-before relation, and a read in E returns the value of the write ordered last before it by this happens-before relation. Because of the way $\xrightarrow{\text{xo(T)}}$ is constructed, every read in E appears in $\xrightarrow{\text{xo(T)}}$ and vice versa, and hence, by Lemma 1, the proposition will be proved.

The proof proceeds by contradiction. Suppose the above claim is not true. Then, either $\xrightarrow{\text{xo(T)}}$ is not a happens-before relation for P, or else a read in E does not return the value of the last write ordered before it by $\xrightarrow{\text{xo(T)}}$. Let t' be the maximum value such that for all $t < t'$, $\xrightarrow{\text{xo(t)}}$ could have lead to a $\xrightarrow{\text{xo(T)}}$ that is a happens-before relation, and every read that appears in $\xrightarrow{\text{xo(t)}}$ returns the value of the last write ordered before it by this happens-before relation. Denote the set of happens-before relations that could have been produced just before time t' as $H(t'\text{-})$.

The time t' is the earliest time at which it can be detected that the system is not sequentially consistent. Hence at t', some data read or some read-only or read-write synchronization operation R, must have committed such that either (i) R does not appear in any of the happens-before relations in $H(t'\text{-})$ or (ii) the value returned by R is from a write that is not ordered last before it by any of the happens-before relations in $H(t'\text{-})$.

We first prove by contradiction that (i) above is not possible. Suppose R does not appear in any of the happens-before relations in $H(t'\text{-})$. The memory accesses generated by a processor are totally governed by the values its reads return. Before t', all the reads that committed returned values that could have lead to some sequentially consistent execution. Hence, these reads could not have lead to the generation of R. Reads that returned values before t' but did not commit are components of read-write synchronization operations. Condition 4 ensures that a processor cannot generate an access until its previous synchronization accesses are committed. Thus, synchronization operations that returned a value but were not committed before t' also cannot result in the generation of R. Thus, we have proved that R does indeed appear in all the happens-before relations in $H(t'\text{-})$.

In the rest of the proof, we show (again by contradiction) that (ii) above is not possible. The argument for (i) also implies that *all* accesses generated before t' appear in all the happens-before relations in $H(t'\text{-})$. Thus $\xrightarrow{\text{xo(t')}}$ can lead to at least one of the happens-before relations in $H(t'-)$. Let one of these relations be $\xrightarrow{\text{hb}}$. Denote the program order and synchronization order relations corresponding to $\xrightarrow{\text{hb}}$ by $\xrightarrow{\text{po}}$ and $\xrightarrow{\text{so}}$ respectively. Let W' be the write whose value R returns[8]. Since R reads the value written by W', W' must be committed before or at t'. Hence, W' appears in $\xrightarrow{\text{xo(t')}}$ and in $\xrightarrow{\text{hb}}$. Therefore, W' is ordered with respect to R by $\xrightarrow{\text{hb}}$. But by hypothesis, W' is not the last write ordered before R by $\xrightarrow{\text{hb}}$. Let W be the last write ordered before R by $\xrightarrow{\text{hb}}$. (DRF0 ensures that this is unique.) Thus, either $W \xrightarrow{\text{hb}} R \xrightarrow{\text{hb}} W'$ or $W' \xrightarrow{\text{hb}} W \xrightarrow{\text{hb}} R$. We will prove that R cannot return the value written by W' in either of these cases.

We first prove the following simple results. Below, S_i's are synchronization operations.

(a) If $S_i \xrightarrow{\text{hb}} S_j$, and S_j committed before or at t', then S_i committed before S_j.

Proof - If $S_i \xrightarrow{\text{so}} S_j$ and S_i did not commit before S_j, then since S_i appears in $\xrightarrow{\text{so(t')}}$, $\xrightarrow{\text{so(t')}}$ cannot be the same as $\xrightarrow{\text{so}}$, and hence $\xrightarrow{\text{xo(t')}}$ cannot lead to $\xrightarrow{\text{hb}}$, a contradiction.

If $S_i \xrightarrow{\text{po}} S_j$, and if S_i did not commit before S_j, then either S_i will commit later or S_i will not occur in the execution. The former violates condition 4 and the latter implies that $\xrightarrow{\text{xo(t')}}$ cannot lead to $\xrightarrow{\text{hb}}$,

Since $\xrightarrow{\text{hb}}$ is the transitive closure of $\xrightarrow{\text{so}}$ and $\xrightarrow{\text{po}}$, it follows that if $S_i \xrightarrow{\text{hb}} S_j$, then S_i committed before S_j.

(b) If A is a data access that committed before or at t' and $S_i \xrightarrow{\text{hb}} A$, then S_i committed before A was generated.

Proof - Either $S_i \xrightarrow{\text{po}} A$ or $S_i \xrightarrow{\text{hb}} S_j \xrightarrow{\text{po}} A$. Suppose $S_i \xrightarrow{\text{po}} A$ and S_i is not committed before A is generated. Then either S_i commits after A is generated, or S_i does not occur in E. The former violates condition 4 and the latter implies that $\xrightarrow{\text{xo(t')}}$ cannot lead to $\xrightarrow{\text{hb}}$. Hence if $S_i \xrightarrow{\text{po}} A$, S_i is committed before t'. Now suppose that $S_i \xrightarrow{\text{hb}} S_j \xrightarrow{\text{po}} A$. Then from the above argument S_j must have committed before A is generated. Therefore, S_i must have committed before A is generated (result a).

(c) If A_i and A_j are conflicting accesses by different processors such that $A_i \xrightarrow{\text{hb}} A_j$, and A_j commits before or at t', then A_i commits before A_j.

If A_i is a synchronization access, then the result follows from results (a) and (b). If A_i is a data access, then either $A_i \xrightarrow{\text{po}} S_1 \xrightarrow{\text{so}} S_2 \xrightarrow{\text{hb}} A_j$ or $A_i \xrightarrow{\text{po}} S_1 \xrightarrow{\text{so}} A_j$. For the former case, S_2 must commit before A_j is generated (result b), and so S_1 must commit before S_2 (result a), and so A_i must commit before S_2 (condition 5 and because $\xrightarrow{\text{xo(t')}}$ can lead to $\xrightarrow{\text{hb}}$). Thus A_i commits before A_j is generated, and hence before it is committed. A similar argument can be applied to the latter case.

---

8. We assume that a read always returns the value of some write in the augmented execution.

(d) If A_i and A_j are conflicting data accesses by different processors such that $A_i \xrightarrow{hb} A_j$, A_i is a write operation and A_j commits before or at t', then A_i is globally performed before A_j is generated.

Proof - The argument used in result (c) for the case where A_i and A_j are data accesses applies.

We now use the above results to prove that for each of the cases $W \xrightarrow{hb} R \xrightarrow{hb} W'$, and $W' \xrightarrow{hb} W \xrightarrow{hb} R$, R cannot return the value written by W'.

Case I - $W \xrightarrow{hb} R \xrightarrow{hb} W'$

If $R \xrightarrow{po} W'$, then since condition 1 requires intra-processor dependencies to be maintained, R cannot return the value written by W'.

If R and W' are from different processors, then result (c) requires that R commit before t'. This is a contradiction.

Case II - $W' \xrightarrow{hb} W \xrightarrow{hb} R$

We show that (i) W commits before or at t', and (ii) R cannot return the value of a write that committed before W. From result (c) or from conditions 1 and 2, it will follow that W' commits before W, and hence we will conclude that R cannot return the value written by W'.

Suppose $W \xrightarrow{po} R$. If W is not committed before or at t', then since intra-processor dependencies have to be maintained, it is either known at time t' that W will not be generated, or it is known that W cannot affect the value returned by R. Either of these conditions implies that $\xrightarrow{xo(t')}$ cannot generate $\xrightarrow{hb}$. Thus W must be committed before or at t'. Conditions 1 and 2 then imply that R cannot return the value of a write that committed before W.

If R and W are from different processors, then since W is the last write ordered before R, either both R and W are data operations or both are synchronization operations. If they are both data operations, then from result (d) and condition 2, R cannot return the value of a write committed before W. Result (d) also implies that W is committed before t'.

If R and W are both synchronization operations, then W commits before R (result c), and so R is globally performed after W (condition 3), and so R cannot return the value of a write that committed before W (condition 2).

Thus, we have proved that W always commits before t', and R never returns the value of a write committed before W. It follows that R cannot return the value from W' (result c).

From Case I and Case II, R cannot return the value from W'. This contradicts our hypothesis and completes the proof. $\square$

Appendix C: Glossary of key definitions

[Hardware is sequentially consistent if] the result of any execution is the same as if the operations of all the processors were executed in some sequential order, and the operations of each individual processor appear in this sequence in the order specified by its program.

Definition 1: In a multiprocessor system, storage accesses are weakly ordered if (1) accesses to global synchronizing variables are strongly ordered, (2) no access to a synchronizing variable is issued by a processor before all previous global data accesses have been globally performed and if (3) no access to global data is issued by a processor before a previous access to a synchronizing variable has been globally performed.

Definition 2: Hardware is weakly ordered with respect to a synchronization model if and only if it appears sequentially consistent to all software that obey the synchronization model.

Definition 3: A program obeys the synchronization model Data-Race-Free-0 (DRF0), if and only if

(1) all synchronization operations are recognizable by the hardware and each accesses exactly one memory location, and

(2) for any execution on the idealized system (where all memory accesses are executed atomically and in program order), all conflicting accesses are ordered by the happens-before relation corresponding to the execution.

Memory Consistency and Event Ordering in Scalable Shared-Memory Multiprocessors

Kourosh Gharachorloo, Daniel Lenoski, James Laudon, Phillip Gibbons,
Anoop Gupta, and John Hennessy

Computer Systems Laboratory
Stanford University, CA 94305

Abstract

Scalable shared-memory multiprocessors distribute memory among the processors and use scalable interconnection networks to provide high bandwidth and low latency communication. In addition, memory accesses are cached, buffered, and pipelined to bridge the gap between the slow shared memory and the fast processors. Unless carefully controlled, such architectural optimizations can cause memory accesses to be executed in an order different from what the programmer expects. The set of allowable memory access orderings forms the memory consistency model or event ordering model for an architecture.

This paper introduces a new model of memory consistency, called *release consistency*, that allows for more buffering and pipelining than previously proposed models. A framework for classifying shared accesses and reasoning about event ordering is developed. The release consistency model is shown to be equivalent to the sequential consistency model for parallel programs with sufficient synchronization. Possible performance gains from the less strict constraints of the release consistency model are explored. Finally, practical implementation issues are discussed, concentrating on issues relevant to scalable architectures.

1 Introduction

Serial computers present a simple and intuitive model of the memory system to the programmer. A load operation returns the last value written to a given memory location. Likewise, a store operation binds the value that will be returned by subsequent loads until the next store to the same location. This simple model lends itself to efficient implementations—current uniprocessors use caches, write buffers, interleaved main memory, and exploit pipelining techniques. The accesses may even be issued and completed out of order as long as the hardware and compiler ensure that data and control dependences are respected.

For multiprocessors, however, neither the memory system model nor the implementation is as straightforward. The memory system model is more complex because the definitions of "last value written", "subsequent loads", and "next store" become unclear when there are multiple processors reading and writing a location. Furthermore, the order in which shared memory operations are done by one process may be used by other processes to achieve implicit synchronization. For example, a process may set a flag variable to indicate that a data structure it was manipulating earlier is now in a consistent state. Consistency models place specific requirements on the order that shared memory accesses (*events*) from one process may be observed by other processes in the machine. More generally, the consistency model specifies what event orderings are legal when several processes are accessing a common set of locations.

Several memory consistency models have been proposed in the literature: examples include sequential consistency [7], processor consistency [5], and weak consistency [4]. The *sequential consistency* model [7] requires the execution of a parallel program to appear as some interleaving of the execution of the parallel processes on a sequential machine. While conceptually simple, the sequential consistency model imposes severe restrictions on the outstanding accesses that a process may have and effectively prohibits many hardware optimizations that could increase performance. Other models attempt to relax the constraints on the allowable event orderings, while still providing a reasonable programming model for the programmer.

Architectural optimizations that reduce memory latency are especially important for scalable multiprocessor architectures. As a result of the distributed memory and general interconnection networks used by such multiprocessors [8, 9, 12], requests issued by a processor to distinct memory modules may execute out of order. Caching of data further complicates the ordering of accesses by introducing multiple copies of the same location. While memory accesses are atomic in systems with a single copy of data (a new data value becomes visible to all processors at the same time), such atomicity may not be present in cache-based systems. The lack of atomicity introduces extra complexity in implementing consistency models. A system architect must balance the design by providing a memory consistency model that allows for high performance implementations and is acceptable to the programmer.

In this paper, we present a new consistency model called *release consistency*, which extends the weak consistency model [4] by utilizing additional information about shared accesses. Section 2 presents a brief overview of previously proposed consistency models. The motivation and framework for release consistency is presented in Section 3. Section 4 considers equivalences among the several models given proper information about shared accesses. Section 5 discusses potential performance gains for the models with relaxed constraints. Finally, Section 6 discusses implementation issues, focusing on issues relevant to scalable architectures.

CH2887-8/90/0000/0015$01.00 © 1990 IEEE

15

2 Previously Proposed Memory Consistency Models

In this section, we present event ordering requirements for supporting the sequential, processor, and weak consistency models. Although the models discussed in this section have already been presented in the literature, we discuss them here for purposes of completeness, uniformity in terminology, and later comparison. Readers familiar with the first three models and the event ordering terminology may wish to skip to Section 3.

To facilitate the description of different event orderings, we present formal definitions for the stages that a memory request goes through. The following two definitions are from Dubois *et al.* [4, 10]. In the following, P_i refers to processor i.

> **Definition 2.1: Performing a Memory Request**
> A LOAD by P_i is considered *performed with respect to* P_k at a point in time when the issuing of a STORE to the same address by P_k cannot affect the value returned by the LOAD. A STORE by P_i is considered *performed with respect to* P_k at a point in time when an issued LOAD to the same address by P_k returns the value defined by this STORE (or a subsequent STORE to the same location). An access is *performed* when it is performed with respect to all processors.

Definition 2.2 describes the notion of *globally performed* for LOADs.

> **Definition 2.2: Performing a LOAD Globally**
> A LOAD is *globally performed* if it is performed *and* if the STORE that is the source of the returned value has been performed.

The distinction between performed and globally performed LOAD accesses is only present in architectures with non-atomic STOREs. A STORE is atomic if the value stored becomes readable to all processors at the same time. In architectures with caches and general interconnection networks, a STORE operation is inherently non-atomic unless special hardware mechanisms are employed to assure atomicity.

From this point on, we implicitly assume that uniprocessor control and data dependences are respected. In addition, we assume that memory is kept coherent, that is, all writes to the same location are serialized in some order and are performed in that order with respect to any processor. We have formulated the conditions for satisfying each model such that a process needs to keep track of only requests initiated by itself. Thus, the compiler and hardware can enforce ordering on a per process(or) basis. We define *program order* as the order in which accesses occur in an execution of the single process given that no reordering takes place. When we use the phrase *"all previous accesses"*, we mean all accesses in the program order that are before the current access. In presenting the event ordering conditions to satisfy each model, we assume that the implementation avoids deadlock by ensuring that accesses that occur previously in program order eventually get performed (globally performed).

2.1 Sequential Consistency

Lamport [7] defines *sequential consistency* as follows.

> **Definition 2.3: Sequential Consistency**
> A system is sequentially consistent if the result of any execution is the same as if the operations of all the processors were executed in some sequential order, and the operations of each individual processor appear in this sequence in the order specified by its program.

Scheurich and Dubois [10, 11] have described event order restrictions that guarantee sequential consistency. Condition 2.1 presents sufficient conditions for providing sequential consistency (these differ slightly from conditions given in [10]).

> **Condition 2.1: Sufficient Conditions for Sequential Consistency**
> (A) before a LOAD is allowed to perform with respect to any other processor, all previous LOAD accesses must be *globally* performed and all previous STORE accesses must be performed, and
> (B) before a STORE is allowed to perform with respect to any other processor, all previous LOAD accesses must be *globally* performed and all previous STORE accesses must be performed.

2.2 Processor Consistency

To relax some of the orderings imposed by sequential consistency, Goodman introduces the concept of *processor consistency* [5]. Processor consistency requires that writes issued from a processor may not be observed in any order other than that in which they were issued. However, the order in which writes from two processors occur, as observed by themselves or a third processor, need not be identical. Processor consistency is weaker than sequential consistency; therefore, it may not yield 'correct' execution if the programmer assumes sequential consistency. However, Goodman claims that most applications give the same results under the processor and sequential consistency models. Specifically, he relies on programmers to use explicit synchronization rather than depending on the memory system to guarantee strict event ordering. Goodman also points out that many existing multiprocessors (e.g., VAX 8800) satisfy processor consistency, but do not satisfy sequential consistency.

The description given in [5] does not specify the ordering of read accesses completely. We have defined the following conditions for processor consistency.

> **Condition 2.2: Conditions for Processor Consistency**
> (A) before a LOAD is allowed to perform with respect to any other processor, all previous LOAD accesses must be performed, and
> (B) before a STORE is allowed to perform with respect to any other processor, all previous accesses (LOADs and STOREs) must be performed.

The above conditions allow reads following a write to bypass the write. To avoid deadlock, the implementation should guarantee that a write that appears previously in program order will eventually perform.

2.3 Weak Consistency

A weaker consistency model can be derived by relating memory request ordering to synchronization points in the program. As an example, consider a processor updating a data structure within a critical section. If the computation requires several STORE accesses and the system is sequentially consistent, then each STORE will have to be delayed until the previous STORE is complete. But such delays are unnecessary because the programmer has already made sure that no other process can rely on that data structure being consistent until the critical section is exited. Given that all synchronization points are identified, we need only ensure that the memory is consistent at those points. This scheme has the advantage of providing the user with a reasonable programming model, while permitting multiple memory accesses to be pipelined. The disadvantage is that all synchronization accesses must be identified by the programmer or compiler.

The *weak consistency* model proposed by Dubois *et al.* [4] is based on the above idea. They distinguish between ordinary shared accesses and synchronization accesses, where the latter are used to control concurrency between several processes and to maintain the integrity of ordinary shared data. The conditions to ensure weak consistency are given below (slightly different from the conditions given in [4]).

Condition 2.3: Conditions for Weak Consistency
(A) before an ordinary LOAD or STORE access is allowed to perform with respect to any other processor, all previous *synchronization* accesses must be performed, and
(B) before a *synchronization* access is allowed to perform with respect to any other processor, all previous ordinary LOAD and STORE accesses must be performed, and
(C) *synchronization* accesses are sequentially consistent with respect to one another.

3 The Release Consistency Model

This section presents the framework for release consistency. There are two main issues explored in this section—performance and correctness. For performance, the goal is to exploit additional information about shared accesses to develop a memory consistency model that allows for more efficient implementations. Section 3.1 discusses a categorization of shared accesses that provides such information. For correctness, the goal is to develop weaker models that are equivalent to the stricter models as far as the results of programs are concerned. Section 3.2 introduces the notion of properly-labeled programs that is later used to prove equivalences among models. Finally, Section 3.3 presents the release consistency model and discusses how it exploits the extra information about accesses.

3.1 Categorization of Shared Memory Accesses

We first describe the notions of *conflicting accesses* (as presented in [13]) and *competing accesses*. Two accesses are conflicting if they are to the same memory location and at least one of the accesses is a STORE.[1] Consider a pair of conflicting accesses a_1 and a_2 on different processors. If the two accesses are not ordered, they may execute simultaneously thus causing a race condition. Such accesses a_1 and a_2 form a *competing pair*. If an access is involved in a competing pair under any execution, then the access is considered a *competing access*.

A parallel program consisting of individual processes specifies the actions for each process and the interactions among processes. These interactions are coordinated through accesses to shared memory. For example, a producer process may set

---

[1]A read-modify-write operation can be treated as an atomic access consisting of both a load and a store.

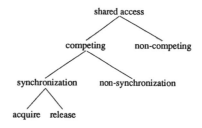

Figure 1: Categorization of shared writable accesses.

a flag variable to indicate to the consumer process that a data record is ready. Similarly, processes may enclose all updates to a shared data structure within lock and unlock operations to prevent simultaneous access. All such accesses used to enforce an ordering among processes are called *synchronization accesses*. Synchronization accesses have two distinctive characteristics: (i) they are competing accesses, with one process writing a variable and the other reading it; and (ii) they are frequently used to order conflicting accesses (i.e., make them non-competing). For example, the lock and unlock synchronization operations are used to order the non-competing accesses made inside a critical section.

Synchronization accesses can further be partitioned into *acquire* and *release* accesses. An acquire synchronization access (e.g., a lock operation or a process spinning for a flag to be set) is performed to gain access to a set of shared locations. A release synchronization access (e.g., an unlock operation or a process setting a flag) grants this permission. An acquire is accomplished by reading a shared location until an appropriate value is read. Thus, an acquire is always associated with a read synchronization access (atomic read-modify-write accesses are discussed in Section 3.2). Similarly, a release is always associated with a write synchronization access.

Not all competing accesses are used as synchronization accesses, however. As an example, programs that use chaotic relaxation algorithms make many competing accesses to read their neighbors' data. However, these accesses are not used to impose an ordering among the parallel processes and are thus considered *non-synchronization* competing accesses in our terminology. Figure 1 shows this categorization for memory accesses.

The categorization of shared accesses into the suggested groups allows one to provide more efficient implementations by using this information to relax the event ordering restrictions. For example, the purpose of a release access is to inform other processes that accesses that appear before it in program order have completed. On the other hand, the purpose of an acquire access is to delay future access to data until informed by another process. The categorization described here can be extended to include other useful information about accesses. The tradeoff is how easily that extra information can be obtained from the compiler or the programmer and what incremental performance benefits it can provide.

Finally, the method for identifying an access as a competing access depends on the consistency model. For example, it is possible for an access to be competing under processor consistency and non-competing under sequential consistency. While identifying competing pairs is difficult in general, the following conceptual method may be used under sequential consistency. Two conflicting accesses b_1 and b_2 on different processes form

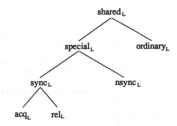

Figure 2: Labels for memory accesses.

a competing pair if there exists at least one legal interleaving where b_1 and b_2 are *adjacent*.

3.2 Properly-Labeled Programs

The previous subsection described a categorization based on the intrinsic properties of an access. We now describe the labelings for an access. The label represents what is asserted about the categorization of the access. It is the responsibility of the compiler or the programmer to provide labels for the accesses. Figure 2 shows possible labelings for memory accesses in a program. The labels shown correspond to the categorization of accesses depicted in Figure 1. The subscript L denotes that these are labels. The labels at the same level are disjoint, and a label at a leaf implies all its parent labels.

The release consistency model exploits the information conveyed by the labels to provide less strict event ordering constraints. Thus, the labels need to have a proper relationship to the actual category of an accesses to ensure correctness under release consistency. For example, the $ordinary_L$ label asserts that an access is non-competing. Since the hardware may exploit the $ordinary_L$ label to use less strict event orderings, it is important that the $ordinary_L$ label be used only for non-competing accesses. However, a non-competing access can be conservatively labeled as $special_L$. In addition, it is important that *enough* competing accesses be labeled as acq_L and rel_L to ensure that the accesses labeled $ordinary_L$ are indeed non-competing. The following definition provides a conceptual model for determining whether enough $special_L$ accesses have been categorized as $sync_L$ (again assuming the sequential consistency model).

> **Definition 3.1: Enough $Sync_L$ Labels**
> Pick any two accesses u on processor P_u and v on processor P_v (P_u not the same as P_v) such that the two accesses conflict, and at least one is labeled as $ordinary_L$. Under any legal interleaving, if v appears after (before) u, then there needs to be at least one $sync_L$ write (read) access on P_u and one $sync_L$ read (write) on P_v separating u and v, such that the write appears before the read. There are *enough* accesses labeled as $sync_L$ if the above condition holds for all possible pairs u and v. A $sync_L$ read has to be labeled as acq_L and a $sync_L$ write has to be labeled as rel_L.

To determine whether all labels are appropriate, we present the notion of properly-labeled programs.

> **Definition 3.2: Properly-Labeled (PL) Programs**
> A program is *properly-labeled (PL)* if the following hold: $(shared\ access) \subseteq shared_L$, $competing \subseteq special_L$, and *enough* (as defined above) $special_L$ accesses are labeled as acq_L and rel_L.

An acq_L or rel_L label implies the $sync_L$ label. Any $special_L$ access that is not labeled as $sync_L$ is labeled as $nsync_L$. In addition, any $shared_L$ access that is not labeled as $special_L$ is labeled as $ordinary_L$. Note that this categorization is based on access and not on location. For example, it is possible that of two accesses to the same location, one is labeled $special_L$ while the other is labeled $ordinary_L$.

Most architectures provide atomic read-modify-write operations for efficiently dealing with competing accesses. The load and store access in the operation can be labeled separately based on their categorization, similarly to individual load and store accesses. The most common label for a read-modify-write is an acq_L for the load and an $nsync_L$ for the store. A prevalent example of this is an atomic test-and-set operation used to gain exclusive access to a set of data. Although the store access is necessary to ensure mutual exclusion, it does not function as either an acquire or a release. If the programmer or compiler cannot categorize the read-modify-write appropriately, the conservative label for guaranteeing correctness is acq_L and rel_L for the load and store respectively (the operation is treated as both an acquire and a release).

There is no unique labeling to make a program a PL program. As long as the above subset properties are respected, the program will be considered properly-labeled. Proper labeling is not an inherent property of the program, but simply a property of the labels. Therefore, any program can be properly labeled. However, the less conservative the labeling, the higher is the potential for performance benefits.

Given perfect information about the category of an access, the access can be easily labeled to provide a PL program. However, perfect information may not be available at all times. Proper labeling can still be provided by being conservative. This is illustrated in the three possible labeling strategies enumerated below (from conservative to aggressive). Only leaf labels shown in Figure 2 are discussed (remember that a leaf label implies all parent labels).

1. If competing and non-competing accesses can not be distinguished, then all reads can be labeled as acq_L and all writes can be labeled as rel_L.

2. If competing accesses can be distinguished from non-competing accesses, but synchronization and non-synchronization accesses can not be distinguished, then all accesses distinguished as non-competing can be labeled as $ordinary_L$ and all competing accesses are labeled as acq_L and rel_L (as before).

3. If competing and non-competing accesses are distinguished and synchronization and non-synchronization accesses are distinguished, then all non-competing accesses can be labeled as $ordinary_L$, all non-synchronization accesses can be labeled as $nsync_L$, and all synchronization accesses are labeled as acq_L and rel_L (as before).

We discuss two practical ways for labeling accesses to provide PL programs. The first involves parallelizing compilers that generate parallel code from sequential programs. Since the compiler does the parallelization, the information about which accesses are competing and which accesses are used for synchronization is known to the compiler and can be used to label the accesses properly.

The second way of producing PL programs is to use a programming methodology that lends itself to proper labeling. For

18

example, a large class of programs are written such that accesses to shared data are protected within critical sections. Such programs are called *synchronized programs*, whereby writes to shared locations are done in a mutually exclusive manner (no other reads or writes can occur simultaneously). In a synchronized program, all accesses (except accesses that are part of the synchronization constructs) can be labeled as $ordinary_L$. In addition, since synchronization constructs are predefined, the accesses within them can be labeled properly when the constructs are first implemented. For this labeling to be proper, the programmer must ensure that the program is synchronized.

Given a program is properly-labeled, the remaining issue is whether the consistency model exploits the extra information conveyed by the labels. The sequential and processor consistency models ignore all labels aside from $shared_L$. The weak consistency model ignores any labelings past $ordinary_L$ and $special_L$. In weak consistency, an access labeled $special_L$ is treated as a synchronization access and as both an acquire and a release. In contrast, the release consistency model presented in the next subsection exploits the information conveyed by the labels at the leaves of the labeling tree.

From this point on, we do not distinguish between the categorization and the labeling of an access, unless this distinction is necessary.

3.3 Release Consistency

Release consistency is an extension of weak consistency that exploits the information about acquire, release, and non-synchronization accesses. The following gives the conditions for ensuring *release consistency*.

> **Condition 3.1: Conditions for Release Consistency**
> (A) before an ordinary LOAD or STORE access is allowed to perform with respect to any other processor, all previous *acquire* accesses must be performed, and
> (B) before a *release* access is allowed to perform with respect to any other processor, all previous ordinary LOAD and STORE accesses must be performed, and
> (C) *special accesses* are processor consistent with respect to one another.

Four of the ordering restrictions in weak consistency are not present in release consistency. The first is that ordinary LOAD and STORE accesses following a release access do not have to be delayed for the release to complete; the purpose of the release synchronization access is to signal that previous accesses in a critical section are complete, and it does not have anything to say about ordering of accesses following it. Of course, the local dependences within the same processor must still be respected. Second, an acquire synchronization access need not be delayed for previous LOAD and STORE accesses to be performed. Since an acquire access is not giving permission to any other process to read/write the previous pending locations, there is no reason for the acquire to wait for them to complete. Third, a non-synchronization special access does not wait for previous ordinary accesses and does not delay future ordinary accesses; a non-synchronization access does not interact with ordinary accesses. The fourth difference arises from the ordering of special accesses. In release consistency, they are only required to be processor consistent and not sequentially consistent. For all applications that we have encountered, sequential consistency and processor consistency (for special accesses) give the same results. Section 4 outlines restrictions that allow

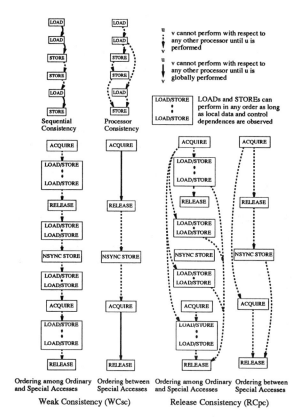

Figure 3: Ordering requirements for different consistency models.

us to show this equivalence. We chose processor consistency since it is easier to implement and offers higher performance.

4 Model Equivalences

The purpose of this section is to provide more insight into the similarities and differences among the consistency models presented in Sections 2 and 3 by showing relations and equivalences among the models.

We have presented four consistency models: sequential consistency (SC), processor consistency (PC), weak consistency with special accesses sequentially consistent (WCsc), and release consistency with special accesses processor consistent (RCpc). Two other models that fit within this framework are weak consistency with special accesses processor consistent (WCpc) and release consistency with special accesses sequentially consistent (RCsc). Figure 3 depicts the event orderings imposed by Conditions 2.1 through 2.3 for SC, PC, WCsc, and Condition 3.1 for RCpc. The WC and RC models have fewer restrictions on ordering than SC and PC, and RC has fewer restrictions than WC. Of course, a hardware implementation has the choice of enforcing the stated conditions directly or imposing some alternative set of conditions that guarantee the executions of programs appear as if the stated conditions were followed.

We define the relations $\geq$ (stricter) and $=$ (equal) for relating the models. If A and B are different consistency models, then relation $A \geq B$ says that results of executions of a program under model A will be in accordance to legal results for the program under model B, but not necessarily vice versa. The stricter relation is transitive. The relation $A = B$ says that for a certain program, models A and B cannot be distinguished based on the results of the program. Given $A \geq B$ and $B \geq A$, we know $A = B$. Some obvious relations that hold for any parallel program are: $SC \geq PC$, $SC \geq WCsc \geq RCsc$, $SC \geq WCpc \geq RCpc$, $PC \geq RCpc$, $WCsc \geq WCpc$, and $RCsc \geq RCpc$. However, the stricter relation does not hold among the following pairs: (PC,WCsc), (PC,RCsc), (PC,WCpc), and (RCsc,WCpc).

Due to the more complex semantics of the weaker models, it is desirable to show that the weaker models are equivalent to the stricter models for certain classes of programs. Such equivalences would be useful. For example, a programmer can write programs under the well defined semantics of the sequential consistency model, and as long as the program satisfies the restrictions, it can safely be executed under the more efficient release consistency model.

Let us first restrict the programs to PL programs under sequential consistency. Given such programs, we have proved the following equivalences: $SC = WCsc = RCsc$. This is done by proving $RCsc \geq SC$ for PL programs and using the relation $SC \geq WCsc \geq RCsc$. Our proof technique is based on an extension of the formalism presented by Shasha and Snir [13]. We have included the proof for $RCsc \geq SC$ in the appendix. A similar proof can be used to show $PC = WCpc = RCpc$ for PL programs under the processor consistency model.

More equivalences can be shown if we restrict programs to those that cannot distinguish between sequential consistency and processor consistency ($SC = PC$). Given a set of restrictions on competing LOAD accesses, it can be shown that $SC = PC$.[2] The restrictions are general enough to allow for all implementations of locks, semaphores, barriers, distributed loops, and task queues that we are interested in. Given competing LOAD accesses have been restricted (therefore, $SC = PC$) and shared accesses are properly labeled to qualify the program as a PL program under SC, it is easily shown that $SC = PC = WCsc = RCsc = WCpc = RCpc$. Therefore, such a program could be written based on the sequential consistency model and will run correctly under release consistency (RCpc).

The above equivalences hold for PL programs only. In some programs most accesses are competing (e.g., chaotic relaxation) and must be labeled as special for proper labeling. While this will make the equivalences hold, the program's performance may not be substantially better on RCsc than on SC. However, such applications are usually robust enough to tolerate a more relaxed ordering on competing accesses. For achieving higher performance in these cases, the programmer needs to directly deal with the more complex semantics of release consistency to reason about the program.

---

[2]Given such restrictions, one can allow an atomic test-and-set used as an acquire to perform before a previous special write access (e.g., unset) has been performed. We are currently preparing a technical report that describes the details.

5 Performance Potentials for Different Models

The main purpose of examining weaker models is performance. In this section, we explore the potential gains in performance for each of the models. Realizing the full potential of a model will generally depend on the access behavior of the program and may require novel architectural and compiler techniques. Our goal is to provide intuition about how one model is more efficient than another.

The performance differences among the consistency models arise from the opportunity to overlap large latency memory accesses with independent computation and possibly other memory accesses. When the latency of an access is hidden by overlapping it with other computation, it is known as access *buffering*. When the latency of an access is hidden by overlapping with other accesses, it is known as access *pipelining*. To do buffering and pipelining for read accesses requires prefetch capability (non-blocking loads).

We provide simple bounds for the maximum performance gain of each model compared to a base execution model. The base model assumes that the processor is stalled on every access that results in a cache miss. It is easily shown that sequential consistency and processor consistency can at best gain a factor of 2 and 3, respectively, over the base model. This gain arises from the opportunity to buffer accesses. In practice though these two models are not expected to perform much better than the base model, since access buffering is not effective when the frequency of shared accesses is high.

The weak and release consistency models can potentially provide large gains over the base model, since accesses and computation in the region between two adjacent synchronization points can be overlapped freely as long as uniprocessor dependences are respected. In this case, the maximum gain over the base model is approximately equal to t_{lat}/t_{ser}, where t_{lat} is the latency of a miss and t_{ser} is the shortest delay between the issue of two consecutive accesses that miss in a cache. Intuitively, this is because ordinary accesses within a region can be pipelined. Unlike the maximum gains for SC and PC, the potential gains for WC and RC are more realizable. For example, several numerical applications fetch and update large arrays as part of their computations. The pipelining of reads and writes in such applications can lead to large performance gains.

The difference in performance between WC and RC arises when the occurrence of special accesses is more frequent. While weak consistency requires ordinary accesses to perform in the region between two synchronization points, release consistency relaxes this by allowing an ordinary access to occur anywhere between the previous acquire and the next release. In addition, an acquire can perform without waiting for previous ordinary accesses and ordinary accesses can perform without waiting for a release. Figure 4 shows an example that highlights the difference between the two models (assume that there are no local dependences).

To illustrate the performance gains made possible by the release consistency model, we consider the example of doing updates to a distributed hash table. Each bucket in the table is protected by a lock. A processor acquires the lock for a bucket first. Next, several words are read from records in that bucket, some computation is performed, and several words are written based on the result of the computation. Finally, the lock is released. The processor then moves on to do the same se-

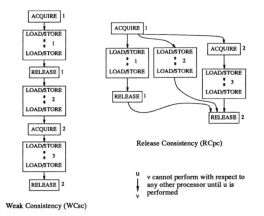

Weak Consistency (WCsc)

Release Consistency (RCpc)

$u \downarrow v$ v cannot perform with respect to any other processor until u is performed

Figure 4: Possible overlap difference between WCsc and RCpc.

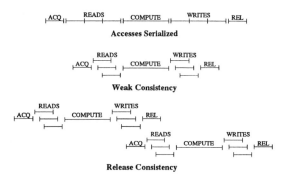

Accesses Serialized

Weak Consistency

Release Consistency

Figure 5: Overlap in processing hash table buckets.

quence of operations on another bucket. Such operations are common in several applications (for example, token hash tables in OPS5 [6]). The locality of data in such an application is low since the hash table can be large and several other processors may have modified an entry from the last time it was accessed. Therefore, the read and write accesses will miss often.

Under sequential consistency, all accesses and computation become serialized. With weak consistency, the reads can be pipelined. Of course, this assumes the architecture allows multiple outstanding reads. All reads need to complete before the computation. Once the computation completes, the writes occur in a pipelined fashion. However, before releasing the lock, all writes need to complete. The lock for the next record can not be acquired until the previous lock is released.

Release consistency provides the most opportunity for overlap. Within a critical section, the overlap is the same as in weak consistency. However, while the release is being delayed for the writes to complete, the processor is free to move on to the next record to acquire the lock and start the reads. Thus, there is overlap between the writes of one critical section and the reads of the next section.

To make the example more concrete, assume the latency of a miss is 40 cycles. Consider read miss, write miss, acquiring a lock, and releasing a lock as misses. Assume t_{ser} is 10 cycles and the computation time is 100 cycles. Assume three read misses and three write misses in each record lookup and update. If all accesses are serialized, each critical section takes 420 cycles. With weak consistency, the read misses before the computation and the write misses after the computation can be pipelined. The three read misses will complete in 60 cycles. The same is true for the write misses. Therefore, the critical section completes in 300 cycles on an implementation with weak consistency. Under release consistency, the same overlap is possible within a critical section. In addition, there is overlap between critical sections. Therefore, the processor can move on to the next critical section every 230 cycles. Figure 5 shows the overlap differences among sequential, weak, and release consistency. The segments shown span the time from the issue to the completion of an access. An access may be initiated by the processor several cycles before it is issued to the memory system.

6 Implementation Issues

The two most important issues from an implementation point of view are correctness and performance. The consistency model determines what a correct implementation of the memory system must provide. The challenge for a correct implementation is to achieve the full performance potential of the chosen consistency model. This section presents practical implementation techniques, focusing on issues relevant to scalable architectures that use caches, distributed memory, and scalable interconnection networks.

In the following subsections, we outline the techniques for ordering accesses under the various consistency models. The problem is split between ordering accesses to the same memory block and those to different memory blocks. General solutions to achieve the proper ordering are given along with the particular solutions employed in the DASH prototype system [8]. Our discussion focuses on invalidation-based coherence protocols, although the concepts can also be applied to update-based protocols.

6.1 Inter-Block Access Ordering and the FENCE Mechanism

As a result of the distribution of the memory and the use of scalable interconnection networks, requests issued by a processor to distinct memory modules may execute out of order. To maintain order among two accesses, we need a mechanism to delay the issue of one access until the previous one has been performed.[3] This requires each processor to keep track of its outstanding accesses. Due to multiple paths and variable delays within the memory system, acknowledge messages from target memories and caches are required to signal the completion of an access.

We refer to the mechanism for delaying the issue of accesses as a *fence* [3, 5, 13]. We define a general set of fence operations and demonstrate how these fence operations can be used to implement the consistency models presented earlier. While

---

[3]There is a subtle difference between delaying issue and delaying an access from being performed with respect to any other processor. Instead of delaying the issue of a write, the processor can delay making the new value visible to other processors. The write is considered performed when the new value is made visible to other processors. This allows write accesses to be pipelined. We are studying hardware techniques that exploit this distinction for write accesses in invalidate-based machines. However, we do not consider such techniques in this paper.

Model	Operation Preceded by Fence	Fence Type	Previous Accesses that must be performed	
			LOAD	STORE
SC	LOAD	full	G	P
	STORE	full	G	P
PC	LOAD	full	P	
	STORE	write	P	P

Figure 6: Fence operations to achieve sequential and processor consistency. P denotes performed while G denotes globally performed.

fence operations are described here as explicit operations, it is possible, and often desirable, to implicitly associate fences with load, store, and special (e.g., acquire, release) accesses.

For generality, we assume that load operations are non-blocking. The processor can proceed after the load is issued, and is only delayed if the destination register of the load is accessed before the value has returned. In contrast, a blocking load stalls the processor until it is performed.

Fence operations can be classified by the operations they delay and the operations they wait upon. Useful operations to delay are: (i) all future read and write accesses (*full fence*); (ii) all future write accesses (*write fence*), and (iii) only the access immediately following the fence (*immediate fence*). Likewise, useful events to wait for are a combination of previous load accesses, store accesses, and (for the weaker models) special accesses.

Figure 6 shows the placement and type of fence operations required to achieve sequential and processor consistency. For example, the first line for SC in the figure indicates that the fence prior to a load is a full fence waiting for all previous loads to globally perform and all previous stores to perform. Figure 7 shows the fence operations necessary to achieve weak consistency (WCsc) and release consistency (RCpc). The implementations outlined are the most aggressive implementation for each model in that only the delays that are necessary are enforced. Conservative implementations are possible whereby hardware complexity is reduced by allowing some extra delays.

To implement fences, a processor must keep track of outstanding accesses by keeping appropriate counters. A count is incremented upon the issue of the access, and is decremented when the acknowledges come back for that access (an acknowledge for a read access is simply the return value). For full and write fences, the number of counters necessary is a function of the number of different kinds of accesses that need to be distinguished. For example, RCpc needs to distinguish four groups of accesses: ordinary, nsync load, acquire, and special store accesses. Therefore, an aggressive implementation requires four counters. However, only two counters are required if special loads are blocking. For immediate fences, the same number of counters (as for full or write fence) is required for each outstanding immediate fence. Therefore, we have to multiply this number by the number of immediate fences that are allowed to be outstanding. Slightly conservative implementations of release consistency may simply distinguish special load accesses from other accesses by using two counters (only one if special loads are blocking) and limit the number of outstanding immediate fences to a small number.

Full fences can be implemented by stalling the processor until the appropriate counts are zero. A write fence can be implemented by stalling the write buffer. The immediate fence, which is only required in release consistency (for an aggressive implementation), requires the most hardware. Each delayed operation requires an entry with its own set of counters. In addition, accesses and acknowledges need to be tagged to distinguish which entry's counters should be decremented upon completion. In the DASH prototype (discussed in Section 6.3), a write fence is substituted for the immediate fence (load accesses are blocking), thus providing a conservative implementation of release consistency.

6.2 Intra-Block Ordering of Accesses

The previous section discussed ordering constraints on accesses to different memory blocks. When caching is added to a multiprocessor, ordering among accesses to the same block becomes an issue also. For example, it is possible to receive a read request to a memory block that has invalidations pending due to a previous write. There are subtle issues involved with servicing the read request while invalidations are pending. Cache blocks of larger than one word further complicate ordering, since accesses to different words in the block can cause a similar interaction.

In an invalidation-based coherence protocol, a store operation to a non-dirty location requires obtaining exclusive ownership and invalidating other cached copies of the block. Such invalidations may reach different processors at different times and acknowledge messages are needed to indicate that the store is performed. In addition, ownership accesses to the same block must be serialized to ensure only one value persists. Unfortunately, the above two measures are not enough to guarantee correctness. It is important to distinguish between dirty cache lines with pending invalidates versus those with no pending invalidates. Otherwise, a processor cache may give up its ownership to a dirty line with invalidates pending to a read or write request by another processor, and the requesting processor would not be able to detect that the line returned was not performed. The requesting processor could then improperly pass through a fence operation that requires all previous loads to be globally performed (if access was a read) or all previous stores to be performed (if access was a write). Consequently, read and ownership requests to a block with pending invalidates must either be delayed (by forcing retry or delaying in a buffer) until the invalidations are complete, or if the request is serviced, the requesting processor must be notified of the outstanding status and acknowledges should be forwarded to it to indicate the completion of the store. The first alternative provides atomic store operations. The second alternative doesn't guarantee atomicity of the store, but informs the requesting processor when the store has performed with respect to all processors. In the next subsection, we will discuss the specific implementation technique used in DASH.

The issues in update-based cache coherence schemes are slightly different. In an update-based scheme, a store operation to a location requires updating other cache copies. To maintain coherence, updates to the same block need to be serialized at a central point and updates must reach each cache in that order. In addition, SC-based models are difficult to implement because copies of a location get updated at different times (it is virtually impossible to provide atomic stores). Consequently, a load may return a value from a processor's cache, with no indication of whether the responsible store has performed with respect to all

Model	Operation Preceded by Fence	Fence Type	Previous Accesses that must be Performed			
			LOAD	STORE	SPECIAL LD	SPECIAL ST
WCsc	first LOAD/STORE after SPECIAL	full			P	P
	SPECIAL LD	full	P	P	G	P
	SPECIAL ST	full	P	P	G	P

Model	Operation Preceded by Fence	Fence Type	Previous Accesses that must be Performed					
			LOAD	STORE	NSYNC LD	ACQUIRE	NSYNC ST	RELEASE
RCpc	first LOAD/STORE after ACQUIRE	full				P		
	NSYNC LD	immediate			P	P		
	ACQUIRE	full			P	P		
	NSYNC ST	immediate			P	P	P	P
	RELEASE	immediate	P	P	P	P	P	P

Figure 7: Fence operations to achieve weak consistency and release consistency. P denotes performed while G denotes globally performed.

processors. For this reason, PC-based models are an attractive alternative for update-based coherence schemes.

6.3 The DASH Prototype

The DASH multiprocessor [8], currently being built at Stanford, implements many of the features discussed in the previous sections. The architecture consists of several processing nodes connected through a low-latency scalable interconnection network. Physical memory is distributed among the nodes. Each processing node, or *cluster*, is a Silicon Graphics POWER Station 4D/240 [2] consisting of four high-performance processors with their individual caches and a portion of the shared memory. A bus-based snoopy scheme keeps caches coherent within a cluster while inter-cluster coherence is maintained using a distributed directory-based protocol. For each memory block, the directory keeps track of remote clusters caching it, and point-to-point messages are sent to invalidate remote copies of the block.

Each cluster contains a directory controller board. This directory controller is responsible for maintaining cache coherence across the clusters and serving as the interface to the interconnection network. Of particular interest to this paper are the protocol and hardware features that are aimed at implementing the release consistency model. Further details on the protocol are given in [8].

The processor boards of the 4D/240 are designed to work only with the simple snoopy protocol of the bus. The base, single-bus system implements a processor consistency model. The single bus guarantees that operations cannot be observed out of order, and no acknowledgements are necessary. Read operations are blocking on the base machine.

In the distributed DASH environment, the release consistency model allows the processor to retire a write after it has received ownership, but before the access is performed with respect to all other processors. Therefore, a mechanism is needed to keep track of outstanding accesses. In DASH, this function is performed by the remote access cache (RAC). Corresponding to each outstanding access, the RAC maintains a count of invalidation acknowledges pending for that cache block and keeps track of the processor(s) associated with that access. In addi-

tion, the RAC maintains a counter per processor indicating the number of RAC entries (i.e., outstanding requests) in use by each processor.

To ensure proper intra-block ordering, the RAC detects accesses to blocks with pending invalidates by snooping on the cluster bus. In case of a local processor access, the RAC allows the operation to complete, but adds the new processor to the processor tag field of the RAC. Thus, the processor that has a copy of the line now shares responsibility for the block becoming performed. For remote requests (i.e., requests from processors on a different cluster) the RAC rejects the request. The RAC does not attempt to share a non-performed block with a remote processor because of the overhead of maintaining the pointer to this remote processor and the need to send an acknowledgement to this processor when the block has been performed. Rejecting the request is not as desirable as queuing the requests locally, but this would require extra buffering.

To ensure proper inter-block ordering, DASH again relies on the acknowledges in the protocol and the RAC. The per processor counter indicates the number of outstanding requests for each processor. When this count is zero, then the processor has no outstanding operations and a fence operation can complete. There are two types of fence operations in DASH: a full fence and a write fence. The full fence is implemented by stalling the processor until all previous memory operations are performed (i.e., the RAC count is zero for that processor). The less restrictive write fence is implemented by stalling the output of the processor's write-buffer until all previous memory operations are performed. This effectively blocks the processor's access to the second level cache and cluster bus.

DASH distinguishes lock and unlock synchronization operations by physical address. All synchronization variables must be partitioned to a separate area of the address space. Each unlock (release) operation includes an implicit write fence. This blocks the issuing of any further writes (including the unlock operation) from that processor until all previous writes have been performed. This implicit write fence provides a sufficient implementation for release consistency. The explicit forms of full and write fence operations are also available. These allow the programmer or compiler to synthesize other consistency models.

23

7 Concluding Remarks

The issue of what memory consistency model to implement in hardware is of fundamental importance to the design of scalable multiprocessors. In this paper, we have proposed a new model of consistency, called release consistency. Release consistency exploits information about the property of shared-memory accesses to impose fewer restrictions on event ordering than previously proposed models, and thus offers the potential for higher performance. To avoid having the programmer deal directly with the more complex semantics associated with the release consistency model, we presented a framework for distinguishing accesses in programs so that the same results are obtained under RC and SC models. In particular, we introduced the notion of properly-labeled (PL) programs and proved the equivalence between the SC and the RCsc model for PL programs. This is an important result since programmers can use the well defined semantics of sequential consistency to write their programs, and as long as the programs are PL, they can be safely executed on hardware implementing the release consistency model.

To implement the various consistency models, we propose the use of fence operations. Three different kinds of fence operations – full fence, write fence, and immediate fence – were identified. Careful placement of these multiple types of fences enabled us to minimize the duration for which the processor is blocked. We also discussed subtle ordering problems that arise in multiprocessors with caches and provided solutions to them. Finally, practical implementation techniques were presented in the context of the Stanford DASH multiprocessor.

We are currently building the prototype for the DASH architecture, which supports the release consistency model. We are using a simulator for the system to quantify the performance differences among the models on real applications and to explore alternative implementations for each model. We are also exploring compiler techniques to exploit the less strict restrictions of release consistency. Finally, we are investigating programming language and programming environment enhancements that allow the compiler to gather higher level information about the shared accesses.

8 Acknowledgments

We would like to thank Rohit Chandra for several useful discussions, and Jaswinder Pal Singh and Sarita Adve for their comments on the paper. We also wish to thank the reviewers for their helpful comments. This research was supported by DARPA contract N00014-87-K-0828. Daniel Lenoski is supported by Tandem Computer Incorporated. Phillip Gibbons is supported in part by NSF grant CCR-86-10181 and DARPA contract N00014-88-K-0166.

References

[1] Sarita Adve and Mark Hill. Personal communication. March 1990.

[2] Forest Baskett, Tom Jermoluk, and Doug Solomon. The 4D-MP graphics superworkstation: Computing + graphics = 40 MIPS + 40 MFLOPS and 100,000 lighted polygons per second. In *Proceedings of the 33rd IEEE Computer Society International Conference – COMPCON 88*, pages 468–471, February 1988.

[3] W. C. Brantley, K. P. McAuliffe, and J. Weiss. RP3 processor-memory element. In *Proceedings of the 1985 International Conference on Parallel Processing*, pages 782–789, 1985.

[4] Michel Dubois, Christoph Scheurich, and Fayé Briggs. Memory access buffering in multiprocessors. In *Proceedings of the 13th Annual International Symposium on Computer Architecture*, pages 434–442, June 1986.

[5] James R. Goodman. Cache consistency and sequential consistency. Technical Report no. 61, SCI Committee, March 1989.

[6] Anoop Gupta, Milind Tambe, Dirk Kalp, Charles Forgy, and Allen Newell. Parallel implementation of OPS5 on the Encore multiprocessor: Results and analysis. *International Journal of Parallel Programming*, 17(2):95–124, 1988.

[7] Leslie Lamport. How to make a multiprocessor computer that correctly executes multiprocess programs. *IEEE Transactions on Computers*, C-28(9):241–248, September 1979.

[8] Dan Lenoski, James Laudon, Kourosh Gharachorloo, Anoop Gupta, and John Hennessy. The directory-based cache coherence protocol for the DASH multiprocessor. In *Proceedings of the 17th Annual International Symposium on Computer Architecture*, May 1990.

[9] G. F. Pfister, W. C. Brantley, D. A. George, S. L. Harvey, W. J. Kleinfelder, K. P. McAuliffe, E. A. Melton, V. A. Norton, and J. Weiss. The IBM research parallel processor prototype (RP3): Introduction and architecture. In *Proceedings of the 1985 International Conference on Parallel Processing*, pages 764–771, 1985.

[10] C. Scheurich and M. Dubois. Correct memory operation of cache-based multiprocessors. In *Proceedings of the 14th Annual International Symposium on Computer Architecture*, pages 234–243, June 1987.

[11] Christoph Scheurich. *Access Ordering and Coherence in Shared Memory Multiprocessors*. PhD thesis, University of Southern California, May 1989.

[12] G. E. Schmidt. The Butterfly parallel processor. In *Proceedings of the Second International Conference on Supercomputing*, pages 362–365, 1987.

[13] Dennis Shasha and Marc Snir. Efficient and correct execution of parallel programs that share memory. *ACM Transactions on Programming Languages and Systems*, 10(2):282–312, April 1988.

Appendix A: Proof for SC = RCsc

In this appendix we present a proof of the equivalence between SC and $RCsc$ for PL programs (with respect to SC). For brevity, we will use the terms RC to denote $RCsc$ and PL to denote PL programs properly-labeled with respect to SC. We begin with a few definitions.

An *execution* of a program on an implementation defines a pair, (T, EO), as follows.

- The *per-processor trace*, T, is a set of traces, one for each processor, showing the instructions executed by the processor during the execution. The order among instructions in the trace is adjusted to depict program order for each processor.

- The execution order, EO, specifies the order in which conflicting accesses are executed. (Recall from section 3 that two accesses, u and v, *conflict* if and only if u and v are to the same location and one is a STORE.) EO fully specifies the results of a program, since any sequential execution of the accesses in an order that extends the execution order (i.e., topological sort) will give the same result.

The *delay relation*, D, is an ordering constraint among instructions within a processor as imposed by some event ordering. For example, the delay relation for RC enforces Condition 3.1, as well as local data and control dependences. These notions of execution order, conflicting accesses, and delay relation were developed previously in [13]. To prove various equivalences, we extend the notions presented in [13] to handle conditionals, non-atomic writes, and consistency models other than SC (we are preparing a technical report on this). Although writes are not atomic, we can assume that conflicting accesses are totally ordered by EO since the implementations we are considering provide cache coherence (i.e., all processors observe two writes to the same location in the same order). Also we make the common assumption that accesses are only to words of memory: each read access returns the value written by some (single) write access.

The execution order EO on an implementation is considered legal if $EO \cup D$ is acyclic. The graph corresponding to $EO \cup D$ is called the *precedence graph*, G, of the execution. Thus a cycle in G denotes an impossible execution. An instruction x *reaches* an instruction y in an execution if there is a (directed) path from x to y in the precedence graph of the execution.

We partition EO into two disjoint sets, EO_s and EO_o, where EO_s defines the execution order among any two (conflicting) special accesses and E_o defines the execution order among any two (conflicting) accesses where at least one is an ordinary access. Likewise, G is partitioned into G_s and G_o.

Given these preliminary definitions, we now proceed with the proof. We first assume that special accesses are not affected by ordinary accesses. This permits us to claim that $EO_{s:SC} = EO_{s:RC}$ follows if $T_{SC} = T_{RC}$. We will later describe how this restriction can be lifted. In lemma 1, we show that if the same per-processor trace can occur on both SC and RC, then the program results are the same. This lemma is then used to prove the main theorem, which shows that $SC = RC$ for all PL programs. The difficulty in extending the lemma to the main theorem is in showing that any legal trace on RC may occur on SC despite any conditional branches or indirect addressing. Note that $SC \geq RC$ for any program, so it suffices to show that $RC \geq SC$.

Lemma 1: Consider an execution $E = (T_{RC}, EO_{RC})$ on RC of a PL program. If there exists a trace on SC such that $T_{SC} = T_{RC}$, then there is a corresponding execution on SC with the same results (i.e., $EO_{SC} = EO_{RC}$).
Proof: Since the event ordering on special accesses is SC for both implementations, and special accesses are not affected by ordinary accesses, $G_{s:SC} = G_{s:RC}$ is a legal precedence graph for special accesses on SC. We will show there exists a legal execution on SC, based on $G_{s:SC}$, such that $EO_{o:SC} = EO_{o:RC}$.

Let u and v be two conflicting accesses from T_{SC}, such that u is an ordinary access. If u and v are on the same processor, then the execution order, EO, between the two is determined by local dependences and is enforced in the same way on SC and RC.

If u and v are on different processors, then the two accesses need to be ordered through special accesses for the program to be a PL program. Access v can be either an ordinary or a special access. Consider the case where v is an ordinary access. For u and v to be ordered, there is either (a) a release REL_u and an acquire ACQ_v

such that REL_u reaches ACQ_v in $G_{s:SC}$ or (b) a release REL_v and an acquire ACQ_u such that REL_v reaches ACQ_u in $G_{s:SC}$. If (a) holds, then u before v, $uEOv$, is the only possible execution order on SC. The same is true on RC, since $vEOu$ will lead to a cycle in the precedence graph. This is because clauses (A) and (B) of Condition 3.1 are upheld. Likewise, a symmetric argument can be used if (b) holds. The same correspondence between SC and RC can be shown for the case where v is a special access. Thus the execution order EO between u and v is the same on SC and RC.

Since $EO_{s:SC} = EO_{s:RC}$, and this execution order determines an E_o that is the same for both SC and RC, we have shown that $EO_{SC} = EO_{RC}$. $\square$

Therefore, $RC \geq SC$ for a program if, for every execution of a program on RC, there is an execution on SC such that the traces are the same.

How can the traces for a program on SC and RC differ? There are two possible sources for any discrepancies between traces: conditional control flow (affecting which instructions are executed) and indirect addressing (affecting the location accessed by a read or write instruction). In what follows, we consider only conditionals. Extending the argument to handle programs with indirect addressing is trivial, and omitted in this proof.

We will prove that $SC = RC$ for PL programs as follows. We must show that there exists an execution on SC in which the outcome of each conditional is the same. A conditional for which we have shown this correspondence will be designated *proven*, otherwise it will be called *unproven*. Initially, all conditionals in the trace on RC are *unproven*. We will construct the trace on SC inductively in a series of stages, where at each stage, we show that an unproven conditional occurs the same way on SC. Once all conditionals are proven, the traces must be equal and we can apply lemma 1.

Theorem 2: $SC = RC$ for PL programs.
Proof: Let P be a PL program. Consider any execution $E = (T_{RC}, EO_{RC})$ on RC. Let G_{RC} be the precedence graph for E. By the definition of a precedence graph, any instruction that affected another instruction in E, e.g., affected the existence of a write access or the value returned on a read access, reaches that instruction in G_{RC}.

As indicated above, we proceed in a series of stages, one for each conditional. At each stage, we construct an execution on SC such that some unproven conditional and all previously proven conditionals have the same outcome on SC and RC.

We begin with stage 1. The proof for stage 1 will be shown using a series of claims. As we shall see, the proof for each remaining stage is identical to stage 1.

Since G_{RC} is acyclic, there is at least one unproven conditional, u_1, that is not reached by any other unproven conditional. Let p_{u_1} be the processor that issued u_1. Let A_1 be the set of instructions that reach u_1 in G_{RC}. Although A_1 is only a subtrace (not even a prefix) of the entire execution E, we will show that the set A_1, constructed in this way, can be used to prove u_1.

Let A_{1s} be the special accesses in A_1. We have the following characterization of A_{1s}.

Claim 1: All special accesses program ordered prior to an access in A_{1s} are themselves in A_{1s}. There are no special accesses within any branch of an unproven conditional, u, where u is program ordered prior to an access in A_{1s}.
Proof: We first show that the claim holds for acquires. Any acquire program ordered prior to an access, x, in A_1 reaches x and hence will itself be in A_{1s}. There are no acquires within any branch of an unproven conditional program ordered prior to an access in A_{1s} since no access after such a conditional can complete prior to the conditional itself.

We claim that the last program ordered access in A_1 for each processor (other than p_{u_1}) is a special access. This fact can be shown by contradiction. Let z_1, an ordinary access, be the last program

25

ordered access for some processor in A_1 (other than p_{u_1}). Since z_1 is in A_1, there is a path, $z_1, z_2, \ldots, u_1$, in G_{RC}. No access in A_1 is locally dependent on z_1 since it is the last program ordered access on its processor. Since P is a PL program, a release below z_1 is needed to order the access ahead of z_2 on SC. However, there is no release below z_1 in A_1. Thus the only way for z_1 to affect z_2 on RC would be in a competing manner that was prevented on SC. This can happen only if some acquire above either z_1 or z_2 were missing in A_{1s}, which contradicts the claim of the previous paragraph.

Claim 1 follows since program order is preserved on RC for special accesses. □

Given this characterization of A_{1s}, we show that there is an execution on SC such that special accesses are the same as in A_1. In other words, we show that both implementations have the same G_s for A_1. This will be used to show that the results returned by read accesses are the same and hence the outcome of conditional u_1 is the same.

Claim 2: There is a prefix of an execution on SC such that the special accesses are precisely the accesses in A_{1s} and the execution order among these special accesses is identical to $EO_{s:RC}$.
Proof: The special accesses in A_{1s} are self-contained, i.e., there are no acquires in A_{1s} that are waiting on releases not in A_{1s}. By claim 1, there is an execution on SC such that all special accesses in A_{1s} occur. Since special accesses are SC on both implementations, the same execution order among these special accesses is possible on both. To complete the proof, we argue that no other special access (i.e., not in $A1_s$) can be forced to occur prior to an access in $A1_s$ in every execution on SC that includes $A1_s$. How can a special access be forced to occur on SC? Either the special access is program ordered prior to some access in A_{1s} or it is a release satisfying an acquire that is not satisfied in A_{1s}. But the former case contradicts claim 1 and the latter case contradicts A_{1s} being self-contained. Thus there is an execution on SC and a point in this execution in which the special accesses performed are precisely the accesses in $A1_s$, and the execution order among these special accesses is identical to $EO_{s:RC}$. □

Claim 3: There is an execution on SC in which the outcome of u_1 is the same as in E.
Proof: Since A_1 consists of all instructions that affect u_1 in E, the outcome of u_1 in the full execution E is determined by only the accesses in A_1. Thus it suffices to show that (a) there is an execution E_{SC} on SC in which the instructions in A_1 occur, (b) all read accesses in A_1 return the same results in E_{SC} as in E, and (c) the outcome of u_1 in E_{SC} is determined by only the accesses in A_1.

The accesses in A_1 will occur on SC since none of them are within an unproven conditional. This follows from the fact that if an access within a conditional can reach u_1, then so can its conditional (since RC enforces control dependence).

Consider the prefix execution, E_1, constructed in claim 2, and let EO_{1s} be the execution order among special accesses in A_1. Since E_1 is a prefix of a PL program, EO_{1s} determines $EO_{o:SC}$ for the accesses in A_1.

We claim that EO_{1s} determines $EO_{o:RC}$ for the accesses in A_1. We must show that the instructions in E_1 that are not in A_1 have no effect on the results returned by read accesses in A_1. Consider a write access, w_1, in E_1 that reaches a read access, r_1, in A_1 on SC, but does not reach it in G_{RC}. Since r_1 is in A_1, it cannot be reached on G_{RC} by an unproven conditional. Thus any local dependence chain from w_1 to r_1, inclusive, does not include any instruction within an unproven conditional. Hence, if there is a local dependence on SC, then there will be one on RC. Moreover, if w_1 is ordinary, then it must be followed by a release on SC. Since all accesses complete on RC prior to a release, w_1 must be in A_1 and reach the release in G_{RC}. Since EO_{1s} is the execution order for both SC and RC, w_1 must reach r_1 in G_{RC}. Similarly, if w_1 is a special access, it must reach r_1 in G_{RC}. In either case, we have a contradiction.

Therefore, the results returned by read accesses in A_1 on SC depend only on other accesses in A_1. Thus we can view the traces as being the same. Hence by lemma 1, all read accesses in A_1 up to the last special access on p_{u_1} return the same results in E_{SC} as in E.

Finally, the outcome of conditional u_1 depends on the values read by p_{u_1}. These read accesses can be ordinary or special. Since P is a PL program, an ordinary read access affecting u_1 returns the value of a write access, w_1, that is ordered by local dependence or through an acquire. A special read access affecting u_1 is already shown to return the correct value. Thus the outcome of u_1 is the same as in E. □

Stage $k > 1$. Inductively, we can assume that $k-1$ unproven conditionals have been shown to correspond on SC and RC, such that there is a kth unproven conditional, u_k, that is not reached by any other unproven conditional. At this stage, we add to the current subtrace all instructions that can reach u_k. Let A_k be this new set of instructions. As before, although A_k is not a complete trace on SC (or even a prefix), we can argue that there is at least one execution on SC such that (1) the same G_s occurs on A_k in both SC and RC, and thus (2) the outcome of u_k is the same as in E. The arguments are identical to those in claims 1–3 above, where $u_1, \ldots, u_{k-1}$ are no longer unproven conditionals.

Therefore, by induction, there is an execution on SC such that the outcome of all conditionals is the same as in E. Since all unprovens correspond, we know that the full traces are equal. Thus there exists a valid trace T_{SC} of P on SC such that $T_{SC} = T_{RC}$. Hence by lemma 1, there exists an execution on SC such that $E_{SC} = E_{RC}$, i.e., the results are the same. This shows that $RC \geq SC$ for P. Since $SC \geq RC$, it follows that $RC = SC$ for P. □

We have assumed for the above proof that special accesses are not affected by ordinary accesses. This is used in the proof, for example, when we assume in lemma 1 that $EO_{s:SC} = EO_{s:RC}$ follows if $T_{SC} = T_{RC}$. In general, however, an ordinary access can affect a special access, e.g., it can be to the same location. Our proof can be extended to handle this general case in which special accesses are affected by ordinary accesses, as follows. Consider special read accesses, conditional branches, and accesses with indirect addressing all to be initially unproven. As above, include one new unproven at each stage, until all are proven. Since we are proving special read accesses along the way, we ensure the correspondence among special accesses between SC and RC at each stage (i.e., $EO_{s:SC} = EO_{s:RC}$). Therefore, theorem 2 holds for general PL programs.

Adve and Hill [1] have proved a similar equivalence between sequential consistency and their version of weak ordering.

Synchronization with Multiprocessor Caches *

Joonwon Lee   *Umakishore Ramachandran*

School of Information and Computer Science
Georgia Institute of Technology
Atlanta, Georgia 30332 USA
e-mail: joon@sybil.gatech.edu, rama@gatech.edu

Abstract

Introducing private caches in bus-based shared memory
multiprocessors leads to the cache consistency problem
since there may be multiple copies of shared data. However, the ability to snoop on the bus coupled with the fast
broadcast capability allows the design of special hardware
support for synchronization. We present a new lock-based
cache scheme which incorporates synchronization into the
cache coherency mechanism. With this scheme high-level
synchronization primitives as well as low-level ones can
be implemented without excessive overhead. Cost functions for well-known synchronization methods are derived
for invalidation schemes, write update schemes, and our
lock-based scheme. To accurately predict the performance
implications of the new scheme, a new simulation model
is developed embodying a widely accepted paradigm of
parallel programming. It is shown that our lock-based
protocol outperforms existing cache protocols.

1 Introduction

Cache memories have been used to reduce memory access latency in uniprocessors. In bus-based shared memory multiprocessors they may additionally reduce bus contention. However, private caches introduce the cache coherence problem [8]. The shared bus enables each cache
controller to monitor the bus traffic and initiate appropriate actions to keep the shared data coherent. A group
of cache coherence schemes called *snooping cache protocols*
use this feature [13, 16, 18, 19, 24]. They are implemented
in hardware and may not be visible to the programmer.

Most snooping cache protocols (Section 2) do not take
into account synchronization requests that usually precede
shared data accesses. Therefore, strong coherence among
multiple copies is blindly enforced resulting in possibly
unnecessary bus traffic for invalidation and data transfer.
Usually, access to shared data is acquired via synchronization methods such as locks, semaphores, and barriers.
Thus there is additional delay in accessing the synchronization variables and then acquiring the actual data.

In this paper, we present a cache coherence protocol supporting lock primitives (Section 3). Our scheme
utilizes locking information provided by the software
(e.g. compiler) to distinguish between shared-locks and
exclusive-locks. We construct a distributed hardware-
assisted FIFO queue of processors waiting for a given lock.
With this scheme, the cache mechanism emerges as a visible part of the architecture since programmers should understand it to develop efficient parallel programs.

Efficient interprocessor synchronization and mutual exclusion are imperative to assure good performance for parallel programs. Therefore, we must evaluate the synchronization efficiency of cache protocols (Section 4).

Evaluating a multiprocessor system is a challenging
task. Trace driven simulation has been used for multiprocessor evaluation [1, 11, 12, 25], but tracing parallel
programs has so far been restricted to a small number
of processors. Furthermore, the trace is affected by the
host multiprocessor's architectural characteristics such as
cache protocol, synchronization primitives, and interconnection
network. As Bitar [4] points out using traces generated by software makes it difficult to verify the validity
of the predicted results. Therefore, we have developed a
new method for the evaluation of cache protocols. Our
simulation model and some results are presented in Section 5.

2 Snooping Caches

Hardware cache coherency schemes for shared-bus multiprocessors have evolved into two categories, namely, *invalidation* schemes and *write update* schemes.

In invalidation schemes [13, 16], a write to a cached
line results in invalidating copies of this line present in
other caches. If writes to cached data always trigger invalidations, the bus is easily saturated with even a few
participating processors [27]. To reduce the invalidation
rate, Goodman developed the *write once* protocol [13] in
which only the first write to a cached data updates main
memory, and is used as a cue by other caches for invalidating their own copies. The Berkeley protocol [16] assumes
an invalidation line on the bus to explicitly invalidate peer
caches. Since an invalidation is induced even with a first

---

*This work is supported in part by NSF grant MIP-8809268

CH2887-8/90/0000/0027$01.00 © 1990 IEEE

W-Run length	Invalidation Scheme	W-Update Scheme	Competitive Snoopy
1	8.0	1.0	1.0
3	2.67	1.0	1.0
8	1.0	1.0	1.0
9	0.89	1.0	1.78
10	0.8	1.0	1.6
20	0.4	1.0	0.8

Table 1: Cost for cache coherency.

write to data that is not being shared, there still exist redundant invalidations. These schemes lead to repeated invalidations and frequent data transfers when data is actively shared by many processors.

In write update schemes [18, 24], writes are broadcast and caches with matching entries update their corresponding cache lines. Using a probabilistic simulation model, Archibald and Baer [2] have shown that write update schemes outperform invalidation schemes. However, using trace driven simulation, Eggers and Katz [11] have shown that neither scheme dominates entirely. The performance of both schemes is sensitive to the sharing pattern. Particularly important is the length of the uninterrupted sequence of write requests interspersed with reads to a shared cache line by one processor (referred to as a *write-run* in [11]). The *length* of a write-run is the number of writes in that write-run. A write-run is terminated when another processor reads or writes the same cache line. Every new write-run requires an invalidation and data transfer. When write-runs are short the invalidation scheme generates frequent invalidations and the write update scheme generates equally frequent updates. Since the total cost for invalidation plus data transfer is much higher than the update of one word, invalidation schemes are inferior for this sharing pattern. For long write-runs, write update schemes perform poorly in comparison to invalidation schemes because of frequent write broadcasts. Repeated updates are clearly redundant given long write-runs. The optimal strategy would be to drop cache lines from all processors other than the writing processor. Thus the performance of both schemes critically depends on the sharing pattern.

In [15], a dynamic cache scheme called *competitive snoopy caching* is introduced. Among several variants presented in the paper, "Limited Block Snoopy Caching" is the most practical. First, the protocol begins by operating like a write update scheme. But, when the length of the write-run exceeds a threshold the cache scheme switches to the invalidation strategy. An important feature of this protocol is *read snarfing* which allows caches to grab a cache line that is being transferred on the bus. This feature allows several readers to acquire a cache line in a single bus transaction following a long write-run. This cache scheme guarantees a lower bound for any sequence of memory requests when the threshold is equal to the block size.

Let p be the block size, which is also the threshold. Let

n be the number of writes among a sequence σ of requests to a single shared address, l_i be the length of i-th write-run, and $\bar{l}$ be the average write-run length. If there are k write-runs $\bar{l} = n/k$. For simplicity of analysis, let n be a multiple of k. Since there are k write-runs the invalidation scheme costs $k \times C_{IX}$ where C_{IX} is the cost for invalidating and transferring a block between processors. The subscripts of C denote the type of transaction: I for invalidation, X for block transfer, W for write update. Note that C_I is usually much smaller than C_W. The write update scheme, regardless of the write-run lengths, costs nC_W where C_W is the cost for one word update of matching cache lines. Since C_{IX} is roughly $p \times C_W$, the total cost of the invalidation scheme is $p/\bar{l}$ times that of the write update scheme. Hence when the write-run length is short and the block size is large, the invalidation scheme generates more bus traffic for cache coherency. If $\bar{l} > p$, the invalidation scheme outperforms the write update scheme by the factor $\bar{l}/p$. Let a be the number of write-runs whose lengths are larger than the threshold p. If $\bar{l}'$ is the average length of such write-runs then the total number of writes in these write-runs is $a\bar{l}'$. Since n is the total number of writes in the whole sequence σ and since $p \leq \bar{l}'$, it follows that $ap \leq n$. The upper bound for the total cost of the competitive snoopy scheme is

$$nC_W + aC_{IX} = nC_W + apC_W$$
$$\leq 2nC_W$$

Thus in the worst case, the competitive snoopy scheme is inferior by a constant factor, namely 2, for any memory request sequence. Table 1 shows the cost relative to the write update scheme for processing the sequence σ by each of the schemes when the block size p is 8.

The protocols considered thus far treat cache coherence problem in isolation and do not consider synchronization issues. Bitar and Despain [5] propose a scheme in which the cache accepts lock and unlock commands from the processor in addition to the traditional read and write requests. On receiving a lock request, the cache broadcasts a write on the bus. If the write is allowed, the cache sets the state to locked and allows the processor to use the line. Otherwise, the line is in use by another cache. So, the requesting cache stores the address of the line in a special register called the *busy-wait* register and the cache holding the lock sets its cache line state to *lock-wait* indicating there is at least one waiting processor. Upon receiving an unlock request, a cache changes its cache line state to invalid and broadcasts unlock if its state was lock-wait. This lock scheme combines lock-based synchronization with the line transfer, thus performing locking in zero time. This scheme does not distinguish between read lock and write lock requests. Since reads are a large portion of shared data access, this scheme limits potential concurrency.

In [14], Goodman et al. suggest a synchronization primitive, QOSB, which can be used by the programmer for high level synchronization operations. They present an efficient implementation of this primitive by exploiting the hardware cache consistency protocol of the multiprocessor. The first lock requester becomes the owner of the

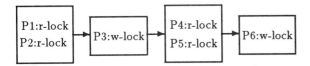

Figure 1: A waiting queue of lock requests

lock. The next requester allocates a new cache line (the *shared line*) and the address of the requesting processor is stored in main memory as the head of a queue of lock requesters. Since the data field of the shared line is invalid, this space can be used to store the address of the next requester. To know when to respond to a new requester, a tail queue pointer is also needed. Therefore, whenever a new requester appears, memory accesses are required to maintain these two queue pointers. These memory accesses can be eliminated if the primitive is implemented for a single bus multiprocessor. Like Bitar and Despain, Goodman only implements exclusive locks.

3   Lock Based Cache Protocol

At about the same time the QOSB primitive was developed, we designed a lock-based cache protocol [22] supporting exclusive and non-exclusive locks. Our lock based protocol (LBP) improves on the schemes discussed above. We chose lock primitives because of their generality. Like the queueing mechanism used in QOSB, a distributed queue is constructed using participating cache lines. In our scheme, a sharable lock is distinguished from an exclusive lock. Sharable locks enhance concurrency and are needed to efficiently implement other synchronization operations.

The processor and the cache together form a node of the shared memory multiprocessor. Each node is assigned a unique id which we refer to in this paper as *node-id*. The handshake between the cache and the bus is explained as follows. The cache entertains six requests from the processor: read, write, read-lock, write-lock, read-unlock, and write-unlock. Read and write are deemed as accesses to non-shared data and the cache processes them as would a uniprocessor cache. The granularity of a lock is a cache line. Processors must wait until the current request is satisfied before generating new requests.

Consider the sequence of lock requests, P1:read-lock, P2:read-lock, P3:write-lock, P4:read-lock, P5:read-lock, P6:write-lock, as shown in Figure 1. The first requester (P1) obtains a read-lock, and the following requester (P2) shares the lock since the lock type is *read*. P3 waits for the lock because its lock type is *write*. P4 and P5 wait after P3 to ensure fairness, even though the current lock held by P1 and P2 is sharable. A *peer-group* is a group of read-lock requesters who concurrently share a lock ({P1,P2} and {P4, P5} are peer-groups). To implement a queue, each directory entry of a cache line has a *next-node* field

States	Meaning
INVALID	The line is invalid
WO	Write lock owner.
WOT	WO at the tail.
WOV	Waiting for a write lock.
WOVT	WOV at the tail.
R	Read lock holder.
RV	Waiting for a read lock.
RO	Read lock owner.
ROT	RO at the tail.
ROV	Waiting for a read lock ownership.
ROVT	ROV at the tail
O	Unlocked, but still an owner.
OT	O at the tail.

Table 2: States of a cache line

containing the node-id of the next waiting cache if any. When a lock is released, the cache sends a *wake* signal to the next waiting cache (if any). Caches with waiting states must monitor the signals on the bus for the line address and their node-id. Note that the protocol described here assumes a single process per processor. In [22], we describe the multiprocessing case and discuss implementation issues on standard buses.

The possible states of a cache line are summarized in Table 2, where **R,W** are used to specify the lock type, **T** to signify the tail of the queue, **V** to indicate waiting state, and **O** for the ownership. State transitions are triggered by processor requests and/or bus activities. Note that the cache controllers only respond to lock and unlock requests on the bus since simple reads and writes are deemed to be for private lines. Therefore, the states in Table 1 apply only for shared lines obtained through lock requests. In the discussion to follow, we use lock and line interchangeably since lock acquisition is merged with the cache line transfer.

An owner cache has the latest copy of the line, so it provides the line to the other caches when requested. The line is written back to memory when a write-lock owner releases the lock. There is at most one owner of a lock even when the lock is shared. A lock state with a **T** suffix denotes that the cache is at the tail of the waiting queue and should respond to subsequent requests for that lock. Only the first requester within a peer-group can be a tail or an owner. A shared lock is released when the size of the peer-group reaches zero, so caches with read-lock ownership or awaiting ownership keep the size of the peer-group in a *count* field. The ownership persists even after the line is unlocked at the owner cache. Assigning read-lock ownership to the first requester may result in unnecessary cache entries since it is likely that the read-lock owner will be the first to release the lock. However, the alternative choice of giving ownership to the last one in a peer-group could generate more bus traffic to transfer the count variable to the new owner. The width of the count field is determined by the number of nodes in the system. Alternatively, the width may be determined by the maximum

state	next-node	count

Figure 2: Tag fields of a cache line

membership we would like to allow in a peer group. Each cache line has a directory entry (tag) with the fields as shown in Figure 2.

Figure 3 illustrates the state transitions. When a processor requests a read-lock, the cache broadcasts it on the bus resulting in one of following responses:

- The block came from the main memory (denoted as *hit(M)* in the state transition diagram). It means that the line is not locked by any cache. The memory system provides the line, and the cache changes the state to ROT since it is the first requester.

- The block came from another cache (denoted as *hit* in the state transition diagram). The current read-lock owner sends the cache line allowing the requester to share the lock. The receiving cache changes its state to R.

- A *wait* signal is detected on the bus. A peer cache in state ROVT sends this signal with its own node-id. Since the *wake* signal (to be discussed shortly) is addressed to the first requester in a peer-group, this node-id is necessary for the waiting nodes to receive the signal correctly. The receiving cache stores this node-id in the next-node field, and changes its state to RV.

- A *wait(T)* signal is detected on the bus. The signal comes from a cache in state WOVT or WOT, and signifies that the tail state is transferred to the requester. Therefore, the receiving cache changes its state to ROVT.

When a cache receives *read-unlock* from the processor, the state of the line is one of R, ROT, or RO. A cache line in the R state is simply changed to the state INVALID, and a read-unlock signal is broadcast on the bus to inform the owner to decrease the count. If the state is ROT or RO, it is changed to OT or O respectively after decrementing the count. The cache is still the owner even after its own processor releases the lock and is responsible for sending a wake signal when the count goes to zero. Even though we assume a single process per processor, a processor may request a lock after releasing a lock, i.e, it may request a lock when the state of the line is OT or O. This case is not shown in Figure 3 since it is treated as a sub-case of multiple processes per processor. Another simple solution without increasing hardware complexity is to allow the processor to be an owner again. In this case, the fairness between processors cannot be guaranteed.

In case of a write lock, it is not necessary for the owner to keep the count since only one writer is allowed at a time. If a wait(T) signal is detected after broadcasting a write-lock, the state is changed from INVALID to WOVT. However, it ceases to be at the tail when any subsequent

R : Bus Response
B : Bus Activity
P : Processor Request

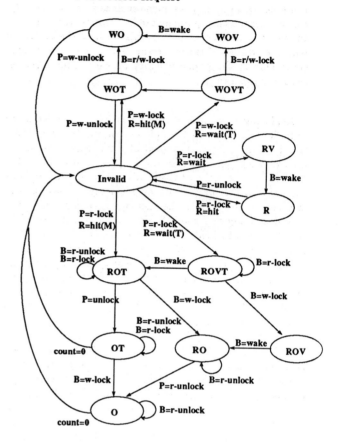

Figure 3: State Transitions

request for a lock is observed on the bus. On receiving an appropriate wake signal, the cache controller changes waiting states, WOV, WOVT, to owner states, WOT, WO respectively, and allows the processor to use the line. It is not necessary to broadcast a write-unlock. On receiving a write-unlock request from the processor, the cache changes the state of the line to INVALID, sends a wake signal enclosing the cache line to the next requester (if any) as indicated by the next-node field, and writes the line back to memory.

Bus signals include: read-lock, write-lock, read-unlock, hit, hit(M), wait, wait(T), and wake. The wait signal is sent from the tail cache to the lock requester when the lock is unavailable. The wait(T) signal additionally transfer the tail state to the requester. The wake signal is sent to notify that the lock is released to a cache whose node-id was stored in the next-node field of the tag entry for the line. Our scheme requires 13 states in the cache controller compared to 4 in most other protocols, and a larger cache tag memory to implement the distributed hardware queue.

Cache line replacement becomes tricky for lock-based protocols including ours. If the line being replaced either owns a lock or is waiting for a lock then special attention is required. In the latter case, the best strategy would be to delete this node from the queue of waiting requesters for this lock. In a bus-based scheme such as ours this strategy can be fairly easily implemented. Prior to replacement, the cache controller broadcasts this event on the bus along with the address of the successor. The predecessor (cache controller) in the queue updates its cache line entry on receiving this event.

Replacing a cache line that owns a lock is a bit more complicated. The most simple and straightforward solution is to disallow replacement of a cache line that owns a lock. However, this solution may be feasible only if a fully associative or a set-associative caching strategy is in use. If a direct mapped caching scheme is used then it is necessary to modify the memory system to hold the lock status, tag and count fields of the cache line in addition to the data field. We believe this can be done with a little added complexity to the cache controller, minimal change to the memory system, and support from the compiler. The compiler can allocate additional memory space for every shared read/write data structure for holding the auxiliary information. For instance, if the data block is 4 words, one word may be reserved by the compiler for storing the auxiliary information. The memory system has a bit for every block that indicates whether the block is locked or not, which is returned with every memory request. When a cache line is replaced, the cache controller checks the status of the cache line. If it is locked, then the cache controller writes back the data field along with the auxiliary information to the memory system. When the block is reloaded from the memory, the cache controller extracts the auxiliary information returned in the data field and stores it in the cache line. When a processor makes a lock request and the block comes from the memory, the cache controller checks the lock bit. If it is set then it is an indication that some other cache currently holds the lock. Therefore, the requesting cache has to retry the lock request at a later time.

The preceding description is only conceptual. In an actual implementation, it is not necessary that the lock bit in memory be out of band data. It is perfectly reasonable, and in fact practically feasible, to keep the lock bit in band. The compiler has to preallocate this space in the cache line and the cache controllers have to agree on the location of this lock bit in the cache line. Keeping the lock bit in band allows the use of conventional RAMs and eliminates the need for any special purpose memory system design.

In the next section, we see how our lock-based protocol aids synchronization and mutual exclusion in a parallel programming environment.

4 Synchronization Issues

Efficient synchronization is imperative for multiprocessors since parallel programs tend to generate repeated requests for mutual exclusion, barrier, and operations on shared data structures. The inefficiency caused by synchronization is twofold: wait times at synchronization points and the intrinsic overhead of the synchronization operations. Reducing waiting time is the province of the programmers. Reducing synchronization overhead is a task for the computer architect. Hardware support for synchronization comes in various forms such as a special-purpose coprocessor (e.g. Sequent SLIC [3]), a combining network [6, 10], and a special bus for interprocessor communication [26]. Recently, researchers have been interested in incorporating synchronization into snoopy cache schemes [5, 14, 22].

In the following subsections, we consider how efficiently various cache schemes (including our own) support synchronization. Three synchronization scenarios are considered. In the first (parallel lock) we assume n processors are simultaneously competing for the same lock. The second scenario (serial lock) assumes that locks are requested only serially. Finally we consider barrier notify. Similar to Goodman's QOSB primitive, a binary semaphore can be implemented very efficiently with our scheme while other schemes require mutual exclusion and queue construction.

4.1 Lock

If the machine supports an atomic test_and_set primitive then mutual exclusion can be implemented as in [20]. However, implementation of the test_and_set on traditional cache schemes can create additional penalties due to the *ping-pong* effect [9]. Since the 'set' part of the test-and-set primitive involves a write to a shared data, a spin-lock may cause each contending processor to invalidate (or update) other caches continuously. The following method avoids the ping-pong effect by busy-waiting on the cache memory without modification.

```
repeat
    while(LOAD(lock_variable) = 1) do nothing;
    /* spin without modification */
until(test_and_set(lock_variable) = 0);
```

But, it still generates considerable bus traffic when a lock is released since all the waiting processors try to modify the cache line, thus invalidating (or updating) the corresponding cache line of the other caches.

Suppose n processors are competing for a lock at the same time (labeled 'parallel lock' in Table 3). After loading the lock variable, each processor executes test_and_set, thus generating n invalidations and $n-1$ block transfers if the invalidation scheme is used. When the first lock holder releases the lock, it invalidates other copies of the lock variable. This invalidation is followed by $(n-1)$ block transfers. Now $n-1$ processors are competing for the lock. So, total cost to service all the n processors with

Scenario	LBP	W-Invalidate	W-Update	Competitive
parallel lock	$2nC_b$	$n^2C_X + \frac{n(n+3)}{2}C_I$	$\frac{n(n+3)}{2}C_W$	$2n(C_X + C_I)$
serial lock	$2nC_b$	$n(C_X + 2C_I)$	$2nC_W$	$n(C_X + 2C_I)$
barrier notify	C_b	$C_I + (n-1)C_X$	C_W	$C_I + C_X$

Table 3: Overhead of Synchronization Primitives.

the invalidation scheme is

$$\sum_{i=1}^{n}(iC_X + iC_I + (i-1)C_X + C_I)$$

where the first term inside the summation is for loading the lock variable, the second and the third terms are the result of test_and_set executed simultaneously by i processors, and the last term is for unlocking. Simplifying the summation we get $n^2C_X + \frac{n(n+3)}{2}C_I$. With the write update scheme, invalidation is replaced with write update. The cost in this case is given by

$$\sum_{i=1}^{n}(iC_W + C_W)$$

where the first term is for test_and_set and the next one is for unlocking. Both of these schemes have a complexity of $O(n^2)$. The constant factor of the invalidation scheme is larger than the write update scheme. The total cost with our scheme is $2n$ primitive bus transactions ($2nC_b$) since each processor issues lock and unlock commands on the bus. The read snarfing feature of the competitive snoopy caching allows an efficient implementation of the parallel lock. An unlock operation results in one invalidation followed by one line transfer to all the waiting requesters. The first cache which successfully performs test_and_set invalidates all the other caches. This invalidation triggers another line transfer for loading the lock variable into all the remaining caches. So, the total cost for this scheme is $2n(C_X + C_I)$.

The other extreme of lock competition is when all the n processors are serialized, i.e., only one processor requests the lock at one time. With the invalidation scheme this situation costs $n(C_X + 2C_I)$ since each processor executes load, test_and_set, and unlock. For the write update scheme it costs $2nC_W$, and for the competitive snoopy caching it costs $n(C_X + 2C_I)$. This case is termed as 'serial lock' in Table 3.

A lock request is with or without an argument. When a process needs mutual exclusion for a specific variable, the variable is specified as an argument. Even when there is not a specific variable to be locked, an argument is used if there are more than one critical sections in an epoch of parallel computation. A lock request with an argument needs twice the accesses to cache lines, one for the synchronization variable, and one for the actual data. The QOSB primitive and our cache scheme merge the two

```
init_barrier(cnt, flag);
    cnt = n;
    flag = 0;
end init_barrier;

barrier(cnt, flag)
    lock(cnt)
    cnt = cnt - 1;
    if (cnt = 0) then
        write(flag, 1);
        unlock(cnt);
    else
        unlock(cnt);
        while(flag = 0) do;
    endif;
end barrier;
```

Figure 4: Barrier implementation with snooping cache schemes

accesses into one for a cache line, and hence would show even more impressive performance than the other schemes for such requests. In Table 3 lock requests are assumed to be without arguments.

4.2 Barrier

Barrier requires all participating processors to synchronize at a certain point (the barrier). Traditional implementation of the barrier uses a counter which may become a hot-spot[1]. In [28] a software combining method is suggested to eliminate the hot-spot where processors contend to increment the counter. This method has a nice scalability property ($O(\log_2 n)$ overhead). But, considering the limit[2] on the scalability of bus-based systems (certainly below 100), the benefit of dispersing the hot-spot is offset by the overhead for shared memory access with the software combining approach. In [23], Sohi et al. describe a restricted form of fetch-and-add, namely, fetch-and-increment that allows all the participating pro-

---

[1] A specific memory location is contended for by many processors simultaneously.

[2] The electrical characteristics of the bus as well as the traffic, limits the number of processors which can be attached to a shared bus.

```
init_barrier(cnt, flag);
    cnt = n;
    write_lock(flag);
end init_barrier;

barrier(cnt, flag)
    write_lock(cnt)
    cnt = cnt − 1;
    if (cnt = 0) then
        write_unlock(flag);
        write_unlock(cnt);
    else
        write_unlock(cnt);
        read_lock(flag);
    endif;
end barrier;
```

Figure 5: Barrier implementation with LBP

cessors to perform the operation in a single bus transaction. Brooks implemented the "Butterfly barrier" with busy-waiting locks [7]. This scheme requires $2 \log_2 n$ lock operations for each processor. A more realistic implementation of the barrier with bus-based snooping caches is given in Figure 4. Processors arriving before the last one keep reading their copies of *flag* variable in their respective cache memories. When the last arrival induces a write to the flag variable, other copies are invalidated or updated according to the cache coherency protocol being used. So, the cost for notifying other processors of the last arrival is $C_I + (n − 1)C_X$ for the invalidation scheme and C_W for the write update scheme. With the read snarfing feature, the competitive snoopy caching executes barrier notification with a cost of $C_I + C_X$.

Barrier implementation with our cache scheme is given in Figure 5. In our scheme the 'wake' operation for a peer-group enables the *notify* phase to execute in one bus transaction. For the *counting* phase simple mutual exclusion is used since it is unlikely that the contention for the counting variable would cause too much overhead with an efficient lock operation. However, note that the degree of contention for the counting phase depends to a large extent on the type of work that has been farmed out to the processors before the barrier. If all the processors take roughly the same amount of time to complete their respective computations then it is likely that the contention will be high. Under such circumstances the scheme proposed by Sohi et al. [23] may prove to be quite efficient.

While synchronization issues are important, it is somewhat artificial to look at them in isolation from the point of view of system performance. To know the relative performance of cache protocols, we need to study the completion times of parallel programs with a workload comprised of private and shared data accesses interspersed with synchronization requests.

5 Performance Evaluation

Evaluating multiprocessors is difficult because of the interaction between the processors and the lack of a standard suite of benchmark applications. Recently real multiprocessor traces have become available. In [1] a tracing facility called ATUM2 is used for capturing the traces of parallel programs. However, it does not generalize for a variety of architectures due to its requirement of special hardware support and its limited scalability. Eggers and Katz [11, 12] measured multiprocessor cache protocols with traces of a set of parallel programs. Since the traces are generated on a per processor basis by software method, they are more scalable than the ATUM2. Traces gathered by software tools are prone to problems such as omission of operating system calls, oversimplification of the execution times of various instructions, and manifestation of architectural characteristics in the traces. Such problems may result in distorting the execution pattern of parallel algorithms. Note that such distortions may not necessarily lead to erroneous results in so far as measuring invalidation rate or performance related to the invalidation rate. However, as Bitar [4] points out, trace driven simulation may not be effective in capturing the high-level interactions between processors for hypothetical architectures.

We present a new simulation model for the measurement of multiprocessors. This model represents a dynamic scheduling paradigm believed to be the kernel of several parallel programs [21]. The basic granularity is a task. A large problem is divided into atomic tasks, and dependencies between tasks are checked. Tasks are inserted into a work queue of executable tasks honoring such dependencies, thus making the work queue non-FIFO in nature. Each processor takes a task from the queue and processes it. If a new task is generated as a result of the processing, it is inserted into the queue. All the processors execute the same code until the task queue is empty or a predefined finishing condition is met. If there is a need to synchronize all the processors at some point, then a barrier operation is used. Figure 6 shows the pseudo code that each processor executes.

To simulate the memory reference pattern of each processor during task execution, a probabilistic model similar to the one developed by Archibald and Baer [2] is incorporated into our model. Additional features in our model are synchronization primitives, differentiation of synchronization variables from other variables, and different evaluation metrics. Many parameters are fixed not only because their effects are well studied in [2] but also our primary concern was to measure the effect of various synchronization mechanisms on protocol performance. The values of the parameters used in the simulation are summarized in Table 4. The degree of sharing will be fairly low during the execution of a task than during queue operation. So, 0.03 and 0.5 are assumed for the degree of sharing for these two cases respectively. Real traces [11, 25] show that the read ratio ranges from 0.6 to 0.9 depending on the application of traced programs. In [2] simulation was done varying

```
finished = false;
new_task = empty;
loop
    lock(queue);
    if (new_task ≠ empty) then
        insert_queue(new_task);
    end if;
    task = delete_queue();
    unlock(queue);
    new_task = execute(task);
    if (need_synchronization) barrier();
    check_if_finished(finished);
until(finished)
```

Figure 6: Programming paradigm with dynamic scheduling

Parameters	value
ratio of shared accesses	0.03, 0.5*
number of shared blocks	32
cache hit-ratio	0.95
read ratio	0.85
main memory cycle time	4 cache cycles
block size	4 words
cache size	1024 blocks
lock ratio	50%

* 0.03: task execution, 0.5: queue access

Table 4: Summary of parameters used in simulation

the read ratio from 0.7 to 0.85. In our simulation the read ratio is set to 0.85. Shared accesses are secured by lock primitives with a probability *lock-ratio*. The nature of the lock can be read (sharable) or exclusive depending on the type of shared access. The ratio of lock requests to shared accesses is from 50% to 70% in some applications [1, 17] and below 10% in other applications [11]. In the results reported a lock-ratio of 50% is assumed[3]. For invalidation and write update schemes, the lock primitive is implemented as test_test_and_set. Another important parameter is the grain size of parallelism. The grain size is decided by the number of data memory references during the execution of a task. Cache schemes evaluated are Berkeley protocol [16] as an invalidation scheme, Dragon [18] protocol as a write update scheme, Bitar and Despain's method [5], and our lock-based protocol. The problem size is 160 tasks, and the results are the average of 5 runs. Measured metrics are completion time in number of cycles, processor utilization, and the average length of the bus queue.

Figure 7 shows the completion time of each cache scheme for the grain size 100 (fine to medium grain) with-

out barrier synchronization. BD denotes the Bitar and Despain's scheme, and LBP is our scheme. The unit metric is 10,000 cycles. The Berkeley protocol shows an anomalous loss of efficiency as the number of processors n increases beyond 8. This loss of efficiency happens because the bus is already saturated (the measured average length of the bus queue supports this argument) and thus, useful work is delayed by queue access activity of each processor. This effect is the multiprocessor equivalent of thrashing induced by the greedy scheduling discipline. All the other schemes also show slowdown in speed-up with more than 8 processors. With 8 processors LBP completes in 20480 cycles while BP, the second best one next to LBP, completes in 25149 cycles. This performance gap grows as n increases. The performance gap between BP and LBP is due to increased concurrency provided by read-locks of LBP during the task execute phase of the simulation model (Figure 6).

Figure 8 depicts the performance with a large grain size of 500. The steep loss of efficiency with Berkeley protocol disappears in this case because the long processing time outweighs the overhead of queue access. Though the grain size is multiplied by 5, the completion times for all the schemes do not scale down by quite as much, which is to be expected because there is a constant overhead for accessing the queue. When n is 8 the performance gap between LBP and BP is 14303 cycles, which is more than three times the gap when the grain size is fine to medium.

The effect of barrier synchronization is shown in Figures 9 and 10. Irrespective of the protocol, the net effect of the barrier is to synchronize the queue access of all the processors thus aggravating the contention for this shared resource (see Figure 6). Hence for a given grain size, the inclusion of the barrier results in longer completion times for all the protocols (compare Figures 7 and 9, and Figures 8 and 10). With respect to Figures 8 and 10, Dragon protocol outperforms Berkeley protocol by larger gaps with barrier than when there is no barrier. The same is true in Figures 7 and 9, except for the anomalous behavior of Berkeley protocol beyond 8 processors in Figure 7. The reason for these gaps is evident from the cost functions developed in Section 4.1: Even though the barrier itself does not lead to significant performance gap, simultaneous lock requests (see 'parallel lock' in Table 3) after the barrier entails considerable expense for the Berkeley protocol as compared to the Dragon protocol, especially with large n. With $n = 8$ and fine to medium grain parallelism, Dragon is better than Berkeley by 8% when barrier is not used, and by 32% when barrier is used. The case when the grain size is large (500) shows a similar trend. LBP outperforms BD by a larger margin with barrier synchronization. When the grain size is fine to medium (100), LBP is better than BP by 4669 cycles if barrier is not required, and by 9249 cycles with barrier. The efficiency of LBP for barrier operation comes from the sharable lock that enables the notification to be done in one bus transaction.

---

[3] Varying the lock-ratio produces only a small difference in performance because the degree of sharing is quite low during task execution.

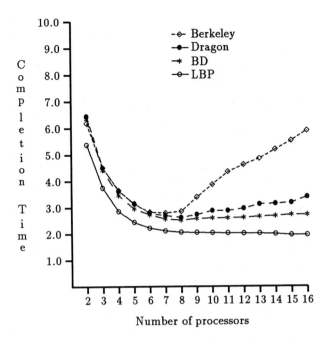

Figure 7: Performance of cache schemes (grain size = 100, without barrier)

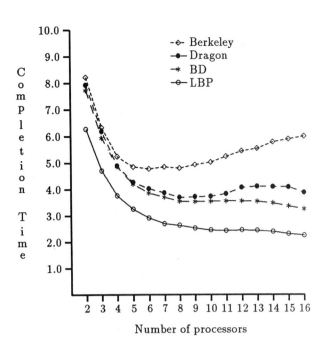

Figure 9: Performance of cache schemes (grain size = 100, with barrier)

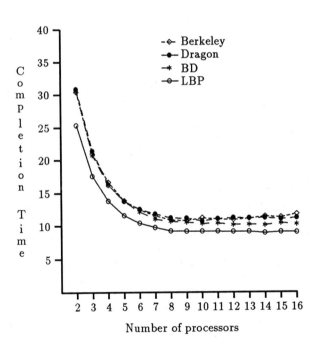

Figure 8: Performance of cache schemes (grain size = 500, without barrier)

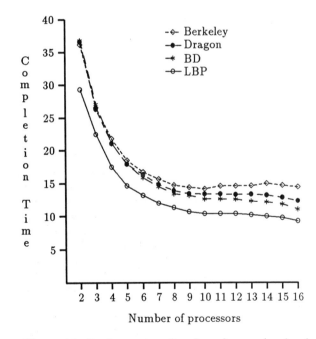

Figure 10: Performance of cache schemes (grain size = 500, with barrier)

35

6 Discussion and Conclusions

We presented a new lock-based scheme which incorporates cache coherency strategy with synchronization. Lock operations were used as the underlying primitives for cache coherency. As a waiting mechanism, a distributed queue was constructed in hardware using the cache line of each lock requester. Memory accesses for queue pointers were eliminated by storing the link information in the tag of the cache memory. The protocol distinguishes sharable lock from exclusive locks thus allowing increased concurrency for simultaneous readers. The invalidation, the write update, and the lock-based schemes were analyzed for synchronization operations to identify the source of inefficiency. For the evaluation of each cache scheme a new simulation model was developed which represents a widely used paradigm for parallel programming. The simulation results show that our scheme outperforms others by a considerable margin in the test cases.

There are several dimension in which our work can be extended in the future. The fetch-and-add [10] primitive is a powerful synchronization primitive and its utility has been demonstrated in combining multistage networks. It would be interesting to compare the performance and hardware complexity of the fetch-and-add primitive in a bus-based environment against our protocol. We showed earlier that read snarfing is a useful feature for synchronization. Detailed simulation study for examining the overall performance of read snarfing on snoopy cache protocols is another area of future research. VLSI implementation of cache schemes such as invalidate, update, Bitar and Despain, QOSB primitive, and ours is also being pursued to quantify the cost in terms of circuit complexity and understand the delay characteristics of the different cache protocols.

Acknowledgment

We thank Jim Goodman for his several constructive criticisms and suggestions. We thank our colleagues, H. Venkateswaran and Phil Hutto for reading earlier drafts of this paper.

References

[1] Anant Agarwal and Anoop Gupta. Memory-reference characteristics of multiprocessor applications under MACH. In *Proceedings of ACM SIGMETRICIS Conference*, pages 215–225, May 1988.

[2] James Archibald and Jean-Loup Baer. Cache coherence protocols: evaluation using a multiprocessor model. *ACM Transactions on Computer Systems*, pages 278–298, Nov. 1986.

[3] Bob Beck, Bob Kasten, and Shreekant Thakkar. VLSI assist for a multiprocessor. *Proceedings of the Second International Conference on Architectural Support for Programming Languages and Operating Systems*, pages 10–20, 1987.

[4] Philip Bitar. A critique of trace-driven simulation for shared-memory multiprocessors. *ISCA'89 Workshop: Cache and Interconnect Architectures in Multiprocessors*, 1989.

[5] Phillip Bitar and Alvin M. Despain. Multiprocessor cache synchronization : Issues, innovations, evolution. In *Proceedings of the 13th Annual International Symposium on Computer Architecture*, pages 424–433, June 1986.

[6] W. C. Brantley, K. P. McAuliffe, and J. Weiss. RP3 processor-memory element. In *Proceedings of the 1985 International Conference on Parallel Processing*, pages 782–789, Aug. 1985.

[7] E. D. Brooks. The Butterfly barrier. *International Journal of Parallel Programming*, pages 295–307, Aug. 1986.

[8] Lucien M. Censier and Paul Feautrier. A new solution to coherence problem in multicache systems. *IEEE Transactions on Computers*, C-27(12):1112–1118, Dec. 1978.

[9] M. Dubois, C. Scheurich, and F. Briggs. Synchronization, coherence, and event ordering in multiprocessors. *IEEE Computer*, pages 9–21, Feb. 1988.

[10] Jan Edler, Allan Gottlieb, Clyde P. Kruskal, Kevin P. McAuliffe, Larry Rudolph, Marc Snir, Patricia J. Telen, and James Wilson. Issues related to MIMD shared-memory computers : the NYU Ultracomputer approach. In *Proceedings of the 12th Annual International Symposium on Computer Architecture*, pages 126–135, June 1985.

[11] Susan J. Eggers and Randy H. Katz. A characterization of sharing in parallel programs and its application to coherency protocol evaluation. In *Proceedings of the 15th Annual International Symposium on Computer Architecture*, pages 373–382, June 1988.

[12] Susan J. Eggers and Randy H. Katz. Evaluating the performance of four snooping cache coherency protocols. In *Proceedings of the 16th Annual International Symposium on Computer Architecture*, pages 2–15, June 1989.

[13] James R. Goodman. Using cache memory to reduce processor-memory traffic. In *Proceedings of the 10th Annual International Symposium on Computer Architecture*, pages 124–131, June 1983.

[14] James R. Goodman, Mary K. Vernon, and Philip J. Woest. Efficient synchronization primitives for large-scale cache-coherent multiprocessor. Technical Report TR-814, Univ. of Wisconsin at Madison, Jan. 1989.

[15] Anna R. Karlin, Mark S. Manasse, Larry Rudolph, and Daniel D. Sleator. Competitive snoopy caching. *Algorithmica*, 3:79–119, 1988.

[16] R. H. Katz, S. J. Eggers, D. A. Wood, C. L. Perkins, and R. G. Sheldon. Implementing a cache consistency protocol. In *Proceedings of the 12th Annual International Symposium on Computer Architecture*, pages 276–283, June 1985.

[17] Zhiyuan Li and Walid Abu-sufah. A technique for reducing synchronization overhead in large scale multiprocessor. In *Proceedings of the 12th Annual International Symposium on Computer Architecture*, pages 284–291, 1985.

[18] E. McCreight. *The Dragon Computer System: An early overview.* Xerox Corp., Sept. 1984.

[19] M. Papamarcos and J. Patel. A low overhead solution for multiprocessors with private cache memories. In *Proceedings of the 11th Annual International Symposium on Computer Architecture*, pages 348–354, June 1984.

[20] James L. Peterson and Abraham Silberschatz. *Operating System Concepts*, pages 337–340. Addison-Wesley, 1983.

[21] Constantine D. Polychronopoulos. *Parallel Programming and Compilers*, pages 113–158. Kluwer Academic Publishers, 1988.

[22] Umakishore Ramachandran and Joonwon Lee. Processor initiated sharing in multiprocessor caches. Technical Report GIT-ICS-88/43, Georgia Institute of Technology, Nov. 1988.

[23] G. S. Sohi, J. E. Smith, and J. R. Goodman. Restricted fetch-and-ϕ operations for parallel processing. In *International Conference on Supercomputing*, June 1989. Crete, Greece.

[24] C. P. Thacker and L. C. Stewart. Firefly: A multiprocessor workstation. In *Proceedings of the Second International Conference on Architectural Support for Programming Languages and Operating Systems*, pages 164–172, Oct. 1987.

[25] Wolf-Dietrich Weber and Anoop Gupta. Analysis of cache invalidation patterns in multiprocessors. In *Proceedings of the Third International Conference on Architectural Support for Programming Languages and Operating Systems*, pages 243–256, 1988.

[26] W. A. Wulf and C. G. Bell. C.mmp - a multi-mini processor. In *Proceedings of the Fall Joint Computer Conference*, pages 765–777, Dec. 1972.

[27] W. C. Yen, D. W. L. Yen, and King-Sun Fu. Data coherence problems in multicache system. *IEEE Transactions on Computers*, c-34, No. 1:56–65, Jan. 1985.

[28] P. C. Yew, N. F. Tzeng, and D. H. Lawrie. Distributing hot-spot addressing in large-scale multiprocessor. *IEEE Transactions on Computers*, pages 388–395, April 1987.

Session 1B: Multiprocessor Network Issues

Dynamic Processor Allocation in Hypercube Computers

Po-Jen Chuang and Nian-Feng Tzeng

The Center for Advanced Computer Studies
University of Southwestern Louisiana
Lafayette, LA 70504

Abstract —— Fully recognizing various subcubes in a hypercube computer efficiently is nontrivial due to the specific structure of the hypercube. We propose a method with much less complexity than the multiple-GC strategy in generating the search space, while achieving complete subcube recognition. This method is referred to as a *dynamic* processor allocation scheme because the search space generated is dependent upon the dimension of the requested subcube dynamically, rather than being predetermined and fixed. The basic idea of this strategy lies in collapsing the binary tree representations of a hypercube successively so that the nodes which form a subcube but are distant would be brought close to each other for recognition. The strategy can be implemented efficiently by using shuffle operations on the leaf node addresses of binary tree representations. Extensive simulation runs are carried out to collect experimental performance measures of interest of different allocation strategies. It is shown from analytic and experimental results that this strategy compares favorably in many situations to any other known allocation scheme capable of achieving complete subcube recognition.

1. INTRODUCTION

Due to its numerous interesting properties [1], the hypercube topology has been drawing considerable attention from researchers of different fields in recent years. Based on this topology, many prototypes and commercial systems have been built or marketed, e.g., Cosmic Cube [2], Intel iPSC/1 [3] and iPSC/2, Connection Machine [4], Ametek S/14 [5], N-Cube/10 [6], the FPS T-Series [7], and the MARK-III prototype research machine [8]. They exhibit a high potential for the parallel execution of various algorithms, and may deliver as good performance as typical supercomputers at a much lower cost.

Considered in this paper is a hypercube system where the resources are the processor nodes forming subcubes of various sizes; an incoming task incident on the system is analyzed for decomposability and the number of processors required for the task is determined. For an efficient management of processor allocation, a subcube, instead of an arbitrary number of processors, is allocated to the task, even though the number of processors actually required may be arbitrary. Specifically, a k-dimensional subcube is allocated to the task that requires

This work was supported in part by the NSF under Grant MIP-8807761 and by the Louisiana Board of Regents' R&D Program Component under Grant 86-USL(2)-127-03.

p processors, where 2^k is the smallest integer such that $p \leq 2^k$. The job of a processor allocator is to find a free subcube with a size just sufficient to meet the need of the task.

The recognition of various subcubes in a hypercube system using the buddy strategy is simple and straightforward, but tends to result in poor subcube recognition ability. Later, a modified buddy strategy [13] is proposed to enhance subcube recognition ability. Chen and Shin [9] proposed the Gray Code (GC) strategy to allocate processors in a hypercube. It is shown that, compared with the buddy strategy, the GC strategy not only has a better subcube recognition ability but also reduces the fragmentation to some extent. They illustrated that the subcube recognition ability using a single GC would be twice as much as that of the buddy strategy [9]. They also proposed the use of multiple GC's to achieve full recognition of all the subcubes of any sizes. It is proved that $C(n, \lfloor n/2 \rfloor)$ GC's are sufficient to accomplish complete subcube recognition (i.e., to recognize all possible subcubes) in an n-cube, where $C(n, l)$ is the combination of n taking l at a time.

The method of determining various GC's required is, however, fairly involved so that the GC's have to be predetermined off-line and incorporated in the processor allocation algorithm [9]. If, due to some reason (such as system reconfiguration after some nodes become faulty), the size of the hypercube changes, one has to redetermine the GC's. Moreover, these $C(n, \lfloor n/2 \rfloor)$ GC's are determined independent of the required subcube dimension, k, and in the worst case, a total number of $C(n, \lfloor n/2 \rfloor)$ GC's should be searched. That is, when this multiple-GC strategy is used, the entire search space is predetermined and fixed, independent of the dimension of the subcube needed by an incoming task (thus, termed a *static* processor allocation scheme).

Another processor allocation scheme, called the free-list strategy, is introduced recently [14]. It maintains lists of free subcubes, with one list for one dimension. A requested subcube is allocated from a free list of the available subcubes. The allocation process is simple, but the deallocation procedure is very complicated. Like the multiple-GC strategy, it can fully recognize all subcubes.

Here, we give a method with much less complexity than the multiple-GC strategy in generating the search space, while still achieving complete subcube recognition. The search space so generated is determined not only by n (for an n-cube) but also by k (the dimension of the

CH2887-8/90/0000/0040$01.00 © 1990 IEEE

subcube needed by an incoming task). Additionally, our method compares favorably in many situations to other allocation schemes in terms of the mean search time, an experimental performance measure. The basic idea of this method is an extension of the buddy strategy [10]. We observe that, due to the specific interconnection pattern in a hypercube, the buddy system fails to recognize all the subcubes. In other words, the nodes that are actually "buddies" (form a subcube) have been "estranged" in the classical buddy approach. Hence, we propose to "reunite" the otherwise "estranged" buddies by "collapsing" the binary tree representation of the hypercube so that the nodes which form a subcube but are distant would be brought close to each other. It will be shown that by repeating the process of collapsing subtrees of the binary tree representation, one can bring about reunion of all estranged buddies for recognition. Since its search space is not predetermined and is dynamically changed according to k, this method is referred to as a *dynamic* processor allocation scheme.

This paper is organized as follows. Section 2 gives useful notations and related work on hypercube processor allocation. Section 3 presents the proposed allocation strategy based on tree collapsing. An efficient implementation of the proposed strategy is introduced in Section 4. Section 5 compares the multiple-GC strategy and the proposed strategy in terms of the worst-case storage and time complexities. Also provided and discussed in this section are the simulated performance measures of interest, such as the mean search time for one allocation attempt, the completion time of a sequence of allocation, and hypercube processor utilization of different allocation strategies. Concluding remarks are given in Section 6.

2. NOMENCLATURE AND RELATED WORK

An n-dimensional hypercube, denoted by H_n, comprises 2^n nodes, each with n connection links serving as communication channels directly to n immediate neighbors. Nodes in H_n are numbered from 0 to 2^n-1 by n-bit binary numbers $(x_{n-1} \cdots x_i \cdots x_0)$, as their addresses. For convenience, x_i is referred to as the ith direction of the binary representation of an address. A node and any of its immediate neighbors have exactly one bit different in their addresses. A k-dimensional subcube in H_n, denoted by S_k, comprises 2^k nodes such that all the nodes have exactly $n-k$ bits identical in their addresses, with the rest k bits being *don't care*. Each address bit of a subcube is denoted by 0, 1 or *, where * is a *don't care* symbol. For example, the notation for a 2-dimensional subcube in H_5 that consists of nodes 10001, 10011, 11001, and 11011 is 1*0*1. It is easy to derive that the number of distinct S_k's in H_n is $C(n,k) \times 2^{n-k}$.

The levels of an n-level binary tree are numbered from 0 to $n-1$, with the root node at level 0 and the leaf nodes at level $n-1$. Definitions 1 and 2 given below facilitate subsequent explanation.

Definition 1: A *binary tree representation* of H_n, denoted by T_n, is an $(n+1)$-level binary tree with param-

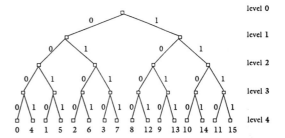

Fig. 1. A binary tree representation (T_4) with a parameter $\langle t_0, t_1, t_2, t_3 \rangle = \langle 0,2,3,1 \rangle$.

eter $\langle t_0, t_1, \cdots, t_{n-1} \rangle$ such that each leaf node represents a cube processor whose address comprises such a bit string that its $(n-1-t_i)$th direction, $0 \leq i \leq n-1$, is the ith bit of the bit sequence along the path from the root to the node (i.e., the ith parameter element, t_i, specifies the $(n-1-t_i)$th direction of the binary representation of the processor address), where $\langle t_0, t_1, \cdots, t_{n-1} \rangle$ is a permutation of $\{0,1,\cdots,n-1\}$.

Each nonleaf node, say node A, at level l (> 0) of T_n is similarly numbered, with its l defined directions being the bit sequence along the path from the root to node A and the other $n-l$ directions being *don't care*. Apparently, node A corresponds to a subcube of dimension $n-l$, i.e., the subcube which contains such 2^{n-l} leaf nodes with node A as their common ancestor. A binary tree representation is uniquely characterized by its parameter, so T_n with parameter $\langle t_0, t_1, \cdots, t_{n-1} \rangle$ is denoted by $T_n \langle t_0, t_1, \cdots, t_{n-1} \rangle$ henceforth. A binary tree representation of H_4, $T_4 \langle 0,2,3,1 \rangle$, is shown in Fig. 1, where the parameter elements denote respectively the 3rd, 1st, 0th, and 2nd directions of the binary representation of processor addresses. The leftmost two nodes at level 2 correspond respectively to the 2-dimensional subcubes 0*0* and 0*1*. In general, for a given $T_n \langle t_0, t_1, \cdots, t_{n-1} \rangle$, if the address of subcube S_k associated with a node at level $n-k$ is $x_{n-1} x_{n-2} \cdots x_j \cdots x_0$, x_j is a *don't care* bit if $j = n-1-t_i$, with i satisfying $n-k \leq i \leq n-1$. For example, the addresses of S_4's associated with the nodes at level 2 of $T_6 \langle 1,3,4,5,0,2 \rangle$ are $*x_4*x_2**$, where $x_4 x_2 \in \{00, 01, 10, 11\}$.

Clearly, there are $n!$ distinct binary tree representations of H_n, since there are $n!$ distinct parameters which are the permutations of $\{0,1,\cdots,n-1\}$. Without an appropriate procedure to determine the search space, one would have to exhaustively examine all these $n!$ trees in order to guarantee complete subcube recognition, yielding an intractable situation.

Definition 2: The *primary binary tree representation* of H_n, denoted by PT_n, is $T_n \langle 0,1,2,\cdots,n-1 \rangle$, i.e., the leaf nodes of PT_n have addresses 0 through 2^n-1, starting from the leftmost node to the rightmost one.

Fig. 2 gives an example of PT_4.

The processors in H_n must be allocated to incident tasks in such a way that processor utilization is maximized (or equivalently, a task is assigned an available sub-

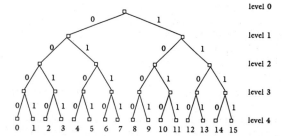

Fig. 2. The primary binary tree representation of H_4.

cube whenever such a subcube exists). Due to the special structure of a hypercube, it is nontrivial to detect the availability of a subcube. To accomplish this, ways of exploiting the ideas used in conventional memory allocation approaches have been focused, giving rise to two major types of strategies — the buddy strategies and the Gray code strategies. The former type includes the simple buddy strategy and the modified buddy strategy [13], which are based on the buddy system [10]; whereas the latter type contains the single Gray code strategy and the multiple Gray codes strategy [9]. Any of these strategies performs a linear search on a list of allocation bits by means of the first-fit search process. Recently, a free-list strategy is proposed [14], where a separate list is used for keeping all the free subcubes of a certain dimension. In what follows, we briefly review these strategies.

2.1. The Buddy and Modified Buddy Strategies

Since H_n has 2^n processors, it requires 2^n allocation bits to keep track of the availability of all the processors. An allocation bit with 0 (or 1) indicates that the corresponding processor is available (or unavailable).

The buddy strategy [9] can be easily explained by the primary binary tree representation of H_n. When an incoming task needs an S_k, this strategy searches level $n-k$ of the primary binary tree from left to right and allocates the first available subcube (associated with a node in the level) to the task. Clearly, only 2^{n-k} S_k's can be recognized, where $1 \leq k \leq n-1$. The strategy is proved to be optimal in the sense that it can always accommodate any input task sequence $\{I_i\}_{i=1}^k$ if and only if $\sum_{i=1}^k 2^{|I_i|} \leq 2^n$, where $|I_i|$ is the dimension of a subcube required to accommodate task I_i.

The modified buddy strategy [13] can also be illustrated by the primary binary tree representation of H_n. The ith partner of a node at level l (> 0) $x_{n-1}x_{n-2}\cdots x_{i+1}x_i x_{i-1}\cdots x_{n-l}$ for any $n-l \leq i \leq n-1$ is defined as the node $x_{n-1}x_{n-2}\cdots x_{i+1}1x_{i-1}\cdots x_0$ if $x_i = 0$, or undefined if $x_i = 1$ (note that the $n-l$ tailing *don't care* bits in the binary address representation of the node are disregarded.) The nearest partner of a node is the ith partner of the node, where i is the smallest integer. A node is free if and only if all of its descendants are free. When a k-dimensional subcube is requested, this strategy searches level $n-k+1$ of the primary binary tree, from left to right, for the first free node and its nearest free partner. If found, it allocates the subcube

formed by the two $(k-1)$-dimensional subcubes corresponding to the two free nodes. This strategy is shown to be able to recognize $(n-k+1)\times 2^{n-k}$ distinct S_k's [13]. An extension to the strategy is also provided: if two free nodes forming an available S_k are unavailable at level $n-k+1$, the higher levels are searched to get more S_k's. Totally, as many as $(k\times(n-k)+1)\times 2^{n-k}$ distinct S_k's can then be recognized.

2.2. The GC and Multiple-GC Strategies

A GC is a sequence of binary numbers where any two successive numbers have only one different bit. The Chen and Shin's allocation strategy [9] is based on the binary reflected Gray Code (BRGC), the best known GC. The strategy is similar to the buddy strategy except that the allocation bits are stored in the BRGC sequence.

The GC strategy [9] can be explained by a binary tree with the addresses of leaf nodes denoted by BRGC. According to the property of BRGC, any two adjacent nodes (including the leftmost and rightmost pair, which enables a circular search) in the $(n-k+1)$th level form an S_k even if they may not have the same immediate predecessor. When an S_k is requested, this strategy searches from left to right for *two* available adjacent nodes in *level* $n-k+1$ rather than for *an* available node in *level* $n-k$. Therefore, it recognizes twice as many subcubes as the buddy strategy.

Since a GC cannot recognize all the subcubes in a hypercube and different GC's recognize different sets of subcubes, Chen and Shin have proved that, for complete subcube recognition, $C(n, \lfloor n/2 \rfloor)$ GC's are needed and sufficient [9]. Fully recognizing all the subcubes of any dimension is unachievable unless $C(n, \lfloor n/2 \rfloor)$ GC's are employed. Although a method is devised to identify such GC's, the process is so complicated that it has to be done off-line in practical implementation, as suggested in [9]. Besides, storage needed for keeping these GC's is quite large.

2.3. The Free List Strategy

This strategy maintains lists of free subcubes available in the hypercube, with one list for a dimension [14]. An incoming request for dimension k gets allocated by assigning the first element in the free list of dimension k, if the list is not empty; otherwise, by decomposing an available subcube with dimension $> k$. Although the allocation steps are simple, the strategy involves a quite complicated deallocation process whenever a subcube is released, in order to guarantee its correctness. Specifically, the deallocation process has to: (1) merge the released subcube with any other subcube to form a bigger cube, or generate another available cube of the same dimension; (2) search all subcubes of the newly produced cube and remove them from their corresponding lists; and (3) repeat the first two steps until nothing can be done further.

Although this strategy assures full subcube recognition, its time and storage complexities in the worst case can be very high, and will be much higher than $O(n^3)$

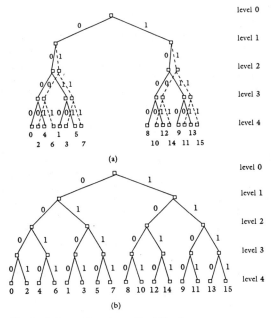

level 0
level 1
level 2
level 3
level 4

(a)

level 0
level 1
level 2
level 3
level 4

(b)

Fig. 3. A C-transform ξ_1 on T_4 of Fig. 1.
    (a) the collapsing of T_4 at level 1 after (i), and
    (b) the collapsed tree — another binary tree
        representation with $<t_0,t_1,t_2,t_3> = <0,3,1,2>$.

claimed in [14] for H_n, because the list for dimension k can grow as much as $O(2^{n-k})$. (The claimed complexity is derived by assuming the list length to be $O(n)$, which is observed from simulation under light traffic.)

3. PROPOSED ALLOCATION STRATEGY

So far, only two allocation strategies achieve complete subcube recognition, namely, the multiple-GC strategy and the free-list strategy. In the following, we introduce a new recognition-complete allocation strategy based on tree collapsing, termed the *TC strategy*, which exhibits better performance in many situations as compared to the other two recognition-complete allocation strategies. Before presenting the TC strategy, we give a definition.

Definition 3: A *Collapsing Transform (C-transform)* is a transform which operates on a binary tree representation of H_n (i.e., T_n) and produces a *collapsed tree*. A C-transform at level i, denoted by ξ_i, involves (i) collapsing T_n such that the left and right subtrees of every node at level i are clustered together without changing their relative locations (the left descendant stays left, while the right one stays right) and then (ii) swapping the incoming links of the two inner nodes in every block of four nodes at level $i+2$ throughout level n.

The result of performing ξ_1 on $T_4<0,2,3,1>$ of Fig. 1 is shown in Fig. 3. Fig. 3(a) illustrates the tree collapsing at level 1 after (i), and then the incoming links of leaf nodes 2 and 4, 3 and 5, etc., are swapped, so are those of the two inner nodes in every block of four nodes at level 3, yielding the collapsed tree $T_4<0,3,1,2>$ given in Fig. 3(b). From the way the collapsed trees are generated, we have the following lemma immediately.

Lemma 1: Given $T_n<t_0,t_1,\cdots,t_{n-1}>$, if the parameter of the collapsed tree T_n' derived by applying ξ_j, $0 \leq j \leq n-1$, to T_n is $<t_0',t_1',\cdots,t_{n-1}'>$, then
(i) $t_i' = t_i$, where $0 \leq i < j$,
(ii) $t_i' = t_{i+1}$, where $j \leq i < n-1$, and
(iii) $t_{n-1}' = t_j$.

Actually, $<t_0',t_1',t_2',\cdots,t_{n-1}'>$ results from $<t_0,t_1,t_2,\cdots,t_{n-1}>$ by operating left rotation on t_i, where $j \leq i \leq n-1$ for a certain j. As an instance, the parameters of the collapsed tree derived from applying ξ_1 to $T_6<1,3,4,5,0,2>$ are $<1,4,5,0,2,3>$.

3.1. Algorithm for Collapsed Trees Generation

Our allocation approach is realized by recognizing the fact that in the buddy strategy the nodes forming subcubes are not adjacent to each other, and only when they are brought adjacent to each other would complete subcube recognition become achievable. The following algorithm performs C-transforms successively on binary tree representations, starting with the primary one until nodes of every possible subcube of the desired dimension are brought together in one of the tree representations. It serves as the basis of the TC strategy.

Algorithm G

Input:
    the primary binary tree representation (stored in primary_tree) of H_n and the dimension of a subcube to be allocated, k, where primary_tree, new_tree, pre_tree are binary tree data structures.

Procedure main(n, k, primary_tree);
begin
    if ($k = 0$ or $k = n$) then stop;
    for $i := n-k-1$ downto 0
        call collapse(i, primary_tree, new_tree);
        call subsequent_collapse(i, 0, new_tree);
    endfor
end;

Procedure subsequent_collapse(pre_level, pre_step, pre_tree);
begin
    $step :=$ pre_step+1;   /* advancing one step */
    if $step \geq k$ then return
    else
        for $i :=$ pre_level to $n-k-1$
            call collapse(i, pre_tree, new_tree);
            call subsequent_collapse(i, step, new_tree);
        endfor
    endif
end

There is no need for performing the C-transform when $k = 0$ or $k = n$. The routine collapse(i, old_tree, new_tree) performs ξ_i on old_tree and stores the resultant collapsed tree in new_tree; whereas the routine subsequent_collapse(pre_level, pre_step, new_tree) generates subsequent collapsed trees recursively from new_tree by using the collapse routine. According to Algorithm G, the possible C-transforms for a given n

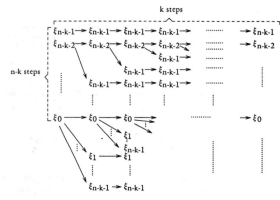

Fig. 4. The possible C-transforms performed in Algorithm G for any given n and k.

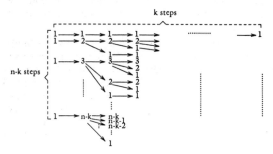

Fig. 5. The numbers of C-transforms in Fig. 4 (counted step by step).

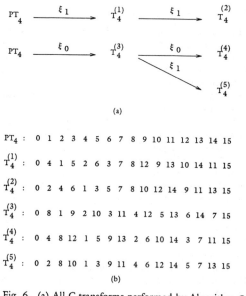

Fig. 6. (a) All C-transforms performed by Algorithm G for $n=4$ and $k=2$.
(b) The leaf nodes of collapsed trees.
(The parenthesized numbers indicate the collapsing order.)

and k are depicted in Fig. 4, where the C-transforms in one column are performed by one step of Algorithm G and totally there are k steps (from step 0 to step $k-1$). The numbers of C-transforms in Fig. 4 counted step by step are given in Fig. 5.

Definition 4: Two binary tree representations of H_n, T_n and T_n', are *overlapped at level $n-k$* if there exist k-dimensional subcubes S_k and S_k' associated respectively with the nodes at levels $n-k$ of T_n and T_n' such that $S_k = S_k'$. Otherwise, T_n and T_n' are *nonoverlapped at level $n-k$*.

Theorem 1: In Algorithm G, (i) the total number of C-transforms performed is $C(n, k) - 1$, and (ii) the primary and collapsed trees are pairwise nonoverlapped at level $n-k$.

A proof of this theorem can be found in Appendix. The result of performing Algorithm G on the case of $n = 4$ and $k = 2$ is given in Fig. 6. The number of produced trees is 5, which equals $C(4, 2) - 1$, and each four leaf nodes associated with any node at level 2 of PT_4 or of any produced T_4 form a distinct S_2.

3.2. The Tree Collapsing Strategy

From Theorem 1, it is easy to derive that all the nodes at level $n-k$ of PT_n and of all produced T_n's correspond to $C(n, k) \times 2^{n-k}$ distinct S_k's (which are all the possible distinct subcubes with size k). If the buddy

strategy is applied to *all* of these binary tree representations, fully recognizing all S_k's can be achieved. Therefore, we propose the following tree collapsing strategy.

Processor Allocation:
Step 1. Set $k := |I_j|$, where $|I_j|$ is the dimension of a subcube required to accommodate task I_j.
Step 2. Search level $n-k$ of the primary binary tree from left to right and find the first available subcube (the allocation bits of the nodes of the subcube, i.e., of the leaf nodes corresponding to a node at the level $n-k$, are all 0's), if any, then go to Step 4.
Step 3. Perform Algorithm G and search level $n-k$ of one produced collapsed tree (if any) at a time, from left to right, until the first available subcube is found. If an available subcube is found, go to the next step; otherwise, go to Step 5.
Step 4. Set the corresponding allocation bits of the available subcube to 1's, and then allocate the subcube to task I_j. Stop.
Step 5. Attach I_j to the task queue and wait until a subcube is released.

Processor Relinquishment:
Reset allocation bits of the released subcube to 0's.

The proposed TC strategy can fully recognize all subcubes of any given dimension. It is a dynamic processor allocation strategy, as its search space varies when the subcube dimension changes. Apparently, the TC strategy is also optimal in the sense that it can always accommodate any input task sequence $\{I_i\}_{i=1}^{k}$ if and only if $\sum_{i=1}^{k} 2^{|I_i|} \leq 2^n$, where $|I_i|$ is the dimension of a subcube required to accommodate task I_i, as in the buddy strategy mentioned earlier.

4. EFFICIENT IMPLEMENTATION

For a direct implementation of the TC strategy, there must be a large store for keeping binary tree structures as well as a long execution time for carrying out C-transforms. To reduce implementation complexity, let us examine closely the effect of a C-transform on the leaf nodes of a binary tree representation. It is easy to observe that collapsing a binary tree at a certain level changes the sequence of leaf node addresses exactly the same way as *performing a perfect shuffle* [11] on the leaf node addresses. A *perfect shuffle* on a block of elements means viewing those elements as two equal decks, with the first half constituting one deck and the other half constituting the other deck, and then shuffle them perfectly so that the elements from the two decks alternate to form the resulting block. Since the sequence of leaf node addresses of a binary tree representation in our case uniquely defines the tree itself, any collapsed tree produced by performing a C-transform can also be derived by carrying out an appropriate perfect shuffle operation on the leaf node addresses; there is a need to keep track of only the sequence of leaf node addresses, not the entire binary tree representation.

4.1. An Implementation

For the subsequent discussion, we provide the following definition.

Definition 5: A *Shuffle Transform (S-transform)* on a sequence of 2^n elements, denoted by σ_i, $0 \leq i \leq n-1$, is a transform on the elements in such a way that a perfect shuffle is performed individually on every successive disjoint block each with 2^{i+1} elements.

Fig. 7 gives an example of performing σ_2 on a sequence of 2^4 elements, indexed from 0000 to 1111. These elements consist of two disjoint 2^3-element blocks and the result comes from carrying out a perfect shuffle on each block separately. Note that every element after σ_i is moved from index ψ to the index equal to left-rotating the rightmost $i+1$ bits of ψ, as the perfect shuffle is performed on 2^{i+1}-element blocks individually. For instance, element 9 is moved from index 1010 to 1100 after σ_2.

It is easy to verify that the C-transform and the S-transform are equivalent. For a binary tree representation T_n, a node at level i corresponds to a set of 2^{n-i} leaf nodes. We can treat every set of such leaf nodes as a block when transform σ_{n-i-1} is performed on the T_n leaf node address sequence to yield another address sequence identical to that of a collapsed tree derived from applying ξ_i to T_n. As an example, the leaf node address sequence of the collapsed tree derived from applying ξ_1 to T_4 (shown in Fig. 3) can result also from performing σ_2 on the leaf node address sequence of T_4, as shown in Fig. 7.

Compared with C-transforms, S-transforms need less memory for storing the data structures (one-dimensional arrays versus binary trees) and take a shorter time for execution. More importantly, it is possible to carry out σ_i very fast. For example, desired S-transforms on an address can be performed by using shift/rotating and

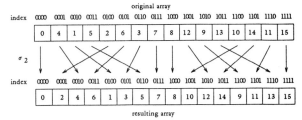

Fig. 7. Performing σ_2 on a sequence of 2^4 numbers corresponding to the leaf node addresses shown in Fig. 1.

logic (e.g., AND) operations. This fact makes possible that the TC strategy on-line generates the search space in response to incoming tasks. In practice, we may design a simple circuit involving shift registers and simple control to have multiple addresses performed at a time. S-transforms are thus considered in the implementation of our TC strategy.

Algorithm G is revised as follows to fit the implementation using S-transforms. The binary tree representation is replaced by an array storing leaf node addresses of the tree, and an equivalent S-transform is performed each time when a C-transform is required. For example, the subroutine call collapse(i, pb_tree, new_tree) in Algorithm G would be replaced by routine shuffle($n-i-1$, pb_ary, new_ary), which performs σ_{n-i-1} on the array of leaf node addresses in pb_tree, i.e., pb_ary, to get a shuffled array new_ary. The revised Algorithm G is referred to as Algorithm G' in our later discussion.

To implement the TC strategy by using S-transforms, initially an array keeping the leaf nodes of the primary binary tree (rather than the primary binary tree itself) is given. Certain steps in the tree collapsing strategy described in the previous section need to be modified. Instead of searching level $n-k$ of the primary binary tree and the collapsed trees for an available subcube (at Step 2 and Step 3 of the allocation procedure given in Section 3.2), we now search the initial array and the shuffled arrays to determine the least integer m such that every jth number in an array, $m \times 2^k \leq j \leq (m+1) \times 2^k - 1$, corresponds to a free processor (and an available subcube is found). Also, Algorithm G performed at Step 3 is substituted by Algorithm G'.

4.2. Implementation Considerations

The TC strategy can be carried out either centrally by a host processor or in a distributed manner using several processors, as explained below.

Centralized Allocation Scheme

In a centralized scheme, a copy of 2^n allocation bits (which initially are all 0's) and an array of 2^n numbers (for indicating the processor addresses which initially are from 0 to $2^n - 1$) are kept in the host processor, and only the host processor is responsible for allocation. (An allocation bit being 0 (or 1) means that its corresponding processor is available (or unavailable).) When a request for an S_k is made, the host processor starts to search the allocation bits block by block (one block here contains 2^k

bits) to find out the first block with all 0's, then sets those bits to 1, and assigns to the request the S_k whose addresses correspond to the selected block bits. Otherwise, Algorithm G' is performed to derive shuffled arrays. These shuffled arrays are then searched one by one. When a shuffled array is searched, one block of 2^k elements is taken from this array at a time and their corresponding allocation bits are examined. If they all are found to be 0's, this block is selected and its corresponding subcube S_k is assigned to the request. When no subcube of the required size is available to an request, the request is queued until processor relinquishment makes room for it. When an S_k is released, the corresponding bits are reset to 0's.

Distributed Allocation Scheme

In a distributed scheme, multiple processors are involved in allocation since some parallelism can be extracted from Algorithm G' and executed by several processors in parallel. Requests for subcubes are managed by a host processor, which keeps the array of allocation bits. On receiving a request, the host processor supplies a copy of the allocation bits to each of those processors involved in executing the allocation program, and also provides it with information as to what sequence of S-transforms is to be carried out. Those processors then start to perform the sequences of S-transforms individually and follow the allocation procedure to find out if a required S_k is available. The processor first coming out with an available subcube notifies the host processor, which then aborts the unfinished S-transforms and searches being executed by the other processors. The array of allocation bits is thus updated by the host processor accordingly.

The processors involved in performing the allocation job can be predetermined or can be dynamically chosen by the host processor upon the arrival of each request. In the former way, processors are initially selected and dedicated solely to executing the allocation program; they are excluded from executing incoming tasks. The number of processors available for executing incoming tasks is thus reduced, leading to degraded system utilization. On the other hand, those involved processors in the latter way are chosen arbitrarily as long as their corresponding allocation bits are 0's, because they work independently and need not communicate with one another during the entire course of performing the allocation job (and it is easy to see from Fig. 4 that they need to communicate only with the host processor). On completing the allocation of a request, they are set free (by the host processor) and may participate in executing the current incoming task. The allocation job can be carried out in parallel this way without reducing the number of processors available for serving incoming tasks. However, since the processors participating in the allocation job are arbitrary and not fixed, each time the host processor needs to send to each participating processor the allocation bit array and the sequence of S-transforms to be performed. The allocation program also has to be sent over, unless it is kept in every processor of H_n (which apparently yields considerable storage overhead).

5. PERFORMANCE COMPARISON

There are three allocation strategies able to achieve complete recognition of all subcubes, namely, the multiple-GC strategy [9], our TC strategy, and the free-list strategy [14]. Unlike the first two, the free-list strategy involves a very complicated deallocation procedure in order to guarantee the correctness of the free lists maintained, whenever a subcube is released. The overall time complexity claimed in [14] is $O(n^3)$, derived by assuming the list length to be $O(n)$. In fact, the claimed value reflects at best only the "observed" worst case under their simulation conditions. Consider a request for subcube S_k in H_n. Theoretically, the list length can grow as large as $O(2^{n-k})$, when only one or two lists are nonempty, say the lists for 0 or 1 dimension. This gives rise to the time complexity of at least $O(n^2 2^{n-k})$. The exact time complexity, however, is fairly difficult to estimate. Hence, we analyze only the first two strategies to derive their time and storage complexities under the worst situation. Then, the performance measures of interest of the three strategies obtained through simulation runs are provided and compared.

5.1. Worst Case Analysis

It is clear from [9] that the multiple-GC strategy needs storage to keep $C(n, \lfloor n/2 \rfloor)$ GC's and the arrays of allocation bits, whereas ours needs far less storage to keep $k+2$ arrays (the original array of PT_n leaf node addresses, k shuffled arrays, and an array of allocation bits). For example, assume that one word is used for each address of 10-cube nodes, then, the multiple-GC strategy requires about 252 K words storage, whereas the TC strategy requires less than 12 K words.

For the multiple-GC strategy, to achieve complete subcube recognition, $C(n, \lfloor n/2 \rfloor)$ appropriate GC's must be generated off-line at the initialization step. When n (the dimension of the target hypercube) changes, the GC's should be redetermined. At each allocation, the entire search space has to be examined in case the required subcube is not found, independent of the dimension of the subcube requested. For each GC, one needs to check up to 2^{n-k+1} blocks, with each containing 2^k elements. Totally, in the worst case $C(n, \lfloor n/2 \rfloor) \times 2^{n-k+1}$ blocks in the search space must be checked, giving rise to search time complexity $C(n, \lfloor n/2 \rfloor) \times 2^{n-k+1} \times \eta(2^k)$, where $\eta(2^k)$ (a function of 2^k) is the time required for a linear search over one block of size 2^k.

For the TC strategy, no initialization step is needed, but the search space is generated each time a request comes up. Assume that each shuffle takes $\phi(2^n)$ time units (a function of system size), then, to generate the search space requires $(C(n, k) - 1) \times \phi(2^n)$ time units, where 1 accounts for the original PT_n array. For each address array, up to 2^{n-k} blocks are searched. Since there are $C(n, k)$ arrays in the search space, totally $C(n, k) \times 2^{n-k}$ blocks are examined in the worst case, yielding search time $C(n, k) \times 2^{n-k} \times \eta(2^k)$.

We plot the search times of the two strategies for H_{10} as a function of k in Fig. 8, where $\eta(2^k)$ is assumed to be 2^k. It is obvious that the TC strategy always has a

46

far less search time. The search space generation time for the TC strategy under the situation of $\phi(2^n) = 2^n$ is also shown in the figure. The time for allocating an arbitrary subcube using the TC strategy is the search time plus the search space generation time. From the figure, it is clear that the multiple-GC strategy takes a considerably longer time, unless k is close to $\lfloor n/2 \rfloor$ where both strategies have about the same time complexity. Notice that, as mentioned earlier, a simple circuit involving shift registers can be employed to greatly reduce the search space generation time. The cost of this circuit is low and may compare favorably to that of storage necessary for keeping the GC's in the multiple-GC strategy.

5.2. Simulation Results

The simulation model used for comparing the three strategies is described below. Task allocation is carried out centrally by a dispatching processor exclusive from the simulated hypercube, so that a request for all of the hypercube nodes is allowed. Initially, the simulated hypercube is empty, and 100 tasks are generated and queued at the dispatcher. The dimensions of the subcubes requested by the 100 tasks are assumed to follow a given distribution. The residence times of allocated subcubes are assumed to have a uniform distribution. At each unit time, the dispatcher attempts to allocate the task at the top of the queue. If the dispatcher fails to identify an available subcube of the desired dimension for the task, it reattempts in the subsequent time units until a free subcube is obtained, i.e., an FCFS scheduling discipline is followed. When an available subcube is allocated to the task, the task is removed from the queue and the next task is served at the following unit time. No new task is generated during the simulation.

Under the above simulation model, we collect such performance measures as the completion time (Ξ — the time taken to finish all the 100 tasks), processor utilization (the percentage of a processor being utilized per unit time) over the period Ξ, and the mean search time for each allocation attempt. To allocate a task in H_n, both the multiple-GC and TC strategies perform searches over the allocation (i.e., status) bits, whereas the free-list strategy[1] involves comparisons between pairs of n-character strings (which are kept in linear lists and each string element can be "0", "1", or "x"). In our simulation, we assume that the time to examine an allocation bit is the same as that to compare a pair of n-character strings, with each taking a cycle. (Note that, practically, to look up a bit may be faster.) The simulation results are averaged over 20 independent runs.

The results for task allocation in H_5 are shown in Table I. Subcube sizes requested by the 100 tasks are governed by two distributions — the uniform and decreasing distributions. The uniform distribution seems to well reflect the situations where the nature of tasks to be executed is unknown. By contrast, the decreasing distribution indicates that the probability of requesting a larger subcube is lower. (The probability of requesting

i-dimensional subcubes, p_i, $0 \le i \le n$, is shown under the table.) This may better reflect the cases where most tasks have reasonable parallelism but are not suitable for fine-grain partition. The residence time distribution of $uniform(5,10)$ indicates that the time is uniformly distributed between 5 and 10 time units. The 10 GC's used by the multiple-GC strategy are those given in [9]. The results shown in the table are reasonably accurate. As an instance, for the first value 368.8 provided in the table, given 95% confidence, the calculated confidence interval half-width over the 20 replications is 13.5, meaning that we are 95% confident that the true result would fall into the interval 368.8 ± 13.5, or equivalently, $368.8 \pm 3.7\%$. This simulated value has only less than 4% error.

It is interesting to observe from the table that the completion time and processor utilization are virtually identical for the three strategies, with negligible differences resulting possibly from the simulation variation. We speculated that all allocation strategies which have the complete subcube recognition ability would lead to pretty much identical processor utilization (and hence, the same completion time). The speculation is supported by the simulated data provided in [14], although the free-list strategy was claimed to be superior to the multiple-GC strategy by the authors there. In fact, from their simulated data, one cannot discriminate the performance of the two strategies because all discrepant amounts are so small that they fall well within tolerable simulation accuracy. What remains to be compared is the mean search time per allocation attempt; the strategy involving the least search time is the best. The search times for our TC strategy are consistently the lowest, and the free-list strategy the highest, even though an optimistic assumption on the comparison times is assumed for the free-list strategy. This is because the free-list strategy needs a very complicated deallocation process. From the simulated data, the residence time seems to have only slight impacts on the mean search time for any allocation strategy. Conversely, the requested subcube pattern has considerable influences on the mean search time, especially for the free-list strategy. The last column gives the expected number of shuffles per allocation attempt. The time complexity of the TC strategy has to take this into account. If a shuffle operation takes one cycle, the TC-strategy would have higher time complexity than the multiple-GC strategy, but still much lower than the free-list strategy. (Recall that the multiple-GC strategy needs extra storage for the GC's used.) However, when a simple circuit is designed for shuffle operations, contribution due to these operations can be kept small and the TC strategy is then likely to have lower time complexity than the multiple-GC strategy.

Simulation runs for H_{10} are also conducted and the results are listed in Table II. In this case, we compare only the free-list and TC strategies, because to generate a proper set of 252 GC's needed for the multiple-GC strategy is not a trivial job (the difficulty in producing an appropriate set of GC's is inherent to the multiple-GC

---

[1]The procedure for the free-list strategy was provided by J. Kim and C. R. Das.

Table I. Simulation results for task allocation in H_5.

Residence time distribution	Subcube size distribution	Completion time			Processor utilization			Search time			NS
		MGC*	FL*	TC	MGC	FL	TC	MGC	FL	TC	
uniform (5,10)	uniform	368.8	368.6	370.0	67.1	67.2	66.9	62.3	191.1	24.4	2.5
	decreasing**	160.7	159.0	159.6	57.6	58.3	58.0	99.9	345.3	27.6	1.9
uniform (20,30)	uniform	1095.6	1094.8	1095.7	75.0	75.1	75.0	62.2	185.6	25.7	3.0
	decreasing	432.6	433.9	432.6	73.3	73.1	73.3	100.5	398.4	31.9	2.8

*MGC: Multiple-GC, FL: Free-List, NS: number of shuffles.
**$p_0 = 0.488$, $p_1 = 0.202$, $p_2 = 0.132$, $p_3 = 0.092$, $p_4 = 0.054$, $p_5 = 0.032$.

Table II. Simulation results for task allocation in H_{10}.

Residence time distribution	Subcube size distribution	Completion time		Processor utilization		Search time		NS
		FL*	TC	FL	TC	FL	TC	
uniform (5,10)	uniform	233.5	232.7	57.3	57.5	2165.7	2240.8	42.0
	decreasing**	67.2	67.3	35.4	35.2	13165.6	1700.1	23.6
uniform (20,30)	uniform	637.3	635.3	69.7	69.9	2562.6	2163.0	42.2
	decreasing	133.4	133.3	58.4	58.4	15461.5	1766.0	31.1

*FL: Free-List, NS: number of shuffles.
**$p_0 = 0.367$, $p_1 = 0.153$, $p_2 = 0.120$, $p_3 = 0.099$, $p_4 = 0.080$, $p_5 = 0.061$, $p_6 = 0.045$, $p_7 = 0.031$, $p_8 = 0.020$, $p_9 = 0.014$, $p_{10} = 0.010$.

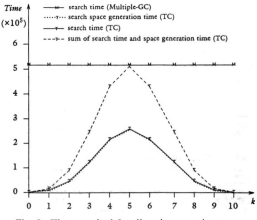

Fig. 8. Time required for allocating an S_k in H_{10} (in the worst case).

strategy.) Again, both strategies lead to almost the same completion time and processor utilization. Also, it can be seen that the TC strategy always has a lower search time, except when the distribution of requested subcube dimensions is uniform and the residence time distribution is *uniform*(5,10). When the decreasing subcube distribution is concerned, the mean search time of the free-list strategy is significantly larger. For either strategy, the change in residence times has much less impacts on the mean search time than the change in requested subcube patterns.

6. CONCLUDING REMARKS

In this paper, we have introduced a new hypercube processor allocation strategy. The strategy involves collapsing the binary tree representations of a hypercube successively, dubbed the tree collapsing (TC) strategy. The TC strategy generates its search space dynamically in response to an incoming request, as compared to the multiple-GC strategy [9] where the search space is fixed and predetermined, irrespective of the requested subcube size. It is proved to achieve complete subcube recognition. To facilitate the implementation of the TC strategy, shuffle transforms on the leaf node addresses of a binary tree representation are suggested. Since shuffle transforms can be realized by shift/rotating plus logic operations efficiently, it is possible to design a simple circuit to fast carry out such transforms.

The TC strategy is compared with the other two allocation strategies capable of accomplishing complete subcube recognition known thus far, namely, the multiple-GC strategy [9] and the free-list strategy [14]. The worst-case storage and time complexities are analytically shown to be higher by the multiple-GC strategy than by the TC strategy. Extensive simulation runs are also conducted to produce performance measures of interest of the three strategies. From the experimental results, it is observed that all the three strategies give rise to virtually the same completion time (of a sequence of 100 tasks) as well as processor utilization measures. However, the mean search time of the TC strategy is often less than those of the other two strategies.

After repeated allocation and relinquishment of subcubes, a fragmented hypercube happens in which even if there are sufficient hypercube processors available, they do not form a subcube large enough for an incoming task. When a sequence of incoming tasks requests a wide variety of subcube sizes, a fragmented hypercube is likely to arise frequently and would become serious. To deal with this fragmentation problem, a *task migration* approach that can be incorporated into the GC strategy nicely was proposed [12]. It might be interesting to consider task migration or other alternative techniques for resolving fragmentation caused by the TC strategy.

APPENDIX

Before the proof of Theorem 1 is given, three lemmas which characterize properties of collapsed trees generated by Algorithm G are provided next. These lemmas are useful for proving the second part of Theorem 1.

Suppose that S_k and S_k' are subcubes in H_n with addresses $x_{n-1}x_{n-2} \cdots x_1 x_0$ and $x_{n-1}' x_{n-2}' \cdots x_1' x_0'$ respectively, and $x_{i_1}, \cdots, x_{i_k}$ and $x_{i_1}', \cdots, x_{i_k}'$ are *don't care* bits. It is easy to verify that $S_k \neq S_k'$ if $\{i_1, i_2, \cdots, i_k\} \neq \{i_1', i_2', \cdots, i_k'\}$ (as they contain different sets of leaf nodes). Therefore, we have the following lemma.

Lemma 2: Given $T_n < t_0, t_1, \cdots, t_{n-1} >$ and $T_n' < t_0', t_1', \cdots, t_{n-1}' >$, T_n and T_n' are overlapped at level $n-k$ if and only if $\{t_i \mid n-k \leq i \leq n-1\} = \{t_i' \mid n-k \leq i \leq n-1\}$.

Clearly, there are 2^{n-k} nodes at level $n-k$ of T_n (or T_n'). Consider the two sets $\Upsilon_k = \{S_k \mid S_k$ is associated with a node at level $n-k$ of $T_n\}$ and $\Upsilon_k' = \{S_k \mid S_k$ is associated with a node at level $n-k$ of $T_n'\}$. If T_n and T_n' are overlapped at level $n-k$, then $\Upsilon_k = \Upsilon_k'$, since totally there are 2^{n-k} subcubes with dimension k and with the *don't care* bits at the same k directions in their addresses.

48

Lemma 3: A sequence of C-transforms $\xi_{i_1}, \xi_{i_2},$ $\cdots, \xi_{i_j}, \cdots, \xi_{i_l}$ operated upon a binary tree representation T_n $(= T_n^{(0)})$ produces collapsed trees $T_n^{(1)}, T_n^{(2)}, \cdots,$ $T_n^{(j)}, \cdots,$ and $T_n^{(l)}$, where $0 \le i_j \le n - k - 1$ for $1 \le j \le l$. Then, $T_n^{(0)}, T_n^{(1)}, T_n^{(2)}, \cdots,$ and $T_n^{(l)}$ are pairwise nonoverlapped at level $n - k$ if $v - u \le k$ for any u and v, $0 \le u < v \le l$.

As an instance, PT_n and the k collapsed trees produced from applying the first row of C-transforms given in Fig. 4 (i.e., k ξ_{n-k-1}'s) to PT_n as well as its subsequent collapsed trees are pairwise nonoverlapped at level $n-k$, since the levels at which C-transforms are carried out are all lower than $n-k$ and the total number of C-transforms performed is k. The same result applies likewise to any other row (i.e., sequence) of C-transforms given in Fig. 4.

Lemma 4: Two distinct sequences of C-transforms $\xi_{i_1}, \xi_{i_2}, \cdots, \xi_{i_j}, \cdots, \xi_{i_l}$ and $\xi_{i_1'}, \xi_{i_2'}, \cdots, \xi_{i_j'}, \cdots, \xi_{i_l'}$ operated upon a binary tree representation T_n produce respectively two sets of collapsed trees $\{T_n^{(1)}, T_n^{(2)}, \cdots, T_n^{(j)}, \cdots, T_n^{(l)}\}$ and $\{T_n^{(1)\prime}, T_n^{(2)\prime}, \cdots, T_n^{(j)\prime}, \cdots, T_n^{(l)\prime}\}$, where $1 \le l \le k$ and $0 \le i_j, i_j' \le n - k - 1$ for $1 \le j \le l$, and where for $p \le r$, $i_p \le i_r$ and $i_p' \le i_r'$. Then, any two collapsed trees with one from each set are nonoverlapped at level $n - k$ if $i_1 \ne i_1'$.

For example, consider the two sets of collapsed trees produced from applying the first two rows of C-transforms shown in Fig. 4 to PT_n. Any collapsed tree in one set and any collapsed tree in the other set are nonoverlapped at level $n - k$, because all the C-transforms in a row (i.e., a sequence) are performed at the same level (which implies that a C-transform at the higher level is not performed ahead of that at the lower level), with the C-transform in one row starting with level $n-k-1$ and in the other row starting with a different level, level $n-k-2$.

With these lemmas, we prove Theorem 1 below.

Proof of Theorem 1: (i) Let $[1, 2, \cdots, m]$ denote a sequence of m numbers. Three operators Ω, Ψ, and Δ are defined as follows.

$$[1, 2, \cdots, m] \Omega [1, 2, \cdots, n] = [1, 2, \cdots, m, 1, 2, \cdots, n]$$
$$\Psi(m) = [1, 2, \cdots, m]$$
$$\Psi([1, 2, \cdots, m]) = \Psi(1) \Omega \Psi(2) \Omega \cdots \Omega \Psi(m)$$
$$\Psi^r(x) = \Psi^{r-1}(\Psi(x))$$

where $r > 1$ and x is a number or a sequence
$$\Delta(\Psi(m)) = \Delta([1, 2, \cdots, m]) = \sum_{i=1}^{m} i$$

Assume that A_k^i denotes the sum of the numbers in the ith column in Fig. 5, then we have
$$A_k^1 = n - k = C(n-k, 1)$$
$$A_k^2 = \Delta(\Psi(n-k)) = 1 + 2 + \cdots + (n-k) = C(n-k+1, 2)$$
$$A_k^3 = \Delta(\Psi^2(n-k)) = \Delta(\Psi(1) \Omega \Psi(2) \Omega \cdots \Omega \Psi(n-k))$$
$$= C(2, 2) + C(3, 2) + \cdots + C(n-k+1, 2) = C(n-k+2, 3)$$
(It is easy to verify by induction that $C(q, q) + C(q+1, q) + \cdots + C(p, q) = C(p+1, q+1)$, where p and q are numbers and $p \ge q$.)
$$A_k^4 = \Delta(\Psi^3(n-k)) = \Delta(\Psi^2(1)\Omega\Psi^2(2)\Omega \cdots \Omega\Psi^2(n-k))$$
$$= C(3, 3) + C(4, 3) + \cdots + C(n-k+2, 3) = C(n-k+3, 4)$$
From the above, we can derive $A_k^i = C(n-k+i-1, i)$.

Now, given n and k, by induction we can prove that the total number of C-transforms performed in Algorithm G, δ_k, equals $C(n, k) - 1$ as follows.
Base: $\delta_1 = A_1^1 = n - 1 = C(n, 1) - 1$, true
Induction: if $\delta_{l-1} = C(n, l-1) - 1$ holds, that is
$$A_{l-1}^1 + A_{l-1}^2 + A_{l-1}^3 + \cdots + A_{l-1}^{l-1}$$
$$= C(n-l+1, 1) + C(n-l+2, 2) + C(n-l+3, 3) + \cdots$$
$$+ C(n-1, l-1)$$
$$= C(n, l-1) - 1,$$

then δ_l
$$= A_l^1 + A_l^2 + A_l^3 + \cdots + A_l^{l-1} + A_l^l$$
$$= C(n-l, 1) + C(n-l+1, 2) + C(n-l+2, 3) + \cdots$$
$$+ C(n-2, l-1) + C(n-1, l)$$
$$= \delta_{l-1} - 1 - (C(n-l+1, 1) + C(n-l+2, 2) + \cdots$$
$$+ C(n-2, l-2)) + C(n-1, l)$$
$$= \delta_{l-1} - 1 - (\delta_{l-1} - C(n-1, l-1)) + C(n-1, l)$$
$$= C(n, l) - 1.$$

(ii) Algorithm G has the following facts (as shown in Fig. 4): (1) the highest level to perform C-transforms is $n-k-1$; (2) the maximum length of any sequence of the C-transforms is k; (3) for each sequence, the C-transform is always performed earlier at the lower level than at the higher level; and (4) any two distinct sequences of C-transforms $\xi_{i_1}, \xi_{i_2}, \cdots, \xi_{i_k}$ and $\xi_{i_1'}, \xi_{i_2'}, \cdots, \xi_{i_k'}$ operated upon the primary binary tree representation produce a set of collapsed trees $\{T_n^{(1)}, \cdots, T_n^{(m)}, T_n^{(m+1)}, \cdots, T_n^{(k)}, T_n^{(m+1)\prime}, \cdots, T_n^{(k)\prime}\}$, where m is the least integer such that $i_1 = i_1'$, $i_2 = i_2'$, $\cdots$, $i_m = i_m'$.

(a) From (1), (2) and Lemma 3, it is clear that the collapsed trees produced during any sequence are pairwise nonoverlapped at level $n-k$.

(b) From (1), (2), (3) and (4) and Lemma 4, we reach that any two collapsed trees respectively from the two sets $\{T_n^{(m+1)}, \cdots, T_n^{(k)}\}$ and $\{T_n^{(m+1)\prime}, \cdots, T_n^{(k)\prime}\}$ are nonoverlapped at level $n-k$ since $i_{m+1} \ne i_{m+1}'$.

According to (a) and (b) above, the theorem is proved.

REFERENCES

[1] Y. Saad and M. H. Schultz, "Topological Properties of Hypercubes," *IEEE Trans. on Computers*, pp. 867-872, July 1988.

[2] C. L. Seitz, "The Cosmic Cube," *CACM*, vol. 28, No. 1, pp. 22-23, Jan. 1985.

[3] Intel Corporation, *A New Direction in Scientific Computing*, Order #28009-001, Intel Corporation, 1985.

[4] W. D. Hillis, *The Connection Machine*, Cambridge, MA: The MIT Press, 1985.

[5] Ametek System 14 User's Guide: C Edition, Ametek Computer Research Division, Arcadia, California, 1986.

[6] J. P. Hayes et al., "A Microprocessor-Based Hypercube Supercomputer," *IEEE Micro*, vol. 6, pp. 6-17, Oct. 1986.

[7] H. L. Gustafson, S. Hawkinson, and K. Scott, "The Architecture of a Homogeneous Vector Supercomputer," *Proc. 1986 Int'l Conf. Parallel Processing*, Aug. 1986, pp. 649-652.

[8] J. C. Peterson et al., "The Mark III Hypercube-Ensemble Concurrent Computer," *Proc. 1985 Int'l Conf. Parallel Processing*, Aug. 1985, pp. 71-73.

[9] M.-S. Chen and K. G. Shin, "Processor Allocation in an N-Cube Multiprocessor Using Gray Codes," *IEEE Trans. on Computers*, C-36, 12, pp. 1396-1407, Dec. 1987.

[10] K. C. Knowlton, "A Fast Storage Allocator," *CACM*, vol. 8, No. 10, pp. 623-625, Oct. 1965.

[11] H. S. Stone, "Parallel Processing with the Perfect Shuffle," *IEEE Trans. on Computers*, vol. C-20, pp. 153-161, Feb. 1971.

[12] M.-S. Chen and K. G. Shin, "Task Migration in Hypercube Multiprocessors," *Proc. 16th Annual Int'l Symp. Computer Architecture*, May 1989, pp. 105-111.

[13] A. Al-Dhelaan and B. Bose, "A New Strategy for Processor Allocation in an N-cube Multiprocessor," *Proc. Phoenix Conf. Comp. and Comm.*, Mar. 1989, pp. 114-118.

[14] J. Kim, C. R. Das, and W. Lin, "A Processor Allocation Scheme for Hypercube Computers," *Proc. 1989 Int'l Conf. Parallel Processing*, Aug. 1989, pp. II 231-238.

A New Approach to Fast Control of $r^2 \times r^2$ 3-Stage Benes Networks of $r \times r$ Crossbar Switches

Abdou Youssef

Department of Elect. Eng. & Comput. Sci.
The George Washington University
Washington, DC 20052

Bruce Arden

College of Engineering and Applied Science
University of Rochester
Rochester, NY 14627

ABSTRACT

The routing control of Benes networks has proven to be costly. This paper introduces a new approach to fast control of $N \times N$ 3-stage Benes networks of $r \times r$ crossbar switches as building blocks, where $N = r^2$ and $r \geq 2$. The new approach consists of setting the leftmost column of switches to an apropriately chosen configuration so that the network becomes self-routed while still able to realize a given family of permutations. This approach requires that, for any given family of permutations, a configuration for the leftmost column be found. Such a family is called compatible and the configuration of the leftmost column is called the compatibility factor. In this paper, compatibility is characterized and a technique to determine compatibility and the compatibility factor is developed. The technique is used to show the compatibility and find the compatibilty factor of Ω-realizable permutations, the permutations needed to emulate a hypercube, and the families of permutations required by FFT, bitonic sorting, tree computations, multidimensional mesh and torus computations, and multigrid computations. An $O(\log^2 N)$ time routing algorithm for the 3-stage Benes will also be developed. Finally, as only 3 compatibility factors are required by the above families of permutations, it will be proposed to replace the first column by 3 multiplexed connections yielding a self-routing network with strong communication capabilities.

§1. Introduction

Reconfigurable multistage interconnection networks have been the focus of intensive research due to their central role in the design and performance of large parallel processing systems [5], [6], [9], [18], [24]. The effectiveness of these networks depend on the efficiency of their routing control and the permutations they realize. Some of these networks, called banyan multistage networks, have efficient routing control but do not realize all permutations [1], [10], [14], [21], [23]. Benes networks, however, realize all permutations but have inefficient routing control [5], [16]. Controlling Benes networks involves either computing the switch configurations of permutations in advance and storing them, or computing them at run time. The first way is costly in space for large systems, while the second is costly in time as setting the switches to realize a given permutation takes $O(N \log N)$ sequential time [22] and $O(N)$ parallel time [11], where N is the number of input terminals of the network.

Two different approaches have been introduced to bypass this control complexity. The first, due to Nassimi and Sahni [15], consists of using destination addresses in a specified manner, and allows for the realization of a subset of permutations in optimal time. The second, due to Lenfant [13], identifies families of frequently used permutations, and develops a specialized control algorithm for each family to realize the permutations of the family efficiently. The first approach produces optimal control but allows for the realization of only a small fraction of permutations. The second approach is limited to a few families.

This paper introduces a new approach to controlling 3-stage Benes networks of r^2 input terminals, r^2 output terminals and $r \times r$ crossbar switches, for arbitrary $r \geq 2$ (Fig. 1). These networks can have up to 1024 input/output terminals as the current technology can provide 32×32 crossbar switches. IBM's GF11 [4] is an example of a 3-stage benes-connected parallel system of 24×24 crossbar switches and 576 processors.

The new approach of routing control consists of setting the first stage of the network to a fixed configuration so that the remaining network can be self-routed and can realize a given family of permutations. This approach requires that, for a given family of permutations, the family be examined to determine if there exists a configuration to which the first column of the network can be set so that the remaining network realizes the family (such a family is said to be compatible). This approach combines the advantages of the aforementioned two approaches in having optimal control for numerous large families of permutations.

In this paper compatibility is characterized and a technique to determine compatibility is developed. The technique is used to show the compatibility of the families of permutations required by many interesting classes of problems such as FFT, bitonic sorting, tree computations, multidemensional mesh and torus computations, and multigrid computations. Additional useful families of permutations, such as the permutations realizable by the omaga network, are also shown to be compatible.

The rest of the paper is organized as follows. The next section gives some definitions and fundamental concepts. Compatibility is characterized in Section 3. Section 4 shows the compatibility of several families of permutations. Section 5 identifies the families of permutations required by several interesting classes of problems and shows their compatibility. Finally, Section 6 gives an implementation of the new control scheme and draws some conclusions

CH2887-8/90/0000/0050$01.00 © 1990 IEEE

regarding the possibility of replacing the leftmost column of the 3-stage Benes network with some fixed interconnetions which leads to self-routed networks of powerful communication capibilities.

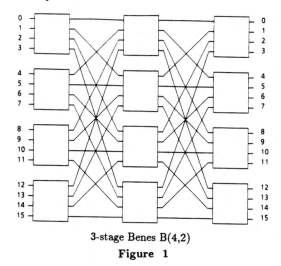

3-stage Benes B(4,2)
Figure 1

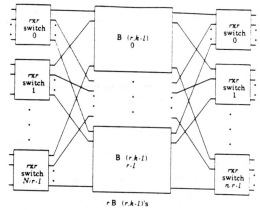

The recursive structure of the Benes network
Figure 2

§2. Definitions and Fundamental Concepts

A Benes network [5], denoted here $B(r,k)$, of r^k input terminals, r^k output terminals, and $r \times r$ crossbar permutation switches as building blocks (where $r \geq 2$), is defined recursively as shown in Fig. 2. For $k = 1$, the network is simply the $r \times r$ crossbar switch. For $k \geq 2$, the connectivity between the leftmost column and the middle $B(r, k-1)$ networks is a permutation that maps (i.e., links) the q-th output port of the p-th switch to the p-th input terminal of the q-th $B(r, k-1)$ for $q = 0, 1, ..., r-1$ and $p = 0, 1, ..., r^{k-1}-1$. The inverse of this permutation connects the output terminals of the middle $B(r, k-1)$ networks to the input ports of the rightmost column. Note that $B(r, k)$ has $2k-1$ columns of r^{k-1} crossbar switches each. An interesting special case is when $k = 2$. The network $B(r, 2)$ has then 3 columns as illustrated in Fig. 1.

The $B(r, 2)$ networks for arbitrary r are the focus of this paper and referred to as *3-stage Benes networks*. Let $N = r^2$ throughout this paper. The columns of $B(r, 2)$ are numbered 0, 1, 2 from left to right, and will often be referred to as left, middle and right column, respectively. Each column has r switches numbered $0, 1, ..., r-1$ from top to bottom. The ports of each column are numbered $0, 1, ..., N-1$, from top to bottom. The q-th port of the p-th switch in any column is then labeled $pr + q$. The connectivity between the left column and middle column is a permutation f where $f(pr+q) = qr+p$, for $p = 0, 1, ..., r-1$ and $q = 0, 1, ..., r-1$. The connectivity between the middle column and the right column is f^{-1} which happens to be equal to f.

Let $R_N = \{0, 1, ..., N-1\}$, $R_r = \{0, 1, ..., r-1\}$, and S_N be the set of permutations of R_N. Every number $x \in$ R_N is uniquely expressed as $pr + q$ for some p and q, where $0 \leq p \leq r-1$ and $0 \leq q \leq r-1$. Let H be the subset of permutations that are realizable by any column of switches of $B(r, 2)$. Observe that H is a subgroup of the symmetric group S_N, and $h \in H$ if $h(pr + q) = pr + q'$ for some q' function of p and q. Let then $q' = t(p, q) = h(pr + q) \bmod r$. Denote by $t(p, .)$ the mapping from R_r to R_r such that $t(p, .)(q) = t(p, q)$. Clearly, $t(p, .)$ is a permutation of R_r.

If $h \in H$, a column of $B(r, 2)$ is said to be *set to h* if the switches are set so that input port $pr + q$ is connected to output port $h(pr + q)$. Equivalently, for $0 \leq p \leq r-1$, the p-th switch of the column is set in such a way that its q-th input port is connected to its $t(p, q)$-th output port.

A permutation ϕ in S_N is *realizable* by $B(r, 2)$ if the switches of $B(r, 2)$ can be set such that the input terminal i is connected to the output terminal $\phi(i)$, for $i = 0, 1, ..., N-1$. A permutation is said to be *h-realizable* for some h in H if it is realizable by $B(r, 2)$ with the left column set to h. A family of m permutations in S_N is said to be *compatible* if there is some permutation $h \in H$ such that all the permutations in the family are h-realizable. The permutation h is then called a *compatibility factor* of the family.

Every path from an input terminal s to an output terminal d in $B(r, 2)$, denoted $s \to d$, goes through six ports $(x_1, x_2, x_3, x_4, x_5, x_6)$, where $x_1 = s$, x_2 is an output port of the left column, x_3 is an input port of the middle column, and so on. Note that $x_3 = f(x_2)$ and $x_5 = f(x_4)$, and therefore, the path is fully decided by x_2 and x_4. Two paths $(x_1, x_2, x_3, x_4, x_5, x_6)$ and $(y_1, y_2, y_3, y_4, y_5, y_6)$ are said to *conflict* if $x_i = y_i$ for some i.

If the left column is set to some configuration h in H, where $h(pr + q) = pr + t(p, q)$, and if the path $(x_1, x_2, x_3, x_4, x_5, x_6)$ between an input terminal $s = x_1 = pr + q$ and an output terminal $d = x_6 = lr + n$ is realizable with the left column set to h, then $x_2 = h(x_1) = pr + t(p, q)$, $x_3 = f(x_2) = t(p, q)r + p$, $x_4 = t(p, q)r + p'$ for some $p' \in R_r$, and $x_5 = f(x_4) = p'r + t(p, q)$. As x_5

51

and x_6 are linked to the same switch in the right column, it follows that $p' = l$. Thus we have:

$$x_1 = pr + q, \quad x_2 = pr + t(p,q),$$
$$x_3 = t(p,q)r + p, \quad x_4 = t(p,q)r + l,$$
$$x_5 = lr + t(p,q), \text{ and } x_6 = d = lr + n.$$

Therefore, if the left column is set to some configuration h in H, there exists a unique path between every input terminal and every output terminal. That path can be determined using the output terminal address [12] as follows: Each switch in the middle column, when receiving a request to connect to some output terminal $lr + n$, links the incoming request to its l-th output port, and each switch in the right column links the incoming request to its n-th output port. Therefore, $B(r,2)$ becomes self-routed when the left column is set to a configuration h in H. Consequently, if a family of permutations is compatible, where one compatibility factor is some h in H, the left column of the 3-stage Benes network can be set to h and the resulting network can realize all the permutations of the family in a self-routed fashion. This is the primary motivation behind our approach.

The main focus of this paper is to determine if a given family of permutations is compatible, and if so, to find one compatibility factor. Compatibility is characterized and various families of permutations that arise from many important classes of problems are identified and shown compatible, and their compatibility factors are found. These compatibility factors (permutations) can then be stored.

When a 3-stage Benes-based computer system executes an algorithm whose communication requirements can be fulfilled by a compatible family of permutations, the left column is first set to the family's compatibility factor (if already found and stored) for the entire duration of the algorithm, allowing then for fast, self-routed realization of the permutations, and leading to speedy execution of the algorithm. Note that the amount of memory required to store the compatibilty factors is very small in comparison with the amount of memory needed to store the setting of the switches for all the $N!$ permutations.

§3. Characterization of Compatibility

In this section, necessary and sufficient conditions for a permutation to be h-realizabale will be given and then a compatibility characterization theorem is concluded which gives necessary and sufficient conditions for a given family of permutations to be compatible. This characterization will be used to show the compatibilty of several interesting families of permutations.

3.1 Lemma. *If the left column is set to some configuration $h \in H$, where $h(pr + q) = pr + t(p,q)$, and if s and s' are two distinct input terminals and d and d' two distinct output terminals, where $s = pr + q$, $s' = p'r + q'$, $d = lr + n$, and $d' = l'r + n'$, then the paths $s \to d$ and $s' \to d'$ conflict if and only if $t(p,q) = t(p',q')$ and $l = l'$.*

Proof. Let the path $(s \to d) = (x_1, x_2, x_3, x_4, x_5, x_6)$ and $(s' \to d') = (y_1, y_2, y_3, y_4, y_5, y_6)$. Since $x_1 \neq y_1$, it follows

that $h(x_1) \neq h(y_1)$ and $f(h(x_1)) \neq f(h(y_1))$, and hence $x_2 \neq y_2$ and $x_3 \neq y_3$. We have also $x_6 \neq y_6$. Therefore, the two paths conflict if and only if $x_4 = y_4$ or $x_5 = y_5$. As $x_5 = f(x_4)$ and $y_5 = f(y_4)$, we have $x_4 = y_4$ if and only if $x_5 = y_5$. So the two paths conflict if and only if $x_4 = y_4$. It was shown in the preceding section that $x_4 = t(p,q)r + l$, and $y_4 = t(p',q')r + l'$. Hence, $x_4 = y_4$ if and only if $t(p,q) = t(p',q')$ and $l = l'$. ∎

3.2 Theorem. *Let h be in H where $h(pr + q) = pr + t(p,q)$. Let also ϕ be a permutation in S_N, and $\alpha(p,q) = \lfloor \frac{\phi(pr+q)}{r} \rfloor$. ϕ is h-realizable if and only if for every two distinct input terminals $s = pr + q$ and $s' = p'r + q'$, $\alpha(p,q) = \alpha(p',q')$ implies that $t(p,q) \neq t(p',q')$.*

Proof. Let $s = pr + q$ and $s' = p'r + q'$ be two arbitrary distinct input terminals, and let $\phi(s) = d = lr + n$ and $\phi(s') = d' = l'r + n'$, where $l = \alpha(p,q)$ and $l' = \alpha(p',q')$. Clearly, $d \neq d'$. If ϕ is h-realizable, then the paths $s \to d$ and $s' \to d'$ do not conflict in $B(r,2)$ with the left column set to h. After the preceding lemma, we must have either $t(p,q) \neq t(p',q')$ or $l \neq l'$. Therefore, if $\alpha(p,q) = \alpha(p',q')$, then $t(p,q) \neq t(p',q')$.

Conversely, if for every two distinct input terminals $s = pr + q$ and $s' = p'r + q'$, $\alpha(p,q) = \alpha(p',q')$ implies that $t(p,q) \neq t(p',q')$, then by the preceding lemma, for every two distinct input terminals s and s', the paths $s \to \phi(s)$ and $s' \to \phi(s')$ do not conflict in $B(r,2)$ with the left column set to h. Consequently, ϕ is h-realizable. ∎

3.3 The Compatibility Characterization Theorem.

Let $\{\phi_1, \phi_2, ..., \phi_m\}$ be a family of permutations in S_N, and $\alpha_i(p,q) = \lfloor \frac{\phi_i(pr+q)}{r} \rfloor$, for $i = 1, 2, ..., m$. The family $\{\phi_1, \phi_2, ..., \phi_m\}$ is compatible if and only if there is a mapping $t: R_r \times R_r \to R_r$ such that:
(i) $t(p,.)$ is a permutation of R_r for every p in R_r.
(ii) If for some $p, p', q, q' \in R_r$ there exists i such that $\alpha_i(p,q) = \alpha_i(p',q')$ and $p \neq p'$, then $t(p,q) \neq t(p',q')$.

Proof. Assume first that $\phi_1, \phi_2, ..., \phi_m$ are compatible, and that h is a compatibility factor. Let t be such that $h(pr + q) = pr + t(p,q)$. Clearly, $t(p,.)$ is a permutation of R_r for every p. To show (ii), assume that for some p, p', q, q' in R_r there exists i such that $\alpha_i(p,q) = \alpha(p',q')$ and $p \neq p'$. Let $s = pr + q$ and $s' = p'r + q'$. Clearly $s \neq s'$ because $p \neq p'$. Since ϕ_i is h-realizable, $s \neq s'$ and $\alpha_i(p,q) = \alpha_i(p',q')$, it follows that $t(p,q) \neq t(p',q')$, after Theorem 3.2.

Conversely, assume that there is a mapping $t : R_r \times R_r \to R_r$ that satisfies (i) and (ii). Let h be the mapping from R_N to R_N such that $h(pr + q) = pr + t(p,q)$. Since $t(p,.)$ is a permutation of R_r for every p, h must a permutation in H. For every i, ϕ_i will be shown h-realizable using Theorem 3.2. Let $s = pr + q$ and $s' = p'r + q'$ such that $s \neq s'$ and $\alpha_i(p,q) = \alpha_i(p',q')$. Since $s \neq s'$, we have $p \neq p'$ or $q \neq q'$. If $p \neq p'$, it follows from (ii) that $t(p,q) \neq t(p',q')$. If $p = p'$, then $q \neq q'$ and therefore $t(p,q) \neq t(p,q')$ because $t(p,.)$ is a permutation. So in both cases $t(p,q) \neq t(p',q')$. After Theorem 3.2, ϕ_i is h-realizable. ∎

It can be seen from the proof of the previous theorem

52

that when there is a mapping t that satisfies the conditions (i) and (ii) of the theorem, one compatibility factor of the family is a permutation $h \in H$ where $h(pr+q) = pr + t(p,q)$.

It is worthwhile to note that Theorem 3.3 can be mapped into a graph-theoretic problem, namely, the node coloring problem. Let $\phi_1, \phi_2, ..., \phi_m$ be m permutations in S_N. Let G = (V,E) be the following undirected graph: V = $R_r \times R_r$ and E = $\{((p,q),(p',q'))|p = p' \text{ or } (\exists i)(\alpha_i(p,q) = \alpha_i(p',q'))\}$. The theorem can now be stated as follows: $\phi_1, \phi_2, ..., \phi_m$ are compatible if and only if G can be r-colored such that no two adjacent nodes have the same color. To prove this, let $t(p,q)$ be the color of node (p,q). It is clear that t satisfies condition (i) and (ii) of Theorem 3.3 if and only if t r-colors G in such a way that no two adjacent nodes have the same color.

The general coloring problem is NP-complete, but it remains open whether these graphs have any peculiarities that open the door to a fast (i.e., polynomial) algorithm to r-color them. Such an algorithm would automate deciding compatibility and finding a compatibility factor.

Using this graph formulation, it can be shown that not every family of permutations is compatible. Take for example $r = 2$, (and hence $N = 4$ and $R_r = \{0,1\}$), $\phi_1 = (0\ 1\ 2)(3)$ and $\phi_2 = (0)(1\ 2\ 3)$. It can be shown that $\alpha_1(0,0) = \alpha_1(1,0) = 0$, $\alpha_1(0,1) = \alpha_1(1,1) = 1$, $\alpha_2(0,0) = \alpha_2(1,1) = 0$, and $\alpha_2(0,1) = \alpha_2(1,0) = 1$. The corresponding graph G is depicted in Fig. 3. Since G has a 3-clique, it cannot be 2-colored and, therefore, ϕ_1 and ϕ_2 are not compatible.

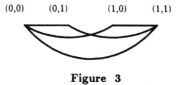

(0,0)   (0,1)   (1,0)   (1,1)

Figure 3

§4. Compatible Families of Permutations

Various families of permutations will be shown compatible in this section. In particular, two large families of permutations, namely, the family of *pseudo bit translations* and the *L-family*, will be defined and shown to be compatible. The permutations realizable by the omega network Ω_N will also be shown compatible. In the next section, the families of permutations required by many application areas will be shown to be subfamilies of these three families and hence compatible. In the remainder of the paper, r is assumed to be a power of two ($r = 2^k$), and therefore, $N = r^2 = 2^{2k}$.

Every number $x = pr + q$ in R_N can be expressed in binary as $x = x_{2k-1}x_{2k-2}...x_0$ and conveniently also as $x = p_{k-1}p_{k-1}...p_0 q_{k-1}q_{k-2}...q_0$, where $p = p_{k-1}p_{k-2}...p_0$ and $q = q_{k-1}q_{k-2}...q_0$. The bit positions $0, 1, ..., k-1$ of x (i.e., the k least significant bits) are said to form the *q-wing* of x, and the bit positions $k, k+1, ..., 2k-1$ (i.e., the k most significant bits) the *p-wing* of x. For $i = 0, 1, ..., k-1$, bits p_i and q_i are called *siblings*. Also, p_i is the *p-sibling* of

q_i and q_i the *q-sibling* of p_i.

If π is a permutation of $\{0, 1, ..., 2k-1\}$, then f_π denotes a permutation in S_N, called a *bit permutation*, such that $f_\pi(x_{2k-1}x_{2k-2}...x_0) = x_{\pi(2k-1)}x_{\pi(2k-2)}...x_{\pi(0)}$. A bit permutation f_π manipulates the bits of its parameter x, moving the i-th bit of x to bit position $\pi^{-1}(i)$, for $i = 0, 1, ..., 2k-1$. A *pseudo bit translation* is a bit permutation f_π that satisfies the following condition: f_π moves a bit from the q-wing to the p-wing if and only if f_π moves the p-sibling of that bit to the q-wing.

4.1 Theorem. *All pseudo bit translations are compatible and their compatibility factor is h such that $h(pr + q) = pr + (p \oplus q)$, where $p \oplus q$ is the bitwise XOR of p and q.*

Proof. Let $t(p,q) = p \oplus q$. It is enough to show that t satisfies the conditions (i) and (ii) of Theorem 3.3.

(i) $t(p,.)$ is a permutation since $t(p,.)(q) = t(p,.)(q') \Rightarrow t(p,q) = t(p,q') \Rightarrow p \oplus q = p \oplus q' \Rightarrow q = q'$.

(ii) Assume that for some p, p', q, $q' \in R_r$ there is a pseudo bit translation ϕ such that $\alpha_\phi(p,q) = \alpha_\phi(p',q')$ and $p \neq p'$. We need to show that $t(p,q) \neq t(p',q')$. Let E be the set of bit positions of the q-wing that are moved to the p-wing by ϕ. Since ϕ is a pseudo bit translation, E must also be the set of p-wing bit positions that move to the q-wing.

$\alpha_\phi(p,q) = \alpha_\phi(p',q') \Rightarrow [(\forall i \notin E)(p_i = p'_i)$ and $(\forall i \in E)(q_i = q'_i)] \Rightarrow q \oplus q'$ has 0's in all bit positions $i \in E$.

$p \neq p' \Rightarrow (\exists i_0)(p_{i_0} \neq p'_{i_0}) \Rightarrow p \oplus p'$ has '1' in bit position i_0. Clearly $i_0 \in E$ because $\forall i \notin E$ we have $p_i = p'_i$. Therefore $(p \oplus p') \oplus (q \oplus q')$ has '1' in bit position i_0. Consequently, $t(p,q) \oplus t(p',q') = (p \oplus q) \oplus (p' \oplus q') = (p \oplus p') \oplus (q \oplus q') \neq 0$. Hence, $t(p,q) \neq t(p',q')$. ∎

Fig. 4-a shows the setting of the left column for pseudo bit translations.

Next we define the *L-family* and show it to be compatible. For every permutation ϕ in S_N, let $\alpha_\phi(p,q) = \lfloor \frac{\phi(pr+q)}{r} \rfloor$ = the leftmost k bits of $\phi(pr+q)$. The *L-family* of permutations in S_N is the set

$L = \{\phi \in S_N|$ if $\alpha_\phi(p,q) = \alpha_\phi(p',q')$ and $p \neq p'$, then p and p' agree in all but one bit position, and q and q' agree in at least one bit position$\}$

To show that the L-family is compatible, the set of switches of the left column (i.e., the set R_r of the switch labels) is partitioned into two subsets E_k and F_k, which will be defined recursively such that the binary representations of any two numbers in each subset disagree in at least two bit positions. Let $E_1 = \{0\}$, $F_1 = \{1\}$ and recursively $E_i = 0E_{i-1} \cup 1F_{i-1}$ and $F_i = 0F_{i-1} \cup 1E_{i-1}$, where $aE_{i-1} = \{ax_{i-2}...x_0|\ x_{i-2}...x_0 \in E_{i-1}\}$ for $a=0$ or 1, and aF_{i-1} is defined similarly. For example, $0E_1 = \{00\}$, $0F_1 = \{01\}$, $1E_1 = \{10\}$, $1F_1 = \{11\}$, and consequently, $E_2 = \{00, 11\}$ and $F_2 = \{01, 10\}$.

It can be easily shown by induction on $i = 1, 2, ..., k$ that $E_i \cup F_i = \{0, 1, ..., 2^i - 1\}$ (in decimal), $E_i \cap F_i = \emptyset$ and for $i > 1$, any two numbers in each of the sets E_i and F_i disagree in at least two bit positions. In particular, $E_k \cap F_k = \emptyset$ and $E_k \cup F_k = \{0, 1, ..., r-1\} = R_r$

4.2 Theorem. *The L-familiy is compatible and its compatibility factor is h such that $h(pr+q) = pr+q$ if $p \in E_k$ and $h(pr+q) = pr+\overline{q}$ if $p \in F_k$, where $\overline{q}$ is the bitwise complement of q.*

Proof. Let $t(p,q) = q$ if $p \in E_k$ and $t(p,q) = \overline{q}$ if $p \in F_k$. It will be shown that t satisfies the two conditions (i) and (ii) of Theorem 3.3.

(i) $t(p,.)$ is a permutation because $t(p,q) = t(p,q') \Rightarrow [q = q'$ or $\overline{q} = \overline{q'}] \Rightarrow q = q'$.

(ii) Assume that for some p, p', q, $q' \in R_r$ there is a permutation $\phi \in L$ such that $\alpha_\phi(p,q) = \alpha_\phi(p',q')$ and $p \neq p'$. By definition of L, it follows that p and p' agree in all but one bit position, and q and q' agree in at least one bit position. Consequently, p and p' cannot both be in the same E_k or F_k. Assume without loss of generality that $p \in E_k$ and $p' \in F_k$. Then $t(p,q) = q$ and $t(p',q') = \overline{q'}$. As q and q' agree in at least one bit position, q and $\overline{q'}$ must disagree in at least one bit position, and therefore, $t(p,q) \neq t(p',q')$. ∎

Fig. 4-b shows the setting of the left column for the L-family.

In addition to the above two families, two more families will be shown compatible, namely, the set H and the set of permutations realizable by the omega network Ω_N [10].

4.3 Theorem. *For every h and $g \in H$, g is h-realizable. In particular, H is compatible and its compatibilty factor can be any arbitrary permutation $h \in H$.*

Proof. Let h and g be two permutations in H, and let I

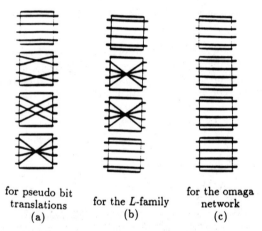

for pseudo bit   for the omaga
translations   for the L-family   network
(a)   (b)   (c)

The configurations of the left column
for various families

Figure 4

be the identity permutation which is also in H. As H is a subgroup of S_N, $h^{-1}g \in H$. Set the left column of $B(r,2)$ to h, the middle column to I and the right column to $h^{-1}g$. This setting realizes the permutation $hfIfh^{-1}g$ which is equal to g (recall that $f = f^{-1}$ and hence $fIf = ff = I$). It follows that $B(r,2)$ can realize g with its left column set

to h. ∎

4.4 Theorem. *The permutations realizable by the omega network Ω_N of N input terminals, N output terminals, and 2×2 crossbar switches as building blocks, are compatible and their compatibility factor is the identity permutation.*

Proof. Let $t(p,q) = q$. It will be shown that t satisfies conditions (i) and (ii) of Theorem 3.3.

(i) Since $t(p,.)(q) = t(p,q) = q$, $t(p,.)$ is the identity permutation of R_r.

(ii) Assume that for some p, p', q, and q' in H there is a permutation ϕ realizable by Ω_N such that $\alpha_\phi(p,q) = \alpha_\phi(p',q')$ and $p \neq p'$. It will be proved next that $t(p,q) \neq t(p',q')$. It was shown in [10] that a permutation ψ is realizable by Ω_N if and only if $(\forall s = s_{2k-1}s_{2k-2}...s_0 \in R_N)(\forall s' = s'_{2k-1}s'_{2k-2}...s'_0 \in R_N)(\forall l < \log N = 2k-1)$ (if $s \neq s'$ and $d_{2k-1}d_{2k-2}...d_{l+1} = d'_{2k-1}d'_{2k-2}...d'_{l+1}$, then $s_l s_{l-1}...s_0 \neq s'_l s'_{l-1}...s'_0$), where $\psi(s) = d_{2k-1}d_{2k-2}...d_0$ and $\psi(s') = d'_{2k-1}d'_{2k-2}...d'_0$. This will be used to show that $t(p,q) \neq t(p',q')$.

Let $s = pr + q$, $s' = p'r + q'$ and $l = k-1$. Thus $p = s_{2k-1}...s_k$, $q = s_{k-1}...s_0$, $p' = s'_{2k-1}...s'_k$ and $q' = s'_{k-1}...s'_0$. Let also $\phi(s) = d_{2k-1}d_{2k-2}...d_0$ and $\phi(s') = d'_{2k-1}d'_{2k-2}...d'_0$. Then $\alpha_\phi(p,q) = d_{2k-1}d_{2k-2}...d_k$ and $\alpha_\phi(p',q') = d'_{2k-1}d'_{2k-2}...d'_k$.

$\alpha_\phi(p,q) = \alpha_\phi(p',q') \Rightarrow d_{2k-1}d_{2k-2}...d_k = d'_{2k-1}d'_{2k-2}...d'_k$. $p \neq p' \Rightarrow s \neq s'$. As ϕ is realizable by Ω_N, it follows that $s_{k-1}s_{k-2}...s_0 \neq s'_{k-1}s'_{k-2}...s'_0$ which implies that $q \neq q'$, that is $t(p,q) \neq t(p',q')$.

Therefore, by Theorem 3.3, all the permutations realizable by Ω_N are h-realizable, where $h(pr+q) = pr+t(p,q) = pr+q$, that is, the identity permutation. ∎

Fig. 4-c shows the setting of the left column for the Ω_N-realizable permutations.

§5. Applications

In this section the families of permutations of several problems are identified and shown to be subfamilies of the families in the last section, and hence compatible.

5.1 The Fast Fourier Transform

To compute FFT in the way described in [19], two permutations are needed: The shuffle (S) and the exchange (E), where $S(x_{2k-1}x_{2k-2}...x_0) = x_{2k-2}...x_0x_{2k-1}$ and $E(x_{2k-1}x_{2k-2}...x_0) = x_{2k-1}x_{2k-2}...x_1\overline{x_0}$. However, at the end of the computation, the components of the resulting vector are in bit reversed order. To restore the order, the bit reversal permutation (ρ) is needed, where $\rho(x_{2k-1}x_{2k-2}...x_0) = x_0x_1...x_{2k-2}x_{2k-1}$. Thus, the overall family of permutations needed by FFT is $\{S, E, \rho\}$.

5.1 Theorem. *The permutations needed by FFT are compatible.*

Proof. As $S(p_{k-1}p_{k-2}...p_0q_{k-1}...q_0) = p_{k-2}...p_0q_{k-1}...q_0p_{k-1}$, it follows that S moves only one bit from the q-wing to the p-wing, namely bit q_{k-1}, and only one bit from the p-wing to the q-wing, namely, p_{k-1}. As these two bits are siblings, S is a pseudo bit translation. The bit reversal ρ moves every bit of the q-wing to the p-wing and every bit of the p-wing to the q-wing. Therefore, ρ is trivially a pseudo bit translation. After Theorem 4.1, S and ρ are h-realizable where $h(pr + q) = pr + p \oplus q$. Since $E \in H$, E must be h-realizable for the same h, after Theorem 4.3. ∎

5.2 Bitonic Sorting

Although parallel sorting algorithms of $O(\log N)$ time have been found [2], they are not practical due to the extremely large multiplicative constant factor of $\log N$. Bitonic Sorting, though of time complexity $O(\log^2 N)$, is a practical parallel algorithm [19].

As shown in [19], N numbers can be sorted using a sorting network of $\frac{\log_2 N(\log_2 N+1)}{2}$ stages of comparison switches and based on Batcher's bitonic sorter [3]. Simulating this sorting network on 3-stage Benes networks involves realizing the interconnections (i.e., permutations) between the columns of the sorting network, as well as the columns of switches themselves.

Bitonic sorting and the sorting network based on the bitonic sorter are briefly reviewed next, and the permutations required to simulate the sorting network on $B(r,2)$ are identified and shown to be compatible.

A sequence of real numbers $a_0, a_1, ... a_{N-1}$ is *bitonic* if
(1) there exists i such that $\{a_0, a_1, ..., a_i\}$ is increasing, and $\{a_{i+1}, ..., a_{N-1}\}$ is decreasing; or if
(2) the sequence can be shifted cyclically so that (1) is satisfied.

An $N \times N$ bitonic sorter is a recursive network where, for $N = 2$, it is a 2×2 comparison switch that takes two input numbers and puts the smaller in the upper output port and the larger in the lower output port (as in Fig. 5-a), or vice versa (as in Fig. 5-b), according to a control bit. For larger N, it is as depicted in Fig. 6. It is shown in [3] and [19] that if the input is a bitonic sequence, then this network sorts the input in increasing order. If the switches of the network of Fig. 6 are replaced by switches of the type in Fig. 5-b, the network sorts the bitonic input in decreasing order.

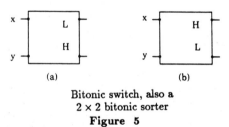

(a)   (b)

Bitonic switch, also a
2×2 bitonic sorter
Figure 5

A full sorting network that sorts any sequence of $N = 2^m$ numbers can be built in m steps, where the i-th step is a column of $\frac{N}{2^i}$ $2^i \times 2^i$ bitonic sorters as shown in Fig. 7. The network works as follows. The first step sorts pairs of numbers into alternately increasing and decreasing pairs so that each sequence of 4 numbers is bitonic. The second step sorts these bitonic sequences into alternately increasing and decreasing sequences so that each sequence of 8 numbers is bitonic. And so on to the last step which receives a bitonic

sequence of length N. Since the last step is an $N \times N$ bitonic sorter, it can sort the incoming sequence. Fig. 8 shows an 8×8 sorting network where the shaded switches place the larger item on the top output, and the blank switches place the smaller on top.

The operations of the sorting network can be viewed as a sequence of data permutations. First the items are permuted by the first column of comparison switches, second they are permuted by the interconnection between the first column and the second column, and then permuted by the second column of switches, and so on. Therefore, the simulation of the sorting network on $B(r,2)$ is done by executing the above sequence of permutations on $B(r,2)$ in order, assuming that the input and output terminals of $B(r,2)$ are N processing elements $pe_0, pe_1, ..., pe_{N-1}$.

Note that when simulating a column of comparison switches (column j, say), more than permuting is required. Assume the numbers coming to this column are $b_0, b_1, ... b_{N-1}$ from top to bottom. Then, in our simulation, these numbers are in $pe_0, pe_1, ... pe_{N-1}$, respectively, when column j is due to be simulated. At comparison switch i of column j, the incoming numbers are b_{2i} and b_{2i+1}. Hence, in simulation, these numbers are in pe_{2i} and pe_{2i+1}, respectively. To be able to do comparison in the simulation, each of pe_{2i} and pe_{2i+1} must have both b_{2i} and b_{2i+1}, for $i = 0, 1, ..., N - 1$. This can be accomplished by first executing the exchange permutation on the numbers, and then if switch i of the sorting network is in state (a) (as in Fig. 5-a), pe_{2i} keeps $\min(b_{2i}, b_{2i+1})$, while pe_{2i+1} keeps

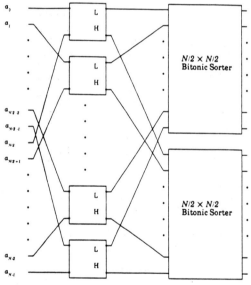

The structure of the bitonic sorter
Figure 6

$\max(b_{2i}, b_{2i+1})$. If the comparison switch is in state (b), the opposite is done. Note that the states of the comparison switches of the sorting network can be known *a priori*.

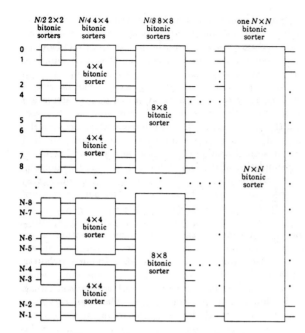

The general structure of the $N \times N$
sorting network based on bitonic sorters

Figure 7

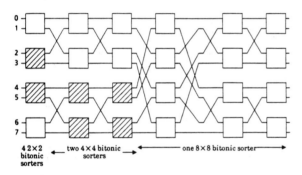

An 8×8 sorting network

Figure 8

The interconnection permutations between the successive columns of the sorting network are identified in the following lemma.

5.2 Lemma. *The inter-column interconnections of the sorting network form the set*

$$\{S_i | 0 \le i \le m-2\} \cup \{U_i S_{i+1} | 0 \le i \le m-2\}$$

where

$$S_i(x_{m-1}...x_0) = x_{m-1}...x_{m-i}x_{m-i-2}...x_0 x_{m-i-1}$$

---

and

$$U_i(x_{m-1}...x_1 x_0) = x_{m-1}...x_{m-i}x_0 x_{m-i-1}...x_1.$$

Proof. Observe first that S_0 is the perfect shuffle on $\{0, 1, ..., 2^m - 1\}$, S_1 is the perfect shuffle within two segments which are $\{0, 1, ..., 2^{m-1} - 1\}$ and $\{2^{m-1}, 2^{m-1} + 1, ..., 2^m - 1\}$, and in general, S_i is the perfect shuffle within 2^i contiguous segments of length 2^{m-i} each. Similarly, U_0 is the perfect unshuffle (i.e, the inverse of S_0) on $\{0, 1, ..., 2^m - 1\}$, and U_i is the perfect unshuffle (i.e., $U_i = S_i^{-1}$) within the same 2^i contiguous segments which S_i shuffles. A close inspection of the bitonic sorter in Fig. 6 shows that the leftmost interconnection is the perfect shuffle S_0, and the interconnection between the first column and the other 2 $\frac{N}{2} \times \frac{N}{2}$ bitonic sortes is the unshuffle U_0. The leftmost interconnection of these 2 $\frac{N}{2} \times \frac{N}{2}$ bitonic sorters must then be S_1. It follows then that the interconnection between the first two columns is $U_0 S_1$. It can be easily shown by induction that the remaining interconnections are $U_1 S_2, U_2 S_3, ...U_{m-2}S_{m-1}$, due to the recursive structure of the bitonic sorter.

As described earlier, the sorting network (Fig. 7) has at the i-th block (from the left) $\frac{N}{2^i}$ $2^i \times 2^i$ bitonic sorters, whose interconnections are then
$S_{m-i}, U_{m-i}S_{m-i+1}, U_{m-i+1}S_{m-i+2}, ..., U_{m-2}S_{m-1}$,
for $i = 2, 3, ..., m$. Note that the first block is just the first column of comparison switches and has no interconnections. It follows that the interconnections of the sorting network are
$$\cup_{2 \le i \le m}\{S_{m-i}, U_{m-i}S_{m-i+1}, U_{m-i+1}S_{m-i+2}, ...U_{m-2}S_{m-1}\}$$
which is equal to $\{S_i | 0 \le i \le m-2\} \cup \{U_i S_{i+1} | 0 \le i \le m-2\}$. ∎

5.3 Theorem. *The permutations required by bitonic sorting are compatible.*

Proof. Note that $m = 2k$ and that for $i \ge k$, $S_i(x)$ does not alter the k most significant bits of x, and therefore, S_i is in the set H. Note also that
$$(x_{m-1}...x_0)U_i S_{i+1} = S_{i+1}(x_{m-1}...x_{m-i}x_0 x_{m-i-1}...x_1)$$
$$= x_{m-1}...x_{m-i}x_0 x_{m-i-2}...x_1 x_{m-i-1}$$
and therefore $U_i S_{i+1}$ does not alter the k most significant bits if $i \ge k$. Hence, for $i \ge k$, $U_i S_{i+1} \in H$. The exchange permutation E needed to simulate the columns of the sorting network is also in H. After Theorem 4.3, H is compatible and its compatibility factor is arbitrary. Consequently, it suffices to show that the remaining permutations $S_0, S_1, ..., S_{k-1}, U_0 S_1, U_1 S_2, ..., U_{k-1}S_k$ are compatible. In fact, they will be shown to be in the L-family.
For all $i < k$, $S_i(p_{k-1}...p_0 q_{k-1}...q_0) =$
$p_{k-1}...p_{k-i}p_{k-i-2}...p_0 q_{k-1}...q_0 p_{k-i-1}$. Let $\alpha_i(p, q)$ be the leftmost bits of $S_i(p_{k-1}...p_0 q_{k-1}...q_0)$, that is, $\alpha_i(p, q) = p_{k-1}...p_{k-i}p_{k-i-2}...p_0 q_{k-1}$.
$[\alpha_i(p, q) = \alpha_i(p', q')$ and $p \ne p'] \Rightarrow [p$ and p' agree in all but bit position $k-i-1$, and q and q' agree in at least bit position $k-1] \Rightarrow S_i \in L$.
Similarly, for $i < k$, we have $(p_{k-1}...p_0 q_{k-1}...q_0)U_i S_{i+1} =$
$p_{k-1}...p_{k-i}q_0 p_{k-i-2}...p_0 q_{k-1}...q_1 p_{k-i-1}$.

56

Let $\alpha_i(p,q)$ be the k leftmost bits of

$$(p_{k-1}...p_0 q_{k-1}...q_0) U_i S_{i+1},$$

that is, $\alpha_i(p,q) = p_{k-1}...p_{k-i}q_0 p_{k-i-2}...p_0$.
$[\alpha_i(p,q) = \alpha_i(p',q')$ and $p \neq p'] \Rightarrow [p$ and p' agree in all but bit position $k-i-1$, and q and q' agree in at least bit position $0] \Rightarrow U_i S_{i+1} \in L$.
Therefore, all the permutations required by bitonic sorting are compatible and their compatibility factor is h of Theorem 4.2. ∎

5.3 Tree Computations

Many parallel computations require full binary tree structures. These include semigroup computations such as addition and multiplication of N numbers, finding the maximum or minimum of N numbers, logical *and* and logical *or* operations on N boolean values, and any other associative operators.

If these algorithms are to run on 3-stage Benes systems, then the tree communication structure has to be emulated by permutations as explained next. Assume a full binary tree of $N-1$ nodes, where $N = 2^{2k}$. The nodes are labeled by level in a standard way where the root is labeled 1 and every internal node i has node $2i$ as its left child and node $2i+1$ as its right child. In the top-down tree communication, each node may send data to its chidren. In the bottom-up communication, each node may send data to its parent. The top-down communication can be accomplished in two steps, where each step can be carried out on $B(r,2)$ by a permutation. In the first step the parents send data to their left children, and in the second step the parents send data to the right children. As the shuffle permutation S maps i to $2i$ for all $i \leq \frac{N}{2}-1$, S can then carry out the first step. In the second step, where every node $i \leq \frac{N}{2}-1$ may send to node $2i+1 = E(2i)$, the permutation SE, which is the composition of S and the exchange E, can carry out the communication because $(i)SE = E(S(i)) = E(2i) = 2i+1$.

Similarly, the bottom-up communication can be accomplished by two steps, where in the first step the left children send data to their parents, and in the second the right children send data to the parents. The first step can be carried out by the unshuffle permutation U, where $U(x_{2k-1}x_{2k-2}...x_1x_0) = x_0 x_{2k-1}x_{2k-2}...x_1$ (in particular, $U(2i) = i$ for $i \leq \frac{N}{2}-1$). The second step where $2i+1$ has to map to $i = U(2i) = U(E(2i+1) = (2i+1)EU$ can be done by the composition EU.

Therefore, the permutations required are
$$\{S, SE, U, EU\},$$
which will be shown to be in the L-family and hence compatible.

5.4 Theorem. *The permutations required by tree computations are compatible.*

Proof. From the definitions of S, SE, U and EU, it can be easily seen that $\alpha_S(p,q) = \alpha_{SE}(p,q) = p_{k-2}p_{k-3}...p_0 q_{k-1}$, $\alpha_U(p,q) = q_0 p_{k-1}p_{k-2}...p_1$, and $\alpha_{EU}(p,q) = \overline{q_0}p_{k-1}p_{k-2}...p_1$, where $p = p_{k-1}p_{k-2}...p_0$ and $q = q_{k-1}q_{k-2}...q_0$.

$\alpha_S(p,q) = \alpha_S(p',q')$ clearly implies that
$$p_{k-2}p_{k-3}...p_0 q_{k-1} = p'_{k-2}p'_{k-3}...p'_0 q'_{k-1}$$
and, therefore, p and p' agree in the right $k-1$ bit positions, and q and q' agree in bit position $k-1$. If in addition $p \neq p'$, then p and p' must agree in all but one position because they can disagree in only bit position $k-1$. Therefore, S is in L. As $\alpha_S(p,q) = \alpha_{SE}(p,q)$, it follows that SE is in L too.

Similarly, $\alpha_U(p,q) = \alpha_U(p',q')$ clearly implies that
$$q_0 p_{k-1}p_{k-2}...p_1 = q'_0 p'_{k-1}p'_{k-2}...p'_1$$
and, therefore, p and p' agree in the left $k-1$ bit positions, and q and q' agree in bit position 0. If in addition $p \neq p'$, then p and p' must agree in all but one position. Therefore, U is in L.
A similar proof would show that EU is in L. It follows then that all the four permutations are compatible after Theorem 4.2. ∎

5.4 Multidimensional Torus and Mesh Computations

Toruses and meshes are very useful structures in image processing and scientific computing. The permutations required to emulate these structures on $B(r,2)$ will be shown to be realizable by the omega network Ω_N and therefore compatible.

An n-dimensional $l_1 \times l_2 \times ... \times l_n$ mesh (resp. torus) is a graph where the set of nodes is $R_{l_1} \times R_{l_2} \times ... \times R_{l_n}$ (recall that $R_z = \{0,1,...,z-1\}$) and any two nodes $(x_1, x_2, ..., x_n)$ and $(x'_1, x'_2, ..., x'_n)$ form an edge if and only if there exists some j such that $(\forall i \neq j)(x_i = x'_i)$ and $x_j = x'_j + 1$ or $x_j = x'_j - 1$ (in the torus case, $+$ and $-$ are modulo l_j). Note that the only difference between meshes and toruses is that toruses have "wrap around" edges.

The communication in toruses and meshes is usually done along one dimension at a time, and also in the same direction. That is, in a communication step there exist some j and $a = 1$ or -1 such that every node $(x_1, x_2, ..., x_{j-1}, x_j, x_{j+1}, ..., x_n)$ may send data to node $(x_1, x_2, ..., x_{j-1}, x_j + a, x_{j+1}, ..., x_n)$, where in the case of torus the addition in the j-th dimension is modulo l_j. Therefore, a communication step in a mesh or torus can be carried out by a permutation $f_j^{(a)}$ such that $f_j^{(a)}(x_1, x_2, ..., x_n) = (x_1, x_2, ..., x_{j-1}, (x_j + a) \bmod l_j, x_{j+1}, ..., x_n)$, where $j = 1, 2, ..., n$ and $a = 1$ or -1.

These permutations will be shown to be realizable by Ω_N when each l_j is a power of two for all $j = 1, 2, ..., n$, and the number of nodes $l_1 \times l_2 \times ... \times l_n = N = 2^{2k}$. To do so we need the following two lemmas which are presented without proof because the first is straightforward and the second follows from the first. They will be used in the following subsection also.

5.5 Lemma. *Let m be a positive integer and $a = 2^i$ or -2^i, where $0 \leq i \leq m-1$. Let also x and x' be two m-bit binary numbers. If $(x + a) \bmod 2^m$ and $(x' + a) \bmod 2^m$ agree in the l most significant bits, then x and x' agree in the l most significant bits.*

5.6 Lemma. Let $m_1, m_2, ..., m_n$ be n positive integers, j an integer in $\{1, 2, ..., n\}$ and $a = 2^i$ or -2^i, where $0 \le i \le m_j - 1$. Let also $x = (x_1, x_2, ..., x_n)$ and $x' = (x'_1, x'_2, ..., x'_n)$ where $(\forall c = 1, 2, ..., n)(x_c$ and x'_c are m_c-bit binary numbers). View the binary representation of x (resp. x') as the concatenation of the binary representations of $x_1, x_2, ..., x_n$ (resp., $x'_1, x'_2, ..., x'_n$). If $(x_1, x_2, ..., x_{j-1}, (x_j + a) \mod 2^{m_j}, x_{j+1}, ..., x_n)$ and $(x'_1, x'_2, ..., x'_{j-1}, (x'_j + a) \mod 2^{m_j}, x'_{j+1}, ..., x'_n)$ agree in the most significant l bits, then x and x' agree in the most significant l bits.

5.7 Theorem. The permutations of multidimensional toruses and meshes of 2^{2k} nodes are compatible.

Proof. Assume the torus (or mesh) is an n-dimensional $2^{m_1} \times 2^{m_2} \times ... \times 2^{m_n}$ torus (or mesh), where $m_1 + m_2 + ... m_n = 2k$. It will be shown that $(\forall j = 1, 2, ..., n)(\forall a = -1, 1)(f_j^{(a)}$ is realizable by $\Omega_N)$. Using the characterization in [10] of permutations realizable by Ω_N, it is enough to show that for all j and a

$(\forall s, s' \in R_N)(\forall l = 1, 2..., 2k - 1)($ if $s \ne s'$ and $d_{2k-1}...d_{l+1} = d'_{2k-1}...d'_{l+1}$, then $s_l s_{l-1}...s_0 \ne s'_l s'_{l-1}...s'_0)$

where

$s = s_{2k-1}...s_0 = (x_1, x_2, ..., x_n)$,
$s' = s'_{2k-1}...s'_0 = (x'_1, x'_2, ..., x'_n)$,
$f_j^{(a)}(s) = d_{2k-1}...d_0$
$= (x_1, ..., x_{j-1}, (x_j + a) \mod 2^{m_j}, x_{j+1}, ..., x_n)$
$f_j^{(a)}(s') = d'_{2k-1}...d'_0$
$= (x'_1, ..., x'_{j-1}, (x'_j + a) \mod 2^{m_j}, x'_{j+1}, ..., x'_n)$.

After Lemma 5.6, $d_{2k-1}...d_{l+1} = d'_{2k-1}...d'_{l+1}$ yields that $s_{2k-1}...s_{l+1} = s'_{2k-1}...s'_{l+1}$, which in turn implies that $s_l s_{l-1}...s_0 \ne s_l s_{l-1}...s_0$ because $s \ne s'$. ∎

5.5 Hypercube Computations

Hypercubes are a special case of multidimesional toruses. Specifically, a hypercube of dimension n is the n-dimensional $2 \times 2 \times ... \times 2$ torus. In particular, the node labels $(x_1, x_2, ..., x_n)$'s are binary and $(x_j + 1) \mod 2 = (x_j - 1) \mod 2 = \overline{x_j}$. Consequently, $f_j^{(a)}(x_1, x_2, ..., x_n) = (x_1, ...x_{j-1}, \overline{x_j}, x_{j+1}, ...x_n)$, whether $a = 1$ or -1.

5.8 Theorem. The permutations of the hypercube of dimension $2k$ are compatible.

Proof. Since the hypercube is a torus, the theorem follows from Theorem 5.7. ∎

5.6 Multigrid Computations

A grid is a two-dimensional mesh. Multigrid computations are common in image processing [20] and scientific computing [7], [8]. The communications in these computations are between nodes that differ in only one dimension by 2^i for $i = 0, 1, 2, ...$ In terms of permutations, the permutations required by a $2^k \times 2^k$ multigrid computations are:
$f_{i,1}^{(1)}(x_1, x_2) = (x_1 + 2^i, x_2)$, $f_{i,1}^{(-1)}(x_1, x_2) = (x_1 - 2^i, x_2)$,
$f_{i,2}^{(1)}(x_1, x_2) = (x_1, x_2 + 2^i)$, and $f_{i,2}^{(-1)}(x_1, x_2) = (x_1, x_2 - 2^i)$,
for $i = 0, 1, 2, ..., k - 1$, where $+$ and $-$ are modulo 2^k.

5.9 Theorem. The permutations of $2^k \times 2^k$ multigrid computations are compatible.

Proof. The proof can be easily carried out using Lemma 5.6 and following the same line of reasoning as in Theorem 5.7. ∎

§6. Conclusions

A new approach to controlling 3-stage Benes networks has been developed. It consists of finding a configration to which the leftmost column can be set so that a given family of permutations can be realized in a self-routed fashion, leading to fast communication and speedy execution of algorithms. The speedup is high when the compatible family of permutations is large. Compatibility, that is, the existence of an appropriate configuration for the leftmost column, was characterized and a technique to show compatibility was derived from the characterization theorem. Various interesting families of permutations were shown compatible and an appropriate configuration of the leftmost column was found for each family. The unsolved case is how to proceed when the permutations cannot be functionally defined (as in FFT and bitonic sorting) but are irregular as in sparse linear systems. More generally, the problem of deciding compatibility in polynomial time remains open.

The implementation of the new approach of routing control is straightforward and can be integrated into the instruction set of the system. A one-bit flag is needed. For each known compatible family, its compatibilty factor h is stored in memory. Before a certain algorithm starts to run, if the family of permutations required by the algorithm is compatible, the compatibility factor is loaded to the leftmost column of the network and the flag is set to 1. Otherwise, the flag is set to 0. If the system has already an instruction REALIZE-PERM that takes a permutation (or a pointer to it) as operand and sets the network to it, then when the flag is set to 0, the same execution takes place; otherwise, the permutation is realized in the self-routed mode using destination addresses. This implementation shows the utility of the new control scheme when the algorithms require compatible permutations.

Among the families that were shown compatible was the family of permutations required by bitonic sorting. One consequence to this is a new $O(\log^2 N)$ routing control algorithm for 3-stage Benes networks: As sorting destination addresses brings the sources to their destinations, a permutation can be realized on the 3-stage Benes in as many passes as needed by bitonic sorting, that is $\frac{\log N(\log N+1)}{2} = O(\log^2 N)$. Another consequence is that the leftmost column of the 3-stage Benes network can be replaced by the interconnection (i.e., configuration) that is the compatibility factor of the permutations of bitonic sorting. The resulting network is cheaper and self-routed, and realizes any permutation in $O(\log^2 N)$ passes. It also realizes the permutations of bitonic sorting and tree computations in a single pass.

Along the same lines, the leftmost column can be replaced by the three compatibility factors (i.e., interconnections) that have been identified as needed by many interesting problem areas. Some multiplexers can be added to choose one of the three interconnections as required. Then every one of the computation areas discussed in this paper and shown to need a compatible family of permutations can be run efficiently on the resulting self-routed network.

§7. References

[1] D. P. Agrawal and J. -S. Leu, "Dynamic accessibility testing and path length optimization of multistage interconnection networks," *IEEE Trans. Comput.*, C-34, pp. 255–266, Mar. 1985.

[2] M. Ajtai, J. Kanlos and E. Szemeredi, "Sorting in clog *n* parallel steps," *Combinatorica* 3, pp. 1-19, 1983.

[3] K. E. Batcher, "Sorting networks and their applications," *1968 Spring Joint Comput. Conf., AFIPS Conf.* Vol. 32, Washington, D.C.: Thompson, 1968, pp. 307–314.

[4] J. Beetem, M. Denneau, and D. Weingarten, "The GF11 Supercomputer," *The 12th ann. Int'l Sump. on Comp. Arch.*, 1985, pp. 108–113.

[5] V. E. Benes, *Mathematical theory on connecting networks and telephone traffic,* Academic Press, New York, 1965.

[6] L. N. Bhuyan and D. P. Agrawal, "Design and performance of generalized interconnection networks," *IEEE Trans. Comput.*, pp. 1081–1090, Dec. 1983.

[7] A. Brandt, "Multigrid Solvers on parallel computers," in *Elliptic Problem Solvers* (M. Schultz, ed.), New York, pp. 39–83, 1981.

[8] T. F. Chan and Y. Saad, "Multigrid algorithms on the Hypercube multiprocessor," *IEEE Trans. Comput.*, vol. C-35, pp. 969–977, Nov. 1986.

[9] T. Feng, "A survey of interconnection networks," *Computer,* Vol. 14, pp. 12–27, Dec. 1981.

[10] D. K. Lawrie, "Access and alignment of data in an arrary processor," *IEEE Trans. Comput.*, C-24, pp. 1145–1155, Dec. 1975.

[11] K. Y. Lee, "On the rearrangeability of $2(\log_2 N) - 1$ stage permutation networks," *IEEE Trans. Comput.*, C-34, pp. 412–425, May 1985.

[12] K. Y. Lee, "A Nerw Benes Network Control Algorithm," *IEEE Trans. Comput.*, C-36, pp. 768–772, May 1987.

[13] J. Lenfant, "Parallel permutations of data: A Benes network control algorithm for frequently used permutations," *IEEE Trans. Comput.*, C-27, pp. 637–647, July 1978.

[14] G. F. Lev, N. Pippenger and L. G. Valiant, "A fast parallel algorithm for routing in permutation networks," *IEEE Trans. Comput.*, C-,30 pp. 93–100, Feb. 1981.

[15] D. Nassimi ans S. Sahni, "A self-routing Benes network and parallel permutation algorithms," *IEEE Trans. Comput.*, C-30, pp. 332–340, May 1981.

[16] D. C. Opferman and N. T. Tsao-Wu, "On a class of rearrangeable switching networks, Parts I and II," *Bell Syst. Tech. J.,* pp. 1579–1618, May-June 1971.

[17] M. C. Pease, "The indirect binary n-cube multiprocessor array," *IEEE Trans. Comput.*, C-26, pp. 458–473, May 1976.

[18] H. J. Siegel and S. Smith, "Study of multistage interconnection networks," *Proc. Fifth Annual Symp. Comp. Arch.,* pp. 223–229, Apr. 1978.

[19] H. S. Stone, "Parallel processing with the perfect shuffle," *IEEE Trans. Comput.*, C-20, pp. 153–161, Feb. 1971.

[20] Q. F. Stout, "Hypercubes and Pyramids," in *Pyramidal Systems for Computer Vision*, edited by V. Cantoni and S. Levialdi, Springer-Verlag, Berlin, 1986.

[21] T. H. Szymanski and V. C. Hamacher, "On the permutation Capibility of multistage interconnection networks," *IEEE Trans. Comput.*, C-36, pp. 810–822, July 1987.

[22] A. Waksman, "A permutation network," *JACM,* Vol. 15, No. 1 pp. 159–163, Jan 1968.

[23] C. Wu and T. Feng, "On a class of multistage interconnection networks," *IEEE Trans. Comput.*, C-29, pp. 694–702, Aug. 1980.

[24] A. Youssef, *Properties of multistage interconnection networks,* Ph.D. dissertation, Princeton University, Feb. 1988.

Virtual-Channel Flow Control[1]

William J. Dally

Artificial Intelligence Laboratory and
Laboratory for Computer Science
Massachusetts Institute of Technology
Cambridge, Massachusetts 02139

Abstract

Network throughput can be increased by dividing the buffer storage associated with each network channel into several virtual channels [DalSei]. Each physical channel is associated with several small queues, virtual channels, rather than a single deep queue. The virtual channels associated with one physical channel are allocated independently but compete with each other for physical bandwidth. Virtual channels decouple buffer resources from transmission resources. This decoupling allows active messages to pass blocked messages using network bandwidth that would otherwise be left idle. Simulation studies show that, given a fixed amount of buffer storage per link, virtual-channel flow control increases throughput by a factor of 3.5, approaching the capacity of the network.

1 Introduction

Interconnection Networks

The processing nodes of a concurrent computer exchange data and synchronize with one another by passing messages over an interconnection network [AthSei, BBN86, Dally89, Seitz85]. The interconnection network is often the critical component of a large parallel computer because performance is very sensitive to network latency and throughput and because the network accounts for a large fraction of the cost and power dissipation of the machine.

An interconnection network is characterized by its topology, routing, and flow control [Dally89b]. The topology of a network is the arrangement of nodes and channels into a graph. Routing specifies how a packet chooses a path in this graph. Flow control deals with the allocation of channel and buffer resources to a packet as

---
[1] The research described in this paper was supported in part by the Defense Advanced Research Projects Agency under contracts N00014-80-C-0622 and N00014-85-K-0124 and in part by a National Science Foundation Presidential Young Investigator Award with matching funds from General Electric Corporation and IBM Corporation.

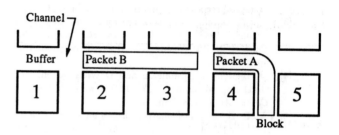

Figure 1: Packet B is blocked behind packet A while all physical channels remain idle.

it traverses this path. This paper deals only with flow control. It describes a method for allocating resources to packets using virtual channels [DalSei]. This method can be applied to any topology and routing strategy.

The Problem

The throughput of interconnection networks is limited to a fraction (typically 20%-50%) of the network's capacity [Dally87] because of coupled resource allocation.

Interconnection networks are composed of two types of resources: buffers and channels. Typically, a single buffer is associated with each channel. Once a packet, A, is allocated the buffer, no other packet, B, can use the associated channel until A releases the buffer. If packet A becomes blocked while holding the buffer, the channel is idled even though there may be other packets in the network that can make productive use of the channel.

This situation is illustrated in Figure 1. In the figure, the network is depicted as a network of streets where each block corresponds to a buffer and each intersection represents one or more channels that connect buffers. Packet A holds buffers 4N (north of block 4) and 4E and is blocked. Packet B is unable to make progress even though all physical channels it requires, (3N to 4N) and (4N to 5N), are idle because Packet A holds

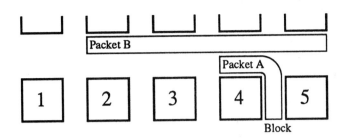

Figure 2: Virtual channels provide additional buffers (lanes) allowing Packet B to pass blocked Packet A.

buffer 4N which is coupled to channel (3N to 4N).

Virtual Channel Flow Control

Virtual channels decouple resource allocation by providing multiple buffers for each channel in the network. If a blocked packet, A, holds a buffer associated with a channel, another buffer is available allowing other packets to pass A. Figure 2 illustrates the addition of virtual channels to the network of Figure 1. Packet A remains blocked holding buffers 4N.1 and 4E.1. In Figure 2, however, Packet B is able to make progress because alternate buffer 4N.2 is available allowing it access to channel (3N to 4N).

Adding virtual channels to an interconnection network is analogous to adding lanes to a street network. A network without virtual channels is composed of one-lane streets. In such a network, a single blocked packet blocks all following packets. Adding virtual channels to the network adds lanes to the streets allowing blocked packets to be passed.

In addition to increasing throughput, virtual channels provide an additional degree of freedom in allocating resources to packets in the network. This flexibility permits the use of scheduling strategies, such as routing the oldest packet first, that reduce the variance of network latency.

The most costly resource in an interconnection network is physical channel (wire) bandwidth. The second most costly resource is buffer memory. Adding virtual channel flow control to a network makes more effective use of both of these resources by decoupling their allocation. The only expense is a small amount of additional control logic.

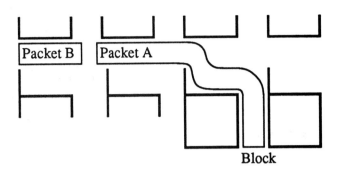

Figure 3: Output queueing or partitioned input queues provide one stage of decoupling. However, long packets (such as Packet A) continue to couple resources and cannot be passed.

Background

The use of virtual channels for flow control builds on previous work in using virtual channels for deadlock avoidance and in using output queueing or split input queues for partial resource decoupling. Virtual channels were introduced in [DalSei] for purposes of deadlock avoidance. A cyclic network can be made deadlock-free by restricting routing so there are no cycles in the channel dependency graph and then adding virtual channels to reconnect the network.

A single stage of resource decoupling is provided by output queueing [KHM87]. By performing the queueing in the output of a switch rather than the input, arriving packets are able to pass blocked messages arriving on the same input. Tamir [Tamir88] has shown how to achieve the same single-stage resource decoupling by partitioning the switch's input queue. This single stage resource decoupling is effective only if an entire packet fits in a single node. As shown in Figure 3 , when a long packet is blocked, it backs up into the output stage of the previous node preventing any following packet from passing it. Extending our roadway analogy, output queueing provides a "turning lane".

Summary

The next section introduces the notation and assumptions that will be used throughout this paper. Section 3 describes virtual channel flow control in detail. The results of simulating networks using virtual channel flow control are described in Section 4.

2 Preliminaries

Topology

An interconnection network consists of a set of **nodes**, N, and a set of **channels**, $C \subseteq N$. Each channel is unidirectional and carries data from a source node to a destination node. A bidirectional network is one where $(n1, n2) \in C \Rightarrow (n2, n1) \in C$.

Routing

A packet is assigned a route through the network according to a **routing relation**, $R \subseteq C \times N \times C$, given the channel occupied by the head of the packet and the destination node of the packet, the routing relation specifies a (possibly singleton) set of channels on which the packet can be routed.

Flow Control

Communication between nodes is performed by sending **messages**. A message may be broken into one or more **packets** for transmission. A packet is the smallest unit of information that contains routing and sequencing information. A packet contains one or more flow control digits or **flits**. A flit is the smallest unit on which flow control is performed. Information is transferred over physical channels in physical transfer units or **phits**. A phit is usually the same size or smaller than a flit.

The flow control protocol of a network determines (1) how resources (buffers and channel bandwidth) are allocated and (2) how packet collisions over resources are resolved. A resource collision occurs when a packet, P, is unable to proceed because some resource it needs (usually a buffer) is held by another packet. Collisions may be resolved by (1) blocking P in place, (2) buffering P in a node prior to where the collision occurs, (3) dropping P , or (4) misrouting P to a channel other than the one it requires. The technique described in this paper is applicable to all of these flow control strategies but is most appropriate for networks that use blocking or limited buffering to resolve collisions.

The flow control strategy allocates buffers and channel bandwidth to flits. Because flits have no routing or sequencing information, the allocation must be done in a manner that keeps the flits associated with a particular packet together. This may be done by associating a set of buffers and some control state together into a virtual channel. A virtual channel or lane is allocated to a packet and the buffers of the lane are allocated in

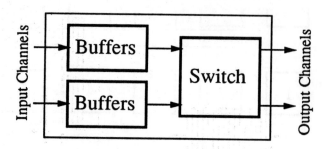

Figure 4: Node organization. Each network node contains a set of buffers for each input channel and a switch.

a FIFO manner to the flits of that packet.

Most networks associate only a single lane with each channel. This paper describes a method for improving the performance of networks by associating several lanes with each channel. This method makes no assumptions about how wires are allocated.

Wormhole Routing

The technique described here is particularly suitable for use in networks that use wormhole routing [Dally87]. Wormhole routing refers to a flow-control protocol that advances each flit of a packet as soon as it arrives at a node (pipelining) and blocks packets in place when required resources are unavailable. Wormhole routing is attractive in that (1) it reduces the latency of message delivery compared to store and forward routing, and (2) it requires only a few flit buffers per node. Wormhole routing differs from virtual cut-through routing [KerKle] in that with wormhole routing it is not necessary for a node to allocate an entire packet buffer before accepting each packet. This distinction reduces the amount of buffering required on each node making it possible to build fast, inexpensive routers.

3 Virtual Channel Flow Control

Structure

Each node of an interconnection network contains a set of buffers and a switch[2] In this paper, we assume that the buffers are partitioned into sets associated with each input channel, an input-buffered node, as shown in Figure 4. An output-buffered switch [KHM87, Tamir88]

---

[2]Each node also contains driver and receiver circuits to communicate across the physical wires and control logic.

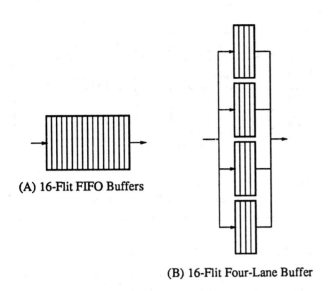

(A) 16-Flit FIFO Buffers

(B) 16-Flit Four-Lane Buffer

Figure 5: (A) Conventional nodes organize their buffers into FIFO queues restricting routing. (B) A network using virtual-channel flow control organizes its buffers into several independent lanes.

can be considered to be an input buffered switch with a non- blocking first stage by associating the buffers on the output of each stage with the inputs of the next stage.

A conventional network organizes the flit buffers associated with each channel into a first-in, first-out (FIFO) queue as shown in Figure 5A. This organization restricts allocation so that each flit buffer can contain only flits from a single packet. If this packet becomes blocked, the physical channel is idled because no other packet is able to acquire the buffer resources needed to access the channel.

A network using virtual channel flow control organizes the flit buffers associated with each channel into several lanes as shown in Figure 5B. The buffers in each lane can be allocated independently of the buffers in any other lane. This added allocation flexibility increases channel utilization and thus throughput. A blocked message, even one that extends through several nodes, holds only a single lane idle and can be passed using any of the remaining lanes.

Operation

In a network using virtual channel flow control, flow control is performed at two levels. At the packet level packets are assigned to virtual channels or lanes. At the flit level channel bandwidth, switch bandwidth, and individual buffers are allocated to flits.

Lane assignment is performed by the node (node A) at the transmitting end of the physical channel. For each of its output channels, this node keeps track of the state of each lane buffer at the opposite end of the channel. For each lane, the state information includes whether the lane is assigned, and if assigned, how many empty buffers it contains. A packet in an input buffer on node A selects a particular output channel based on its destination and the routing algorithm in use. The flow-control logic then assigns this packet to any free lane of the selected channel. If all lanes are in use, the packet is blocked.

Maintaining lane state information on the transmitting end of the channel allows lane assignment to be performed on a single node. No additional internode communication is required to maintain this information as it is already required for flit-level flow control.

Once a lane is assigned to a packet, flit-level flow control is used to advance the packet across the switch and physical channel. To advance from the input buffer on the transmitting node (node A) to the input buffer on the receiving node (node B), a flit must gain access to (1) a path through the switch to reach the output of node A, and (2) the physical channel to reach the input of node B. Typically either the switch is non-blocking, and thus always available, or a few flits of buffering are provided at the output of node A so that switch and channel resources do not have to be allocated simultaneously.

When the last flit of a message (the tail flit) leaves a node the lane assigned to that packet is deallocated and may be reassigned to another packet.

Allocation Policies

Flit-level flow control across the physical channel involves allocating channel bandwidth among lanes that (1) have a flit ready to transmit and (2) have space for this flit at the receiving end. Any arbitration algorithm can be used to allocate this resource including random, round-robin, or priority.

Deadline scheduling [LiuLey] can be implemented by allocating channel bandwidth based on a packet's deadline or age – earliest deadline or oldest age first. Scheduling packets by age reduces the variance of message latency. Deadline scheduling provides several classes of delivery service and reduces the variance within each class.

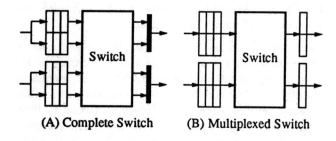

(A) Complete Switch   (B) Multiplexed Switch

Figure 6: (A) Adding virtual channels increases switch complexity if a complete switch is used. (B) using a multiplexed switch leaves switch complexity unchanged.

Implementation Issues

Virtual channel flow control can be integrated into existing switch designs by replacing FIFO buffers with multi-lane buffers. When this replacement is made, however, the switch must be modified to deal with a larger number of inputs and outputs, and the flow control protocol between nodes must be modified to identify lanes.

Increasing the number of virtual channels multiplexed on each physical channel increases the number of inputs and outputs that must be switched at each node. If the switch handles each of these inputs and outputs separately as shown in Figure 6(A), the switch complexity will increase significantly. Increasing the switch complexity is not required, however. The average data rate out of the set of lanes associated with a given physical channel is limited to the bandwidth of the channel. Thus it is sufficient to provide a single switch input for each physical input and output channel as shown in Figure 6(B). With this organization, a small (one or two flit) output buffer is desirable to decouple switch allocation from physical channel allocation. Individual lanes are multiplexed onto the single path through the switch in the same manner that they are multiplexed over the single physical channel between the nodes.

Any network that uses blocking or buffering flow control must, for each channel, send information in the reverse direction to indicate the availability of buffering on the receiving node. These acknowledgment signals can be transmitted on separate wires [DalSon] or, in a bidirectional network, they can be transmitted out-of-band on a channel in the opposite direction [Inmos].

In a network using multi-lane buffers, two effects increase the acknowledgment traffic. First, a few bits must be added to each acknowledgment signal to iden-

tify the lane being acknowledged. Second, because a lane buffer is typically smaller than a channel FIFO, the use of block acknowledgments to amortize the cost of the signal over several flits is restricted[3].

Even with these effects, acknowledgment signal bandwidth is still a small fraction of forward bandwidth. In a network with 32-bit flits, 15 lanes per channel, and no block acknowledgment, 4 bits must be sent along the reverse channel for each flit transmitted along the forward channel, a 12.5% overhead. An additional 12.5% overhead is required to identify the lane associated with each flit sent in the forward direction. Such a scheme could be realized by a physical channel consisting of an 9-bit forward path (8-bit phits) and a 1-bit reverse path. Every four channel cycles a 32-bit flit is transmitted over the forward path along with its 4-bit lane identifier and a 4-bit acknowledgment code is transmitted over the reverse path. Efficiency can be improved further by increasing the flit size or using block acknowledgments.

4   Experimental Results

To measure the effect of virtual channel flow control on network performance (throughput and latency) we have simulated a number of networks holding the total buffer storage per node constant and varying the number of lanes per channel. If lanes are added, the depth of each lane is proportionally reduced.

The simulator is a 3000 line C program that simulates interconnection networks at the flit-level. A flit transfer between two nodes is assumed to take place in one time unit. The network is simulated synchronously moving all flits that have been granted channels in one time step and then advancing time to the next step. The simulator is programmable as to topology, routing algorithm, and traffic pattern.

Throughput is measured by applying to each network input a saturation source that injects a new packet into the network whenever a lane is available on its input channel. Throughput is given as a fraction of network capacity. A uniformly loaded network is operating at capacity if the most heavily loaded channel is used 100% of the time.

Latency is measured by applying a constant rate source to each input and measuring the time from packet creation until the last flit of the packet is accepted at the destination. Source queueing time is included in the

---

[3]A block acknowledgments signals the availability of a block (several flits) of storage in a single action rather than signalling each flit separately

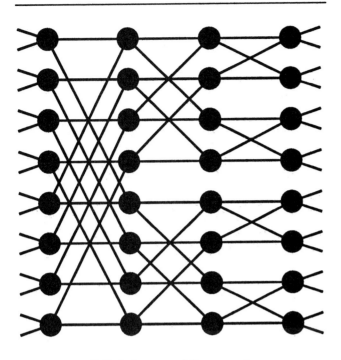

Multistage Network

Figure 7: A 2-ary 4-fly network.

latency measurement.

Multistage Networks

Multistage (k-ary n-fly) networks have kn inputs connected to kn outputs by n-stages of kn-1 k x k -switches. For example, a 2-ary 4-fly is shown in Figure 7. Because of their simplicity, simulations of multistage networks were used to evaluate virtual channel flow control. The method is in no way specific to multistage networks. It is equally applicable to other topologies including direct networks such as k-ary n- cubes, and trees.

Throughput

Figure 8 shows the saturation throughput versus the number of lanes per channel for radix-2 multistage networks (2-ary n- flys). Data is shown for networks with dimensions of 4,6,8, and 10. Each network simulated has 16 flits of storage per channel. The number of lanes per channel was varied from 1 (conventional network) to 16 in powers of two.

The simulations were run with packet length fixed at

20 flits and uniformly distributed random packet destinations. Channel bandwidth was allocated randomly to lanes.

The results show that adding lanes to a network greatly increases its throughput, particularly for large networks. The radix 10 (1024-input) network shows a throughput gain of 250%, throughput more than tripled, with the addition of lanes. The first few lanes results in most of the improvement with diminishing returns for larger numbers of lanes. Increasing from 8 to 16 lanes gives only a 14% improvement for the radix 10 network. This suggests that 4 to 8 lanes per channel is adequate for most networks.

Adding lanes holding the total storage constant gives a far greater throughput improvement than does increasing the total amount of buffering with a single lane (see [Mailhot]).

Latency

Figure 9 shows the average packet latency versus offered traffic for radix-2 dimension- 8 multistage networks (2-ary 8-flys). As above, each network simulated has 16 flits of storage per node, and the number of lanes per node was varied from 1 to 16 in powers of two.

The results show that adding lanes has little effect on latency below the saturation throughput of a conventional network. The curves lie on top of each other below a traffic of 0.2. Above this point the latency of a conventional network is infinite (no data for 1 lane) and the addition of lanes extends the latency curve smoothly for each network simulated until it reaches its saturation throughput.

Each network's departure from the smooth latency curve as saturation is reached is smoother than shown in this figure. The abrupt transition shown in the figure is due to the coarse spacing of data points at 10% increments in network load.

Scheduling Algorithm

Figure 10 shows the effect of the channel scheduling algorithm on latency. The figure shows two latency histograms, one for a random assignment of channel bandwidth to packets, and the other for oldest-packet-first channel bandwidth allocation (deadline scheduling). Both curves are for 2-ary 6- fly networks with random traffic operating at 50% capacity. The histograms have been truncated at 128 cycles latency.

The use of deadline scheduling reduced the average latency slightly, from 74.4 cycles to 71.8 cycles and dra-

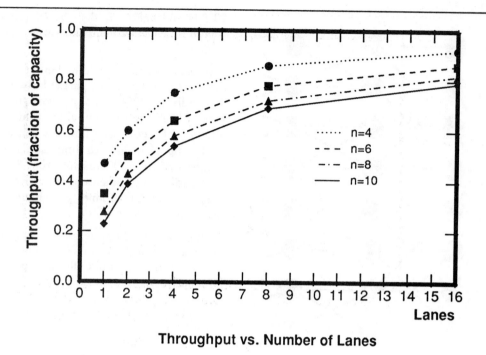

Throughput vs. Number of Lanes

Figure 8: Throughput vs. number of lanes for radix-2 multistage networks under random traffic. Throughput increases rapidly as lanes are added with diminishing returns for larger numbers of lanes. For the dimension-10 network throughput with 16 lanes is 3.5 times the throughput with a single lane.

matically reduced the variation in latency. With deadline scheduling 4619 packets, over one quarter of all packets delivered during the simulation, had a latency of 23 cycles, the minimum possible for this network. The deadline curve also shows smaller peaks of 949, 277, and 93 packets at 43, 63, and 83 cycles that are due to packets that had to wait one or more entire packet delays (about 20 cycles) before being able to proceed. These peaks stand out from the background level that slopes from about 100 packets per cycle at 24 cycles latency to about 30 packets per cycle at 128 cycles latency.

In contrast to the sharp peaks of the deadline curve, the random curve shows broad peaks at 43 and 83 cycles. The random curve also has a higher background level except in the region from 24 cycles to 36 cycles. The two curves cross over at 36 cycles. The data suggest that deadline scheduling can be useful in reducing average message latency and in making message latency more predictable.

The experiment shown here was run with all packets having the same deadline (their birth time). The same scheduling algorithm can be used to provide different classes of service by giving some packets tighter deadlines than others. This would be useful, for example,

in a switch that handles both voice and data where the voice traffic has a tight deadline and should be dropped if it cannot make its deadline.

5 Conclusion

The performance of interconnection networks can be improved by organizing the buffers associated with each network channel into several lanes or virtual channels rather than a single FIFO queue. Associating several lanes with each physical channel decouples the allocation of virtual channels to packets from the allocation of physical channel bandwidth to flits. This decoupling allows active messages to pass blocked messages dramatically improving network throughput.

The use of virtual channel flow control also allows flexibility in allocating physical channel bandwidth. By decoupling resource allocation, a channel's bandwidth need not be allocated to the "next packet in line". Instead, this bandwidth may be allocated on the basis of packet type, age, or deadline. The use of deadline scheduling may be particularly important in networks where one class of packets must be delivered in a bounded amount of time.

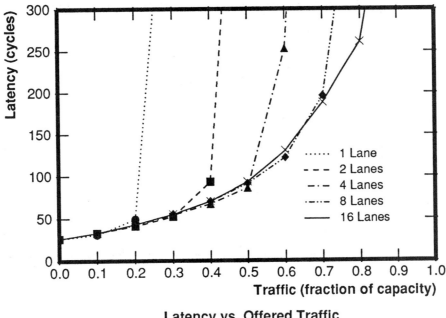

Latency vs. Offered Traffic

Figure 9: Latency vs. offered traffic for 2-ary 8-flys under random traffic. Adding lanes to the network has little effect on latency below saturation throughput for a single lane. Above this point, the latency curves for multiple lanes are extended smoothly until they reach their saturation throughput levels.

Several indirect (2-ary n-fly) networks have been simulated to measure the performance of virtual channel flow control. These simulations show that with the total amount of buffer storage per node held constant, adding lanes increased throughput by a significant factor. For a 2-ary 10-fly network (1024 input butterfly), the throughput with 16 lanes per channel is 3.5 times the throughput with a single lane.

Simulations also indicate that adding lanes has little effect on latency below saturation throughput and extend the latency curve smoothly as throughput is improved. The use of deadline scheduling reduces average latency by a small amount and makes latency much more predictable.

The critical resources in an interconnection network are wire bandwidth and buffer memory. Virtual channel flow control is a method for allocating these critical resources in a more efficient manner. With network switches constructed using VLSI circuits, the cost of adding the small amount of control state and logic required to implement multiple lanes per channel is well worth the cost.

Acknowledgment

I thank Steve Ward, Anant Agarwal, Tom Knight, and Charles Leiserson for many discussions about interconnection networks and their analysis. Appreciation is due to the referees for many helpful comments and suggestions. Finally, I thank all the members of the MIT Concurrent VLSI Architecture group and especially Scott Wills, Dave Chaiken, and Waldemar Horwat for their help with and contributions to this paper.

References

[AthSei] Athas, W.C., and Seitz, C.L., "Multicomputers: Message-Passing Concurrent Computers," IEEE Computer, Vol 21, No 8, August 1988, pp. 9-24.

[BBN86] BBN Advanced Computers, Inc., Butterfly Parallel Processor Overview, BBN Report No 6148, March 1986.

[Dally87] Dally, W.J. "Wire-Efficient VLSI Multiprocessor Communication Networks," Proceedings of the Stanford Conference on Advanced Research in VLSI, Paul Losleben, ed., MIT Press, March 1987, pp. 391-

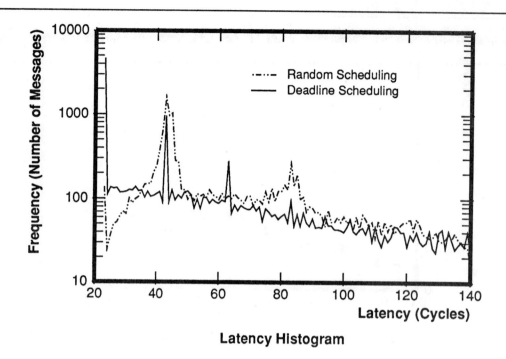

Latency Histogram

Figure 10: Latency histogram for a 2-ary 6-fly network with random traffic at 50% capacity using deadline (oldest first) and random scheduling of physical channels. The histogram for deadline scheduling has a sharp peak at 23 and smaller peaks at 43, 63, and 83. The curve for random scheduling shows a broad peak at 43.

415.

[Dally89a] Dally, W.J., et. al., "The J- Machine: a Fine-Grain Concurrent Computer," Information Processing 89, Elsevier North Holland, 1989.

[Dally89b] Dally, W.J., "Network and Processor Architecture for Message-Driven Computing," in VLSI and Parallel Processing, R. Suaya and G. Birtwistle eds., Morgan Kaufmann, to appear 1989.

[DalSei] Dally, W.J. and Seitz, C.L., "Deadlock Free Message Routing in Multiprocessor Interconnection Networks," IEEE Transactions on Computers, Vol C-36, No 5, May 1987, pp. 547-553.

[DalSon] Dally, W.J., and Song, P., "Design of a Self-Timed VLSI Multicomputer Communication Controller", Proceedings IEEE International Conference on Computer Design, ICCD-87, October 1987, pp 230-234.

[Inmos] Inmos Limited, IMS T424 Reference Manual, Order No 72 TRN 006 00, Bristol, UK, November 1984.

[KerKle] Kermani, P., and Kleinrock, L., "Virtual Cut-Through: A New Computer Communication Switching Technique," Computer Networks, Vol 3, 1979, pp. 267-286.

[KHM87] Karol, M.J., Hluchyj, M.G., and Morgan, S.P., "Input Versus Output Queueing on a Space-Division Packet Switch," IEEE Transactions on Communications, Vol COM- 35, No 12, December 1987, pp. 1347- 1356.

[LiuLey] Liu and Leyland, "Scheduling Algorithms for Multiprogramming in a Hard Real-Time Environment," Journal of the ACM, Vol 20, No 1, January 1973, pp. 46- 61.

[Mailhot] Mailhot, J.N., A Comparative Study of Routing and Flow-Control Strategies in k- ary n-cube Networks, Massachusetts Institute of Technology, SB Thesis, May 1988.

[Seitz85] Seitz, C.L., "The Cosmic Cube," Communications of the ACM, Vol 28, No 1, January 1985, pp. 22-33.

[Tamir88] Tamir, Y., and Frazier, G.L., "High-Performance Multi-Queue Buffers for VLSI Communication Switches," 15th annual ACM/IEEE Symposium on Computer Architecture, June 1988, pp. 343-354.

Session 2A: Special-Purpose Architectures

Supporting Systolic and Memory Communication in iWarp

Shekhar Borkar, Robert Cohn, George Cox, Thomas Gross,
H. T. Kung, Monica Lam, Margie Levine, Brian Moore, Wire Moore,
Craig Peterson, Jim Susman, Jim Sutton, John Urbanski, and Jon Webb

School of Computer Science
Carnegie Mellon University
Pittsburgh, Pennsylvania 15213

Intel Corporation, CO4-01
5200 N.E. Elam Young Pkwy
Hillsboro, Oregon 97124

Abstract

iWarp is a parallel architecture developed jointly by Carnegie Mellon University and Intel Corporation. The iWarp communication system supports two widely used interprocessor communication styles: *memory communication* and *systolic communication*. This paper describes the rationale, architecture, and implementation for the iWarp communication system.

The sending or receiving processor of a message can perform either memory or systolic communication. In memory communication, the entire message is buffered in the local memory of the processor before it is transmitted or after it is received. Therefore communication begins or terminates at the local memory. For conventional message passing methods, both sending and receiving processors use memory communication. In systolic communication, individual data items are transferred as they are produced, or are used as they are received, by the program running at the processor. Memory communication is flexible and well suited for general computing; whereas systolic communication is efficient and well suited for speed critical applications.

A major achievement of the iWarp effort is the derivation of a common design to satisfy the requirements of both systolic and memory communication styles. This is made possible by two important innovations in communication: (1) program access to communication and (2) logical channels. The former allows programs to access data as they are transmitted and to redirect portions of messages to different destinations efficiently. The latter increases the connectivity between the processors and guarantees communication bandwidth for classes of messages. These innovations have provided a focus for the iWarp architecture. The result is a communication system that provides a total bandwidth of 320 MBytes/sec and that is integrated on a single VLSI component with a 20 MFLOPS plus 20 MIPS long instruction word computation engine.

The research was supported in part by Defense Advanced Research Projects Agency (DOD) monitored by the Space and Naval Warfare Systems Command under Contract N00039-87-C-0251.

Authors' affiliations: R. Cohn, T. Gross, H. T. Kung, and J. Webb are with Carnegie Mellon University; S. Borkar, G. Cox, M. Levine, B. Moore, W. Moore, C. Peterson, J. Susman, J. Sutton, and J. Urbanski are with Intel; M. Lam, who was a Ph.D. student at Carnegie Mellon University, is now with Computer Systems Laboratory, Stanford University, Stanford, CA 94305

1. Introduction

iWarp [5] is a distributed parallel computing system under joint development by Carnegie Mellon University and Intel Corporation since 1986. The architecture is derived from the original Warp architecture developed by Carnegie Mellon [2]. The building block of an iWarp system is the *iWarp cell*, made out of a single-chip *iWarp processor* (or *iWarp component*) connected to a local memory. Parallel systems of different scales and topologies can be built cost-effectively by simply linking together iWarp cells. Figure 1 illustrates one possible configuration.

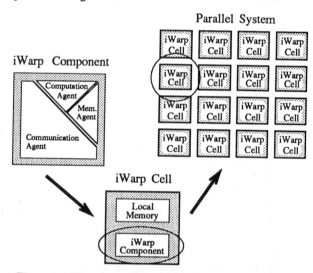

Figure 1. iWarp cell: a building block for parallel systems

The iWarp processor integrates both a high-speed computation and communication capability in a single component. The processor is a powerful computation engine that employs instruction-level parallelism to allow simultaneous operation of multiple functional units. What makes iWarp unique, however, is its interprocessor communication capability. An iWarp processor can simultaneously communicate with a number of other iWarp processors at very high speeds. More importantly, the iWarp processor has a highly flexible communication mechanism that can support different programming models, including the tightly coupled computing found in systolic arrays and the message passing style of computation found in distributed memory machines. These communication capabilities allow the effective use of iWarp for a wide range of applications.

CH2887-8/90/0000/0070$01.00 © 1990 IEEE

The iWarp component consists of three autonomous subsystems, as depicted in Figure 1. The *computation agent*, which executes programs, can deliver 20 (or 10) MFLOPS for single (or double) precision calculations plus 20 MIPS for integer/logic operations. The *communication agent*, which implements the iWarp's communication system, can sustain an aggregate intercell communication bandwidth of 320 MBytes/sec by using four input and four output busses. The *memory agent*, which provides a high-bandwidth interface to the local memory, can transfer streams of data into or out of the communication agent at a rate of 160 MBytes/sec.

The first silicon of the iWarp component was fabricated in December 1989. It consists of approximately 650,000 transistors and measures about 1.4cm (551mil) on a side. Figure 2 shows a photo of the component, together with a floor plan that highlights the major units. The iWarp component operates at a frequency of 20 MHz, with the exception that the data is transferred between processors at twice that frequency (40 MHz). Three iWarp demonstration systems will be delivered to Carnegie Mellon by the Fall of 1990. Each of these systems consists of an 8×8 torus of iWarp cells, delivering more than 1.2 GFLOPS. The system can be readily expanded to include up to 1,024 cells for an aggregate computing power of over 20 GFLOPS and communication bandwidth of 160 GBytes/sec.

The software for the initial iWarp systems includes optimizing compilers for C and FORTRAN as well as parallel program generators such as Apply [11] for image processing. A resident run-time system on each cell supports systolic and memory communication. Included in this run-time system are the message-passing services of the Nectar communication system, originally developed for Carnegie Mellon's Nectar network [3].

This paper describes in depth the rationale, concepts, and realization of the iWarp communication agent. In particular, we describe the common design to support both systolic and memory communications, and the innovative architectural features needed to efficiently support these different types of communication.

This paper complements earlier iWarp papers on other topics: iWarp overview [5], architecture and compiler tradeoffs for the computation agent [6], and networks that can be formed on an iWarp array [9]. General discussions on interprocessor communication methods can be found in [14], which describes a taxonomy of communication methods and uses iWarp communication methods as part of the examples. Further discussions on systolic communication can be found in [12].

The organization of the paper is as follows. We first describe the fundamental differences between systolic and memory communication and point out that these two styles of communication each has its own merit. We then discuss the two unique architectural concepts in the iWarp communication system: (1) program access to communication and (2) logical channels. These innovations were motivated originally by systolic communication needs, but as described in Section 3, they are also useful in improving the performance of memory communication. We discuss the details of the iWarp communication system in Sections 4 through 7, starting with the physical intercell connections, the implementation of logical channels, routing and bandwidth reservation, and finally, communication agent interaction with the computation and the memory agents. We close the paper with some performance figures on the latency of communication, and some concluding remarks.

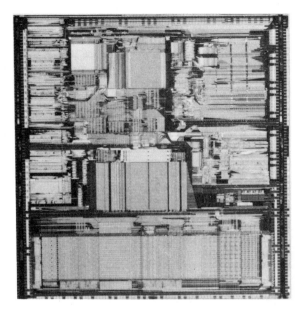

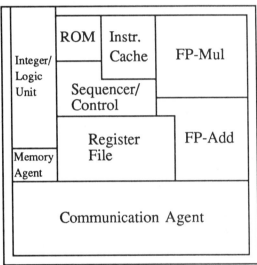

Figure 2. Photo and floor plan of iWarp component

2. Systolic vs. memory communication

An iWarp cell is said to perform *systolic communication* if the program has direct access to the input or output port of a message queue as the message is being sent or received; it is said to perform *memory communication* otherwise. The sending and receiving cells of the same message do not necessarily use the same communication style; that is, one cell may perform systolic communication while the other performs memory communication. In the following we motivate and elaborate on these two styles of intercell communication.

2.1. Memory communication

In conventional message passing, messages are delivered from the local memory of the sending cell to the local memory of the receiving cell. That is, a message is first built in the local memory of the sending cell and then delivered (as a unit) to that of the receiving cell. Only when the full message is available in the local memory of the receiving cell is it ready to be operated upon by its program. Thus, in conventional message passing, both the sending and receiving cells perform memory communication.

In memory communication, the program running on the cell is insulated from communication. In the case of a sending cell, the program just needs to build the message in its local memory. After the complete message has been built, delivering it over the network is handled independently by some network software. Similarly, in the case of a receiving cell, the program is not involved in receiving the message, and will operate on the data in the message only after the entire message has been delivered to the local memory by the network software.

Memory communication has the advantage that communication is decoupled from computation. While the message is being delivered and buffered through memory, the program at the sending or receiving cell can operate autonomously on its local data. Moreover, communication protocols can be developed independently from the program to handle communication-specific issues such as deadlock avoidance and recovery from transmission failures. This makes memory communication the method of choice for applications which do not assume detailed knowledge about intercell communication. For these applications, message passing which uses memory communication at both sending and receiving cells is widely used.

2.2. Systolic communication

Systolic communication was motivated by systolic algorithms. In a systolic algorithm, an array of cells perform computations on long data streams flowing through the array. To achieve high efficiency, each cell processes the data immediately as each item arrives. We can view all data sent along each directed connection in a systolic array as belonging to one message. However, instead of waiting until all the data in the message have arrived, each cell operates on the data items within a message as they arrive individually. It then sends the results of the computation to other cells on-the-fly as data of out-going messages. Therefore, each cell performs systolic communication as defined in the beginning of this section.

Systolic communication has the following advantages over memory communication:

- *Fine-grain communication.* The program at the sending cell can send out data items individually as soon as they are produced; similarly the program at the receiving cell can use data items individually as soon as they are received. This allows programs to communicate and synchronize with each other at word-level rather than message-level granularity. The message routing and header information overheads are not paid with each unit of synchronization. This low communication cost makes it possible for the cells to cooperate in fine-grain parallel processing.

- *Reduced access to local memory.* Incoming and outgoing data need not be buffered in the cell's local memory unless it is required by the computation. Since memory access is typically a bottleneck in the cell's performance, the reduced access to local memory may translate into increased computation performance.

- *Increased instruction-level parallelism.* At each cell, systolic inputs and outputs provide additional parallel sources of operands for instructions. These operands can help keep the multiple functional units busy and increase instruction-level parallelism. Optimizing compilers for wide-word instruction set architectures, such as the compilers for Warp and iWarp [6, 15], have been developed to take advantage of this instruction-level parallelism.

- *Reduced size for local memory.* Avoiding buffering data in the local memory also reduces the memory size requirement for some applications.

However, systolic communication is harder to use than memory communication with respect to the flexibility of data access by a cell's program. The local memory of a cell can be accessed *randomly*, while message queues in the communication agent can only be accessed *sequentially*. Consequently, in systolic communication, one must make sure that the reads and writes of message queues are properly sequenced. That is, whenever the cell's program reads from an input queue, the right data item will appear at the front of the queue. Similarly, whenever the program writes a data item to an output queue, one must make sure that when the data item emerges from the front of an input queue of the receiving cell, that cell's program will be ready to read it.

Furthermore, in systolic communication after an item has been sent, it will no longer be available on the sending cell and cannot be re-transmitted. Therefore the communication system must guarantee reliable transmission.

3. Two iWarp architectural innovations in communication

iWarp has two important architectural innovations: *program access to communication*, and *logical channels*. These innovations were motivated by the desire to support systolic communication.

In addition, iWarp has many of the more "traditional" architectural features [5] found in previous distributed memory machines [4, 17], such as support for non-neighborhood communication, message routing hardware, word-level flow control between neighboring cells and spooling (a DMA-like mechanism). Together, the traditional features and our two innovations make iWarp an effective processor for both systolic and memory communications.

3.1. Program access to communication

iWarp's communication is unique in that its low level communication mechanisms are exposed and accessible by programs. First, the communication agent supports word-level flow control between connecting cells and transfers messages word by word to implement wormhole routing [7, 8]. Exposing this mechanism to the computation agents allows programs to communicate systolically. Second, a communication agent can automatically route messages to the appropriate destination without the intervention of the computation agent. By allowing the computation agent to modify the routing of messages in midstream, the program can implement some common message operations such as message concatenation or distribution efficiently.

3.1.1. Program access to communication data

To implement systolic communication, iWarp allows programs running on the computation agent to have direct access to the inputs and outputs of message queues in the communication agent. These locations can be bound to special registers, called *gates*, in the register space of the instruction set architecture. Reading from the gate corresponds to receiving data from the queue; similarly, writing to the gate corresponds to sending data to the queue. Data are transferred in FIFO order and reading from an empty queue or sending to a full queue will block the operation.

Applications typically use message queues to smooth the flow of data between cells and to delay one stream of data with respect to others. The size of such queues is application-specific and can be larger than the message queues that the communication agent can provide in hardware. iWarp overcomes this problem by providing the option of extending the queue into the local memory of the cell. Although using this mechanism increases the demand for memory bandwidth, it is a software transparent method for providing queues that are too long to implement with dedicated buffer space.

Besides supporting systolic communication, the ability for the program to access message queues directly can also speed up memory communication. In conventional message passing for distributed memory machines, messages are usually copied from the user space to system space at the sending cell, transmitted, and then copied from system space to user space at the receiving cell. Reliable and safe service routines are used to transfer messages between the system spaces. We call this *station-to-station* delivery [5]. Making copies of data back and forth between the application and the system spaces incurs considerable overhead.

Direct access to message queues can be used to optimize the communication protocol. That is, the application can transmit the data itself using an application-specific protocol; the data are sent directly between the user spaces of the sending and receiving cells. We call this *door-to-door* delivery.

To implement door-to-door delivery, the application program at the receiving cell needs to read the message header before the entire message is buffered in the local memory. Using the information in the header, the program will explicitly control the memory allocation and tell the communication system where to deposit messages.

These details can be readily handled by parallel program generators such as Apply [10] and AL [18]. The extra protection provided by service routines for station-to-station communication is not needed by such tools, since the programs generated by the tools can be trusted to be correct in their interactions with the run-time system. Furthermore, parallel program generators can achieve additional efficiency by computing and communicating concurrently, with the use of instruction-level parallelism in iWarp.

3.1.2. Program access to data routing

Under normal operation, the communication agent establishes a route between the sender and the receiver, and all the data in the message follow the same route. In iWarp, the program may alter this route in the middle of a message so that the rest of the data can be forwarded to another cell, along another route. Program access to data routing reduces the need to buffer data in memory.

The importance of this mechanism can be illustrated by the "GetRow" and "PutRow" I/O methods [1], which have been extensively used on Warp for image processing applica-

tions. GetRow is an input method of distributing data (e.g., a row of an image) to a group of cells. All the cells participating in the GetRow operation are linked together by pathways. The first cell, the left-most cell in Figure 3 (a), sends out the data as a single outgoing message to cells to the right. Each receiving cell in turn takes its portion of the message, and then forwards the remainder, if any, to cells to the right. To avoid buffering through the local memory of the receiving cell, the destination for the remaining message is altered. More precisely, after having read its portion of the incoming message, the program at the cell will instruct the communication agent to redirect the remaining portion of the message to the next cell. This redirection eliminates the need for the cell to buffer up the remaining portion of the message before forwarding it to the next cell. Note that the first cell does not have to know how many cells will receive the data that it sends out, nor how the data will be distributed among them.

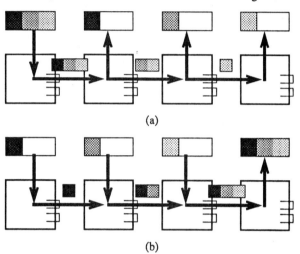

(a)

(b)

Figure 3. (a) GetRow and (b) PutRow on iWarp

Corresponding to GetRow is the "PutRow" output method of concatenating multiple messages from a group of cells to form one long message. All the cells participating in the PutRow operation are linked by a set of pathways. In PutRow, the last cell, the right-most cell in Figure 3 (b), receives the data from all the other cells. Each of the other cells sends out its data as a separate outgoing message to the next cell. After having sent out its message, the program at the cell, without closing the message, will peel off the header of the incoming message and instruct the communication agent to redirect the incoming message as the remaider of the original outgoing message.

3.2. Logical channels

iWarp's second innovation in communication is logical channels. They have two important functions. First, in mapping computations onto iWarp arrays, logical channels provide a higher degree of connectivity than that achievable by physical means. Second, they provide a mechanism for delivering guaranteed communication bandwidth for classes of messages.

3.2.1. Increasing connectivity

When mapping computations onto iWarp arrays, it is desirable for the cells to be highly interconnected. However, the number of physical connections is limited by hard constraints such as the number of available pins and pads on the iWarp component. Logical channels overcome this problem by providing multiple "logical" connections over the same physical connection. In iWarp, multiple logical channels can time-multiplex a physical bus at word-level granularity (see Section 5). Up to forty logical channels can be multiplexed over the eight external and five internal physical busses in each cell.

A high degree of connectivity is useful for systolic communication. In systolic communication, a cell may need to have simultaneous connections to several cells. Without logical channels, algorithms that require more physical connections than those provided in hardware cannot be implemented. Consider, for example, mapping a hexagonal systolic array onto a 2-dimensional grid of iWarp processors. Whereas the X and Y connections of the hexagonal array map directly onto those of the iWarp array, each of the diagonal connections of the hexagonal array can be implemented on the iWarp array with one horizontal and one vertical channel.

In general, a high degree of connectivity is required when mapping computations onto a physical array which has quite a different intercell communication topology. Even when the computation and the physical array have exactly the same communication topology, extra connections may still be needed to route around congested or faulty cells. Extensive simulation has shown that a moderate number of logical channels (on the order of 10) can be highly effective in avoiding faulty cells [16].

3.2.2. Delivering guaranteed communication bandwidth

Logical channels can be used to guarantee communication bandwidth for special classes of messages between a set of selected cells. The time-multiplexing of logical channels onto physical busses uses a fair schedule. Therefore some minimum bandwidth is guaranteed to be available to each logical channel, and thus to the messages carried by the channel, since the total number of logical channels sharing the same physical bus is bounded. Moreover, the multiplexing of logical channels to physical busses is designed such that idle logical channels do not consume any physical bandwidth. That is, when a logical channel is inactive, the physical bandwidth reserved for it is not wasted and can be used by other logical channels.

The ability to deliver guaranteed communication bandwidth is important for both systolic and memory communication. The need in the case of systolic communication is obvious. The connection for systolic communication requires some guaranteed minimum performance to ensure effective low cost fine-grain communication. A systolic connection may exist for an indefinitely long period of time, possibly for the duration of an entire application program. If connections exclude other communication on the same bus, then cells engaged in systolic communication can potentially lock out all other messages by monopolizing the connections. It is important that some bandwidth be made available for memory communication to support system-related functions such as monitoring.

Guaranteeing communication bandwidth in the case of memory communication is less clear but nonetheless important. Messages received and sent using memory communication will complete in a bounded amount of time for a given available communication bandwidth. Provided that at least one connection from any cell to any cell can be made at any one time, all messages will eventually arrive at their destinations. However, there is little guarantee as to when a par-

ticular message will be delivered. Reserving a set of logical channels for a class of messages guarantees that some minimum bandwidth is reserved for them. For example, it is useful to guarantee that special system messages can be delivered in a timely fashion. This is especially useful for debugging and diagnostic purposes.

Reserving communication resources in iWarp is modeled by the notion of *pathways*, each being a chain of linearly connected logical channels (see Section 6). Logical channels in a given set of pathways can be reserved to transport a class of messages between the cells connected by the pathways. Conversely, all these messages are confined to use only those logical channels within the pathways, guaranteeing the availability of the rest of the resources for other usages. Figure 4 shows some examples of networks of pathways within a 2-dimensional system, where each arrow denotes a reserved logical channel.

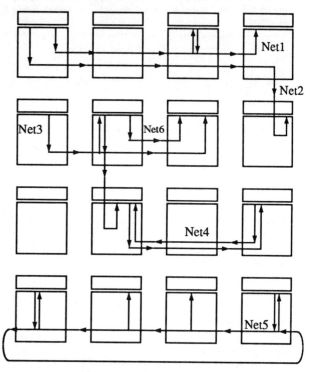

Figure 4. Examples of networks of pathways reserved in a 2-dimensional iWarp array

4. Physical busses

In the next few sections, we describe the architecture and implementation of the iWarp communication system and, in particular, show how they implement the two communication concepts described in Section 3. We describe the system in a bottom-up fashion. We start with the physical connections and the logical channels, then proceed to describe how logical channels guarantee minimum communication bandwidth for classes of messages. Lastly, we describe how the low level communication mechanisms are made accessible to the computation and memory agents.

Each processor is connected via eight external busses to the outside world, each delivering a bandwidth of 40 MBytes/sec. The busses are unidirectional; four are input busses and the other four are output busses. We refer to these external busses as XRight, YUp, XLeft, and YDown as shown in Figure 5. The subscripts "in" and "out" are attached when necessary to distinguish between input and output busses.

The design of the physical busses is a tradeoff between performance goals and implementation constraints. The component is limited by the number of pins in the package and the switching speed of the signals. Each of the eight external busses consists of eight data lines and five control lines. The data busses are unidirectional because they can operate at higher frequencies than bidirectional busses. The unit of transfer over a bus is a 32-bit data word; it takes four phases of 25 ns each to complete a transfer. That is, the external interface of the communication agent operates at a frequency of 40 MHz, yielding a bandwidth of 40 MBytes/sec for each bus.

The partitioning of the total 64 data lines into byte parallel busses is motivated by the desire to provide a high peak bandwidth per bus. Dividing the data lines into more, yet narrower, busses would increase the connectivity of the system. However, narrower busses reduce the available bandwidth for an individual message, and penalize programs that need only a low dimension of connectivity. Instead of taking this approach, we achieve both high individual bus bandwidth and high connectivity by the use of logical channels, as described below.

Internal to each processor, the communication agent interfaces with the computation agent through four unidirectional busses, two in and two out, each with a bandwidth of 40 MBytes per second. It interfaces with the memory agent via a bidirectional bus that can deliver 160 MBytes per second.

Each bus is complete in the sense that it contains all the necessary control lines to transfer data between two adjacent cells. This includes the ability of the receiver to provide status information to the transmitter, and vice versa. Thus the busses are completely independent. For example, there is no need to connect $XRight_{in}$ to the same neighbor cell as $XRight_{out}$. This feature is necessary to create, for example, a special-purpose hexagonal array in which each cell is connected to six neighboring cells, as seen in Figure 6.

5. Implementation of logical channels

A logical channel is a unidirectional connection: it can be an external connection between neighboring cells, or an internal connection between a communication agent and either the computation or the memory agent in the same cell. Multiple logical channels are time-multiplexed onto a single physical bus at word-level granularity. A logical channel is referred to as a logical output channel for the transmitter and as a logical input channel for the receiver. Each logical input channel has a dedicated queue implemented in hardware (see Figure 7 (b)). The communication agent supports up to twenty logical input channels and twenty logical output channels simultaneously.

5.1. Management of logical channels

Channels are jointly managed by the two end cells. There are two phases in managing logical channels—static channel allocation and dynamic channel assignment. First, logical channels on each cell are statically *allocated* among the different physical busses. Before execution begins, the set of logical input channels for one cell is divided up among the different input directions, thereby creating disjoint groups of logical channels for each physical bus. That is, each logical

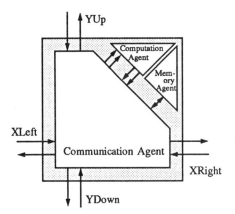

Figure 5. Physical busses

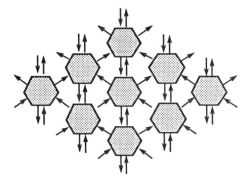

Figure 6. Hexagonal array

input channel on a cell is allocated either to one of the neighbor cells or left unallocated so that this cell can use it to initiate a message. When a logical input channel is allocated to a neighbor cell, that neighbor cell allocates a matching, logical output channel.

Figure 7 shows a possible allocation of logical input channels in a 2-dimensional array of iWarp cells: the cell shown has allocated four logical input channels to its right, left, and lower neighbors and two logical input channels to its upper neighbor. It has allocated six channels to generate messages. Two of those currently directed at the computation agent, for systolic communication, two are used for memory communication, and the remaining two are unused at this point in time. Also, this cell has four logical output channels to each of its right and upper neighbors, and six logical output channels to its left and lower neighbors. It can use these channels in any way that it sees fit, as described above. Each cell can use up to 20 logical input channels and 20 logical output channels at any given point in time.

For the second phase of dynamic channel assignment, the transmitter of each physical bus is responsible for managing the logical channels allocated to the bus. The transmitter can initiate communication using any of its pre-allocated free logical channels without first consulting the receiver. This design minimizes the time needed to initiate communication. More specifically, when a cell wants to connect one of its logical input channels with a logical output channel in a specific direction, it *assigns* a free logical output channel from the set of channels allocated to it. This assignment is implemented by linking the logical input channel to the logical output channel, via a 20×20 *logical crossbar* in the communication agent.

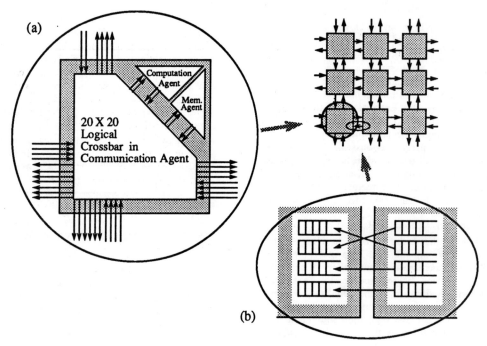

(a)

(b)

Figure 7. Logical channels

5.2. Multiplexing onto a physical bus

The multiplexing of logical channels over a physical bus is designed to maximize utilization; when only one logical channel is active, it must be able to take advantage of the full bandwidth of the physical bus. For example, the bandwidth should not be wasted on trying to send data to a full queue. It is undesirable to use schemes which require the receiver to supply an ack/nack (acknowledge or not acknowledge) signal to the transmitter to indicate whether the transfer is successful.

On iWarp, the transmitter keeps a count of the free slots in each of the receiver's queues. With every word it sends along a logical channel, the transmitter decrements the free space counter for the logical channel. Every time the receiver removes data from one of its input queues, it informs the transmitter with a dequeue signal that contains the index of the logical output channel from which a word was read. The transmitter then increments the free space counter for its corresponding logical input channel. The queue size of eight 32-bit words is designed to tolerate the feedback delay so that the maximum bandwidth can be used for a single logical channel.

The logical channel manager includes a round robin scheduler that multiplexes data from the logical channels over the physical bus. To preserve bandwidth, only those logical channels that have a non-empty input queue and non-full output queue participate in the scheduling decision. That is, logical channels that are currently idle do not waste any physical bus bandwidth. Consequently, if only one of the logical channels allocated to the same bus is active, it can utilize the full bandwidth of 40 MBytes/sec. of the underlying physical bus.

6. Routing and bandwidth reservation

The logical channels in the communication agent of an iWarp cell are statically divided into two pools. The first pool, called the *reservation pool*, is to implement "pathways" which can be reserved over a long period of time for transporting classes of messages with some guaranteed bandwidth. The second pool, called the *open pool*, is to implement traditional message passing. For this pool, there is no reservation of pathways; the logical channels are dynamically acquired and released for transporting each message. As described in Section 3.2.2, these messages do not hold onto resources indefinitely. It is well known that by dedicating a pool for such messages, it is possible to guarantee that there is no deadlock to prevent these messages from being delivered.

Although the usages between the two pools are different, they use the same basic hardware mechanism. For example, the same hardware is used to route pathways for the reservation pool and messages for the open pool. In the following we first describe the support for the reservation pool, then show briefly how the same mechanism implements the open pool.

6.1. The reservation pool

Intercell communication using the reservation pool consists of two phases: (1) reserving the logical channels for communication, and (2) sending the data as messages on those reserved channels. The reservation is done *dynamically* by setting up "pathways". This can be likened to a railway transportation system: first connect the track segments (logical channels) to form a pathway from a source to a destination, and then run trains (messages) over the pathway.

6.1.1. Setting up a pathway

A *pathway* is a unidirectional connection, built out of logical channels, that leads from a source cell to a destination cell. Pathways are created using wormhole routing [7, 8]. The source cell generates a header containing a destination address and additional routing information. As the header is passed along from the source to the destination according to the route specified, the logical channels are linked up to build the

76

pathway. It is not necessary for the pathway to be completely established before messages over the pathway are sent; the sending cell can start sending a message as soon as the pathway header leaves the cell.

6.1.2. Pathway markers

Each data word that is transmitted between cells can carry with it a tag. If a tag is present, we call the data word plus tag a *marker*; the absence of a tag indicates a normal data item. Markers are recognized by the communication system. There are two markers for pathways, the *pathway begin marker*, which includes a data field that carries pathway routing, and the *pathway end marker*.

6.1.3. Specifying pathway route

iWarp uses "street-sign" routing. Pathway begin markers have a default course of travel. For example, markers arriving on a logical input channel allocated to the XLeft bus default to continuing onto a logical output channel leaving via the XRight bus, and vice versa. Similarly, markers arriving on the YUp bus default to continuing onto the YDown bus, and vice versa.

The source cell can change this default course of travel by including in the header the addresses of all the cells at which a different action is to be taken. There are two possible actions: the pathway has either reached the destination, or it has to "turn a corner" and head in the specified direction. This is analogous to city street navigation where each cell is a street intersection. The scheme is to follow the road in the same direction until you reach the destination, or make a turn when you come to a particular corner. For each corner turned, the pathway must include a word in the header containing the cell address and the direction to turn, in the order in which the cells are reached.

Street-sign routing takes advantage of the underlying topology of the system. By incorporating the concept of a default direction, headers can be kept short. A header contains only the addresses of those cells where a specific action is to take place (i.e., corner turning points and destination). Therefore the header takes less time to generate, and fewer routing decisions have to be made during the routing. In addition, a shorter header means a smaller overhead to the load of the communication system.

6.1.4. Pathway routing by communication agent

All begin markers arriving at the communication agent are matched against a small content-addressable memory, called the *match CAM*. The computation agent can "program" the communication agent by loading different values into this match CAM.

One of the uses of the match CAM is pathway routing. At initialization time, the run-time system on each cell preloads the match CAM with the address of this cell. Upon receiving a pathway begin marker, the communication agent presents the data field of the marker to the match CAM. If the marker does not match, the pathway continues in the default direction. If the marker matches, the current cell is either the destination, or the pathway must turn a corner. The information on the action taken is encoded in the marker. If the destination is reached, the computation agent is notified of the arrival of a new pathway. If a corner turning operation is specified, part of the matching marker indicates the new direction. The communication agent discards this marker and converts the next word (i.e., the destination or the next corner at which to turn) into a new pathway begin marker and directs the pathway to follow the specified direction.

The pathway header also indicates the reservation pool from which the free logical channel should be drawn. Therefore, to continue a pathway in a certain direction, the communication agent must assign a free logical output channel among those belonging to the reservation pool and allocated to the specified direction. If such an outgoing logical channel is not available, then this request is blocked and repeated until a logical channel becomes available.

If a pathway header reaches the last cell of the array without reaching its destination, then the communication system on this cell can notice the situation and take appropriate action, for example, report an error or discard the data. However, if the topology of the system is a ring or a torus, there is no "last" cell. One way to avoid the "Flying Dutchman" problem (i.e., the pathway header circulating around without ever reaching a destination) is to set up the match CAM of each cell to detect pathways originated by the cell itself.

6.1.5. Dismantling a pathway

Pathways are long-lived in the sense that they exist until explicitly taken down. To dismantle a pathway, i.e., to free up the resources reserved by this pathway, the source cell sends a pathway end marker over the pathway. As this marker is seen by each cell along the pathway, the logical channels used in each cell are returned to the set of free channels.

6.1.6. Joint cells and bandwidth reservation via pathways

A cell that is both a source and destination cell of two or more pathways is called a *joint cell* for the pathways. In Figure 8, Cells 1, 3 and 6 are joint cells.

At a joint cell, the computation agent can configure the communication agent to *link* together a pair of incoming and outgoing pathways. The output pathway is called the *default output pathway* for the input pathway. Any message arriving on the input pathway which is not intended for the cell is automatically forwarded by the communication agent to the default outgoing pathway. However, when a message destined for the joint cell arrives, the communication agent will notify the computation agent to process or route the message. Therefore messages can be sent over a single pathway, or multiple pathways via joint cells.

As stated earlier, pathways are built to reserve bandwidth for classes of messages which are to be sent over the pathways. In Figure 8, there is one pathway connecting Cell 0 to Cell 1, and another one connecting Cell 1 to Cell 5. Over these two pathways two classes of messages can be sent simultaneously, one from Cell 0 to Cell 1 and one from Cell 1 to Cell 5. Via the joint cell (i.e., Cell 1) messages from Cell 0 to Cell 5 can be sent over the two pathways. These two pathways reserve a set of logical channels solely for communication between cells 0, 1 and 5. Conversely, messages designated to use these pathways will not use other resources, and as a result will not block out other messages which critically depend on the other resources. For example, if a message from Cell 0 to Cell 5 passes through Cell 1 in Figure 8, then Cell 1 cannot send messages over the pathway from Cell 1 to Cell 5 until the ongoing message is complete.

Figure 8 also illustrates the use of the FIFO buffers in the communication agent to implement message queues. These FIFO buffers are associated with logical channels, and reserving the channels links the buffers together. So if Cell 4 wants to send a message to Cell 7, the buffers in all intermediate cells implement a single message queue for this communication.

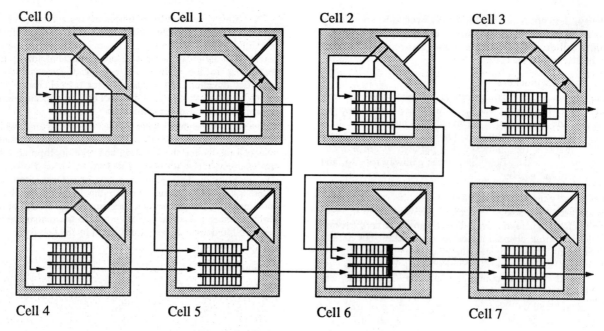

Figure 8. Pathways and joint cells examples

6.1.7. Message routing over pathways

A message header contains the address of the destination cell and information needed to route the message over a given set of pathways. For each joint cell at which the message's route is to depart from the default, the header must include the cell address and information to identify the intended output pathway.

In the simple case of sending a message over a single pathway, the destination of a message is the destination of the pathway. The message simply follows the twists and turns of the pathway route until the destination is reached.

Routing messages over multiple pathways requires special attention at joint cells. When the header of a message arrives at a joint cell, the cell performs one of the following three actions:

1. *Forwarding the message by hardware.* If the destination in the header does not match in the match CAM, the communication agent forwards the message onto the default output pathway.

2. *Receiving the message.* If the destination in the header matches in the match CAM, the communication agent *splits* the incoming pathway from the default outgoing pathway, and notifies the computation agent. After receiving the notification, the computation agent reads the message header, recognizes that the message is intended for the cell, and starts processing the message. After the message is consumed, the computation agent restores the link between the incoming pathway and the default outgoing pathway.

3. *Routing the message by software.* Continuing onto a pathway other than the default requires software intervention. As above, the communication agent notifies the computation agent that the address on the header matches the cell's, the computation agent then interprets the header and instructs the communication agent to direct the message onto a specific outgoing pathway.

In summary, routing of messages over reserved pathways is not completely supported in hardware, unless the pathways form a chain so that the default outgoing pathway can be take at every joint cell. If another outgoing pathway other than the default one is desired, the computation agent at the joint cell must serve as a smart router. The computation agent can, in fact, perform arbitrarily complex computation on the beginning of the message before forwarding the rest of the message onto another cell. The usefulness of this scheme is illustrated by the GetRow and PutRow examples in Section 3.1.2.

6.2. The open pool

The open pool is reserved for message passing. Data sent using the open pool of logical channels are encapsulated as *routing* messages. Each of these messages has its own routing information in the header. These messages are routed in a similar manner as pathways; therefore the routing is completely supported in hardware. To the routing hardware, these messages are identical to pathways, except that the logical channels are assigned from among the open pool instead of the reservation pool.

7. Communication agent interaction with computation and memory agents

There are two types of interaction between the communication agent and the rest of the system: data and control. Data in a message can be accessed directly by the computation agent or it can be spooled through memory by the memory agent. On the control side, the computation agent informs the communication agent of the events it is interested in and the communication agent notifies the computation agent when an event occurs. In addition, the computation agent can redirect messages by changing the connection of the pathways in the communication agent's logical crossbar.

7.1. Data interface to computation agent

In the computation agent's register address space there are special locations called *systolic gates*. There are two input gates and two output gates. Under program control, these gates can be bound to different logical channels in the communication agent. Reading from an input gate corresponds to receiving data from the message queue associated with the logical channel bound to the gate. Similarly, writing to an output gate corresponds to sending data to the queue.

Since these gates are in the processor's register space, an input gate can be used as a source operand of an instruction, and an output gate can be used as a result register of an instruction. Any read of an input gate implies an input operation, and any write to an output gate implies an output operation. Specifying input and output instructions implicitly through the use of these special registers greatly reduces the instruction word width. For example, a three-address arithmetic operation using input and output gates as operands will imply two input operations, the arithmetic operation itself and one output operation. If any of the input queues is empty or if the output queue is full, the instruction execution is stalled until the condition of the queues changes. In the long instruction word of iWarp, all four systolic gates may be used in one instruction. The iWarp hardware can execute all four input/output operations in two 50 ns clock cycles.

Through the systolic gates, data can be transferred between the computation and communication agents at the rate of 160 MBytes per second. As computation can be specified in the same (long) instruction word of the machine, this high communication rate can be accompanied by an equally impressive computation rate. The additional data operands supplied by the input and output gates help reduce the memory bottleneck and increase the utilization of the functional units. Using systolic communication requires more programming effort to ensure that cells do not stall frequently on empty or full message queues; however, a well-designed systolic algorithm can be extremely efficient.

7.2. Data interface to the memory agent

The memory agent transfers, or spools, data directly from the message queues in the communication agent into consecutive locations in the memory, and vice versa. It is like a DMA device, with special hardware to keep the state and to sequence the spooling operation. The memory agent steals memory and computation cycles when spooling data in or out of memory. The memory agent is useful for memory communication transfers as well as for simulating large queues for systolic communication by buffering data in memory.

There are eight 64-bit spooling gates that can be dynamically reconfigured for either input or output and can be bound to the logical channels in the communication agent. The bandwidth of the memory bus is 160 MBytes/second, while each physical bus within the communication agent has a bandwidth of only 40 MBytes/second. Spooling one message queue at peak rate consumes one quarter of the total memory and computation bandwidth. The memory agent can spool eight different message queues "concurrently" by interleaving the transfers at double word granularity over the 64-bit memory bus. The ability of the spooling unit to dynamically select the next logical channel on a word by word basis is especially useful when multiple messages are being spooled into (or out of) memory. It is likely that the data words of the messages will arrive at varying rates, either because of contention on the physical busses or because systolic messages

come directly from the computation agent. Dynamically selecting the next spool ensures that cell memory bus bandwidth is never wasted.

Besides using a counter based termination condition, as in the case of DMA, spooling to memory can also terminate on receiving a message end marker. This is important for spooling data that was generated by systolic communication, because the number of words in a message may not be known in advance. Since spooled messages can be of arbitrary size, a mechanism is needed to ensure that a spooled message does not overflow its buffer. The current spool address is checked against an address limit register to prevent this from happening.

Once spooled to memory, the computation agent can access the data randomly using regular memory operations. Similarly, it can first prepare the message in memory before requesting the memory agent to spool out the message. This implements memory communication.

The computation agent can also access data spooled in memory in a FIFO manner as if the data just arrived over a logical channel systolically. This is achieved by connecting a systolic input gate to a logical input channel that is bound to an output spooling gate. As the computation agent reads data from the systolic input gate, data are spooled from memory and buffered in the queue associated with the logical channel. This allows the computation agent to use implicit input operations to consume the data that were buffered in memory. Similarly, the data generated by the program can first be spooled into memory from an outgoing message queue by connecting an outgoing systolic gate to an input spooling gate.

It is not necessary to wait for the entire message to be received before it can be spooled out as described above. Thus, as the tail buffer of the message is spooled in, the head buffer can be spooled out to the computation agent. This mechanism of buffering through memory extends the length of the message queues in the communication agent, at a cost of one clock cycle per word. This extension in memory is necessary for those programs that will deadlock if the queues at the receiving cell are too short [13]. Also, a long queue reduces stalling. Since a spooled message can be read from the systolic gates in the same manner as a message received directly from another cell, the decision to buffer a message in memory can be delayed until run time.

7.3. Control interface to the computation agent

The computation agent can inform the communication agent of events that are of interest by storing the appropriate information into the communication agent's match CAM. The communication agent notifies the computation agent of these events when they take place by storing the information in status registers.

Sample events that are of interest to the computation agent are:

- Arrival of a pathway begin marker

- Arrival of a pathway end marker

- Arrival of a message begin marker

- Arrival of a message end marker

- Arrival of an application marker

Some of these events can be registered on a per-logical channel basis; for others, they are either registered for all logical channels or not at all. An application marker is a tagged data word that can be found anywhere within a message. It is used by the application program to mark those points within a message that demand special attention by the computation agent.

When an event occurs for which the computation agent wishes to be notified, the communication agent posts this event by setting the appropriate status register. These registers are monitored by the master sequencer of the computation agent and result in a control transfer to an appropriate service routine.

The computation agent can also instruct the communication agent to modify the connections of existing pathways. One example is the joining of two pathways, as discussed in Section 6.1.6, or to route around a faulty cell.

8. Communication latency summary

When a program creates a pathway, the originating cell's computation agent asks the local communication agent for a logical channel in the direction of the destination. If a logical channel is available, this request takes 150 ns to complete. Next, the computation agent must generate and send a pathway begin marker, which takes 100 ns. The creation of additional addresses for corner turning (if required) takes 50 ns per address. At this point, the computation agent can send messages on the pathway. Tearing down a pathway requires that a pathway end marker be generated and sent; this takes 100 ns. Note, however, that the above numbers assume that the relevant data (i.e., data field of begin marker, additional addresses for corner turning, etc.) are already in registers. In practice, the run-time system imposes additional overheads such as retrieving values from a configuration table, checking for valid cell addresses, and updating various tables.

The communication agent of every intermediate cell in the pathway must decide if the incoming pathway begin marker matches on this cell or must be forwarded. If the marker does not match, it will take 200 ns to forward to the next cell. If the marker matches for corner turning, it will take 250 ns to discard the current marker, convert the next data word into a new marker and forward the new marker to the next cell. Joining two pathways is inexpensive; after the join instruction is issued, it will take 100 ns for the first data word to leave the joint cell for the next cell. Once the pathways are joined together, there is no additional latency involved for data passing through a joint cell.

Generating a message begin marker is fast because all the necessary resources are reserved at the time when the underlying pathway was created. The message begin marker and the message end marker are generated in 100 ns each. This time does not include any run-time system overhead to look up the destination address in the message header, or to maintain bookkeeping tables. The latency of a message header is the same as the latency of a pathway header (200 ns, plus 50 ns for corner turning) if the message is routed by the communication agent.

9. Conclusions

An iWarp system is a distributed memory machine, supporting two very different styles of communication, systolic and memory communication, fully and efficiently. Housed in one system, the two styles of communication can be easily intermixed to adapt to the application needs.

The iWarp communication architecture provides a wealth of communication services. As a systolic array, iWarp allows data to stream through the cells at high data rates, with each cell cooperating at word-level granularity. This basic systolic functionality is enriched by a set of features that simplify programming without reducing efficiency. Processors can communicate with non-neighboring cells directly without involving programs at intervening cells. An iWarp system can efficiently implement intercell communication topologies which are quite different from that of the hardware interconnect in the system. This capability is also useful in routing data around faults and congestion. The size of input queues can be extended indefinitely by spooling through memory, a decision that can be made dynamically and is totally transparent to the program. By redirecting data messages, a cell can have messages or portions of them forwarded to an appropriate destination automatically. This is especially useful for overlapping the input/output phase of a systolic algorithm with computation.

As a message passing machine, iWarp routes messages between cells efficiently using wormhole routing. Its "street-sign" routing minimizes routing overhead by imposing a default direction at each hop of the routing. On iWarp, it is possible to reserve communication bandwidth for specific classes of messages. This management of the bandwidth is important to implement system functions such as monitoring. iWarp can implement "door-to-door" delivery by allowing data to be stored into the user's data space directly without buffering through system space.

This myriad of communication functionalities is provided using only a few communication mechanisms in iWarp. The two unique iWarp architectural features are logical channels and program access to the communication system. Having only a small number of basic new ideas keeps the design simple and easily optimized, and more importantly, makes it possible to integrate the communication agent with the computation and memory agents in a single VLSI component.

The iWarp hardware supports a high communication bandwidth, and more importantly, the iWarp architecture can translate this raw data rate into a high communication rate between programs through the various layers of communication abstraction. First, iWarp has a peak communication bandwidth of 320 MBytes per second; the bandwidth for each bus is 40 MBytes per second. This bandwidth can be fully utilized by one logical channel if it is the only active channel. That is, reserving a logical channel only guarantees that the bandwidth is available when needed. Dedicated communication hardware routes the messages through the system with a minimum latency. To realize the efficiency at the program level, iWarp has a unique, high bandwidth interface between communication and computation. Data can be spooled into memory at a rate of 160 MBytes per second, or four messages can be accessed directly via long instructions at a rate of 40 Mbytes per second. This high bandwidth is made possible by the integration of the communication and computation units into a single component.

The complete iWarp communication architecture is designed to deliver a high effective program communication rate to both systolic and memory communication models. Integrating this communication capability with a computation engine that delivers 20 MFLOPS and 20 MIPS into a single component, iWarp is a powerful building block for large-scale distributed memory machines.

Acknowledgements

We appreciate the contributions of Dave Nedwek and An Nguyen, of Intel Corp. to the design and implementation of the iWarp communication system. We also thank Abu Noaman and David Yam of Carnegie Mellon University for assistance in design validation and performance evaluation.

References

1. Annaratone, M., Bitz, F., Clune, E., Kung, H. T., Maulik, P., Ribas, H., Tseng, P. and Webb, J. Applications and Algorithm Partitioning on Warp. COMPCON Spring '87, IEEE Computer Society, 1987, pp. 272-275.

2. Annaratone, M., Arnould, E., Gross, T., Kung, H. T., Lam, M., Menzilcioglu, O. and Webb, J. A. "The Warp Computer: Architecture, Implementation, and Performance". *IEEE Transactions on Computers C-36*, 12 (December 1987), 1523-1538.

3. Arnould, E. A., Bitz, F. J., Cooper, E. C., Kung, H. T., Sansom, R. D. and Steenkiste, P. A. The Design of Nectar: A Network Backplane for Heterogeneous Multicomputers. Proceedings of Third International Conference on Architectural Support for Programming Languages and Operating Systems (ASPLOS III), ACM, April, 1989, pp. 205-216.

4. Athas, W. C. and Seitz, C. L. "Multicomputers: Message-Passing Concurrent Computers". *Computer 21*, 8 (August 1988), 9-24.

5. Borkar, S., Cohn, R., Cox, G., Gleason, S., Gross, T., Kung, H. T., Lam, M., Moore, B., Peterson, C., Pieper, J., Rankin, L., Tseng, P. S., Sutton, J., Urbanski, J. and Webb, J. iWarp: An Integrated Solution to High-Speed Parallel Computing. Proceedings of Supercomputing '88, IEEE Computer Society and ACM SIGARCH, Orlando, Florida, November, 1988, pp. 330-339.

6. Cohn, R., Gross, T., Lam, M. and Tseng, P. S. Architecture and Compiler Tradeoffs for a Long Instruction Word Microprocessor. Proceedings of Third International Conference on Architectural Support for Programming Languages and Operating Systems (ASPLOS III), ACM, April, 1989, pp. 2-14.

7. Dally, William J. *A VLSI Architecture for Concurrent Data Structures*. Kluwer Academic Publishers, 1987.

8. Dally, W. J., and Seitz, C. L. "The Torus Routing Chip". *Distributed Computing 1*, 4 (1986), 187-196.

9. Gross, T. Communication in iWarp Systems. Proceedings of Supercomputing '89, November, 1989, pp. 436 - 445.

10. Hamey, L. G. C., Webb, J. A., and Wu, I. C. "An Architecture Independent Programming Language for Low-Level Vision". *Computer Vision, Graphics, and Image Processing 48* (1989), 246-264.

11. Hamey, L. G. C., Webb, J. A., and Wu, I. C. Low-level Vision on Warp and the Apply Programming Model. In *Parallel Computation and Computers for Artificial Intelligence*, Kluwer Academic Publishers, 1987, pp. 185-199. Edited by J. Kowalik.

12. Kung, H. T. Systolic Communication. Proceedings of the International Conference on Systolic Arrays, San Diego, California, May, 1988, pp. 695-703.

13. Kung, H. T. "Deadlock Avoidance for Systolic Communication". *Journal of Complexity 4*, 2 (June 1988), 87-105. (A revised version also appears in Conference Proceedings of the 15th Annual International Symposium on Computer Architecture, June 1988, pp. 252-260)..

14. Kung, H. T. Network-Based Multicomputers: Redefining High Performance Computing in the 1990s. Proceedings of Decennial Caltech Conference on VLSI, MIT Press, Pasadena, California, March, 1989, pp. 49-66.

15. Lam, M. *A Systolic Array Optimizing Compiler*. Ph.D. Th., Carnegie Mellon University , May 1987. The thesis is published by Kluwer Academic Publishers, Boston, Massachusetts, 1988.

16. Menzilcioglu, O., Kung, H. T. and Song, S. W. Comprehensive Evaluation of a Two-Dimensional Configurable Array. Proceedings of the Nineteenth International Symposium on Fault-Tolerant Computing, 1989, pp. 93-100.

17. Seitz, C. L., Athas, W. C., Flaig, C. M., Martin, A. J., Seizovic, J., Steele, C. S. and Su, W-K. The Architecture and Programming of the Ametek Series 2010 Multicomputer. The Third Conference on Hypercube Concurrent Computers and Applications., Pasadena, California, January, 1988, pp. 33-36.

18. Tseng, P. S. *A Parallelizing Compiler for Distributed Memory Parallel Computers*. Ph.D. Th., Carnegie Mellon University , May 1989.

Monsoon: an Explicit Token-Store Architecture

Gregory M. Papadopoulos
Laboratory for Computer Science
Masachusetts Institute of Technology

David E. Culler
Computer Science Division
University of California, Berkeley

Abstract

Dataflow architectures tolerate long unpredictable communication delays and support generation and coordination of parallel activities directly in hardware, rather than assuming that program mapping will cause these issues to disappear. However, the proposed mechanisms are complex and introduce new mapping complications. This paper presents a greatly simplified approach to dataflow execution, called the *explicit token store* (ETS) architecture, and its current realization in *Monsoon*. The essence of dynamic dataflow execution is captured by a simple transition on state bits associated with storage local to a processor. Low-level storage management is performed by the compiler in assigning nodes to slots in an *activation frame*, rather than dynamically in hardware. The processor is simple, highly pipelined, and quite general. It may be viewed as a generalization of a fairly primitive von Neumann architecture. Although the addressing capability is restrictive, there is exactly one instruction executed for each action on the dataflow graph. Thus, the machine oriented ETS model provides new understanding of the merits and the real cost of direct execution of dataflow graphs.

1 Introduction

The Explicit Token Store (ETS) architecture is an unusually simple model of dynamic dataflow execution that is realized in *Monsoon*, a large-scale dataflow multiprocessor[27]. A Monsoon processor prototype is operational at the MIT Laboratory for Computer Science, running large programs compiled from the dataflow language Id. A full-scale multiprocessor system is under development[6] in conjunction with Motorola Inc. Formulation of the ETS architecture began in 1986 as an outgrowth of the MIT Tagged-Token Dataflow Architecture (TTDA) and was based on a family of design goals — some evolutionary, some revolutionary, and some reactionary.

The fundamental properties of the TTDA that we wanted to retain included a large synchronization namespace, inexpensive synchronization, and tolerance to memory and communication latency[9]. These properties do not improve peak performance, but they dictate how much of it is actually delivered on complex applications[5]. To obtain high performance on a parallel machine lacking these features, a program must be partitioned into a small number of processes that operate almost entirely on local data and rarely interact[10,21]. However, if highly parallel machines are to be used in solving problems more complex than what is addressed on current supercomputers, it is likely they will have to be programmed in a very high level language with little explicit programmer management of parallelism[7,8], and the behavior of these complex applications may be very dynamic. Together, these observations suggest that we cannot expect to achieve a perfect mapping for many applications that we will want to execute on a highly parallel machine, so we are studying the design of processors that tolerate an imperfect mapping and still obtain high performance.

Tagged-token dataflow machines achieve this tolerance through sophisticated matching hardware, which dynamically schedules operations with available operands[2,20,29]. When a token arrives at a processor, the tag it carries is checked against the tags present in the token-store. If a matching token is found, it is extracted and the corresponding instruction is enabled for execution; otherwise, the incoming token is added to the store. This allows for a simple non-blocking processor pipeline that can overlap instructions from closely related or completely unrelated computations. It also provides a graceful means of integrating asynchronous, perhaps misordered, memory responses into the normal flow of execution. However, the matching operation involves considerable complexity on the critical path of instruction scheduling[18]. Although progress has been made in matching hardware[20,29], our goal was to achieve the benefits of matching with a fundamentally simpler mechanism.

The more subtle problem with the matching paradigm is that failure to find a match *implicitly* allocates resources within the token store. Thus, in mapping a portion of the computation to a processor, an unspecified commitment is placed on the token store of that processor and, if this resource becomes overcommitted, the program may deadlock[1]. If the match is to be performed rapidly, we cannot assume this resource is so plentiful that it can be wasted. The worst-case token storage requirement can be determined on a per-code-block basis with sophisticated compiler analysis, but the "bottom line" is that this complex mechanism fails to simplify resource management. Thus, engineering and management concerns led us to consider how to make the token-store *explicit* in the dataflow model.

The result is a simple architecture that directly executes dataflow graphs, yet can be understood as a variation on a (fairly primitive) von Neumann machine. It is simple enough to build and serves to clarify many aspects of dataflow execution.

The sequel describes the ETS architecture and its realization in Monsoon. Section 2 outlines the basic execution model. Section 3 describes the Monsoon implementation. Sections 4 and 5 provide preliminary measurements of programs on this machine and reflections on the evolution of dataflow architectures.

2 ETS Architecture

The central idea in the ETS model is that storage for tokens is dynamically allocated in sizable blocks, with detailed usage of locations within a block determined at compile time. When a function is invoked, an *activation frame* is allocated explicitly, as part of the calling convention, to provide storage for all tokens generated by the invocation. Arcs in the graph for the function are statically mapped onto slots in the frame by coloring the graph, much like modern register assignment[12]. The basic structure of an executing program is illustrated in Figure 1. A *token* comprises a value, a pointer to the instruction to execute (IP), and a pointer to an activation frame (FP). The latter two form the *tag*. The instruction fetched from location IP specifies an opcode (*e.g.*, SUB), the offset in the activation frame where the match will take place (*e.g.*, FP+3), and one or more destination instructions that will receive the result of the operation (*e.g.*, instructions IP+1 and IP+2). An input port (left/right) is specified with each destination.

Each frame slot has associated *presence bits* specifying the disposition of the slot. The dynamic dataflow *firing rule* is realized by a simple state transition on these presence bits, as illustrated in Figure 1. If the slot is empty, the value on the token is deposited in the slot (making it full) and no further processing of the instruction takes place. If it is full, the value is extracted (leaving the slot empty) and the corresponding instruction is executed, producing one or more new tokens. Observe, each token causes an instruction to be initiated, but when an operand is missing the instruction degenerates to a store of the one available operand. Initially, all slots in a frame are empty and upon completion of the activation they will have returned to that state. The graphs generated by the compiler include an explicit release of the activation frame upon completion of the invocation.

The ETS activation frame is obviously similar to a conventional call frame. The differences are that presence-bits are associated with each slot and that an executing program generates a *tree* of activation frames, rather than a stack, because a procedure may generate parallel calls where the caller and the callees execute concurrently. The concurrent callees may themselves generate parallel calls, and so on. For loops, several frames are allocated, so that many iterations can execute concurrently[1,13], and reused efficiently. Graphs are compiled such that a frame is not reused until the previous uses of it are complete.

The ETS execution model is easily formalized in terms of a linear array of locations, M, such that the ith location, M[i], contains $q.v$, where v is a fixed size value and q is the **status** of location M[i]. The status and value parts of a location may be manipulated independently. The one operation defined on the status part is an atomic read-modify-write, $M[i].q \leftarrow S(M[i].q)$, where S is a simple transition function. Three atomic operations are defined on the value part: *read, write, exchange*. In addition to the store, the state of the machine includes a set of tokens. The pair of pointers FP.IP is a valid data value, so indirect references and control transfers are possible. Every token in the set of unprocessed tokens represents an operation that is ready to be executed. Thus, a parallel machine step involves selecting and processing some subset of the unprocessed tokens. This generates a set of updates to the store and new unprocessed tokens. The model is inherently parallel, as any number of operations may be performed in a step. Of course, in realizing the model, additional constraints will have to be imposed.

ETS instructions are essentially a 1-address form, in that one operand is the value carried on the token and the second is the contents of the location specified by a simple effective address calculation, *e.g.*, FP + r. The value part of the token functions as the accumulator, IP as the program counter, and FP as an index register. The unusual quality of the ETS instruction is that it may also specify a simple synchronization operation and multiple successors. The synchronization component is merely a state transition on the presence bits associated with the memory operand. However, the state transition affects the behavior of the instruction as a whole, possibly nullifying the continuation.

The simplest continuation is a single successor in the same code-block, specified relative to IP; this corresponds to a node with a single output arc. The fork continuation allows multiple tokens to be produced each carrying the result value and FP from the input token, but with different IPs, derived from that on the input token by a simple offset. To represent conditionals, the offset is selected based on one of the input values. To support the function call and return mechanism, the *Extract Tag* operation places the tag for a node (FP.IP+s), where s is a relative instruction offset, into the value part of the result token and *Send* uses the value part of one input as a result tag. Thus, program code is re-entrant.

The ETS is a dataflow architecture, in that it directly executes dynamic dataflow graphs. Operations in a tagged-token dataflow architecture correspond one-

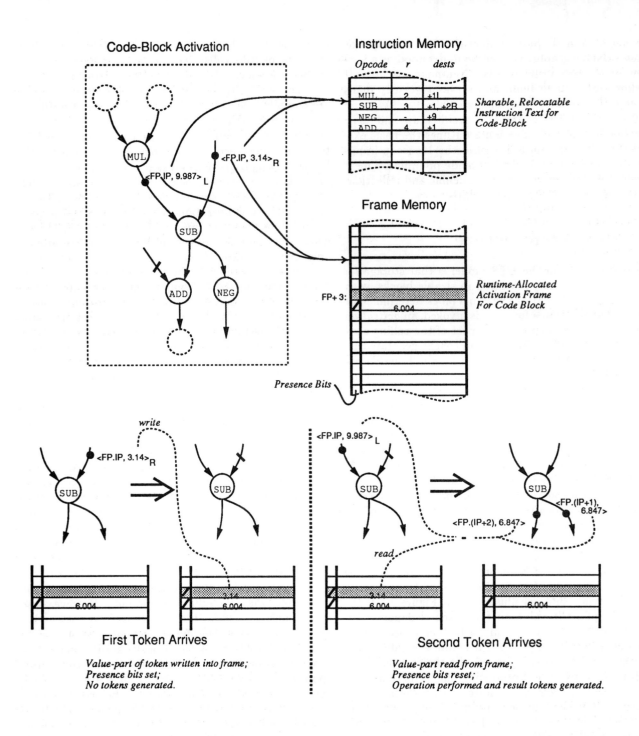

Figure 1: ETS Representation of an Executing Dataflow Program

to-one with operations in the ETS architecture. The data-driven scheduling mechanism is much simpler in the latter case, because the rendezvous point for the two operands is defined by a simple address calculation, rather than hash and match logic. However, making the token store explicit also makes the execution model more general. Using other state transitions on the presence-bits, it directly supports important extensions to the dynamic dataflow model, including loop constants, I-structures, and accumulators. By simply ignoring the presence bits, (multiple) imperative control threads are supported, as well. The overall execution schedule of an ETS program depends on a variety of run-time factors, however, by using dataflow graphs as a programming methodology, we are guaranteed that all execution schedules produce the same result.

3 Monsoon

Monsoon is a general purpose multiprocessor that incorporates an explicit token store. A Monsoon machine includes a collection of pipelined processing elements (PE's), connected via a multistage packet switch network to each other and to a set of interleaved I-structure memory modules (IS's), as shown in Figure 2. Messages in the interprocessor network are simply tokens—precisely the format used within the PE and IS. Thus, the hardware makes no distinction between inter- and intra-processor communication.

The ETS model suggests a natural form of locality; a given activation frame resides entirely on one PE. A code-block activation is dynamically bound to a particular processing element at invocation-time and executes to completion on that PE. Each concurrent iteration of a loop is assigned a separate activation frame, and these frames may be on separate PEs. This strategy reduces network traffic without squandering fine-grain parallelism—the parallelism within an activation is used to keep the processor pipeline full. The policy of mapping an activation frame to a single PE implies that interprocessor token traffic is only generated by data structure reads and writes and transmission of procedure arguments and return values. The interprocessor network is therefore appropriately sized to handle this fraction (less than 30%) of the total number of tokens produced during the course of a computation.

A Monsoon PE is a highly pipelined processor. On each processor cycle a token may enter the top of the pipeline and, after eight cycles, zero, one or two tokens emerge from the bottom[1]. In the process, an instruction is fetched from instruction memory, which reads or

---

[1] A processor *cycle* usually corresponds to a single processor clock, but may extend to multiple clocks during certain operations that cause a pipeline stall, *e.g.*, a frame-store exchange or a floating point divide. Tokens advance from one stage to the next only at cycle boundaries.

writes a word in the data memory called *frame-store.* One of the output tokens can be *recirculated, i.e.,* immediately placed back into the top of the pipeline. Tokens produced by the pipeline that are not recirculated may be inserted into one of two token queues or delivered to the interprocessor network and automatically routed to the correct PE.

3.1 Machine Formats

A Monsoon token is a compact descriptor of computation state comprising a tag and a value. A value can be a 64-bit signed integer, an IEEE double precision floating point number, a bit field or boolean, a data memory pointer, or a tag.

As in the ETS, a Monsoon tag encodes two pointers: one to the instruction to execute and one to the activation frame that provides the context in which to attempt execution of that instruction. However, since activation frames do not span PEs, the frame pointer and instruction pointer are conveniently segmented by processing element, TAG = PE:(FP.IP), where PE is the processing element number and IP and FP are *local* addresses on processor PE. Tags and values are both 64-bit quantities and each is appended with eight additional bits of run-time type information. A token is therefore a 144-bit quantity. For tags, the size of the PE field is eight bits, and FP and IP are 24 bits each. The machine automatically routes tokens to the specifed PE, whereupon instruction IP is fetched and frame FP is accessed. The most significant bit of the instruction pointer encodes a PORT bit which, for two-input operations, establishes the left/right orientation of the operands. All activation frame references are local and are considered non-blocking—activation frame reads and writes can take place within the processor pipeline without introducing arbitrary waits.

A data structure pointer encodes an address on a processing element or I-structure memory module. Pointers are represented in a "normalized" format as the segmented address PE:OFFSET, where PE denotes the processing element or I-structure module number and OFFSET is a local address on the PE or module. Additionally, pointers contain *interleave information,* which describes how the data structure is spread over a collection of modules. The interleave information describes a *subdomain*[4], *i.e.,* collection of 2^n processors or memory modules which starts on a modulo 2^n PE number boundary. If $n = 0$ then increments to the pointer will map onto the same PE. If $n = 1$ then increments to the pointer alternate between PE and PE+1, and so on.

Following the ETS model, the instruction dictates the offset in the frame, the kind of matching operation that will take place (*i.e.*, the state transition function on a word in frame-store), the operation performed in the ALU and the way that new result tokens will be formed. All Monsoon instructions are of uniform, 32-

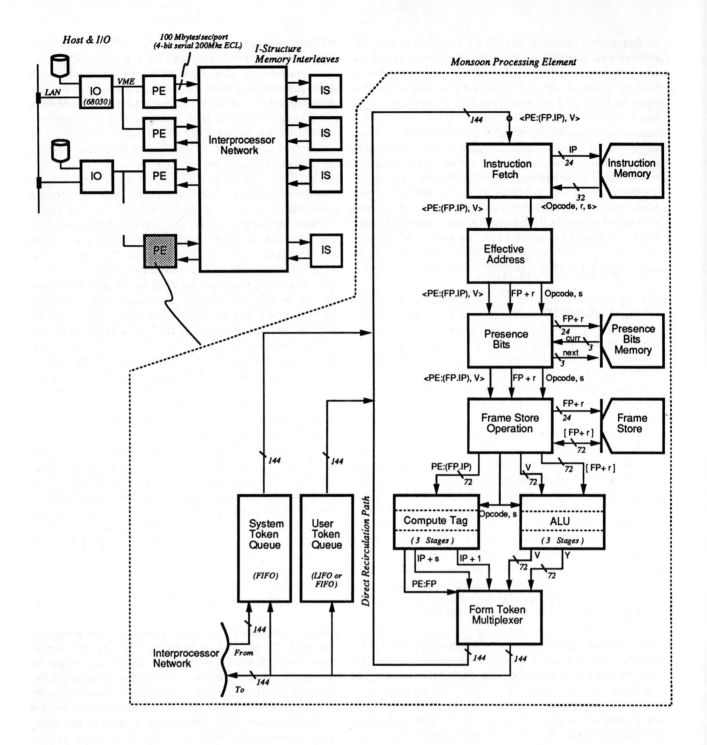

Figure 2: Monsoon Processing Element Pipeline

bit format, with a 12-bit opcode, a 10-bit operand, and a 10-bit destination field. The operand field, r, can be used as a frame-relative address in local frame store, $FP + r$, or as an absolute local address, to access literal constants and procedure linkage information kept in low memory by convention. The operand and destination fields can be combined to form a 20-bit address, as well. Every instruction can have up to two destinations, encoded as an adjustment to IP with an explicit PORT value. When an operand specifier is used, one of the destinations is $IP + 1$. The opcode completely determines the interpretation of the other two fields. There are three presence (or status) bits associated with each word of memory to support data-driven scheduling.

3.2 Pipeline operation

The right-hand portion of Figure 2 describes the internal pipeline of the Monsoon processor, which operates as follows. (1) The IP from the incoming token is used as an address into local instruction memory. (2) The effective address of a location in frame-store is computed ($FP + r$ or r). (3) The three presence bits associated with this frame-store location are read, modified (by a table lookup), and written back to the same location. The state transition function represented by the lookup depends on the port bit on the incoming token and the instruction opcode. It produces the new presence bits and two control signals for subsequent pipeline stages: one dictates whether the operation on the value part of the associated frame-store location is a read, write, exchange or no-op, and the other suppresses the generation of result tokens. For example, when the first token for a two-input operator is processed, the lookup specifies a write to the frame-store and supression of results. (4) Depending on the result of the lookup, the value part of the specified frame-store location is ignored, read, written, or exchanged with the value on the token.

The ALU represents three stages and operates in parallel with tag generation. (5) The value on the token and the value extracted from the frame-store are sorted into left and right values using the port bit of the incoming token. It is also possible to introduce the incoming tag as one of the ALU operands. (6,7) The operands are processed by one of the function units: a floating point/integer unit, a specialized pointer/tag arithmetic unit, a machine control unit or a type extract/set unit. Concurrent with the final ALU processing, two new result tags are computed by the next address generators. (8) Finally, the form-token stage creates result tokens by concatenating the computed tags with the ALU result. During inter-procedure communication (*i.e.* call and return values and structure memory operations) the result tag is actually *computed by* the ALU. The form-token multiplexor therefore allows the ALU result to be the tag of one of the tokens. An extra result

value, a delayed version of the "right" value, is also available to the form-token multiplexor. This stage detects whether PE of a result token tag is equal to the present processing element number. If not, the token is forwarded to the network and routed to the correct processing element or I-structure module. One of the (local) result tokens may be recirculated directly to the instruction fetch stage. If two local tokens are created, one of the result tokens is placed onto either the system or user token queue. If no tokens are created then a token is dequeued from one of the token queues for processing.

Consider the processing of a two-input operator. Either the left or right token may be processed first. The first token to be processed enters the pipeline and fetches the instruction pointed to by IP. During the effective address stage the location in frame-store where the match will take place is computed. The associated set of presence bits are examined and found to be in the empty state. The presence state is thus set to full and the incoming value is written into the frame-store location during the frame-store stage. Further processing of the token is suppressed because the other operand has yet to arrive. This "bubbles" the pipeline for the remaining ALU stages; no tokens are produced during form-token, permitting a token to be removed from one of the token queues for processing.

The second token to be processed enters the pipeline and fetches the same instruction. It therefore computes the same effective address. This time, however, the presence state is found to be full, so the frame-store location (which now contains the value of the first token) is read and both values are processed by the ALU. Finally, one or two result tokens are created during the form-token stage.

4 Evaluation

A single processor Monsoon prototype has been operational at the MIT Laboratory for Computer Science since October 1988 and a second prototype is due to be delivered to the Los Alamos National Laboratories for further evaluation. Except for an interprocessor network connection, the prototype employs the synchronous eight stage pipeline and 72-bit datapaths presented in Section 3. The memory sizes are fairly modest: 128KWords (72 bits) of frame-store and 128KWords (32 bits) of instruction memory. The prototype was designed to process six million tokens per second, although we typically clock at one-half this rate for reliability reasons. The processor is hosted via a NuBus adapter in a Texas Instruments Explorer lisp machine. The compiler and loader are written in Common Lisp and run on the host lisp machine whereas the runtime activation and heap memory management kernels are written in Id and execute directly on Monsoon.

Runtime management has been a particular challenge for large programs because, lacking an I-structure memory module, all activation frames and heap data structures are drawn from the same frame-store memory. We presently use 128 word activation frames. Free activation frames are kept on a shared free-list, so the frame *alloc* and *release* operators expand to three instructions each. Half of the frame-store memory is dedicated to the heap and managed by *allocate* and *deallocate* library routines. Two experimental memory managers have been developed for the prototype: a simple first-fit manager (with coalescing) and a more sophisticated buddy system that permits simultaneous allocations and deallocations against the various free-lists.

In spite of the serious memory limitations, some surprisingly large codes have been executed on Monsoon, including GAMTEB, a monte carlo histogramming simulation of photon transport and scattering in carbon cylinders. This code is heavily recursive and relatively difficult to vectorize. On Monsoon, a 40,000 particle simulation executed a little over one billion instructions. For comparison purposes, a scalar Fortran version of GAMTEB executes 40,000 particles in 250 million instructions on a CRAY-XMP. We have found that about 50% of Monsoon instructions were incurred by the memory management system (the Fortran version uses static memory allocation). The remaining overhead of about a factor of two when compared with Fortran is consistent with our experience with other codes on the MIT tagged token dataflow architecture [3]. We are encouraged by these preliminary data and expect marked future improvements in the memory management system and the overall dynamic efficiency of compiled code.

One of the non-scientific codes we have experimented with is a simulated annealing approach to the traveling salesperson problem, written in Id, but exercising user-defined object managers. The following statistics are typical of an iteration from a tour of fifty cities.

Fifty City TSP Tour on Monsoon		
Instruction Class	Total Cycles	Percentages
Fanouts and Identities	27,507,282	39.25
Arithmetic Operations	6,148,860	8.77
ALU Bubbles	20,148,890	28.75
I-Fetch Operations	3,590,992	5.12
I-Store Operations	285,790	0.41
Other Operations	8,902,202	12.70
Idles	3,503,494	5.00

Fanout and identities are used for replicating data values and termination detection. These are roughly equivalent to move instructions in von Neumann machines. Arithmetic operations include both integer and floating point operations. ALU bubbles occur when the first-arriving operand of a two-input operator is written into a frame slot and and further processing of instruction is suppressed. Idling occurs during a cycle where no tokens are produced and the token queues are empty.

The current Monsoon compiler is a retargeted version of the Id to TTDA graph compiler[30] and essentially follows a transliteration of TTDA instructions into the Monsoon instruction set. It performs the static assignment of nodes to frame slots, but takes little advantage of the additional power of the ETS model. As such, we view the current application base as a proof of principle more than as a statement of potential performance.

We are now working with the Motorola Microcomputer Division and the Motorola Cambridge Research Center to develop multiprocessor Monsoon prototypes. The new processors are similar to the first prototype but are faster, (10 million tokens per second) have somewhat larger frame storage, (256KWords to 1MWord) and, significantly, have dedicated I-structure memory modules (4MWords) and a high-speed multistage packet switch (100 Mbytes/sec/port). Versions comprising eight processors and eight memory modules and four Unix-based I/O processors should be operational in the Spring of 1991. Motorola will also be supporting a Unix-based single processor/single memory module workstation for Id program development.

The ETS activation frame functions much like a conventional register set and, by ignoring the presence-bits, can be accessed as such. Of course, a *single* instruction of a three-address von Neumann processor could read two registers, perform an operation and write the result register, whereas Monsoon takes three instructions to accomplish the same action. Monsoon permits only a single frame-store operation per cycle. In a very real sense, the value part of a token corresponds to an accumulator—it can be loaded, stored, or operated upon, in combination with the local frame. However, from a hardware engineering viewpoint, the single port access to frame-store is an important restriction, since the frame-store simultaneously holds *thousands* of activation frames; three-port access would be prohibitively expensive. Competitive implementations of a Monsoon-like processor would certainly employ a cache of local frame memory; nonetheless, the single port frame-store suggests what might be an inherent inefficiency in the ETS model.

The future architectural development of Monsoon will continue to explore fundamental improvements in dynamic instruction efficiency. Part of this work addresses a basic mismatch in the Monsoon pipeline, that is characteristic of dataflow architectures. Each two-input instruction requires two operations against frame-store, and thus two processor cycles, but only utilizes the ALU with the arrival of the second token. As suggested by the statistics above, approximately 30% of the ALU cycles are consumed by this mismatch (ALU bubbles). Observe, that a sequence of instructions that produce one local result at each step follows the direct recirculation path, thus occupying one of eight processor interleaves. The new version of Monsoon provides a 3 × 72-bit four-port (two read, two write) temporary register set for each interleave. For simple arithmetic expressions, the temporary set can improve the dynamic instruction efficiency (the number cycles required to compute the expression) by a factor of two. Note, the temporaries are valid only as long as a thread has a recirculating token; when a token is first popped from a queue, the values of the temporaries are indeterminate. The temporaries are also invalidated when performing a split-phase read. These temporaries are very similar to the register set in Iannucci's hybrid architecture [23].

5 Related Work

In our view, the beauty of the ETS model and its realization in Monsoon lies in its simplicity, not its novelty. It draws heavily on developments in dynamic and static dataflow architectures, yet demystifies the dataflow execution model be providing a simple, concrete, machine-oriented formulation — one simple enough to build. Activation frames are certainly not a new idea. The use of presence-bits to detect enabled operations is represented in the earliest static dataflow architectures[15,16,28]. In those designs, instructions and operand slots were combined into an instruction template, which was delivered to a function unit when it was determined that the operand slots were full. Presence detection was performed by an autonomous unit, functioning asynchronously with the rest of the system, rather than simply treated as a stage in an instruction pipeline. Also, the utilization of the activity store was poor, because storage was preallocated for every operand slot in the entire program, even though the fraction of these containing data at any time is generally small. Other drawbacks included the complex firing rule of the merge operator, the need for acknowledgement arcs to ensure one token per arc, loss of parallelism due to artificial dependences, and the inability to support general recursion.

Tagged-token architectures addressed these problems by naming each activity in terms of its role in the computation, rather than by the resources used to perform the activity. Iteration and recursion is easily implemented by assigning new names for each activation of the loop or function. This eliminated the troublesome merge operator, the acknowledgement arcs, and the artificial dependences. Storage for operands was allocated "as needed" via the matching mechanism. In our own efforts to refine the MIT Tagged-Token Dataflow Architecture, the association between the name for an activity and the resources devoted to performing the activity became ever more immediate. Once state information was directly associated with each activation, it was a small step to eliminate the matching store. However, before it made sense to represent storage for operands directly, it was necessary to ensure that the utilization would be reasonable. This involved developments in compilation of loops[13], as well as frame-slot mapping.

A separate line of development generalized the static model by dynamically splicing the graph to support recursion[32]. VIM[17] advances these ideas by separating the program and data portions of the instruction template, so the splicing operations could be implemented by allocating an operand frame and providing a form of token indirection. Representation of iteration in this context presents problems and is generally eliminated in favor of tail-recursion.

The ETS model pulls these three areas together in an elegant fashion. The power of the tagged-token approach is provided with a simple mechanism, expressed in familiar terms. The mechanism is quite close to that which is used to support I-structures and provides a uniform means fo representing synchronizing data structure operations. Since the instruction determines how the operand store is accessed, it is straightforward to realize imperative control threads as well.

Graph reduction architectures provide an additional reference point, contemporary with the development of dataflow architectures and addressing a similar class of languages[14,25]. The function application mechanism under a reduction model closely resembles graph splicing, in that a copy of the function body is produced and arguments substituted where formal parameters appear. The copy of the function body can be viewed as an activation frame, the slots of which contain references to chunks of computation that will eventually be reduced to a value. In this sense, state information is associated with each slot in the frame to indicate whether it is reduced or not. Parallel graph reduction architectures require additional mechanisms for recording requests made for a value while it is being reduced. By demanding values before they are actually needed, data-driven scheduling can be simulated[24]. The rather primitive ETS mechanism can be used to support demand-driven execution as well[22], although we have not pursued that direction extensively. A detailed comparison between the two execution models is beyond the scope of this paper.

Several researchers have suggested that dataflow and von Neumann machines lie at two ends of an architectural spectrum[11,19,23,26]. In reflecting upon the development of Monsoon, our view is somewhat different. Dataflow architectures and modern RISC machines represent orthogonal generalizations of the single accumulator "von Neumann" machine. The mainstream architectural trend enhances the power of a single execution thread with multiple addresses per operation. Dataflow graphs essentially represent multiple 1-address execution threads, with a very simple synchronization paradigm. Having made the transition from propagating values through graphs to "virtual" processors, we can begin to address the question of what is the best processor organization to "virtualize." Certainly there are gains to be made by incorporating more powerful operand specification, but this must be weighed against additional complexity in synchronization. Recently, attention has been paid to multi-threaded variants of a full 3-address load/store architecture to tolerate latency on a cache miss[31]. The proposed techniques range from a four-port register file to complete replication of the data path. Thus, considerable complexity is contemplated to address only the latency aspect of parallel computing. It is not obvious that a simple, inexpensive synchronization mechanism can be provided in this context. It is likely that the optimal building block for scalable, general purpose parallel computers will combine the two major directions of architectural evolution, but may not be extreme in either direction.

Acknowledgements

This work reflects considerable contributions of many members and past members of the Computation Structures Group, led by Prof. Arvind, including R. S. Nikhil, Andy Boughton, Ken Traub, Jonathan Young, Paul Barth, Stephen Brobst, Steve Heller, Richard Soley, Bob Iannucci, Andy Shaw, Jack Costanza, and Ralph Tiberio. Special thanks to our growing user community, including Olaf Lubeck of LANL, and to Motorola Inc. for their continuing support.

The research was performed primarily at the MIT Laboratory for Computer Science and partly at the University of California, Berkeley. Funding for the project is provided in part by the Advanced Projects Agency of the Department of Defense under the Office of Naval Research contract N00014-84-K-0099.

References

[1] Arvind and D. E. Culler. Managing Resources in a Parallel Machine. In *Proc. of IFIP TC-10 Working Conference on Fifth Generation Computer Architecture, Manchester, England*. North-Holland Publishing Company, July 1985.

[2] Arvind and D. E. Culler. Dataflow Architectures. In *Annual Reviews in Computer Science*, volume 1, pages 225–253. Annual Reviews Inc., Palo Alto, CA, 1986. Reprinted in Dataflow and Reduction Architectures, S. S. Thakkar, editor, IEEE Computer Society Press, 1987.

[3] Arvind, D. E. Culler, and K. Ekanadham. The Price of Asynchronous Parallelism: an Analysis of Dataflow Architectures. In *Proc. of CONPAR 88*, Univ. of Manchester, September 1988. British Computer Society — Parallel Processing Specialists. (also CSG Memo No. 278, MIT Lab for Computer Science).

[4] Arvind, D. E. Culler, R. A. Iannucci, V. Kathail, K. Pingali, and R. E. Thomas. The Tagged Token Dataflow Architecture. Technical Report FLA memo, MIT Lab for Computer Science, 545 Tech. Sq, Cambridge, MA, August 1983. Revised October, 1984.

[5] Arvind, D. E. Culler, and G. K. Maa. Assessing the Benefits of Fine-Grain Parallelism in Dataflow Programs. *The Int'l Journal of Supercomputer Applications*, 2(3), November 1988.

[6] Arvind, M. L. Dertouzos, R. S. Nikhil, and G. M. Papadopoulos. PROJECT DATAFLOW, a Parallel Computing System Based on the Monsoon Architecture and the Id Programming Language. Technical Report CSG Memo 285, MIT Lab for Computer Science, 545 Tech. Sq, Cambridge, MA, 1988.

[7] Arvind and K. Ekanadham. Future Scientific Programming on Parallel Machines. *The Journal of Parallel and Distributed Computing*, 5(5):460–493, October 1988.

[8] Arvind, S. K. Heller, and R. S. Nikhil. Programming Generality and Parallel Computers. In *Proc. of the Fourth Int'l Symp. on Biological and Artificial Intelligence Systems*, pages 255–286, Trento, Italy, September 1988. ESCOM (Leider).

[9] Arvind and R. A. Iannucci. Two Fundamental Issues in Multiprocessing. In *Proc. of DFVLR - Conference 1987 on Parallel Processing in Science and Engineering, Bonn-Bad Godesberg, W. Germany*, June 1987.

[10] R. G. Babb II, editor. *Programming Parallel Processors*. Addison-Wesley Pub. Co., Reading, Mass., 1988.

[11] L. Bic. A Process-Oriented Model for Efficient Execution of Dataflow Programs. In *Proc. of the 7th Int'l Conference on Distributed Computing*, Berlin, West Germany, September 1987.

[12] G. Chaitin, M. Auslander, A. Chandra, J. Cocke, M. Hopkins, and P. Markstein. Register Allocation via Coloring. *Computer Languages*, 6:47–57, 1981.

[13] D. E. Culler. *Managing Parallelism and Resources in Scientific Dataflow Programs*. PhD thesis, MIT Dept. of Electrical Engineering and Computer Science, Cambridge, MA, June 1989. To appear as MIT Lab for Computer Science TR446.

[14] J. Darlington and M. Reeve. ALICE - A Multi-Processor Reduction Machine for Parallel Evaluation of Applicative Languages. In *Proc. of the 1981 Conference on Functional Programming and Computer Architecture*, pages 65–76, 1981.

[15] J. B. Dennis. Data Flow Supercomputers. *IEEE Computer*, pages 48–56, November 1980.

[16] J. B. Dennis and D. P. Misunas. A Preliminary Architecture for a Basic Dataflow Processor. In *Proc. of the 2nd Annual Symp. on Computer Architecture*, page 126. IEEE, January 1975.

[17] J. B. Dennis, J. E. Stoy, and B. Guharoy. VIM: An Experimental Multi-User System Supporting Functional Programming. In *Proc. of the 1984 Int'l Workshop on High-Level Computer Architecture*, pages 1.1–1.9, Los Angeles, CA, May 1984.

[18] D.D. Gajski, D.A. Padua, David J. Kuck, and R.H. Kuhn. A Second Opinion of Data Flow Machines and Languages. *IEEE Computer*, 15(2):58–69, February 1982.

[19] V. G. Grafe, J. E. Hoch, and Davidson G.S. Eps'88: Combining the Best Features of von Neumann and Dataflow Computing. Technical Report SAND88-3128, Sandia National Laboratories, January 1989.

[20] J. Gurd, C.C. Kirkham, and I. Watson. The Manchester Prototype Dataflow Computer. *Communications of the Association for Computing Machinery*, 28(1):34–52, January 1985.

[21] J. L. Gustafson, G. R. Montry, and R. E. Benner. Development of Parallel Methods for a 1024-Processor Hypercube. *SIAM Journal on Scientific and Statistical Computing*, 9(4), July 1988.

[22] S. K. Heller. Efficient lazy data-structures on a dataflow machine. Technical Report LCS/MIT/TR-438, MIT Lab for Computer Science, 545 Tech. Sq, Cambridge, MA, 1988. (PhD Thesis, Dept. of EECS, MIT).

[23] R. A. Iannucci. A Dataflow/von Neumann Hybrid Architecture. Technical Report TR-418, MIT Lab for Computer Science, 545 Tech. Sq, Cambridge, MA, May 1988. (PhD Thesis, Dept. of EECS, MIT).

[24] R. M. Keller and F. C. Lin. Simulated Performance of a Reduction-Based Multiprocessor. *IEEE Computer*, pages 70–82, July 1984.

[25] R. M. Keller, G. Lindstrom, and S. Patil. A Loosely-Coupled Applicative Multi-Processing System. In *Proc. of the National Computer Conference*, volume 48, pages 613–622, New York, NY, June 1979.

[26] R. S. Nikhil and Arvind. Can Dataflow Subsume von Neumann Computing? In *Proc. of the 16th Annual Int'l Symp. on Computer Architecture*, Jerusalem, Israel, May 1989. To appear.

[27] G. M. Papadopoulos. Implementation of a General Purpose Dataflow Multiprocessor. Technical Report TR432, MIT Lab for Computer Science, 545 Tech. Sq, Cambridge, MA, September 1988. (PhD Thesis, Dept. of EECS, MIT).

[28] J. Rumbaugh. A Data Flow Multiprocessor. *IEEE Transactions on Computers*, C-26(2):138–146, February 1977.

[29] T. Shimada, K. Hiraki, and K. Nishida. An Architecture of a Data Flow Machine and its Evaluation. In *Proc. of CompCon 84*, pages 486–490. IEEE, 1984.

[30] K. R. Traub. A Compiler for the MIT Tagged-Token Dataflow Architecture. Technical Report TR-370, MIT Lab for Computer Science, 545 Tech. Sq, Cambridge, MA, August 1986. (MS Thesis, Dept. of EECS, MIT).

[31] W. Weber and A. Gupta. Exploring the Benefits of Multiple Hardware Contexts in a Multiprocessor Architecture: Preliminary Results. In *Proc. of the 1989 Int'l Symp. on Computer Architecture*, pages 273–280, Jerusalem, Israel, May 1989.

[32] K. Weng. An Abstract Implementation for a Generalized Data Flow Language. Technical Report MIT/LCS/TR-228, MIT Lab for Computer Science, 545 Tech. Sq, Cambridge, MA, 1979. (PhD Thesis, Dept. of EECS, MIT).

The K2 Parallel Processor:
Architecture and Hardware Implementation

MARCO ANNARATONE, MARCO FILLO, KIYOSHI NAKABAYASHI[†] AND MARC VIREDAZ

Integrated Systems Laboratory, Swiss Federal Institute of Technology
Gloriastrasse 35, 8092 Zurich, Switzerland

and

[†] *NTT Communications and Information Processing Laboratories, Tokyo 180, Japan*

Abstract

K2 is a distributed-memory parallel processor designed to support a multi-user, multi-tasking, time-sharing operating system and an automatically parallelizing FORTRAN compiler. This paper presents the architecture and the hardware implementation of K2, and focuses on the architectural features required by the operating system and the compiler. A prototype machine with 24 processors is currently being developed.

1 Introduction

Distributed-memory parallel processors (DMPPs) feature different interconnection topologies (i.e., tori, hypercubes, linear arrays, just to mention DMPPs that were built and commercialized) and different parallelism grain-size, i.e., from the 64 vector processors of the MIMD iPSC/2[1] to the 65,536 simple processors of the SIMD Connection Machine CM-2[2]. Efficient interconnection topologies, communication mechanisms, etc., have been researched and debated in recent years. Conversely, system software issues have not been as aggressively addressed. We believe this is one of the reasons why DMPPs have not achieved a significant commercial success so far. For this reason we have concentrated our research on automatically parallelizing compilers (APCs), interactive symbolic debuggers, and multi-user operating systems. Considering such features within the development of a DMPP modifies profoundly the design space and forces the architectural parameters mentioned above to be evaluated under a new perspective.

This paper presents the architecture and the hardware implementation of K2, a DMPP designed to support a FORTRAN APC and a multi-user, multi-tasking, time-sharing operating system. In the paper we first critique current

This research was supported in part by ETH grant number 0.330.066.23/4, in part by the Mikrotechnik Kredit.

Permission to copy without fee all or part of this material is granted provided that the copies are not made or distributed for direct commercial advantage, the ACM copyright notice and the title of the publication and its date appear, and notice is given that copying is by permission of the Association for Computing Machinery. To copy otherwise, or to republish, requires a fee and/or specific permission.

DMPPs. Second, we present the architecture of K2. Then, we analyze the different design alternatives and justify our choices. The hardware implementation and the project status are finally discussed. Throughout the paper we also refer to our ongoing research on the compiler and the operating system.

2 A Critique of DMPPs

DMPPs such as the Connection Machine (CM) [2], NCUBE [3], Intel iPSC/2 [1], Warp [4] and iWarp [5], and various Transputer-based computers like the Meiko M40 [6] are *attached processors*: there is a host between the user and the DMPP. The host is a Symbolics or a Vax in the CM, a SUN in the NCUBE, a SUN with dedicated I/O processors in Warp, and a SUN (remote) and an 80386 (local) on the iPSC/2. Such approach dates back to the Solomon [7] and ILLIAC IV [8] DMPPs, and has also been used to connect array processors to mini or mainframe computers.

These DMPPs run single-user or, at most, provide *space sharing* (iPSC, NCUBE, and CM): programmers can concurrently use *non-overlapping* sections of the DMPP topology.

On these machines jobs may run on the attached processor in batch-mode, similarly to what was done on Cray computers running under COS. Batch processing makes it unrealistic to run interactive programs, and tends to favor post-mortem debugging. Interactive use and debugging is possible on some DMPPs only by locking the machine. This is not a practical solution since debugging sessions can last hours if not days, and running the application on a simulator to check the functional correctness of the code has a limited usefulness.

As some experts have realized, a single-user, single-task DMPP is unlikely to fulfill the market requirements in the years to come. In a recent paper by Gordon Bell [9] one reads:

> "The lack of multiprogramming ability today may dictate using these machines [i.e., high-performance DMPPs] on only one or a few very large jobs at the same time, and hence *making*

the cost per job quite high, thus diminishing the performance/price advantage." [emphasis added]

In the above DMPPs the user interface and the software development environment reside on the host. The host runs the sequential part of the application; this may result in a communication bottleneck between the host and the attached processor that for the CM-1 or the iPSC/2, for instance, can be severe.

The above DMPPs do not have APCs. An APC takes as input, source code developed for uniprocessors and performs the following tasks: (1) domain decomposition on the DMPP topology, (2) code optimization and parallelization, and (3) code generation for all the nodes including interprocessor communication operations. APCs are already available on shared-memory multiprocessors—the KAP FORTRAN compiler [10] for the Sequent Symmetry or the Alliant FORTRAN compiler [11] are two examples. The major hurdle in the implementation of an APC for DMPPs is the domain decomposition. Nonetheless, the development of an APC is an essential step towards more usable DMPPs, since programmers should not be expected to manually decompose the data-structures (much like they are not expected to allocate registers in uniprocessors).

From the above considerations, we can derive the system features that should be supported by a new architecture:

- A time-sharing, multi-user, multi-tasking operating system. This eases interactive debugging, and generally decreases the cost per job. This implies:

  - a disk subsystem with enough bandwidth to support paging activities, process swapping, and large-files transfer (see also below).

  - large local storage to decrease the load on the interprocessor communication channels [12], and to accommodate the working sets of several large-sized processes. For instance, finite-element analysis of three-dimensional semiconductor structures requires data sets in excess of 320 Mbyte [13]; trace-driven cache simulations need data-sets of more than 150 Mbyte to be able to capture a few hundred milliseconds of RISC microprocessor activity [14].

  - memory protection and virtual memory support on each node.

- Efficient execution of APC-generated parallel programs.

- Higher communication bandwidth between the serial part and the parallel part of the code by avoiding the attached processor design paradigm.

3 Overview of the K2 architecture

K2 has been designed to support the execution of application software and the execution of system software. While

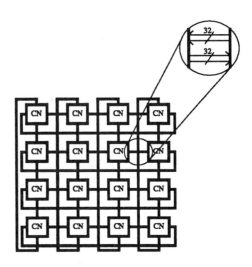

Figure 1: The K2 user-level machine abstraction.

much is known about efficient topologies and communication mechanisms for parallel application code, the same cannot be said for parallel system software. Our decision was to design a topology well known to perform efficiently on application code, and to enhance it to support system-related activities.

Figure 1 shows the K2 *user-level machine abstraction*, which consists of a torus of computation nodes (CNs). CNs are interconnected by point-to-point (32-bit wide) bidirectional channels, hereafter referred to as *user channels*. The advantages of this topology (when the DMPP has a limited number of processors, as in our case) are well-known. By summarizing the results from the works of Dally [15], Vitányi [16], and Johnsson [17], a two-dimensional topology represents a natural choice when the processing elements are 256 or less (Dally), or 64 or less (Johnsson). This consensus can be found in the marketplace as well. In fact, the Warp machine (a linear array of processors) has evolved into iWarp (a two-dimensional torus); moreover, many hypercube users "flatten" the topology and work on tori embedded in the hypercube [18, 19, 20, 21, 22].

The K2 *system-level machine abstraction* is shown in figure 2. Each row (or column) of CNs is connected to an input/output node (ION) to which terminals and disks are attached. The connection between each ION and a row (or column) of CNs is a serial token-ring, referred to as *system channel*. An identical token-ring serves all IONs and connects them to an Ethernet gateway.

All nodes are intended to run both user and system processes. The CNs are dedicated to computation-intensive parallel jobs, while the IONs run light-weight jobs such as editing, mail, etc. In addition, although the OS activities are distributed over all CNs and IONs, the latter are primarily used as file servers and disk caches.

In the following sections we elaborate on the two major architectural features in the design of K2, i.e., the user channels and the system channels.

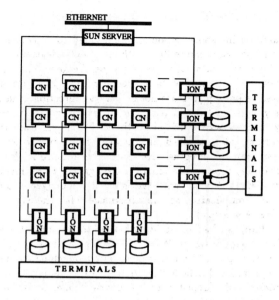

Figure 2: The K2 system-level machine abstraction.

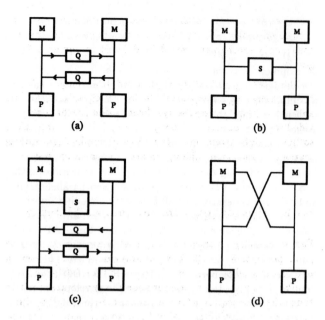

Figure 3: Four user channel architectures. (M: local memory; P: processor; Q: queue; S: shared-memory.)

3.1 The user channels

CNs communicate with one another in two different domains: user and system. While the former is typical of all DMPPs available today, the latter is unique to K2. Communication among processors in the user *and* system domains cannot be efficiently supported by a single interconnection paradigm. In fact, application-related information is highly deterministic, and its flow within the torus is mainly dictated by the programmer of the parallel task (or by the APC). This is not the case for system-related communication, as we shall discuss in detail in section 3.2. Because precise control over the interprocessor communication *and* synchronization is generally possible in the user domain, processors can communicate without resorting to the asynchronous, interrupt-based policy which characterizes message-passing architectures. That is, neighboring processors can exchange data by simply copying them from their own local memory to dedicated hardware channels. This mechanism, also used in Warp and iWarp, has two major advantages:

1. The communication is totally supported in hardware. Hence, no kernel activity is required either to send or to receive data, unlike in message-passing architectures.

2. If queue channels are used, self-synchronizing communication can efficiently be achieved through hardware blocking. Processors reading from an empty queue or writing to a full queue will stall until the queue status changes.

Such a mechanism, unlike message-passing, lacks automatic routing and transparent forwarding. However, the low-dimensionality of the topologies featuring it makes the manual routing of information manageable by the programmer. This consideration does not apply to higher-dimensionality topologies (e.g., hypercubes): in this case automatic routing and transparent forwarding must be provided. Moreover, this issue becomes less important with the availability of an APC.

3.1.1 Alternative user channel architectures

Before committing to a specific user channel architecture, we evaluated four different alternatives. They are shown in figure 3. Figure 3(a) shows the "Warp/iWarp" channel architecture; it provides a simple and clear programming model (based on send and receive) and automatic process synchronization through queue blockage. This model features the highest interprocessor bandwidth when sending and receiving raw data. However, sharing of read/write data structures can be done only by physically moving them from processor to processor. The shared-memory model in figure 3(b) is more efficient, as long as the sharing of data structures is limited to two neighboring processors, but it lacks the simple programming model of the previous one and an automatic process synchronization mechanism (locks must be checked before accessing writable shared resources).

The architecture in figure 3(c) merges the previous two together: shared data structures do not have to be physically copied between neighboring processors, and automatic process synchronization is accomplished by enqueueing and dequeueing pointers to the shared structures. Two disadvantages are higher costs and a clumsy programming model. In fact, variable definition would be similar to that found in shared-memory multiprocessors (e.g., SHARED and PRIVATE) but with access semantics similar to DMPPs (i.e., send and receive). Neither architecture 3(b) nor 3(c) copes well with variables that are normally local to processors and become occasionally shared; the data allocation strategy and the consistency mechanism would be difficult to implement elegantly.

The fourth architecture (figure 3(d)), although it solves the problems just mentioned, lacks a programming model and the automatic process synchronization mechanism provided by the queues. Finally, it requires the processors to have a tight coupling of their logical-to-physical address mapping, something difficult to accomplish in practice.

3.1.2 User channel throughput and latency

Fast local communication throughput is essential to achieve good performance. We have quantified this parameter in one of our studies [23]: the time to send a double-precision number to a neighbor processor should be no greater than 16 times the time required for a local double-precision multiplication or addition. Decreasing the communication throughput penalizes performance, while increasing it does not result in appreciable performance improvement. Note that this holds true in a single-task environment, which was the assumption in the study cited above. In our case, the multitasking requirements call for the fastest queue flush on process switch. In addition, fast channels are required by the APC under development. In fact, the APC avoids some deficiencies typical of current shared-memory APCs (notably KAP [10]) by carrying out run-time data-dependency analysis and construction of interprocessor communications. This allows, for instance, to parallelize fast-Fourier transform code, a task which KAP is unable to do because it limits its parallelization to a compile-time analysis of the code. Since the run-time portion of the compiler requires substantial amount of information exchange among processors, its efficiency depends heavily on the speed of the user channels. Even with the 0.5 communication/computation ratio of a CN, the average overhead introduced by the compiler run-time activities on an 8 × 8 K2 is about 20%, with a best case of 2% (in a fluid-dynamics simulation) and a worst case of 30% (in a binary FFT program) [24].

Another justification for high-throughput, low-latency channels comes from the need to support fast communication between the serial and parallel parts of an application. K2's multi-tasking makes it possible to have a CN in charge of running the sequential part of the application, and switch back and forth between this task and the one belonging to the parallel part. In this way we have reached the goal of eliminating the "host-attached processor" structure and its inherent communication bottleneck. The serial part of the application now runs *within* the parallel part, and can therefore communicate with it using the high bandwidth of the user channels. The resulting minimum bandwidth (i.e., that between the CN running the serial part and the surrounding CNs) features 50 Mbyte/s throughput for outgoing data and 200 Mbyte/s for incoming data (limited to maximum 4 Kbyte bursts).

3.1.3 The K2 user channel architecture

Based on the above reasoning, we decided to implement the model shown in figure 3(a) with some extra features.

First, the status of a queue can be checked. That is, the hardware queues allow both blocking and non-blocking access. Second, queues are not strictly unidirectional; in fact, they can also be read (only in supervisor mode, however) by the processor *writing* into them. Whenever the current process context is saved, the queues will be flushed out and their contents saved as part of it. This feature is also useful in the implementation of a debugger for the machine. Without it, the implementation of the debugger would be rather complicated, as the experience with the Warp machine showed [25].

Third, we had to decide whether to implement several virtual queues (as in iWarp [5]) on top of the physical one or not. Support of multi-tasking on the machine can be accomplished either by having virtual queues assigned to each process and mapped onto the physical one, or by having the physical queue assigned to a single process at any given time. In the first case, the total depth of the physical queue is subdivided into all processes active at a given time (i.e., those that are either running or in fast wait), and a process switch does not require flushing of the queues to local memory but simply performing a pointer exchange. In the second case the depth of the virtual queue is identical to that of the physical one, but queue flush is required at any process switch. Given the limited size of the queues and their fast access time, a complete flushing of the queues to local memory does not represent a significant overhead even when the quantum of the process switch is relatively small (e.g., every 20,000 instructions), and therefore the second solution has been implemented.

3.2 The system channels

The design of the user channels has been tailored to the characteristics of the application software running on the CNs: strong locality, predefined occurrence of communication activities, and relatively high computation/communication ratio. To define similar figures—even qualitatively—for the system domain one must resort to some educated guess. Research on multi-user, multi-tasking operating systems for DMPPs has just started, and hard facts are not yet available.

It is fair to assume, however, that the data locality will strongly depend on the design of the file system, that communication will be stochastic in nature and will largely prevail over computation. If even one of the above assumptions held true, the communication mechanism implemented in the user domain would be highly inadequate. Its synchrony, its assumption of local communication, and its inflexibility cannot be used to support largely asynchronous activities typical of file transfers, paging, and process swapping. Moreover, the transfer of system-related information has a granularity which may go from the size of a page to small parcels of information such as acknowledgements, requests for services, etc. Finally, system-related information may

Table 1: Characteristics of the user channels and the system channels.

PARAMETER	USER CHANNELS	SYSTEM CHANNELS
Info carried	Application	System
Communication mechanism	Raw data	Message passing
Routing type	Manual	Automatic
Routing done by	CPU	SNIK
Medium	Parallel wires	Coax and optical fiber
Type	Blocking and non-blocking	Non-blocking
Throughput per channel (peak)	$400Mb/s$	$100Mb/s$
Latency: CPU reg. to CPU reg. SNIK to SNIK	$160ns$	$1.5\mu s$ (min)

Table 2: Metrics of the prototype K2.

UNIT	CHIP COUNT	FOOTPRINT cm^2 $[in^2]$	MAX POWER CONS. (W)
PE-CN	160	846 [131.1]	115
PE-ION	190	860 [133.3]	115
SNIK	85	754 [116.8]	30
User channels	120	517 [80.1]	50
Disk controller	48	308 [47.7]	35
CN	365	2117 [328.1]	195
ION	323	1922 [308.7]	180

have quite different priorities (from panic signals to character outputs), and the queues of the user channels only support "first-in, first-out."

These reasons justify the implementation of a dedicated communication network, which is shown in figure 2. Here, a collection of token-rings provides the necessary decoupling from the communication activities going on in the user domain.

Given the above requirements, the semantics of this network has to differ significantly from that of the user channels. This network provides, in fact:

- Message passing with automatic routing and transparent forwarding. Messages are packetized and routed automatically through the sytem channels by specialized units called Serial Network Interface Controllers (SNIKs) present on both CNs and IONs.

- Overlapping communication and computation is fully supported. Messages flow across the system channels without disturbing the local computation of the CNs they traverse; SNIKs reroute messages and alert the processing element (PE) only when an incoming message is destined for it.

- Communication is non-blocking, and the PE can interrogate its own SNIK about incoming messages.

- All messages may carry an associated priority.

Finally, table 1 summarizes the main characteristics of both communication networks.

4 Hardware implementation

K2 consists of two units:

- A computation node (CN), which includes a processing element (PE), four outgoing and four incoming 32-bit wide user channels, and a SNIK.

- An input/output node (ION), which includes a processing element (PE), a SNIK, a disk controller and terminal interfaces, but no user channels.

The processing element of the ION is identical to that of the CN, except that its local storage is four times larger, since these nodes are intended to implement an intelligent disk cache mechanism to increase the performance of the paging system. Therefore, four basic units were designed, i.e., the PE, the user channels, the SNIK, and the disk controller. The machine that we describe here is the "prototype K2," and has a simplified design. First, a 4×4 torus of CNs is implemented. Second, CNs and IONs do not have on-board cache memories.

The CN block diagram is shown in figure 4(a), while the ION block diagram is shown in figure 4(b). The CN consists of an AMD Am29000 microprocessor with AMD Am29027 floating-point co-processor (FPC), separate instruction (0.5 Mbyte) and data (2 Mbyte) memories with error detection and correction, four pairs of 32-bit wide user channels, and the SNIK unit.

The ION architecture is similar to that of the CN with few major differences. First, the user channels are not present. Second, the local memory is increased to 2 Mbyte for instructions and 8 Mbyte for data. An intelligent mass storage controller (MSC) interfaces directly to the PE through a dual-port memory and provides a peripheral SCSI interface with a peak throughput of about 4 Mbyte/s.

The metrics for the various units are given in table 2. Figures 5 and 6 show the prototype boards of the PE-CN and of the SNIK, respectively. The manufacturing of the printed-circuit boards has been contracted outside. The design, schematic entry, chip placement and board routing was carried out at the Laboratory.

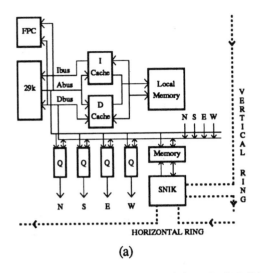
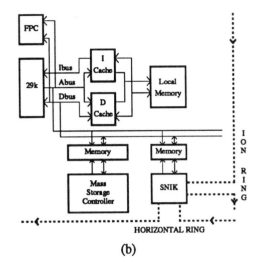

(a)   (b)

Figure 4: Block-diagram of CN (a) and ION (b). Cache memories are not included in the prototype K2.

4.1 Processing element

The choice of the CPU and the structure of the local memory system were the fundamental issues in the design of the PE.

4.1.1 The choice of the CPU

We decided to use a commercial CPU, rather than a custom processor, because of the obvious advantages both in hardware design (support chips and development tools), and in software development (availability of assemblers, compilers and debuggers).

When the CPU was chosen (May 1988), there were four high performance microprocessors in the market or about to enter it: the AMD Am29000, the Motorola MC88100, the SPARC, and the MIPS R2000. The last two were not considered for other than technical reasons. The remaining two, i.e., the 29000 and 88100 CPUs, follow quite different design philosophies and a detailed analysis of both is outside the scope of this study. The CPUs' architectural characteristics which influenced the evaluation are shown in table 3.

Eventually, what tipped the scale in favor of the 29000 was the interface to the user channels. As already pointed out in section 3.1.2, the CPU architecture should allow a fast access mechanism to the user channels (whose references are non-cacheable), and their prompt blocking/unblocking.

With the 29000, mapping the channels onto the virtual address space does not cause any performance degradation since the on-chip TLB performs address translation as one of the pipeline stages. Instead, in the 88100 the mapping of the channels onto virtual space slows down their access since they must be addressed through the off-chip CMMU. More importantly, the 88000 CPU to CMMU handshake protocol introduces an access overhead for non-cacheable data of at least 5 extra cycles.

A further consideration on this topic came from the efficiency in interrupt servicing during user channel blockage.

Table 3: Main characteristics of the AMD Am29000 and the Motorola MC88100 at the time of evaluation.

PARAMETER	Am29000	MC88100
Clock freq.	25MHz	20MHz
Bus arch.	3 buses	4 buses
Bus protocol	simple, pipelined, burst	synchronous
On-chip reg.	192	32
Instr. cache	8 Kbyte (casc.), 2-way set-assoc.[†]	16 ÷ 64 Kbyte, 4-way set-assoc. off-chip (88200)
Data cache	8 Kbyte (casc.), 2-way set-assoc.[†]	16 ÷ 64 Kbyte, 4-way set-assoc. off-chip (88200)
Branch target buffer	128 entries, on-chip	N.A.
FPU	off-chip (29027)	on-chip
MMU	on-chip	off-chip (88200)

[†] Since then AMD decided to drop the development of the cache chips.

As we shall see later in section 4.2, the 29000 provides a hardware mechanism to handle exception recovery, while the 88100 must resort to software emulation.

4.1.2 The design of the memory system

Four alternative structures of the local memory were considered:

- Instruction and data cache based system (I&D CACHE), with split caches and a two-way interleaved DRAM local memory.

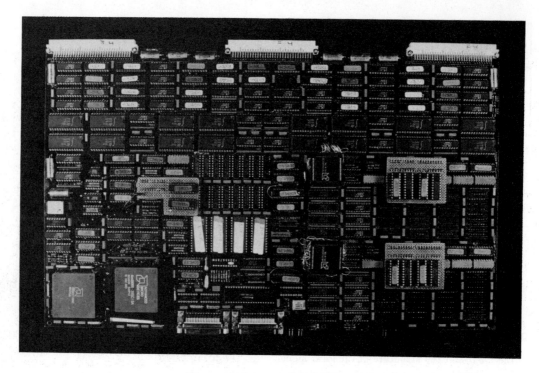

Figure 5: The PE-CN board.

- Instruction cache and DRAM local memory (I CACHE).
- Video-DRAM memory without caches (VRAM).
- Separate DRAM memory banks for instructions and data, no caches (SPLIT MEMORY).

The four memory structures listed above were compared using a 29000 instruction-set simulator. Table 4 shows the assumed memory access speeds. Such figures were used as input parameters to the simulator, and the same table shows the resulting performance in Am29000 MIPS (million instructions per second). The five benchmark programs (B1 to B5) are integer compute-intensive sections of parallel programs developed on the K2 simulator [26]. The figures relative to I&D CACHE should be considered as optimistic, since the simulator does not model a cache-based memory system. Those of I CACHE are more realistic; our studies have indeed demonstrated that it is possible to achieve hit ratios very close to 100% on the instruction, even for small caches and regardless of their organization [14]. To limit the chip count and because of the unavailability of the AMD 29000 cache chip, the two cache-based memory structures were discarded. A VRAM-based is expensive and it requires a complex circuit to accommodate error correction circuitry. Therefore the SPLIT MEMORY system was chosen for the prototype K2.

4.2 User channels

User channels are more complicated than simple FIFOs. To allow flushing of the queues on process switch, the outgoing channels can be *read* by the sending processor when in supervisor mode. Furthermore, a dedicated circuitry had to

Table 4: Performance comparison of the four memory structures.

MEMORY ACCESS	ACCESS CYCLES			
	I&D CACHE	I CACHE	VRAM	SPLIT MEMORY
Instr. b.i.	2	2	6	5
Instr. b.s.	1	1	1	2
Data b.i.	2	6	4	6
Data b.s.	1	1	1	2

TEST PROGRAM	PERFORMANCE (AM29000 MIPS)			
	I&D CACHE	I CACHE	VRAM	SPLIT MEMORY
B1	23.02	20.58	17.38	13.48
B2	23.92	21.48	19.94	13.48
B3	23.23	19.12	18.35	14.10
B4	20.15	14.12	14.73	12.08
B5	22.87	20.71	18.43	13.81

Instr. (data) b.i.: Burst initialization: number of cycles to access the first instruction (data) of a sequence.
Instr. (data) b.s.: Burst steady-state: number of cycles to access one instruction (data) during burst access.

be included to allow blocking without affecting kernel activities. Our fast blocking scheme consists of not issuing the data transfer acknowledge to the processor whenever the queue is empty (on read) or full (on write). In this case the processor does not terminate the access and introduces wait-cycles indefinitely until the queue changes its state (to not-empty or to not-full, respectively).

A similar mechanism was implemented on Warp, which however had no interrupt-driven kernel activities running on top of the application. The presence of a multi-user, multi-tasking operating system kernel on K2 called for a special hardware solution to allow the processor to sense and serve interrupts while blocked on the queues. If an interrupt comes when the processor is blocked, the processor can leave its state by means of a trap, serve the interrupt, and come back to the channel access it could not complete.

This can be easily implemented on the 29000, because when a trap occurs the processor saves the current bus cycle information (necessary to resume the channel access) into special registers. The access to the blocked channel will be automatically resumed according to this information when the interrupt return is executed at the end of the trap handler.

4.3 SNIK

Figure 7 shows the block-diagram of the Serial Network Interface Controller (SNIK). The SNIK utilizes a Motorola MC68030 microprocessor, with its own local boot ROM and program/data memory. The choice of a microprocessor, as opposed to a controller, can be justified by the added versatility of the former, which makes it easier to evaluate several different communication strategies.

The physical connection to the system network is implemented through two pairs of AMD "Transparent Asynchronous Transmitter/Receiver Interfaces" (TAXI), which perform the parallel (8-bit) to serial conversion on transmission and vice versa on reception. These chips communicate on balanced lines implemented either by coaxial cables or by optical fibers.

The 68030 is in charge of packet routing and "corner turning" (i.e., hopping from a horizontal ring to a vertical ring or vice versa), checksum calculation and test, and packet acknowledgement. FIFOs between the 68030 and the TAXI chips perform flow control. A large finite-state machine (FSM) between the FIFOs and the TAXI chips interprets the incoming packets and buffers them if they are destined for the local PE or if a corner-turn is required. The sender is also responsible for removing the packets from the ring. The FSM also implements the token-passing protocol and various error detection mechanisms.

Figure 8 quantifies the performance of a single K2 token-ring by showing the ratio between the effective ring throughput and the worst-case latency as a function of the number of processors on the ring and the size of the packet(s) sent. The worst-case latency is defined as the elapsed time from when the first byte of a packet is ready to be sent through the ring to when it is stored into the receiving SNIK, under

Figure 6: The SNIK board. Note on the right side of the board the four connector pairs for the token-rings.

the assumption that all nodes are transmitting, and that a SNIK is ready again to send a new packet just after it released the token.

The simulation was carried out assuming that (1) each node sends one and only one packet every time it receives the token, (2) all packet bodies have the same size, (3) each packet travels the longest possible distance on the ring before reaching the receiving node.

The figure shows that the throughput/latency ratio is maximized for a packet body of around 92 bytes; scenarios striving for high throughput (or low latency) may require a different size of packet body. Figure 9(a) shows the curves relative to the effective throughput (in Mbyte/s), while figure 9(b) shows those relative to the worst-case latency (in ms). A size of 512 bytes already insures an effective throughput close to that of the physical medium (12.5 Mbyte/s). On the other hand, the worst-case latency quickly becomes unacceptable, since already for 512 bytes it can be of 0.5ms or longer. These figures provide a higher bound on the expected performance of each token-ring. In practice, the software communication layers will be largely responsible for the overall performance, as experienced with TCP/IP and similar communication protocols.

5 Project status

The status of the project as of March 1990 is as follows:

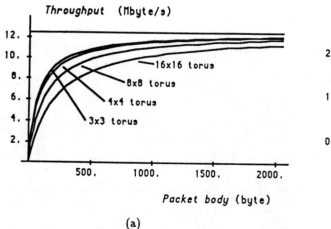

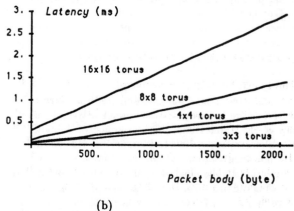

(a)   (b)

Figure 9: Communication performance of a single K2 token-ring. Effective throughput (a), and worst-case latency (b) vs. size of packet body for a 3×3, 4×4, 8×8, and 16×16 K2 torus. Each token-ring has 4, 5, 9, and 17 processors, respectively.

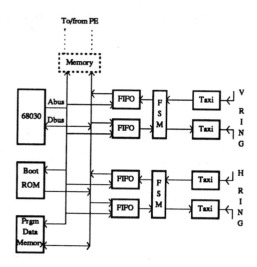

Figure 7: Block-diagram of SNIK.

- The PE and user channels of the CN and the PE of the ION have been designed, manufactured and tested. They run at full speed (50 MHz clock for the finite-state machines, 25 MHz for the AMD Am29000 microprocessor).

- The SNIK has been designed, manufactured and tested. It runs at full-speed (25 MHz for the processor, 12.5 MHz for the TAXI chips). Its communication software has been designed, written and tested.

- The disk controller has been designed, manufactured and partially tested. Its software has been designed and partially written.

- The design of the system backplane, chassis, power supply distribution and cooling systems is being completed.

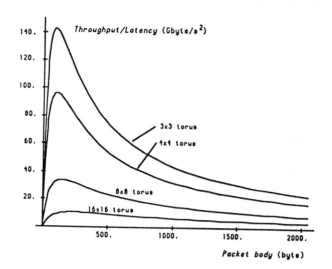

Figure 8: Communication performance of a single K2 token-ring. Effective throughput over worst-case latency vs. size of packet body for a 3×3, 4×4, 8×8, and 16×16 K2 torus. Each token-ring has 4, 5, 9, and 17 processors, respectively.

The following steps have to be carried out:

1. Integrating CN-PE, the user channels, and SNIK on one board, manufacturing and testing.

2. Integrating ION-PE, the SNIK, and the disk controller on one board, manufacturing and testing.

3. Manufacturing of 16 CNs (plus spares) and 8 IONs (plus spares).

4. Manufacturing of the system chassis, backplane, and final system integration.

We plan to have the hardware operational by the first quarter of 1991.

6 Concluding remarks

The decoupling between the communication networks in the user and system domain, their different communication mechanisms, the aggressive design of the user channels and of the I/O subsystem, and the elimination of the host-attached processor design style are not justified solely on performance grounds. They were found to be essential components in the efficient implementation of the distributed operating system and of the automatically parallelizing compiler, as part of a global solution.

Distributed-memory parallel processors will no longer be confined to restricted niches of users only when time-sharing, multi-user, multi-tasking operating systems and conventional programming methodologies will become available on them. The K2 project is the first attempt to merge the programming environment typical of minicomputers and mainframes and the computational power offered by parallel processing into a single framework.

Acknowledgements

We thank other members of the team, namely Georg zur Bonsen, Claude Pommerell, Roland Rühl, and Peter Steiner. The K2 project has been greatly helped by a group of dedicated undergraduate students: Felix Äbersold, Marc Brandis, Mirko Bulinsky, Pascal Dornier, Olivier Gemoets, Michael Halbherr, Alain Kaegi, Roland Lüthi, John Prior, Stefan Sieber, Markus Tresch, and Othmar Truniger.

Peter Beadle developed the first version of the K2 simulator. Peter Lamb gave us useful suggestions on several software-related aspects. We acknowledge the help from Norbert Felber. Special thanks go to Wolfgang Fichtner and Walter Seehars for their continuous support. The comments of the anonymous reviewers helped us to improve the quality of the paper.

References

[1] P. Close. The iPSC/2 node architecture. In *Concurrent Supercomputing*, pages 43–49. Intel Scientific Computers, 1988.

[2] Thinking Machines Corporation. Connection machine model cm-2 technical summary. Technical Report HA87-4, Thinking Machines Corporation, April 1987.

[3] J.P. Hayes, T. Mudge, and Q.F. Stout. A microprocessor-based hypercube supercomputer. *IEEE Micro*, pages 6–17, October 1986.

[4] M. Annaratone, E. Arnould, T. Gross, H.T. Kung, M. Lam, O. Menzilcioglu, and J.A. Webb. The Warp Computer: Architecture, Implementation, and Performance. *IEEE Trans. on Computers*, December 1987.

[5] S. Borkar et al. iWarp: an integrated solution to high-speed parallel computation. In *Proc. Supercomputing 88*, November 1988.

[6] The MEIKO Computing Surface, 1988. Meiko Inc., USA.

[7] D.L. Slotnick et al. The Solomon computer. In *Proc. AFIPS - Joint Computer Conference*, volume 22, pages 97–107, 1962.

[8] G.H. Barnes et al. The Illiac IV computer. *IEEE Trans. on Computers*, C-17(8):746–757, August 1968.

[9] G. Bell. The future of high performance computers in science and engineering. *Communications of the ACM*, 32(9):1091–1101, September 1989.

[10] M. Wolfe. Automatic detection of concurrency for shared memory multiprocessors. Technical report, Kuck and Associates Inc., October 1987. 1987 ESUG meeting.

[11] FX/SERIES Architecture Manual, January 1986. Alliant Computer Systems Co. - 300-00001-B.

[12] H. T. Kung. Memory requirements for balanced computer architectures. In *Proc. 13th Symposium on Computer Architecture*, pages 49–54. IEEE-ACM-IPSJ, June 1986.

[13] J. Buergler, P. Conti, G. Heiser, S. Paschedag, and W. Fichtner. Three dimensional simulation of complex semiconductor device structures. In *International Symposium on VLSI Technology, Systems and Applications*, pages 106–110. IEEE, 1989.

[14] M. Annaratone and R. Ruehl. Efficient cache organizations for distributed-memory parallel processors. Technical report, Integrated Systems Laboratory, Swiss Federal Institute of Technology, 1989.

[15] W. J. Dally. Wire-efficient VLSI multiprocessor communication networks. VLSI Memo 86-345, Massachusetts Institute of Technology, Cambridge, Massachusetts, October 1986.

[16] P. M. B. Vitányi. Locality, communication, and interconnect length in multicomputers. *SIAM J. Comput.*, 17(4):659–672, August 1988.

[17] S. L. Johnsson. Communication efficient basic linear algebra computations on hypercube architectures. *J. of Parallel and Distributed Processing*, 4(2):133–172, April 1987.

[18] V. Cherkassy and R. Smith. Efficient mapping and implementation of matrix algorithms on a hypercube. *The Journal of Supercomputing*, 2, 7-27, 2(1):7–27, September 1988.

[19] P. Sadayappan and F. Ercal. Nearest-neighbor mapping of finite element graphs onto processor meshes. *IEEE Transactions on Computers*, C-36(12):1408–1424, December 1987.

[20] J. L. Gustafson, G. R. Montry, and R. E. Benner. Development of parallel methods for a 1024-processor hypercube. *SIAM J. Sci. Stat. Comput.*, 9(4):609–638, July 1988.

[21] S. C. Eisenstat, M. T. Heath, C. S. Henkel, and C. H. Romine. Modified cyclic algorithms for solving triangular systems on distributed-memory multiprocessor. *SIAM J. Sci. Stat. Comput.*, 9(3):589–600, May 1988.

[22] D. M. Nicol and F. H. Willard. Problem size, parallel architecture, and optimal speedup. *Journal of Parallel and Distributed Computing*, 5:404–420, 1988.

[23] M. Annaratone, C. Pommerell, and R. Rühl. Interprocessor communication speed and performance in distributed-memory parallel processors. In *Proc. 16th Symposium on Computer Architecture*. IEEE-ACM, May 1989.

[24] M. Ruehl and M. Annaratone. Parallelization of FORTRAN code on distributed-memory parallel processors. In *Proc. ACM International Conference on Supercomputing*, Amsterdam, June 1990.

[25] B. Bruegge and T. Gross. A program debugger for a systolic array: design and implementation. In *Proc. SIGPLAN/SIGOPS Workshop on Parallel and Distributed Debugging*, pages 174–182, Madison, Wisconsin, May 1988. published as SIGPLAN Notices, vol. 24, n. 1, January, 1989.

[26] P. Beadle, C. Pommerell, and M. Annaratone. K9: A simulator of distributed-memory parallel processors. In *Proc. Supercomputing 89*, Reno, Nevada, November 1989. ACM.

Session 2B: Shared-Memory Multiprocessors

APRIL: A Processor Architecture for Multiprocessing

Anant Agarwal, Beng-Hong Lim, David Kranz, and John Kubiatowicz
Laboratory for Computer Science
Massachusetts Institute of Technology
Cambridge, MA 02139

Abstract

Processors in large-scale multiprocessors must be able to tolerate large communication latencies and synchronization delays. This paper describes the architecture of a rapid-context-switching processor called APRIL with support for fine-grain threads and synchronization. APRIL achieves high single-thread performance and supports virtual dynamic threads. A commercial RISC-based implementation of APRIL and a run-time software system that can switch contexts in about 10 cycles is described. Measurements taken for several parallel applications on an APRIL simulator show that the overhead for supporting parallel tasks based on *futures* is reduced by a factor of two over a corresponding implementation on the Encore Multimax. The scalability of a multiprocessor based on APRIL is explored using a performance model. We show that the SPARC-based implementation of APRIL can achieve close to 80% processor utilization with as few as three resident threads per processor in a large-scale cache-based machine with an average base network latency of 55 cycles.

1 Introduction

The requirements placed on a processor in a large-scale multiprocessing environment are different from those in a uniprocessing setting. A processor in a parallel machine must be able to tolerate high memory latencies and handle process synchronization efficiently [2]. This need increases as more processors are added to the system.

Parallel applications impose processing and communication bandwidth demands on the parallel machine. An efficient and cost-effective machine design achieves a balance between the processing power and the communication bandwidth provided. An imbalance is created when an underutilized processor cannot fully exploit the available network bandwidth. When the network has bandwidth to spare, low processor utilization can result from high network latency. An efficient processor design for multiprocessors provides a means for hiding latency. When sufficient parallelism exists, a processor that rapidly switches to an alternate thread of computation during a remote memory request can achieve high utilization.

Processor utilization also diminishes due to synchronization latency. Spin lock accesses have a low overhead of memory requests, but busy-waiting on a synchronization event wastes processor cycles. Synchronization mechanisms that avoid busy-waiting through process blocking incur a high overhead.

Full/empty bit synchronization [22] in a rapid context switching processor allows efficient fine-grain synchronization. This scheme associates synchronization information with objects at the granularity of a data word, allowing a low-overhead expression of maximum concurrency. Because the processor can rapidly switch to other threads, wasteful iterations in spin-wait loops are interleaved with useful work from other threads. This reduces the negative effects of synchronization on processor utilization.

This paper describes the architecture of APRIL, a processor designed for large-scale multiprocessing. APRIL builds on previous research on processors for parallel architectures such as HEP [22], MASA [8], P-RISC [19], [14], [15], and [18]. Most of these processors support *fine-grain interleaving* of instruction streams from multiple threads, but suffer from poor single-thread performance. In the HEP, for example, instructions from a single thread can only be executed once every 8 cycles. Single-thread performance is important for efficiently running sections of applications with low parallelism.

APRIL does not support cycle-by-cycle interleaving of threads. To optimize single-thread performance, APRIL executes instructions from a given thread until it performs a remote memory request or fails in a synchronization attempt. We show that such *coarse-grain multithreading* allows a simple processor design with context switch overheads of 4–10 cycles, without significantly hurting overall system performance (although the pipeline design is complicated by the need to handle pipeline dependencies). In APRIL, thread scheduling is done in software, and unlimited virtual dynamic threads are supported. APRIL supports full/empty bit synchronization, and provides tag support for *futures* [9]. In this paper the terms process, thread, context, and task are used equivalently.

0

CH2887-8/90/0000/0104$01.00 © 1990 IEEE

By taking a systems-level design approach that considers not only the processor, but also the compiler and run-time system, we were able to migrate several non-critical operations into the software system, greatly simplifying processor design. APRIL's simplicity allows an implementation based on minor modifications to an existing RISC processor design. We describe such an implementation based on Sun Microsystem's SPARC processor [23]. A compiler for APRIL, a run-time system, and an APRIL simulator are operational. We present simulation results for several parallel applications on APRIL's efficiency in handling fine-grain threads and assess the scalability of multiprocessors based on a coarse-grain multithreaded processor using an analytical model. Our SPARC-based processor supports four hardware contexts and can switch contexts in about 10 cycles, which yields roughly 80% processor utilization in a system with an average base network latency of 55 cycles.

The rest of this paper is organized as follows. Section 2 is an overview of our multiprocessor system architecture and the programming model. The architecture of APRIL is discussed in Section 3, and its instruction set is described in Section 4. A SPARC-based implementation of APRIL is detailed in Section 5. Section 6 discusses the implementation and performance of the APRIL run-time system. Performance measurements of APRIL based on simulations are presented in Section 7. We evaluate the scalability of multithreaded processors in Section 8.

2   The ALEWIFE System

APRIL is the processing element of ALEWIFE, a large-scale multiprocessor being designed at MIT. ALEWIFE is a cache-coherent machine with distributed, globally-shared memory. Cache coherence is maintained using a directory-based protocol [5] over a low-dimension direct network [20]. The directory is distributed with the processing nodes.

2.1   Hardware

As shown in Figure 1, each ALEWIFE node consists of a processing element, floating-point unit, cache, main memory, cache/directory controller and a network routing switch. Multiple nodes are connected via a direct, packet-switched network.

The controller synthesizes a global shared memory space via messages to other nodes, and satisfies requests from other nodes directed to its local memory. It maintains strong cache coherence [7] for memory accesses. On exception conditions, such as cache misses and failed synchronization attempts, the controller can choose to trap the processor or to make the processor wait. A multithreaded processor reduces the ill effects of the long-latency acknowledgment messages resulting from a strong cache coherence protocol. To allow experimentation with other programming models, the controller provides special mechanisms for bypassing the coherence protocol and facilities for preemptive interprocessor interrupts and block transfers.

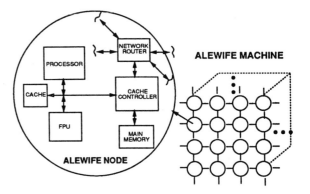

Figure 1: ALEWIFE node.

The ALEWIFE system uses a low-dimension direct network. Such networks scale easily and maintain high nearest-neighbor bandwidth. However, the longer expected latencies of low-dimension direct networks compared to indirect multistage networks increase the need for processors that can tolerate long latencies. Furthermore, the lower bandwidth of direct networks over indirect networks with the same channel width introduces interesting design tradeoffs.

In the ALEWIFE system, a context switch occurs whenever the network must be used to satisfy a request, or on a failed synchronization attempt. Since caches reduce the network request rate, we can employ coarse-grain multithreading (context switch every 50–100 cycles) instead of fine-grain multithreading (context switch every cycle). This simplifies processor design considerably because context switches can be more expensive (4 to 10 cycles), and functionality such as scheduling can be migrated into run-time software. Single-thread performance is optimized, and techniques used in RISC processors for enhancing pipeline performance can be applied [10]. Custom design of a processing element is not required in the ALEWIFE system; indeed, we are using a modified version of a commercial RISC processor for our first-round implementation.

2.2   Programming Model

Our experimental programming language for ALEWIFE is Mul-T [16], an extended version of Scheme. Mul-T's basic mechanism for generating concurrent tasks is the future construct. The expression (future X), where X is an arbitrary expression, creates a task to evaluate X and also creates an object known as a *future* to eventually hold the value of X. When created, the future is in an *unresolved*, or *undetermined*, state. When the value of X becomes known, the future *resolves* to that value, effectively mutating into the value of X. Concurrency arises because the expression (future X) returns the future as its value without waiting for the future to resolve. Thus, the computation containing (future X) can proceed concurrently with the evaluation of X. All tasks execute in a shared address-space.

The result of supplying a future as an operand of some

operation depends on the nature of the operation. *Non-strict* operations, such as passing a parameter to a procedure, returning a result from a procedure, assigning a value to a variable, and storing a value into a field of a data structure, can treat a future just like any other kind of value. *Strict* operations such as addition and comparison, if applied to an unresolved future, are suspended until the future resolves and then proceed, using the value to which the future resolved as though that had been the original operand.

The act of suspending if an object is an unresolved future and then proceeding when the future resolves is known as *touching* the object. The touches that automatically occur when strict operations are attempted are referred to as *implicit* touches. Mul-T also includes an *explicit* touching or "strict" primitive (touch X) that touches the value of the expression X and then returns that value.

Futures express control-level parallelism. In a large class of algorithms, data parallelism is more appropriate. Barriers are a useful means of synchronization for such applications on MIMD machines, but force unnecessary serialization. The same serialization occurs in SIMD machines. Implementing data-level parallelism in a MIMD machine that allows the expression of maximum concurrency requires cheap fine-grain synchronization associated with each data object. We provide this support in hardware with *full/empty bits*.

We are augmenting Mul-T with constructs for data-level parallelism and primitives for placement of data and tasks. As an example, the programmer can use future-on which works just like a normal future but allows the specification of the node on which to schedule the future. Extending Mul-T in this way allows us to experiment with techniques for enhancing locality and to research language-level issues for programming parallel machines.

3 Processor Architecture

APRIL is a pipelined RISC processor extended with special mechanisms for multiprocessing. This section gives an overview of the APRIL architecture and focuses on its features that support multithreading, fine-grain synchronization, cheap futures, and other models of computation.

The left half of Figure 2 depicts the user-visible processor state comprising four sets of general purpose registers, and four sets of Program Counter (PC) chains and Processor State Registers (PSR). The PC chain represents the instruction addresses corresponding to a thread, and the PSR holds various pieces of process-specific state. Each register set, together with a single PC-chain and PSR, is conceptually grouped into a single entity called a *task frame* (using terminology from [8]). Only one task frame is active at a given time and is designated by a current frame pointer (FP). All register accesses are made to the active register set and instructions are fetched using the active PC-chain. Additionally, a set of 8 global registers that are always accessible (regardless of the FP) is provided.

Registers are 32 bits wide. The PSR is also a 32-bit register and can be read into and written from the general reg-

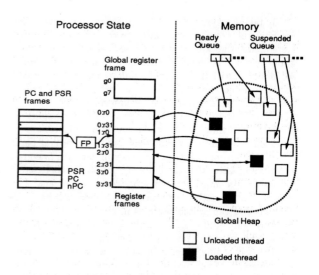

Figure 2: Processor State and Virtual Threads.

isters. Special instructions can read and write the FP register. The PC-chain includes the Program Counter (PC) and next Program Counter (nPC) which are not directly accessible. This assumes a single-cycle branch delay slot. Condition codes are set as a side effect of compute instructions. A longer branch delay might be necessary if the branch instruction itself does a compare so that condition codes need not be saved [13]; in this case the PC chain is correspondingly longer. Words in memory have a 32 bit data field, and have an additional synchronization bit called the *full/empty* bit.

Use of multiple register sets on the processor, as in the HEP, allows rapid context switching. A context switch is achieved by changing the frame pointer and emptying the pipeline. The cache controller forces a context switch on the processor, typically on remote network requests, and on certain unsuccessful full/empty bit synchronizations.

APRIL implements *futures* using the trap mechanism. For our proposed experimental implementation based on SPARC, which does not have four separate PC and PSR frames, context switches are also caused through traps. Therefore, a fast trap mechanism is essential. When a trap is signalled in APRIL, the trap mechanism lets the pipeline empty and passes control to the trap handler. The trap handler executes in the same task frame as the thread that trapped so that it can access all of the thread's registers.

3.1 Coarse-Grain Multithreading

In most processor designs to date (e.g. [8, 22, 19, 15]), multithreading has involved cycle-by-cycle interleaving of threads. Such fine-grain multithreading has been used to hide memory latency and also to achieve high pipeline utilization. Pipeline dependencies are avoided by maintaining instructions from different threads in the pipeline, at the price of poor single-thread performance.

In the ALEWIFE machine, we are primarily concerned

with the large latencies associated with cache misses that require a network access. Good single thread performance is also important. Therefore APRIL continues executing a single thread until a memory operation involving a remote request (or an unsuccessful synchronization attempt) is encountered. The controller forces the processor to switch to another thread, while it services the request. This approach is called *coarse-grain multithreading*. Processors in message passing multicomputers [21, 27, 6, 4] have traditionally taken this approach to allow overlapping of communication with computation.

Context switching in APRIL is achieved by changing the frame pointer. Since APRIL has four task frames, it can have up to four threads loaded. The thread that is being executed resides in the task frame pointed to by the FP. A context switch simply involves letting the processor pipeline empty while saving the PC-chain and then changing the FP to point to another task frame.

Threads in ALEWIFE are virtual. Only a small subset of all threads can be physically resident on the processors; these threads are called *loaded threads*. The remaining threads are referred to as *unloaded threads* and live on various queues in memory, waiting their turn to be loaded. In a sense, the set of task frames acts like a cache on the virtual threads. This organization is illustrated in Figure 2. The scheduler tries to choose threads from the set of loaded threads for execution to minimize the overhead of saving and restoring threads to and from memory. When control eventually passes back to the thread that suffered a remote request, the controller should have completed servicing the request, provided the other threads ran for enough cycles. By maximizing local cache and memory accesses, the need for context switching reduces to once every 50 or 100 cycles, which allows us to tolerate latencies in the range of 150 to 300 cycles with 4 task frames (see Section 8).

Rapid context switching is used to hide the latency encountered in several other trap events, such as synchronization faults (or attempts to load from "empty" locations). These events can either cause the processor to suspend execution (wait) or to take a trap. In the former case, the controller holds the processor until the request is satisfied. This typically happens on local memory cache misses, and on certain full/empty bit tests. If a trap is taken, the trap handling routine can respond by:

1. *spinning* – immediately return from the trap and retry the trapping instruction.

2. *switch spinning* – context switch without unloading the trapped thread.

3. *blocking* – unload the thread.

The above alternatives must be considered with care because incorrect choices can create or exacerbate starvation and thrashing problems. An extreme example of starvation is this: all loaded threads are spinning or switch spinning on

an exception condition that an unloaded thread is responsible for fulfilling. We are investigating several possible mechanisms to handle such problems, including a special controller initiated trap on certain failed synchronization tests, whose handler unloads the thread.

An important aspect of the ALEWIFE system is its combination of caches and multithreading. While this combination is advantageous, it also creates a unique class of thrashing and starvation problems. For example, forward progress can be halted if a context executing on one processor is writing to a location while a context on another processor is reading from it. These two contexts can easily play "cache tag", since writes to a location force a context switch and invalidation of other cached copies, while reads force a context switch and transform read-write copies into read-only copies. Another problem involves thrashing between an instruction and its data; a context will be blocked if it has a load instruction mapped to the same cache line as the target of the load. These and related problems have been addressed with appropriate hardware interlock mechanisms.

3.2   Support for Futures

Executing a Mul-T program with futures incurs two types of overhead not present in sequential programs. First, strict operations must check their operands for availability before using them. Second, there is a cost associated with creating new threads.

Detection of Futures   Operand checks for futures done in software imply wasted cycles on every strict operation. Our measurements with Mul-T running on an Encore Multimax show that this is expensive. Even with clever compiler optimizations, there is close to a factor of two loss in performance over a purely sequential implementation (see Table 3). Our solution employs a tagging scheme with hardware-generated traps if an operand to a strict operator is a future. We believe that this hardware support is necessary to make futures a viable construct for expressing parallelism. From an architectural perspective, this mechanism is similar to dynamic type checking in Lisp. However, this mechanism is necessary even in a statically typed language in the presence of dynamic futures.

APRIL uses a simple data type encoding scheme for automatically generating a trap when operands to strict operators are futures. This implementation (discussed in Section 5) obviates the need to explicitly inspect in software the operands to every compute instruction. This is important because we do not want to hurt the efficiency of all compute instructions because of the possibility an operand is a future.

Lazy Task Creation   Little can be done to reduce the cost of task creation if future is taken as a command to create a new task. In many programs the possibility of creating an excessive number of fine-grain tasks exists. Our solution to this problem is called *lazy task creation* [17]. With lazy task creation a future expression does not create a new task, but computes the expression as a local procedure call, leaving behind a marker indicating that a new task could have been created. The new task is created only when some processor becomes idle and looks for work, *stealing* the continuation of that procedure call. Thus, the user can specify the maximum possible parallelism without the overhead of creating a large number of tasks. The race conditions are resolved using the fine-grain locking provided by the full/empty bits.

3.3 Fine-grain synchronization

Besides support for lazy task creation, efficient fine-grain synchronization is essential for large-scale parallel computing. Both the dataflow and data-parallel models of computation rely heavily on the availability of cheap fine-grain synchronization. The unnecessary serialization imposed by barriers in MIMD implementations of data-parallellism can be avoided by allowing fine-grain word-level synchronization in data structures. The traditional test&set based synchronization requires extra memory operations and separate data storage for the lock and for the associated data. Busy-waiting or blocking in conventional processors waste additional processor cycles.

APRIL adopts the full/empty bit approach used in the HEP to reduce both the storage requirements and the number of memory accesses. A bit associated with each memory word indicates the state of the word: full or empty. The load of an empty location or the store into a full location can trap the processor causing a context switch, which helps hide synchronization delay. Traps also obviate the additional software tests of the lock in test&set operations. A similar mechanism is used to implement I-structures in dataflow machines [3], however APRIL is different in that it implements such synchronizations through software trap handlers.

3.4 Multimodel Support Mechanisms

APRIL is designed primarily for a shared-memory multiprocessor with strongly coherent caches. However, we are considering several additional mechanisms which will permit explicit management of caches and efficient use of network bandwidth. These mechanisms present different computational models to the programmer.

To allow software-enforced cache coherence, we have loads and stores that bypass the hardware coherence mechanism, and a *flush* operation that permits software writeback and invalidation of cache lines. A loaded context has a *fence counter* that is incremented for each dirty cache line that is flushed and decremented for each acknowledgement from memory. This fence counter may be examined to determine if all writebacks have completed. We are proposing a block-transfer mechanism for efficient transfer of large blocks of data. Finally, we are considering an interprocessor-interrupt mechanism (IPI) which permits preemptive messages to be sent to specific processors. IPIs offer reasonable alternatives to polling and, in conjunction with block-transfers, form a primitive for the message-passing computational model.

Type	Format	Data transfer	Control flow
Compute	op s1 s2 d	d ← s1 op s2	PC+1
Memory	ld *type* a d	d ← mem[a]	PC+1
	st *type* d s	mem[a] ← s	PC+1
Branch	j*cond* offset		if *cond* PC+offset else PC+1
	jmpl offset d	d ← PC	PC+offset

Table 1: Basic instruction set summary.

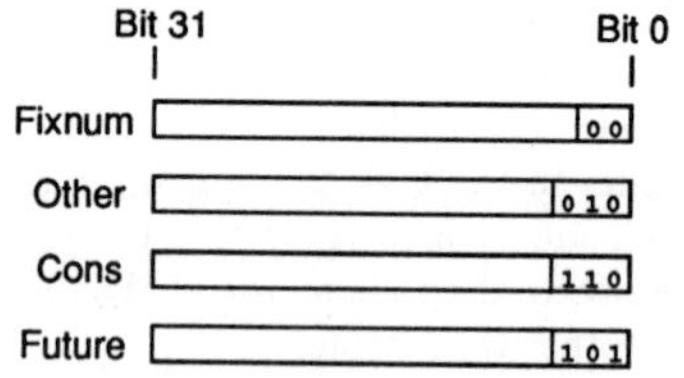

Figure 3: Data Type Encodings.

Although each of these mechanisms adds complexity to our cache controller, they are easily implemented in the processor through "out-of-band" instructions as discussed in Section 5.

4 Instruction Set

APRIL has a basic RISC instruction set augmented with special memory instructions for full/empty bit operations, multithreading, and cache support. The attraction of an implementation based on simple SPARC processor modifications has resulted in a basic SPARC-like design. All registers are addressed relative to a current frame pointer. Compute instructions are 3-address register-to-register arithmetic/logic operations. Conditional branch instructions take an immediate operand and may increment the PC by the value of the immediate operand depending on the condition codes set by the arithmetic/logic operations. Memory instructions move data between memory and the registers, and also interact with the cache and the full/empty bits. The basic instruction categories are summarized in Table 1. The remainder of this section describes features of APRIL instructions used for supporting multiprocessing.

Data Type Formats APRIL supports tagged pointers for Mul-T, as in the Berkeley SPUR processor [12], by encoding the pointer type in the low order bits of a data word. Associating the type with the pointer has the advantage of saving an additional memory reference when accessing type information. Figure 3 lists the different type encodings. An important purpose of this type encoding scheme is to support hardware detection of futures.

Name	Type	Reset f/e bit	EL[1] trap	CM[2] response
ldtt	1	No	Yes	Trap
ldett	2	Yes	Yes	Trap
ldnt	3	No	No	Trap
ldent	4	Yes	No	Trap
ldnw	5	No	No	Wait
ldenw	6	Yes	No	Wait
ldtw	7	No	Yes	Wait
ldetw	8	Yes	Yes	Wait

[1]Empty location. [2]Cache miss.

Table 2: Load Instructions.

Future Detection and Compute Instructions Since a compute instruction is a *strict* operation, special action has to be taken if either of its operands is a future. APRIL generates a trap if a future is encountered by a compute instruction. Future pointers are easily detected by their non-zero least significant bit.

Memory Instructions Memory instructions are complex because they interact with the full/empty bits and the cache controller. On a memory access, two data exceptions can occur: the accessed location may not be in the cache (a cache miss), and the accessed location may be empty on a load or full on a store (a full/empty exception). On a cache miss, the cache/directory controller can trap the processor or make the processor wait until the data is available. On full/empty exceptions, the controller can trap the processor, or allow the processor to continue execution. Load instructions also have the option of setting the full/empty bit of the accessed location to empty while store instructions have the option of setting the bit to full. These options give rise to 8 kinds of loads and 8 kinds of stores. The load instructions are listed in Table 2. Store instructions are similar except that they trap on full locations instead of empty locations.

A memory instruction also shares responsibility for detecting futures in either of its address operands. Like compute instructions, memory instructions also trap if the least significant bit of either of their address operands are non-zero. This introduces the restriction that objects in memory cannot be allocated at byte boundaries. This, however, is not a problem because object allocation at word boundaries is favored for other reasons [11]. This trap provides support for implicit future touches in operators that dereference pointers, *e.g.*, car in LISP.

Full/Empty Bit Conditional Branch Instructions Non-trapping memory instructions allow testing of the full/empty bit by setting a condition bit indicating the state of the memory word's full/empty bit. APRIL provides conditional branch instructions, Jfull and Jempty, that dispatch on this condition bit. This provides a mechanism to explicitly control the action taken following a memory instruction that would normally trap on a full/empty exception.

Frame Pointer Instructions Instructions are provided for manipulating the register frame pointer (FP). FP points to the register frame on which the currently executing thread resides. An INCFP instruction increments the FP to point to the next task frame while a DECFP instruction decrements it. The incrementing and decrementing is done modulo the number of task frames. RDFP reads the value of the FP into a register and STFP writes the contents of a register into the FP.

Instructions for Other Mechanisms The special mechanisms discussed in Section 3.4, such as FLUSH are made available through "out-of-band" instructions. Interprocessor-interrupts, block-transfers, and FENCE operations are initiated via memory-mapped I/O instructions (LDIO, STIO).

5 An Implementation of APRIL

An ALEWIFE node consists of several interacting subsystems: processor, floating-point unit, cache, memory, cache and directory controller, and network controller. For the first round implementation of the ALEWIFE system, we plan to use a modified SPARC processor and an unmodified SPARC floating-point unit.[1] There are several reasons for this choice. First, we have chosen to devote our limited resources to the design of a custom ALEWIFE cache and directory controller, rather than to processor design. Second, the register windows in the SPARC processor permit a simple implementation of coarse-grain multithreading. Third, most of the instructions envisioned for the original APRIL processor map directly to single or double instruction sequences on the SPARC. Software compatibility with a commercial processor allows easy access to a large body of software. Furthermore, use of a standard processor permits us to ride the technology curve; we can take advantage of new technology as it is developed.

Rapid Context Switching on SPARC SPARC processors contain an implementation-dependent number of overlapping register windows for speeding up procedure calls. The current register window is altered via SPARC instructions (SAVE and RESTORE) that modify the Current Window Pointer (CWP). Traps increment the CWP, while the trap return instruction (RETT) decrements it. SPARC's register windows are suited for rapid context switching and rapid trap handling because most of the state of a process (*i.e.*, its 24 local registers) can be switched with a single-cycle instruction. Although we are not using multiple register windows for procedure calls within a single thread, this should not significantly hurt performance [25, 24].

To implement coarse-grain multithreading, we use two register windows per task frame – a user window and a trap window. The SPARC processor chosen for our implementation has eight register windows, allowing a maximum of four

---

[1]The SPARC-based implementation effort is in collaboration with LSI Logic Corporation.

hardware task frames. Since the SPARC does not have multiple program counter (PC) chains and processor status registers (PSR), our trap code must explicitly save and restore the PSRs during context switches (the PC chain is saved by the trap itself). These values are saved in the trap window. Because the SPARC has a minimum trap overhead of five cycles (for squashing the pipeline and computing the trap vector), context switches will take at least this long. See Section 6.1 for further information.

The SPARC floating-point unit does not support register windows, but has a single, 32-word register file. To retain rapid context switching ability for applications that require efficient floating point performance, we have divided the floating point register file into four sets of eight registers. This is achieved by modifying floating-point instructions in a context dependent fashion as they are loaded into the FPU and by maintaining four different sets of condition bits. A modification of the SPARC processor will make the CWP available externally to allow insertion into the FPU instruction.

Support for Futures We detect futures on the SPARC via two separate mechanisms. Future pointers are tagged with their lowest bit set. Thus, direct use of a future pointer is flagged with a *word-alignment trap*. Furthermore, a strict operation, such as subtraction, applied to one or more future pointers is flagged with a modified *non-fixnum trap*, that is triggered if an operand has its lowest bit set (as opposed to either one of the lowest *two* bits, in the SPARC specification).

Implementation of Loads and Stores The SPARC definition includes the Alternate Space Indicator (ASI) feature that permits a simple implementation of APRIL's many load and store instructions (described in Section 4). The ASI is available externally as an eight-bit field. Normal memory accesses use four of the 256 ASI values to indicate user/supervisor and instruction/data access. Special SPARC load and store instructions (LDASI and STASI) permit use of the other 252 ASI values. Our first-round implementation uses different ASI values to distinguish between flavors of load and store instructions, special mechanisms, and I/O instructions.

Interaction with the Cache Controller The cache controller in the ALEWIFE system maintains strong cache coherence, performs full/empty bit synchronization, and implements special mechanisms. By examining the processor's ASI bits during memory accesses, it can select between different load/store and synchronization behavior, and can determine if special mechanisms should be employed. Through use of the Memory Exception (MEXC) line on SPARC, it can invoke synchronous traps corresponding to cache misses and synchronization (full/empty) mismatches. The controller can suspend processor execution using the MHOLD line. It passes condition information to the processor through the Coprocessor Condition bits (CCCs), permitting the full/empty conditional branch instructions (Jfull and Jempty) to be implemented as coprocessor branch instructions. Asynchronous

traps (IPI's) are delivered via the SPARC's asynchronous trap lines.

6 Compiler and Run-Time System

The compiler and run-time system are integral parts of the processor design effort. A Mul-T compiler for APRIL and a run-time system written partly in APRIL assembly code and partly in T have been implemented. Constructs for user-directed placement of data and processes have also been implemented. The run-time system includes the trap and system routines, Mul-T run-time support, a scheduler, and a system boot routine.

Since a large portion of the support for multithreading, synchronization and futures is provided in software through traps and run-time routines, trap handling must be fast. Below, we describe the implementation and performance of the routines used for trap handling and context switching.

6.1 Cache Miss and Full/Empty Traps

Cache miss traps occur on cache misses that require a network request and cause the processor to context switch. Full/empty synchronization exceptions can occur on certain memory instructions described in Section 4. The processor can respond to these exceptions by *spinning*, *switch spinning*, or *blocking* the thread. In our current implementation, traps handle these exceptions by switch spinning, which involves a context switch to the next task frame.

In our SPARC-based design of APRIL, we implement context switching through the trap mechanism using instructions that change the CWP. The following is a trap routine that context switches to the thread in the next task frame.

```
rdpsr psrreg ; save PSR into a reserved reg.
save          ; increment the window pointer
save          ; by 2
wrpsr psrreg ; restore PSR for the new context
jmpl  r17     ; return from trap and
rett  r18     ; reexecute trapping instruction
```

We count 5 cycles for the trap mechanism to allow the pipeline to empty and save relevant processor state before passing control to the trap handler. The above trap handler takes an additional 6 cycles for a total of 11 cycles to effect the context switch. In a custom APRIL implementation, the cycles lost due to PC saves in the hardware trap sequence, and those in calling the trap handler for the PSR saves/restores and double incrementing the frame pointer could be avoided, allowing a four-cycle context switch.

6.2 Future Touch Trap

When a future touch trap is signalled, the future that caused the trap will be in a register. The trap handler has to decode the trapping instruction to find that register. The future is resolved if the full/empty bit of the future's value slot is set to full. If it is resolved, the future in the register is replaced with the resolved value; otherwise the trap routine can decide to *switch spin* or *block* the thread that trapped. Our future touch trap handler takes 23 cycles to execute if the future is resolved.

If the trap handler decides to block the thread on an unresolved future, the thread must be unloaded from the hardware task frame, and an alternate thread may be loaded. Loading a thread involves writing the state of the thread, including its general registers, its PC chain, and its PSR, into a hardware task frame on the processor, and unloading a thread involves saving the state of a thread out to memory. Loading and unloading threads are expensive operations unless there is special hardware support for block movement of data between registers and memory. Since the scheduling mechanism favors processor-resident threads, loading and unloading of threads should be infrequent. However, this is an issue that is under investigation.

7 Performance Measurements

This section presents some results on APRIL's performance in handling fine-grain tasks. We have implemented a simulator for the ALEWIFE system written in C and T. Figure 4 illustrates the organization of the simulator. The Mul-T compiler produces APRIL code, which gets linked with the run-time system to yield an executable program. The instruction-level APRIL processor simulator interprets APRIL instructions. It is written in T and simulates 40,000 APRIL instructions per second when run on a SPARCServer 330. The processor simulator interacts with the cache and directory simulator (written in C) on memory instructions. The cache simulator in turn interacts with the network simulator (also written in C) when making remote memory operations. The simulator has proved to be a useful tool in evaluating system-wide architectural tradeoffs as it provides more accurate results than a trace driven simulation. The speed of the simulator has allowed us to execute lengthy parallel programs. As an example, in a run of **speech** (described below), the simulated program ran for 100 million simulated cycles before completing.

Evaluation of the ALEWIFE architecture through simulations is in progress. A sampling of our results on the performance of APRIL running parallel programs is presented here. Table 3 lists the execution times of four programs written in Mul-T: **fib**, **factor**, **queens** and **speech**. **fib** is the ubiquitous doubly recursive Fibonacci program with 'future's around each of its recursive calls, **factor** finds the largest prime factor of each number in a range of numbers and sums them up, **queens** finds all solutions to the n-queens chess problem for $n = 8$ and **speech** is a modified Viterbi graph search algorithm used in a connected speech recognition system called SUMMIT, developed by the Spoken Language Systems Group at MIT. We ran each program on the Encore Multimax, on APRIL using normal task creation, and on APRIL using lazy task creation. For purposes of comparison, execution time has been normalized to the time taken to execute a

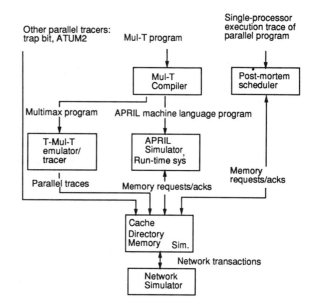

Figure 4: Simulator Organization.

sequential version of each program, *i.e.*, with no futures and compiled with an optimizing T-compiler.

The difference between running the same sequential code on T and on Mul-T on the Encore Multimax (columns "T seq" and "Mul-T seq") is due to the overhead of future detection. Since the Encore does not support hardware detection of futures, an overhead of a factor of 2 is introduced, even though no futures are actually created. There is no overhead on APRIL, which demonstrates the advantage of tag support for futures.

The difference between running sequential code on Mul-T and running parallel code on Mul-T with one processor ("Mul-T seq" and 1) is due to the overhead of thread creation and synchronization in a parallel program. This overhead is very large for the **fib** benchmark on both the Encore and APRIL using normal task creation because of very fine-grain thread creation. This overhead accounts for approximately a factor of 28 in execution time. For APRIL with normal futures, this overhead accounts for a factor of 14. Lazy task creation on APRIL creates threads only when the machine has the resources to execute them, and performs much better because it has the effect of dynamically partitioning the program into coarser-grain threads and creating fewer futures. The overhead introduced is only a factor of 1.5. In all of the programs, APRIL consistently demonstrates lower overhead due to support for thread creation and synchronization over the Encore.

Measurements for multiple processor executions on APRIL (2 – 16) used the processor simulator without the cache and network simulators, in effect simulating a shared-memory machine with no memory latency. The numbers demonstrate that APRIL and its run-time system allow par-

Program	System	T seq	Mul-T seq	1	2	4	8	16
fib	Encore	1.0	1.8	28.9	16.3	9.2	5.1	
	APRIL	1.0	1.0	14.2	7.1	3.6	1.8	0.97
	Apr-lazy	1.0	1.0	1.5	0.78	0.44	0.29	0.19
factor	Encore	1.0	1.4	1.9	0.96	0.50	0.26	
	APRIL	1.0	1.0	1.8	0.90	0.45	0.23	0.12
	Apr-lazy	1.0	1.0	1.0	0.52	0.26	0.14	0.09
queens	Encore	1.0	1.8	2.1	1.0	0.54	0.31	
	APRIL	1.0	1.0	1.4	0.67	0.33	0.18	0.10
	Apr-lazy	1.0	1.0	1.0	0.51	0.26	0.13	0.07
speech	Encore	1.0	2.0	2.3	1.2	0.62	0.36	
	APRIL	1.0	1.0	1.2	0.60	0.31	0.17	0.10
	Apr-lazy	1.0	1.0	1.0	0.52	0.27	0.15	0.09

Table 3: Execution time for Mul-T benchmarks. "T seq" is T running sequential code, "Mul-T seq" is Mul-T running sequential code, 1 to 16 denote number of processors running parallel code.

allel program performance to scale when synchronization and task creation overheads are taken into account, but when memory latency is ignored. The effect of communication in large-scale machines depends on several factors such as scheduling, which are active areas of investigation.

8 Scalability of Multithreaded Processor Systems

Multithreading enhances processor efficiency by allowing execution to proceed on alternate threads while the memory requests of other threads are being satisfied. However, any new mechanism is useful only if it enhances *overall system performance*. This section analyzes the system performance of multithreaded processors.

A multithreaded processor design must address the trade-off between reduced processor idle time and increased cache miss rates, network contention, and context management overhead. The private working sets of multiple contexts interfere in the cache. The added interference misses coupled with the higher average traffic generated by a higher utilized processor impose greater bandwidth demands on the interconnection network. Context management instructions required to switch the processor between threads also add to the overhead. Furthermore, the application must display sufficient parallelism to allow multiple thread assignment to each processor.

What is a good performance metric to evaluate multithreading? A good measure of system performance is system power, which is the product of the number of processors and the average processor utilization. Provided the computation of processor utilization takes into account the deleterious effects of cache, network, and context-switching overhead, the processor utilization is itself a good measure.

We have developed a model for multithreaded processor utilization that includes the cache, network, and switching

overhead effects. A detailed analysis is presented in [1]. This section will summarize the model and our chief results. Processor utilization U as a function of the number of threads resident on a processor p is derived as a function of the cache miss rate $m(p)$, the network latency $T(p)$, and the context switching overhead C:

$$U(p) = \begin{cases} \frac{p}{1+T(p)m(p)} & \text{for } p < \frac{1+T(p)m(p)}{1+Cm(p)} \\ \frac{1}{1+Cm(p)} & \text{for } p \geq \frac{1+T(p)m(p)}{1+Cm(p)} \end{cases} \quad (1)$$

When the number of threads is small, complete overlapping of network latency is not possible. Processor utilization with one thread is $1/(1 + m(1)T(1))$. Ideally, with p threads available to overlap network delays, the utilization would increase p-fold. In practice, because the miss rate and network latency increase to $m(p)$ and $T(p)$, the utilization becomes $p/(1 + m(p)T(p))$.

When it is possible to completely overlap network latency, processor utilization is limited only by the context switching overhead paid on every miss (assuming a context switch happens on a cache miss), and is given by $1/(1 + m(p)C)$.

The models for the cache and network terms have been validated through simulations. Both these terms are shown to be the sum of two components: one component independent of the number of threads p and the other linearly related to p (to first order). Multithreading is shown to be useful when p is small enough that the fixed components dominate.

Let us look at some results for the default set of system parameters given in Table 4. The analysis assumes 8000 processors arranged in a three dimensional array. In such a system, the average number of hops between a random pair of nodes is $nk/3 = 20$, where n denotes network dimension and k its radix. This yields an average round trip network latency of 55 cycles for an unloaded network, when memory latency and average packet size are taken into account. The fixed miss rate comprises first-time fetches of blocks into the cache, and the interference due to multiprocessor coherence invalidations.

Parameter	Value
Memory latency	10 cycles
Network dimension n	3
Network radix k	20
Fixed miss rate	2%
Average packet size	4
Cache block size	16 bytes
Thread working set size	250 blocks
Cache size	64 Kbytes

Table 4: Default system parameters.

Figure 5 displays processor utilization as a function of the number of threads resident on the processor when context switching overhead is 10 cycles. The degree to which

112

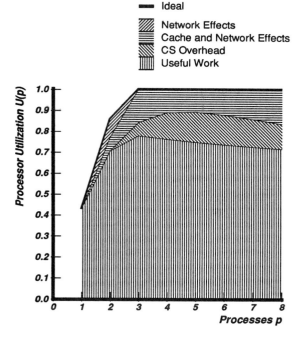

Figure 5: Relative sizes of the cache, network and overhead components that affect processor utilization.

the cache, network, and overhead components impact overall processor utilization is also shown. The ideal curve shows the increase in processor utilization when both the cache miss rate and network contention correspond to that of a single process, and do not increase with the degree of multithreading p.

We see that as few as three processes yield close to 80% utilization for a ten-cycle context-switch overhead which corresponds to our initial SPARC-based implementation of APRIL. This result is similar to that reported by Weber and Gupta [26] for coarse-grain multithreaded processors. The main reason a low degree of multithreading is sufficient is that context switches are forced only on cache misses, which are expected to happen infrequently. The marginal benefits of additional processes is seen to decrease due to network and cache interference.

Why is utilization limited to a maximum of about 0.80 despite an ample supply of threads? The reason is that *available network bandwidth limits the maximum rate at which computation can proceed.* When available network bandwidth is used up, adding more processes will not improve processor utilization. On the contrary, more processes will degrade performance due to increased cache interference. In such a situation, for better system performance, effort is best spent in increasing the network bandwidth, or in reducing the bandwidth requirement of each thread.

The relatively large ten-cycle context switch overhead does not significantly impact performance for the default set of parameters because utilization depends on the product of context switching frequency and switching overhead, and the switching frequency is expected to be small in a cache-based system. This observation is important because it allows a simpler processor implementation, and is exploited in the design of APRIL.

A multithreaded processor requires larger caches to sustain the working sets of multiple processes, although cache interference is mitigated if the processes share code and data. For the default parameter set, we found that caches greater than 64 Kbytes comfortably sustain the working sets of four processes. Smaller caches suffer more interference and reduce the benefits of multithreading.

9 Conclusions

We described the architecture of APRIL – a coarse-grain multithreaded processor to be used in a cache-coherent multiprocessor called ALEWIFE. By rapidly switching to an alternate task, APRIL can hide communication and synchronization delays and achieve high processor utilization. The processor makes effective use of available network bandwidth because it is rarely idle. APRIL provides support for fine-grain tasking and detection of futures. It achieves high single-thread performance by executing instructions from a given task until an exception condition like a synchronization fault or remote memory operation occurs. Coherent caches reduce the context switch rate to approximately once every 50–100 cycles. Therefore context switch overheads in the 4–10 cycle range are tolerable, significantly simplifying processor design. By providing hardware support only for performance-critical operations and migrating other functionality into the compiler and run-time system, we were able to simplify the processor design even further.

We described a SPARC-based implementation of APRIL that uses the register windows of SPARC as task frames for multiple threads. A processor simulator and an APRIL compiler and run-time system have been written. The SPARC-based implementation of APRIL switches contexts in 11 cycles. APRIL and its associated run-time system practically eliminate the overhead of fine-grain task creation and detection of futures. For Mul-T, the overhead reduces from 100% on an Encore Multimax-based implementation to under 5% on APRIL. We evaluated the scalability of multithreaded processors in large-scale parallel machines using an analytical model. For typical system parameters and a 10 cycle context-switch overhead, the processor can achieve close to 80% utilization with 3 processor resident threads.

10 Acknowledgements

We would like to acknowledge the contributions of the members the ALEWIFE research group. In particular, Dan Nussbaum was partly responsible for the processor simulator and run-time system and was the source of a gamut of ideas, David Chaiken wrote the cache simulator, Kirk Johnson supplied the benchmarks, and Gino Maa and Sue Lee wrote the network simulator. We appreciate help from Gene Hill, Mark Perry, and Jim Pena from LSI Logic Corporation for the SPARC-based implementation effort. Our design was influenced by Bert Halstead's work on multithreaded processors. Our research benefited significantly from discussions with Bert Halstead, Tom Knight, Greg Papadopoulos, Juan Loaiza, Bill Dally, Steve Ward, Rishiyur Nikhil, Arvind, and John Hennessy. Beng-Hong Lim is partly supported by an Analog Devices Fellowship. The research reported in this paper is funded by DARPA contract # N00014-87-K-0825 and by grants from the Sloan Foundation and IBM.

References

[1] Anant Agarwal. Performance Tradeoffs in Multithreaded Processors. September 1989. MIT VLSI Memo 89-566, Laboratory for Computer Science.

[2] Arvind and Robert A. Iannucci. *Two Fundamental Issues in Multiprocessing.* Technical Report TM 330, MIT, Laboratory for Computer Science, October 1987.

[3] Arvind, R. S. Nikhil, and K. K. Pingali. I-Structures: Data Structures for Parallel Computing. In *Proceedings of the Workshop on Graph Reduction, (Springer-Verlag Lecture Notes in Computer Science 279)*, September/October 1986.

[4] William C. Athas and Charles L. Seitz. Multicomputers: Message-Passing Concurrent Computers. *Computer*, 21(8):9–24, August 1988.

[5] David Chaiken, Craig Fields, Kiyoshi Kurihara, and Anant Agarwal. Directory-Based Cache-Coherence in Large-Scale Multiprocessors. June 1990. To appear in IEEE Computer.

[6] W. J. Dally et al. Architecture of a Message-Driven Processor. In *Proceedings of the 14th Annual Symposium on Computer Architecture*, pages 189–196, IEEE, New York, June 1987.

[7] Michel Dubois, Christoph Scheurich, and Faye A. Briggs. Synchronization, coherence, and event ordering in multiprocessors. *IEEE Computer*, 9–21, February 1988.

[8] R.H. Halstead and T. Fujita. MASA: A Multithreaded Processor Architecture for Parallel Symbolic Computing. In *Proceedings of the 15th Annual International Symposium on Computer Architecture*, pages 443–451, IEEE, New York, June 1988.

[9] Robert H. Halstead. Multilisp: A Language for Parallel Symbolic Computation. *ACM Transactions on Programming Languages and Systems*, 7(4):501–539, October 1985.

[10] J. L. Hennessy and T. R. Gross. Postpass Code Optimization of Pipeline Constraints. *ACM Transactions on Programming Languages and Systems*, 5(3):422–448, July 1983.

[11] J. L. Hennessy et al. Hardware/Software Tradeoffs for Increased Performance. In *Proc. SIGARCH/SIGPLAN Symp. Architectural Support for Programming Languages and Operating Systems*, pages 2–11, March 1982. ACM, Palo Alto, CA.

[12] M. D. Hill et al. Design Decisions in SPUR. *Computer*, 19(10):8–22, November 1986.

[13] Mark Horowitz et al. A 32-Bit Microprocessor with 2K-Byte On-Chip Instruction Cache. *IEEE Journal of Solid-State Circuits*, October 1987.

[14] R.A. Iannucci. Toward a Dataflow/von Neumann Hybrid Architecture. In *Proceedings of the 15th Annual International Symposium on Computer Architecture*, Hawaii, June 1988.

[15] W. J. Kaminsky and E. S. Davidson. Developing a Multiple-Instruction-Stream Single-Chip Processor. *Computer*, 66–78, December 1979.

[16] D. Kranz, R. Halstead, and E. Mohr. Mul-T: A High-Performance Parallel Lisp. In *Proceedings of SIGPLAN '89, Symposium on Programming Languages Design and Implementation*, June 1989.

[17] Eric Mohr, David A. Kranz, and Robert H. Halstead. Lazy task creation: a technique for increasing the granularity of parallel tasks. In *Proceedings of Symposium on Lisp and Functional Programming*, June 1990. To appear.

[18] Nigel P. Topham, Amos Omondi and Roland N. Ibbett. Context Flow: An Alternative to Conventional Pipelined Architectures. *The Journal of Supercomputing*, 2(1):29–53, 1988.

[19] Rishiyur S. Nikhil and Arvind. Can Dataflow Subsume von Neumann Computing? In *Proceedings 16th Annual International Symposium on Computer Architecture*, IEEE, New York, June 1989.

[20] Charles L. Seitz. Concurrent VLSI Architectures. *IEEE Transactions on Computers*, C-33(12), December 1984.

[21] Charles L. Seitz. The Cosmic Cube. *CACM*, 28(1):22–33, January 1985.

[22] B.J. Smith. A Pipelined, Shared Resource MIMD Computer. In *Proceedings of the 1978 International Conference on Parallel Processing*, pages 6–8, 1978.

[23] SPARC Architecture Manual. 1988. SUN Microsystems, Mountain View, California.

[24] P. A. Steenkiste and J. L. Hennessy. A Simple Interprocedural Register Allocation Algorithm and Its Effectiveness for LISP. *ACM Transactions on Programming Languages and Systems*, 11(1):1–32, January 1989.

[25] David W. Wall. Global Register Allocation at Link Time. In *SIGPLAN '86, Conference on Compiler Construction*, June 1986.

[26] Wolf-Dietrich Weber and Anoop Gupta. Exploring the Benefits of Multiple Hardware Contexts in a Multiprocessor Architecture: Preliminary Results. In *Proceedings 16th Annual International Symposium on Computer Architecture*, IEEE, New York, June 1989.

[27] Colin Whitby-Strevens. The Transputer. In *Proceedings 12th Annual International Symposium on Computer Architecture*, IEEE, New York, June 1985.

PLUS:
A Distributed Shared-Memory System

Roberto Bisiani and Mosur Ravishankar
School of Computer Science
Carnegie Mellon University
Pittsburgh, PA 15213

Abstract.

PLUS is a multiprocessor architecture tailored to the fast execution of a single multithreaded process; its goal is to accelerate the execution of CPU-bound applications. PLUS supports shared memory and efficient synchronization. Memory access latency is reduced by non-demand replication of pages with hardware-supported coherence between replicated pages. The architecture has been simulated in detail and the paper presents some of the key measurements that have been used to substantiate our architectural decisions. The current implementation of PLUS is also described.

1. Introduction.

Shared memory is one of the most popular parallel processing models because of the ready availability of bus-based shared-memory systems. Bus-based systems are relatively easy to build, but, because of their limited bus-bandwidth, do not perform well with fast processors, large number of processors, or algorithms that have a poor cache hit-ratio. In fact, most shared memory systems are limited to 10-20 processors or to slow processors and their main application is executing a non-parallel multi-user Unix load. On the other hand, the system we are building, called PLUS, is aimed at efficiently executing a single multithreaded process by using distributed memories, hardware supported memory coherence and synchronization mechanisms.

In order to maintain reasonable memory performance with a large number of fast processors it is necessary to distribute the memory among the processors and connect them with a scalable communication mechanism. The implementation of such a physically distributed, but logically shared, memory system is difficult, because communication latency hinders fast access to remote memories. The operations that cause performance degradation are *remote memory access* and *synchronization*.

This research is sponsored by the Defense Advanced Research Projects Agency, DoD, through ARPA Order 5167, and monitored by the Space and Naval Warfare Systems Command under contract N00039-85-C-0163. Views and conclusions contained in this document are those of the authors and should not be interpreted as representing official policies, either expressed or implied, of the Defense Advanced Research Projects Agency or of the United States Government. Part of the implementation is sponsored by AppleComputer, Inc.

Caching is the key to implementing fast remote memory access. Usually, caching is performed by hardware on demand, together with a protocol that guarantees memory coherence. In order to be effective in a medium/large system, this requires a substantial amount of fast and expensive hardware. PLUS relies on software-controlled, non-demand caching of data among multiple memories, and a simple protocol implemented in hardware to insure memory coherence. This mechanism is described in Section 2.

The latency of synchronization operations often cannot be reduced by caching, because these operations require exclusive access to synchronization variables. Systems that use caching with invalidation must ensure no other cache has a copy of the synchronization variable before performing the synchronization. PLUS makes it possible to hide the elapsed time between the start of a synchronization operation and its completion by providing separate mechanisms for each. This mechanism and its uses are described in Section 3.

This paper is mainly concerned with architectural issues, see [4] for a description of the software environment.

Although PLUS is aimed at the execution of a single, multithreaded program, some of the ideas proposed in this paper can be applied to a general-purpose, multiuser system.

2. Memory Access.

Memory access protocols can be described according to the kind of ordering they enforce and the caching mechanisms they use. We will touch on these questions in general before we describe PLUS's protocol.

2.1 Strong and Weak Ordering.

Most programmers take for granted that the result of a sequence of write operations performed by a processor will be immediately observable by any other processor exactly in the same order as it was performed. On a bus-based system, all write operations can be easily made visible to all the processors either by immediately announcing them on the bus (as in a write-through protocol) or by announcing them only when necessary (as with copy-back protocols). These systems are *sequentially consistent* [16] and *strongly ordered* [8], and let programmers use ordinary read/write memory operations to implement synchronization operations.

When there are multiple physical memory units and there is no global communication medium, enforcing strong ordering requires time consuming protocols. Fortunately, a weaker form of ordering, in which actions performed by one processor do not immediately have to become visible to all the other processors, is usually sufficient.

Typically, a parallel program alternates between a long sequence of normal read and write operations on shared data structures and synchronization operations (e.g. P and V). Enforcing strong ordering among normal read and write operations is not necessary, if the programmer understands that a synchronization operation should be used whenever two concurrent computations have to obey a specific order in accessing the shared data. A memory system with these characteristics is said to implement *weak ordering*. See [18, 8] for a formal definition.

When a system implements a weak-ordering model, programmers must *explicitly* flag synchronization operations for the system to implement them correctly. For example, a buffer shared between a producer and a consumer process is usually associated with a flag that is set when the buffer is full and cleared when it is empty. In a weakly ordered system, if the flag and buffer are allocated in separate memory modules and only normal read and write operations are used, it is possible for the consumer to observe the flag as full *before* the writes to the buffer have completed. For a weakly ordered system to work correctly, operations on the flag must be strongly ordered. We believe most programs will port to a weakly ordered system without any change. For example, we have examined the code of the Mach operating system kernel and found that a synchronization had been implemented as a normal access only in one case.

In general, a computation only needs to insure the ordering of *some* of its actions in relation to a *few* other selected computations. This is very hard to express and very hard to implement in the general case, but possible in some special cases. For example, if the data that are accessed in a critical region are all stored in a cache line, the QOSB, Test_and_Set and Unset operations proposed for the Wisconsin Multicube [12] guarantee correct behavior without strict ordering. This is due to the fact that these operations return the cache line upon successful locking, the semaphore is part of the line *and* a cache line is guaranteed to be coherent by the caching protocol.

Another form of weak ordering, called *release consistency,* has been proposed for the DASH multiprocessor [10]. Under this model only certain kinds of synchronization operations enforce a specific ordering, allowing for more flexibility than in the weak-ordering model.

PLUS provides three ways of improving the performance of synchronization operations. First, an explicit *fence* operation (see Section 2.3) is available to implement strong ordering of synchronization operations when necessary (as opposed to the more restrictive approach of always enforcing strong ordering at synchronization time). Second, PLUS splits an atomic read-modify-write operation into an *issue* primitive and a *verify* primitive that reads the result; the execution of the operation can proceed concurrently with other computation. Finally, in contrast to other RISC systems, the set of read-modify-write operations comprises rather complicated operations.

2.2 Caching Mechanisms.

In order to obtain good performance, a bus-based system has to maintain multiple copies of read/write data and minimize the number of write operations. In pursuing these goals, snooping protocols have evolved from simple write-through to the increasingly sophisticated write-once [11], write-invalidate [15] and write-update [17] protocols.

For example, the DRAGON [17] protocol achieves very good performance, because it keeps multiple copies of shared data even if the data are being written by more than one processor, thus avoiding the ping-ponging of shared data. As a consequence, it has far fewer write misses (fewer by a factor of six, compared to a simple *write-through-with-invalidate* protocol, for one of the applications evaluated in [1]). The DRAGON protocol broadcasts an update only if other caches indicate (with a bus signal) that the line is shared, as opposed to simpler protocols that either blindly broadcast every write or blindly invalidate all copies on the first write.

Protocols that use fewer write operations are beneficial in centralized-memory bus systems, because they use less memory and bus bandwidth. In a distributed-memory non-bus-based system both memory and communication bandwidth grow with the number of processors, so it is not always necessary for a protocol to minimize the frequency of writes.

Moreover, since latency in moving data is much larger in distributed-memory systems than in bus-based systems, using a protocol that does not invalidate other copies, but instead updates them, is very useful in minimizing the cost of cache misses.

PLUS uses a write-update protocol in which all writes to shared data are propagated to all the copies. The latency of write operations does not stall the processor, because multicast operations to update the copies are carried out independently by dedicated hardware.

2.3 PLUS's Coherence and Caching Mechanism.

PLUS caching mechanism is an extension of the mechanisms described in [2,3]. Each PLUS node (see Figure 2-1) contains one processor with its cache, some local memory and a memory-coherence manager that is linked to other nodes through a fast interconnection network. The local memory is used both as main memory and as a cache for data in other nodes' memories. Note that any data in the local memory may also be cached in the processor cache. In order to avoid confusion, we use the terminology *replicated data* to mean data stored in more than one node's local memory, and *cached data* to mean data stored in the processor cache.

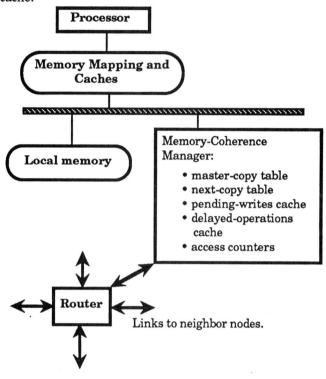

Figure 2-1: A PLUS Node.

PLUS uses a non-demand, write-update coherence protocol for the replicated data. The unit of replication is a page (whose size is dictated by the memory management system of the off-the-shelf CPU, 4 Kbytes in the current implementation). However, the unit of memory access and coherence maintenance is one (32-bit) word. Pages are replicated at the request of software, but the coherence manager hardware is aware of this replication and automatically keeps copies coherent. The rest of this Section describes the replicated memory structure and the implementation of coherent read and write operations.

A virtual page corresponds to a list of physical pages replicated on different nodes. The first item of this list is called the *master* copy. (An unreplicated page *only* has the master copy). A node maps each virtual page to the most convenient physical copy, i.e. the closest copy. The global address of a physical page is a *<node-id, page-id>* pair and is generated directly by the memory-mapping mechanism of the processor.

The operating system kernel orders the copy-list to minimize the network path length through all the nodes in the list. On each node, the replication structure is made visible to the coherence manager via the *master* and *nextcopy* tables, which are maintained by the operating system. For each locally replicated physical page, the master table identifies the global physical page address of the master copy, and the next-copy table identifies the successor, if any, of the local copy along the copy-list.

Read operations are implemented as follows. The *node-id* field of the translated physical address determines which node is addressed, and the page-id field specifies the page within that node. If the local node is indicated, the local memory is read. Otherwise, the coherence manager sends a read request to its counterpart in the specified remote node, waits for the response, and passes the returned data to the processor.

Write operations are more complicated, because they must take effect on every copy. Writes are always performed first on the master copy and then propagated down the ordered copy-list. This insures that all copies eventually contain the same data when all writes issued by all processors have completed. (This property is called *general coherence* [18]). The coherence manager handles writes as described below.

If the physical address indicates a remote node, the coherence manager sends a write request to that node (note that the remote node might not be the master). Otherwise, it checks the master table to determine the master-copy location. If the master copy is local, it carries out the write on the local memory, and sends an *update* request to the next copy, if any (determined by looking up the next-copy table). If the master copy is not local, it sends a write request to the node that has the master copy.

A coherence manager, that receives a write request, also goes through the process of making sure the write begins at the master copy. A coherence manager, that receives an update request, updates its memory and sends another update request to the next copy, if any. Finally, the last copy in the copy-list returns an acknowledge to the processor that originated the write operation, thus completing that operation. General coherence is guaranteed since copies of a given location are always written in the same order.

Write operations do not block the issuing processor while they propagate through the copies and a processor can issue several writes before blocking. However, reading a location that is currently being written blocks until the write completes. This is achieved by remembering the address of incomplete write operations in the pending-writes cache of the coherence manager and guarantees strong ordering within a single processor independently of replication (in the absence of concurrent writes by other processors). There is no such guarantee with respect to another processor. In particular, actions by one processor may be observed out of order by other processors.

When strong ordering is necessary between processors, e.g. for correct synchronization, a processor must use a *fence* operation, which causes the coherence manager to block any subsequent write by the processor, until all its earlier ones have completed (this is implemented by waiting until the pending-writes cache is empty). The processor can then proceed with the synchronization operation. A similar technique was proposed for the RP3 [6] multiprocessor. Three kinds of fence operations have been described in [10]: *write-fences* that block all subsequent writes, *full fences* that block all subsequent reads and writes, *immediate fences* that block only the next operation. PLUS implements explicit write fences that wait for all previous writes. A more aggressive implementation could use immediate fences. PLUS *does not* enforce full fences as part of synchronization operations, as in DASH. Instead, the user can explicitly issue the fence operation when appropriate (see Section 3-1).

Note that contents of a processor's local memory can be cached in the processor's primary cache. In order for writes to eventually propagate to all copies, all writes by a processor must be visible to its coherence manager. Hence, replicated pages must be cached with a write-through policy. At the remote site, a snooping protocol on the node bus ensures coherency between memory and cache whenever the coherence manager carries out a write or update operation.

2.4 Memory Mapping.

Since PLUS executes one multithreaded process at a time, all nodes use the same virtual memory space and, because of replication, different nodes might map the same virtual page to different physical copies.

Although the page tables could be fully shared, it is more efficient if each node maintains its own page tables. These tables do not have to contain all the possible mappings but only those that are actively used by the node. If a node accesses a page that is not mapped by the local page tables, the exception handler checks in a centralized table if the mapping is legal and then updates the local tables. This *lazy evaluation* of page tables limits the amount of interference caused by dynamic memory allocation and requires less memory than if the tables were fully replicated.

Software is responsible for page placement and replication policies, but the hardware helps in performing them. Deleting a copy is akin to removing a page in a paging operating system, since all the nodes that have a copy of the page must update their address translation tables and flush their TLBs. Replicating a page can be done almost entirely as a background activity: first the new entry is added to the copy-list at a convenient point, and then the hardware copies the data from the previous copy. (Note that the copy operation can be overlapped with writes to the same page by any processor in the system, without destroying the page integrity.) When the new page has been fully written, each node can update the address translation tables to use the new copy. Page migration is achieved simply by creating a copy and then deleting the old one.

Page replication and migration can be used in three ways, possibly at the same time:

- If the access pattern is known to the programmer it is possible to request a memory layout that minimizes network traffic and latency (for example by means of language-level pragmas).
- If the access pattern is not data dependent, it can be measured during one run of the application and the results of the measurement used to optimally allocate memory in subsequent runs.
- If the access pattern is unknown, it is possible to use competitive algorithms [5] that try to optimize memory references by replicating or migrating pages. The basic idea is to keep track of remote references, and, when the cumulative cost of remote references to a page exceeds the cost of creating a page copy, actually create a copy locally. In PLUS, competitive algorithms are supported by hardware that counts the number of references from each processor to each page and interrupts the node processor if any counter overflows.

Stack and code areas are usually not replicated, and can be kept in local physical memory.

2.5 Evaluation of Replication.

The performance of PLUS depends critically on the application and there is currently no set of parallel benchmarks that cover a wide spectrum of applications. In order to evaluate the design before starting the implementation, we have used a few applications that we knew very well and that stress the characteristics of the architecture. These include a production system applications, a shortest-path program, and a speech recognition system. We also carried out some experiments with synthetic loads as reported in [2]. We built a PLUS simulator that is driven by an application program in C language. A library package provides functions to create simulated shared memory and to allocate it on the nodes specified by the user. When the program reads or writes data allocated in shared memory, the simulator emulates the actions of the coherence manager and the network. Caching, coherence management, routing and memory access are simulated and instrumented in detail. From the instruction stream, the simulator also computes an approximate estimate of execution time between simulated shared memory references. Unfortunately, such a detailed simulation cannot be performed for systems larger than about 100 processors, because of the time and memory space needed.

The Single Point Shortest Path problem is a good example that requires many synchronization operations.

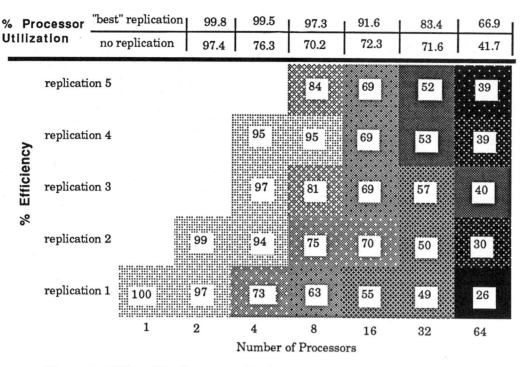

% Processor Utilization		99.8	99.5	97.3	91.6	83.4	66.9
	"best" replication	99.8	99.5	97.3	91.6	83.4	66.9
	no replication	97.4	76.3	70.2	72.3	71.6	41.7

Figure 2-1: Effect of Replication on Total % Efficiency (graph) and % Processor Utilization (top table) for the Single Point Shortest Path Application.

The problem involves finding the minimum cost to traverse a graph from one vertex to any other vertex. Both sequential and concurrent algorithms for this problem work by propagating the distance cost from one vertex and updating it until no more updates are possible.

Number of Copies	Reads Local/Remote	Writes Local/Remote	Ratio Total/ Update
1	1.25	3.40	6.18
2	1.70	1.18	2.91
3	1.84	0.70	2.24
4	2.14	0.45	1.89
5	2.32	0.36	1.68

Table 2-1 Effect of Replication on Messages.

The basic step in a concurrent implementation consists in choosing a vertex from a queue of vertices to be examined and computing the cost of moving to each of its neighbors. If the new cost is better than the cost stored at the vertex, the cost is updated and the vertex is queued for further expansion. When there are no more vertices to expand, the algorithm terminates. Each step requires three kinds of synchronization operations: extracting a vertex from the queue, locking a vertex in order to update its cost atomically, and inserting a vertex into the queue. Each step takes about 20 µs of processing time (not including synchronization), on a 20 MHz Motorola 88000 and requires an average of eight synchronization operations.

Our implementation uses multiple queues since, owing to queue bandwidth limitation, a single queue introduces serialization and requires long remote accesses. The vertices are evenly distributed among the nodes and there is one queue associated with each node. If a processor extracted work only from its queue, some processors would remain idle for part of the time, especially if the ratio of number of vertices to the number of processors is low. For a better load balance each processor must extract work from other queues when its local queue is empty. The shared memory model and the ability to replicate data are very helpful in this case. We have replicated the queues and vertices on more than one processor and found a substantial performance increase due to better load balancing. Figure 2-1 shows the efficiency of the algorithm and the *utilization*, i.e. ratio of average useful processor time to elapsed time for different levels of replication. With no replication, the utilization decreases substantially when more than 2 processors are used; while with replication it remains high until the number of processors exceeds 32. When more than 32 processors are used, most processors are idle waiting for work, since the problem is not large enough to occupy all processors.

Table 2-1 shows how the ratio of local to remote operations changes with replication in the 16-processor case of Figure 2-1. An increase in replication causes a drop in the number of remote reads and an increase in the number of remote writes and updates. Such a tradeoff is usually beneficial because of the overall decrease in remote read latency.

As replication increases, so does the total number of network messages (last column in Table 2-1) and a larger percentage of them is used to update copies. In this application there were no bad consequences, because the network was only lightly loaded. In general, however, uncontrolled replication can result in the system getting flooded with update requests, slowing down useful computation.

3. Synchronization.

Caching is only marginally useful in improving the latency of synchronization operations, since these operations always involve competitive and exclusive accesses to a variable.

For example, synchronization operations can severely degrade the performance of a system that uses a snooping coherence protocol. Constructs such as *test-and-test-and-set* were invented to minimize the overhead caused by the interference between the coherence protocol and the synchronization operations.

3.1 PLUS's Delayed Operations.

PLUS provides several variants of interlocked read-modify-write memory operations. Like writes, these operations take effect at all copies of the addressed location, beginning with the master and propagating down the copy-list. However, the master, in addition to executing the operation atomically and forwarding update requests to the next copy, also returns the old contents of memory to the originating node. Since this result always has to come from the master copy, there can be a substantial delay between the initiation of the

operation and the availability of its result.

PLUS allows the user or the compiler to hide this latency by separating the initiation of an operation from the checking of its result, as described in [2].

We call these operations *delayed operations*, since the execution of the operation overlaps regular processing, as is the case of delayed branches. The processor can continue with normal instruction execution in the meantime. PLUS also lets a processor have more than one delayed operation in progress at any time (8 in the current implementation), thereby further reducing their average latency.

In PLUS, synchronization instructions return an identifier that the program can later use to retrieve the result of the operation. This identifier is simply the address of a location in the delayed-operations cache. This location is automatically allocated when the processor executes a delayed operation and deallocated when it reads the result. If the result is not available when the processor reads it, the read blocks (since the software can inspect the status of these locations, it is also possible to implement a non-blocking read).

There is no implicit fence operation associated with these delayed operations. Instead, there is a separate, explicit fence operation available to the programmer. It is the responsibility of the programmer or the compiler to use these primitives to implement synchronization correctly. This scheme leaves substantial room for speed improvement through code scheduling and selective use of the fence operation. (For instance, there is usually no need to issue a fence before a P operation).

The delayed operations available in the current implementation of PLUS are described in Table 3-1. The cost of a delayed operation comprises three components: the time taken by the processor to issue the operation, the

Operation	Description	Execution cycles by the coherence manager
xchng	Return current value and write 30-bit unsigned word.	39
cond-xchng	Return current value of memory. If top bit set, write 30-bit unsigned word.	39
fetch-and-add	Return current value of memory. Increment memory by given signed word.	39
fetch-and-set	Return the current value and set top bit.	39
queue	(Addressed location contains offset in addressed page to tail of queue.) Return current word at tail. If top bit of tail clear, write given word there, set top bit, and increment the offset (modulo maximum queue size) to next word in queue.	52
dequeue	(Addressed location contains offset in addressed page to head of queue.) Return current word at head. If top bit of head set, clear it and increment the offset (modulo maximum queue size) to next word in queue.	52
min-xchng	Return current value, store given value if smaller than the original value.	52
delayed-read	Return current value, no modification	39

Table 3-1: PLUS's Delayed Operations.

time taken by the coherence manager to execute the operation and obtain the result (the processor is not involved in this), and the time taken by the processor to read the result. The first step takes approximately 25 cycles (each cycle in the current PLUS implementation takes 40ns). The time to perform the second step can be divided into communication time and processing time. The round trip communication time between two adjacent nodes is about 24 cycles; if the nodes are not adjacent each extra hop adds 4 cycles (these numbers were measured on the router used in the current implementation). The processing time depends on the operation; an estimate based on the detailed hardware design is shown in Table 3-1. The last step, the processor reading the result, takes about 10 cycles, assuming the result is available. As a comparison, the cost of a remote (blocking) read is about 32 cycles plus the round-trip network delay.

Appendix) we see that, although a single kind of primitive is used (fetch-and-add), it must be used three times to correctly perform a queuing operation. As we saw before, there is a substantial delay until the result of each synchronization operation is available. If we execute a number of synchronization primitives in short succession, the issuing processor will be idle most of the time, and hiding this latency will be hard.

Performance can be improved if more powerful primitives such as the queue and dequeue operations in Table 3-1 are used. These primitives reduce the total number of read-modify-write operations compared to queues implemented with simpler primitives. We believe that a reasonable set of complicated synchronization operations is a better choice for distributed-memory systems. We evaluated different sets of synchronization operations by writing various algorithms and measuring their performance on our simulator. The

```
/* lock variable "lock" initialized to 0, i.e. busy,
   variables QP and DQP contain offsets within page to tail and head of queue,
   QP and DQP initialized to 0 and all queue words initially empty (top bit clear) */


LOCK: if(fadd(lock, 1) != 0) {    /* lock unavailable, queue myself for obtaining lock */
          while (queue(QP, myID) & 0x80000000);  /* spin if queue is full, unlikely */
          wait();                 /* go to sleep until someone wakes me up and gives me the lock */
      }                           /* my thread has lock */
    — — — — — — — — — — — — — — — — — — — — — — — —

UNLOCK:  if (fadd(lock, -1) > 1)  {/* some other thread waiting for lock, pop its ID from queue */
             while (! ((k = dequeue(DQP)) & 0x80000000)); /* loop if queue is empty */
             wake_up(k &= 0x7fffffff);  /* k == ID of next process in queue, wake it up; */
         }                            /* thread k now has lock */
```

Table 3-2: Lock with Queue.

3.2 Complex is Better.

It is often argued that simpler operations are better: the implementation is simpler and faster and the user has an easier time mastering them. In principle, many existing primitives like test-and-set and fetch-and-add are, alone, sufficient to implement all synchronization operations. (See [12] for a summary of state-of-the-art synchronization primitives). However, we should keep in mind that speed is the main concern in synchronization and not ease of use. Hardware synchronization primitives should not be used directly by users and should be either encapsulated in higher level constructs or directly generated and optimized by a compiler.

If we look at the implementation of queue operations with a fetch-and-add (see the paper by Gottlieb et.al.[13],

synchronization operations available in PLUS are part of the delayed operations, which are listed in Table 3-1. These operations allow the implementation of many common synchronization data structures, such as semaphores, queues, lists barriers and high-contention locks. For example, Table 3-2 shows the code for implementing a lock in such a way that contenders, failing to acquire the lock, can queue themselves up for obtaining it, without flooding the system with unsuccessful attempts. In terms of operations over the network, this mechanism has the same complexity as Goodman's QOSB mechanism, but is not bound to a particular cache implementation.

Delayed operations are also used for purposes other than synchronization:

• The *min-xchng* operation is useful in load balancing algorithms that need a global approximation of the minimum or maximum value of some variable.

• The *delayed-read* operation is like an ordinary read, except that it proceeds asynchronously and the result can be retrieved later. Since several such operations can be in progress simultaneously, this is useful for hiding the latency of remote read operations. However, it needs careful, handcrafted code or a clever optimizing compiler. We do not currently have such a compiler.

3.3 Software Pipelining and Context Switching.
Delayed synchronization allows two latency-avoidance

able to make good use of delayed synchronization in many cases.

Context switching is an extremely attractive way of hiding latency and a few systems based on fast context switching have been built [14] or proposed [19]. The usefulness of context switching depends mostly on the ratio between the context switch time and the time between context switches. If a context switch were to cost only a few processor cycles, it would solve all latency problems, and could be used whenever remote memory is accessed. Unfortunately, this is not possible with off-the-shelf processors.

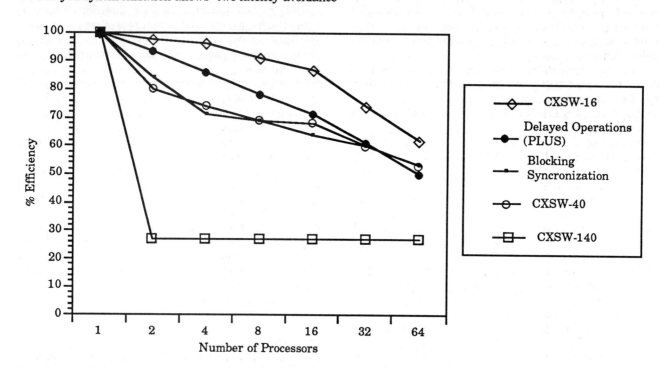

Figure 3-1: Efficiency of the Beam Search Application
with Different Synchronization Costs.

techniques: software pipelining and context switching.

Software pipelining is typically implemented by the compiler but, in some cases, it can be exploited directly by the programmer. For example, we programmed a primitive that returns a pointer to a free element in a queue with very little latency, because it eagerly asks for a new element every time the user consumes the previous element (the first time it is called, it retrieves two elements). In another case we have been able to issue a number of lock requests in advance, so that part of the latency was absorbed by the computation.

Although we do not have a compiler that takes advantage of delayed synchronization, we have been

3.4 Evaluation of Delayed Operations.
We show the performance of a beam search algorithm that searches a Hidden Markov Model representation of the speech process (a directed graph) and returns the most likely sequence of words. Beam search requires a very fine-grain parallel decomposition and a substantial amount of synchronization. Typically, a processor must dequeue one vertex from the list of vertices to be processed, lock all the vertices that follow it and finally queue a new vertex. This inner loop can be coded in about 70 RISC instructions and requires about 10 memory references per iteration, which cause about 3 cache misses if the cache line contains four words. (The

algorithm has spatial locality but almost no temporal locality.)

Queue operations on a central queue cause too much serialization, owing to bandwidth limitation at the queue. As with the shortest-path problem, the queue is split into local queues, one at each processor, to avoid this bottleneck. In this case, because of the highly data-dependent behavior of beam search, it is likely that some queues will become empty before others and some processors will remain idle and create a load imbalance. This load imbalance can be overcome by sharing a queue among a number of processors instead of keeping them all disjoint.

Figure 3-1 compares the performance with different context switching overheads and with delayed operations. The *blocking synchronization* curve has been computed by running a program that waits for synchronization primitives to return a result before proceeding. The *delayed operations* curve has been computed by explicitly programming the pipelining of synchronization operations:

•the next vertex is dequeued in parallel with the processing of the current state;

•the locking of all next vertices is performed in parallel.

The programming burden of these changes was easily hidden in two macros, so the code is not very different from the blocking-synchronization case. The context-switch curves were computed by simulating a context switch every time a synchronization operation was issued. The cost of the context switch was set to 16, 40 and 140 processor cycles (the curves in Figure 3-1 are labeled with this cost).

As expected, very fast context switching has the best performance but delayed operations are more effective than a context switching mechanism with a 40-cycle overhead. To put things in perspective, a state-of-the-art RISC processor might need to save and restore about 15 registers. If this operation can be performed entirely in cache, a context switch would cost about 40 cycles (including the instructions necessary to decide which is the new context). If the processor misses in cache, it would cost about 140 cycles because of the bus and memory latency (we are assuming a four-word line fetch takes 15 cycles). Future commercial processors might include wide busses between registers and local memory. In this case the save/restore operation could be completed in fewer cycles and the performance of the top curve of Figure 3-1 might become possible.

The results in Figure 3-1 are more pessimistic than those reported by Weber and Gupta in [19]. This is probably due to two factors. First, our application has a very short inner loop. Second, our assumptions about network delay and interface overhead (sending and receiving a message) are more conservative than theirs.

4. Related Work.

PLUS represents a specific trade-off in the space of distributed-memory architectures that range from large-granularity LAN-based machines, to message-passing machines, to hierarchical-bus machines to full-fledged directory-based shared-memory machines.

Operating system researchers have devised techniques to implement shared memory across distributed systems, for example by means of shared memory servers [9]. The problem with these solutions is that, regardless of network and processor speed, they result in large software overhead because the basic mechanism is paging. Faster networks will improve the performance of these systems to the point where the physical transfer of a page will take a negligible amount of time but the software overhead (a few milliseconds on one-Vax-MIP machines) will remain. Of course the usability of such systems depends heavily on the application.

Intelligent message coprocessors that relieve the main processor of the task of sending a message are now common in message passing machines. Nevertheless, the overhead to send and receive a message is still larger than 10 µseconds for state-of-the-art systems. Most of this overhead is again due to software. PLUS also uses hardware to interface processor and network, but the hardware does not require any software interface, e.g. a send function, because it is triggered directly by a memory reference.

Multiple-bus systems like the Wisconsin Multicube and Encore's extension of the Multimax, which employ an extended form of snoopy caching, and directory-based systems like DASH and the proposed SCI standard are all true shared-memory systems, and all employ sophisticated caches and cache-coherence protocols. PLUS relies on software-controlled non-demand replication of pages to achieve the same goals without the high hardware cost. We believe that in many single-user applications PLUS will perform as well as any of these machines.

5.Current Implementation.

The current implementation of PLUS uses a general purpose Motorola 88000 processor (25 MHz) with 32 Kbytes of cache and 8 or 32 Mbytes of main memory at each node. The memory is organized in two interleaved banks to sustain the burst bandwidth needed for cache line accesses. Global memory mapping, coherence management and atomic operations are performed by a hardware module that is implemented with Xilinx PLD's and PAL's. (It is possible to implement this module in a single ASIC device.) In this implementation, each node can have up to 8 writes and 8 delayed operations in progress. The interconnection network uses a mesh router designed at Caltech [7]. Each router has five pairs of I/O links: one for the processor and one for each of its mesh neighbors. Links operate at 20 Mbyte/second in each direction. SCSI devices, audio peripherals and host computers can be attached to each node. The implementation of PLUS is at an advanced stage. A one-node prototype has been running since November 1989, and we expect to have a working multinode system in the Summer of 1990.

Acknowledgments.

Some ideas were originated by discussions with Lawrence Butcher and Andreas Nowatzyk. Raj Reddy and Duane Adams have been, as always, instrumental to the survival of this project. We are also extremely grateful to George White of Apple Computer, Inc. for his support. The first prototype was built with the help of John Figueroa of On Target Associates.

References

1. Agarwal, A., Simoni, R., Hennessy, J., and Horowitz, M. An Evaluation of Directory Schemes for Cache Coherence. In *15th Int. Symp. on Comp. Arch.*, IEEE, May 1988, pp. 280-289.

2. Bisiani, R., Nowatzyk, A., and Ravishankar, M. Coherent Shared Memory on a Message Passing Machine. Tech. Rept. CMU-CS-88-204. School of Computer Science, Carnegie Mellon University, December, 1988.

3. Bisiani, R. and Forin, A. Multilanguage Parallel Programming of Heterogeneous Machines. *IEEE Trans. on Comp.* 37, 8 (August 1988), 930-945 .

4. Bisiani, R. and Ravishankar, M. Shared-Memory Programming on the PLUS Distributed-Memory System. In *The Fifth Distributed Memory Computing Conference*, IEEE, Charleston, SC, April 1990.

5. Black, D.L., Gupta, A., and Weber, W. Competitive Management of Distributed Shared Memory. In *Compcon '89*, IEEE, Spring 1989.

6. Brantley, W.C., McAuliffe, K.P., and Weiss, J. RP3 Processor-Memory Element. In *1985 International Conference on Parallel Processing*, IEEE Computer Society, 1985, pp. 782-789.

7. Dally, W.J. and Seitz, C.L. Deadlock-Free Message Routing in Multiprocessor Interconnection Networks. *IEEE Trans. on Computers C-36*, 5 (May 1987), 547-553.

8. Dubois, M., Scheurich, C., and Briggs, F. Memory Access Buffering in Multiprocessors. In *13th Int. Symp. on Comp. Arch.*, IEEE, June 1986, pp. 434,442.

9. Forin, A., Barrera, J., and Sanzi, R. The Shared Memory Server. In *Intl. Winter USENIX Conference*, USENIX Association, San Diego, CA, February 1989, pp. 229-244.

10. Gharachorloo, K., Lenoski, D., Laudon, J., Gupta, A., and Hennessy, J. Memory Consistency and Event Ordering in Scalable Shared-Memory Multiprocessors. Tech. Rept. CSL-TR-89-405. Computer Systems Laboratory, Stanford University, November, 1989.

11. Goodman, J.R. Using Cache Memory to Reduce Processor Memory Traffic. In *10th Int. Symp. on Comp. Arch.*, IEEE, June 1983, pp. 124-131.

12. Goodman, J.R., Vernon, M.K., and Woest, P.J. Efficient Synchronization Primitives for Large-scale Coherent Multiprocessors. In *3rd ASPLOS*, IEEE, Boston, April 1989, pp. 64-73.

13. Gottlieb, A. The NYU Ultracomputer - Designing an MIMD Shared Memory Parallel Computer. *IEEE Trans. on Computers C-32*, 2 (February 1983), 175-189.

14. Jordan, H.F. Performance Measurements on HEP - a Pipelined MIMD Computer. In *10th Int. Symp. on Comp. Arch.*, IEEE Computer Society, June 1983, pp. 207-212.

15. Katz, R.H., Eggers, S.J., Wood, D.A., Perkins, C.L., and Sheldon, R.G. Implementing a Cache Consistency Protocol. In *12th Int. Symp. on Comp. Arch.*, IEEE, Boston, June 1985, pp. 276-283.

16. Lamport, L. Solved Problems, Unsolved Problems and Non-Problems in Concurrency. *Operating Systems Review 19*, 4 (October 1985), 34-44.

17. McCreight, E. The Dragon Computer System: An Early Overview. Tech. Rept. Xerox Corp., September, 1984.

18. Scheurich, C.E. *Access Ordering and Coherence in Shared-memory Multiprocessors*, Ph.D. dissertation, Also published as Tech, Rep. No. CENG 89-19, Computer Engineering - University of Southern Califirnia, May 1989.

19. Weber, W. and Gupta, A. Exploring the Benefits of Multiple Hardware Contexts in a Multiprocessor Architecture: Preliminary Results. In *16th Int. Symp. on Comp. Arch.*, IEEE, June 1989, pp. 273-280.

Adaptive Software Cache Management for Distributed Shared Memory Architectures

*John K. Bennett**
*John B. Carter***
*Willy Zwaenepoel***

*Department of Electrical and Computer Engineering
**Department of Computer Science
Rice University
Houston, TX 77251-1892

Abstract

An *adaptive* cache coherence mechanism exploits semantic information about the expected or observed access behavior of particular data objects. We contend that, in distributed shared memory systems, adaptive cache coherence mechanisms will outperform static cache coherence mechanisms. We have examined the sharing and synchronization behavior of a variety of shared memory parallel programs. We have found that the access patterns of a large percentage of shared data objects fall in a small number of categories for which efficient software coherence mechanisms exist. In addition, we have performed a simulation study that provides two examples of how an adaptive caching mechanism can take advantage of semantic information.

1 Introduction

We are developing Munin [4], a system that will allow programs written for shared memory multiprocessors to be executed efficiently on distributed memory machines. What distinguishes Munin from previous distributed shared memory systems [6, 12, 14] is the means by which memory coherence is achieved. Instead of a single memory coherence mechanism for all shared data objects, Munin will employ several different mechanisms, each appropriate for a different category of shared data object. We refer to this technique of providing multiple coherence mechanisms as *adaptive caching*. Adaptive caching maintains coherence

This work was supported in part by the National Science Foundation under Grants CDA-8619893 and CCR-8716914.

based on the expected or observed access behavior of each shared object and on the size of cached items. We contend that adaptive caching provides an efficient abstraction of shared memory on distributed memory hardware. Since coherence in distributed shared memory systems is provided in software, we expect the overhead of providing multiple coherence mechanisms to be offset by the increase in performance that such mechanisms will provide.

For adaptive caching to perform well, it must be possible to characterize a large percentage of all accesses to shared data objects by a small number of categories of access patterns for which efficient coherence mechanisms can be developed. In a previous paper [4], we have identified a number of categories, and described the design of efficient coherence mechanism for each. In this paper, we show that these categories capture the vast majority of the accesses to shared data objects in a number of shared memory parallel programs. We also show, through simulation, the potential for performance improvement of adaptive caching compared to static coherence mechanisms.

In Section 2 of this paper, we briefly reiterate the main results of our previous paper [4]. We describe the categories of access patterns, provide examples, and give a brief description of how each category can be handled efficiently. Section 3 describes the programs that we study in this paper, our technique for logging the accesses to shared memory by these programs, the method by which we analyze these logs to discover common access patterns, and the results of our logging study. Section 4 describes a simulation study that provides two examples of how an adaptive caching mechanism can take advantage of semantic information. We discuss previous work in this area in Section 5. Finally, we draw conclusions in Section 6.

CH2887-8/90/0000/0125$01.00 © 1990 IEEE

2 Categories of Sharing

2.1 Intuitive Definitions

We have identified the following categories of shared data objects: *Write-once*, *Write-many*, *Producer-Consumer*, *Private*, *Migratory*, *Result*, *Read-mostly*, and *Synchronization*. We classify all shared data objects that do not fall into one of these categories as *General Read-Write*.

Write-once objects are read-only after initialization. *Write-many* objects frequently are modified by several threads between synchronization points. For example, in Quicksort, multiple threads concurrently modify independent portions of the array being sorted. *Producer-Consumer* objects are written (produced) by one thread and read (consumed) by a fixed set of other threads. *Private* objects, though declared to be shared data objects, are only accessed by a single thread. Many parallel scientific programs exhibit "nearest neighbors" or "wavefront" communication whereby the only communication is the exchange of boundary elements between threads working on adjacent sub-arrays. The boundary elements are *Producer-Consumer* and the interior elements are *Private*. *Migratory* objects are accessed in phases, where each phase corresponds to a series of accesses by a single thread. Shared objects protected by locks often exhibit this property. *Result* objects collect results. Once written, they are only read by a single thread that uses the results. *Read-mostly* objects are read significantly more often than they are written. *Synchronization* objects, such as locks and monitors, are used by programmers to force explicit inter-thread synchronization points. Synchronization events include attempting to acquire a lock, acquiring a lock, and releasing a lock. The remaining objects, which we cannot characterize by any of the preceding classes, are called *General Read-Write*. The categories define a hierarchy of types of shared data objects. When we identify an object's sharing category, we use the most specific category possible under the following order (from most specific to least specific): *Synchronization*, *Private*, *Write-once*, *Result*, *Producer-Consumer*, *Migratory*, *Write-many*, *Read-mostly*, and *General Read-Write*.

2.2 Coherence Mechanisms

We have developed memory coherence techniques that can efficiently support these categories of shared data objects. A brief description of these mechanisms may provide insight into why these particular categories are chosen. A separate paper describes our complete set of coherence mechanisms in more detail [4].

Write-Many objects appear in many parallel programs wherein several threads simultaneously access and modify a single shared data object between explicit synchronization points in the program. If the programmer knows that individual threads access independent portions of the data, and the order in which individual threads are scheduled is unimportant, the program can tolerate a controlled amount of inconsistency between cached portions of the data. The programmer uses explicit synchronization (such as a lock or monitor) to denote the points in the program execution at which such inconsistencies are not tolerable. We refer to this controlled inconsistency as *loose coherence* [4], as contrasted with *strict coherence*, in which no inconsistency is allowed. Strict and loose coherence are closely related to the concepts of *strong* and *weak ordering* of events as described by Dubois, et al [7]. Strong and weak ordering define a relation on the ordering of events (such as accesses to shared memory) in a system, while strict and loose coherence are operational definitions of the coherence guarantees that a system provides. Maintaining strict coherence unnecessarily is inefficient and introduces *false sharing*. The effects of false sharing can often be reduced by algorithm restructuring or careful memory allocation, but these efforts impose significant additional work on the programmer or compiler, are not possible for all algorithms, and are architecture dependent.

Delayed updates, based on loose coherence, allow *Write-many* objects to be handled efficiently. When a thread modifies a *Write-many* object, we delay sending the update to remote copies of the object until remote threads could otherwise indirectly detect that the object has been modified. In this manner, by enforcing only loose coherence, we avoid unnecessary synchronization that is not required by the program's semantics, and reduce the number of network packets needed for data motion and synchronization.

If the system knows that an object is shared in *Producer-Consumer* fashion, it can perform *eager object movement*. Eager object movement moves objects to the node at which they are going to be used in advance of when they are required. In the nearest neighbors example, this involves propagating the boundary element updates to where they will be required. In the best case, the new values are always available before they are needed, and threads never wait to receive the current values.

We propose to handle *Synchronization* objects with distributed locks. More elaborate synchronization objects, such as monitors and atomic integers, can be built on top of this. When a thread wants to acquire or test a global lock, it performs the lock operation on a local proxy for the distributed lock, and the local lock server arbitrates with the remote lock servers to perform the lock operation. Each lock has a queue associated with it that contains a list of the servers that need the lock. This queue facilitates efficient exchange of lock ownership. This mechanism is similar to that proposed by Goodman, et al [9].

Several categories of shared data objects can be handled in a straightforward fashion. *Private* objects are only accessed by one thread, so keeping them coherent is trivial. Replication is used for *Write-once* objects. *Read-mostly* objects are also candidates for replication since reads predominate writes. A *Migratory* object can be handled efficiently by migrating a single copy of the object among the processors that access it. *Result* objects are handled by maintaining a single copy and propagating updates to this copy. Finally, *General Read-Write* objects are handled by a standard coherence mechanism.

3 Logging Study

3.1 Programs

We have studied six shared memory parallel programs written in C++ [17] using the Presto programming system [5] on the Sequent Symmetry shared memory multiprocessor [13]. The selected programs are written specifically for a shared memory multiprocessor so that our results are not influenced by the program being written with distribution in mind and accurately reflect the memory access behavior that occurs when programmers do not expend special effort towards distributing the data across processors. Presto programs are divided into an initialization phase, during which the program is single-threaded, and a computation phase.

The six programs are: Matrix multiply, Gaussian elimination, Fast Fourier Transform (FFT), Quicksort, Traveling salesman problem (TSP), and Life. Matrix multiply, Gaussian elimination, and Fast Fourier Transform are numeric problems that distribute the data to separate threads and access shared memory in predictable patterns. Quicksort uses divide-and-conquer to dynamically subdivide the problem. Traveling salesman uses central work queues protected by locks to control access to problem data. Life is a "nearest-neighbors" problem in which data is shared only by neighboring processes.

As a measure of the "quality" of these parallel programs, Figure 3.1 shows a speedup plot for each of the six programs. The programs exhibit nearly linear speedup for small numbers of processors. The decrease in speedup seen for larger numbers of processors is due primarily to the unavailability of processors and the effects of bus contention.

3.2 Logging Technique

We collect logging information for a program by modifying the source and the run-time system to record all accesses to shared memory (13 microseconds to record each access). The program modifications are currently done by hand. A call to a logging object is added to the program source after every statement that accesses shared memory. The Presto run-time system is modified so that thread creations and destructions are recorded, as are all synchronization events. The end of each program's initialization phase is logged as a special event so that our analysis tool can differentiate between the initialization and the computation phase.

A program executed with logging enabled generates a series of log files, one per processor. Each log entry contains an *Object ID*, a *Thread ID*, the *Type of Access*, and the *Time of Access*. Examples of *Type of Access* include creation, read, write, and lock and monitor accesses of various types. *Time of Access* is the absolute time of the access, read from a hardware microsecond clock, so the per-processor logs can be merged to form a single global log.

We can specify the granularity with which to log accesses to objects. The two supported granularities

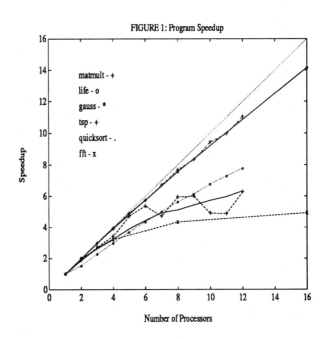

FIGURE 1: Program Speedup

matmult - +
life - o
gauss - *
tsp - +
quicksort - .
fft - x

Speedup

Number of Processors

are *object* and *element*. At object granularity, an access to any part of an object is logged as an access to the entire object. At element granularity, an access to a part of an object is logged as an access to that specific part of the object. For example, the log entry for a read of an element of a matrix object indicates only that the matrix was read at object granularity, but indicates the specific element that was read at element granularity.

Our study of sharing in parallel programs distinguishes itself from similar work [8, 15, 18] in that it studies sharing at the programming language level, and hence is relatively architecture-independent, and in that our selection of parallel programs embodies a wider variation in programming and synchronization styles.

An important difference between our approach and previous methods [1, 16] is that we only log accesses to shared memory, not all accesses to memory. Non-shared memory, such as program code and local variables, generally does not require special handling in a distributed shared memory system. A useful side effect of logging only accesses to shared memory is that the log files are much more compact. This allows us to log the shared memory accesses of relatively long-running programs in their entirety, which is important because the access patterns during initialization are significantly different from those during computation.

Logging in software during program execution combines many of the benefits of software simulation [16] and built-in tracing mechanisms [1], without some of the problems associated with these techniques. As with software simulation, with software logging it is easy to change the information that is collected during a particular run of the program. For example, if only the accesses to a particular object are of interest, such as the accesses to the lock protecting a central queue, only the logging associated with that object need be enabled. On the other hand, software-based logging does not slow down program execution to the extent that software simulation of the program and architecture does. Unlike with address tracing techniques, it is possible to collect higher-order information about particular accesses. For example, we can log an attempt to acquire a monitor, successful acquisition of the monitor, or sleeping on a monitor condition variable. This information is not easily recreated from a standard address trace.

The flexibility, power and low overhead of our system does not come without cost. Only accesses to shared memory performed by the applications program and run-time system are collected, so our system suffers from what Agarwal refers to as *omission*

distortion [1], the inability of a system to record the complete address stream of a running program. The omission distortion is not significant in this study because we are not trying to determine how any particular cache coherence mechanism will perform, but rather are attempting to characterize patterns of sharing that are common in parallel applications programs. Also, because only accesses to shared memory are collected, our logs may experience *temporal distortion* in the sense that periods with frequent accesses to shared memory will be slowed down to a greater extent than periods when accesses to shared memory are infrequent. The temporal distortion is limited by synchronization events, which constrain the relative ordering of events.

3.3 Analysis

We now formalize the intuitive definitions of the different categories of shared data objects given in Section 2 for the purpose of the log analysis.

Objects that are accessed by multiple threads between consecutive synchronization events sufficiently often (default: during 50% of the inter-synchronization periods) are categorized as *Write-Many*. Whenever a thread synchronizes, the analysis program examines each object that the thread has modified since it last synchronized to determine if another thread has accessed the same object during that period.

A producer-consumer phase for a particular object *Obj* is characterized by the following sequence of events. Thread *A* writes *Obj* and synchronizes (thread *A* may access *Obj* additional times). Then some other threads read *Obj* before *A* writes it again. The analysis program counts the number of accesses to an object that occur in producer-consumer phases, and if this number exceeds a specified percentage of all accesses to the object (default: 75%), then the object is declared to be *Producer-Consumer*.

Migratory objects are accessed in long runs. A *run* or *write-run* [8] is a sequence of accesses to a single object by a single thread. For the purposes of our analysis, the minimum length of a long run is variable (default: 8). An object is declared to be migratory if the percentage of all accesses to it that are contained in long runs exceeds a threshold (default: 85%).

Read-Mostly objects are primarily read (default: 75%). *Write-once*, *Result*, *Private*, and *Synchronization* objects can be easily identified using their intuitive definitions (see Section 2.1).

We have developed a tool to analyze the shared memory access logs in the manner just described. The tool detects common access patterns and identifies objects according to the characteristic kind of sharing that they exhibit. It also collects statistics specific to each category of shared data object, such as the average number of consumers for a *Producer-Consumer* object, the average run length of a *Migratory* object, and the average number of accesses to a *Write-Many* object between consecutive synchronization events. We have experimented with different values for the various thresholds, and the results do not appear to be very sensitive to variations in these thresholds.

3.4 Results

The results of our analysis are summarized in Tables 1 through 7. Odd-numbered tables present results from analysis runs where data was logged "by object." Even-numbered runs present results where data was logged "by element."

Tables 1 and 2 give the relative frequency of each type of shared access for each of the programs studied. These tables indicate the potential advantages of a memory coherence mechanism that is able to support both object and element granularity over a mechanism that supports only one level of granularity. With object-level logging, *Write-Many* accesses dominate other forms of shared data access (81.4, 100, 99.1, 99.2, and 47.3 percent), except for Matrix Multiply (only 2.8 percent). The other sharing category into which a large portion of the accesses fall at object-level granularity is *Write-Once* (18.6 percent in FFT, 97.2 percent in Matrix Multiply, and 23.9 percent in TSP). Parallel programs in which the granularity of sharing is fine tend to have their underlying fine grained behavior masked when the logging is performed on a per-object basis. With per-element logging, Matrix Multiply retains its *Write-Once* behavior, indicating that these are the inherent results. However, the access behavior of other programs are considerably different when examined per element. The best example of this unmasking is the Life program, where 82.4 percent of the shared data is in fact *Private* (the interior elements of the board) and 16.8 percent is *Producer-Consumer* (the edge elements).

The results in Tables 1 and 2 can be related to user-level objects in the programs as follows:

- The input arrays in Matrix Multiply exhibit *Write-Once* behavior, and references to these arrays dominate all other forms of access regardless of the granularity of logging. Accesses to the output matrix show up as *Result* when logged by element.

- Edge elements in the Life program exhibit *Producer-Consumer* behavior when shared ac-

Type	FFT	Qsort	Gauss	Life	Mult	TSP
Private						
RdMostly						
WriteOnce	18.6				97.2	23.9
Result						
Prod/Cons						
Migratory						15.0
WriteMany	81.4	100	99.1	99.2	2.8	47.3
Synch			.9	.8		12.4
GeneralRW						1.4

Table 1   Percent of Shared Access (By Object)

Type	FFT	Qsort	Gauss	Life	Mult	TSP
Private	.7	2.8	29.5	82.4	1.6	
RdMostly			30.0			13.2
WriteOnce	17.9		1.7		95.8	25.5
Result			3.7		2.6	
Prod/Cons			10.0	16.8		
Migratory	73.4	.8	2.6			40.8
WriteMany	8.0	96.4	21.6			4.4
Synch			.9	.8		12.0
GeneralRW						4.1

Table 2   Percent of Shared Access (By Element)

cesses are logged by element. Internal elements are *Private*.

- In TSP, the input array containing the path weights is *Write-Once*. At object granularity, the work queue is accessed in a migratory fashion, since it is a single object protected by a lock. The different partially computed tours are treated as one single object, and thus accesses to them are categorized as *Write-Many*. At element granularity, the partially computed tours are treated as independent objects and also exhibit *Migratory* behavior.

- At object granularity, the input coefficient array in Gaussian Elimination exhibits *Write-Many* behavior. At element granularity, access behavior to this array is less well-defined, indicating the different manner in which row, column, and pivot elements are accessed.

- The array being sorted in Quicksort exhibits *Write-Many* sharing at both object and element granularity. This is because of how Quicksort is implemented. The programmer knows that different threads access independent parts of the array, so accesses to the array are not synchronized.

- The input sample array in FFT exhibits *Write-Many* sharing behavior at object granularity. At element granularity, this array exhibits *Migratory* behavior because elements are passed between workers in phases. The ω array, an array of numeric coefficients that is initialized at the start of the algorithm and used extensively thereafter, is *Write-Once*. A temporary array, which is used to re-order the input array (in parallel) so that the elements required by each worker thread are contiguous, is *Write-Many*.

These observations correspond closely to our expectations, based on an informal understanding of how the programs access shared memory.

Tables 3 and 4 illustrate the dramatic differences between element and object granularity. These tables record the average size of the data element being accessed for each type of access for each of the programs. The objects at object granularity are generally arrays or matrices, and are thus relatively large. The 4-byte elements in Quicksort, Gaussian Elimination, Life, and Matrix Multiply are long integers. The 16-byte elements in FFT are complex numbers, represented by a pair of 8-byte double precision floating point numbers. Except for the TSP program, which uses fairly large arrays to store partial solutions, the elements being accessed are quite small. Thus, if coherence is maintained strictly on a per-object basis, the coherence protocol moves much larger units of

memory than the program requires. However, several large objects can be handled easily on a per-object basis. For example, the *Write-Once* (e.g., the input arrays in Matrix Multiply) objects can be replicated. It is therefore advantageous that the coherence protocol knows the size of the shared data objects, and their internal elements, in addition to their sharing behavior.

Tables 5 and 6 present data specific to *Write-Many* objects. The average number of different objects accessed between synchronization points indicates the average number of delayed updates that will be queued up at a time. If this number is small, as the data indicate, managing the queue of delayed updates may not require significant overhead. The remaining *Write-Many* data are also encouraging. *Write-Many* objects are written about one-half as many times as they are read. Large numbers of accesses occur between synchronization points. We call a series of accesses to a single object *by any thread* between two synchronization points in a particular thread a "no-synch run." The large size of the no-synch runs indicate that delayed updates offers substantial performance improvement. No-synch runs differ from Eggers's "write-runs" in that they do not end when a remote thread accesses the object, but rather whenever a thread synchronizes. Intuitively, write-runs end when a standard coherence mechanism, such as write-invalidate and write-update, would ensure consistency. No-synch runs end when the programmer *requires* consistency.

Table 7 presents the data recorded for locks, and contains both good and bad news. The good news is that the same thread frequently reacquires the same lock, which can be handled locally. Another piece of good news is that usually the number of threads

Type	FFT	Qsort	Gauss	Life	Mult	TSP
Private						
RdMostly						
WriteOnce	16K				4.9K	324
Result						
Prod/Cons						
Migratory						12K
WriteMany	32K	4K	2.5K	5K	2.5K	24K
GeneralRW						40

Table 3   Avg Access Size (bytes) (By Object)

Type	FFT	Qsort	Gauss	Life	Mult	TSP
Private	16	4	4	4	4	
RdMostly				4		12
WriteOnce	16		4		4	168
Result			4	4		
Prod/Cons			4	4		
Migratory	16	4	4			114
WriteMany	16	4	4			1.5K
GeneralRW						29

Table 4   Avg Access Size (bytes) (By Element)

	FFT	Qsort	Gauss	Life	Mult	TSP
Avg No Diff Objs Accsd Btwn Synchs	1	2	1.7	1	2	1.5
Avg No of Local Accs Btwn Synchs	8.3K	160	510	3.1K	38	20
Avg No of Loc Writes Btwn Synchs	3.5K	36	110	320	37	12
Avg No of Rmt Accs Btwn Synchs	48K	52K	17K	9.4K	2.4K	47
Avg No of Rmt Writes Btwn Synchs	21K	10K	3.6K	970	12K	28

Table 5   Write-Many Data (By Object)

	FFT	Qsort	Gauss	Life	Mult	TSP
Avg No Diff Objs Accsd Btwn Synchs	96	20	5.5			1.0
Avg No of Local Accs Btwn Synchs	817	127	36			1.3
Avg No of Loc Writes Btwn Synchs	375	35	74			1.1
Avg No of Rmt Accs Btwn Synchs	1.5K	1.5K	1.9K			2.6
Avg No of Rmt Writes Btwn Synchs	750	720	610			2.4

Table 6 Write-Many Data (By Element)

waiting on the same lock is quite small, indicating that lock arbitration will not require excessive network traffic. The bad news, in terms of being able to achieve the same performance on distributed memory multiprocessors as on shared memory multiprocessors, is that we observe small delays between attempts to acquire a lock and lock acquisition. Even an optimized distributed lock scheme requiring only a single message to release and reacquire the lock will be hard pressed to exhibit this small delay for feasible network latencies in a distributed system.

The general results of our analysis can be summarized as follows:

1. There are very few *General Read-Write* objects. Coherence mechanisms exist that can support the other categories of shared data objects efficiently, so a cache coherence protocol that adapts to the expected or observed behavior of each shared object will outperform one that does not.

2. The conventional notion of an object often does not correspond to the appropriate granularity of data decomposition for parallelism. Often it is

	FFT	Qsort	Gauss	Life	Mult	TSP
Avg dt Btwn Lock and Acquire (µsec)			83	1900		350
Pct This Acquire Same Thrd as Last			41	47		25
Avg No of Thrds Waiting on Same Lock			0	.6		.4

Table 7 Lock Data

appropriate to maintain coherence at the object level, but sometimes it is more appropriate to maintain coherence at a level smaller or larger than an object. Thus, a cache coherence protocol that adapts to the appropriate granularity of data decomposition will outperform one that does not.

4 Simulation Study

To test our hypothesis that adaptive caching mechanisms can outperform standard static caching mechanisms, we simulate two memory coherence mechanisms (write-invalidate and write-update) and two coherence mechanisms that are well-suited for particular types of sharing. All simulation runs are fed identical input streams from the logs generated from actual running programs. The simulation model allows us to select the cache coherence mechanism and set the cache line size for each run. It assumes an infinite cache so no replacement is performed except as required for coherence. The simulation collects information such as: the total number of shared memory accesses, the number of transactions, the total amount of data transmitted (bandwidth consumed), and the number of cache misses. For the discussion below, when the term *line size* is used in the context of a distributed shared memory system, it refers to the minimum granularity of memory that the system handles.

In the first simulation, we compare write-invalidate and write-update with our delayed update mechanism. With delayed updates, whenever the updates are propagated, the remote caches are updated rather than invalidated, so the worst case performance of this mechanism should be equivalent to that of a standard write-update cache. However, if multiple accesses to a single shared variable occur between user-specified synchronization points, delayed updates can significantly improve on a standard write-update mechanism.

The delayed update mechanism is particularly useful when the size of the elementary shared data items is smaller than the cache line size, and there can be a significant amount of false sharing. On the other hand, it must be recognized that false sharing can be minimized by prudent memory allocation by the compiler and/or the programmer. Since the programs used in these simulations are not optimized to avoid false sharing, the following results for write-invalidate and write-update must be interpreted as an upper bound on the negative effects of false sharing.

131

Table 8 presents the results of simulating the performance of the parallel Quicksort algorithm. The adaptive caching mechanism significantly reduces the amount of bus traffic required to maintain coherence. Compared to write-invalidate, the delayed update mechanism reduces the amount of bus traffic by 31%, 38%, and 52% for 4, 16, and 64 byte cache lines, respectively. Compared to write-update, the delayed update mechanism reduces the amount of bus traffic by 35%, 73%, and 86% for 4, 16, and 64 byte cache lines, respectively. The improvement is caused by the fact that Quicksort performs many writes to shared data objects between synchronization points, so many updates to the same data object are combined before they are eventually propagated. These results are a conservative estimate of the benefits of a delayed update mechanism, because updates to different data objects being sent to the same remote cache were counted as separate transfers. An efficient delayed update mechanism would coalesce updates to the same cache.

In the second simulation, we compare the standard coherence mechanisms with a write-invalidate mechanism that brings an entire object into the cache whenever any portion of it is accessed. This mechanism helps to alleviate object fragmentation caused by a cache line that is too small to hold an entire object. Both the cache line size and the basic object size that we examine are fairly small, but the results are valid whenever the objects used in a computation are larger than a single cache line. Larger cache line sizes are being proposed, but there will always be problems with very large objects that cannot fit into a single line, such as programs that manipulate rows or columns of a matrix.

Table 9 presents the results of this simulation for the parallel FFT. Since the majority of the data objects accessed by the FFT algorithm are complex variables (consisting of a pair of eight-byte double precision floating point variables), a cache line size of less than 16 bytes is inefficient, but the adaptive mech-

Coherence Mechanism	Linesize	Transfers (1000's)	Data Copied (kilobytes)
Adapts to Object Size	4	11.5	188
	16	11.5	188
	64	3.36	218
Write-Invalidate	4	46.9	188
	16	11.7	188
	64	3.41	218
Write-Update	4	45.2	181
	16	11.3	181
	64	6.00	384

Table 9   Simulation of FFT

anism overcomes this by automatically loading the entire complex data object when any part of it is accessed. The adaptive coherence mechanism requires the same amount of bandwidth as the write-invalidate mechanism, but when the cache line size is 4 bytes, it does so with 25% as many messages (thus, the average message is 4 times as large). The slight differences between write-invalidate and the adaptive scheme for cache line sizes larger than 4 bytes are caused by the relatively few accesses to objects that are even larger than complex variables, such as threads and monitors.

These two examples provide evidence that adaptive cache coherence mechanisms can significantly improve upon the performance of standard cache coherence mechanisms in a distributed shared memory system where all coherence is performed in software and network latencies are relatively high.

5   Related Work

Archibald and Baer discuss a variety of cache coherence protocols [3], most of which are variations of *write-invalidate* and *write-update*. Each works well in some instances and poorly in others. For example, when a single data item is frequently read and written by multiple processors (*fine-grained sharing*), a write-update cache tends to outperform a write-invalidate cache because the data item always resides in the local caches, and the needless cache misses and reloads after each invalidation are avoided. On the other hand, write-invalidate caches outperform write-update caches when one processor is performing most of the reads and writes of a particular data item or when a data item migrates between processors (*sequential sharing*). This is because after the invalidation associated with the first write to a data item, a write-invalidate cache does not needlessly broadcast the new value during subsequent writes.

Coherence Mechanism	Line size	Transfers (1000's)	Data Copied (kilobytes)
Delayed Update	4	19.6	87.7
	16	5.48	78.5
	64	1.65	106
Write-Invalidate	4	28.5	114
	16	8.81	141
	64	3.39	217
Write-Update	4	30.2	121
	16	14.9	239
	64	11.5	734

Table 8   Simulation of Quicksort

Archibald described a cache coherence protocol that attempts to adapt to the current reference pattern and dynamically choose to update or invalidate the other copies of a shared data object depending on how they are being used [2]. His protocol is designed for hardware implementation, and therefore is fairly simple and not as aggressive in its attempts to adapt to the expected access behavior as what we propose. Nevertheless, his simulation study indicates that even a simple adaptive protocol can enhance performance.

Other adaptive caching schemes have been proposed, including competitive snoopy caching [10] and read-broadcast [11]. Each appears to be appropriate for particular types of sharing behavior, and we plan to examine them in more detail as our work continues.

Weber and Gupta attempt to link the observed invalidation patterns back to high-level applications program objects [18]. They distinguished several distinct types of shared data objects: *Code and read-only*, *Mostly-read*, *Migratory*, *Synchronization*, and *Frequently read/written*. The first four of their categories have corresponding categories in our classification and are handled similarly. *Frequently read/written* data had the worst invalidation behavior and their coherence protocols could not handle them efficiently. They advised that this type of data object be avoided if at all possible. Our approach is more aggressive. We have identified two types of shared data objects (*Write-Many* and *Producer-Consumer*) that would fall into Weber-Gupta's *Frequently read/written* category, yet can be handled efficiently by an appropriate protocol.

Eggers and Katz analyze the sharing characteristics of four parallel programs [8]. Two of the applications exhibited a high percentage of *sequential sharing* while the other two exhibited a high degree of *fine-grained sharing*. This indicates that neither write-broadcast nor write-invalidate is clearly better for all applications. The observed low contention for shared data objects led them to conclude that write-invalidate outperforms write-broadcast on the average, but one major cause of their low contention is their programming methodology (SPMD). Each process executes on an independent piece of data, and the only contention occurs at the central task queue. Thus, most computation occurs without contention, which favors write-invalidate.

6   Conclusions

We have characterized several distinct categories of shared data access: *Write-once*, *Write-many*, *Producer-Consumer*, *Private*, *Migratory*, *Result*, *Read-mostly*, *Synchronization*, and *General Read-Write*. We have briefly described efficient memory coherence mechanisms for each of these categories. By studying logs of shared memory accesses of a variety of parallel programs, we have shown that a large percentage of shared memory accesses fall in these categories. These results support our contention that adaptive cache coherence techniques that are designed to exploit the anticipated or observed access behavior of a particular data object can significantly outperform standard cache coherence mechanisms, at least in the context of a distributed shared memory system. We have also described two simulations studies to further support this hypothesis.

Acknowledgements

The authors would like to thank the referees and the members of the Rice computer systems group (Elmootazbellah Elnozahy, Jerry Fowler, David Johnson, Pete Keleher, and Mark Mazina) for their helpful suggestions. Trung Diep assisted with the acquisition and plotting of program speedup data.

References

[1] Anant Agarwal, Richard L. Sites, and Mark Horowitz. ATUM: A new technique for capturing address traces using microcode. In *Proceedings of the 13th Annual International Symposium on Computer Architecture*, pages 119–127, June 1986.

[2] James Archibald. A cache coherence approach for large multiprocessor systems. In *International Conference on Supercomputing*, pages 337–345, November 1988.

[3] James Archibald and Jean-Loup Baer. Cache coherence protocols: Evaluation using a multiprocessor simulation model. *ACM Transactions on Computer Systems*, 4(4):273–298, November 1986.

[4] John K. Bennett, John B. Carter, and Willy Zwaenepoel. Munin: Distributed shared memory based on type–specific memory coherence. In *Proceedings of the 1990 Conference on Principles and Practice of Parallel Programming*, March 1990.

[5] Brian N. Bershad, Edward D. Lazowska, and Henry M. Levy. PRESTO: A system for object-oriented parallel programming. *Software—*

Practice and Experience, 18(8):713–732, August 1988.

[6] Jeffrey S. Chase, Franz G. Amador, Edward D. Lazowska, Henry M. Levy, and Richard J. Littlefield. The Amber system: Parallel programming on a network of multiprocessors. In *Proceedings of the Twelfth ACM Symposium on Operating Systems Principles*, pages 147–158, December 1989.

[7] Michel Dubois, Christoph Scheurich, and Fayé A. Briggs. Synchronization, coherence, and event ordering in multiprocessors. *IEEE Computer*, 21(2):9–21, February 1988.

[8] Susan J. Eggers and Randy H. Katz. A characterization of sharing in parallel programs and its application to coherency protocol evaluation. In *Proceedings of the 15th Annual International Symposium on Computer Architecture*, pages 373–383, May 1988.

[9] James R. Goodman, Mary K. Vernon, and Philip J. Woest. Efficient synchronization primitives for large-scale cache-coherent multiprocessor. In *Proceedings of the 3rd International Conference on Architectural Support for Programming Languages and Systems*, April 1989.

[10] A. R. Karlin, M. S. Manasse, L. Rudolph, and D.D. Sleator. Competitive snoopy caching. In *Proceedings of the 16th Annual IEEE Symposium on the Foundations of Computer Science*, pages 244–254, 1986.

[11] Kai Li. Private communication. March 1990.

[12] Kai Li and Paul Hudak. Memory coherence in shared virtual memory systems. *ACM Transactions on Computer Systems*, 7(4):321–359, November 1989.

[13] Tom Lovett and Shreekant Thakkar. The Symmetry multiprocessor system. In *Proceedings of the 1988 International Conference on Parallel Processing*, pages 303–310, August 1988.

[14] Umakishore Ramachandran and M. Yousef A. Khalidi. An implementation of distributed shared memory. *Distributed and Multiprocessor Systems Workshop*, pages 21–38, 1989.

[15] Richard L. Sites and Anant Agarwal. Multiprocessor cache analysis using ATUM. In *Proceedings of the 15th Annual International Symposium on Computer Architecture*, pages 186–195, June 1988.

[16] K. So, F. Darema-Rogers, D. George, V.A. Norton, and G.F. Pfister. PSIMUL: A system for parallel simulation of the execution of parallel programs. Technical Report RC11674, IBM Research, 1986.

[17] Bjarne Stroustrup. *The C++ Programming Language*. Addison-Wesley, 1987.

[18] Wolf-Dietrich Weber and Anoop Gupta. Analysis of cache invalidation patterns in multiprocessors. In *Proceedings of the 3rd International Conference on Architectural Support for Programming Languages and Systems*, pages 243–256, April 1989.

PANEL: Big Science Versus Little Science -- Do You Have to Build It?

Panelists

David. R. Ditzel, Sun Microsystems
John L. Hennessy, Stanford University
Bernie Rudin, IBM - Kingston
Alan Jay Smith, University of California-Berkeley
Stephen L. Squires, DARPA
Zeke Zalcstein, National Science Foundation

Moderated by Mark D. Hill, University of Wisconsin-Madison

Research can be called *big science* if projects have numerous researchers, large funding, significant infrastructure, and plans to build complex tools or prototypes. Most experimental physicists practice big science, as do computer architects who build prototype software-hardware systems.

Conversely, research can be called *little science* when projects have few researchers, modest funding, little special infrastructure, and no plans to build complex tools or prototypes. Most mathematicians practice little science, as do computer architects who study aspects of a design and build confidence in their proposals with models or simulations.

A very simple model contrasting the two approaches is illustrated below, where money flows from governments (GOV) to academia (EDU) which produce ideas for industry (COM) to make better products for all (POP). A key difference is whether governments fund a few, large research projects or many, smaller ones.

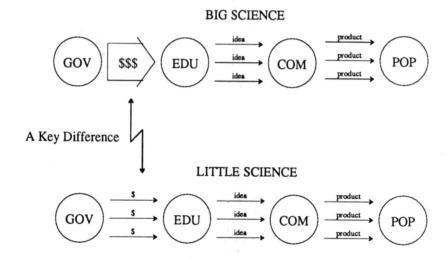

The goal of this session is explore whether, when and why universities should do big or little science. Panelists may discuss why big science wastes money, exploits graduate students and makes research too short range. They may argue that little science produces results that are too deep and narrow, oblivious to global systems issues, not properly validated, and too out of touch with reality to ever be practical. Panelists may also find some advantages to both kinds of science.

Panelists include members from government, academia and industry, who are also members of the general population. To keep the discussion lively, nothing said necessarily represents the opinion of any government agency, university or corporation with whom panelists are affiliated.

Session 3A: Cache Memory

An Empirical Evaluation of
Two Memory-Efficient Directory Methods

Brian W. O'Krafka   A. Richard Newton

Department of Electrical Engineering and Computer Sciences
University of California, Berkeley

Abstract

This paper presents an empirical evaluation of two memory-efficient directory methods for maintaining coherent caches in large shared memory multiprocessors. Both directory methods are modifications of a scheme proposed by Censier and Feautrier [5] that does not rely on a specific interconnection network and can be readily distributed across interleaved main memory. The schemes considered here overcome the large amount of memory required for tags in the original scheme in two different ways. In the first scheme each main memory block is sectored into sub-blocks for which the large tag overhead is shared. In the second scheme a limited number of large tags are stored in an associative cache and shared among a much larger number of main memory blocks. Simulations show that in terms of access time and network traffic both directory methods provide significant performance improvements over a memory system in which shared-writeable data is not cached. The large block sizes required for the sectored scheme, however, promotes sufficient false sharing that its performance is markedly worse than using a tag cache.

1 Introduction

General purpose multiple instruction stream, multiple data stream (MIMD) multiprocessors [8] offer an attractive way to accelerate many computationally intensive tasks. MIMD multiprocessors are attractive because they are a general purpose solution that can also be exploited as high performance multiprogrammed computers. The particular class of shared bus, shared memory multiprocessors has gained commercial acceptance by offering high performance at reduced cost for applications with modest amounts of exploitable parallelism. By supporting the shared memory programming paradigm, these machines are usually much easier to program than those supporting message passing because the programmer does not have to worry about distributing data across multiple memories.

The success of shared bus multiprocessors is largely due to the efficient caching techniques made possible because of the shared bus [Bec87]. Effective caching techniques are important in multiprocessor design because the provision of a cache at each processor masks the often severe access delay to main memory through an interconnection network. Unfortunately, computers with two or more caches require techniques for ensuring that the caches remain consistent: all changes to a piece of data must eventually be reflected in all cached copies. It is now fairly well-understood how to enforce cache consistency in shared bus multiprocessors by exploiting their broadcast capabilities [EgK88], but shared bus architectures support relatively few processors (probably 50 or less), and it is unclear how to enforce consistency in more scalable, non-bus architectures.

This paper investigates the use of directory methods for maintaining cache coherence in large shared memory multiprocessors. In particular, it investigates two memory-efficient variations of Censier and Feautrier's directory method [5]. The different schemes are evaluated using execution driven simulations of three benchmark programs, two of which are computer-aided design tools for VLSI circuits.

This paper is organized as follows. Section 2 reviews previous work in cache coherence. Section 3 presents the specifications of the consistency schemes that are evaluated using the methodology described in Section 4. Section 5 summarizes the simulation results, from which conclusions are drawn in Section 6.

Throughout this paper we consider multiprocessors that use *weak ordering*, as defined in [16], as their standard of correctness. The directory methods described here are readily applicable in multiprocessors for which a different coherence standard is desired.

2 Previous Work

Cache consistency methods proposed to date may be divided into four classes: those in which shared writeable data is uncached, "snooping" protocols (for shared-bus systems), directory schemes, and software assisted techniques [2]. The first three classes are categorized as hardware based techniques. Hardware techniques enforce consistency in a manner that requires no special cache control instructions to be inserted in program object code. Software techniques, on the other hand, rely on a sophisticated compiler to determine how to manage the memory hierarchy at compile time and generate appropriate cache control instructions.

It is now fairly well-understood how to build memory hierarchies and provide hardware supported cache coherency in shared-bus multiprocessors [7]. Hardware enforced coherency is attractive because it requires little software support and operates transparently to the programmer. Unfortunately, shared-bus architectures support relatively few processors, and it is unclear how to enforce consistency in larger, non-bus architectures.

The Ultracomputer [11], RP3 [15], and Cedar [9] multiprocessors deal with the consistency problem using software methods. Only recently has work been reported on the investigation of hardware coherence methods for large non-bus machines. In addition, few results have been reported characterizing the behavior of parallel programs running on large numbers of processors. [1] used traces from a four processor VAX multiprocessor to compare directory methods to snooping bus protocols, in the context of shared-bus multiprocessors. Three recent research efforts–work by Wilson at CMU [21], the Wisconsin Multicube [10] and work by Carlton at Berkeley [4]–have concentrated on extensions to shared-bus schemes based on collections of busses connected in trees, meshes or cubes. So far, no extensive simulations have been performed to evaluate these designs.

CH2887-8/90/0000/0138$01.00 © 1990 IEEE

138

3 Four Schemes for Enforcing Cache Coherence

In this section four hardware-based approaches to enforcing cache consistency in large shared memory multiprocessors are presented. The schemes are:

- Shared writeable data is uncached.

- Censier and Feautrier's directory method.

- A sectored version of Censier and Feautrier's scheme.

- A version of Censier and Feautrier's scheme with a limited number of tags stored in an associative tag cache.

The first two schemes were selected to provide comparison data for the others.

3.1 No Caching of Shared Writeable Data

In this coherence technique, shared writeable data is tagged un-cacheable. The memory controllers must bypass their caches and access main memory for all references to non-cacheable data. In this scheme the main memory must be able to handle cache requests for block contents and cache requests to displace blocks. Since up to 40% of all references can be to shared writeable data, this method offers the poorest performance of the four schemes, but provides a useful reference point for evaluating the others.

3.2 Censier and Feautrier's Directory Method

In this scheme physical memory is divided into blocks of fixed size. Each block of main memory is associated with a directory entry (or tag) containing 1 bit per cache, a single bit indicating whether or not the block is modified, and a lock bit (Figure 1). Using the notation of

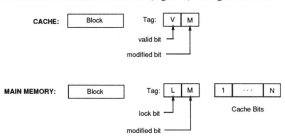

Figure 1: Tags for Basic Censier and Feautrier Protocol

[2], a block is always in one of these three states:

1. ABSENT: no cache holds a copy (all cache bits in the directory entry are 0, and the modified bit is 0; lock bit is 0);

2. PRESENT: one or more caches hold copies, and the block is un-modified (one or more cache bits in the directory entry are 1, and the modified bit is 0; lock bit is 0);

3. PRESENTM: exactly one cache has a copy and it is modified (exactly one cache bit is 1 and modified bit is 1; lock bit is 0);

4. LOCKED: an operation on this block is currently in progress (lock bit is 1);

In like manner, each cache block is associated with a cache directory entry consisting of a valid bit and a modified bit (Figure 1). Cache blocks may be in one of these states:

1. INVALID: the contents of the cache block are invalid (valid bit is 0);

2. VALID: the contents of the cache block are valid and unmodified (valid bit is 1 and modified bit is 0);

3. VALIDM: the contents of the cache block are valid and modified (valid bit is 1 and modified bit is 1). This state implies that this cache has the only valid copy of the block in the entire multiprocessor.

The cache consistency protocol is defined by the set of actions taken by the memory controllers and the main memory for each different combination of processor request, cache block state, and main memory state.

If a processor issues a read and the local cache block of the data is valid, no main memory access is needed and the data is simply read from the cache. If a block for the referenced data does not exist, a block must be assigned and its old data displaced to main memory. The missed reference is then handled as if the block was invalid: a read transaction is issued to the main memory. If the main memory block is in an unmodified state, the block contents are returned to the requesting memory controller. If the main memory block is modified, the block contents are read from the single "owning" cache, written to main memory, and forwarded to the requestor. In all of these cases the cache and main memory entries have their states updated to VALID and PRESENT, respectively.

When a processor issues a write, it can only be satisfied locally if the local cache block is VALIDM. If the local cache state is VALID, an invalidate transaction is sent to the main memory which, if other caches have copies (ie: main memory state is PRESENT or PRESENTM), issues invalidations to them. If, however, the local cache misses or the block is invalid, the controller issues an invalidate-fetch transaction to the main memory. A fetch is required here so that the portion of the block untouched by the write is made valid. The main memory sends invalidations to caches with copies and if the block is modified, fetches the current data, updates itself, and forwards the data to the requestor. The states of cache and main memory blocks are updated to VALIDM and PRESENTM, respectively.

We assume for this and the other coherence schemes that references to synchronization variables bypass the cache completely and are always handled at the main memory.

Block displacements are always sent to the main memory which clears the appropriate cache bit. If a cache displaces a VALIDM block, the block contents must be written back and the main memory state changed to ABSENT.

The Censier and Feautrier scheme is well-suited to large multiprocessors because it does not depend on the use of broadcasts (and hence does not depend on a particular network), and permits the main memory and its directory to be interleaved. Although the communication overhead could be excessive if many blocks reside in many caches, the scheme's greatest drawback is the severe memory overhead introduced by the large number of cache bits in the main memory tags. As an example, a system with 100 processors requires a 102 bit tag, dictating a block size in excess of 125 bytes for tag overhead to be less than 10%. Systems built using this consistency scheme are not easily expanded because the tag length is dependent on the number of processors.

Several variations of the basic protocol have been suggested for reducing the tag size. In one variation, processors are clustered onto a set of busses so only the clusters holding copies of a block need to be recorded. In another variation [2], the array of cache bits is eliminated and an extra bit is used to indicate if one or more caches have copies.

The basic Censier and Feautrier protocol is modified so that whenever a block must be invalidated from the main memory a broadcast is used. The communication requirements of this variation can be reduced at the expense of a slightly larger tag by adding a small number, say i, of multiprocessor identifiers which would hold the addresses of caches holding copies of the associated block [1]. If the number of copies ever exceeds i, either broadcasting is used or one of the cached copies is invalidated and its identifier reused. This scheme should work well if the average number of copies of a block are low, as suggested by the empirical results of [1]. One of the schemes evaluated in this paper exploits this empirical observation in a similar way.

3.3 Sectored Censier and Feautrier Directory Method

Another way to reduce tag overhead is to increase the block size but maintain finer granularity for invalidations by dividing blocks into sub-blocks. Finer granularity is needed to reduce the number of cache misses caused by the invalidation of a large block because of a write to a small portion of it. It also allows a block to be referenced without transferring its entire contents. This idea is similar to sectored cache schemes for uniprocessor memory systems [12].

With sectored blocks, the Censier and Feautrier protocol is modified as follows. In the main memory directory, each sub-block is given a tag large enough to hold a processor number, plus a modified bit. The array of cache bits is associated with an entire block. A cache bit set to one now indicates that the associated cache holds one or more valid sub-blocks. In the cache directories, the valid and modified bits are now distributed among the sub-blocks. Figure 2 illustrates the new tag scheme.

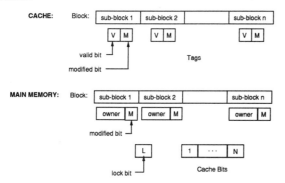

Figure 2: Tag Scheme for Sectored Censier and Feautrier Protocol

As before, different protocol actions are taken depending on sub-block state in the caches and at the main memory. In the caches, sub-blocks can be VALID, VALIDM or INVALID, depending on their respective valid and modified bits in the same way that cache block state is determined in the original scheme. At the main memory, the state of a sub-block is determined as follows:

1. ABSENT: no caches hold any portion of the block containing the sub-block (all cache bits for the containing block are zero; lock bit is 0);

2. PRESENT: one or more caches hold portions of the block containing the sub-block (one or more cache bits for the containing block are 1, and the modified bit for the sub-block is 0; lock bit is 0);

3. PRESENTM: exactly one cache holds a valid copy of the sub-block, and it is modified (one or more cache bits for the containing

block are 1, the modified bit for the sub-block is 1, and its "owner" tag holds the address of the cache holding the modified copy; lock bit is 0);

4. LOCKED: an operation on this block is currently in progress (lock bit is 1);

Protocol actions as a function of cache and main memory state are the same as those for the original protocol with only a minor modification to the way main memory state is updated with a displacement: in the new scheme all sub-blocks must be checked so that those which are PRESENTM and "owned" by the displacing cache are correctly updated.

[12] investigated the use of sectored blocks in the context of small, microprocessor on-chip caches and found that sectoring substantially increased the number of cache misses. In the study reported here, however, the cache sizes are much larger and it was felt that misses resulting from sharing and accesses to synchronization variables would dominate any extra misses due to sectoring. The results in Section 5 support this reasoning.

The original Censier and Feautrier protocol is a subset of this scheme in which each block has only one sub-block. The original Censier and Feautrier scheme requires N bits per tag per sub-block, where N is the number of processors. In the sectored scheme, $(N+1)/n + \log N + 1$ bits per tag per sub-block are needed, where n is the number of sub-blocks in a block. For $N = 512$ and $n = 32$, the original scheme requires 512 bits per tag per sub-block while the sectored scheme only requires 26. Tag size can be further reduced by a factor of 2 to 10 if processors are clustered onto busses so that only cluster addresses are needed. While the modified scheme requires less memory for tags, it requires slightly higher communication overhead because invalidations are sent to all caches holding portions of the affected block, some of which may not hold valid copies of the affected sub-block (this phenomenon is known as *false sharing*). Although the tags in the new scheme are still dependent on the number of processors in the system, the reduced tag overhead should make it possible to build a machine with tag sizes allocated for the worst case number of processors.

3.4 Censier and Feautrier's Directory Method Using Tag Caches

In this scheme the amount of tag memory is reduced by using a quantity of tags much smaller than the number of main memory blocks; the tags are stored in an associative tag cache indexed by block address [2]. More specifically, two caches of different tag sizes are provided at each bank of the distributed main memory: a large cache with small tags capable of holding the identifiers of a small number of cached copies (Figure 3), and a small cache with full-sized tags (Figure 1).

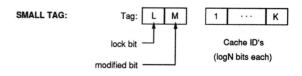

Figure 3: Small Tag Fields

The coherence protocol for this scheme is similar to the basic Censier and Feautrier protocol with the exception that tags must be allocated from a tag cache as needed; when no tags are free, a cached block must be invalidated and its tag re-allocated. When a block is first referenced, it is allocated a small tag. When the number of copies of a block exceed the number of copies supported by the small tags, a large tag is allocated and the small tag is freed. In this study a least-recently-used displacement strategy was used to select tags for re-allocation.

This scheme exploits the following characteristics of data sharing in a multiprocessor:

1. Tags are only needed to record the locations of blocks residing in caches. If the total number of cache blocks is much smaller than the total number of main memory blocks, tag overhead can be greatly reduced. For example, a 64 processor machine with 32 kilobyte caches and 32 megabytes of distributed main memory requires only 1600 kilobytes of full length tags (66 bits in length, plus 32 bit association tags) to store directory information for the $64 \times 32k \div 16 = 128k$ cache blocks. Alternatively, 25000 kilobytes of full length tags are needed if one tag is provided per main memory block.

2. It has been empirically observed [1] that most blocks of shared writeable data are not intensively shared, so tags with a small number of cache identifiers should be sufficient most of the time. However, a small number of blocks may be shared by many caches and some means must be provided to efficiently support them.

4 Evaluation Methodology

The four consistency methods of Section 3 were evaluated using execution driven simulations of three benchmark programs. In this section the methods, assumptions, and goals of the evaluation are described. Evaluation results are presented in Section 5. This study uses two figures of merit: average communication requirements and average memory access time. Average communication requirements are presented as the average number of bytes transferred across the network, normalized with respect to the number of data references made by a cpu. Average memory access time is presented as the average number of normalized time units required to satisfy a single memory reference, to data, by one processor. Here a normalized time unit is the time required to reference data in a local cache.

For the rest of this report the names of the cache consistency schemes are abbreviated as follows:

1. NOCACHE or N: shared writeable data is not cached;

2. CANDF or F: basic Censier and Feautrier scheme;

3. SECTORED or S: sectored Censier and Feautrier scheme;

4. TCACHE or T: Censier and Feautrier scheme with tag caches;

Most simulation studies of computer memory systems have used address traces collected from real machines running a set of benchmark programs [19, 20]. Of these studies, most of those considering multiprocessors have dealt with relatively few processors, typically under 10 [1, 3, 7]. For large numbers of processors, trace driven methods become cumbersome because of the large amount of storage required to hold the traces. As an example, traces for 64 processors with one million 32 bit references per processor require 256 megabytes of storage in uncompressed form. The quantity and ordering of synchronization references may be dependent on the particular machine on which traces are gathered, severely restricting the architectures that can be analyzed. The motivation for trace driven simulation is also reduced because multiprocessor memory systems require more complex simulation models, thus relatively little extra simulation time is required to simulate the

processors executing the code. For these reasons, a simulator was developed to perform simulations of complete multiprocessors in sufficient detail to evaluate the performance of different memory systems. Although considerable effort was required to develop the simulator, and simulations take somewhat longer than when traces are used, it requires much less storage and does not depend on using an existing machine to collect traces.

The simulation study involved simulations of three benchmark programs on four multiprocessor architectures supporting the cache coherency techniques of the preceding section. Each simulation required the following steps:

1. Compile the shared memory benchmark program into 68020 assembler using the *HPUX* C compiler (available on Hewlett Packard series 350 workstations).

2. Convert the assembly code into the pre-decoded format required by the simulator. A global 32 bit virtual address space (Figure 4) was used. In a global address space, to each piece of logical piece of data there corresponds exactly one virtual address; if two or more processes reference the same data they must use identical virtual addresses. This type of address space was chosen to avoid

MSB				LSB
PROCESS ID	SEGMENT	BLOCK	SUB-BLOCK	BYTE
8 BITS	3 BITS		17 BITS	4 BITS

Figure 4: Components of an Address

the problems associated with "synonyms"—two or more distinct virtual addresses corresponding to the same data [19].

3. Prepare a netlist of the architecture to be simulated, providing specifications for and interconnections among a set of CPU's, memory controllers and main memories.

4. Run the simulation.

In this section the simulator, the simulation models and the benchmark programs are described. The operating system support required for the simulations is also described, along with details of the four multiprocessor architectures.

4.1 The Simulator and Simulation Models

The multiprocessor simulator was constructed in a modular fashion, with a core providing message passing facilities for a simulator shell and collection of architectural models. The models include a 68020/68881 CPU, four different memory controllers, a network model, four main memories and a statistics gathering module. The following subsections describe each of the simulator components.

4.1.1 Message Passing Core

The message passing core provides a set of functions that operate on *messages*, which are characterized by a *message type*, the *data* which they contain, and the *time* at which they are to arrive. The data passed in a message can be anything expressible as a structure in the C programming language, the language in which the simulator is written. Messages are created and sent between instances of simulator models, characterized by a set of input ports, output ports and message handlers for the different message types that can be received. A priority queue was used to deliver messages in proper order.

4.1.2 68020/68881 CPU

The model of the 68020/68881 CPU supports a large subset of the Motorola 68020/68881 instruction set in sufficient detail to permit the assembler output from a C compiler to be simulated correctly with reasonable efficiency. The model has the following characteristics:

1. It models the execution of a large subset of the 68020/68881 instruction set.

2. There is full modelling of byte, word, long word and 64 bit floating point operands, including support for 1, 2, 3 and 4 byte alignments.

3. The processor stalls only on read misses and synchronization references.

4. Pipelining was modelled approximately as follows:

   - Instructions and data are stored in the same cache.

   - Instructions can be prefetched simultaneously with data accesses; Instruction fetches stall the processor only when they resulted in a cache miss. This approximates the use of a large instruction buffer between the cache and the processor.

   - A single fixed delay of 2 cache cycles, independent of instruction, was used to model the delay between data references.

4.1.3 Memory Controllers for the NOCACHE, SECTORED, CANDF and TCACHE Schemes

These models simulate the four coherence protocols of Section 3, using fully associative LRU caching with variable block size. Instances of these models have two pairs of input and output ports: one pair to communicate with a CPU and one pair to communicate with a multiprocessor interconnection network. A single delay is used to model the time between receiving a message from the CPU or network and issuing another one. This delay corresponds to the time to process a cache hit. In these models it was assumed that displacements are buffered so that the controllers never have to wait for a displacement to complete.

4.1.4 Network Model

A multistage indirect binary N-cube network was modelled [18] by interconnecting $\frac{N}{2} \log N$ 2 by 2 switch modules, where N is the number of processors. Two networks were used: one to connect N processors to N main memory banks, and one to connect the memory banks to the processors. The following network characteristics were assumed:

- Each processor is assigned a unique identifier between 0 and $N-1$, inclusive.

- N is a power of 2.

- Memory is interleaved N ways.

- Interleaving is done on the lower order $\log_2 N$ address bits of the block address field (Figure 4).

- Conflicting network transactions are resolved using round robin scheduling.

- All network transactions are assigned lengths in bytes according to the following rules:

  - 4 bytes for transaction type and originating cpu;

  - 4 bytes for virtual address;

  - a suitable number of bytes for data (eg. 4 bytes for one word, 16 bytes for a sub-block, etc.);

- Each port at a switch node is assumed to be 4 bytes wide.

- Delay through a network node is modelled in terms of unit delays, in which one "packet" of data can be handled per unit delay. "packet" here denotes an amount of data equivalent to one port width. A unit delay was assumed to be the same as the cache cycle time.

- If an arriving network transaction is destined to an output that is unblocked, it is routed with only one unit delay.

- Up to four transactions (of any type) can be buffered per each output port at a switch element. Handshaking between switching elements prevents buffer overflows.

4.1.5 Main Memories for the NOCACHE, SECTORED, CANDF and TCACHE Schemes

These models simulate large interleaved main memories supporting the four coherence protocols. Since virtual addresses are sent from the memory controllers they perform virtual to real address translation. A single delay is used to model main memory access time. Actions involving the sending of more than one reply transaction (eg. the sending of invalidations) require one delay interval between transaction.

4.2 Operating System Support

As part of the simulation process it was necessary to provide partial operating system support in the form of a kernel and a set of utility functions to perform such things as input, output and interprocess synchronization. The stub of a UNIX-like operating system was written to minimize the difficulty of simulating existing parallel programs written for the DYNIX operating system on a Sequent multiprocessor. Support was limited to applications written in the C programming language.

A simple kernel was required to start up the child processes forked by a parent. At the beginning of a simulation of an N processor system, a single processor begins executing the benchmark program (the parent) while the $N-1$ free processors execute the kernel. The kernel begins by examining a globally shared queue of processes ready to be started. If this queue is empty, the kernel indicates that its respective processor is available for work on another shared queue holding a list of free processors. Whenever a process is forked by the parent process, it is assigned to a free processor if one is available, or an entry is made in the ready queue. Processors are suspended while the wait for processes to become available on the ready queue.

A standard library of commonly used functions such as *printf, scanf* and *strcpy* was provided. Each function was implemented in one of two ways: as compiled simulator code or as C code which is assembled and linked with the benchmark assembly code in Step 2 of the simulation sequence at the beginning of this chapter. Although the functions implemented as simulator code do not accurately model operating system references, they were used relatively infrequently in the computationally intensive portions of the benchmarks.

Locking synchronization primitives *s_lock* and *s_unlock* were implemented as spin locks built upon test-and-set and clear synchronization instructions.

The implementation of *s_wait_barrier* was chosen to improve simulation efficiency. Instead of building the barrier functions using the lock mechanism described above, the implementation of Figure 5 was used. Here a barrier structure is composed of:

```
s_init_barrier(barrier b, int n) {
    s_init_lock(b.lock);
    b.n = n;
    b.cnt = 0;
}

s_wait_barrier(barrier b) {
    s_lock(b.lock);
    b.cnt = b.cnt + 1;
    if (b.cnt != b.n) {
    /* myid identifies calling cpu */
        b.id_list[b.cnt] = myid;
        s_unlock(b.lock);
        suspend;
    }
    else {
        b.cnt = 0;
        for (i = 0; i < b.n - 1; i++) {
            restart(b.id_list[i]);
        }
    }
    s_unlock(b.lock);
}
```

Figure 5: Implementation of a Barrier

- *lock*: a lock to prevent more than one process from modifying the structure at a time;

- *cnt*: a counter to indicate the number of processors that have reached the barrier;

- *n*: the number of processors which will check in at the barrier;

- *id_list*: a list of the identifiers of the processors checked in at the barrier;

The implementations of "suspend" and "restart" simply stop and restart the affected processor without performing any context switch; for simplicity the possibility of interrupts or multiple parallel programs sharing a processor was neglected.

4.3 Benchmarks

The benchmarks are:

1. *ssim*, a parallel simulation of a simple stochastic model of a multiprocessor. The program executes the statically defined schedule of a synchronous data flow [13] representation of a simple multiprocessor.

2. *genie*, a parallel topological array compactor used in the layout of VLSI circuits. It uses an algorithm based on simulated annealling– a probabilistic optimization technique [6].

3. *verf*, a parallel verifier of combinational logic circuits [14].

Some characteristics of the benchmarks, including program size, memory usage and reference behavior are shown in Table 1. These benchmarks were all originally written and debugged on the Sequent shared memory multiprocessor. The benchmarks are computation intensive and require little operating system intervention throughout their execution.

Table 1: Benchmark Characteristics

Benchmark	Lines	Memory			No. of Refs.	
		code	local	shared	parent	child
ssim	470	15k	200k	750	280k	90k
genie	2300	46k	12k	1.5M	9M	523k
verf	2600	47k	68k	460k	2M	760k

Table 2: Default Parameters of Simulated Architectures

MODEL[a]	PARAMETER	VALUE
CPU	Delay	1
NOCACHE Controller	Delay	1
	Cache Size	128kB
	Block Size	16B
NOCACHE Main Memory	Delay	10
CANDF Controller	Delay	1
	Cache Size	128kB
	Block Size	16B
CANDF Main Memory	Delay	10
SECTOR Controller	Delay	1
	Cache Size	128kB
	Block Size	64B
	Sub-Block Size	16B
SECTOR Main Memory	Delay	10
TCACHE Controller	Delay	1
	Cache Size	128kB
	Block Size	16B
TCACHE Main Memory	Delay	10
	Small Tag Length	1
	No. Small Tags	128k
	No. Large Tags	4k

[a]All models assume a network delay of 10.

4.4 Simulated Architectures

Table 2 shows the default parameters chosen for the four multiprocessor architectures for which simulations were performed. Unless specified otherwise, these parameters were used for all of the simulation results in the next section. 64 processors were used for all simulations. It was assumed that for each benchmark the entire program could reside in main memory.

5 Simulation Results

Simulation results are presented in the following eight subsections. The first two subsections present comparison data for all four coherence schemes. Subsection 5.3 presents results that show the effect of cache size on system performance. Subsections 5.4 and 5.5 present more detailed results for the sectored and tag cache directory methods. The last three subsections present results investigating invalidation traffic, synchronization traffic and the inherent parallelism of the benchmarks.

5.1 Reference Characteristics

Table 3 shows the cpu reference characteristics and cache hit ratios for simulations using the default parameters of Section 4. Since different

Table 3: Simulation Statistics

Benchmark and Scheme		f_n [a]	f_s [b]	f_{sy} [c]	f_{sw} [d]	h_s [e]	h_n [f]	h_i [g]
ssim	n	0.01	0.37	0.01	0.26	-	0.984	0.996
	f	0.01	0.37	0.02	0.25	0.987	0.984	0.997
	s	0.02	0.36	0.02	0.26	0.987	0.990	0.997
	t	0.01	0.37	0.02	0.25	0.987	0.984	0.997
verf	n	0.02	0.39	0.01	0.21	-	0.995	0.999
	f	0.03	0.39	0.01	0.21	0.952	0.996	0.999
	s	0.02	0.38	0.02	0.22	0.956	0.996	0.999
	t	0.03	0.38	0.01	0.21	0.967	0.996	0.999
genie	n	0.04	0.40	0.02	0.18	-	0.997	0.999
	f	0.03	0.39	0.03	0.19	0.973	0.997	0.999
	s	0.03	0.38	0.04	0.21	0.977	0.996	0.999
	t	0.03	0.39	0.03	0.19	0.981	0.997	0.999

[a] f_n is the fraction of references to non-shared writeable data.
[b] f_s is the fraction of references to shared writeable data.
[c] f_{sy} is the fraction of references to synchronization variables.
[d] f_{sw} is the fraction of references to shared writeable data that are writes.
[e] h_s is the hit ratio for references to shared writeable data.
[f] h_n is the hit ratio for references to non-shared writeable data.
[g] h_i is the hit ratio for references to instructions.

coherence schemes result in different dynamic referencing behavior at synchronization points, the breakdown of references for a given benchmark varies slightly. As expected, hit ratios for shared writeable data are lower than for data that is not shared writeable.

5.2 Overall Comparison

Figures 6 and 7 show the average access time (in cache cycles) and average network traffic (in bytes per cpu data reference) of the four coherence schemes. The per-process access time for each caching scheme was calculated by dividing the run-time of the process by the total number of cpu reads, writes (data only) and synchronization operations, and subtracting the cpu delay between accesses (see Section 4.1.2). Time spent sleeping at a barrier was subtracted from the total run-time. Per process average network traffic was calculated as the total number of bytes sent over the network divided by the total number of cpu reads, writes (data only) and synchronization operations. The numbers reported here are averages of the per-process average access time and network traffic for all child processes. The results of Figures 6 and 7, and all other results presented in this section, were derived from the portions of the simulations immediately following the forking of all child processes.

For all benchmarks the CANDF, SECTOR and TCACHE schemes provide substantial reductions in access time and network traffic over NOCACHE. Among the three superior schemes, CANDF and TCACHE perform similarly and considerably better than SECTOR. Although caching shared writeable data is very effective at reducing access time, the access times for CANDF and TCACHE range from 4 to 40 cache cycles, which is still unacceptable for high performance multiprocessing. Results in Subsection 5.7 suggest that the reason access times remain high is the presence of contention among synchronization references at barriers.

5.3 Cache Size Effects

Figures 8 and 9 show the effects of cache size on access time and network traffic for the CANDF scheme.

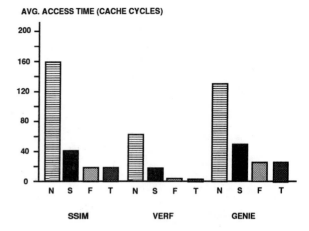

AVG. ACCESS TIME (CACHE CYCLES)

Figure 6: Access Time with Default Parameters

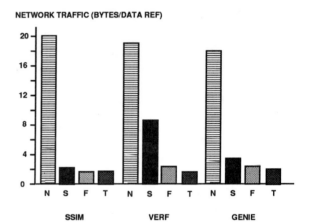

NETWORK TRAFFIC (BYTES/DATA REF)

Figure 7: Network Traffic with Default Parameters

Figure 8 shows that for the benchmarks considered, increasing the cache size results in little change in access time. Network traffic (Figure 9), on the other hand, noticeably increases for smaller cache sizes for the larger benchmarks. Access time does not vary as much as network traffic because displacements, which are a major source of network traffic for smaller cache sizes, do not stall the processor.

5.4 Performance of Sectored Scheme

The effects of cache size and block size on access time and network traffic are shown in Figures 10 and 11. The numbers beneath the bars in the figures indicate cache size and block size in bytes. Varying cache and block size has little effect on the small benchmark (*ssim*). For the larger benchmarks, increasing cache or block size results in moderate increases in access time. This is most likely due to increases in false sharing. As block size is increased, it becomes more likely for different caches to hold copies of blocks with disjoint sets of valid sub-blocks. This results in a greater number of unnecessary invalidations being sent to caches that do not have valid copies of the affected sub-block. As cache size is increased, blocks remain in caches longer so more copies of a cached block are likely to accumulate, drawing more redundant

144

AVG. ACCESS TIME (CACHE CYCLES)

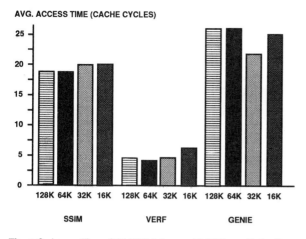

Figure 8: Access Time of CANDF Scheme with Different Cache Sizes

NETWORK TRAFFIC (BYTES/DATA REF)

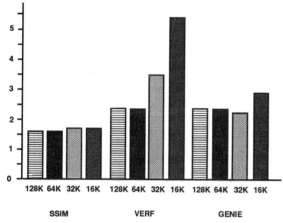

Figure 9: Network Traffic of CANDF Scheme with Different Cache Sizes

invalidation traffic. The effect of false sharing on network traffic is even more pronounced. Figure 11 shows that block size has a much larger impact than cache size on network traffic.

Although the absolute values of access time and network traffic are considerably better than those obtained without caching shared write-able data, they are considerably worse than those obtained for the CANDF and TCACHE schemes.

5.5 Performance of Tag Caching Scheme

Figures 12 and 13 show the effects of cache size and the number of full-size tags on TCACHE performance. The numbers beneath the bars in the figures show cache size and number of full-size tags (available to all 64 processors). Varying the cache size and number of tags has little effect on access time and network traffic except for the *verf* example. For *verf* the results obtained for different caches sizes in Subsection 5.3 indicate that miss traffic rises substantially when cache size is reduced from 64 to 32 kilobytes. The decrease in traffic when the number of

AVG. ACCESS TIME (CACHE CYCLES)

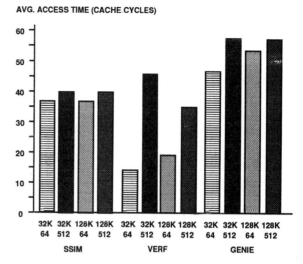

Figure 10: Access Time for Sectored Scheme

full tags is reduced from 4096 to 256 appears to be due to changes in invalidation behavior: when fewer full tags are available, data that is shared by several processors is invalidated more frequently when full tags are reused. For the *verf* example it appears that the premature invalidations caused by fewer available full tags has a beneficial effect by reducing false sharing.

In all cases the results are very close to those obtained for the CANDF scheme, in which an unlimited number of full tags are provided. The results add further support to the observation in [1] that very few blocks of data require more than one cache tag.

5.6 Invalidation Traffic

Figure 14 shows the number of invalidations issued per shared write for the CANDF and TCACHE schemes, and the SECTOR scheme with block sizes of 64 and 512 bytes. The figure shows that significantly more invalidations are issued in the SECTOR schemes because of false sharing. The CANDF and TCACHE results are similar, although the premature invalidations in TCACHE appear to reduce the total number of invalidations relative to CANDF.

5.7 Synchronization Traffic

The impact of synchronization traffic is illustrated in Figure 15, in which the fraction of network transactions due to synchronization references is shown for the four coherence schemes (with their default parameters). As expected, the fraction of synchronization traffic becomes more pronounced when shared writeable data is cached. Synchronization traffic is most extreme for *ssim* and *genie*, which both make extensive use of a small number of barriers. This suggests that the absolute average access times in Figure 6 are poor because of serialization at barrier points. If this is true, acceptable performance for the benchmarks considered may only be achievable by combining synchronization references [17] in hardware or software, or by drastically changing the structure of the programs so that they do not require barriers.

NETWORK TRAFFIC (BYTES/DATA REF)

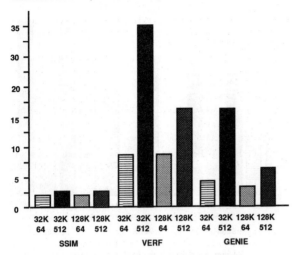

Figure 11: Network Traffic for Sectored Scheme

AVG. ACCESS TIME (CACHE CYCLES)

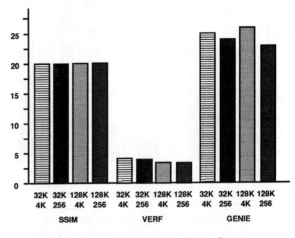

Figure 12: Access Time for Tag Caching Scheme

5.8 Inherent Parallelism of Benchmarks

A final set of simulation results were used to find the amount of parallelism in the benchmarks by comparing the execution times obtained for 4 and 64 simulated processors. The speedups from 4 to 64 processors for the three benchmarks were: 1.2 for *ssim*, 6.0 for *verf* and 6.3 for *genie*. Here speedup is the ratio of execution times for the two cases, with execution times measured from the beginning of parallel execution. The results were obtained using the CANDF scheme with a 128kB cache. The results of Subsection 5.7 suggest that more efficient support for handling concurrent access to locks and barriers may permit much better speedups with little modification to the original programs.

6 Conclusions

Two memory-efficient directory methods for scalable shared memory multiprocessors have been compared using instruction-level simulations of three benchmark programs. Both directory methods are variations of Censier and Feautrier's scheme [5]. The first (SECTOR) reduces directory tag overhead by using large sectored data blocks; the second (TCACHE) reduces tag overhead by using two tag sizes and by storing a much smaller number of them in an associative cache. For both schemes the amount of memory required to store directory tags can be reduced to 20% or less of the total main memory size for multiprocessors with up to 512 processors. Two other cache coherence schemes were used as reference points: a scheme in which shared writeable data is uncached (NOCACHE), and Censier and Feautrier's original scheme (CANDF).

As expected, caching shared writeable data using either the SECTOR or TCACHE schemes is effective at substantially reducing average memory access time and average network traffic for real multiprocessor applications in a shared memory multiprocessor; access time and network traffic were reduced by factors of 2 to 6, depending on the benchmark. Although the SECTOR scheme compares favorably to memory systems that do not cache shared writeable data, it performs substantially worse than the TCACHE scheme, and requires more tag memory for large numbers of processors. In addition, an examina-

NETWORK TRAFFIC (BYTES/DATA REF)

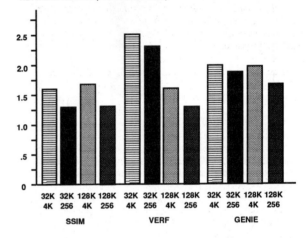

Figure 13: Network Traffic for Tag Caching Scheme

INVALS PER SHARED WRITE

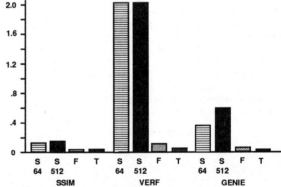

Figure 14: Invalidation Traffic of Sectored and Tag Caching Schemes

146

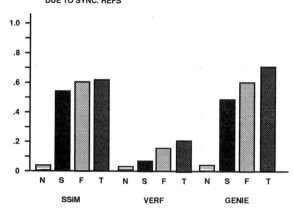

**FRACTION OF NETWORK TRANSACTIONS
DUE TO SYNC. REFS**

Figure 15: Fraction of Traffic Due to Synchronization References

tion of invalidation traffic shows that the SECTOR scheme generates a much larger number of invalidations by promoting false sharing with its large block size. Although the number and size of available directory tags is restricted in the TCACHE scheme, it performed as well as Censier and Feautrier's scheme with an unlimited number of full sized tags.

The simulations also show that increasing cache size above 32 kilobytes has little effect on access time and network traffic for the TCACHE and CANDF schemes. This was probably due to the fact that any reductions in miss ratio were minimal compared to the component of delay caused by synchronization traffic.

Although the TCACHE scheme performed much better than the NO-CACHE scheme, the absolute values of average access time were still unacceptably high, on the order of 4 to 40 cache cycles. The fraction of traffic due to synchronization references (which always bypass the cache) suggested that much of this delay is probably due to contention at barriers, which were heavily used in two of the three benchmarks. This indicates that for a multiprocessor cache memory system to be fully exploited, contention at barriers and other intensely shared locks must be reduced by program restructuring or sophisticated synchronization support, such as combining.

There remain many ways in which this study can be expanded. First, more benchmarks, especially those with greater parallelism, should be investigated. Simulations using more processors should also be performed to see if the conclusions of this study scale. A comparison of the coherence schemes considered here and several of the software methods is needed to determine if complex hardware support is really necessary. Analytic models should be developed and compared with these simulation results to refine current, and guide future, shared memory multiprocessor designs. Lastly, and ultimately, some multiprocessor hardware must be implemented to reveal the subtle and not-so-subtle effects that are frequently not revealed by simulation.

Acknowledgements

The authors would like to thank Alan Smith for comments on portions of this work, and to the anonymous reviewers for their helpful remarks. Funding was provided for this project by the Natural Sciences and Engineering Research Council of Canada, Digital Equipment Corporation, Hewlett Packard, and the Defense Advanced Research Projects Agency (under contract N00039-C-87-0182).

References

[1] A. Agarwal et al. An evaluation of directory schemes for cache coherence. In *Proceedings of the International Symposium on Computer Architecture*, pages 280–289, May 1988.

[2] J. Archibald and J-L. Baer. An economical solution to the cache coherence problem. In *Proceedings of the International Symposium on Computer Architecture*, pages 355–362, 1984.

[3] T. Axelrod et al. A simulator for MIMD performance prediction: Application to the S-1 MkIIa multiprocessor. *Parallel Computing*, 1:237–274, 1984.

[4] M. Carlton. private communication.

[5] L. M. Censier and P. Feautrier. A new solution to coherence problems in multicache systems. *IEEE Transactions on Computers*, C-27(12):1112–1118, Dec. 1978.

[6] S. Devadas and A. R. Newton. Topological optimization of multiple level array logic. *IEEE Transactions on Computer-Aided Design*, Nov. 1987.

[7] S. J. Eggers and R. H. Katz. A characterization of sharing in parallel programs and its application to coherency protocol evaluation. In *Proceedings of the International Symposium on Computer Architecture*, pages 373–383, June 1988.

[8] M. J. Flynn. Some computer organizations and their effectiveness. *IEEE Transactions on Computers*, C-21(9):948–960, Sept. 1972.

[9] D. Gajski et al. Cedar–a large scale multiprocessor. In *Proceedings of the International Conference on Parallel Processing*, pages 514–529, August 1983.

[10] J. R. Goodman and P. J. Woest. The Wisconsin Multicube: A new large-scale cache-coherent multiprocessor. In *Proceedings of the International Symposium on Computer Architecture*, pages 422–433, May 1988.

[11] A. Gottlieb et al. The NYU Ultracomputer–designing an MIMD shared memory parallel computer. *IEEE Transactions on Computers*, C-32(2):175–189, Feb. 1983.

[12] M. D. Hill and A. J. Smith. Experimental evaluation of on-chip microprocessor cache memories. In *Proceedings of the International Symposium on Computer Architecture*, pages 158–166, June 1984.

[13] E. A. Lee and D. G. Messerschmitt. Static scheduling of synchronous data flow programs for digital signal processing. *IEEE Transactions on Computers*, C-36(1):24–35, Jan. 1987.

[14] H. T. Ma et al. Logic verification algorithms and their parallel implementation. In *Proceedings of the Design Automation Conference*, pages 283–290, July 1987.

[15] G. F. Pfister et al. The IBM research parallel processor prototype (RP3): Introduction and architecture. In *Proceedings of the International Symposium on Computer Architecture*, June 1985.

[16] C. Scheurich and M. Dubois. Correct memory operation of cache-based multiprocessors. In *Proceedings of the International Symposium on Computer Architecture*, pages 234–243, June 1987.

[17] J. T. Schwartz. Ultracomputers. *ACM Transactions on Programming Languages and Systems*, 2(4):484–521, Oct. 1980.

[18] H. J. Siegel. *Interconnection Networks for Large-Scale Parallel Processing*. Lexington Books, 1985.

[19] A. J. Smith. Cache memories. *Computing Surveys*, 14(3):473–530, Sept. 1982.

[20] H. S. Stone. *High-Performance Computer Architecture*. Addison-Wesley Publishing Company, 1987.

[21] A. W. Wilson Jr. Hierarchical cache/bus architecture for shared memory multiprocessors. In *Proceedings of the International Symposium on Computer Architecture*, pages 244–252, June 1987.

The Directory-Based Cache Coherence Protocol
for the DASH Multiprocessor

Daniel Lenoski, James Laudon, Kourosh Gharachorloo,
Anoop Gupta, and John Hennessy

Computer Systems Laboratory
Stanford University, CA 94305

Abstract

DASH is a scalable shared-memory multiprocessor currently being developed at Stanford's Computer Systems Laboratory. The architecture consists of powerful processing nodes, each with a portion of the shared-memory, connected to a scalable interconnection network. A key feature of DASH is its distributed directory-based cache coherence protocol. Unlike traditional snoopy coherence protocols, the DASH protocol does not rely on broadcast; instead it uses point-to-point messages sent between the processors and memories to keep caches consistent. Furthermore, the DASH system does not contain any single serialization or control point. While these features provide the basis for scalability, they also force a reevaluation of many fundamental issues involved in the design of a protocol. These include the issues of correctness, performance and protocol complexity. In this paper, we present the design of the DASH coherence protocol and discuss how it addresses the above issues. We also discuss our strategy for verifying the correctness of the protocol and briefly compare our protocol to the IEEE Scalable Coherent Interface protocol.

1 Introduction

The limitations of current uniprocessor speeds and the ability to replicate low cost, high-performance processors and VLSI components have provided the impetus for the design of multiprocessors which are capable of scaling to a large number of processors. Two major paradigms for these multiprocessor architectures have developed, *message-passing* and *shared-memory*. In a message-passing multiprocessor, each processor has a local memory, which is only accessible to that processor. Interprocessor communication occurs only through explicit message passing. In a shared-memory multiprocessor, all memory is accessible to each processor. The shared-memory paradigm has the advantage that the programmer is not burdened with the issues of data partitioning, and accessibility of data from all processors simplifies the task of dynamic load distribution. The primary advantage of the message passing systems is the ease with which they scale to support a large number of processors. For shared-memory machines providing such scalability has traditionally proved difficult to achieve.

We are currently building a prototype of a scalable shared-memory multiprocessor. The system provides high processor performance and scalability though the use of coherent caches and a directory-based coherence protocol. The high-level or-

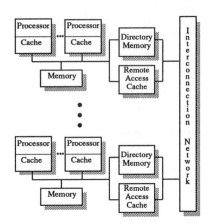

Figure 1: General architecture of DASH.

ganization of the prototype, called DASH (Directory Architecture for SHared memory) [17], is shown in Figure 1. The architecture consists of a number of processing nodes connected through a high-bandwidth low-latency interconnection network. The physical memory in the machine is distributed among the nodes of the multiprocessor, with all memory accessible to each node. Each processing node, or *cluster*, consists of a small number of high-performance processors with their individual caches, a portion of the shared-memory, a common cache for pending remote accesses, and a directory controller interfacing the cluster to the network. A bus-based snoopy scheme is used to keep caches coherent within a cluster, while inter-node cache consistency is maintained using a distributed directory-based coherence protocol.

The concept of directory-based cache coherence was first proposed by Tang [20] and Censier and Feautrier [6]. Subsequently, it has been been investigated by others ([1],[2] and [23]). Building on this earlier work, we have developed a new directory-based cache-coherence protocol which works with distributed directories and the hierarchical cluster configuration of DASH. The protocol also integrates support for efficient synchronization operations using the directory. Furthermore, in designing the machine we have addressed many of the issues left unresolved by earlier work.

In DASH, each processing node has a directory memory corresponding to its portion of the shared physical memory. For each memory block, the directory memory stores the identities

CH2887-8/90/0000/0148$01.00 © 1990 IEEE

of all remote nodes caching that block. Using the directory memory, a node writing a location can send point-to-point invalidation or update messages to those processors that are actually caching that block. This is in contrast to the invalidating broadcast required by the snoopy protocol. The scalability of DASH depends on this ability to avoid broadcasts. Another important attribute of the directory-based protocol is that it does not depend on any specific interconnection network topology. As a result, we can readily use any of the low-latency scalable networks, such as meshes or hypercubes, that were originally developed for message-passing machines [7].

While the design of bus-based snoopy coherence protocols is reasonably well understood, this is not true of distributed directory-based protocols. Unlike snoopy protocols, directory-based schemes do not have a single serialization point for all memory transactions. While this feature is responsible for their scalability, it also makes them more complex and forces one to rethink how the protocol should address the fundamental issues of correctness, system performance, and complexity.

The next section outlines the important issues in designing a cache coherence protocol. Section 3 gives an overview of the DASH hardware architecture. Section 4 describes the design of the DASH coherence protocol, relating it to the issues raised in section 2. Section 5 outlines some of the additional operations supported beyond the base protocol, while Section 6 discusses scaling the directory structure. Section 7 briefly describes our approach to verifying the correctness of the protocol. Section 8 compares the DASH protocol with the proposed IEEE-SCI (Scalable Coherent Interface) protocol for distributed directory-based cache coherence. Finally, section 9 presents conclusions and summarizes the current status of the design effort.

2 Design Issues for Distributed Coherence Protocols

The issues that arise in the design of any cache coherence protocol and, in particular, a distributed directory-based protocol, can be divided into three categories: those that deal with correctness, those that deal with the performance, and those related to the distributed control of the protocol.

2.1 Correctness

The foremost issue that any multiprocessor cache coherence protocol must address is correctness. This translates into requirements in three areas:

Memory Consistency Model: For a uniprocessor, the model of a correct memory system is well defined. Load operations return the last value written to a given memory location. Likewise, store operations bind the value returned by subsequent loads of the location until the next store. For multiprocessors, however, the issue is more complex because the definitions of "last value written", "subsequent loads" and "next store" become less clear as there may be multiple processors reading and writing a location. To resolve this difficulty a number of memory consistency models have been proposed in the literature, most notably, the sequential and weak consistency models [8]. Weaker consistency models attempt to loosen the constraints on the coherence protocol while still providing a reasonable programming model for the user. Although most existing systems

utilize a relatively strong consistency model, the larger latencies found in a distributed system favor the less constrained models.

Deadlock: A protocol must also be deadlock free. Given the arbitrary communication patterns and finite buffering within the memory system there are numerous opportunities for deadlock. For example, a deadlock can occur if a set of transactions holds network and buffer resources in a circular manner, and the consumption of one request requires the generation of another request. Similarly, lack of flow control in nodes can cause requests to back up into the network, blocking the flow of other messages that may be able to release the congestion.

Error Handling: Another issue related to correctness is support for data integrity and fault tolerance. Any large system will exhibit failures, and it is generally unacceptable if these failures result in corrupted data or incorrect results without a failure indication. This is especially true for parallel applications where algorithms are more complex and may contain some non-determinism which limits repeatability. Unfortunately, support for data integrity and fault-tolerance within a complex protocol that attempts to minimize latency and is executed directly by hardware is difficult. The protocol must attempt to balance the level of data integrity with the increase in latency and hardware complexity. At a minimum, the protocol should be able to flag all detectable failures, and convey this information to the processors affected.

2.2 Performance

Given a protocol that is correct, performance becomes the next important design criterion. The two key metrics of memory system performance are latency and bandwidth.

Latency: Performance is primarily determined by the latency experienced by memory requests. In DASH, support for cachable shared data provides the major reduction in latency. The latency of write misses is reduced by using write buffers and by the support of the release consistency model. Hiding the latency for read misses is usually more critical since the processor is stalled until data is returned. To reduce the latency for read misses, the protocol must minimize the number of inter-cluster messages needed to service a miss and the delay associated with each such message.

Bandwidth: Providing high memory bandwidth that scales with the number of processors is key to any large system. Caches and distributed memory form the basis for a scalable, high-bandwidth memory system in DASH. Even with distributed memory, however, bandwidth is limited by the serialization of requests in the memory system and the amount of traffic generated by each memory request.

Servicing a memory request in a distributed system often requires several messages to be transmitted. For example, a message to access a remote location generates a reply message containing the data, and possibly other messages invalidating remote caches. The component with the largest serialization in this chain limits the maximum throughput of requests. Serialization affects performance by increasing the queuing delays, and thus the latency, of memory requests. Queuing delays can become critical for locations that exhibit a large degree of sharing. A protocol should attempt to minimize the service time at all queuing centers. In particular, in a distributed system no central resources within a node should be blocked while inter-node communication is taking place to service a request. In this way serialization is limited only by the time of local, intra-node operations.

The amount of traffic generated per request also limits the effective throughput of the memory system. Traffic seen by the global interconnect and memory subsystem increases the queueing for these shared resources. DASH reduces traffic by providing coherent caches and by distributing memory among the processors. Caches filter many of the requests for shared data while grouping memory with processors removes private references if the corresponding memory is allocated within the local cluster. At the protocol level, the number of messages required to service different types of memory requests should be minimized, unless the extra messages directly contribute to reduced latency or serialization.

2.3 Distributed Control and Complexity

A coherence protocol designed to address the above issues must be partitioned among the distributed components of the multiprocessor. These components include the processors and their caches, the directory and main memory controllers, and the interconnection network. The lack of a single serialization point, such as a bus, complicates the control since transactions do not complete atomically. Furthermore, multiple paths within the memory system and lack of a single arbitration point within the system allow some operations to complete out of order. The result is that there is a rich set of interactions that can take place between different memory and coherence transactions. Partitioning the control of the protocol requires a delicate balance between the performance of the system and the complexity of the components. Too much complexity may effect the ability to implement the protocol or ensure that the protocol is correct.

3 Overview of DASH

Figure 2 shows a high-level picture of the DASH prototype we are building at Stanford. In order to manage the size of the prototype design effort, a commercial bus-based multiprocessor was chosen as the processing node. Each node (or *cluster*) is a Silicon Graphics POWER Station 4D/240 [4]. The 4D/240 system consists of four high-performance processors, each connected to a 64 Kbyte first-level instruction cache, and a 64 Kbyte write-through data cache. The 64 Kbyte data cache interfaces to a 256 Kbyte second-level write-back cache through a read buffer and a 4 word deep write-buffer. The main purpose of this second-level cache is to convert the write-through policy of the first-level to a write-back policy, and to provide the extra cache tags for bus snooping. Both the first and second-level caches are direct-mapped.

In the 4D/240, the second-level caches are responsible for bus snooping and maintaining consistency among the caches in the cluster. Consistency is maintained using the Illinois coherence protocol [19], which is an invalidation-based ownership protocol. Before a processor can write to a cache line, it must first acquire exclusive ownership of that line by requesting that all other caches invalidate their copy of that line. Once a processor has exclusive ownership of a cache line, it may write to that line without consuming further bus cycles.

The memory bus (MPBUS) of the 4D/240 is a pipelined synchronous bus, supporting memory-to-cache and cache-to-cache transfers of 16 bytes every 4 bus clocks with a latency of 6 bus clocks. While the MPBUS is pipelined, it is not a split transaction bus. Consequently, it is not possible to efficiently interleave long duration remote transactions with the short duration local

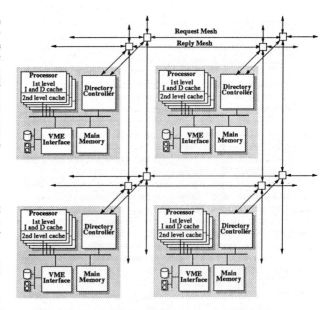

Figure 2: Block diagram of sample 2 x 2 DASH system.

transactions. Since this ability is critical to DASH, we have extended the MPBUS protocol to support a retry mechanism. Remote requests are signaled to retry while the inter-cluster messages are being processed. To avoid unnecessary retries the processor is masked from arbitration until the response from the remote request has been received. When the response arrives, the requesting processor is unmasked, retries the request on the bus, and is supplied the remote data.

A DASH system consists of a number of modified 4D/240 systems that have been supplemented with a directory controller board. This directory controller board is responsible for maintaining the cache coherence across the nodes and serving as the interface to the interconnection network.

The directory board is implemented on a single printed circuit board and consists of five major subsystems as shown in Figure 3. The *directory controller* (DC) contains the directory memory corresponding to the portion of main memory present within the cluster. It also initiates out-bound network requests and replies. The *pseudo-CPU* (PCPU) is responsible for buffering incoming requests and issuing such requests on the cluster bus. It mimics a CPU on this bus on behalf of remote processors except that responses from the bus are sent out by the directory controller. The *reply controller* (RC) tracks outstanding requests made by the local processors and receives and buffers the corresponding replies from remote clusters. It acts as memory when the local processors are allowed to retry their remote requests. The *network interface* and the local portion of the network itself reside on the directory card. The interconnection network consists of a pair of meshes. One mesh is dedicated to the request messages while the other handles replies. These meshes utilize *wormhole routing* [9] to minimize latency. Finally, the board contains *hardware monitoring logic* and miscellaneous control and status registers. The monitoring logic samples a variety of directory board and bus events from which usage and performance statistics can be derived.

The directory memory is organized as an array of directory

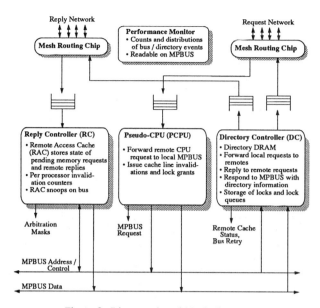

Figure 3: Directory board block diagram.

entries. There is one entry for each memory block. The directory entries used in the prototype are identical to that originally proposed in [6]. They are composed of a single state bit together with a bit vector of pointers to clusters. The state bit indicates whether the clusters have a read (shared) or read/write (dirty) copy of the data. The bit vector contains a bit for each of the sixteen clusters supported in the prototype. Associating the directory with main memory allows the directory to be built with the same DRAM technology as main memory. The DC accesses the directory memory on each MPBUS transaction along with the access to main memory. The directory information is combined with the type of bus operation, address, and result of the snooping within the cluster to determine what network messages and bus controls the DC will generate.

The RC maintains its state in the *remote access cache* (RAC). The functions of the RAC include maintaining the state of currently outstanding requests, buffering replies from the network and supplementing the functionality of the processors' caches. The RAC is organized as a snoopy cache with augmented state information. The RAC's state machines allow accesses from both the network and the cluster bus. Replies from the network are buffered in the RAC and cause the waiting processor to be released for bus arbitration. When the released processor retries the access the RAC supplies the data via a cache-to-cache transfer.

3.1 Memory Consistency in DASH

As stated in Section 2, the correctness of the coherence protocol is a function of the memory consistency model adopted by the architecture. There is a whole spectrum of choices for the level of consistency to support directly in hardware. At one end is the *sequential consistency* model [16] which requires the execution of the parallel program to appear as some interleaving of the execution of the parallel processes on a sequential machine. As one moves towards weaker models of consistency, performance

gains are made at the cost of a more complex programming model for the user.

The base model of consistency provided by the DASH hardware is called *release consistency*. Release consistency [10] is an extension of the weak consistency model first proposed by Dubois, Scheurich and Briggs [8]. The distinguishing characteristics of release consistency is that it allows memory operations issued by a given processor to be observed and complete out of order with respect to the other processors. The ordering of operations is only preserved before "releasing" synchronization operations or explicit ordering operations. Release consistency takes advantage of the fact that while in a critical region a programmer has already assured that no other processor is accessing the protected variables. Thus, updates to these variables can be observed by other processors in arbitrary order. Only before the lock release at the end of the region does the hardware need to guarantee that all operations have completed. While release consistency docs complicate programming and the coherence protocol, it can hide much of the overhead of write operations.

Support for release consistency puts several requirements on the system. First, the hardware must support a primitive which guarantees the ordering of memory operations at specific points in a program. Such fence [5, 10] primitives can then be placed by software before releasing synchronization points in order to implement release consistency. DASH supports two explicit fence mechanisms. A *full-fence* operation stalls the processor until all of its pending operations have been completed, while a *write-fence* simply delays subsequent write-operations. A higher performance implementation of release consistency includes implicit fence operations within the releasing synchronization operations themselves. DASH supports such synchronization operations yielding release consistency as its base consistency model. The explicit fence operations in DASH then allow the user or compiler to synthesize stricter consistency models if needed.

The release consistency model also places constraints on the base coherence protocol. First, the system must respect the local dependencies generated by the memory operations of a single processor. Second, all coherence operations, especially operations related to writes, must be acknowledged so that the issuing processor can determine when a fence can proceed. Third, any cache line owned with pending invalidations against it can not be shared between processors. This prevents the new processor from improperly passing a fence. If sharing is allowed then the receiving processor must be informed when all of the pending invalidates have been acknowledged. Lastly, any operations that a processor issues after a fence operation may not become visible to any other processor until all operations preceding the fence have completed.

4 The DASH Cache Coherence Protocol

In our discussion of the coherence protocol, we use the following naming conventions for the various clusters and memories involved in any given transaction. A *local cluster* is a cluster that contains the processor originating a given request, while the *home cluster* is the cluster which contains the main memory and directory for a given physical memory address. A *remote cluster* is any other cluster. Likewise, *local memory* refers to the main memory associated with the local cluster while *remote memory* is any memory whose home is not the local.

The DASH coherence protocol is an invalidation-based ownership protocol. A memory block can be in one of three states as indicated by the associated directory entry: (i) *uncached-remote*, that is not cached by any remote cluster; (ii) *shared-remote*, that is cached in an unmodified state by one or more remote clusters; or (iii) *dirty-remote*, that is cached in a modified state by a single remote cluster. The directory does not maintain information concerning whether the home cluster itself is caching a memory block because all transactions that change the state of a memory block are issued on the bus of the home cluster, and the snoopy bus protocol keeps the home cluster coherent. While we could have chosen not to issue all transactions on the home cluster's bus this would had an insignificant performance improvement since most requests to the home also require an access to main memory to retrieve the actual data.

The protocol maintains the notion of an *owning cluster* for each memory block. The owning cluster is nominally the home cluster. However, in the case that a memory block is present in the dirty state in a remote cluster, that cluster is the owner. Only the owning cluster can complete a remote reference for a given block and update the directory state. While the directory entry is always maintained in the home cluster, a dirty cluster initiates all changes to the directory state of a block when it is the owner (such update messages also indicate that the dirty cluster is giving up ownership). The order that operations reach the owning cluster determines their global order.

As with memory blocks, a cache block in a processor's cache may also be in one of three states: invalid, shared, and dirty. The shared state implies that there may be other processors caching that location. The dirty state implies that this cache contains an exclusive copy of the memory block, and the block has been modified.

The following sections outline the three primitive operations supported by the base DASH coherence protocol: read, read-exclusive and write-back. We also discuss how the protocol responds to the issues that were brought up in Section 2 and some of the alternative design choices that were considered. We describe only the normal flow for the memory transactions in the following sections, exception cases are covered in section 4.6.

4.1 Read Requests

Memory read requests are initiated by processor load instructions. If the location is present in the processor's first-level cache, the cache simply supplies the data. If not present, then a cache fill operation must bring the required block into the first-level cache. A fill operation first attempts to find the cache line in the processor's second-level cache, and if unsuccessful, the processor issues a read request on the bus. This read request either completes locally or is signaled to retry while the directory board interacts with the other clusters to retrieve the required cache line. The detailed flow for a read request is given in Figure 7 in the appendix.

The protocol tries to minimize latency by using cache-to-cache transfers. The local bus can satisfy a remote read if the given line is held in another processor's cache or the remote access cache (RAC). The four processor caches together with the RAC form a five-way set associative (1.25 Mbyte) cluster cache. The effective size of this cache is smaller than a true set associative cache because the entries in the caches need not be distinct. The check for a local copy is initiated by the normal snooping when the read is issued on the bus. If the cache line is present in the shared state then the data is simply transferred over the bus to the requesting processor and no access to the

remote home cluster is needed. If the cache line is held in a dirty state by a local processor, however, something must be done with the ownership of the cache line since the processor supplying the data goes to a shared state in the Illinois protocol used on the cluster bus. The two options considered were to: (i) have the directory do a sharing write-back to the home cluster; and (ii) have the RAC take ownership of the cache line. We chose the second option because it permits the processors within a cluster to read and write a shared location without causing traffic in the network or home cluster.

If a read request cannot be satisfied by the local cluster, the processor is forced to retry the bus operation, and a request message is sent to the home cluster. At the same time the processor is masked from arbitration so that it does not tie up the local bus. Whenever a remote request is sent by a cluster, a RAC entry is allocated to act as a placeholder for the reply to this request. The RAC entry also permits merging of requests made by the different processors within the same cluster. If another request to the same memory block is made, a new request will not be sent to the home cluster; this reduces both traffic and latency. On the other hand, an access to a different memory block, which happens to map to a RAC entry already in use, must be delayed until the pending operation is complete. Given that the number of active RAC entries is small the benefit of merging should outweigh the potential for contention.

When the read request reaches the home cluster, it is issued on that cluster's bus. This causes the directory to look up the status of that memory block. If the block is in an uncached-remote or shared-remote state the directory controller sends the data over the reply network to the requesting cluster. It also records the fact that the requesting cluster now has a copy of the memory block. If the block is in the dirty-remote state, however, the read request is forwarded to the owning, dirty cluster. The owning cluster sends out two messages in response to the read. A message containing the data is sent directly to the requesting cluster, and a sharing writeback request is sent to the home cluster. The sharing writeback request writes the cache block back to memory and also updates the directory. The flow of messages for this case is shown in Figure 4.

As shown in Figure 4, any request not satisfied in the home cluster is forwarded to the remote cluster that has a dirty copy of the data. This reduces latency by permitting the dirty cluster to respond directly to the requesting cluster. In addition, this forwarding strategy allows the directory controller to simultaneously process many requests (i.e. to be multithreaded) without the added complexity of maintaining the state of outstanding requests. Serialization is reduced to the time of a single intra-cluster bus transaction. The only resource held while inter-cluster messages are being sent is a single entry in the originating cluster's RAC.

The downside of the forwarding strategy is that it can result in additional latency when simultaneous accesses are made to the same block. For example, if two read requests from different clusters are received close together for a line that is dirty remote, both will be forwarded to the dirty cluster. However, only the first one will be satisfied since this request will force the dirty cluster to lose ownership by doing a sharing writeback and changing its local state to read only. The second request will not find the dirty data and will be returned with a *negative acknowledge* (NAK) to its originating cluster. This NAK will force the cluster to retry its access. An alternative to the forwarding approach used by our protocol would have been to buffer the read request at the home cluster, have the home send

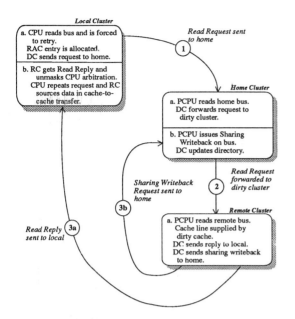

Figure 4: Flow of Read Request to remote memory with directory in dirty-remote state.

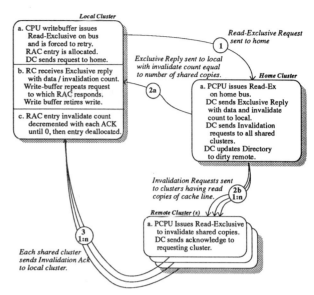

Figure 5: Flow of Read-Exclusive Request to remote memory with directory in shared-remote state.

a flush request to the owning cluster, and then have the home send the data back to the originating cluster. We did not adopt this approach because it would have increased the latency for such reads by adding an extra network and bus transaction. Additionally, it would have required buffers in the directory to hold the pending transaction, or blocking subsequent accesses to the directory until the first request had been satisfied.

4.2 Read-Exclusive Requests

Write operations are initiated by processor store instructions. Data is written through the first-level cache and is buffered in a four word deep write-buffer. The second-level cache can retire the write if it has ownership of the line. Otherwise, a read-exclusive request is issued to the bus to acquire sole ownership of the line and retrieve the other words in the cache block. Obtaining ownership does not block the processor directly; only the write-buffer output is stalled. As in the case of read requests, cache coherence operations begin when the read-exclusive request is issued on the bus. The detailed flow of read-exclusive request is given in the appendix in Figure 9 and is summarized below.

The flow of a read-exclusive is similar to that of a read request. Once the request is issued on the bus, it checks other caches at the local cluster level. If one of those caches has that memory block in the dirty state (it is the owner), then that cache supplies the data and ownership and invalidates its own copy. If the memory block is not owned by the local cluster, a request for ownership is sent to the home cluster. As in the case of read requests, a RAC entry is allocated to receive the ownership and data.

At the home cluster, the read-exclusive request is echoed on the bus. If the memory block is in an uncached-remote or shared-remote state the data and ownership are immediately sent

back over the reply network. In addition, if the block is in the shared-remote state, each cluster caching the block is sent an invalidation request. The requesting cluster receives the data as before, and is also informed of the number of invalidation acknowledge messages to expect. Remote clusters send invalidation acknowledge messages to the requesting cluster after completing their invalidation. As discussed in Section 3.1, the invalidation acknowledges are needed by the requesting processor to know when the store has been completed with respect to all processors. The RAC entry in the requesting cluster persists until all invalidation acknowledges have been received. The receipt of the acknowledges generally occurs after the processor itself has been granted exclusive ownership of the cache line and continued execution. Figure 5 depicts this shared-remote case.

If the directory indicates a dirty-remote state, then the request is forwarded to the owning cluster as in a read request. At the dirty cluster, the read-exclusive request is issued on the bus. This causes the owning processor to invalidate that block from its cache and to send a message to the requesting cluster granting ownership and supplying the data. In parallel, a request is sent to the home cluster to update ownership of the block. On receiving this message, the home sends an acknowledgment to the new owning cluster. This extra acknowledgment is needed because the requesting cluster (the new owning cluster) may give up ownership (e.g. due to a writeback) even before the home directory has received an ownership change message from the previous owner. If these messages reach the home out of order the directory will become permanently inconsistent. The extra acknowledgment guarantees that the new owner retain ownership until the directory has been updated.

Performance of the read and write operations is closely related to the speed of the MPBUS and the latency of inter-cluster communication. Figure 6 shows the latencies for various mem-

Read Operations	
Hit in 1st Level Cache	1 pclock
Fill from 2nd Level Cache	12 pclock
Fill from Local Cluster	22 pclock
Fill from Remote Cluster	61 pclock
Fill from Dirty Remote, Remote Home	80 pclock

Fill operations fetch 16 byte cache blocks and empty the write-buffer before fetching the read-miss cache block.

Write Operations	
Hit on 2nd Level Owned Block	3 pclock
Owned by Local Cluster	18 pclock
Owned in Remote Cluster	57 pclock
Owned in Dirty Remote, Remote Home	76 pclock

Write operations only stall the write-buffer, not the processor, while the fill is outstanding.
Write delays assume Release Consistency (i.e. they do not wait for remote invalidates to be acknowledged).

Figure 6: Latency for various memory system operations in processor clocks. Each processor clock in the prototype is 40 ns.

ory operations in the DASH prototype assuming no network or bus contention. The figure illustrates the one-to-one relationship between the latency of an operation and its corresponding number of network hops and bus transactions. In DASH, the network and directory board overhead is roughly equal to the CPU overhead to initiate a bus transaction. Thus, if an intracluster bus transaction takes roughly 20 processor clocks then an inter-cluster transaction that involves two clusters, (i.e. three bus transactions) takes roughly 60 processor clocks, and a three cluster transaction takes 80 processor clocks.

4.3 Writeback Requests

A dirty cache line that is replaced must be written back to memory. If the home of the memory block is the local cluster, then the data is simply written back to main memory. If the home cluster is remote, then a message is sent to the remote home which updates the main memory and marks the block uncached-remote. The flow of a writeback operation is given in the appendix in Figure 8.

4.4 Bus Initiated Cache Transactions

CPU initiated transactions have been described in the preceding sections. The protocol also includes transitions made by the slave caches that are monitoring their respective buses. These transitions are equivalent to those in a normal snoopy bus protocol. In particular, a read operation on the bus will cause a dirty cache to supply data and change to a shared state. Dirty data will also be written back to main memory (or the RAC if remote). A read-exclusive operation on the bus will cause all other cached copies of the line to be invalidated. Note that when a valid line in the second-level cache is invalidated, the first-level cache is also invalidated so that the processor's second-level cache is a superset of the first-level cache.

4.5 Support for Memory Consistency

As discussed in section 3.1, DASH supports the release consistency model. Memory system latency is reduced because the

semantics of release consistency allows the processor to continue after issuing a write operation. The write-buffer within the processor holds the pending operation, and the write-buffer is allowed to retire the write before the operation has completed with respect to all processors. The processor itself is allowed to continue while the write-buffer and directory controller are completing the previous operations. Ordering of memory accesses is only guaranteed between operations separated by a releasing synchronization operation or an explicit fence operation. Upon a write-fence (explicit or implicit), all previous read and write operations issued by this processor must have completed with respect to all processors before any additional write operations can become visible to other processors.

DASH implements a write fence by blocking a processor's access to its second-level cache and the MPBUS until all reads and writes it issued before the write fence have completed. This is done by stalling the write-fence (which is mapped to a store operation) in the processor's write-buffer. Guaranteeing that preceding reads and writes have been performed without imposing undue processor stalls is the challenge. A first requirement is that all invalidation operations must be acknowledged. As illustrated in Figure 5, a write operation to shared data can proceed after receiving the exclusive reply from the directory, but the RAC entry associated with this operation persists until all of the acknowledges are received by the reply controller (RC). Each RAC entry is tagged with the processor that is responsible for this entry and each processor has a dedicated counter in the RC which counts the total number of RAC entries in use by that processor. A write fence stalls until the counter for that processor is decremented to zero. At this point, the processor has no outstanding RAC entries, so all of its invalidation acknowledges must have been received.

We observe that simply using a per processor counter to keep track of the number of outstanding invalidations is not sufficient to support release consistency. A simple counter does not allow the processor cache to distinguish between dirty cache lines that have outstanding invalidates from those that do not. This results in another processor not being able to detect whether a line returned by a dirty cache has outstanding invalidates. The requesting processor could then improperly pass through a fence operation. Storing the pending invalidate count on a per cache line basis in the RAC, and having the RAC snoop bus transactions, allows cache lines with pending invalidates to be distinguished. The RAC forces a reject of remote requests to such blocks with a NAK reply. Local accesses are allowed, but the RAC adds the new processor to its entry for the line making this processor also responsible for the original invalidations. Write-back requests of a line with outstanding invalidations are blocked by having the RAC take dirty ownership of the cache block.

In the protocol, invalidation acknowledges are sent to the local cluster that initiated the memory request. An alternative would be for the home cluster to gather the acknowledges, and, when all have been received, send a message to the requesting cluster indicating that the request has been completed. We chose the former because it reduces the waiting time for completion of a subsequent fence operation by the requesting cluster and reduces the potential of a hot spot developing at the memory.

4.6 Exception Conditions

The description of the protocol listed above does not cover all of the conditions that the actual protocol must address. While enumerating all of the possible exceptions and protocol responses would require an overly detailed discussion, this section introduces most of the exception cases and gives an idea of how the protocol responds to each exception.

One exception case is that a request forwarded to a dirty cluster may arrive there to find that the dirty cluster no longer owns the data. This may occur if another access had previously been forwarded to the dirty cluster and changed the ownership of the block, or if the owning cluster performs a writeback. In these cases, the originating cluster is sent a NAK response and is required to reissue the request. By this time ownership should have stabilized and the request will be satisfied. Note that the reissue is accomplished by simply releasing the processor's arbitration mask and treating this as a new request instead of replying with data.

In very pathological cases, for example when ownership for a block is bouncing back and forth between two remote clusters, a requesting cluster (some third cluster) may receive multiple NAK's and may eventually time-out and return a bus error. While this is undesirable, its occurrence is very improbable in the prototype system and, consequently, we do not provide a solution. In larger systems this problem is likely to need a complete answer. One solution would be to implement an additional directory state which signifies that other clusters are queued for access. Only the first access for a dirty line would be forwarded while this request and subsequent requests are queued in the directory entry. Upon receipt of the next ownership change the directory can respond to all of the requests if they are for read only copies. If some are for exclusive access then ownership can be granted to each in turn on a pseudo-random basis. Thus, eventually all requests will be fulfilled.

Another set of exceptions arise from the multiple paths present in the system. In particular, the separate request and reply networks together with their associated input and output FIFO's and bus requesters imply that some messages sent between two clusters can be received out of order. The protocol can handle most of these misorderings because operations are acknowledged and out-of-order requests simple receive NAK responses. Other cases require more attention. For example, a read reply can be overtaken by an invalidate request attempting to purge the read copy. This case is handled by the snooping on the RAC. When the RAC sees an invalidation request for a pending read, it changes the state of that RAC entry to invalidated-read-pending. In this state, the RC conservatively assumes that any read reply is stale and treats the reply as a NAK response.

4.7 Deadlock

In the DASH prototype, deadlocks are eliminated through a combination of hardware and protocol features. At the hardware level, DASH consists of two mesh networks, each of which guarantees point-to-point delivery of messages without deadlocks. However, this by itself is not sufficient to prevent deadlocks because the consumption of an incoming message may require the generation of another outgoing message. This can result in circular dependencies between the limited buffers present in two or more nodes and cause deadlock.

To address this problem, the protocol divides all messages into request messages (e.g. read and read-exclusive requests and invalidation requests) and reply messages (e.g. read and read-exclusive replies and invalidation acknowledges). Furthermore, one mesh is dedicated to servicing request messages while the

other handles reply messages. Reply messages are guaranteed to be consumed at the destination, partly because of their nature and partly because space for the reply data is preallocated in the RAC. This eliminates the possibility of request-reply circular dependencies and the associated deadlocks.

However, the protocol also relies on request messages that generate additional requests. Because of the limited buffer space, this can result in deadlocks due to request-request circular dependencies. Fairly large input and output FIFO's reduce the probability of this problem. If it does arise, the directory hardware includes a time-out mechanism to break the possible deadlock. If the directory has been blocked for more than the time-out period in attempting to forward a request it will instead reject the request with a NAK reply message. Once this deadlock breaking mode is entered enough other requests are handled similarly so that any possible deadlock condition that has arisen within the request network can be eliminated. As in cases discussed earlier, this scheme relies on the processor's ability to reissue its request upon receiving a NAK.

4.8 Error Handling

The final set of exceptions arise in response to error conditions in the hardware or protocol. The system includes a number of error checks including ECC on main memory, parity on the directory memory, length checking of network messages and inconsistent bus and network message checking. These checks are reported to processors through bus errors and associated error capture registers. Network errors and improper requests are dropped by the receiver of such messages. Depending upon the type of network message that was lost or corrupted, the issuing processor will eventually time-out its originating request or some fence operation which will be blocked waiting for a RAC entry to be deallocated. The time-out generates a bus-error which interrupts the processor. The processes using the particular memory location are aborted, but low level operating system code can recover from the error if it is not within the kernel. The OS can subsequently clean up the state of a line by using back-door paths that allow direct addressing of the RAC and directory memory.

5 Supplemental Operations

During the evolution of the DASH protocol, several additional memory operations were evaluated. Some of these operations are included in the DASH prototype, while others were not included due to hardware constraints or a lack of evidence that the extension would provide significant performance gains.

The first major extension incorporated into the DASH protocol was support for synchronization operations. The sharing characteristics of synchronization objects are often quite different from those of normal data. Locks, barriers, and semaphores can be highly contended. Using the normal directory protocol for synchronization objects can lead to hot spots. For example, when a highly contended lock is released, all processor caches containing the lock are invalidated; this invalidation results in the waiting processors rushing to grab the lock. DASH provides special *queue-based lock* primitives that use the directory memory to keep track of clusters waiting for a lock. Using the directory memory is natural since it is already set up to track queued clusters, and the directory is normally accessed in read-modify-write cycles that match the atomic update necessary for locks. An unlock of a queue-based lock while clusters are waiting results in a grant of the lock being sent to one of the waiting clusters. This grant allows the cluster to obtain the lock without any further network messages. Thus, queue-based locks reduce the hot spotting generated by contended locks and reduce the latency between an unlock operation and subsequent acquisition of the lock. This and other synchronization primitives are discussed in detail in [17].

Another set of operations included in the prototype help hide the latency of memory operations. Normally, when a read is issued the processor is stalled until the data comes back. With very fast processors, this latency can be tens to hundreds of processor cycles. Support for some form of prefetch can clearly help. DASH supports both *read prefetch* and *read-exclusive prefetch* operations [17]. These operations cause the directory controller to send out a read or read-exclusive request for the data, but do not block the processor. Thus, the processor is able to overlap the fetching of the data with useful work. When the processor is ready to use the prefetched data, it issues a normal read or read exclusive request. By this time the data will either be in the RAC or the prefetch will be outstanding, in which case the normal read or read-exclusive is merged with the prefetch. In either case, the latency for the data will be reduced. Ideally, we would have liked to place the prefetched data directly in the requesting processor's cache instead of the RAC, but that would have required significant modifications to the existing processor boards.

There are some variables for which a write-update coherence protocol is more appropriate than the DASH write-invalidate protocol [3]. The prototype system provides for a single word *update write* primitive which updates memory and all the caches currently holding the word. Since exclusive ownership is not required, the producer's write buffer can retire the write as soon as it has been issued on the bus. Update-writes are especially useful for event synchronization. The producer of an event can directly update the value cached by the waiting processor reducing the latency and traffic that would result if the value was invalidated. This primitive is especially useful in implementing barriers, as an update-write can be used by the last processor entering the barrier to release all waiting processors. Update operations conform to the release consistency memory model, but require explicit fence operations when used for synchronization purposes.

6 Scalability of the DASH Directory

The DASH directory scheme currently uses a full bit-vector to identify the remote clusters caching a memory block. While this is reasonable for the DASH prototype, it does not scale well since the amount of directory memory required is the proportional to the product of the main memory size and the number of processors in the system. We are currently investigating a variety of solutions which limit the overhead of directory memory. The most straightforward modification is the use of a limited number of pointers per directory entry. Each directory pointer holds the cluster number of a cluster currently caching the given line. In any limited pointer scheme some mechanism must exist to handle cache blocks that are cached by more processors then there are pointers. A very simple scheme resorts to a broadcast in these cases [1]. Better results can be obtained if the pointer storage memory reverts to a bit vector when pointer overflow occurs. Of course, a complete bit vector is not possible, but if

each bit represents a *region* of processors the amount of traffic generated by such overflows can be greatly reduced relative to a broadcast.

Other schemes to scale the directory rely on restructuring of directory storage. Possible solutions include allowing pointers to be shared between directory entries, or using a cache of directory entries to supplement or replace the normal directory [18, 13]. A directory structured as a cache need not have a complete backing memory since replaced directory entries can simply invalidate their associated cache entries (similar to how multi-level caches maintain their inclusion property). Recent studies [13] have shown that such *sparse-directories* can maintain a constant overhead of directory memory compared with a full-bit vector when the number of processors grows from 64 to 1024. A sparse directory using limited pointers and a coarse vector only increases the total traffic by only 10-20% and should have minimal impact on processor performance. Furthermore, such directory structures require only small changes to the coherence protocol given here.

7 Validation of the Protocol

Validation of the DASH protocol presents a major challenge. Each cluster in DASH contains a complex directory controller with a large amount of state. This state coupled with the distributed nature of the DASH protocol results in an enormous number of possible interactions between the controllers. Writing a test suite that exercises all possible interactions in reasonable time seems intractable. Therefore, we are using two less exhaustive testing methods. Both these methods rely on the software simulator of DASH that we have developed.

The simulator consists of two tightly coupled components: a low-level DASH system simulator that incorporates the coherence protocol, and simulates the processor caches, buses, and interconnection network at a very fine level of detail; and Tango [11], a high-level functional simulator that models the processors and executes parallel programs. Tango simulates parallel processing on a uniprocessor while the DASH simulator provides detailed timing about latency of memory references. Because of the tight coupling between the two parts, our simulator closely models the DASH machine.

Our first scheme for testing the protocol consists of running existing parallel programs for which the results are known and comparing the output with that from the DASH simulator. The drawback of using parallel programs to check the protocol is that they use the memory system and synchronization features in "well-behaved" ways. For example, a well-written parallel program will not release a lock that is already free, and parallel programs usually don't modify shared variables outside of a critical section. As a result, parallel applications do not test a large set of possible interactions.

To get at the more pathological interactions, our second method relies on test scripts. These scripts can be written to provide a fine level of control over the protocol transitions and to be particularly demanding of the protocol. While writing an exhaustive set of such test scripts is not feasible, we hope to achieve reasonable test coverage with a smaller set of scripts by introducing randomness into the execution of the scripts.

The randomness idea used is an extension of the Berkeley Random Case Generation (RCG) technique [22] used to verify the SPUR cache controller design. Our method, called Intelligent Case Generation (ICG), is described in detail in [14]. Each script is a self-contained test sequence which executes a number of memory operations on a set of processors. Each script consists of some initialization, a set of test operations, and a check for proper results. Like RCG, multiple, independent scripts run simultaneously and interact in two ways. First, a processor randomly chooses which of the multiple active scripts it is going to pick its next action from. Therefore, execution of the same set of scripts will be interleaved in time differently upon each run. Second, while each script uses unique memory locations, these locations may be in the same cache line. Scripts interact by changing the cache state of cache lines used by other scripts.

ICG extends RCG in three ways. First, instead of simple two step scripts (a write followed by a read), ICG supports multi-step scripts in which some steps are executed in series and some are allowed to execute in parallel. Second, ICG provides a finer level of control over which processors execute which steps of a script and introduces randomness into the assignment process. Finally, ICG allows for a more flexible assignment of test addresses so that particular scripts do not have to be written to interact. Using ICG to dynamically assign addresses results in different scripts interacting at different times during a run, and results in the same script using various combinations of local and remote memory.

Of course, the hardware itself will also serve as a verification tool. The hardware can run both parallel programs and test scripts. While debugging protocol errors on the hardware will be difficult, the sheer number of cycles executed will be a demanding test of the protocol.

8 Comparison with Scalable Coherent Interface Protocol

Several protocols that provide for distributed directory-based cache coherence have been proposed [15, 21]. The majority of these protocols have not been defined in enough detail to do a reasonable comparison with the DASH protocol. One exception is the IEEE P1596 - Scalable Coherent Interface (SCI) [12]. While still evolving, SCI has been documented in sufficient detail to make a comparison possible. SCI differs from DASH, however, in that it is only an interface standard, not a complete system design. SCI only specifies the interfaces that each processor should implement, leaving open the actual node design and exact interconnection network.

At the system level, a typical SCI system would be similar to DASH with each processing node containing a processor, a section of main memory, and an interface to the interconnection network. Both systems rely on coherent caches maintained by distributed directories and distributed memories to provide scalable memory bandwidth. The major difference lies in how and where the directory information is maintained. In SCI, the directory is a distributed sharing list maintained by the processor caches themselves. For example, if processors A, B, and C are caching some location, then the cache entries storing this location will form a doubly-linked list. At main memory, only a pointer to the processor at the head of the linked list is maintained. In contrast, DASH places all the directory information with main memory.

The main advantage of the SCI scheme over DASH is that the amount of directory pointer storage grows naturally with the number of processors in the system. In DASH, the maximum number of processors must be fixed beforehand, or the system

must support some form of limited directory information. On the other hand, the SCI directory memory would normally employ the same SRAM technology used by the processor caches while the DASH directory is implemented in main memory DRAM technology. Another feature of SCI is that it guarantees forward progress in all cases, including the pathological "live-lock" case alluded to in section 4.6.

The primary disadvantage of the SCI scheme is that the distribution of the individual directory entries increases the complexity and latency of the directory protocol, since additional directory update messages must be sent between processor caches. For example, on a write to a shared block cached by $N + 1$ processors (including the writing processor), the writer must perform the following actions: (i) detach itself from the sharing list; (ii) interrogate memory to determine the head of the sharing list; (iii) acquire head status from the current head; and (iv) serially purge the other processor caches by issuing invalidation requests and receiving replies indicating the next processor in the list. Altogether, this amounts to $2N + 8$ messages including N serial directory lookups. In contrast, DASH can locate all sharing processors in a single directory lookup and invalidation messages are serialized only by the network transmission rate. Likewise, many read misses in SCI require more inter-node communication. For example, if a block is currently cached, processing a read miss requires four messages since only the head can supply the cache block. Furthermore, if a miss is replacing a valid block in the processor's cache, the replaced block must be detached from its sharing list.

Recently, the SCI working committee has proposed a number of extensions to the base protocol that address some of these shortcomings. In particular, the committee has proposed additional directory pointers that allow sharing lists to become sharing trees, the support for request forwarding, and the use of a clean cached state. While these extensions reduce the differences between the two protocols, they also add complexity. The fundamental question is what set of features leads to better performance at a given complexity level. As in the design of other hardware systems, this requires a careful balance between optimizing the performance of common operations without adding undue complexity for uncommon ones. The lack of good statistics on scalable shared memory machines, however, makes the identification of the common cases difficult. Thus, a complete comparison of the protocols is likely to require actual implementations of both designs and much more experience with this class of machines.

9 Summary and Status

Distributed directory-based coherence protocols such as the DASH protocol allow for the scalability of shared-memory multiprocessors with coherent caches. The cost of scalability is the added complexity of directory based schemes compared with existing snoopy, bus-based coherence protocols. The complexity arises primarily from the lack of a single serialization point within the system and the lack of atomic operations. Additional complexity stems simply from the larger set of components that interact to execute the protocol and the deeper hierarchy within the memory system.

Minimizing memory latency is of paramount importance in scalable systems. Support for coherent caches is the first step in reducing latency, but the memory system must also be optimized towards this goal. The DASH protocol attempts to minimize latency through the use of the release consistency model, cache-to-cache transfers, a forwarding control strategy and special purpose operations such as prefetch and update write. Adding these latency reducing features must, of course, be traded off with the complexity needed to support them. All of the above features were added without a significant increase in the complexity of the hardware.

Verification of a complex distributed directory-based cache coherence protocol is a major challenge. We feel that verification through the use of test scripts and extensive random testing will provide an acceptable level of confidence. The design effort of the prototype is currently in the implementation phase. A functional simulator of the hardware is running as well as a gate level simulation of the directory card. We plan to have a 4 cluster, 16 processor system running during the summer of 1990. This prototype should serve as the ultimate verification of the design and provide a vehicle to fully evaluate the design concepts discussed in this paper.

10 Acknowledgments

The DASH project team is composed of a number of graduate students and faculty within the Computer System Laboratory at Stanford. Many related topics are being researched and the results of much of this work has influenced the design of the DASH architecture and coherence protocol. Besides the authors, a number of others have directly contributed to the development of DASH. In particular, we would like to thank Wolf-Dietrich Weber for creating the DASH simulator, Helen Davis and Stephen Goldschmidt for modifying their Tango simulator to interact with the DASH simulator, and Bruce Kleinman for developing the DASH protocol verifier. Likewise, we want to recognize research engineer Dave Nakahira who has made significant contributions to the design of the DASH hardware. We also wish to thank Valid Logic Systems who has donated the CAE software used to develop the DASH prototype.

This research is supported by DARPA contract N00014-87-K-0828. Dan Lenoski is supported by Tandem Computers Incorporated.

References

[1] A. Agarwal, R. Simoni, J. Hennessy, and M. Horowitz. An evaluation of directory schemes for cache coherence. In *Proc. of the 15th Annual Int. Sym. on Computer Architecture*, pages 280–289, June 1988.

[2] J. Archibald and J.-L. Baer. An economical solution to the cache coherence problem. In *Proc. of the 12th Int. Sym. on Computer Architecture*, pages 355–362, June 1985.

[3] J. Archibald and J.-L. Baer. Cache coherence protocols: Evaluation using a multiprocessor simulation model. *ACM Trans. on Computer Systems*, 4(4):273–298, 1986.

[4] F. Baskett, T. Jermoluk, and D. Solomon. The 4D-MP graphics superworkstation: Computing + graphics = 40 MIPS + 40 MFLOPS and 100,000 lighted polygons per second. In *Proc. of the 33rd IEEE Computer Society Int. Conf. – COMPCON 88*, pages 468–471, February 1988.

[5] W. C. Brantley, K. P. McAuliffe, and J. Weiss. RP3 processor-memory element. In *Proc. of the 1985 Int. Conf. on Parallel Processing*, pages 782–789, 1985.

[6] L. Censier and P. Feautrier. A new solution to coherence problems in multicache systems. *IEEE Trans. on Computers*, C-27(12):1112–1118, December 1978.

[7] W. J. Dally. Wire efficient VLSI multiprocessor communication networks. In *Stanford Conference on Advanced Research in VLSI*, 1987.

[8] M. Dubois, C. Scheurich, and F. Briggs. Memory access buffering in multiprocessors. In *Proc. of the 13th Annual Int. Sym. on Computer Architecture*, pages 434–442, June 1986.

[9] C. M. Flaig. VLSI mesh routing systems. Technical Report 5241:TR:87, California Institute of Technology, May 1987.

[10] K. Gharachorloo, D. Lenoski, J. Laudon, P. Gibbons, A. Gupta, and J. Hennessy. Memory consistency and event ordering in scalable shared-memory multiprocessors. In *Proc. of the 17th Annual Int. Sym. on Computer Architecture*, June 1990.

[11] S. R. Goldschmidt and H. Davis. Tango introduction and tutorial. Technical Report CSL-TR-90-410, Stanford University, January 1990.

[12] P1596 Working Group. P1596/Part IIIA - SCI Cache Coherence Overview. Technical Report Revision 0.33, IEEE Computer Society, November 1989.

[13] A. Gupta and W.-D. Weber. Reducing memory and traffic requirements for scalable directory-based cache coherence schemes. Technical Report CSL-TR-90-417, Stanford University, March 1990.

[14] B. Kleinman. *DASH Protocol Verification*, EE-391 Class Project Report, December 1989.

[15] T. Knight. Architectures for artificial intelligence. In *Int. Conf. on Computer Design*, 1987.

[16] L. Lamport. How to make a multiprocessor computer that correctly executes multiprocess programs. *IEEE Trans. on Computers*, C-28(9):241–248, September 1979.

[17] D. Lenoski, J. Laudon, K. Gharachorloo, A. Gupta, J. Hennessy, M. Horowitz, and M. Lam. Design of the Stanford DASH multiprocessor. Technical Report CSL-TR-89-403, Stanford University, December 1989.

[18] B. O'Krafka and A. R. Newton. An empirical evaluation of two memory-efficient directory methods. In *Proc. of the 17th Annual Int. Sym. on Computer Architecture*, June 1990.

[19] M. S. Papamarcos and J. H. Patel. A low overhead coherence solution for multiprocessors with private cache memories. In *Proc. of the 11th Annual Int. Sym. on Computer Architecture*, pages 348–354, June 1984.

[20] C. K. Tang. Cache design in the tightly coupled multiprocessor system. In *AFIPS Conf. Proc., National Computer Conf., NY, NY*, pages 749–753, June 1976.

[21] J. Willis. Cache coherence in systems with parallel communication channels & many processors. Technical Report TR-88-013, Philips Laboratories - Briarcliff, March 1988.

[22] D. A. Wood, G. A. Gibson, and R. H. Katz. Verifying a mulitprocessor cache controller using random case generation. Technical Report 89/490, University of California, Berkeley, 1988.

[23] W. C. Yen, D. W. Yen, and K.-S. Fu. Data coherence problem in a multicache system. *IEEE Trans. on Computers*, C-34(1):56–65, January 1985.

Appendix A: Coherence Transaction Details

```
if (Data held locally in shared state by processor or RAC)
    Other cache(s) supply data for fill;

else if (Data held locally in dirty state by processor or RAC) {
    Dirty cache supplies data for fill and goes to shared state;
    if (Memory Home is Local)
        Writeback Data to main memory;
    else
        RAC takes data in shared-dirty state;
}

else if (Memory home is Local) {
    if (Directory entry state != Dirty-Remote)
        Memory supplies read data;
    else {
        Allocate RAC entry, mask arbitration and force retry;
        Forward Read Request to Dirty Cluster;
        PCPU on Dirty Cluster issues read request;
        Dirty cache supplies data and goes to shared state;
        DC sends shared data reply to local cluster;
        Local RC gets reply and unmasks processor arbitration;
        Upon local processor read, RC supplies data and the
            RAC entry goes to shared state;
        Directory entry state = Shared-Remote;
    }
}

else /* Memory home is Remote */ {
    Allocate RAC entry, mask arbitration and force retry;
    Local DC sends read request to home cluster;
    if (Directory entry state != Dirty-Remote) {
        Directory entry state = Shared-Remote, update vector;
        Home DC sends reply to local RC;
        Local RC gets reply and unmasks processor arbitration;
    else {
        Home DC forwards Read Request to dirty cluster;
        PCPU on dirty cluster issues read request and DC sends
            reply to local cluster and sharing writeback to home;
        Local RC gets reply and unmasks processor arbitration;
        Home DC gets sharing writeback, writes back dirty data,
            Directory entry state = Shared-Remote, update vector;
    }
    Upon local processor read, RC supplies the data and the
        RAC entry goes to shared state;
}
```

Figure 7: Normal flow of read request bus transaction.

```
if (Memory Home is Local) {
    Writeback data is written back into main memory;
}
else /* Memory Home is Remote */ {
    Writeback request sent to home;
    Writeback data is written back into main memory;
    Directory entry state = Uncached-Remote, update vector;
}
```

Figure 8: Normal flow of a write-back request bus transaction.

```
if (Data held locally in dirty state by processor or RAC)
    Dirty cache supplies Read-Exclusive fill data and
        invalidates self;

else if (Memory Home is Local) {
    switch (Directory entry state) {

        case Uncached-Remote :
            Memory supplies data, any locally cached copies
                are invalidated;
            break;

        case Shared-Remote :
            RC allocates an entry in RAC with DC specified
                invalidate acknowledge count;
            Memory supplies data, any locally cached copies are
                invalidated;
            Local DC sends invalidate request to shared clusters;
            Dir. entry state = Uncached-Remote, update vector;
            Upon receipt of all acknowledges RC deallocates RAC
                entry;
            break;

        case Dirty-Remote :
            Allocate RAC entry, mask arbitration and force retry;
            Forward Read-Exclusive Request to dirty cluster;
            PCPU at dirty cluster issues Read-Ex request,
                Dirty cache supplies data and invalidates self;
            DC in dirty cluster sends reply to local RC;
            Local RC gets reply from dirty cluster and unmasks
                processor arbitration;
            Upon local processor re-Read-Ex, RC supplies data,
                RAC entry is deallocated and
                Dir. entry state = Uncached-Remote, update vector;
    }
}
else /* Memory Home is Remote */ {
    RC allocates RAC entry, masks arbitration and forces retry;
    Local DC sends Read-Exclusive request to home;
    switch (Directory entry state) {

        case Uncached-Remote :
            Home memory supplies data, any locally cached copies
                are invalidated, Home DC sends reply to local RC;
            Directory entry state = Dirty-Remote, update vector;
            Local RC gets Read-Ex reply with zero invalidation
                count and unmasks processor for arbitration;
            Upon local processor re-Read-Ex, RC supplies data and
                RAC entry is deallocated;
            break;

        case Shared-Remote :
            Home memory supplies data, any locally cached copies
                are invalidated, Home DC sends reply to local RC;
            Home DC sends invalidation requests to sharing
                clusters;
            Directory entry state = Dirty-Remote, update vector;
            Local RC gets reply with data and invalidate acknow-
                ledge count and unmasks processor for arbitration;
            Upon local processor re-Read-Ex, RC supplies data;
            Upon receipt of all acknowledges RC deallocates RAC
                entry;
            break;

        case Dirty-Remote :
            Home DC forwards Read-Ex request to dirty cluster;
            PCPU at dirty cluster issues Read-Ex request,
                Dirty cache supplies data and invalidates self;
            DC in dirty cluster sends reply to local RC with
                acknowledge count of one and sends Dirty Transfer
                request to home;
            Local RC gets reply and acknowledge count and unmasks
                processor for arbitration;
            Upon local processor re-Read-Ex, RC supplies data;
            Upon receipt of Dirty Transfer request, Home DC
                sends acknowledgment to local RC,
                Home Dir. entry state = Dirty-Remote, update vector;
            Upon receipt of acknowledge RC deallocates RAC entry;
    }
}
```

Figure 9: Normal flow of read-exclusive request bus transaction.

The Performance Impact of
Block Sizes and Fetch Strategies

Steven Przybylski

MIPS Computer Systems,
928 Arques Ave, Sunnyvale, CA 94086

Abstract

This paper explores the interactions between a cache's block size, fetch size and fetch policy from the perspective of maximizing system-level performance. It has been previously noted that given a simple fetch strategy the performance optimal block size is almost always four or eight words [10]. If there is even a small cycle time penalty associated with either longer blocks or fetches, then the performance-optimal size is noticeably reduced. In split cache organizations, where the fetch and block sizes of instruction and data caches are all independent design variables, instruction cache block size and fetch size should be the same. For the workload and write-back write policy used in this trace-driven simulation study, the instruction cache block size should be about a factor of two greater than the data cache fetch size, which in turn should equal to or double the data cache block size. The simplest fetch strategy of fetching only on a miss and stalling the CPU until the fetch is complete works well. Complicated fetch strategies do not produce the performance improvements indicated by the accompanying reductions in miss ratios because of limited memory resources and a strong temporal clustering of cache misses. For the environments simulated here, the most effective fetch strategy improved performance by between 1.7% and 4.5% over the simplest strategy described above.

1. Introduction

Over the last several years, designers have been increasingly concerned with the growing gap between the cycle times of dynamic RAMs and microprocessor CPUs. This concern has spurred interest in increasing cache block sizes to minimize impact of a relatively long main memory latency. Though there have been several studies published to date that explore the characteristics of caches with longer block sizes [2, 12, 15, 16, 18, 20, 21], the studies have generally failed to explore the performance implications of some of the more significant design decisions.

This paper expands on a section in a previous work [10]. In that article, the dependency of performance on the block size was graphed as a function of the main memory characteristics. The conclusion was that each memory system, as characterized by its latency and transfer rate, implies a performance-optimal block size that is independent of the CPU characteristics, including the cycle time. That analysis was limited by underlying assumptions of the study. In particular, exactly one block was fetched from main memory on a cache miss, the CPU was stalled until the fetch was complete, and there was no assumed cycle time degradation with increasing block size. In this paper we will relax each of these constraints in turn and thereby examine their impact on the best block size and the resulting performance level.

In recognition of the fact that the ultimate measure of a memory hierarchy is the performance obtained by the computer of which it is a part, execution time is the primary metric used in this paper to compare different cache organizations and fetch policies. The use of this metric is especially important in the study of policies that rely on parallelism between CPU execution and memory activity to presumably improve performance. Miss ratios alone are inadequate for judging their effectiveness because not all misses are created equal. In the presence of a complicated fetch strategy individual misses can have widely varying contributions to the total cycle count, depending on the exact state of the machine at the time. As a result, the relationship between the number of misses and the execution time is not necessarily straightforward. In this study, different system configurations are compared using a trace-driven simulator which accurately keeps track of activity at all levels in the memory hierarchy during every machine cycle.

After describing the terminology and experimental method in Sections 2 and 3, we reproduce in Section 4 the results from the previous paper as a baseline for comparison. In Section 5, we examine the effects of a cycle time penalty for long block sizes. If the additional multiplexors and control needed to implement a longer block size degrades the cycle time of the CPU from the simple, single word block size case, then there clearly will be an impact on the tradeoff between latency and transfer

CH2887-8/90/0000/0160$01.00 © 1990 IEEE

160

period that determines the optimal block size.

An important realization is that the amount of data that is fetched from memory need not be equal to a block. It can, in fact, be either more or less. Machines that prefetch instructions are fetching several blocks per cache miss. Section 6 asks the question: how are the optimal block size and fetch size related as a function of the memory characteristics. In contrast, Section 7 asks the question: what is the benefit of more complicated fetch strategies that try to overlap CPU execution with main memory fetches. Finally, Section 8 summarizes and concludes the paper.

2. Terminology

The literature on caches is confused with respect to the definitions of some important terms. The following definitions are unambiguous, consistent with the majority of the literature and appropriate for the discussion of block sizes and fetch strategies.

Block:
A block is the unit of data in the cache associated with a tag. An *n-way* set associative cache with *m* sets has $n \times m$ blocks. Block sizes are always binary values – that is, powers of teo – and typically range from one word[1] to 128 words.

Sub-block:
A sub-block is the unit of data that is associated with a valid bit. Sub-blocks are smaller than or equal to blocks, and are generally either one byte, one word or one block long. In write-back caches, dirty bits are typically also associated with sub-blocks.

Fetch Size:
The fetch size is the quantity of data fetched from memory at one time. The only hard constraint is that it be an integral number of sub-blocks, though in reality it is typically a binary number of blocks. That the most common fetch size is one block contributes to common usage of block size for fetch size and the blurred distinction between the two.

Fetch Policy:
The fetch policy is the algorithm used to determine when a main memory read is to occur, which words are to be fetched, what order they will be returned in, and at what point the CPU will be allowed to continue execution if it is stalled. Designs that prefetch on a cache miss have a fetch size greater than one block, and resume execution as soon as the missed sub-block or block is returned from memory.

(Read) Cache Miss Ratio:
Most researchers define the cache miss ratio as the ratio of read misses and write misses to the number of memory references. However, it is widely recognized that reads (instruction fetches and loads) and writes (stores) have greatly differing frequencies, policies, and hit and miss penalties [7, 17]. In the light of the shift that is occurring in analysis of memory

hierarchies away from miss ratios and towards overall system-level performance, we define the read cache miss ratio and write cache miss ratio separately. When used without qualification, *miss ratio* refers to the read miss ratio.

3. Experimental Method

All the results presented in this paper were generated with a trace-driven simulator stimulated by eight large address traces. This section briefly describes the simulator and the traces. Both are characterized at great length in other documents [11, 10]. The first of these publications also includes a detailed analysis supporting the credibility of conclusions based on this method.

A proper study of memory hierarchies in which the metric for comparison is execution time requires a simulator that accurately accounts for time at all levels of the hierarchy. Specifically, the simulator used here allows the user to specify the duration of reads and writes to the tag and data portion of caches and write buffers, as well as the minimum separation between operations. In addition, latency and transfer delays between levels of the hierarchy can be varied to allow for complete and realistic system models. A wide variety of fetch strategies and an equally broad spectrum of write strategies are provided for.

The second prerequisite is a set of system models to be used in the simulations. The cache design space is incredibly diverse. Including the often overlooked temporal parameters, there are literally tens of independent design variables per level in a memory hierarchy. Since it is impossible to explore the entire design space in any one study, we limit ourselves by fixing most of the parameters at common values that are consistent with the ranges of the free variables of the experiment. For instance, we have restricted ourselves to a single-level, split instruction/data cache. A realistic base system was chosen as the reference. In each of the experiments to follow, three or more design parameters are changed simultaneously over a portion of the design space while all of the others remain fixed.

The base system is characteristic of a system built around a 25MHz RISC CMOS processor. Throughout this study, we will uniformly assume that the caches determine the CPU cycle time. The single level of caching contains 64KB in each of the instruction and data caches. Both are direct-mapped and have default block and fetch sizes of 4 words. The sub-block size is uniformly one word. The data cache is a write-back cache with a four entry write buffer, each entry being one block wide. The datapath into and out of the write buffer is equal in width to the backplane. Both ports cycle at the CPU cycle rate, and they can operate simultaneously. Writes into the cache take two cycles, and the write miss policy is to fill the sub-block written to with the written data but not to fetch the rest of the block from main memory. With these choices, both write hits and misses are relatively quick. An aggressive write policy minimizes the write's

---
[1]For convenience, a word is defined to be 32 bits.

contribution to the overall execution time and allows us to concentrate on the read effects.

The caches are connected by a one word wide bus capable of block transfers at a rate of one word per cycle. The cache read miss penalty is one cycle to get the address to the memory, several cycles of memory latency, then several cycles to transfer the data back into the cache. The main memory is characterized by a 180ns combined decode and access time, plus a 120ns gap between operations. The default fetch strategy is to stall the CPU on a read miss until the entire fetch is complete and the cache is loaded (demand fetch only [4]). During the loading of the cache, the requested datum is shunted off into a buffer and passed to the CPU on the last cycle of the memory transfer so that no additional overhead is needed to get the datum out of the cache.

The first four of the eight traces used to stimulate this model are drawn from the VAX architecture. They are concatenations of several 400,000 reference long snapshots taken on a VAX 8200. They include operating system references and true multiprogramming activity. The traces were preprocessed to collapse adjacent byte references to the code segment into long word (32b) references, and to transform quad word references into the appropriate sequence of long word references. The warm-start boundary is set to 450,000 references for all four traces. All addresses are virtual addresses. The generation and detailed characteristics of these traces are documented elsewhere [1, 2].

The second four traces are derived from the MIPS R2000 architecture. They are interleaved uniprocess, virtual address traces of a variety of optimized C programs. Though they do not include any operating system references, the individual uniprocess traces were randomly interleaved with the same distribution of context switches as were observed in the VAX traces. Each uniprocess trace was captured from the middle of the program's execution so that its steady state behaviour would be measured. However, the interleaved traces are prepended by references, also appropriately interleaved, to all the data and code that the individual programs touched prior to the beginning of tracing. In this way, the caches are completely loaded at the warm-start boundary. At that point, the caches' contents are identical to what would be observed if all the programs were traced from their beginnings. Except for the lack of operating systems references, miss activity observed over the final one million references of each trace is identical to that which would be observed in a real system running these programs interleaved in that way. This is true regardless of the cache size or other characteristics. Unlike in most simulation studies, the validity of the miss rates and performance statistics generated from these traces is not limited cache sizes smaller than the touched data set, but instead extends to much larger cache sizes. Furthermore, the size of the traces implies that the 95% confidence interval around the measured miss ratio as an estimate of the real miss ratio is less than plus or minus 0.01%, even for cache sizes greater than 2MB [8].

Though there are significant quantitative differences in the behaviour of the two sets of traces, qualitatively they are very similar. By using the geometric mean of the results from all eight traces, the goal is to produce results that are more generally applicable. The preparation and characteristics of all the traces, and the differences between the two sets, are described in detail elsewhere [11].

4. Equal Block Size and Fetch Size

We will begin by reproducing as a basis for comparison the results presented previously [10]. In this section we assume that the fetch size is equal to the block size, and that the fetch strategy is the very simple one described above. Given these assumptions, we attempt to determine the best choice for the block size as a function of the memory and cache characteristics.

The fetch size is unique among the organizational parameters in that it affects the performance of the computer system through two related mechanisms. The most obvious is through the miss ratio: as the fetch size increases, the miss ratio decreases due to the spatial locality of programs. The probability that an item will be referenced soon decreases with the distance from the most recent reference. With increasing fetch size the mean utility of the words being fetched also drops. When the mean utility of the fetched words drops below the mean utility of the words that are being replaced, the miss ratio starts to rise again. The mean utility of data in the cache is primarily a function of the cache size: smaller caches only contain things that were used recently and so have a high likelihood of being used again. For each cache size, there is an optimum fetch size that minimizes the miss ratio.

There is another secondary effect on the average utility of data in the cache that is dependent on the block size: if the cache size is constant, then as the block size increases the number of blocks decreases. As the number of tags is reduced there is less opportunity to hold a lot of widely distant data in the cache. Also, with longer blocks, a write miss knocks out of the cache more potentially useful data than in the case of shorter blocks. As a result, increasing the block size along with the fetch size reduces the fetch size at which the miss penalty is minimized.

The second mechanism through which the fetch size affects performance is via the miss penalty. A longer fetch takes more time, and increases the cache miss penalty. Thus for small fetch sizes, the two effects are in opposition: increasing the fetch size decreases the miss ratio but increases the miss penalty. The point at which those two effects are balanced defines the minimum execution time as a function of the fetch size. This size is inevitably less than the fetch size that minimizes the miss ratio. This effect is illustrated in Figure 4-1. For the model simulated here – the default 64KB caches, and a 260ns latency, one word per cycle memory system – the load miss ratio is minimized by a fetch and block size of 32 words, while the instruction cache miss ratio is minimized by a fetch/block size of somewhat more than 64 words. In contrast, the fetch/block size that minimized the execution time was 8 words.

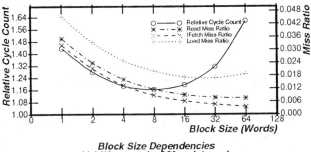

Block Size Dependencies
(1.0 W per cycle, 260 ns latency)
Figure 4-1

Smith has pointed out that if the cache miss penalty is expressed as the sum of a latency (la) and a transfer time – the ratio of the fetch size and the transfer rate (FS/tr) – then the fetch size that minimizes the mean read time – the product of the cache miss penalty and the cache miss ratio – is only dependent on the product of the latency and transfer rates ($la \times tr$), and not on either independently [21]. To first order, the fetch size that minimizes the mean read time also minimizes the execution time. This sole dependence on the memory speed product is verified experimentally by simulating a variety of memory configurations and plotting the performance optimal block size as a function of the product.

Figure 4-2 shows the aggregate relative execution time as a function of the block size of both caches and of the memory characteristics. In this experiment, and in those that follow, the transfer rate is varied from one word per CPU cycle to four words per cycle. For the cycle time chosen for the base system these translate to bandwidths of 25MBps and 400MBps respectively. The latency is similarly varied from 100ns to 420ns. Thus we have a large spectrum of memory systems experimentally represented.

For each pair of memory characteristics, the performance curve has a minimum at the optimum block/fetch size. Fitting a parabola through the lowest three points approximates that non-integral block size and estimates the best performance level attainable with that hypothetical memory system. These minima are plotted in Figure 4-3. They are connected with a lattice that joins points with the same transfer ratio and latency respectively. The conclusions that we can draw from this is that the optimal block size for a split I/D system with identical block and fetch sizes for both caches is typically either four or eight words. If the memory system is particularly unbalanced – that is, with both the transfer rate and latency being either high or low – then the optimum could be either two or sixteen words. More significantly, since the performance curves of Figure 4-2 are very flat near their minima, selecting the block size

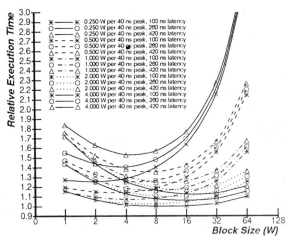

Execution Time vs Memory Parameters
Figure 4-2

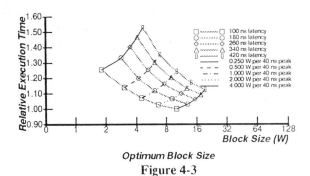

Optimum Block Size
Figure 4-3

incorrectly by a factor of two – four versus eight or vice versa – does not have a very great performance impact.

Smith's assertion is directly verified in Figure 4-4, in which the optimal block/fetch sizes are plotted against the product of the latency and transfer rate. Indeed, as expected, the four line segments, which correspond to the different transfer rates, fall on top of each other, indicating that the optimal block size is a function of the product of the two variables and not of either independently. The dotted line indicates the block size for each memory speed product ($la \times tr$) at which the transfer time equals the latency period. It is interesting to note that for memory systems that favour fast transfers (large la, tr and $la \times tr$) it is best to spend more time waiting on the memory latency. For the reverse situation, when the latency is low with respect to the transfer rate (small la, tr and $la \times tr$), then it is best to spend more than half the time in the transfers.

For larger caches, the web of points in Figure 4-3 shifts to the right somewhat. Figure 4-5 shows the optimal block sizes for a 2MB of cache split equally between the instruction and data caches. One can see that the dependence of the optimal block size on the $la \times tr$ product remains, and for any particular product the optimal binary sized block size can be larger than the 132KB total cache size case by up to a factor of two. For caches smaller than 132KB, the web of points does not shift appreciably to the

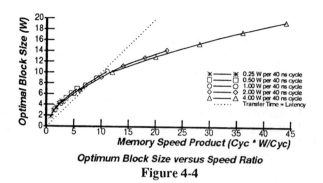

Optimum Block Size versus Speed Ratio

Figure 4-4

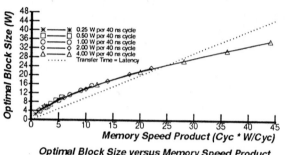

Optimal Block Size versus Memory Speed Product
2MB Cache

Figure 4-5

left and so the optimal block sizes remain essentially unchanged from Figure 4-3.

5. Effects of Cycle Time Penalties

There are two main motivations for changing the metric for evaluating caches from miss ratios to execution time. The first is, of course, relevancy: the system designer, the cache design engineer and their managers are ultimately much more interested in the system's performance than in the cache's miss ratio. The second, more subtle, reason is to expose to the designers the tradeoffs that inherently exist between the temporal and organizational design variables. In this section we examine one of those tradeoffs: the link that exists between the CPU cycle time and the block size. A simple, first order, analysis shows that if the CPU cycle time is not a function of the block size, as in the previous section, then the performance optimal block size is independent of the value of the cycle time. In this section we relax this assumption and explore the behaviour of the performance optimal block size in the situation where there is a dependency between the cycle time and the block size. Again, we will be assuming that the block and fetch sizes of both caches are all identical.

We will examine this tradeoff in very general terms. Instead of assuming a fixed cycle time as a function of the block size, we will assume a small proportional increase in the cycle time for each doubling of the block size. Specifically, we will start by assuming a one percent degradation per doubling: that is a 40ns cycle time for a block size of one, a 40.4ns cycle time for a block size of

two, a 40.804ns cycle time for a block size of four, and so on. This level of degradation is consistent with increasing the fan-in of a multiplexor between the CPU and the caches, or additional loading on cache address lines due to the additional width of the caches' data array.

Figure 5-1 shows the characteristic web of points for this scenario. The unshaded symbols show the reference scenario of no cycle time penalty. For most of the memory systems considered, a two to three percent performance degradation occurs due to an effect of this magnitude. The maximum performance increase of 4.2% occurs at the extreme right had corner of the web, while the minimum (0.7%) occurs at the left hand corner. Interestingly, the cycle time degradation causes a shift in the web of points that is roughly equivalent to a change in the transfer rate. This is intuitively explainable in terms of equivalent influences. Both effects have an increasingly pronounced negative impact on performance as the block size increases.

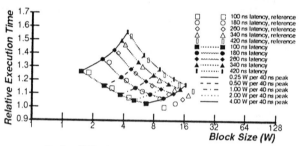

Optimal Block Size: 1% Cycle Time Degradation

Figure 5-1

Figure 5-2 shows the corresponding graph of the optimal block size as a function of the memory speed product. It shows two effects: first, there is a small but noticeable decrease in the optimal block size. Only in a few cases, though, is the binary optimal block size changed. Second, the optimal block size's independence from the individual latency and transfer rate parameters is lost: the line segments no longer line up exactly on top of each other.

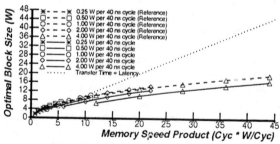

Optimal Block Size versus Memory Speed Product:
1% Cycle Time Degradation

Figure 5-2

When the percentage degradation per doubling is increased to five percent, both these effects are dramatically increased. The performance loss over the default scenario averages around 10% with a range of

1.2% to 15%. Figure 5-3 shows the choice of the optimal block size in this case. The penalty for large block sizes is so extreme here that the optimal block size never exceeds four words.

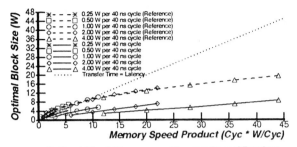

Optimal Block Size versus Memory Speed Product: 5% Cycle Time Degradation
Figure 5-3

Of course, the reality of cache design is dramatically different than this very simplified model. The relationship between a potential CPU's cycle time and the block/fetch size is not well behaved or even monotonic. The selection of different RAMs and multiplexors with different access times for different cache organizations will affect the cycle time in subtle ways. Therefore, the moral of this section is that the designer needs to be aware of the general influence on the optimal block size that results from any additional complexity involved in implementing long block and fetch sizes.

6. Different Block and Fetch Sizes

It is becoming increasingly common to have a fetch size that is larger than the block size [5]. This is typically done in conjunction with a more complicated fetch strategy that allows for early continuation of execution as soon as the requested block is received. We, however, will investigate these two decisions separately in this and the subsequent sections. In this section, the block size and fetch size are allowed to vary independently, but fetches still occur only on misses, and execution is still suspended until the entire fetch is complete.

Formally, the desire to free both the block and fetch size variables comes from the realization that the mean read time, the product of the miss penalty and the miss rate ($(la + FS/tr) \times MR(BS, FS)$), is dependent on the two variables separately. In particular, the miss penalty is only dependent on the fetch size and the memory characteristics. A designer might therefore reasonably select the fetch size that is most closely suited to the memory system and then select the block size that minimizes the miss ratio given that block size.

Recalling the discussion of the influences on the miss ratio in Section 4, we note that as the block size increases there is a slight negative impact on the miss rate because of the reduction in the number of tags. For the default cache size and associativity, and a fetch size of sixteen words, the overall miss ratio increases from 0.0087 to

0.0090 as the block size increases from one word to sixteen words. All of that change occurs in the data cache, since there is no interference between reads and writes in the instruction cache: once a block is loaded by a fetch it must remain in the cache until a cache miss to a conflicting block forces it and all other blocks loaded at the same time to be replaced. In this case, the data cache load miss ratio went from 0.0161 to 0.0173, while the instruction fetch miss ratio was constant at 0.0062

For block sizes greater than the fetch size this degradation in the miss ratio with increasing block size becomes more dramatic and affects both the instruction and data caches. By the time the block size reaches 64 words, the instruction and load miss ratios have reached 0.0084 and 0.0277 respectively, for a combined read miss ratio of 0.013.

Thus, given this fetch strategy, there is no intrinsic advantage to having a block size greater than the fetch size. For the instruction cache, there is no advantage to having a block size smaller than the fetch size. For the data cache, there is a miss ratio preference for a block size that is as small as practical.

Figure 6-1 shows the results of an experiment in which both the block and fetch sizes were varied over the range 1 word to 64 words. For each set of memory characteristics, a two dimensional array of execution times was the result. By fitting parabolas first in one direction and then the other, the optimal non-binary fetch and block size could be estimated along with the best case performance. The figure shows the web of the optimal fetch sizes and performance levels. Again, the hollow symbols indicate the base level case of equal block and fetch sizes.

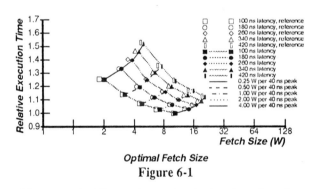

Optimal Fetch Size
Figure 6-1

The most significant observation is that there is only a small increase in the optimal fetch size, and a negligible improvement in the performance level (less than 0.6%). Clearly, selecting equal block and fetch sizes is a very good choice. Figure 6-2 shows the optimal block and fetch size for each memory speed product. The dashed lines again represent the baseline case of enforced equal block and fetch sizes. Freeing up the block and fetch sizes has allowed the fetch size to increase fractionally and the block size to decrease slightly. When restricted to binary sized blocks and fetches, the best case is occasionally equal blocks and fetches, and occasionally fetches of two blocks.

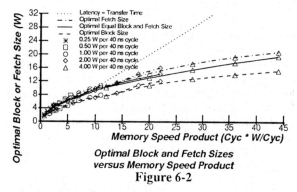

**Optimal Block and Fetch Sizes
versus Memory Speed Product
Figure 6-2**

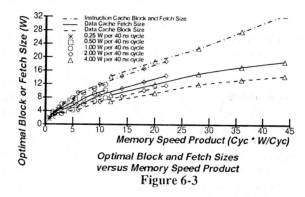

**Optimal Block and Fetch Sizes
versus Memory Speed Product
Figure 6-3**

The question that then arises is why was the optimal block size not significantly smaller than in the default scenario. The answer is write effects. Even though we have selected a write policy that minimizes the performance impact of writes, the block size impact on the read miss ratio was so small that it was overwhelmed by the block size impact on the write performance. Specifically, as the block size was decreased the number of discrete writes to main memory increased since each fetch could replace a number of dirty blocks, each with potentially different tags. Each of these would translate to a separate write to main memory, each with its own latency and overhead. Combining writes from different blocks into block writes requires a significant increase in the complexity of the write buffer and is only somewhat successful. Basically, just as larger fetches make the most of the memory bandwidth for reads, large blocks make the most of it for writes.

There is another important aspect to the interaction between the write policy and block size. For the experiments performed here, the write hit time was a constant two cycles, regardless of the block size. However, with write-through caches, the write hit and miss time are both dramatically minimized for writes equal in size to the block size. In this case, there is no need to check the tags before performing the write into the data portion. For machines with write-through primary caches, this strongly biases the block size towards 1 word. A complete investigation of the interactions between the block size and the write policy is beyond the scope of this paper.

We have noted several times that there are significant behavioural differences between the instruction and data sides of the cache. Given that the block size on the instruction side has no performance impact provided it is less than or equal to the instruction cache fetch size, there are really three free variables in the design of a split cache: the instruction block/fetch size, the data fetch size and the data block size. The optimal size for each of these can be estimated by looking at the instruction and data components to the total execution time observed in the above experiment. Figure 6-3 shows the estimated optimal instruction block and fetch size, data fetch size, and data block size. As expected, the best instruction cache fetch size can be substantially larger than the best combined cache or data cache fetch size.

The conclusion to be drawn here is that the fetch size is properly selected with regard to the memory characteristics, while the block size needs to be selected in conjunction with the write policy. For the write-back data cache and write buffers simulated here, that implies a fairly long block size – usually equal to or slightly less than the fetch size.

7. Complicated Fetch Strategies

In this section we explore the second half of the traditional rationale for longer fetch sizes: the use of more complicated fetch policies facilitates parallelism between CPU execution and memory activity. There are a large number of details involved in fully specifying an involved fetch strategy. The consequence of this complexity is that the complete design space of fetch strategies is large and convoluted. Rather than trying to systematically explore all the various options, we will be presenting simulation results for two of the most effective alternative fetch strategies investigated. Both are fairly aggressive and hardware intensive.

There have been a number of studies of fetch strategies [13, 14, 20], and of prefetching in particular [3, 6, 9, 12, 15, 19]. For the most part, though, these have concentrated on the reduction in the miss rate that stems primarily from the increase in the fetch size or initiation a fetch prior to a miss occurring. Such studies are deceptive because the potential performance improvements indicated by the miss ratio improvements are possible only under very specific temporal conditions. For instance, if prefetched data does not arrive before it is needed, or if a stall occurs because the cache or memory are busy due to a prefetch, then the amount of time saved by the fetch strategy is less than predicted. Furthermore, it is important to realize that the fetch strategy affects performance both through the mean cache miss penalty and through any impact on the cycle time that the additional complexity would entail.

Three of the main design parameters of the fetch strategy are:

1. When will a fetch occur,
2. Which word is returned first from main memory, and
3. At what point is the CPU allowed to continue

execution.

The alternatives for the first design decision are 1) consider initiating a fetch on every memory reference, and 2) fetch only on a cache miss. The two most common alternatives for the second decision are 1) begin with the lowest address, and 2) start with the desired word. From there, the fetch usually proceeds with increasing addresses, wrapping around to the start of the fetch unit if necessary. This is sometimes referred to as a wrapping fetch [7]. The simple approach to the third question is to wait until the entire fetch is complete before resuming execution. A common alternative, though, is to release the CPU from its stall as soon as the data it requires is available. This is often called early-continuation or early restart.

Traditionally, a machine is said to be prefetching data if either 1) a fetch on a cache miss retrieves more than one block of data (fetch size > block size) and CPU execution is resumed after the desired word or block is returned, or 2) a fetch can be initiated even though no cache miss occurred. Smith categorizes these two cases as Class 1 and Class 2 respectively [16], or alternatively as "Prefetch on Fault" and "Prefetch Always" respectively [15].

If fetches are initiated regardless of whether a miss occurred, or if the CPU is allowed to proceed before the fetch is complete, then the next major point of differentiation of fetch strategies is what happens if a miss is encountered while a fetch is in progress. Again, the common simple case is to wait out the current fetch until the bus and memory are again available. A more aggressive alternative is to abort the fetch in progress and start a new one to satisfy the new miss.

So far we have only considered the simplest possible fetch strategy: complete the entire fetch, beginning with the lowest address, before allowing the CPU to continue. In this section we will present data on two additional strategies. The first, called *nbdwf*, fetches one block's worth of data on a cache miss, beginning with the desired word and wrapping around when the end of the block is reached. The CPU is restarted as soon as possible, and the caches are assumed to be dual ported so that CPU references can proceed unhindered by the fetch in progress. If a new miss is encountered, the existing fetch is allowed to complete before a new fetch is initiated. The second strategy, *adwf*, is a more aggressive strategy that greedily tries to satisfy the CPU's immediate needs as quickly as possible. In this case, a miss aborts any fetch in progress, and causes a new fetch to be initiated. The CPU is again restarted as soon as possible. Despite the fact that neither of these fetch strategies are technically prefetching strategies – the block and fetch sizes are identical, and fetches are only initiated on misses – the underlying phenomena behind their observed behaviour apply to most prefetching strategies as well.

Figure 7-1 compares the web of optimal fetch (and block) sizes and attainable performance for the *nbdwf* strategy with that for the default simple strategy. Again we observe that the change in fetch strategy is roughly

equivalent to an increase in the transfer rate. Uniformly across the range of memory systems, only relatively small performance improvements (1.7% to 4.5%) are obtained over the baseline scenario. The optimal fetch sizes are somewhat increased but generally by an amount less than sufficient to increase the best binary fetch size. This is further illustrated when the optimal fetch size is plotted as a function of the memory speed product, as in Figure 7-2.

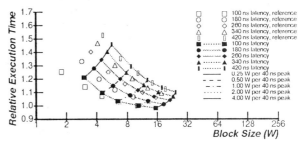

Optimal Block Size: nbdwf Fetch Strategy
Figure 7-1

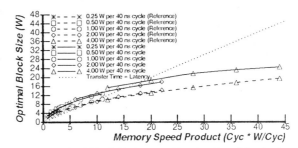

Optimal Block Size versus Memory Speed Product:
nbdwf Fetch Strategy
Figure 7-2

The more aggressive strategy, *adwf*, performed very similarly, though not as well. The performance improvements over the base ranged from 0.8 to 4% across the spectrum of memory characteristics. The shift in the optimal fetch size was even less than shown in Figure 7-2.

There are two main reasons for this relatively poor showing. The first is that the baseline choice of an optimally selected block and fetch size does a very good job of exploiting as much of the locality in the program as possible, given the specific memory system at hand. Second, cache misses are very tightly clustered and correlated. When a strategy has a good chance of fetching something to reduce the miss rate, it frequently lacks the time to do so. Furthermore, when there is a lot of time between misses, it is difficult to know what to fetch.

Complex fetch strategies are at a disadvantage because there is a relatively small region of the design space where they have a significant opportunity for improving on the default case. Consider the maximum possible benefit as a function of backplane utilization. When the utilization is very low, then the processor is not spending very much time in cache misses, so even reducing this component of the execution time by a large fraction will not dramatically improve the system-level performance. At the other extreme, when the backplane utilization is high, there is very little time between misses. Any use of the free bandwidth to the advantage of the miss ratio is likely to be offset by an additional penalty to the next miss. Figure 7-3 illustrates that only in the center region, indicative of a balanced system, do the complicated fetch strategies have enough resources available to them to significantly affect the overall execution time. The figure shows the maximum improvement attained by the two fetch strategies for two cache sizes as a function of the bus utilization, and drives home the realization that even aggressive strategies are of little benefit when the memory hierarchy plays a dominant role in the overall execution time.

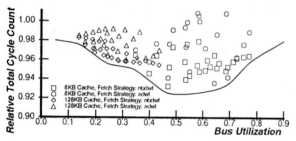

Relative Performance Improvement versus Bus Utilization
Figure 7-3

Above and beyond this limitation of resources, the task of improving on the simple case is made significantly harder by the temporal clustering of cache misses. Figure 7-4 shows this clustering by plotting the cumulative distribution of the interval between cache misses, measured in instructions, as a function of the block/fetch size for the default 128KB (total) split I/D organization. The value for each interval is the probability of two successive misses being separated by less than that number of instructions. As the block size is increased, the probability of short intervals between misses is decreased. However, since spatial and temporal locality are just that – local in nature – the probability of large gaps between misses does not increase as dramatically as we might hope. For example, for a block size of 64W, fully 50% of all misses are encountered within 16 instructions of their predecessors. Regardless of the block size, if a cache and memory system have just finished satisfying a miss, they had better be prepared to handle another soon.

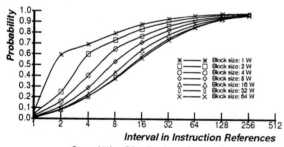

Interval in Instruction References
Cumulative Distribution of the Interval
Between Cache Misses
(128KB Split I/D Cache)
Figure 7-4

8. Conclusions

This paper has investigated several aspects of the selection of the block size, fetch size and fetch strategy. It expanded greatly on a portion of an earlier paper [10]. That paper concluded that if the fetch and block size are kept the same, then for most memory systems, the best binary block size was 4 or 8 words, and that being wrong by one size does not have a large performance impact. It also verified that given certain assumptions, the optimal block size is a function of the product of the memory's latency and transfer rate, and is independent of the CPU cycle time and the individual memory parameters. Because these results are indepedent of the CPU cycle time, they are expressed, where appropriate, in terms of nanoseconds, not CPU cycles.

This paper has made several additional observations. First, it is important to realize that the substantial reduction in miss ratio that is generally attributed to improvements in the block size is really due to increases in the fetch size, and that the two are properly independent. In fact, given a constant fetch size, there is a small increase in the miss ratio with increasing block size, especially in data caches. It does not make sense therefore to have block sizes that are larger than the fetch size. For most fetch strategies, it also does not make sense to have an instruction block size smaller than the instruction fetch size. In general, the fetch size is appropriately selected based on the memory characteristics so that the mean read time is minimized, and the block size should be chosen to best suit the write policy. For the write-back caches with deep write buffers studied here, long block sizes, comparably sized to the fetch size, were most effective at using the available memory bandwidth. Write-through caches' block sizes should be optimized to handle the most common size of write as quickly as possible. In split caches, if the instruction block size is allowed to be different from the data cache block and fetch sizes, then, for the workload measured here, the optimal instruction block size tends to be larger than the appropriate data fetch size by about a factor of two.

Second, if there is any cycle time penalty associated with longer block or fetch sizes, then the performance optimal block size is reduced in size and the independence of the block size of the individual memory characteristics is degraded.

Finally, complicated fetch strategies do not improve much on the simple case of having an equal block and fetch size, and stalling the CPU until the fetch completes. The reasons for this are two fold. First, it is only in well-balanced systems that sufficient resources are available to significantly reduce the memory component of the total execution time; and second, cache misses are temporally clustered. When its clear what should be fetched next, chances are high that the desired data will be needed before the fetch is complete. When there is plenty of time between cache misses, it is unclear what should be profitably fetched next.

It is important to realize that real cache design involves a great many more factors than can be adequately addressed in a paper of this length. Issues of cost, power, availability of components and marketing concerns all significantly perturb machines to design points that may appear to be sub-optimal but which are in fact are best given the circumstances of the design in question. These observations and conclusions are meant as an indicator of general interactions between design variables in the computer design problem. However, given this qualification, all indications are that a simple, straightforward fetch strategy with an appropriately selected block and fetch size does a very good job of making the most of the memory system to reduce the overall execution time of programs.

Acknowledgments

This research was primarily conducted at Stanford University with Professors John Hennessy and Mark Horowitz. The author is profoundly grateful to them for their contribution and support. While at Stanford, the author was funded by Defense Advanced Research Projects Agency contract No. N00014-87-K-0828.

References

1. Agarwal, A., Sites, R., Horowitz, M. ATUM: A New Technique for Capturing Address Traces Using Microcode. Proceedings of the 13th Annual International Symposium on Computer Architecture , Tokyo, Japan, June 1986, pages 119-129.

2. Agarwal, A. *Analysis of Cache Performance for Operating Systems and Multiprogramming*. Ph.D. Thesis, Stanford University, May 1987. Available as Technical Report CSL-TR-87-332.

3. Bennett, B.T., Pomerene, J.H., Puzak T.R., Rechtschaffen, R.N. "Prefetching in a Multilevel Hierarchy". *IBM Technical Disclosure Bulletin 25*, 1 , June 1982, pages 88-89.

4. Cho, J., Smith, A.J., Sachs H. The Memory Architecture and the Cache and memory Management Unit for the Fairchild CLIPPER Processor. Tech. Report UCB/CSD 86/289, Computer Science Division, University of California, Berkeley, April, 1986.

5. Freitas, D. 32-bit Processor Achieves Sustained Performance of 20 MIPS. Proceedings of Northcon , October 1988.

6. Gindele, B.S. "Buffer Block Prefetching Method". *IBM Technical Disclosure Bulletin 20*, 2 , July 1977, pages 696-697.

7. Hennessy, J.L., Patterson, D.A. *Computer Architecture: A Quantitative Approach*. Morgan Kaufmann, San Mateo, CA, 1990.

8. Lapin, L.L. *Probability and Statistics for Modern Engineering*. PWS Publishers, Boston, MA, 1983.

9. Lee, R.L., Yew, P.-C., Lawrie, D.H. Data Prefetching in Shared Memory Multiprocessors. CSRD Report 639, Center for Supercomputing Research and Development, University of Illinios, January, 1987.

10. Przybylski, S., Horowitz, M., Hennessy J. Performance Tradeoffs in Cache Design. Proceedings of the 15th Annual International Symposium on Computer Architecture , June 1988, pages 290-298.

11. Przybylski, S. *Cache and Memory Hierarchy Design: A Performance-Directed Approach*. Morgan Kaufmann, San Mateo, CA, 1990.

12. Rau, B.R. Sequential Prefetch Strategies for Instructions and Data. Tech. Report CSL-TR-77-131, Digital Systems Laboratory, Stanford University, January, 1977.

13. Rau, B.R. *Program Behaviour and the Performance of Memory Systems*. Ph.D. Thesis, Stanford University, 1977.

14. Rau, B.R., Rossman G. The Effect of Instruction Fetch Strategies Upon the Performance of Pipelined Instruction Units. Proceedings of the 4th Annual International Symposium on Computer Architecture , June 1977, pages 80-89.

15. Smith, A.J. "Sequential Program Prefetching in Memory Hierarchies". *IEEE Computer 11*, 12 , December 1978, pages 7-21.

16. Smith, A.J. "Sequentiality and Prefetching in Database Systems". *ACM Transactions on Database Systems 3*, 3 , September 1978, pages 223-247.

17. Smith, A.J. "Characterizing the Storage Process and Its Effects on Main Memory Update". *Journal of the ACM 26*, 1 , January 1979, pages 6-27.

18. Smith, A.J. "Cache Memories". *ACM Computing Surveys 14*, 3 , September 1982, pages 473-530.

19. Smith, A.J. Cache Evaluation and the Impact of Workload Choice. Proceedings of the 12th Annual International Symposium on Computer Architecture , June 1985, pages 64-73.

20. Smith, A.J. "Bibliography and Readings on CPU Cache Memories and Related Topics". *Computer Architecture News 14*, 1 , January 1986, pages 22-42.

21. Smith, A.J. "Line (Block) Size Choice for CPU Cache Memories". *IEEE Transaction on Computers C-36*, 9 , September 1987, pages 1063-1075.

Session 3B: Instruction Sets

Performance Comparison of Load/Store and Symmetric Instruction Set Architetctures

D. Alpert [†] [*]   A. Averbuch [‡]   O. Danieli [†]

[†] National Semiconductor Israel, P.O. Box 3007
Herzelia B. 46104, Israel

[‡] Dept. of Computer Science, School of Mathematical Sciences
Tel-Aviv University
Ramat Aviv, Tel Aviv 69978, Israel
E-Mail: amir@taurus.BITNET or amir@MATH.TAU.AC.IL

Abstract

Is it true that a *Load/Store* architecture is both simpler and faster than a *Symmetric* architecture, or does the *Symmetric* architecture offer a potential performance advantage that can be realized by the use of additional hardware?

In order to answer it quantitatively, we simulated two models that were equal in all aspects except the factor that we measure. We found that the *Load/Store* model executes 12% more instructions but only 4% more cycles.

1 Introduction

Where do we go after RISC ?

Now, that that RISCs processors performance is close to 1 cycle/instruction, how can a computer architect achieve an even better performance ? For a given hardware technology, one may try to execute more than one instruction per cycle (the parallel alternative) or one may try to perform less instructions by executing more powerful instructions.

One way to make the instructions more powerful is to go one step back from the RISC's *Load/Store* architecture and use a *Symmetric* instruction-set which can perform direct operation on memory. In a *Load/Store* instruction-set architecture the only instructions that access memory are LOAD and STORE. Computational instructions can only use registers as operands. A *Symmetric* instruction-set architecture, on the other hand, treats register-operands and memory-operands symmetrically, and has the additional capability to perform direct computation on memory. Example:

Symmetric	*Load/Store*
ADD r1,MEM[r2+disp2]	LOAD MEM[r2+disp1],r3
	ADD r1,r3
	STORE r3,MEM[r2+disp2]

Both architectures have to perform almost the same basic operations. In the above example these are: two to three address calculations, three memory references and one addition. The Symmetric architecture uses a fewer instructions, but the instructions of the *Load/Store* architecture are more streamlined.

The question addressed by this study is: Is it true that the *Load/Store* architecture is both simpler and faster, or does the *Symmetric* architecture offer a potential performance advantage that can be realized by the use of additional hardware?

In the past this was a theoretical question. Design tradeoffs in the early RISCs were based on silicon technology that allows only 50-100 thousand transistors per chip. This silicon area constraint combined with the RISC general trend to push simplicity to the limit, made the Load/Store architecture the natural choice. Today, however, this question is of practical value. Due to the progress in technology, CMOS VLSI chips are ten times denser and it is feasible to implement on silicon a pipelined processor with a capability to perform computations directly on memory.

In order to answer it quantitatively, we simulated two models that were equal in all aspects except the factor that we wanted to measure.

2 Problem Definition

The main tradeoff between *Load/Store* and *Symmetric* architectures is a tradeoff between *path-length*, the number of instructions executed (for a given program) and *CPI*, the average number of cycles per instruction. The following identity represents this tradeoff:

$$\text{Program execution-time} \equiv \text{path-length} \times \text{CPI} / \text{CPU-Frequency}$$

The CPU-frequency is a function of the technology and the micro-architecture: the speed of a gate is a function of technology and the number of gates that have to act sequentially in one cycle is a function of the micro-architecture. Design tradeoffs in this work are based on current CMOS technology. Nevertheless, many of the results reported here can be applied as well to pipeline designed in other technologies.

---

[*]This author is currently in Intel Corporation SC4-59, P.O. Box 58122, Santa Clara, CA 95052, USA

CH2887-8/90/0000/0172$01.00 © 1990 IEEE

The remaining two terms: path-length and CPI, are **both** affected by the selection between *Load/Store* or *Symmetric* architecture. The path-length of the *Symmetric* architecture is of course no longer than that of the *Load/Store* architecture. Measuring the path-length difference between the two, however, is not a trivial task, since there are several other factors that affect the path-length. These are: the operations in the instruction-set, the addressing-modes and the compiler quality.

In order to compute the performance difference between the two models we have to measure the difference in the CPI term too. Assuming a pipeline implementation, the CPI is the sum of three terms:

$$CPI \equiv 1 + \text{pipe-delay} + \text{storage-delay}$$

The "1" term represents the assumption that each instruction stays exactly one cycle at each pipe-stage and therefore the peak throughput is one cycle per instruction when there are no delays.

Pipe-delay is a function of the pipeline structure. It is composed from three components:

$$\text{pipe-delay} \equiv \text{resource-delay} + \text{data-delay} + \text{control-delay}$$

A pipe delay occurs when a pipeline-stage cannot perform its task because it needs a resource that is currently occupied by another stage (resource-delay), or because it needs data that has not been computed yet (data-delay) or because it does not know from where to fetch the next instruction (control-delay).

Storage-delay occurs when the CPU must wait for a memory reference. Modern computers reduce this delay by the use of a memory-hierarchy scheme: registers and caches. The slow-storage is referenced only when the data is *missing* in the fast-storage. The effect of storage-delay is out of the scope of this study. (See [FMM87] for a study on the effect of *Load/Store* architecture vs. *Symmetric* architecture on cache hit ratio). We use the same memory-hierarchy for both architectures and assume 100% hit-rate (no access to slow storage).

3   The Evaluation Environment

When trying to evaluate the contribution of a single architectural feature to the overall performance it is very important to keep all other parameters constant. Our approach is to compare two computers which differ from each other by only one aspect: the capability to perform computations directly on memory. We define two architectures: a *Load/Store* and a *Symmetric* architecture. For each of the two we define an implementation model, simulate a common workload and measure its performance. The performance difference between the models represents the net effect of the additional

direct computations on memory. The evaluation environment we used was developed by the architecture group of National Semiconductor, Israel. Its overall structure looks like this:

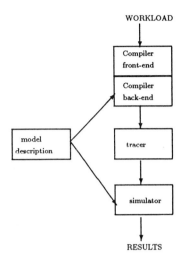

Figure 1: Simulation environment

3.1   The Workload

The workload consists of five programs, written in C. All inputs to all programs were fixed across all runs.

DC- The Unix desk calculator (1938 lines), computing $\sqrt{(e^5)}$ with 10-digit precision.

GREP - Search a 300-line file for a complex regular expression (323 lines).

PTC - Pascal To C translator (9718 lines). This program, representing a compiler like application, translating a 70-line pascal program.

SED - A non-interactive editor (1432 lines). Performing simple text substitutions in a 140 lines file.

SORT - The Unix sorting utility (1384 lines). Sorting 160 decimal numbers.

3.2   The Compiler

The compiler's contribution to the overall performance is an important parameter. The difference between two different compilers can be bigger than the effect we are trying to measure. In this work we use for both models the **same** compiler, the CTP C compiler [Sem86],[BeE88]. This optimizing compiler implements similar optimization techniques to those described by F. Chow in [Cho83]. Its four main parts are: front-end, optimizer, back-end and code-reorder. The description below focuses on the parts that are not identical in both models.

Register Allocation Criteria - The benefits from using a register instead of memory results mainly from the fact that a memory-access might cause a data-cache miss or a pipeline contention. However, the use of a register might involve an overhead that results from the need to save/restore this register before/after it is used or before/after a procedure call.

In the *Symmetric* model, the optimizer has the freedom to choose between a register and memory. It allocates a variable into a register only if the overhead involved in using the register is less than the benefit gained by using the registers.

In the *Load/Store model*, the compiler must load a memory operand into a register before it uses it. This fact makes the optimizer criteria simpler: every variable that is used more than once is a candidate for a register. The LOAD/STORE overhead is spread over all the uses of this variable.

Code Reordering - In order to eliminate as many pipeline delays[1] as possible we added a code-reordering phase at the very end of the compilation process. Both models use the same algorithms (similar to [GiM86]) but the section that describes the pipeline delays is, of course, different for each model. Note that the code-reordering changes only the order of the instructions and not the path-length.

3.3 Tracer and Simulator

The tracer generates a dynamic trace of the instructions that the program executes. It is implemented as a side-effect-free subroutine that the program calls prior to the execution of each instruction. The fact that the instruction set that we used in this study is a sub-set of the Series 32000[2] instruction set eliminates the need to simulate the program's functionality. Instead we actually run the program on a real computer. This greatly simplifies the tracer, making it fast, accurate and reliable.

The simulator inputs are a table-description of the micro-architecture and a dynamic trace of the program. Using a Scoreboard[3] it simulates the flow of instructions in the pipeline and provides, as its output, a cycle-by-cycle detailed description of the program execution.

4 Common to Both Models

The following sections describes the common architecture which we use for the *Load/Store* and the *Symmetric* architectures.

---

[1] See next sections for a detailed description of the pipeline delays in each model.

[2] Trademark of National Semiconductor Corporation. See [Hun87] for Series 32000 Programmer's Reference Manual.

[3] Scoreboard is a hardware-mechanism, used by the CDC 6600, to control the parallel execution of ten functional units [Tho64].

4.1 Instruction Set

In order to avoid significant part of the extra work involved in defining a brand new instruction set (writing a compiler and a functional-simulator), we use an existing instruction set, the Series 32000, as a base line for our instruction set. The Series 32000 is a CISC architecture. It contains many instructions and addressing modes that are infrequently used. In this study we use only the following reduced subset that is appropiate for efficent pipelined implementation:

ADD	Addition
ADDR	Compute the effective address of an operand
AND	Logical and
ASH	Arithmetic shift
BRCOND	Conditional branch
BR	Unconditional branch to PC+displacement
BSR	Branch to subroutine
CMP	Compare
JUMP	Like BR but the destination is a register
LSH	Logical shift
MOV	Move
MOVXI	Sign extended move
MOVZI	Zero extended move
MUL	Multiply
OR	Logical or
QUO	Divide
REM	Compute the reminder
SUB	Subtract
XOR	Logical xor

Table 1: The instruction set

Register	The operand is in register
Register-relative	The operand address is calculated by adding a register and a displacement
Absolute	The operand address is a 32-bit number
Immediate	The operand is a 32-bit immediate

Table 2: The addressing-modes

4.2 Branch Mechanism

The branch issue is related to our comparison because the selection between *Symmetric* architecture and *Load/Store* architecture implies different pipeline implementations, which in turn affect the branch mechanism and the branch delay. Since the branch-mechanism depends on the pipeline structure and we are interested only in the **difference** in branch-delay between the two models we evaluate its effect at the end of this study.

4.3 Registers

Both models use a flat register-file (without a window mechanism) that contains 16 general purpose registers, a stack-pointer (SP) and a program-counter (PC). The major point is that we use the same number of registers for both models. While it is true that a Load/Store architecture needs more registers than a Symmetric architecture, by examining the code of our workload we find out that only when the number of registers is less than 8 does this need of the Load/Store architectures for more register shows up. (The compiler we use does not perform register allocation across procedures, procedure inlining or loop unrolling).

4.4 Two-Operand Instructions

In both architectures, all instructions are two-operand instructions. In computational instructions the second operand is both a source and a destination. For example: the semantics of **ADD r1,r2** is "add **r1** to **r2**".

5 The Load/Store Architecture Model

5.1 The Pipeline Structure

The pipeline for the *Load/Store* architecture is based on the MIPS-X pipeline [HoC87] and is similar to that of many other RISC processors. The basic pipeline structure is:

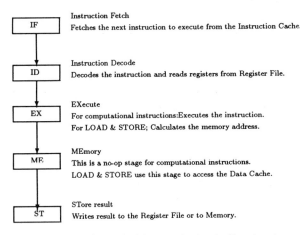

Figure 2: Load/Store architecture basic pipeline structure

The execution *latency* of an instruction is five cycles for most of the instructions and the pipeline's maximal throughput is one instruction per cycle.

5.2 Pipeline Delays

Execution delay - Three instructions: MUL, QUO and REM execute in more than a single cycle and cause an execution-delay. This delay, however, does not affect our comparison because both models execute exactly the same number of MUL, QUO and REM in the same number of cycles. Execution of a MUL takes 10 cycles and QUO and REM are executed in 25 cycles. Table 3 presents the execution delay in our workload:

	DC	GREP	PTC	SED	SORT	MEAN
Delay	0.158	0.0	0.109	0.0	0.014	0.056

Table 3: MUL,QUO and REM execution-delay in CPI

Resource dependency - In this model, a STORE immediately followed by LOAD (Read After Write or RAW) creates a 1-cycle delay. The reason is that the LOAD and the STORE access the DC simultaneously because the STORE writes the DC at the ST-stage and the LOAD reads the DC at the ME-stage. The same type of delay can be found in other implementations ([GiM86], [HoC87],[BeE88]).

Data Dependency - in this pipeline there are two types of interlock: an interlock between two computational instructions (interlock delay) and an interlock between a LOAD instruction and a computational instruction (LOAD delay). Examples:

Interlock Delay	Load Delay
I1:ADD 1,r1	I1:LOAD MEM[r1+d],r2
I2:CMP r1,r2	I2:ADD r2,r3

In order to reduce the delay caused by interlocks we add 3 bypasses to the pipeline. Figure 3 presents the pipe with the new bypasses.

Interlock Delay - Two computational instructions interlock when instruction **I2** reaches the ID-stage and one of its source operands, **opd**, is not ready because it is the destination of a previous instruction **I1** that has not reached the ST-stage yet. The point is, that if **I2** is about to enter EX then **I1** is already done with EX and the result to be stored in **opd** can be used as soon as it becomes available. To do so, the output of the EX-stage is written into *Bypass registers*. The bypass registers, BP1 and BP2, are two registers organized as a queue (FIFO). They allow the destination register of a computational instruction to be used as the source of the next two instructions. Logically, it is fed back

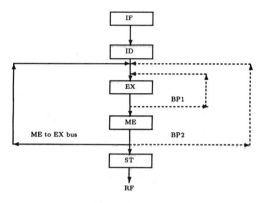

Figure 3: Load/Store pipeline: final structure

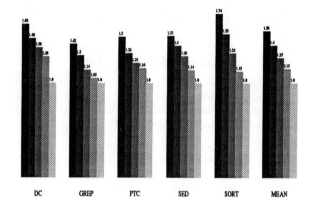

	DC	GREP	PTC	SED	SORT
Instructions	500,152	542,143	685,488	175,644	569,558
Cycles	642,427	570,213	793,665	199,753	640,694

Table 4: Final instructions and cycles count

Figure 4: Load/Store results and evaluation summary

to the EX's input via the dotted lines BP1 or BP2. Physically, special hardware is used to detect that this register is to be read from the bypass registers and not from the RF.

BP2, reduces the interlock delay to a single cycle if the instructions are consecutive and eliminates it if they are not. BP1 together with BP2 eliminate **all** interlocks between computational instructions.

LOAD Delay - This interlock occurs when a LOAD instruction loads a register from memory and one of the next two instructions reads this register. The delay is 2 or 1 cycles respectively. In order to reduce the LOAD delay we need a bus from ME to EX (BP2 is not a bus) to bypass data that arrives from the data-cache to the EX-stage. It reduces the 2-cycle LOAD delay to 1 cycle and eliminates all LOAD delays between a LOAD and a non-consecutive instruction.

5.3 Final Results

Table 4 and figure 4 present a detailed summary of the performance of the *Load/Store* model.

All programs are weighed equally and therefore all right bars are scaled to 1. The five bars represent (left to right) the performance of the:

1. Initial pipeline,

2. Pipeline with BP2,

3. Pipeline with BP2 and BP1,

4. Final pipeline with BP2, BP1 and ME-to-EX.

5. Ideal pipeline with no delay (path-length).

The number on top of each bar are CPI, that means the number of cycles it take to execute the program on the corresponding pipe structure divided by the program path-length. The difference between each two adjacent bars are (left to right) the performance contribution of BP2, BP1 and ME-to-EX. The last difference (right most) is the remaining delay in the final *Load/Store* pipeline. The average cycles per instruction is 1.151 CPI. The extra 0.151 CPI are due to LOAD delay (0.075 CPI), RAW resource-dependency (0.020 CPI) and execution delay (0.056 CPI).

6 The Symmetric Architecture Model

The Symmetric model attempts to speedup execution by three means:

1. Reduce the path-length (instruction count) by using a more powerful instruction set.

2. Eliminate the LOAD delay (the major delay) by using a different pipeline structure.

3. Avoid the introduction of other delays.

The following sections present the Symmetric architecture, explain how it reduces the path-length and analyze its performance.

6.1 Symmetric Instruction-Set Architecture

The *Symmetric* architecture is identical to the *Load/Store* architecture except for the Symmetric model's **extra** capability to operate directly on memory. Its more powerful instruction set creates a potential to reduce the path-length. The following example demonstrates the difference between the two architectures. It shows part of the the *strcmp* routine (from the C run-time library) which compares two null terminated strings pointed by registers **Rq** and **Rp**: The

	Load/Store		Symmetric
Loop:	LOAD MEM[Rp],r1	Loop:	LOAD MEM[Rp],r1
	LOAD MEM[Rq],r2		
	CMP 0, r1		CMP 0,r1
	BNE L_out		BNE L_out
	ADD 1,Rp		ADD 1,Rp
	ADD 1,Rq		ADD 1,Rq
	CMP r2, r1		CMP MEM[Rq], r1
	BEQ Loop		BEQ Loop

Table 5: *Strcmp* body

Symmetric code is one instruction shorter, 12.5%. It code could have been made another instruction shorter by eliminating the LOAD-instruction and using a CMP-instruction with two memory operands but in this study we do not allow memory to memory operations. The rationale behind this restriction is it low impact on the overall performance on one hand and the significant complexity that it saves on the other hand.[4]

6.2 Basic Pipeline Structure

The pipeline we use to implement the Symmetric architecture is similar to the Z80,000 pipeline [Zil84].

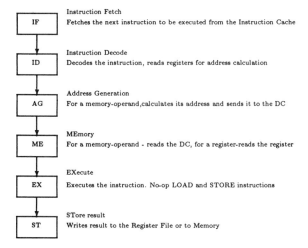

The idea behind this pipeline structure is to exploit the potential parallelism contained in instructions that operate directly on memory by performing an address calculation (at AG) in parallel with an ALU operation (at EX).

6.3 Pipeline Delays

Execution-delay - same as in the *Load/Store* model.

Resource Dependency - Like in the *Load/Store* model, in this model there is a Read-After-Write resource dependency too. The Data-Cache structure is the same as in the *Load/Store* model but in this model a write instruction followed by a read instruction causes a 2-cycles delay which is twice as long as in the *Load/Store* model.

Theoretically, a resource-dependency can be eliminated by incorporating additional hardware resources and performing memory references out-of-order. In this model, as in the *Load/Store* model, we do not introduce any additional hardware and therefore the RAW delay is not removed.

Data Dependencies - There are 3 types of data dependencies: *register interlock*, *AG interlock* and *AG-to-AG interlock*. In order to reduce the delay caused by these interlocks we add 4 bypasses to the pipeline. The pipeline structure with these new bypasses is presented in fig. 5.

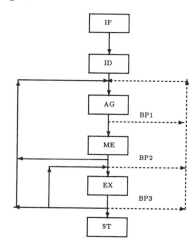

Figure 5: *Symmetric* pipeline: final structure

---

[4]By compiling and simulating the workload without this restriction we found that the average frequency of memory-to-memory instructions is 4.4%. In order to support memory-to-memory instructions at a throughput of 1 instruction per cycle, we have to add to the pipeline a second port to the data-cache and one more adder.

Register interlock - When the source-operand of an instruction is a register, and that register is the destination-operand of the previous instruction, a *register interlock* arises and the pipe is stalled for 1 cycle. The EX-to-EX bypass eliminates all register interlocks. In particular it eliminates all LOAD delays, which account for 80% of the pipeline delays in the *Load/Store* model.

AG-to-AG Interlock - This interlock is similar to the interlock between two computational-instructions in the *Load/Store* model: The adder at the AG-stage computes a result and 1-3 cycles later it needs this result as one of its source-operands. Example: The solution

```
I1: ADDR MEM[r1+1],r1    # Increment r1
I2: CMP 0,MEM[r1+0]      # Use of r1 in address calculation
```

is similar too: "remember" the last three results. "Remembering" means a three register FIFO: BP1, BP2 and BP3. The bypasses are dotted to stress the point that they cannot be used to transfer to the AG-stage results that were computed at the EX or ME stages. Using these bypass-registers, the AG-stage can "read" an operand from the output of AG, ME or EX by reading its own local copy from bypass-register BP1, BP2 or BP3 respectively.

AG Interlock - When an instruction that performs an address-calculation reaches the ID-stage and it cannot read its operand because the register is the destination of one of the three previous instructions, an AG-interlock arises and the pipe is stalled for 1-3 cycles. This interlock is inherent to the pipeline structure because the operand that is needed at the AG-stage is calculated at latter stages: EX (if it is a computation) or ME (result of a LOAD). The best we can do is to reduce it. Instead of waiting until the result is written to the RF, we can read it as soon as it is ready. Two bypasses are needed: One from EX to AG to bypass results of computational instructions and one from ME to AG to bypass the result of LOADs.

6.4 Summary of Results

Table 6 summarizes the performance of the final *Symmetric* model:

	DC	GREP	PTC	SED	SORT
Instructions	467,256	465,161	640,448	142,793	531,296
Cycles	640,864	518,130	804,092	164,086	585,492

Table 6: Instructions and cycles count summary

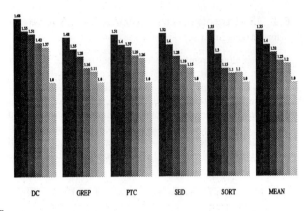

Figure 6: *Symmetric* model: performance summary

The average CPI is 1.199. The AG-interlock, the RAW resource dependency and the execution-delay cause an average delay of 0.055 CPI, 0.084 CPI and 0.060 respectively.

Figure 6 summarizes the evaluation of the *Symmetric* model:

The bars, from left to right, represent the performance results of the following:

1. Plain Pipe.

2. With EX-to-EX Bypass.

3. With AG-to-AG Bypass-Registers.

4. With EX-to-AG Bypass.

5. With ME-to-AG Bypass.

6. Ideal pipe - Path-length.

Note how in two applications, DC and PTC, the final average CPI is much higher than the average because of their high execution-delay. (They execute MUL, QUO and REM relatively frequently).

Note also, that in SORT the fourth bar (left to right) is slightly lower than the fifth bar. This performance degradation is caused by an anomaly of the code-reorganizer and not by the bypass form ME to AG.

7 Control-dependency

Up until this point, all the cycle counts we reported did not include the delay caused by control dependency (branch-delay). In order to make a complete comparison we evaluate the difference in the branch-delay too.

Unconditional Branches - The two model are equal in terms of unconditional branches. There is a 1-cycle delay when the IF-stage waits until a special adder at the ID-stage computes the non-sequential PC.

Conditional Branches - We use a CMP instruction to perform the comparison and set the condition flags. A BRcond instruction computes the branch-target and selects the next-PC according to the flags. As with the unconditional branches, the BRcond computes the non-sequential-PC at the ID-stage. The CMP instruction evaluates the condition at the EX-stage. If the IF-stage waits until the condition is resolved at the EX-stage before it fetches the next instruction then each BRcond results a delay of one cycles in the Load/Store model and three in the *Symmetric* model. Instead, we incorporate a *branch-prediction* mechanism. The two most simple (and common) prediction policies and their delay are:

	Prediction			
	Never-Taken		Always-Taken	
Outcome	L/S	Symm	L/S	Symm
Branch Not-Taken	0	0	1	3
Branch Taken	1	3	1	1

Table 7: Conditional brances delay (in cycles). L/S stands for Load/Store and Symm for Symmetric.

Under the assumption of 15% wrong prediction ([LeS84], [DiM87], [McH86]), the preferable prediction-policy for both models is never-taken. For correct prediction, both models perform equally. For incorrect prediction, the delay in the *Symmetric model* is two cycles longer than the delay in the *Load/Store* model because the EX-stage is two stages ahead. Using *branch-spreading*, we managed to reduce the average delay in the Symmetric model from 3 to 2.81.

In order to compute the overall delay due to conditional branches we have to know their frequency. This information is presented in table 8. Note that both models execute the

	DC	GREP	PTC	SED	SORT	MEAN
L/S	13.36	10.57	11.62	18.79	19.33	14.73
Symm	14.30	12.32	12.44	23.02	20.72	16.56

Table 8: Conditional branch frequency in percentage

same number of conditional-branches but their frequencies is not the same because the *Load/Store* path-length is longer. The average delay due to conditional branches (assuming 85% correct prediction) is therefore:

In the *Load/Store* model: $0.15 \times 1.00 \times 0.1473$ = 0.0221 CPI.
In the *Symmetric* model: $0.15 \times 2.81 \times 0.1656$ = 0.0698 CPI.
The difference between the two models is 0.048 CPI.

8   Comparison Between The Two Models

8.1   The Path-length

In table 9, we see that the use of a more powerful instruction-set reduces the path-length of a *Load/Store* architecture by an average factor of 1.12 (In this section we use a geometric mean whenever we report an average ratio).

	DC	GREP	PTC	SED	SORT
L/S	500,152	542,143	685,488	175,644	569,558
Symm	467,256	465,161	640,448	142,793	531,296
Ratio	1.07	1.17	1.07	1.23	1.07

Table 9: Path-length

The path-length reduction result from the fact that the Symmetric model executes less LOAD and STORE instructions because they are frequently combined with an operator into an operation on memory. A similar result, 10%, was reported in [FMM87].

8.2   Number of Cycles

As explained before, a reduction in the path-length does not necessarily result in a performance gain. More powerful instructions are also more complicated to execute. In order to measure the performance contribution of the *Symmetric* architecture we implemented two pipelines, one for each architecture. Table 10 presents the performance of these pipelines:

	DC	GREP	PTC	SED	SORT
L/S	642,427	570,213	796,831	199,753	640,694
Symm	640,864	518,130	804,092	164,086	585,492
Ratio	1.00	1.10	0.99	1.22	1.09

Table 10: Optimized pipeline performance

The average performance-ratio is to 1.078, smaller than the path-length ratio. This is because the *Load/Store* pipeline executes an average instruction in 1.151 cycles while the *Symmetric* pipeline does so in 1.199 cycles. The extra cycles (in both models) results from data-dependency and resource dependency (in both models the execution delay is the same and branch delay is not included).

8.3   Data-dependency

In the *Load/Store* model, data dependency delay results from LOAD-delay which causes a 1-cycle delay. In the *Symmetric* model data dependency results from AG-interlock, which causes a 1 or 2-cycle delay. Table 11 presents the delay which results from data-dependencies. (The numbers are in CPI units):

	DC	GREP	PTC	SED	SORT
Load/Store	0.076	0.035	0.041	0.116	0.107
Symmetric	0.027	0.063	0.076	0.042	0.066

Table 11: Data dependency delay

The average delay caused by data dependency is 0.075 CPI in the *Load/Store* model and 0.055 CPI in the *Symmetric* model.

8.4 Resource-dependency

The only resource dependency results from contention on the data-cache. Both models use the same data-cache: a two-way set-associative physical cache. A STORE which is immediately followed by a LOAD causes a 1-cycle delay in the *Load/Store* model and two cycles delay in the *Symmetric* model. Table 12 presents the delay which results from resource dependencies:

	DC	GREP	PTC	SED	SORT
Load/Store	0.051	0.017	0.007	0.021	0.004
Symmetric	0.175	0.051	0.063	0.109	0.021

Table 12: Read-after-write delay

The average delay is 0.020 CPI in the *Load/Store* model and 0.084 CPI in the *Symmetric* model. The main reason why the delay in the *Symmetric* model is four times longer than that of the *Load/Store* model is that a contention on the data-cache causes a 2-cycle delay in the *Symmetric* model and only a 1-cycle delay in the *Load/Store* model. In the presence of an optimizing compiler this factor of 2 is further magnified. The compiler reorders the code in order to spread the STORE and the LOAD instructions. Statistically, there are many cases in which the compiler can find only one instruction to insert between the STORE and the LOAD. In these cases the delay in the *Load/Store* model vanishes while in the *Symmetric* model the delay only reduces to one cycle.

8.5 Overall Performance

Table 13 presents the overall performance including the branches-delay:

	DC	GREP	PTC	SED	SORT
L/S	652,451	578,806	808,783	204,704	657,209
Symm	669,033	542,279	837,678	177,998	631,889
Ratio	0.98	1.07	0.97	1.15	1.04

Table 13: Performance with branches-delay

The total number of cycles with branches-delay is computed by adding the number of cycles without branches-delay (reported in table 10), to the number of branches (reported in table 8) multiplied by the average branch-cost (0.15 for

the *Load/Store* model and 0.42 for the *Symmetric*). Taking into account the branches-delay, the performance-ratio between the two models becomes 1.0375.

9   Summary

Two pipeline models, one implementing a *Load/Store* architecture, the other a *Symmetric* architecture were compared under identical simulation environments. The *Symmetric* architecture instructions are more powerful, but also more complex; therefore the pipeline model for the *Symmetric* architecture contains an additional stage with additional adder, more bypasses and extra port to the register file.

Our simulations show that the path-length of the *Load/Store* architecture is 1.12 longer than that of the *Symmetric* architecture. Nevertheless, most of this advantage is lost because of various pipeline delays that reduce the speedup factor from 1.12 to 1.0375. The main delaying contribution is due to resource dependency (0.064 CPI) and control dependency (0.048 CPI).

For more detailes about this study see [Dan88].

References

[BeE88] C. Bendalac and G.Erlich, "CTP - A family of Optimizing Compilers for the NS32532 Microprocessor", *ICCD, 1988 I(1988)*.

[Cho83] F. C. Chow, "A Portable Machine-Independent Global Optimizer-Design and Measurments", *Phd Thesis, Computer System Lab., Stanford, Technical Note No. 83254, 1983*.

[Dan88] O. Danielli, "Performance Comparsion of Load/Store and Symmetric Instruction Set Architectures", *M.Sc Thesis, Dept. of Computer Science, Tel Aviv University, 1988*.

[DiM87] D.R. Ditzel and H.R. McLellan, "Branch Folding in the CRISP Microprocessor: Reducing branch delay to zero", *The 14th Annual International Symposium on Computer Architecture, 2-8, 1987*.

[FMM87] M.J. Flynn, C.L. Mitchell and J.M. Mulder, "And Now a Case for More Complex Instructions Sets", *Computer, 71-83, 1987*.

[GiM86] P.B. Gibbons and S.S. Muchnick, "Efficient Instruction Scheduling for a Pipeline Architecture", *ACM, 11, 1986*.

[HoC87] M. Horowitz and P. Chow, "Architectural Tradeoffs in the Design of MIPS-X", *The 14th Annual International Symposium on Computer Architecture, 300-308, 1987*.

[Hun87] C. Hunter, *Series 32000 programmer's Reference Manual*, Prentice-Hall,1987.

[LeS84] J.K.L Lee and A. Smith, "Branch Prediction Strategies and Branch Target Buffer Design", *Computer 17, 1987.*

[McH86] S. McFarling and J. Hennessy, "Reducing the cost of Branches", *The 13th Annual International Symposium on Computer Architecture, 396-403, 1986.*

[Sem86] N. Semiconductor, *CTP User Manual,* 1986.

[Tho64] J. Thormton, "Parallel Operation in the Control Data 6600", *AFIPS Proc. 26, pp. 33-40, 1964.*

[Zil84] Zilog, *Z80,000 Preliminary Technical Manual,* 1984.

Reducing the Cost of Branches
by Using Registers†

JACK W. DAVIDSON AND DAVID B. WHALLEY

Department of Computer Science
University of Virginia
Charlottesville, VA 22903, U. S. A.

ABSTRACT

In an attempt to reduce the number of operand memory references, many RISC machines have thirty-two or more general-purpose registers (e.g., MIPS, ARM, Spectrum, 88K). Without special compiler optimizations, such as inlining or interprocedural register allocation, it is rare that a compiler will use a majority of these registers for a function. This paper explores the possibility of using some of these registers to hold branch target addresses and the corresponding instruction at each branch target. To evaluate the effectiveness of this scheme, two machines were designed and emulated. One machine had thirty-two general-purpose registers used for data references, while the other machine had sixteen data registers and sixteen registers used for branching. The results show that using registers for branching can effectively reduce the cost of transfers of control.

1. INTRODUCTION

Branch instructions cause many problems for machines. Branches occur frequently and thus a large percentage of a program's execution time is spent branching to different instructions. Branches can result in the pipeline having to be flushed, which reduces its effectiveness and makes pipelines with smaller number of stages more attractive. Furthermore, when the target of a branch instruction is not in the cache, additional delays are incurred as the instruction must be fetched from slower main memory.

This paper describes a technique that can eliminate much of the cost due to branches by using a new set of registers. A field is dedicated within each instruction to indicate a branch register that contains the address of the

†This work was supported in part by the National Science Foundation under Grant CCR-8611653.

next instruction to be executed. Branch target address calculations are performed by instructions that are separate from the instruction causing the transfer of control. By exposing to the compiler the calculation of branch target addresses as separate instructions, the number of executed instructions can be reduced since the calculation of branch target addresses can often be moved out of loops. Much of the delay due to pipeline interlocks is eliminated since the instruction at a branch target is prefetched at the point the address is calculated. This prefetching of branch targets can also decrease the penalty for cache misses.

2. REVIEW

Due to the high cost of branches, there has been much work proposing and evaluating approaches to reduce the cost of these instructions. One scheme that has become popular with the advent of RISC machines is the delayed branch. While the machine is fetching the instruction at the branch target, the instruction after the branch is executed. For example, this scheme is used in the Stanford MIPS [HENN83] and Berkeley RISC [PATT82] machines. Problems with delayed branches include requiring the compiler or assembler to find an instruction to place after the branch and the cost of executing the branch itself.

Branch folding is another technique that reduces the cost of executing branches. This has been implemented in the CRISP architecture [DITZ87b]. Highly encoded instructions are decoded and placed into a wide instruction cache. Each instruction in this cache contains an address of the next instruction to be executed. Unconditional branches are folded into the preceding instruction since the program counter is assigned this new address for each instruction. Conditional branches are handled by having two potential addresses for the next instruction and by inspecting a static prediction bit and the condition code flag to determine which path to take. If the setting of the condition code (the compare) is spread far enough apart from the conditional branch, then the

CH2887-8/90/0000/0182$01.00 © 1990 IEEE

correct instruction can be fetched with no pipeline delay. Otherwise, if the incorrect path is chosen, then the pipeline must be flushed. The problems with this scheme include the complex hardware needed to implement the technique and the large size of the instruction cache since each decoded instruction is 192 bits in length.

An approach to reduce delays due to cache misses is to prefetch instructions into a buffer [RAU77]. The conditional branch instruction causes problems since either one of two target addresses could be used [RISE72]. One scheme involves prefetching instructions along both potential execution paths [LEE84]. This scheme requires more complicated hardware and also must deal with future conditional branch instructions. Other approaches use branch prediction in an attempt to choose the most likely branch target address [LEE84]. If the incorrect path is selected, then execution must be halted and the pipeline flushed.

3. THE BRANCH REGISTER APPROACH

As in Wilke's proposed microprogrammed control unit [WILK83] and the CRISP architecture [DITZ87a], every instruction in the branch register approach is a branch. Each instruction specifies the location of the next instruction to be executed. To accomplish this without greatly increasing the size of instructions, a field within all instructions specifies a register that contains the virtual address of the next instruction to execute.

Examples depicting instructions in this paper are represented using register transfer lists (RTLs). RTLs describe the effect of machine instructions and have the form of conventional expressions and assignments over the hardware's storage cells. For example, the RTL

```
r[3]=r[1]+r[2]; cc=r[1]+r[2]?0;
```

represents a register-to-register integer addition instruction on many machines. The first register transfer stores the sum of the two registers into a third register, while the second register transfer compares the sum of the two registers to set the condition codes. All register transfers within the same RTL represent operations that are performed in parallel.

For instructions specifying that the next instruction to be executed is the next sequential instruction, a branch register is referenced which contains the appropriate address. This register is, in effect, the program counter (PC). While an instruction is being fetched from the instruction cache, the PC is always incremented by the machine to point to the next sequential instruction. If every instruction is thirty-two bits wide, then this operation can always be performed in a uniform manner. Once an instruction has been fetched, the value of the branch register specified in the instruction is used as an address for the

next instruction. At the point the PC is referenced, it will represent the address of the next sequential instruction. An example of this is shown in the RTL below, where b[0] (a branch register) has been predefined to be the PC.

```
r[1]=r[1]+1; b[0]=b[0]; /* go to next seq. inst.
```

Since references to b[0] do not change the address in b[0], subsequent RTLs do not show this default assignment.

If the next instruction to be executed is not the next sequential instruction, then code is generated to calculate and store the virtual address of that instruction in a different branch register and to reference that branch register in the current instruction. Storing the virtual address of a branch target instruction into a branch register also causes the address to be sent to the instruction cache to prefetch the instruction. The prefetched instruction will be stored into an instruction register that corresponds to the branch register receiving the virtual address. The address in the branch register will be incremented to point to the instruction after the branch target. The instruction register i[0], that corresponds to the branch register b[0], which is used as the program counter, is always loaded with the next sequential instruction.

To implement this technique, an organization shown in Figure 1 could be used. During the decode stage of the current instruction, the bit field specifying one of the branch registers is also used to determine which instruction register to use in the decode stage of the next instruction. When a branch register is referenced in an instruction to indicate that a transfer of control is to occur, the next instruction to execute is taken from the corresponding instruction register.

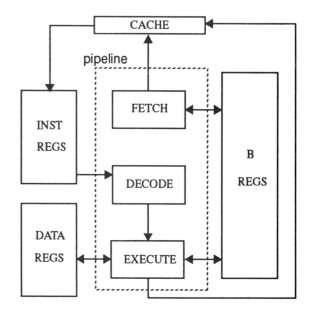

Figure 1: Dataflow for Branch Register Machine

4. CODE GENERATION

The following sections describe how code can be generated to accomplish various transfers of control using branch registers.

Calculating Branch Target Addresses

For all instructions where the next instruction to be executed is not the next sequential instruction, a different branch register from the PC must be specified and the virtual address it contains must have been previously calculated. If we assume a virtual address of thirty-two bits, an address cannot be referenced as a constant in a single instruction. Consequently, most instructions would use an offset from the PC to calculate branch addresses. The compiler knows the distance between the PC and the branch target if both are in the same routine. This is shown in the following RTLs:

```
b[1]=b[0]+(L2-L1);  /* store address of L2
L1: ...
    ...
L2: ...
```

For calls or branch targets that are known to be too far away, the calculation of the branch address requires two instructions. One part of the address is computed by the first instruction and then the other part in the second. Global addresses are calculated in this fashion for programs on the SPARC architecture [SUN87]. An address calculation requiring two instructions is illustrated by the following RTLs:

```
r[5]=HI(L1);        /* store high part of addr
b[1]=r[5]+LO(L1);   /* add low part of addr
    ...
L1: r[0]=r[0]+1;    /* inst at branch target
    ...
```

Unconditional Branches

Unconditional branches are handled in the following manner. First, the virtual address of the branch target is calculated and stored in a branch register. To perform the transfer of control, this branch register is moved into the PC (b[0]), which causes the instruction at the target address to be decoded and executed next. While the instruction at the branch target is being decoded, the instruction sequentially following the branch target is fetched. An example of an unconditional branch is depicted in the following RTLs:

```
b[2]=b[0]+(L2-L1);      /* store addr of L2
L1: ...
    ...
r[1]=r[1]+1; b[0]=b[2]; /*  next inst at L2
    ...
L2: .
```

Conditional Branches

Conditional branches are generated by the following method. First, the virtual address of the branch target is calculated and stored in a branch register. At some point later, an instruction determines if the condition for the branch is true. Three branch registers are used in this instruction. One of two registers is assigned to the destination register depending upon the value of the condition. To more effectively encode this compare instruction, two of the three registers could be implied. For instance, the RTLs in the following example show how a typical conditional branch is handled. The destination branch register is b[7], which is by convention a trash branch register. The other implied branch register, the source register used when the condition is not true, is b[0], which represents the address of the instruction sequentially following the transfer of control instruction. An instruction following this conditional assignment would reference the destination branch register. This is illustrated below.

```
b[2]=b[0]+(L2-L1);      /* store addr of L2
L1: ...
    ...
b[7]=r[5]<0->b[2]|b[0]; /* set branch register
r[1]=r[1]+1; b[0]=b[7]; /* jump to at addr in b[7]
    ...
L2:
```

Function Calls and Returns

Function calls and returns can also be implemented efficiently with this approach. Since the beginning of a function is often an unknown distance from the PC, its virtual address is calculated in two instructions and stored in a branch register. Then, an instruction at some point following this calculation would reference that branch register. To accomplish a return from a function, the address of the instruction following the call would be stored in an agreed-on branch register (for example b[7]). Every instruction that references a branch register that is not the program counter, b[0], would store the address of the next physical instruction into b[7]. If the called routine has any branches other than a return, then b[7] would need to be saved and restored. When a return to the caller is desired, the branch register is restored (if necessary) and referenced in an instruction. An example that illustrates a call and a return on this machine is given in the following RTLs.

```
r[2]=HI(_foo);      /* store high part of addr
b[3]=r[2]+LO(_foo); /* add low part of addr
    ...
r[0]=r[0]+1; b[0]=b[3]; b[7]=b[0];
/* next inst is first inst in foo
    ...
_foo:
    ...
r[0]= r[12]; b[0]=b[7];   /* return to caller
```

Indirect Jumps

For implementation of indirect jumps, the virtual address is loaded from memory into a branch register and then referenced in a subsequent instruction. The following RTLs illustrate how a switch statement might be implemented.

```
r[2]=r[2]<<2;          /* r2 is index in table
r[1]=HI(L01);          /* store high part of L01
r[1]=r[1]+LO(L01);     /* add low part of L01
b[3]=L[r[1]+r[2]];     /* load addr of switch case
    ...
r[0]=r[0]+1; b[0]=b[3]; 
/* next inst is at switch case
L01:  .long Ldst1      /* case label
      .long Ldst2      /* case label
      ...
      ...
```

5. COMPILER OPTIMIZATIONS

Initially, it may seem there is no advantage to the branch register approach. Indeed, it appears more expensive since an instruction is required to calculate the branch target address and a set of bits to specify a branch register is sacrificed from each instruction. However, one only needs to consider that the branch target address for unconditional jumps, conditional jumps, and calls are usually constants. Therefore, the assignment of these addresses to branch registers can be moved out of loops. Because transfers of control occur during execution of other instructions, the cost of these branches disappears after the first iteration of a loop.

Since there is a limited number of available branch registers, often every branch target cannot be allocated to a unique branch register. Therefore, the branch targets are first ordered by estimating the frequency of the execution of the branches to these targets. The estimated frequency of execution of each branch is used, rather than the execution of each branch target instruction, since it is the calculation of the virtual address used by each branch that has the potential for being moved out of loops. If there is more than one branch to the same branch target, then the frequency estimates of each of these branches are added together.

After calculating the estimated frequency of reference, the compiler attempts to move the calculation of the branch target with the highest estimated frequency to the preheader of the innermost loop in which the branch occurs. The preheader is the basic block that precedes the first basic block that is executed in the loop (or the head of the loop). At this point the compiler tries to allocate the calculation of the branch target address to a branch register. If the loop contains calls, then a non-scratch branch register must be used. If a branch register is only associated with branches in other loops that do not overlap with the execution of the current loop, then the branch target calculation for the branch

in the current loop can be allocated to the same branch register. If the calculation for a branch target can be allocated to a branch register, then the calculation is associated with that branch register and the preheader of that loop (rather than the basic block containing the transfer of control) and the estimated frequency of the branch target is reduced to the frequency of the preheader of the loop. Next, the compiler attempts to move the calculation of the branch target with the currently highest frequency estimate out of the loop. This process continues until all branch target calculations have been moved out of loops or no more branch registers can be allocated.

To reduce further the number of instructions executed, the compiler attempts to replace no-operation (noop) instructions, that occur when no other instruction can be used at the point of a transfer of control, with branch target address calculations. These noop instructions are employed most often after compare instructions. Since there are no dependencies between branch target address calculations and other types of instructions that are not used for transfers of control, noop instructions can often be replaced.

Figures 2 through 4 illustrate these compiler optimizations. Figure 2 contains a C function. Figure 3 shows the RTLs produced for the C function for a conventional RISC machine with a delayed branch. Figure 4 shows the RTLs produced for the C function for a machine with branch registers. In order to make the RTLs easier to read, assignments to b[0] that are not transfers of control and updates to b[7] at instructions that are transfers of control are not shown. The machine with branch registers had one less instruction (eleven as opposed to fourteen) due to a noop being replaced with branch target address calculations. Since branch target address calculations were moved out of loops, there was only five instructions inside of the loop for the branch register machine as opposed to six for the machine with a delayed branch.

```
strlen(s)
char *s;
{
    int n = 0;

    if (s)
        for (; *s; s++)
            n++;
    return(n);
}
```

Figure 2: C function

```
      r[1]=L[r[31]+s.];     /* load s
      NZ=r[1]?0;            /* compare s to 0
      PC=NZ==0->L14;        /* delay cond. jump
      r[2]=0;               /* initialize n to 0
      PC=L17;               /* jmp to loop test
      NL=NL;                /* no-op required
L18:r[2]=r[2]+1;            /* increment n
      r[1]=r[1]+1            /* increment s
L17:r[0]=B[r[1]];           /* load character
      NZ=r[0]?0;            /* compare to zero
      PC=NZ!=0->L18;        /* delayed cond. jump
      NL=NL;                /* no-op required
L14:PC=RT;                  /* delayed return
      r[0]=r[2];            /* delay slot filled
```

Figure 3: RTLs for C Function with Delayed Branches

```
      b[1]=b[7];                  /* save ret address
      b[7]=b[0]+(L14-L2);         /* compute exit addr
L2:r[1]=L[r[15]+s.];            /* load s
      b[7]=r[1]==0->b[7]|b[0];    /* test cond.
      r[2]=0; b[0]=b[7];    /* initialize n and jmp
      b[7]=b[0]+(L17-L1);   /* compute entry to loop
L1:b[2]=b[0]+(L18-L18);b[0]=b[7]; /*compute loop
                          /* header and jump to entry
L18:r[2]=r[2]+1                 /* increment n
      r[1]=r[1]+1;                /* increment s
L17:r[0]=B[r[1]];               /* load character
      b[7]=r[0]!=0->b[2]|b[0]; /* compute target
      NL=NL;b[0]=b[7];            /* jump
L14:r[0]=r[2];b[0]=b[1];         /* return
```

Figure 4: RTLs for C Function with Branch Registers

6. REDUCTION OF PIPELINE DELAYS

Most pipeline delays due to branches on conventional RISC machines can be avoided using the branch register approach. For a three-stage pipleline, Figure 5 contrasts the pipeline delays for unconditional transfers of control on machines without a delayed branch, with a delayed branch, and with branch registers. The three stages in the pipeline in this figure are:

1. Fetch (F)
2. Decode (D)
3. Execute (E)

The branch target instruction cannot be fetched until its address has been calculated. For the first two machines, this occurs in the execute stage of the jump instruction. A conventional RISC machine without a delayed branch would have an N-1 delay in the pipeline for unconditional transfersof control where N is the number of stages in the pipeline. The next instruction for the machine with a delayed branch and the machine with branch registers represents the next sequential instruction following the jump instruction. Thus, a RISC machine with a delayed branch, where the branch is delayed for one instruction, would have an N-2 delay in the pipeline. Finding more than one useful instruction to place behind a delayed branch is difficult for most types of programs [MCFA86]. A jump

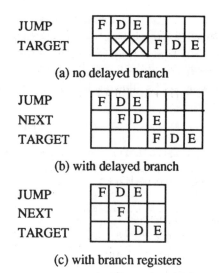

(a) no delayed branch

(b) with delayed branch

(c) with branch registers

Figure 5: Pipeline Delays for Unconditional Transfers of Control

instruction for the machine with branch registers represents an instruction that references a branch register that is not the PC (b[0]). The branch register referenced is used during the decode stage of the jump instruction to determine which one of the set of instruction registers is to be input as the next instruction to be decoded. While the jump instruction is being decoded, the next sequential instruction is being fetched and loaded into i[0], the default instruction register. If b[0] had been referenced, then i[0] would be input to the decode stage. Since a different branch register is referenced for the jump instruction, its corresponding instruction register containing the branch target instruction would be input to the next decode stage. Thus, assuming that the branch target instruction has been prefetched and is available in the appropriate instruction register, the machine with branch registers would have no pipeline delay for unconditional transfers of control regardless of the number of stages in the pipeline.

The example in Figure 6 shows the actions taken by each stage in the pipeline for an unconditional transfer of control in the branch register machine, assuming that the jump sequentially follows the previously executed instruction. The subscript on the actions denotes the stage of the pipeline. During the first cycle, the jump instruction is fetched from memory and the PC is incremented to the next sequential instruction. In the second cycle, the jump instruction is decoded and the next sequential instruction after the jump is fetched from memory. In the third cycle, the jump instruction is executed, the prefetched branch target in i[4] is decoded, and the instruction sequentially following the branch target is fetched. Since the address in a branch register is incremented after being used to prefetch an instruction from the cache, the branch register contains the address of the instruction after the branch target.

$r[1] = r[1] + 1; b[0] = b[4];$

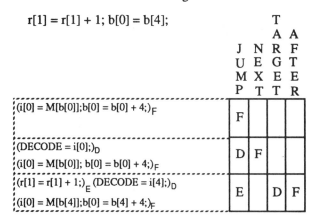

	JUMP	NEXT	TARGET	AFTER
$(i[0] = M[b[0]]; b[0] = b[0] + 4;)_F$	F			
$(DECODE = i[0];)_D$ $(i[0] = M[b[0]]; b[0] = b[0] + 4;)_F$	D	F		
$(r[1] = r[1] + 1;)_E (DECODE = i[4];)_D$ $(i[0] = M[b[4]]; b[0] = b[4] + 4;)_F$	E		D	F

Figure 6: Pipeline Actions for Unconditional Transfer of Control

Figure 7 contrasts the pipeline delays for conditional transfers of control for the same three types of machines. For unconditional transfers of control, the conventional RISC machine without a delayed branch

```
COMPARE   F  D  E
JUMP         F  D  E
TARGET             X  X  F  D  E
```
(a) no delayed branch

```
COMPARE   F  D  E
JUMP         F  D  E
NEXT            F  D  E
TARGET             X  F  D  E
```
(b) with delayed branch

```
COMPARE   F  D  E
JUMP         F  D  E
NEXT            F
TARGET                D  E
```
(c) with branch registers

Figure 7: Pipeline Delays for Conditional Transfers of Control

would have a N-1 pipeline delay and the RISC machine with a delayed branch would have a N-2 pipeline delay for conditional transfers of control. The compare instruction for

the machine with branch registers will assign one of two branch registers to a destination branch register depending upon the result of the condition in the compare. It will also make an assignment between the corresponding instruction registers. The conditional jump instruction is performed by the instruction following the compare instruction that references the destination branch register of the compare instruction. The branch register referenced is used during the decode stage of the conditional jump instruction to cause the corresponding instruction register to be input as the next instruction to be decoded. Therefore, the decode stage of the target instruction cannot be accomplished until the last stage of the compare instruction is finished. This results in an N-3 pipeline delay for conditional transfers of control for a machine with branch registers.

The example in Figure 8 shows the actions taken by each stage of the pipeline for a conditional transfer of control, assuming that the compare instruction sequentially follows the previously executed instruction. During the first cycle, the compare instruction is fetched from memory and the PC is incremented to the next sequential instruction. In the second cycle, the compare instruction is decoded and the jump instruction is fetched from memory. In the third cycle, the compare instruction is executed (resulting in assignments to both b[7] and i[7]), the jump instruction is decoded, and the instruction sequentially following the jump is fetched. If the condition of the compare is not true, then b[7] and i[7] receive the same values from the fetch operation. During the fourth cycle, the jump instruction is executed, either the target instruction or the next instruction after the jump is decoded, and the instruction after the instruction being decoded is fetched.

$b[7] = r[5] < 0 \rightarrow b[3] | b[0];$
$r[1] = r[1] + 1; b[0] = b[7];$

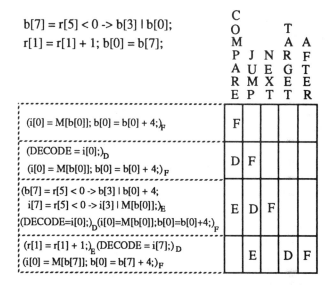

	COMPARE	JUMP	NEXT	TARGET	AFTER
$(i[0] = M[b[0]]; b[0] = b[0] + 4;)_F$	F				
$(DECODE = i[0];)_D$ $(i[0] = M[b[0]]; b[0] = b[0] + 4;)_F$	D	F			
$(b[7] = r[5] < 0 \rightarrow b[3] | b[0] + 4;$ $i[7] = r[5] < 0 \rightarrow i[3] | M[b[0]];)_E$ $(DECODE=i[0];)_D (i[0]=M[b[0]];b[0]=b[0]+4;)_F$	E	D	F		
$(r[1] = r[1] + 1;)_E (DECODE = i[7];)_D$ $(i[0] = M[b[7]]; b[0] = b[7] + 4;)_F$		E		D	F

Figure 8: Pipeline Actions for Conditional Transfer of Control

To avoid pipeline delays, even when the branch target instruction is in the cache, the branch target address must be calculated early enough to be prefetched from the cache and placed in the instruction register before the target instruction is to be input to the decode stage. Assuming there is a one cycle delay between the point that the address is sent to the cache at the end of the execute stage and the instruction is loaded into the instruction register, this would require that the branch target address be calculated at least two instructions previous to the instruction with the transfer of control when the number of stages in the pipeline is three. This is shown in Figure 9.

ADDR CALC	F	D	E	☒		
INST		F	D	E		
JUMP			F	D	E	
NEXT				F		
TARGET					D	E

Figure 9: Prefetching to Avoid Pipeline Delays

7. EXPERIMENTAL EVALUATION

In an attempt to reduce the number of operand memory references, many RISC machines have thirty-two or more general-purpose registers (e.g. MIPS-X, ARM, Spectrum). Without special compiler optimizations, such as inlining [SCHE77] or interprocedural register allocation [WALL86], it is infrequent that a compiler can make effective use of even a majority of these registers for a function. In a previous study [DAVI89a], we calculated the number of data memory references that have the potential for being removed by using registers. We found that 98.5% could be removed by using only sixteen data registers. In order to evaluate the effectiveness of the branch register approach, two machines were designed and emulated. *ease*, an environment which allows the fast construction and emulation of proposed architectures [DAVI89b], was used to simulate both machines. Detailed measurements from the emulation of real programs on a proposed architecture are captured in this environment. This is accomplished by creating a compiler for the proposed machine, collecting information about instructions during the compilation, inserting code to count the number of times sets of basic blocks are executed, and generating assembly code for an existing host machine from the RTLs of the program on the proposed machine. Appendix I lists the set of test programs used for this experiment.

The first machine served as a baseline to measure the effectiveness of the second machine. The baseline machine was designed to have a simple RISC-like architecture. Features of this machine include:

- 32-bit fixed-length instructions
- load and store architecture
- delayed branches
- 32 general-purpose data registers
- 32 floating-point registers
- three-address instructions

Figure 10 shows the instruction formats used in the baseline machine.

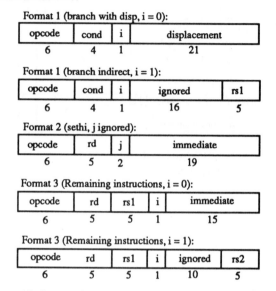

Figure 10: Instruction Formats for the Baseline Machine

The second machine was a modification of the first to handle branches by using branch registers. Features of the branch register machine that differ from the baseline machine include:

- only 16 general-purpose data registers
- only 16 floating-point registers
- 8 branch registers
- 8 instruction registers
- no branch instructions
- a compare instruction with an assignment
- an instruction to calculate branch target addresses
- smaller range of available constants in some instructions

If one ignores floating-point registers, there are approximately the same number of registers on each machine. Figure 11 shows the instruction formats used in the branch register machine. Since the only differences between the baseline machine and the branch register machine are the instructions to use branch registers as opposed to branches, the fewer number of data registers that can be referenced, and the smaller range of constants available, the reports generated by this environment can accurately show the impact of using registers for branches.

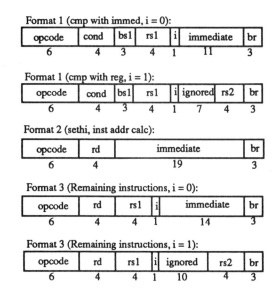

Format 1 (cmp with immed, i = 0):

opcode	cond	bs1	rs1	i	immediate	br
6	4	3	4	1	11	3

Format 1 (cmp with reg, i = 1):

opcode	cond	bs1	rs1	i	ignored	rs2	br
6	4	3	4	1	7	4	3

Format 2 (sethi, inst addr calc):

opcode	rd	immediate	br
6	4	19	3

Format 3 (Remaining instructions, i = 0):

opcode	rd	rs1	i	immediate	br
6	4	4	1	14	3

Format 3 (Remaining instructions, i = 1):

opcode	rd	rs1	i	ignored	rs2	br
6	4	4	1	10	4	3

Figure 11: Instruction Formats for the Branch Register Machine

The branch register machine executed 6.8% fewer instructions and yet performed 2.0% additional data memory references as compared to the baseline machine. The ratio of fewer instructions executed to additional data references for the branch register machine was 10 to 1. Approximately 14% of the instructions executed on the baseline machine were transfers of control. The reduction in the number of instructions executed was mostly due to moving branch target address calculations out of loops. The ratio of transfers of control executed to branch target address calculations was over 2 to 1. Another factor was replacing 36% (2.6 million) of the noops in delay slots of branches in the baseline machine with branch target address calculations at points of transfers of control in the branch register machine. There were also additional instructions executed on the branch register machine to save and restore branch registers. The additional data references on the branch register machine were due to both fewer variables being allocated to registers and saves and restores of branch registers. Table I shows the results from running the test set through both machines.

Machine	Millions of instructions executed	Millions of data references
baseline	183.04	61.99
branch register	170.75	63.22
diff	-12.29	+1.23

Table I: Dynamic Measurements from the Two Machines

By prefetching branch target instructions at the point the branch target address is calculated, delays in the pipeline can be decreased. In the baseline machine, there were 7.95 million unconditional transfers of control and 17.69 million conditional transfers of control. Assuming a pipeline of three stages, not uncommon for RISC machines [GIMA87], then each branch on the baseline machine would require at least a one-stage delay. Also assuming that each instruction can execute in one machine cycle, and no other pipeline delays except for transfers of control, then the test set would require about 208.83 million cycles to be executed on the baseline machine. As shown previously in Figures 5 and 7, the branch register machine would require no delay for both unconditional and conditional branches in a three stage pipeline assuming that the branch target instruction has been prefetched. As shown in Figure 9, the branch target address must be calculated at least two instructions before a transfer of control to avoid pipeline delays even with a cache hit. We estimate that only 13.86% of the transfers of control that were executed would result in a pipeline delay. Thus, the branch register machine would require about 22.09 million (10.6%) fewer cycles to be executed. There would be greater savings for machines having pipelines with more stages. For instance, we estimate that the branch register machine would require about 30.04 million (12.8%) fewer cycles to be executed due to fewer delays in the pipeline alone assuming a pipeline with four stages.

8. HARDWARE CONSIDERATIONS

An instruction cache typically reduces the number of memory references by exploiting the principles of spatial and temporal locality. However, when a particular main memory line is referenced for the first time, the instructions in that line must be brought into the cache and these misses will cause delays. When an assignment is made to a branch register, the value being assigned is the address of an instruction that eventually will likely be brought into the instruction cache.

To take advantage of this knowledge, each assignment to a branch register has the side effect of directing the instruction cache to prefetch the line associated with the instruction address. Prefetch requests could be performed efficiently with an instruction cache that would allow reading a line from main memory at the same time as requests for instruction words from the CPU that are cache hits are honored. This could be accomplished by setting a busy bit in the line of the cache that is being read from memory at the beginning of a prefetch request and setting it to not busy after the prefetch has completed. To handle prefetch requests would require a queuing mechanism with the size of the queue equal to the number of available branch registers. A queue would allow the cache to give priority to cache misses for sequential fetches over prefetch requests which do not require the execution of the program to wait. Directing the instruction cache to bring in instructions before they are used will not decrease the number of cache misses. It will, however, decrease or eliminate the delay of loading the instruction into the cache when it is needed to be fetched and executed.

The machine must determine if an instruction has been brought into an instruction register and thus is ready to be decoded after the corresponding branch register is referenced in the preceding instruction. This can be accomplished by using a flag register that contains a set of bits that correspond to the set of instruction registers. The appropriate bit could be cleared when the request is sent to the cache and set when the instruction is fetched from the cache. Note that this would require the compiler to ensure that branch target addresses are always calculated before the branch register is referenced.

9. FUTURE WORK

There are several interesting areas involving the use of branch registers that remain to be explored. The best cache organization to be used with branch registers needs to be investigated. An associativity of at least two would ensure that a branch target could be prefetched without displacing the current instructions that are being executed. A larger number of words in a cache line may be appropriate in order to less often have cache misses of sequential instructions while instructions at a branch target are being loaded from memory into the instruction cache. Another feature of the cache organization to investigate is the total number of words in the cache. Since instructions to calculate branch target addresses can be moved out of loops, the number of instructions in loops will be fewer. This may improve cache performance in machines with small on-chip caches.

The exact placement of the branch target address calculation can affect performance. The beginning of the function could be aligned on a cache line boundary and the compiler would have information about the structure of the cache. This information would include

- the cache line size
- the number of cache lines in each set
- the number of cache sets in the cache

Using this information the compiler could attempt to place the calculation where there would be less potential conflict between cache misses for sequential instructions and cache misses for prefetched branch targets. By attempting to place these calculations at the beginning of a cache line, the potential for conflict would be reduced.

Prefetching branch targets may result in some instructions being brought into the cache that are not used (cache pollution). Since most branches tend to be taken [LEE84], we have assumed that this penalty would not be significant. By estimating the number of cycles required to execute programs (which includes cache delays) on the branch register machine and the baseline machine, the performance penalty due to cache pollution of unused prefetched branch targets could be determined.

Other code generation strategies could be investigated. For instance, if a fast compare instruction could be used to test the condition during the decode stage [MCFA86], then the compare instruction could update the program counter directly. A bit may be used in the compare instruction to indicate whether to squash [MCFA86] the following instruction depending upon the result of the comparison. Eight branch registers and eight instruction registers were used in the experiment. The available number of these registers and the corresponding changes in the instruction formats could be varied to determine the most cost effective combination.

10. CONCLUSIONS

Using branch registers to accomplish transfers of control has been shown to be potentially effective. By moving the calculation of branch target addresses out of loops, the cost of performing branches inside of loops can disappear and result in fewer executed instructions. By prefetching the branch target instruction when the branch target address is calculated, branch target instructions can be inserted into the pipeline with fewer delays. By moving the assignment of branch registers away from the use of the branch register, delays due to cache misses of branch targets may be decreased. The performance of a small instruction cache, such as the cache for the CRISP architecture [DITZ87a], could also be enhanced since the number of instructions in loops will be fewer. Enhancing the effectiveness of the code can be accomplished with conventional optimizations of code motion and common subexpression elimination. A machine with branch registers should also be inexpensive to construct since the hardware would be comparable to a conventional RISC machine.

11. ACKNOWLEDGEMENTS

The authors wish to thank Anne Holler and Ron Williams for providing many helpful suggestions.

12. REFERENCES

[DAVI89a] J. W. Davidson and D. B. Whalley, *Methods for Saving and Restoring Register Values across Function Calls*, Tech. Rep. 89-11, University of Virginia, November 1989.

[DAVI89b] J. W. Davidson and D. B. Whalley, *Ease: An Environment for Architecture Study and Experimentation*, Tech. Rep. 89-08, University of Virginia, September 1989.

[DITZ87a] D. R. Ditzel and H. R. McLellan, *The Hardware Architecture of the CRISP Microprocessor*, Proceedings of the 14th Annual Symposium on Computer Architecture, Pittsburg, PA, June 1987, 309-319.

[DITZ87b] D. R. Ditzel and H. R. McLellan, *Branch Folding in the CRISP Microprocessor: Reducing Branch Delay to Zero*, Proceedings of the 14th Annual Symposium on Computer Architecture, Pittsburg, PA, June 1987, 2-9.

[GIMA87] C. E. Gimarc and V. Milutinovic, *A Survey of RISC Processors and Computers of the Mid-1980s*, IEEE Computer **20**,9 (September 1987), 59-69.

[HENN83] J. Hennessy and T. Gross, *Postpass Code Optimization of Pipeline Constraints*, ACM Transactions on Programming Languages and Systems **5**,3 (July 1983), 422-448.

[LEE84] J. K. F. Lee and A. J. Smith, *Branch Prediction Strategies and Branch Target Buffer Design*, IEEE Computer **17**,1 (January 1984), 6-22.

[MCFA86] S. McFarling and J. Hennessy, *Reducing the Cost of Branches*, Proceedings of the 13th Annual Symposium on Computer Architecture, Tokyo, Japan, June 1986, 396-403.

[PATT82] D. A. Patterson and C. H. Sequin, *A VLSI RISC*, IEEE Computer **15**,9 (September 1982), 8-21.

[RAU77] B. R. Rau and G. E. Rossman, *The Effect of Instruction Fetch Strategies upon the Performance of Pipelined Instruction Units*, Proceedings of the 4th Annual Symposium on Computer Architecture, Silver Spring, MD, March 1977, 80-89.

[RISE72] E. M. Riseman and C. C. Foster, *The Inhibition of Potential Parallelism by Conditional Jumps*, IEEE Transactions on Computers, **21**,12 (December 1972), 1405-1411.

[SCHE77] R. W. Scheifler, *An Analysis of Inline Substitution for a Structured Programming Language*, Communications of the ACM **20**,9 (September 1977), 647-654.

[SUN87] *The SPARC Architecture Manual*, Sun Microsystems, Mountain View, CA, 1987.

[WALL86] D. W. Wall, *Global Register Allocation at Link Time*, Proceedings of the SIGPLAN Notices '86 Symposium on Compiler Construction, Palo Alto, CA, June 1986, 264-275.

[WILK83] M. Wilkes and J. Stringer, *Microprogramming and the Design of the Control Circuits in an Electronic Digital Computer*, Proceedings of the Cambridge Philosophical Society, Cambridge, England, April 1983.

13. APPENDIX I: TEST PROGRAMS

Class	Name	Description or Emphasis
Utilities	cal	Calendar Generator
	cb	C Program Beautifer
	compact	File Compression
	diff	File differences
	grep	Search for Pattern
	nroff	Text formatter
	od	Octal dump
	sed	Stream editor
	sort	Sort or merge files
	spline	Interpolate Curve
	tr	Translate characters
	wc	Word count
Benchmarks	dhrystone	Synthetic Benchmark
	matmult	Matrix multiplication
	puzzle	Recursion, Arrays
	sieve	Iteration
	whetstone	Floating-Point arithmetic
User code	mincost	VLSI circuit partitioning
	vpcc	Very Portable C compiler

AN INVESTIGATION OF STATIC VERSUS DYNAMIC SCHEDULING

Carl E. Love
University of Colorado at Boulder
2505 Table Mesa Dr. Boulder, Colorado 80303
(303) 499-7421
Email love@boulder.colorado.edu

Harry F. Jordan
University of Colorado at Boulder
Dept. of Electrical Engineering
Campus Box 425 Boulder, Colorado 80309-0425
(303) 492-7927
Email harry@boulder.colorado.edu

Abstract

This paper investigates two techniques for instruction scheduling, dynamic and static scheduling. A decoupled access/execute architecture consists of an execution unit and a memory unit with separate program counters and separate instruction memories. The very long instruction word (VLIW) architecture has only one program counter and relies on the compiler to perform static scheduling of multiple units. To idealize the comparison the VLIW architecture considered had only two units. The instruction sets and execution times for the two architectures were made as nearly the same as possible. The execution times were compared and analyzed to compare the capabilities of static and dynamic instruction scheduling. Both regular and irregular programs were constructed and optimized by hand for each architecture. The experiment showed that the two methods are nearly equally powerful. The decoupled architecture performed better on subroutine calls than the VLIW architecture. It also worked better on programs which switched from memory intensive to computation intensive code. The decoupled architecture was generally better at hiding the floating point latency. The register sharing enabled the VLIW architecture to do more load balancing which resulted in shorter initialization times, and shorter loop iteration times.

Introduction

1.1 Purpose of the Research

A limiting feature of the Von Neumann architecture is that it only allows one instruction issue at a time. The CPU is typically idle while a memory request is serviced. Even if the fetching, decoding and execution of instructions are pipelined, the architecture only allows one instruction to be issued at a time. The purpose of this paper is to investigate two architectures which permit issuing two instructions per cycle. The two architectures are the Decoupled architecture and the Very Long Instruction Word architecture (VLIW). These architectures can issue a memory reference instructions and an execution unit instruction simultaneously for higher throughput. In this way it is possible to issue a request for an operand far enough in advance so that it will be in a register when needed, hence hiding the memory latency. The decoupled architecture uses dynamic scheduling to keep both units busy. Queues synchronize data transmission between access and execute streams so that they need not stay in step. The VLIW architecture requires the compiler to statically place access and execute operations in

each instruction word. The resulting lock-step execution requires the memory latency and instruction execution times to be known by the compiler.

The processor is typically an order of magnitude faster than the memory. If it must wait on memory, it cannot be fully utilized. Issuing memory requests as early as possible reduces processor waiting. It also helps to make the architecture less sensitive to memory latency since operand fetching proceeds in parallel with execution.

The two architectures were investigated to determine which was better at allowing multiple instructions to be issued and which was better at hid the memory latency. To make the comparison fair, the architectures have similar instructions, execution times and memory reference times. The total execution times, processor execution times, instruction wait times, and the time each processor waited on the other were measured by running programs on the two architecture simulators. The investigation was limited to a single execution unit and a single address unit to try and compare the architectural differences directly. Multiple execution and address units introduces questions of how well the code can be parallelized, synchronization etc. These are important issues, but were not the prrimary emphasis of this investigation. The programs were chosen to investigate how the architectures performed on memory intensive programs, computation intensive programs, and programs with a mix of memory and computation. Interrupts were not modeled.

1.2 Review of the Decoupled Architecture and the

VLIW Architecture

Decoupled architectures have been investigated by James E. Smith [1][2][3] [4] and others at the University of Wisconsin. The architecture they studied was based on the CRAY-1 scalar processor. The decoupled CRAY-1 architecture consisted of two processors, a memory processor and an execution processor. The two processors communicate via queues. The queues allow the processors to operate in an asynchronous manner. The queues synchronize two processors. The Livermore loops were run to determine the speedup of the decoupled CRAY-1. The mean speedup was 1.72 for vectorizable loops and 1.40 for nonvectorizable loops. He also found that the decoupled architecture was less sensitive to memory delays.

Joseph Fisher's [5][6][7] approach to extracting parallelism was based on a technique he developed called trace scheduling [7]. The machine uses a single long instruction word (VLIW) to issue multiple memory and execution stream instructions. The machine consisted of eight memory and eight execution units. The memory and execution units were interconnected. Fisher was able to extract more parallelism than was traditionally possible.

192

CH2887-8/90/0000/0192$01.00 © 1990 IEEE

Architectures Investigated

2.1 Description of the Experiment

The study compared dynamic scheduling done by the decoupled architecture with static scheduling done for the VLIW architecture. Both architectures speed up computation by issuing multiple instructions per cycle. The two architectures also hide memory latency by issuing the fetch requests as early as possible. A set of programs which ranged from memory intensive to computation intensive were selected. These programs were run on the two architectures and the execution times were compared. The operand memory and the E-unit and A-unit instruction memories are all separated to avoid contention. Caching would give the effect of separate memories by placing the most likely used items in a separate fast memory, so the assumption of separate memories is a reasonable one.

The queues in the decoupled architecture are some what like having a few extra registers. This advantage is offset in the VLIW architecture by the fact that any registers not used by the address unit can be used by the execution unit. A reason to expect better performance from the decoupled architecture is that the A-unit could get far ahead of the E-unit so that many operands were available for the E-unit. The VLIW architecture might not be able to issue fetch requests early enough to prevent waiting for operands. Static balancing of the work loads by the VLIW compiler is a factor favoring the VLIW architecture. As will be seen, each architecture performed better on three out of the six programs.

2.2 Description of the Decoupled Architecture

The decoupled architecture consists of the E-unit, the A-unit, a store arbiter and the memory. The E-unit performs all floating point operations and type conversions. It is also able to perform integer operations, initialize a register, and move operands to and from registers and the various queues. The A-unit can fetch and store operands for the E-unit and the A-unit, perform integer operations, and move values to and from the queues. The A-unit registers are A0 through A7. The E-unit registers are X0 through X7. Register X0 is used for queue access. Figure 2.1 shows the Decoupled architecture.

The units all communicate via queues. Integer values may be passed directly from the E-unit to the A-unit by the EA queue and from the A-unit to the E-unit by the AE queue. The E-unit and the A-unit each have their own set of branch test instructions that place the outcome of the test in the branch queue of the other unit, i.e. the E branch queue (EB queue) or the A branch queue (AB queue). A branch from queue instruction is executed to decide if a branch was taken by the other unit. Operands fetched by the A-unit for use by the E-unit are placed in the operand queue (OP queue). The E-unit takes the operands from the OP queue and puts values to be stored in the E-unit store queue (S queue). The store addresses for the E-unit operands are produced by the A-unit and placed in the store address queue (SA queue). The A-unit can also store values from its own registers. The A-unit places the operand to be stored in the A-unit store queue (AS queue). The store address is placed in the A-unit address store queue (ASA queue). When both the S and SA queues are not empty,

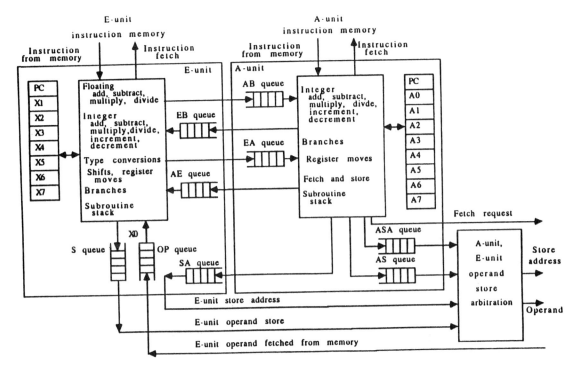

Figure 2.1 Decoupled Architecture

193

the top values are removed and sent to memory. Similarly, if the ASA and AS queues are not empty, the top values are sent to memory. If the S queue, SA queue, AS queue, and the ASA queue are not empty, then the A-unit and E-unit requests alternate. The A-unit store queues allow the A-unit to proceed if the memory bus is busy with an E-unit request. The E-unit store queues allow the store address to be calculated at any time relative to the operand. An instruction needing queue space is delayed if the queue is full. Similarly, an instruction which gets a value from a queue must wait if the queue is empty.

The E-unit has a three register architecture, i.e. $Xk \leftarrow Xi$ (op) Xj, and is responsible for performing arithmetic calculations. It also performs data dependent branch tests. The E-unit contains two sets of branch instructions. One set put a result in the A branch queue, the other set are E-unit only branches. The E-unit can perform add, subtract, multiply and divide on both floating point and integer values. There are register to register move instructions as well as moves to and from the queues. The seven registers $X1$ to $X7$ are general purpose registers. If $X0$ is the source of an operand, the value is taken from the top of the operand queue. If $X0$ is the destination of a result, the value is placed in the E-unit store queue (S queue). For an instruction in which $X0$ is the source of both operands, Xi is the top value and Xj is the next value of the OP queue. The instruction set and execution times for the E-unit are given in Table 2.1. There is a stack of depth seven for subroutine return addresses. It is up to the programmer to save the registers.

Instruction execution times are based on the CRAY-1. Exceptions are integer and floating point divide, integer

multiply, conditional and unconditional jump, jump to subroutine, and return from subroutine. The CRAY-1 uses reciprocal approximation for division. The divide execution time was chosen to be twice that of multiplication. Integer multiply was changed from six minor cycles (mc) to four. The jump mechanism on the CRAY-1 is very complex. Conditional branch for this architecture only requires a comparison and changing the PC if needed. The test can be done in one mc and replacing the PC is a one mc register move. Unconditional jump requires one mc to load the PC. Subroutine jump requires saving the PC on the subroutine stack and replacing it from the instruction, using two mc. Increment and decrement have been made the same as integer add and subtract. Both type conversions have been set at three mc. The movement of a value to or from a queue takes one mc.

The purpose of the A-unit is to perform address calculations, issue fetch requests for the E-unit, and store the E-unit results. It is also used to count loop iterations. It also has a three register architecture. The instruction set contains integer add, subtract, multiply and divide and two sets of conditional branches. There are A-unit only branches and branches that place the test result on the E-unit branch queue. The A-unit can fetch and store E-unit and A-unit operands. The instruction set also includes register moves and moves to and from the queues. The A-unit instruction set and execution times are given in Table 2.2.

The A-unit execution times are the same as in the E-unit. The only instructions in the A-unit not occurring in the E-unit are fetch and store. The time required to initiate a fetch or a store is two mc.

Program stop	PS	0 mc	No operation	NOP	1 mc
Jump indirect via Xi	JP, Xi	1 mc	Jump to K	JP, K	1 mc

Conditional branch to K

		Stack test result				E-unit only		
$Xi = Xj$	EQ, Xi, Xj, K	2 mc				BEQ, Xi, Xj, K	2 mc
$Xi \geq Xj$	GE, Xi, Xj, K	2 mc				BGE, Xi, Xj, K	2 mc
$Xi < Xj$	LT, Xi, Xj, K	2 mc				BLT, Xi, Xj, K	2 mc
$Xi \neq Xj$	NE, Xi, Xj, K	2 mc				BNE, Xi, Xj, K	2 mc
$Xi = 0$	ZR, Xi, K	2 mc				ZR, Xi, K	2 mc
$Xi \neq 0$	NZ, Xi, K	2 mc				BNZ, Xi, K	2 mc
Branch to K if EB-queue is true	BR, K	2 mc					

Arithmetic: $Xk \leftarrow Xi$ op Xj

		Floating point				Integer		
Multiply	MF, Xi, Xj, Xk	7 mc				MI, Xi, Xj, Xk	4 mc
Divide	DF, Xi, Xj, Xk	14 mc				DI, Xi, Xj, Xk	8 mc
Add	AF, Xi, Xj, Xk	6 mc				AI, Xi, Xj, Xk	2 mc
Subtract	SF, Xi, Xj, Xk	6 mc				SI, Xi, Xj, Xk	2 mc
Increment Xi by 1	IN, Xi	2 mc	Decrement Xi by 1	DC, Xi	2 mc
Floating to integer	FI, Xi	3 mc	Integer to floating	IF, Xi	3 mc
Jump to subroutine	JS, K	2 mc	Return from subroutine	RT	1 mc
Set Xi to K	SX, Xi, K	1 mc	Move Xi to Xj	MX, Xi, Xj	1 mc

Move Xi to EA-queue	ME, Xi	1 mc
Move from AE-queue to Xi	MA, Xi	1 mc
Left shift Xi by Xj place	LS, Xi, Xj	2 mc
Right shift Xi by Xj places	RS, Xi, Xj	2 mc

Table 2.1 The Decoupled Architecture E-unit Instructions

Program stop	PS	0 mc		No operation	NOP	1 mc
Jump indirect via Ai	JP, Ai	1 mc		Jump to K	JP, K	1 mc

Conditional branch to K

	Stack test result			E-unit only	
Ai = Aj	EQ, Ai, Aj, K	2 mc		BEQ, Ai, Aj, K	2 mc
Ai ≥ Aj	GE, Ai, Aj, K	2 mc		BGE, Ai, Aj, K	2 mc
Ai < Aj	LT, Ai, Aj, K	2 mc		BLT, Ai, Aj, K	2 mc
Ai ≠ Aj	NE, Ai, Aj, K	2 mc		BNE, Ai, Aj, K	2 mc
Ai = 0	ZR, Ai, K	2 mc		BZR, Ai, K	2 mc
Ai ≠ 0	NZ, Ai, K	2 mc		BNZ, Ai, K	2 mc
Branch to K if AB-queue is true	BR, K	2 mc			

Arithmetic: Ak ← Ai op Aj

Multiply	MI, Xi, Xj, Xk	4 mc		Divide	DI, Xi, Xj, Xk	8 mc
Add	AI, Xi, Xj, Xk	2 mc		Subtract	SI, Xi, Xj, Xk	2 mc
Increment Xi by 1	IN, Ai	2 mc		Decrement Ai by 1	DC, Ai	2 mc
Jump to subroutine	JS, K	2 mc		Return from subroutine	RT	1 mc
Set Ai to K	SA, Ai, K	1 mc		Move Ai to Aj	MA, Ai, Aj	1 mc
Store E-unit value	SE, Ai	2 mc		Fetch E-unit value	FE, Ai	2 mc
Store E-unit value	SE, K	2 mc		Fetch E-unit value	SE, K	2 mc
Store Ai at Aj	SA, Ai, Aj	2 mc		Fetch Ai from Aj	FA, Ai, Aj	2 mc
Store Ai at K	SA, Ai, K	2 mc		Fetch Ai from K	FA, Ai, K	2 mc

Move Ai to AE-queue	MA, Ai	1 mc
Move from EA-queue to Ai	ME, Ai	1 mc

Table 2.2 The Decoupled Architecture A-unit Instructions

When an A-unit fetch is issued, the destination register Ai is locked so it is not used by another instruction until unlocked. The register is unlocked when the operand arrives from memory. If an instruction attempts to use a locked register it is blocked until the register is unlocked.

The memory consists of three parts: two instruction memories and an operand memory. The instruction memories are independent so that there are no conflicts between the two units accessing instructions. Operand memory requires eleven cycles to store a value and eleven cycles to fetch a value. The address and the unit to which the operand is to be sent are included in a fetch request. If the value goes to the A-unit, the destination register must be included in the request. When the memory unit places the value in the A-unit register, the register is unlocked.

2.3 Description of the VLIW Architecture

The VLIW architecture consists of E-unit, A-unit and the memory unit. The E-unit performs floating point operations and type conversions. It can also do integer operations, initialize a register to an integer, and move an operand between registers. The A-unit performs fetch and store and can also do integer operations, register to register moves and initialize a register to an integer. The VLIW architecture has a single program counter and sixteen registers which can be accessed by both E- and A-units. Sixteen registers were chosen so that both architectures would have the same number. Figure 2.2 shows the VLIW architecture.

The compiler is responsible for fetching an operand early enough to be in the target register when the instruction using it is executed. Values to be stored are taken from registers and sent directly to memory. The compiler insures that data precedence is preserved and supplies all synchronizations. For this experiment, the E-unit and A-unit operations in a given instruction could not access the same registers. This restriction could be removed. The subroutine stack length of seven matched that in the decoupled architecture. Since E-unit and A-unit operations are packed into one instruction, only one program counter is needed. The A-unit is responsible for manipulating the program counter by executing jump instructions, conditional branch instructions and subroutine calls.

The E-unit is a three register architecture for arithmetic calculations. The E-unit instructions are add, subtract, multiply, and divide of integer and floating point operands. It can also initialize a register to an integer and perform register moves, type conversions, and arithmetic shifts. The E-unit can access any of the sixteen registers, so it can perform address calculations when not busy doing floating point operations. The E unit performs no branch tests, jumps or subroutine calls. Table 2.3 gives the E-unit instructions and execution times, which have been made to match the decoupled architecture.

The A-unit is a three register architecture which performs address calculations and issues fetch and store requests. It can perform add, subtract, multiply, and divide on integers, register moves, set a register to an integer, unconditional jump, conditional branches, subroutine call, and subroutine return. It can access all sixteen registers, so the compiler can do static load balancing when either the A-unit or the E-unit can do an operation. The subroutine stack is part of the A-unit. The programer must save and restore registers in a subroutine call. A-unit instruction times are the same as in the decoupled architecture. The A-unit instructions and their execution times are given in Table 2.4.

The memory consists of two parts: instruction memory and operand memory. The operand memory requires eleven cycles to fetch or store a value. The instruction memory contains two part instructions. When an instruction is fetched, the left part is sent to the E-unit and the right part to the A-unit.

Program stop	PS	0 mc	No operation	NOP	1 mc

Arithmetic: Xk ← Xi op Xj

	Floating point			Integer	
Multiply	MF, Xi, Xj, Xk	7 mc		MI, Xi, Xj, Xk	4 mc
Divide	DF, Xi, Xj, Xk	14 mc		DI, Xi, Xj, Xk	8 mc
Add	AF, Xi, Xj, Xk	6 mc		AI, Xi, Xj, Xk	2 mc
Subtract	SF, Xi, Xj, Xk	6 mc		SI, Xi, Xj, Xk	2 mc
Increment Xi by 1	IN, Xi	2 mc	Decrement Xi by 1	DC, Xi	2 mc
Floating to integer	FI, Xi	3 mc	Integer to floating	IF, Xi	3 mc
Set Xi to K	SX, Xi, K	1 mc	Move Xi to Xj	MX, Xi, Xj	1 mc

Left shift Xi by Xj places	LS, Xi, Xj 2 mc
Right shift Xi by Xj places	RS, Xi, Xj 2 mc

Table 2.3 The VLIW Architecture E-unit Instructions

Program stop	PS	0 mc	No operation	NOP	1 mc
Jump indirect via Ai	JP, Ai	1 mc	Jump to K	JP, K	1 mc

Conditional branch to K

Xi = Xj	EQ, Xi, Xj, K	2 mc	Xi ≥ Xj	GE, Xi, Xj, K	2 mc
Xi < Xj	LT, Xi, Xj, K	2 mc	Xi ≠ Xj	NE, Xi, Xj, K	2 mc
Xi = 0	ZR, Xi, K	2 mc	Xi ≠ 0	NZ, Xi, K	2 mc

Arithmetic: Xk ← Xi op Aj

	Floating point			Integer	
Multiply	MI, Xi, Xj, Xk	4 mc	Divide	DI, Xi, Xj, Xk	8 mc
Add	AI, Xi, Xj, Xk	2 mc	Subtract	SI, Xi, Xj, Xk	2 mc

Increment Xi by 1	IN, Xi	2 mc	Decrement Xi by 1	DC, Xi	2 mc
Jump to subroutine	JS, K	2 mc	Return from subroutine	RT	1 mc
Set Xi to K	SX, Xi, K	1 mc	Move Xi to Xj	MX, Xi, Xj	1 mc
Store Xi at Xj	SX, Xi, Xj	2 mc	Fetch Xi from Xj	FX, Xi, Xj	2 mc
Store Xi at K	SX, Xi, K	2 mc	Fetch Xi from K	FX, Xi, K	2 mc

Table 2.4 The VLIW Architecture A-unit Instructions

Simulation Results

Programs were chosen to investigate how the two architectures behave on programs ranging from memory intensive (bubble sort) to computation intensive (differential equation). Matrix add and matrix multiply fell between these two extremes. The bisection root finding program and the linked list program were selected to investigate performance on programs which switched from memory intensive to computation intensive execution. The root finding program has a variable number of computations to find each root and a fixed number of memory references for each root. The linked list program had a variable number of memory references followed by a fixed amount of computation. The programs were optimized for each architecture were compiled and optimized by hand. The optimization consisted of loop unrolling and rearranging thee code to obtain the most optimal code possible. It is estimated with about an 85% certainty that a compiler could not improve the programs by more than 10% using loop unrolling, rearranging the code, or other techniques. The above numbers were based on how certain we were that the code was optimal and looking at what the performance improvement would be if a cycle could be removed from the inner loop code. In order to determine how well an architecture executed a program, the data set needed to be large enough so that the program reached a steady state of execution. Short simulations are often distorted by start up time. For example in the matrix multiply, the computation of each element is done in the innermost loop, so matrix dimensions must be large enough that the inner loop accounts for the majority of execution time. The data set was chosen so that the inner loop accounted for at least 95% of the execution time.

The six programs were run on each architecture, and the percentage difference found by taking the difference in the execution times and dividing by the longer one. Figure 3.1 shows the results.

The decoupled architecture on average ran 8.8% faster on three out of six programs. The VLIW architecture ran on average 8.1% faster on the other three programs. The decoupled architecture performed better on problems in which the memory stream was able to get ahead of the execution stream. The VLIW architecture performed better on

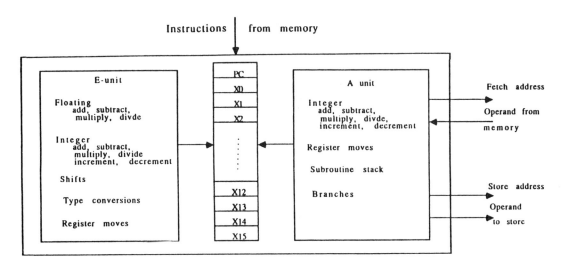

Instructions from memory

Instruction format

E-unit instruction	A-unit instruction

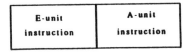

Figure 2.2 VLIW Architecture

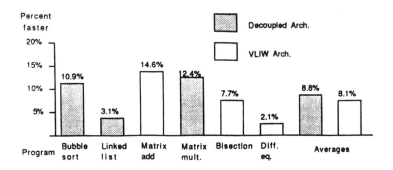

Figure 3.1 Percentage difference in program execution times.

programs for which the compiler could perform some load balancing of the two instruction streams. The details of why one architecture ran faster will be addressed in the following sections.

If an instruction has an associated constant, for example a set register or branch instruction, the constant is placed in the next instruction position. The simulator treats the instruction and constant as one word. Only one fetch is required for either architecture.

3.1 Bubble Sort Program

The bubble sort program sorted n floating point numbers into ascending order. It was found that for n equal to 57 the 95% condition was met. Tables 3.1 and 3.2 show

the loop code for the decoupled and VLIW architectures, respectively.

The decoupled program required 16,543 mc to execute and the VLIW program required 18,576 mc. Thus the decoupled program was 10.9% faster. Data comparison and exchange are done by the E-unit. The E-unit execution time is completely masked by the A-unit in the decoupled architecture, so the execution time is a function only of the A-unit execution time. The memory latency, data comparisons and exchanges were not masked by other work in the VLIW program. (See lines 19 through 23 of the VLIW program.) The instructions done by the A-unit in both programs were the fetch, store and branch instructions. The time required by the decoupled program to execute these instructions for $n = 57$ was: $3n(n-1) + 6(n-1) = 9,912$ mc. The time required for the VLIW program to exe-

Table 3.1 Decoupled bubble sort loop code

A-UNIT INSTRUCTIONS

17.	SA, A3	
18.	1	
19.	FE, A3	FETCH FIRST ITEM
20.	SA, A4	
21.	1	
22.	IN, A3	INCREMENT INNER LOOP COUNT
23.	FE, A3	FETCH NEXT ITEM
24.	STE, A4	STORE SMALLER ITEM
25.	IN, A4	INCREMENT STORE ADDRESS
26.	LT, A3, A1	INNER LOOP SORT
27.	22	
28.	STE, A4	
29.	DC, A1	
30.	NE, A1, A2	OUTER LOOP
31.	17	

E-UNIT INSTRUCTIONS

7.	MV, X0, X2	FETCH FIRST ITEM
8.	MV, X0, X1	FETCH NEXT ITEM
9.	BGE, X2, X1	
10.	15	
11.	MV, X2, X0	MOVE ITEM
12.	MV, X1, X2	TO STORE
13.	JP	
14.	16	
15.	MV, X1, X0	MOVE ITEM TO STORE
16.	BR	INNER LOOP
17.	8	
18.	MV, X2, X0	MOVE ITEM TO STORE
19.	BR	OUTER LOOP
20.	7	

Table 3.2 VLIW bubble sort loop code

	E-UNIT	A-UNIT	
12.	NOP	IN, X11	
13. - 17. ARE ALL NOP'S			
18.	NOP	FE, X1, X11	FETCH NEXT ITEM
19.	IN, X12	GE, X2, X1	COMPARE ITEMS
20.	XXX	29	
21.	NOP	MV, X1, X0	EXCHANGE ITEMS
22.	NOP	MV, X2, X1	
23.	NOP	MV, X0, X2	
24.	IN, X11	ST, X1, X12	STORE SMALL ITEM
25.	SX, X13	GE, X9, X11	INNER LOOP SORT
26.	2	18	
27.	IN, X11	ST, X1, X12	STORE SMALL ITEM
28.	SX, X13	GE, X9, X11	INNER LOOP SORT
29.	2	15	
30.	NOP	JP	
31.	XXX	32	
32.	SX, X11	IN, X12	
33.	1	XXX	
34. - 36. ARE ALL NOPS			
37.	NOP	GE, X2, X1	FINAL ITEM
38.	XXX	42	COMPARISON
39.	NOP	MV, X1, X0	EXCHANGE ITEMS
40.	NOP	MV, X2, X1	
41.	NOP	MV, X0, X2	
42.	NOP	ST, X1, X12	STORE LAST
43.	NOP	IN, X12	TWO ITEMS
44.	NOP	ST, X2, X12	
45.	SX, X12	FE, X1, X13	FETCH INITIAL
46.	0	XXX	TWO ITEMS
47.	DC, X9	FE, X2, X11	
48.	IN, X11	NE, X9, X10	OUTER LOOP
49.	XXX	12	

cute these instructions for n = 57 is: $3((n-1)(n-2)+2) + 12(n-1) = 9,918$ mc. The extra six cycles required by the VLIW program were an overhead incurred when the final loop iteration was unrolled. The decoupled program also needed to perform address calculations which required $2n(n-1) + 4(n-1)$ mc. The VLIW program spent $1.5((n-1)(n-2)+2) + 3(n-1) - 3X$ mc waiting on the memory and $(n-1)(n-2) + 1 + 2(n-1)$ mc doing comparisons, where X is the number of data exchanges. The time spent exchanging data values is given by: $1.5((n-1)(n-2)+2) + 3X(n-1)$. The E-unit was idle during most of the time the A-unit was busy.

From these equations it is evident that the longer execution time for the VLIW program results from a combination of memory latency, data comparisons and exchanges. If memory latency is reduced from 11 mc to 6 mc, the VLIW program would still be slower but only by 389 minor cycles. The decoupled bubble sort program is faster because the data comparisons, exchanges and memory latency are hidden, making the E-unit and A-unit work loads more balanced than in the VLIW program.

3.2 Linked List Program

The linked list program searches two linked lists to find corresponding data items. The two are the function list and the data list. Each node in the function list contains a pointer to the next node, a one or a zero to identify the desired function, and a node identifier. Each node in the data list contains a pointer to the next node, the value at which the function is to be evaluated, and a node identifier. The node identifiers are in order in the function list, but randomized in the data list. The program takes the next item from the function list and searches the data list for the corresponding identifier. The function identifier then selects either the e^x or the $\cos(x)$ function, which is evaluated for the value in the data list.

The total number of nodes (n) to be searched is $n(n+1)/2$, and the number of function evaluations is n for a data set of n nodes. The execution time of the decoupled linked list program is $25n(n+1)/2 + 19n + n(53F_0 + 46F_1) + 1$ mc. The time to perform the node search and execute the functions is $25n(n+1)/2 + 53nF_0 + 46nF_1$ mc, assuming no waiting on the E-unit by the A-unit. The execution time of the VLIW linked list program is $25n(n+1)/2 + 18n + n(165F_0 + 184F_1)$ mc. The time to search the nodes and execute the functions is $25n(n+1)/2 + n(165F_0 + 184F_1)$ mc. The number of times e^x is executed is nF_0. The number of times $\cos(x)$ is executed is nF_1. For the data set used, F_0 was 0.4 and F_1 was 0.6. The programs were run for n equal to 160, which exceeded the steady state criterion.

The decoupled program ran faster by 3.1%. The execution times of the main routines are a function of how fast the A-unit can search the data list. The execution of the two functions depends on the E-unit. After the VLIW program fetches the message identifier from the data list, the next instruction compares the message identifiers. Eleven NOP's had to be inserted between the fetch and the comparison to allow the value to arrive from memory. Three NOP's were inserted to allow the pointer to the next function node to be fetched before it was used. The decoupled program fetches the message identifier and then does a move followed by a comparison of the message identifiers. The move was delayed because an A-unit register was locked due to an earlier fetch. After the move, the A-unit still had to wait for the register which was to receive the message identifier to be unlocked. The A-unit had to wait for the full memory latency before the comparison and had to wait three cycles for the pointer to the next function node. Hence, memory latency for fetching an A-unit value was not masked in either program.

Function execution is approximately the same in both programs. The time to execute an iteration in the decoupled program is the same as in the VLIW program when the time spent waiting for locked registers is included. The decoupled program ran faster because the A-unit finished function execution before the E-unit and was able to fetch the next node in the function list and start searching the data list. The VLIW program had to wait for the function evaluation before fetching the next node. The difference can be attributed to the relaxed synchronization between instructions in the decoupled architecture.

3.3 Matrix Multiply Program

The matrix multiply program multiplies two floating point matrices and stores the result in a third matrix. The execution time of the decoupled program is $15n^3 + 7n^2 + 2n + 15$ mc, where matrices are n x n. The inner loop time is given by $15n^3$ mc. The execution time of the VLIW program is $17n^2(n-1) + 29n^2 + 15n + 11$ mc. The inner loop time is $17n^2(n-1)$ mc. A matrix of size 34 x 34 meets the steady state criterion.

The decoupled program ran faster by 12.4%. The inner loop of the decoupled program required twelve cycles for the A-unit and fifteen cycles for the E-unit. The A-unit could only get seven fetch requests ahead of the E-unit before waiting for the E-unit to dequeue an operand. The inner loop of the VLIW program required seventeen cycles. One address calculation and the loop counter increment which are done by the A-unit in the decoupled program are done by the E-unit in the VLIW program. This reduces the A-unit work load by four cycles, but it has to wait nine cycles for the E-unit. The inner loop of the VLIW program was longer by five cycles. There is no waiting due to memory latency in either program. The difference in execution times can be attributed to better masking of the floating point operations in the decoupled program.

3.4 Matrix Add Program

The matrix add program adds two square matrices of floating point numbers and stores the result in a third matrix. The execution time for the decoupled matrix add is $16(n^2 - 1) + 18$ mc, where matrices are n x n. The loop time is $16(n^2 - 1)$ mc. The execution time for the VLIW program is $14(n^2 - 1) + 22$ mc. The loop time is $14(n^2 - 1)$ mc. The programs were run on matrices of dimension 14 x 14, which met the steady state criterion. The decoupled program initializes two fetch addresses and issues the initial requests before setting up the loop counter and store addresses, as does the VLIW program. Each iteration of the loop issues fetch requests for the next iteration while calculating the current result. Table 3.3 gives the decoupled loop code for the matrix add program, and Table 3.4

gives the VLIW loop code.

Table 3.3 Decoupled matrix add loop code

A-UNIT INSTRUCTIONS

15.	STE, A3	STORE RESULT
16.	IN, A1	INCREMENT A-ARRAY ADDRESS
17.	FE, A1	FETCH NEXT A ITEM
18.	IN, A2	INCREMENT B-ARRAY ADDRESS
19.	FE, A2	FETCH NEXT B ITEM
20.	IN, A3	INCREMENT C-ARRAY ADDRESS
21.	DC, A4	DECREMENT NUM ITERATIONS
22.	NZ, A4	LOOP IF NOT ZERO
23.	15	
24.	STE, A3	STORE FINAL RESULT

E-UNIT INSTRUCTIONS

1.	AF, X0, X0, X0	CALCULATE FIRST RESULT
2.	BR	
3.	7	
4.	AF, X0, X0, X0	CALCULATE I TH RESULT
5.	BR	
6.	4	

Table 3.4 VLIW matrix add loop code

	E-UNIT	A-UNIT	
11.	IN, X11	FE, X0, X10	FETCH NEXT A ITEM
12.	IN, X10	FE, X1, X9	FETCH NEXT B ITEM
13.	AF, X1, X0, X1	NOP	CALCULATE RESULT
14.	DC, X12	ST, X1, X11	STORE RESULT
15.	IN, X9	NZ, X12	LOOP
16.	XXX	11	
17.	NOP	NOP	
18.	AF, X1, X0, X1	IN, X11	FINAL RESULT
19.	NOP	ST, X1, X11	STORE RESULT

The VLIW program ran 14.6% faster. The decoupled program execution time is limited by the A-unit. It takes sixteen cycles for the A-unit to execute one iteration of the loop, which was longer than for the E-unit. In the VLIW program, address calculations are done by both E-unit and A-unit, reducing the loop iteration time by eight cycles. (See lines 11 through 15 of the VLIW program.) The A-unit has to wait for the floating point add, which required six cycles. The total saving is two cycles per iteration. The savings amounted to 392 cycles in the program. Six additional cycles were saved in the initialization. The VLIW program ran faster because of register sharing between the processors and the load balancing in the generated code; this decreased the loop iteration time more than the A-unit used waiting for the E-unit.

3.5 Bisection Root Finder Program

The root finding program uses the bisection method to find the roots of a polynomial. The main program passes the endpoints and maximum iterations to a bisection subroutine. This subroutine finds the root and returns the result to the main program. The bisection subroutine calls a subroutine to evaluate the function, passing the value at which the function is to be evaluated and receiving the result in registers. The execution time of the decoupled bisection program is $130n + 154m - 5$ mc, where n is the number of roots and m is the number of iterations required for the desired accuracy. The inner loop time is

199

instructions and the execution stream instructions couldn't be executed in parallel.

Conclusions

The experiment showed that the two architectures were approximately equal in their ability to issue two instructions per cycle based on the assumption that hand compiled code was equally optimal. If one of the two architectures was fundamentally superior, then the programs run on the two architectures should have indicated which architecture was better. The programs were selected because they represented the types of computations which are frequently found in application programs. The types of computations ranged from memory intensive to computation intensive and the programs included both regular and irregular programs. There wasn't conclusive evidence that the memory intensive programs were better suited for either one of the two architectures. This can be seen by looking at the bubble sort and the matrix add programs. The inner loop of the bubble sort program spent approximately 85% of the time performing memory stream instructions; the decoupled architecture executed this program 10.9% faster that the VLIW. The matrix add program spent about 73% of the time doing memory stream instructions; the VLIW architecture ran the program 14.6% faster. If one of the architectures was fundamentally better on memory intensive programs, then it should have given better performance on both of these two programs. The same behavior can be seen for the computation intensive programs.

The gate counts for the two architectures were estimated. The decoupled architecture required a second PC, a subroutine stack, plus seven queues. It was estimated that the decoupled architecture requires on the order of 50% more gates than the VLIW architecture. The queues would be the only hardware which would have to be designed from scratch, the second PC and subroutine stack could simply be duplicated. It would only be necessary to design two queues, a one bit branch queue and a 32 bit data queue, and then replicate them as needed. The additional design time is expected to be relatively small.

It was extimated that a VLIW compiler would be on the order of two or three times more complex and slower than a decoupled compiler based on the additional work which must be done. The compiler has to arrange the code not only based on the data dependencies but on their execution times as well. The compiler needs to place instructions which require approximately the same time to execute in the same instruction word to avoid having processors idle. This will require examining more possibilities in compiling the code. The compiler needs to know the worst case execution times of the instructions. In addition to the work done by a single stream compiler the decoupled architecture would have to separate the execution stream and memory stream instructions. Branch from queue instructions must be added and the branch address would have to be fixed. This will only add a few percent to the size of the compiler and a few percent to its execution time.

Application programs used to solve problems in science and engineering are typically very large. These programs also tend to have many subroutines. Application programs will typically have some regular computations as well as memory intensive and computation intensive segments of code. The programs chosen for the experiment all have at least one of these characteristics. Based on this information, the behavior of application programs must be extrapolated. There was no indication, based on the programs run, that a given selection of application programs would tend to favor either of the two architectures.

Since there was no clear indication that one of the architectures was superior, the choice of one architecture over the other wouldn't adversely effect the performance of the machine. The choice should be based on how well one approach fits in with the other constraints imposed on the machine. These constraints might include virtual processes, the number of distinct processors, how tightly coupled these processors are and the memory hierarchy. Virtual processes could be handled better by a VLIW architecture with multiple processors. The wide instruction word allows the processes to be scheduled on any available processor, hence making more effective use of the hardware. The processes could be scheduled on any processor since each processor can access any of the registers. The decoupled architecture would be better adapted to a system with distinct processors. The VLIW architecture is tightly coupled and the decoupled architecture is loosely coupled. The decoupled architecture is able to handle varying memory latencies, as in a paged memory system, better than the VLIW architecture. These are only a few of the constraints that might affect the choice of a decoupled or VLIW type architecture.

REFERENCES

[1] Smith, James E., Weiss, Shlomo and Pang, Nicholas "A Simulation Study of Decoupled Architecture Computers", IEEE Transactions on Computers, Vol. C-35, No. 8, pp. 692-702, August 1986.

[2] Smith, James E. "Decoupled Acess/Execute Computer Architectures", ACM Transactions on Computer Systems, pp. 289-308, Vol. 2, No. 4, 1984.

[3] Smith, James E. and Kaminski, Thomas J. "Varieties of Decoupled Acess/ Execute Architectures", 20 th Alerton Conf. on Communication, Control And Computer Proceedings, pp. 577-587, 1982.

[4] Smith, James E. "Decoupled Acess/Execute Computer Architectures", 9 th Annual International Symposium on Computer Architecture, pp. 112-119, April 26-29, 1982.

[5] Fisher, Joseph A. "Very Long Instruction Word Architectures and the ELI-512", The 10 th Annual International Symposium on Computer Architecture, pp. 140-150, IEEE Computer Society and Association for Computing Machinery, June 1983.

[6] Fisher, Joseph A. and Ellis, John R. "Parallel Processing: A Smart Compiler and a Dumb Machine", Proceeding of the ACM SIGPLAN '84 Symposium on Compiler Construction, pp. 37-47, Vol. 19, No. 6, June 1984.

[7] Fisher, Joseph A. "Trace Sceduling: A Technique for Global Microcode Compaction", IEEE Transactions on Computers, pp. 478-490, Vol. C-30, No. 7, July 1981.

[8] Love, Carl E. "An Investigation of Static Versus Dynamic Scheduling", Master's Thesis, Dept. of Electrical Engineering, University of Colorado at Boulder, May 1989.

[9] Love, Carl E. "The Decoupled And VLIW Architecture Simulator Code", Dept. of Electrical Engineering, University of Colorado Internal Report, May 1989.

15m mc. The execution time of the VLIW bisection program is $105n + 301m + 10$ mc. The inner loop time is $301m$ mc. For n equal to fourteen, m must be at least 224 to approximate steady state execution. To insure that m is at least 224, the root tolerance has to be at least five orders of magnitude smaller than the difference in the endpoints.

The VLIW program was faster by 7.7%. The register save time for a subroutine call s counted as initialization time. The decoupled bisection subroutine contained E-unit and A-unit conditional branches, so it is not possible for one unit to get ahead of the other. Only waiting on branch queues in the decoupled program makes the bisection behavior different. The decoupled bisection subroutine has an E-unit conditional branch followed by a branch from the EB-queue. The corresponding A-unit instructions were: branch from the AB-queue, increment A2 and branch if A1 is less than A2. The back to back branches require the E-unit to wait for the A-unit before the next iteration of the loop. This added six cycles to the E-unit loop iteration, which increased the execution time of the decoupled program by 744 cycles over the VLIW program. The above reason accounted for about three quarters of the difference. The rest of the difference was due to a smaller initialization time for the bisection subroutine in the VLIW program because address calculations for parameter block access were done by the E-unit.

3.6 Differential Equation Program

The differential equation program was a 4th order Runge Kutta solution to the equation $dy/dx = xy$. The result was for $x = x_0$ to $x =$ number of iterations times the step size. The number of iterations and the step size were parameters in the programs. The initial values of x and y, x_0 and y_0 respectively, and the step size are fetched from memory. The execution time of the decoupled differential program was given by $195n + 20$ mc where n is the number of steps. The inner loop time was given by $195n$ mc. The execution time for the VLIW was given by $191n + 15$ mc. The loop time was given by $191n$ mc. It was found that for n equal to 20 the steady state criterion was met while also giving a reasonably large execution time.

The decoupled program required 3,918 mc to execute and the VLIW program required 3,835 mc to execute, thus the VLIW program which 2.1% faster. Of the 85 cycles, 83 cycles could be accounted for by the masking of the branch and the two set instruction times by the execution of the E-unit instructions and a 3 cycle shorter shorter initialization time. The time required to execute the two programs was dependent on the E-unit execution times. The sharing of the E-unit work load with the A-unit and the masking of the branch time were the reason for the improved performance of the VLIW program.

3.7 Decoupled Architecture

The decoupled architecture worked better on programs which tended to switch between a memory intensive mode and a computation mode which couldn't be overlapped with the memory intensive mode. For example, the bubble sort program had a memory intensive mode in which the values were fetched, followed by a computation intensive mode which consisted of the data comparisons and exchanges. The VLIW architecture couldn't overlap the data exchanges with work from the memory stream. The decoupled architecture queues allowed the exchange of the data items to be carried on in parallel with the memory stream instructions. The decoupled architecture performed better on programs in which the number of cycles required to execute the memory stream instructions and the execution stream instructions for one loop iteration were roughly

equal, but the number of instructions in each stream differed significantly. For example, the memory stream of the matrix multiply program had six instructions requiring twelve cycles to execute. The execution stream had two instructions requiring thirteen cycles to execute. The difference in the instruction execution times was masked better in the decoupled architecture because it allowed multiple memory stream instructions to be executed while only one execution stream instruction was executed.

The decoupled architecture hid the memory latency better in programs which allowed the memory stream to get ahead of the execution stream. This was because the fetch requests could be issued early enough that they would be in the operand queue when the E-unit need them. Hence the memory latency was completely hidden from the E-unit. This was particularly important when the number of cycles required for the execution stream to execute one iteration of the loop was greater than the number of cycles required for the memory stream to execute one iteration but less than the memory latency.

3.8 VLIW Architecture

The VLIW architecture performed best on programs in which the number of branch instructions and the memory stream instructions exceeded the number of execution stream instructions or vice versa. The improved performance came from the compiler's ability to statically perform load balancing of the workload between the two units. The number of cycles required to execute one iteration of the loop had to be large enough so that it wasn't necessary to insert NOP's into the instruction stream to allow the memory to finish fetching an operand from memory.

Programs which had more memory and branch instructions than execution stream instructions in a loop made it possible for some of the memory address calculations to be done by the E-unit. For the VLIW architecture, the number of cycles saved by moving some of the address calculations to be done by the E-unit had to be greater than the number of cycles the A-unit was forced to wait for the E-unit to finish the floating point computations. For example, in the matrix add program, the three array address calculations and the loop increment instruction were moved to the E-unit. Eight cycles were saved in the A-unit instruction stream by moving these four instructions to the E-unit in the VLIW program. The A-unit had to wait six cycles for the E-unit to finish its instructions. The total savings was two cycles per loop iteration. The movement of the four instructions in the VLIW program resulted in more instructions being issued per cycle than could be issued in the decoupled architecture.

Programs which had more execution stream instructions than memory stream instructions performed better on the VLIW architecture if some of the execution stream instructions could be done by the A-unit. The movement of the instructions resulted in more instructions being executed per cycle. This was the case in the differential equation program.

The sharing of the workload by the two processors led to shorter initialization times as well as smaller loop iteration times as long as the moved instructions could be done in parallel with the other instructions.

The VLIW architecture didn't perform well on programs that required NOP's to be inserted into the loop to allow a fetch to be completed. This was especially true when the memory stream required fewer cycles to execute one iteration of the loop than were required for the execution stream to execute one iteration of the loop. It also didn't perform as well on programs in which the memory stream

Session 4A: Processor Implementations

VAX Vector Architecture

Dileep Bhandarkar
Richard Brunner

Digital Equipment Corporation
Boxboro, Massachusetts
USA

The VAX Architecture has been extended to include an integrated, register-based vector processor. This extension allows both high-end and low-end implementations and can be supported with only small changes by VAX/VMS and VAX/ULTRIX operating systems. The extension is effectively exploited by the new vectorizing capabilities of VAX FORTRAN. Features of the VAX Vector Architecture and the design decisions which make it a consistent extension of the VAX Architecture are discussed.

1. Introduction

For a long time vector processing was mainly available on large, expensive supercomputers such as the Cray-1[1]. More recently, mainframe computers such as the IBM 3090 have also offered vector processing as an optional add-on feature [2]. By 1985, several more affordable "mini supercomputers" such as the Convex C-1, SCS40, and Alliant FX started offering vector processing [3,4,5]. With the availability of low cost, pipelined floating-point arithmetic chips, and the maturation of vectorizing compiler technology, vector processing has become a mainstream technology in scientific computing.

The VAX architecture was originally introduced in 1977[6]. Since then, over ten models with varying price/performance have been introduced as part of the VAX family. All these processors are software compatible. The original architecture effort left room for expanding the instruction set. While the instruction set was extended early in the life of the architecture to add multiprocessing support and new floating-point data types, the architecture has stayed very stable over the last decade. In fact, the only major architectural change was the introduction of the microVAX subset to allow single-chip VLSI implementations [7].

The VAX architecture has now been extended to include integrated vector processing. One of the primary reasons for this extension was to improve the performance of vectorizable applications. The cycles per floating-point operation is a good measure of the efficiency of an architecture for the class of applications that a benchmark represents. For LINPACK, previous VAX processors averaged between 16 to 20 cycles per floating-point operation; our analysis showed that a typical VAX Vector processor could achieve 3 to 4 times improvement in the cycles per floating-point operation. Adding vector processing capability is a very cost effective way of extending the performance range of the VAX architecture in an upward compatible manner.

This paper discusses the design goals and constraints and an overview of the resulting architecture. Details of the VAX Architecture, including the new vector extensions, can be found in the VAX Architecture Reference Manual [8].

2. Architecture Goals

The design of the vector architecture for VAX had some obvious design constraints due to the large installed base of VAX systems. The vector architecture had to be a consistent extension of the existing VAX architecture. Availability of unused opcodes was not a problem, but integration of vector processing with VAX memory management, exception handling, and synchronization to the scalar machine required special attention.

The vector architecture effort started in December 1985. At that time several CPU development projects were well underway. In particular the VAX 6200 and VAX 8800 were too far along to accommodate any changes without major impact on their schedules. Digital decided to target vector processing for the next set of processors that were in design but could tolerate minor changes to support vector processing. This necessitated an approach that required very few changes to the scalar processors. Therefore, vector processing was viewed as an optional feature, where the scalar processor decoded vector instructions and passed them on to its associated vector coprocessor. All processing of vector instructions is handled by the vector processor with mechanisms provided for vector-scalar synchronization and handling of vector exceptions by the scalar processor.

While the architecture had to account for the implementation constraints of on-going projects, it had to be general and flexible enough to allow future, more integrated implementations at high performance. The architecture also had to minimize its impact on existing VAX/VMS and VAX/ULTRIX operating systems.

3. Major Design Decisions

The vector architecture supports the major VAX data types: 32-bit longwords, single precision F_floating, and double precision D_floating and G_floating. The vector architecture provides arithmetic and logical operations that are identical to their scalar counterparts.

The VAX scalar architecture supports full memory to memory operations, where the source as well as destination operands can be in memory. The vector architecture departs from this memory based approach and adopts a vector-register-based design pioneered by the CRAY-1 [1]. The architecture was designed to allow maximum concurrency where several loads, stores, and arithmetic operations could be performed simultaneously. The number of vector registers was chosen to be 16. Each vector register contains 64 elements of 64-bits. Vector length, vector mask, and

vector count register are also provided.

The original VAX architecture features variable length instructions, each with as many operands as needed. A natural way to extend this concept would have been to use one operand specifier for each vector operand. For example, a vector add would be:

VADD vsrc1, vsrc2, vdst

where each operand would specify one vector operand. Like the scalar architecture, two and three operand versions could be provided. This approach requires several operands to be evaluated and more memory accesses. Instead the VAX vector architecture uses a control word to encode vector operand selection information. Thus, a vector add is encoded as:

VADD cntrl

The control word is a 16-bit operand that is fetched by the scalar processor and passed on to the vector processor along with the opcode. Details of the control word are shown later. (However, for ease of use, the assembly language format allows the programmer to write the instruction as: **VADD vsrc1, vsrc2, vdst.**)

Another important design consideration is whether the vector processor operates synchronously or asynchronously with respect to the scalar processor. Asynchronous operation allows the overlap of scalar processing with vector processing as well as the simultaneous execution of more than one vector instruction. On the other hand, asynchronous operation creates some problems such as precision of exceptions and coherency of simultaneous memory accesses. The VAX vector architecture allows asynchronous operation of the vector processor in order to maximize performance. Special instructions are provided for software-controlled explicit synchronization.

4. Basic Architecture

As described earlier, there are 16 vector registers, each of which holds 64 elements; an element is 64-bits. Instructions which operate on longword integers or F_floating-point data, only manipulate the low-order 32-bits of each element -- sometimes referred to as longword elements.

A number of vector control registers, control which elements of a vector register are processed by an instruction. The Vector Length Register (VLR) limits the highest-numbered vector register element that is processed by a vector instruction. The Vector Mask Register (VMR) consists of a 64-bit mask, where each mask bit corresponds to one of the possible element positions in a vector register. When instructions are executed under control of the VMR, only those elements for which the corresponding mask bit is true are processed by the instruction. Vector compare instructions set the value of the VMR.

The Vector Count Register (VCR) receives the number of elements generated by the compressed IOTA instruction, which is similar to COMPRESSED IOTA on the CRAY-2 [9]. (See Appendix A for an example using IOTA.)

All VAX vector instructions use two-byte extended opcodes. Any necessary scalar operands (e.g., base address and stride for vector memory instructions) are specified by standard VAX scalar operand specifiers. The instruction formats allow all VAX vector instructions to be encoded in 7 classes -- these 7 basic instruction groups and their opcodes are shown in Table 1.

Within each class, all instructions have the same number and types of operands. This allows the scalar processor to use block-decoding techniques. The differences in operation between the individual instructions within a class are irrelevant to the scalar processor and need only be known by the vector coprocessor.

Notable aspects of the instruction set are: support for random-strided vector memory data through gather (VGATH) and scatter (VSCAT) instructions; generation of compressed IOTA vectors (through the IOTA instruction) to be used as offsets to the gather and scatter instructions; merging vector registers through the VMERGE instruction; and the ability for any vector instruction to operate under control of the VMR. Appendix A of this paper shows the usage of these instructions in some code examples.

Additional control information for a vector instruction is provided in the vector control word (shown as *cntrl* in Table 1), which is a scalar operand to most vector instructions. The control word operand can be specified using any VAX addressing mode; however, VAX compilers will generally use immediate mode addressing (that is, place the control word within the instruction stream). The format of the vector control word is shown in figure 1.

The Va, Vb, and Vc fields indicate the source and destination vector registers to be used by the instruction. These fields also indicate the specific operation to be performed by a vector compare or convert instruction.

The MOE bit indicates whether the particular instruction operates under control of the VMR.

The MTF bit determines what bit value corresponds to "true" for VMR bits. It allows a compiler to vectorize if-then-else constructs; and example of such code is given in Appendix A of this paper.

The EXC bit is used in vector arithmetic instructions to enable Integer Overflow and Floating Underflow exception reporting.

The MI bit is used in vector memory load instructions to indicate modify-intent.

The MI bit is a useful innovation for systems with write-back caches. It indicates that a majority of memory locations being read by a vector memory load instruction will be subsequently written by vector memory store instructions. When MI is set for a vector memory load instruction, a system with a write-back cache can acquire both read and write ownership of the necessary cache blocks in anticipation of the subsequent store. Without such a mechanism, cache blocks acquired by the load with read ownership would have to be discarded and reacquired with write ownership when the store executed.

Figure 2 shows the encoding for some typical VAX Vector Instructions.

5. Execution Model

With the addition of vector processing, a typical VAX processor consists of a scalar processor and an associated vector coprocessor; the two are referred to as a scalar/vector pair. A VAX multiprocessor system comprises a number of these scalar/vector pairs. Asymmetric configurations can exist where only some of the VAX processors in a multiprocessor system contain a vector coprocessor.

For good performance, the scalar processor operates asynchronously from its vector coprocessor whenever possible; this allows the execution of scalar instructions to be overlapped with the execution of vector instructions. Furthermore, the servicing of interrupts and scalar exceptions by the scalar proces-

15	14	13	12	11			8	7			4	3			0
MOE	MTF	EXC MI	0	Va / Convert Fcn				Vb				Vc / Compare Fcn			

Figure 1: Vector Control Word

Assembler Format:

VVEQLF	**V6, V7**	; If V6[i] = V7[i] then VMR[i] = 1, else VMR[i] = 0
		; (VVEQLF is a VVCMPF pseudo-opcode)
VVADDF/1	**V1, V2, V3**	; V3 = V1 + V2. Do addition under control of VMR
		; with match=1
VSMULF/U	**R4,V4,V5**	; V5 = R4*V4 with underflow exception checking enabled

Instruction Format:

VVCMPF	**cntrl.rw**	; Instruction consists of opcode and control word
VVADDF	**cntrl.rw**	; Instruction consists of opcode and control word
VSMULF	**cntrl.rw, src.rl**	; Instruction consists of opcode, control word, & scalar source

Encoding in Memory:

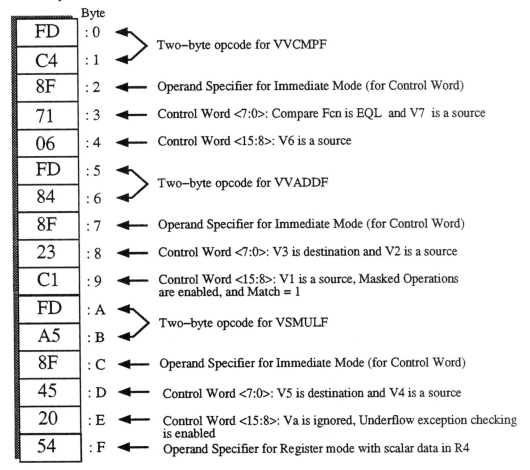

Figure 2: Vector Instruction Encoding

207

Table 1: VAX Vector Instruction Classes

Vector Memory, constant-stride			**Vector-Scalar Double-Precision Arithmetic**		
opcode cntrl, base, stride			*opcode cntrl, scalar*		
VLDL	Load Longword Vector Data		VSADDD	D_floating Add	
VLDQ	Load Quadword Vector Data		VSADDG	G_floating Add	
VSTL	Store Longword Vector Data		VSCMPD	D_floating Compare	
VSTQ	Store Quadword Vector Data		VSCMPG	G_floating Compare	
			VSDIVD	D_floating Divide	
			VSDIVG	G_floating Divide	
Vector Memory, random-stride			VSMULD	D_floating Multiply	
opcode cntrl, base			VSMULG	G_floating Multiply	
			VSSUBD	D_floating Subtract	
VGATHL	Gather Longword Vector Data		VSSUBG	G_floating Subtract	
VGATHQ	Gather Quadword Vector Data		VSMERGE	Merge	
VSCATL	Scatter Longword Vector Data				
VSCATQ	Scatter Quadword Vector Data		**Vector-Vector Arithmetic**		
			opcode cntrl or regnum		
Vector-Scalar Single-Precision Arithmetic			VVADDL	Integer Longword Add	
opcode cntrl, scalar			VVADDF	F_floating Add	
			VVADDD	D_floating Add	
VSADDL	Integer Longword Add		VVADDG	G_floating Add	
VSADDF	F_floating Add		VVBICL	Bit Clear Longword	
VSBICL	Bit Clear Longword		VVBISL	Bit Set Longword	
VSBISL	Bit Set Longword		VVCMPL	Integer Longword Compare	
VSCMPL	Integer Longword Compare		VVCMPF	F_floating Compare	
VSCMPF	F_floating Compare		VVCMPD	D_floating Compare	
VSDIVF	F_floating Divide		VVCMPG	G_floating Compare	
VSMULL	Integer Longword Multiply		VVCVT	Convert	
VSMULF	F_floating Multiply		VVDIVF	F_floating Divide	
VSSLLL	Shift Left Logical Longword		VVDIVD	D_floating Divide	
VSSRLL	Shift Right Logical Longword		VVDIVG	G_floating Divide	
VSSUBL	Integer Longword Subtract		VVMERGE	Merge	
VSSUBF	F_floating Subtract		VVMULL	Integer Longword Multiply	
VSXORL	Exclusive-Or Longword		VVMULF	F_floating Multiply	
IOTA	Generate Compressed IOTA Vector		VVMULD	D_floating Multiply	
			VVMULG	G_floating Multiply	
			VVSLLL	Shift Left Logical Longword	
Vector Control Register Read			VVSRLL	Shift Right Logical Longword	
opcode regnum, destination			VVSUBL	Integer Longword Subtract	
			VVSUBF	F_floating Subtract	
MFVP	Move From Vector Processor		VVSUBD	D_floating Subtract	
			VVSUBG	G_floating Subtract	
Vector Control Register Write			VVXORL	Exclusive-Or Longword	
opcode regnum, scalar					
			VSYNC	Synchronize Vector Memory Access	
MTVP	Move To Vector Processor				

sor does not disturb the execution of the vector coprocessor, which is freed from the complexity of resuming the execution of vector instructions after such events. However, the asynchronous execution does cause the reporting of vector exceptions to be imprecise. Special instructions are provided to ensure synchronous operation when necessary; these are discussed in section 8.

Both scalar and vector instructions are initially fetched from memory and decoded by the scalar processor. If the opcode indicates a vector instruction, the opcode and necessary scalar operands are issued to the vector coprocessor and placed in its instruction queue. The vector coprocessor accesses memory directly for any vector data that it need read or write. For most vector instructions, once the scalar processor successfully issues the vector instruction, it goes on to process other instructions; it does not wait for the vector instruction to complete. An execution model is shown in Figure 3.

When the scalar processor attempts to issue a vector instruction, it checks to see if the vector coprocessor is disabled -- that is, whether it will accept further vector instructions. If the vector coprocessor is disabled, then the scalar processor takes a "vector processor disabled" fault. An operating system handler is then invoked on the scalar processor to examine the various error reporting registers on the vector coprocessor to determine the disabling condition. The vector coprocessor disables itself to report the occurrence of vector arithmetic exceptions or hardware errors. The operating system disables the vector coprocessor by writing to a privileged vector register; this is usually done to indicate the unavailability of the vector coprocessor. If the disabling condition can be corrected, the handler enables the vector coprocessor, and the scalar processor re-issues the faulted vector instruction.

Within the constraint of maintaining the proper ordering among the operations of data-dependent instructions, the architecture explicitly allows the vector coprocessor to execute any number of the instructions in its queue concurrently and retire them out of order. This allows a VAX vector implementation to chain and overlap to the extent best-suited for its technology and cost-performance. In addition, by making this an explicit part of the architecture, software is provided with a programming model that ensures correct results independent of the extent a particular implementation chains or overlaps. This approach differs with respect to some other existing vector ar-

chitectures, such as the IBM S/370 vector architecture [10], which give the appearance of sequential instruction execution.

A VAX vector implementation may have its own memory management hardware, translation buffer, and cache; or it may share those of the scalar processor. For high-end systems, such as the VAX 9000 [11] where the vector and scalar processors are tightly-coupled, the problems of limited chip area and translation buffer and cache coherency can be lessened by allowing high-speed memory management hardware and cache to be shared by both vector and scalar processors. For low-end implementations, such as the VAX 6000-400 [12] where the vector and scalar processors are not so tightly-coupled, there is a performance advantage in allowing separate memory management hardware and cache. Little additional effort is necessary by an operating system to support separate vector memory management hardware and cache.

Due to the time involved in performing VAX memory management exception (MME) checking, a VAX vector implementation, may issue vector memory instructions in either a synchronous or asynchronous mode. In the synchronous mode, once the scalar processor issues a vector memory instruction, it pauses until the vector coprocessor determines whether an MME will be encountered by the instruction. If an MME will occur, then a precise exception is taken on the scalar processor and the appropriate operating system handler is invoked. If no MME will occur, the scalar processor goes on to process other instructions and the vector coprocessor completes the memory instruction. In the case of referencing a unity-strided vector, which occurs most frequently, the MME checking takes only a very short time at the beginning because the vector is contained in two or less pages. (MME checking is done at the page level.) The advantage of this mode is that it is less complicated to implement in hardware. The disadvantage is that it does not allow as much overlapping between the execution of the scalar and vector processors. The first generation of VAX vector processors will use this mode.

In asynchronous mode, the scalar processor does not pause after issuing a vector memory instruction, but goes on to process other vector and scalar instructions. Eventually, the vector coprocessor will begin to execute the vector memory instruction and determine if the instruction will encounter an exception. If an MME will occur, then the scalar processor is notified when it attempts to send some subsequent vector instruction and an imprecise exception is taken on the scalar processor. The appropriate operating system handler is then invoked. The advantage of this mode is that it allows greater overlapping between the execution of the scalar and vector processors. The disadvantage comes in the complexity inherent in saving the partially-completed execution state of the vector coprocessor when the operating system decides to context switch the vector coprocessor rather than service the exception at that time.

6. Context Switching

Because of the asynchronous operation of the vector and scalar processors, the vector context state of a process is physically separate from its scalar context state. Thus, it is possible for an operating system to swap in a new process on to the scalar processor while allowing the vector context of the previous process to remain on the vector coprocessor. When the previous process is *swapped out, the vector coprocessor is disabled by the operating system to prevent other processes from accessing this vector context.

If the subsequent processes do not use the vector coprocessor, then the operating system avoids the overhead of saving and subsequently restoring 8-kilobytes of vector context state for the original process. Of course, if another process does use the vector coprocessor, the operating system will first need to re-enable the vector processor, then save the vector state of the original process, and finally load the vector context of the new process, if any, and make the vector coprocessor available. This full context switch can take a few hundred microseconds on the VAX 6000 Model 400.

Assuming that there are only a few processes which

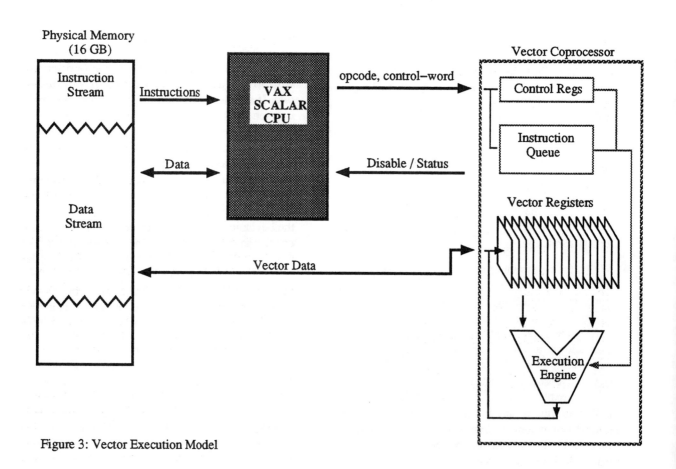

Figure 3: Vector Execution Model

require the vector coprocessor, it is likely that when the original process is rescheduled on to the same scalar / vector pair, the process will find its vector context state still residing on the vector coprocessor.

Utilizing this technique, which is referred to as "cheap vector context switching", both VAX/VMS and VAX/ULTRIX reduce the time required to swap in a process which uses the vector coprocessor.

7. Exceptions

Most of the exceptions encountered by VAX vector instructions are identical to those that occur for VAX scalar instructions. The arithmetic exceptions are exactly the same. The memory management exceptions have been extended to include two new vector exceptions. Details of the VAX exception architecture can be found in [8].

As described in section 5, arithmetic exceptions are reported in an imprecise manner by vector processor disabled faults. The reporting of floating underflow and integer overflow exceptions can be disabled by setting the EXC bit in the vector control word.

An instruction can encounter a vector arithmetic exception in the processing of a vector register element. When that happens, the element in the destination vector register which was to receive the result, the result element, instead receives an encoded floating-point reserved operand. Certain low-order bits within this reserved operand indicate which exception occurred in the attempt to calculate the result element. (By placing a reserved operand in the result element, subsequent attempts to use this element in other vector and scalar instructions will result in a floating-point reserved-operand exception.) Exception information is also recorded in privileged registers and the vector coprocessor disables itself.

After writing the reserved operand into the result element and disabling itself, the vector coprocessor continues to execute the instruction to completion and processes all other vector register elements. This is a major difference from the VAX scalar processor, which when servicing an arithmetic exception, restores all state modified by the instruction to its original state before invoking the exception handler.

As discussed in section 5, due to the time involved in performing memory management exception checking, a VAX Vector implementation may issue vector memory instructions in one of two modes. Independent of the mode, once a vector memory management exception is reported to the scalar processor, the scalar processor takes a normal VAX memory management fault and places exception information on the stack in the same format as for scalar memory management exceptions. Using the same format minimizes the effort needed by an operating system to support vector MME. Depending on the instruction-issue mode, the exception is either precise or imprecise.

Memory management exceptions were extended for vectors to include two new exception parameter bits: vector I/O space reference and vector alignment fault. A vector I/O space reference occurs whenever an attempt is made to load or store vector data to I/O space. Because of the performance degradation of unaligned memory data, a vector alignment fault occurs whenever an element being accessed by a vector memory instruction does not begin at an address which is an integer multiple of the length of the element in bytes. For example, a longword (four byte) element in memory should begin at an address which is an integer multiple of four bytes.

8. Synchronization

For most cases, it is desirable for the vector coprocessor to operate asynchronously with the scalar processor so as to achieve good performance. However, there are cases where the operation of the vector and scalar processors must be synchronized to ensure correct results. Rather than forcing the vector coprocessor to detect and automatically provide synchronization in these cases, the architecture provides software with special instructions to accomplish the synchronization. These are discussed below.

Vector and scalar memory references may be issued simultaneously. Their accesses must be synchronized to prevent conflict when referencing shared memory locations. This synchronization is provided by the MSYNC function of the MFVP instruction. Once the MSYNC function is invoked, the scalar processor does not issue further instructions until all previous vector and scalar memory references have completed.

A vector coprocessor may concurrently execute a number of vector memory instructions using multiple load/store paths to memory. If these multiple instructions are referencing common memory locations, then synchronization is necessary to prevent conflict. The VSYNC instruction provides synchronization to order the conflicting memory accesses of vector-memory instructions issued after VSYNC with those issued before VSYNC. It has no effect on the scalar processor and is ignored by vector implementations which do not execute multiple vector memory instructions in parallel.

Because the vector and scalar processors execute asynchronously, software cannot determine when a vector exception will be reported; yet, there is clearly a need to have exceptions reported at certain checkpoints. For example, exceptions incurred in a procedure must be reported within the context of that procedure before another procedure is called. This exception reporting synchronization is provided by the SYNC function of the MFVP instruction. Once SYNC is invoked, the scalar processor does not issue further instructions until the exceptions of previous vector instructions, if any, are reported.

Software must determine when to use these synchronization instructions to ensure correct results or establish exception checkpoints. Given the necessary sophistication of vectorizing compilers, this requirement is not onerous.

9. Implementations

The first two implementations of the VAX Vector Architecture are found in the VAX 9000 and VAX 6000 Model 400 systems. Each of these systems provide vector processing capability to their respective price-performance ranges. The following paragraphs provide a brief description of the systems. Table 2 shows the performance of the VAX 6000 Model 400 for some standard benchmarks. Performance measurements for the VAX 9000 are currently underway.

VAX 9000

The VAX 9000 is the newest high-end processor in the VAX family [11]. It employs RISC style design techniques at a 16-ns cycle time using advanced ECL gate-array (MCA3) and chip-interconnect (HDSC) technology to achieve scalar performance of 25 to 50 times that of the VAX 11/780. The system is a tightly-coupled multiprocessor with up to four scalar/vector pairs that are connected to each other, a shared main memory, and I/O controllers by a crossbar switch (termed the System Control Unit). The SCU provides high speed, simultaneous transfers at an aggregate bandwidth of 2 gigabytes per second.

With 1-megabit memory chips, the main memory of the system can expand up to 512 megabytes.

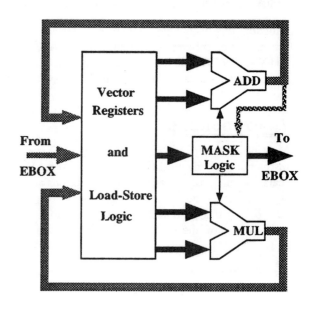

Figure 4: VAX 9000 Vector Processor

The VAX 9000 vector processor (VBOX) connects to the scalar CPU as an additional execution unit; a block diagram of the VBOX is shown in figure 4. The VBOX contains the vector registers, mask logic, and three independent execution units: load/store logic, vector add logic, and vector multiply logic. These three function units can both overlap and chain. Thus the following sequence requires only 1 chime (approximately vector length times cycle time) on the VAX 9000 vector processor:

VVADDD	V1, V2, V3
VVMULD	V3, V4, V5
VSTQ	V5, dst, #8

This organization allows the VBOX to achieve a peak performance of 125 Mflops on double-precision data. The total peak vector performance for a four-processor system is then roughly 500 Mflops. Simulation shows that a uniprocessor with the vector option will achieve about 18 Mflops on 100 x 100 LIN-PACK (Coded BLAS) and 115 Mflops on matrix multiplication.

The VBOX shares a 128-Kbyte data cache with the scalar CPU. When a memory reference for a constant-strided vector load instruction misses in this cache, processor logic not only fetches the missing cache line, but, also prefetches subsequent cache lines in anticipation of their eventual use.

VAX 6000 Model 400

The VAX 6000 Model 400 is the latest model in the VAX 6000 series of bus-based, CMOS-processor systems [12]. It uses the same platform, main memory interconnect and I/O structure as the models 200 and 300. The scalar processor operates at a 28-ns cycle time. The optional vector processor, which operates at a cycle time of 44.5 ns, occupies a bus slot adjacent to the scalar CPU and is connected to it by a short interface cable. The VAX 6000 Model 400 is capable of supporting multiple scalar processors; depending on configuration, it can support up to two scalar/vector pairs. Peak vector performance is 90 Mflops for single-precision data and 45 Mflops for double-precision data.

Performance for some standard benchmarks is shown in Table 2. The table shows, as expected, that speedup increases as the vectorizable content and the opportunity to better utilize the vector registers through more efficient algorithms increases. The LINPACK numbers in the table are based on a pre-release version of the VAX FORTRAN-HPO compiler.

Table 2: VAX 6000 Model 400 Performance
(Double-Precision MFLOPS, Uniprocessor)

	Size	Scalar	Vector	Ratio
LINPACK	100^2	1.2	3.4	2.8
LINPACK	300^2	1.0	10.3	10.3
LINPACK	1000^2	1.5	24.8	16.5
FFT	4096	1.2	14.6	14.2
Convolution	150 x 1500	1.3	30.1	23.2
Matrix Multiply	64^2	1.0	38.3	38.3

The vector processor has its own interconnect to the system memory bus and a private, 1-Mbyte data

cache. It performs its own virtual memory management. It has two independent execution units -- a load/store unit and an arithmetic unit -- which can both overlap and chain. A block diagram of the vector processor is shown in figure 5.

Logically, the arithmetic unit consists of four parallel pipelines; the vector registers are segmented across the pipelines such that every fourth element is accessed by the same pipeline. Physically, the arithmetic unit consists of four pairs of chips, one chip containing an arithmetic pipeline and the other holding one quarter of the vector registers. This intra-instruction parallelism allows the arithmetic unit to execute two arithmetic instructions in the time it takes to execute one load/store instruction. For example, the following executes in one chime:

```
VSMULD     Scalar, V0, V1
VVADDD     V1, V2, V3
VLDQ       dst, #8, V4
```

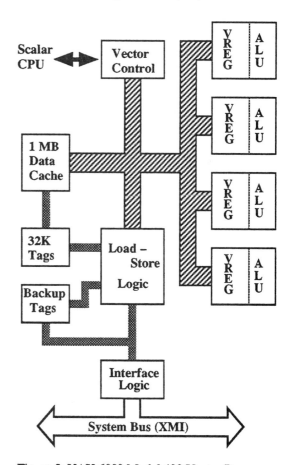

Figure 5: VAX 6000 Model 400 Vector Processor

10. Conclusions

The addition of vector processing capability is a significant extension to the VAX Architecture which will allow VAX users to achieve much better performance in scientific computing. The design of the architecture maximizes the asynchronism between the scalar and vector processors and the parallelism within the vector coprocessor. Yet, the design preserves the existing VAX memory management and exception handling mechanism such that only minimal changes are required to VAX/VMS and VAX/ULTRIX operating systems to support it.

11. Acknowledgments

The VAX vector architecture is based on another vector architecture developed by Dileep Bhandarkar, Dave Cutler, Dave Orbits, Wayne Cardoza, Rich Witek, and Rich Grove [13]. Adaptation of that architecture to VAX processors was largely done by Dileep Bhandarkar, Bob Supnik, and Tryggve Fossum with contributions by Dwight Manley, and Steve Hobbs. Frank Mckeen and Cheryl Wiecek contributed to the asynchronous memory management architecture. Kevin Harris and Brian Koblenz provided the vectorizing compiler perspective. Richard Brunner is currently responsible for architecture control and refinement.

References

[1] R. Russell, "The CRAY-1 Computer System", Comm. ACM, Vol. 21, No. 1, Jan 1978, pp.63-72.

[2] Frank R. Moore and David S. Wehrly, "The IBM 3090 Vector Computer System", COMPCON Spring '86.

[3] Steve Wallach, "The CONVEX C-1 64-bit Supercomputer", COMPCON Spring '86, pp.452-457.

[4] Hanan Potash, "The SCS-40 And Contributing Technologies", COMPCON Spring '86, pp.471-477.

[5] Robert Perron and Craig Mundie, "The Architecture of The Alliant FX/8 Computer", COMPCON Spring '86, pp.390-393.

[6] W.D. Strecker, "VAX-11/780 - A Virtual Address Extension to The DEC PDP-11 Family," AFIPS Conf. Proc. 47, 1978, pp.967-980.

[7] Daniel W. Dobberpuhl, Robert M. Supnik, Richard T. Witek; "MicroVax 78032 Chip, A 32-Bit Microprocessor," Proc. - IEEE International Conference on Computer Design: VLSI in Computers, ICCD '86, pp.414-419.

[8] Richard A. Brunner, "VAX Architecture Reference Manual," Digital Press, 1990.

[9] Cray Research, Inc.; "CRAY-2 Computer System Functional Description," 1985.

[10] W. Buchholz; "The IBM System/370 vector architecture," IBM Systems Journal, Vol 25, no. 1, 1986, pp.51-62.

[11] T. Fossum and D. Fite, "Designing a VAX For High Performance", Proc. COMPCON Spring '90.

[12] D. Fenwick, J. Redford, T. Stanley, D. Williams, "A VLSI Implementation of the VAX Vector Architecture", Proc. COMPCON Spring '90.

[13] D. Bhandarkar et al, "High Performance Issue Oriented Architecture", Proc. COMPCON Spring '90.

Appendix A - Code Examples

Assume in the following examples that all arrays are 8-byte double-precision.

1. MERGE example

```
Do i = 1, 64
    a(i) = b(i) - c(i)
    if (a(i) .gt. 0) then
        b(i) = a(i)
    else
        b(i) = c(i)
    endif
enddo
```

Vectorizes as:

```
VLDQ        b, #8, V0       ;Load vector b
VLDQ        c, #8, V1       ;Load vector c
VVSUBD      V0, V1, V2      ;b-c
VSTQ        V2, a, #8       ;Store vector a
VSLSSD      #^X0, V2        ;Test a(*) and set mask
                            ;in VMR. (VSCMP
                            ;pseudo-op doing Less
                            ;Than Signed test)
VVMERGE     V1, V2, V0      ;Merge a and c into b
                            ;using mask in VMR
VSTQ        V0, b, #8       ;Store vector b
```

2. IF-THEN-ELSE

```
Do i = 1, 64
    if (a(i) .gt. 0) then
        b(i) = c(i)
    else
        b(i) = c(i) / a(i)
    endif
enddo
```

Vectorizes as:

```
VLDQ        a, #8, V0       ;Load vector a
VSLSSD      #^X0, V0        ;Test a(*) and set mask
                            ;in VMR. (VSCMP
                            ;pseudo-op doing Less
                            ;Than Signed test)
VLDQ        c, #8, V1       ;Load vector c
VVDIVD/0    V1, V0, V2      ;Masked divide of c by a
                            ;for VMR[i] = 0
VSTQ/1      V1, b, #8       ;Store "then"part of b(*)
VSTQ/0      V2, b, #8       ;Store "else" part of b(*)
```

3. SCATTER - GATHER - IOTA:

```
Do i = 1, 64
    if (a(i) .eq. 0) then
        b(i) = c(i)/d(i)
    endif
enddo
```

Vectorizes as:

```
VLDQ        a, #8, V0       ;Load vector a
VSEQLD      #^X0 ,V0        ;Test a(*) for zero & set
                            ;mask. (VSCMP pseudo-
                            ;op doing Equal test)
IOTA        #8, V1          ;Make compressed
                            ;vector of offsets; write
```

```
                            ;size of vector to VCR
MFVCR       R0              ;Move VCR into R0
                            ; (MFVP pseudo-op)
MTVLR       R0              ;Load new VLR value
                            ;(MTVP pseudo-op)
VGATHQ      c, V1, V2       ;Gather vector c
                            ;using offsets in V1
VGATHQ      d, V1, V3       ;Gather vector d
                            ;using offsets in V1
VVDIVD      V2, V3, V4      ;Divide c by d
VSCATQ      V4, b, V1       ;Scatter vector b using
                            ;offsets in V1
```

4. DAXPY INNER LOOP

```
Do i = 1,64
    DY(i) = DY(i) + DA * DX(i)
enddo
```

Vectorizes as:

```
VLDQ        DX, #8, V0      ;Load vector DX
VSMULD      DA, V0, V1      ;V1 = DA*DX
VLDQ/M      DY, #8, V2      ;Load vector DY
                            ;with modify intent
VVADDD      V1, V2, V3      ;V3= V1+DY
VSTQ        V3, DY, #8      ;Store vector DY
```

5. SYNCHRONIZATION

```
Do i = 1, 64
    a(i) = b(i) * c(i)
enddo
a(1) = a(1) * d
```

Vectorizes as:

```
VLDQ        b, #8, V0       ;Load vector b
VLDQ        c, #8, V1       ;Load vector c
VVMULD      V0, V1, V2      ;V2 = b * c
VSTQ        V2, a, #8       ;Store vector a
MSYNC       R0              ;Wait for previous
                            ;memory ops to finish
SYNC        R0              ;Synchronize vector
                            ;exceptions
MULD2       d, a            ;Compute new a(1) in
                            ;scalar mode
```

Multiple Instruction Issue in the NonStop Cyclone Processor

Robert W. Horst   Richard L. Harris   Robert L. Jardine

Tandem Computers Incorporated
19333 Vallco Parkway
Cupertino, CA 95014

Abstract

This paper describes the architecture for issuing multiple instructions per clock in the NonStop Cyclone Processor. Pairs of instructions are fetched and decoded by a dual two-stage prefetch pipeline and passed to a dual six-stage pipeline for execution. Dynamic branch prediction is used to reduce branch penalties. A unique microcode routine for each pair is stored in the large duplexed control store. The microcode controls parallel data paths optimized for executing the most frequent instruction pairs. Other features of the architecture include cache support for unaligned double-precision accesses, a virtually-addressed main memory, and a novel precise exception mechanism.

1. Introduction

The NonStop Cyclone system is a fault-tolerant mainframe targeted at transaction processing, query processing and batch. Each system consists of four to sixteen processors that are connected by dual high-speed busses (Figure 1). Sections of four processors may be geographically distributed and interconnected by fiber optic cables. Each processor has its own memory and drives two to four I/O channels. Fault detection is performed primarily by the hardware, and fault recovery is performed by the message-based operating system. The system can tolerate a single fault in a processor, peripheral controller, power supply, or cooling system. Failed components can be serviced on-line without disrupting processing.

Five generations of Tandem computers (NonStop II, TXP, VLX, CLX and Cyclone) are object-code compatible and have been kept current through microcode updates downloaded to writeable control store. The Tandem instruction set has approximately 300 fixed-length (16-bit) instructions, ranging from simple RISC-like instructions to very complex instructions, such as block moves and inter-processor sends, which may take hundreds of clocks to complete. Most operations are zero-address with operands on the top of an eight-word register stack. The basic memory reference instructions are load and store instructions with address displacements relative to a stack pointer or segment base register.

The Cyclone processor is over three times faster than its predecessor. Approximately half of the performance improvement is due to higher clock rates, and the other half is due to the new micro-architecture. Much of the architectural improvement stems from the ability to issue up to two instructions per clock cycle. Other improvements are due to parallel data paths and new designs for the caches and main memory. This paper describes the architectural aspects of the NonStop Cyclone processor. In particular, it concentrates on the features that have been included to support multiple-instruction issue.

2. Overview

In recent years, advances in technology and computer architecture have allowed the design of processors in which simple instructions can be executed in a single clock cycle. Once that point is reached, further architectural performance improvements must be made by executing more

CH2887-8/90/0000/0216$01.00 © 1990 IEEE   216

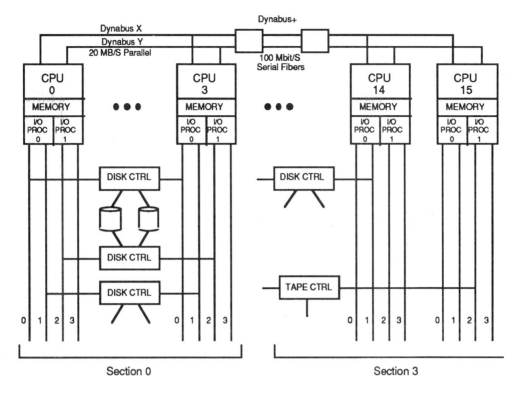

Figure 1. Cyclone System Architecture.

than one instruction per clock. Some previous scientific machines were capable of issuing multiple instructions per clock, but this was done through simultaneous execution of integer and floating point operations. When the instruction set can be partitioned into independent operations that share few resources, then it is possible to design independent function units and to assign each instruction to one of these units. Several instructions can be issued to the function units simultaneously [1].

Issuing multiple integer instructions per clock is more difficult because most integer instructions require use of the same resources. Typically, nearly all instructions access the same register file, and there are many inter-instruction data dependencies. There is no simple partitioning that would easily allow execution of multiple instructions per clock.

Very Long Instruction Word (VLIW) machines use sophisticated compiler technology to generate wide object code to control parallel data paths [2]. Typically, each VLIW implementation has its own unique object code format. While VLIW is useful in some situations, our environment demands object-code compatibility between generations of machines. It was essential to find a way to detect the parallelism at run-time rather than at compile-time.

The term "superscalar" was recently coined to describe machines that issue multiple instructions per clock, yet produce the same results as machines that execute instructions sequentially [3]. At about the same time the NonStop Cyclone system was announced, superscalar microprocessors were announced by Intel and IBM. The primary difference between the Cyclone processor and other superscalar designs is in the selection of which sets of instructions are to be issued simultaneously. Other machines have divided the instruction set into categories, such as branches, memory reference, and execution operators. In those machines, at most one instruction from each category can be issued simultaneously.

During the design of the Cyclone processor, we recognized that there may be many cases where several sequential instructions from the same category (or even the same instruction) should be issued simultaneously. For instance, in our stack-based machine, it is common to sequentially load two literal constants onto the register stack with Load Immediate (LDI) instructions. This pair of instructions, LDI&LDI, could easily be executed in a single clock with appropriate data path flexibility and enough register file ports. However, there was no obvious way to partition the machine into independent function units to which instructions could be assigned. Some pairs could benefit from separate ALUs, while others could benefit from separate partitions for memory reference and ALU. A few operations even suggest a bit-partitioning; one frequent pair has separate instructions to load a full-word literal into a register from left and right half-word literals.

Rather than partitioning the processor into independent function units, we chose to use firmware control and to program the microcode routines for each unique pair individually. In this way, there are no artificial restrictions on which instructions can be paired. In addition, by using microcode control, we do not restrict pairable operators to ones that can execute in a single clock cycle. For instance, instructions that use indirect addressing make two sequential accesses to the data cache and require three clocks to complete. However, it is still beneficial to pair indirect operators with other instructions. It takes three clocks to perform an indirect load, yet takes no more clocks when the indirect load is paired with a branch, immediate, or add instruction.

Once we decided to control pair execution with unique microcode routines, we could decide on a case-by-case basis whether to include the hardware support to be able to execute a pair in a single clock cycle. A hardware performance monitor was built, and instruction-pair frequencies were gathered for transaction processing applications. We then examined the frequencies to determine which hardware would gain the most performance for the least cost.

Figure 2 shows the pairing matrix for some representative instructions. Of the pairs shown, all except those in the last row execute in a single clock. The indirect loads require three clocks. In the current microcode, the full table of 2014 pairs has 38 "first" instructions (out of a possible 64) and 53 "second" instructions (out of a possible 127). In future microcode releases, more pairs may be added for improved performance.

The most important data path additions for the support of pairing were the inclusion of a nine-port register file and two ALUs that could be controlled independently or linked together for double-precision arithmetic. The flexibility of the data paths also turned out to be of great benefit in the execution of long instructions, such as the those that move or scan blocks of data, and those that send or receive messages.

In some cases, we chose not to include data path support for pairing. For instance, support for the pairing of memory reference instructions would have required more than twice the area and cost

SECOND	FIRST INSTRUCTION					
INSTR	BCC	LDI	LOAD	STOR	DADD	RRM
BCC	-	X	X	X	X	X
LDI	X	X	X	X	-	X
LOAD	X	X	-	-	X	X
STOR	X	X	-	-	X	X
DADD	X	X	X	X	-	-
RRM	X	X	X	X	-	X
LOADI	X	X	-	-	X	X

Figure 2. Sample matrix of instruction pairs. X's indicate coded instruction pairs. BCC = conditional branch, LDI = load immediate, LOAD = memory load, STOR = memory store, DADD = double-precision add, RRM = register to register move, LOADI = load indirect.

of a simpler cache. The frequency of successive memory references did not warrant such a cost. Instead, we determined that a greater payoff would result from supporting fast access to unaligned cache data for double-words.

The following sections describe in more detail the support for multiple instruction issue in key parts of the processor: the instruction fetch unit, the control store, the data paths, and the memory.

3. Instruction Fetch Unit

The Cyclone Instruction Fetch Unit (IFU) has four main functions: 1) to fetch instructions from memory, 2) to decode these instructions to determine whether they are candidates for paired execution, 3) to provide the beginning address for microcode execution of the instruction or pair, and 4) to assist in the execution of branching in-structions and exception handling.

The IFU also maintains the macro-instruction pipeline. As shown in Figure 3, each stage (or rank) of this pipeline holds two instructions to support paired execution. During ranks 1 and 2, control store is accessed; during rank 3, operands are fetched; during rank 4, ALU operations are performed; during rank 5, queued stores are completed and certain exception handling is performed.

The IFU design requirements centered around the ability to fetch at least two instructions per cycle. The alternatives were quickly narrowed down to an asynchronous IFU that could fetch two instructions per cycle with a four-instruction queue acting as a buffer between the instruction fetch and execution units. Extensive modeling showed that an instruction fetch rate of less than two instructions per cycle or an instruction queue

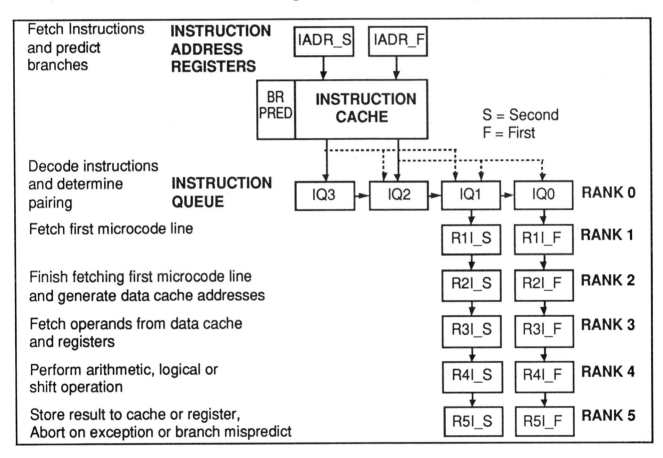

Figure 3. Instruction Fetch Unit Pipeline.

of less than four instructions would result in significant performance degradation, but IFU designs with more capability would not increase overall performance significantly.

The IFU contains an instruction cache, which holds 32K instructions. Two instructions can be fetched in each cycle, whether the address is aligned on an even or an odd instruction address. This cache is similar in structure to the separate data cache, which is described in section 6. A hardware state-machine initiates memory requests and supervises receiving an eight-instruction block from memory when a cache miss occurs. Modeling shows that about half of the time penalty associated with an instruction cache miss is masked by the execution of instructions already in the pipeline and instruction queue.

The instruction queue holds up to four instructions in preparation for decoding and execution. Instructions fetched from the instruction cache are placed directly in the queue. Either one or two instructions are fetched, depending on how much room is left in the queue. The instructions can be placed into any location in the queue, and the queue can shift (due to instruction initiation) on the same cycle as instructions are being fetched. In between instruction cache misses, the instruction queue fills up quickly and remains full with one or two instructions fetched to replace the one or two instructions promoted out of the queue at each instruction initiation. The queue typically becomes empty while the instruction cache is filling or while recovering from a branch misprediction.

The two instructions at the head of the instruction queue (in IQ0 and IQ1) are decoded and used to address two RAMs, called the Entry Point Tables (EPTs). The information in the EPT entries is combined to determine whether the two instructions will proceed into the execution pipeline as a pair or as separate instructions. (The term "instruction family" or just "family" is used to describe the instruction or pair as it proceeds through the execution pipeline.) In addition, the combination of the two EPT entries supplies an initial microcode address for the execution of the instruction family.

When the microcode routine for each family nears completion, the Control Unit signals the IFU that the next family should be initiated. If the next two instructions are pairable, they are both moved into rank 1 of the instruction pipeline, and the instruction queue shifts two positions. If the two instructions are not pairable, one instruction is moved into the first stage of the pipeline, and the instruction queue shifts one position. At the same time, the address of the first word (or only word) of the microcode routine for the family is delivered to the Control Unit.

Because of the depth of the pipeline, any instructions that manipulate the instruction address (such as branches) would seriously degrade performance if the most straightforward microcode implementation were chosen: the simplest branches would be at least seven cycles, and indirect branches would be nine or more cycles. To avoid this problem, the IFU was designed to have its own address adder and a branch prediction mechanism, to allow it to decode branch instructions and calculate the next address (or probable next address) without any assistance from the Control Unit or Data Unit.

Branch instructions contain a self-relative offset. Thus, for unconditional branches, the IFU need only add the address of the branch instruction to the offset extracted from the branch instruction. This addition is done as soon as the branch is fetched from the instruction cache into the instruction queue, and then the next (target) instruction is fetched. The cost of performing this addition is a single cycle, which is usually masked by the execution of instructions already in the pipeline and queue. In the case of unconditional indirect branches, two additional cycles are taken by the IFU to fetch the indirect cell and add its value to the target address.

A dynamic branch prediction mechanism is used for conditional branches. This mechanism relies on the premise that when a particular branch instruction is repeatedly encountered, it will tend to be taken (condition met) or not taken (condition not met) in the same direction each time. An extra bit for each instruction in the instruction cache records the direction of the most recent branch. This branch prediction strategy has been used in other machines, but generally with much smaller instruction caches [4]. Our modeling has shown branch prediction accuracy on many benchmarks, including the ET1 debit-credit benchmark, to range from 85% to 95%. This figure includes the effects of system code and context switching.

The microcode (executed by the Control Unit and Data Unit) has one simple role to play in conditional branches--once the branch instruction reaches Rank 4 of the execution pipeline, the data is finally available to determine whether the branch should actually be taken or not. This data can be either a condition code or the top-of-stack value. The microcode determines the correct branch direction and compares it with the IFU's predicted direction. If they match, the pipeline proceeds without interruption. If they do not match, a branch misprediction has occurred and the microcode signals the IFU to flush the pipeline and start fetching instructions from the other path. In addition, the branch prediction bit in the instruction cache is inverted, so that it will correctly indicate the actual path taken.

A correctly-predicted branch consumes a single cycle in the pipeline, while an incorrectly-predicted branch consumes seven. With 85% to 95% accuracy, the branch prediction mechanism results in an average cost of 1.3 to 1.9 cycles per branch instruction.

In addition, because the branch prediction occurs early in the instruction queue, by the time the branch reaches the head of the queue, it may be a candidate for pairing. In fact, a branch can be paired in three different ways: with its immediate predecessor, with its static successor (when it is predicted to be not taken), or with its dynamic successor (when it is predicted to be taken). The ability to pair branches in these ways leads to an even lower average cost per branch.

Another important aspect of total compatibility with the previous Tandem processors is exception handling. Some exceptions, such as arithmetic overflows, are reported after the execution of the instruction that encounters them, while other exceptions, such as page faults, are reported before the instruction. We wanted to handle all exceptions in such a way that the paired-instruction execution would be transparent.

In the Nonstop Cyclone implementation, a family of two instructions could have zero, one, or two exceptions; in the case of one exception, it could be reported before the family, between the two instructions of the family, or after the family.

Handling exceptions reported before or after the family is relatively easy to do with general mechanisms, but handling exceptions that should be reported between the two instructions of the family is difficult. If unique microcode were required to handle each individual case for every pair of instructions, the amount of microcode would be unmanageable. Instead, most exceptions in instruction pairs are handled in a uniform way: exception handlers are written only for single-instruction families. When an exception is encountered in a paired instruction family, the hardware initiates an "unpaired restart". It aborts the execution of the pair, refetches the first instruction, and issues the two instructions sequentially as single-instruction families. The exceptions are then encountered again and handled correctly in order.

4. Sequencer

The microcode sequencer controls the execution of both long and short instruction algorithms. It also includes extensive microcode to handle interrupts and exceptions. A large control store is required to hold enough microcode to individually code the algorithms for each instruction pair. Figure 4 shows the layout of the control store and its relationship to the entry point logic of the IFU. Fully half of the available addresses are reserved for paired instructions, including the case of a pairable instruction that executes unpaired.

The two instructions at the head of the instruction queue, in IQ0 and IQ1, are used to address separate entry point table RAMs, EPT_F and EPT_S, respectively. Bits from these tables indicate groups of resources required by the instructions; intersections of these bits exclude unpairable combinations. If the instructions are pairable, a control store address is formed from six bits taken from the EPT_F table and seven bits from

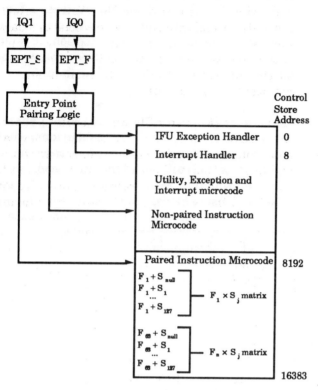

Figure 4. Microcode Layout

the EPT_S table, thus providing for a matrix of 64 "firsts," each a candidate for pairing with up to 127 "seconds." If the first instruction is pairable but resource conflicts exist, the six bits from EPT_F are concatenated with seven 0 bits. Multiple-clock pair algorithms reduce the number of available "seconds" by 1 for each sequential word of microcode that they use. A 13-bit entry point address is taken from EPT_F for instructions that are not pairable. A fourteenth bit is computed by the logic that determines whether to access the paired or non-paired region of control store.

The highly pipelined nature of the processor allows for access of each microinstruction in two stages. The Vertical Control Store (VCS) contains 16K words of 48-bits each. The VCS is responsible for control of the operand access portion of the data unit and also provides microse-

quencer branching control. The Horizontal Control Store (HCS) contains 16K words of 112 bits each. The HCS provides control for the main ALU and register storage functions, as well as a variety of other functions.

The Jump Control Store (JCS) is a copy of the VCS that provides a fast conditional jump mechanism within the sequencer. For a conditional jump in the microcode, the not-taken path is addressed in the VCS while the jump-taken path is simultaneously accessed in the JCS. The outcome of the condition evaluation is used to choose whether the VCS or the JCS is loaded into the control register. The condition evaluation and microcode access overlap considerably, providing a faster branch mechanism than is possible with a serial mechanism.

In addition to the fast conditional jump mechanism, a slower but less expensive "trap" mechanism handles exception conditions related to data cache access. A base address register is combined with a small offset field to vector into a set of utility routines. This trap address supersedes the JCS address of the successor microinstruction, thus implementing a one cycle slower jump for the cost of only a register and an address multiplexer. Traps have the unique feature of acting as a special type of microcode call, saving both the current and successor microcode addresses. This function is needed because the microinstruction that incurred the exception must be re-executed after resolution of the problem.

Duplicate copies of all three control stores (VCS, JCS, HCS) are included for performance and reliability. Two full cycles can be allowed for each access by reading alternate copies of each control store on successive cycles. This technique allows the use of 16Kx16 CMOS RAM modules for the control store, which would ordinarily not be fast enough for the control store of an ECL machine.

The second copy of each control store is also used to recover from RAM failures. Any error detected in one bank is overcome by retrying the access from the other bank, at a cost of two additional cycles to recirculate the addresses. In addition to this error recovery mechanism, spare RAMs are included. An exception handling routine can programmatically substitute a spare in place of a failing device. This mechanism, an extension of the one used in the NonStop VLX processor [5], provides substantial MTBF improvement at a relatively low cost.

5. Data Path

The design of the main data paths was driven by the requirements of the most frequent instructions pairs, tempered by reasonable cost limitations on logic. Two parallel ALUs were included for cases that required independent computation and to accommodate relatively frequent double-word (32-bit) operands.

We found that many pair algorithms could benefit from simple "selector" paths that could read and write the main register file without performing data transformations. The selector paths were also used for the interface to other sections of the processor outside the main data path, such as the integer multiplier, I/O subsystems, and maintenance processor.

A nine-ported register file was needed to support the desired register access flexibility. There are four write ports (two ALUs and two selector paths) and five read ports. Four of the read ports are for operand registers used directly in the ALUs and selector paths, while the fifth read port provides

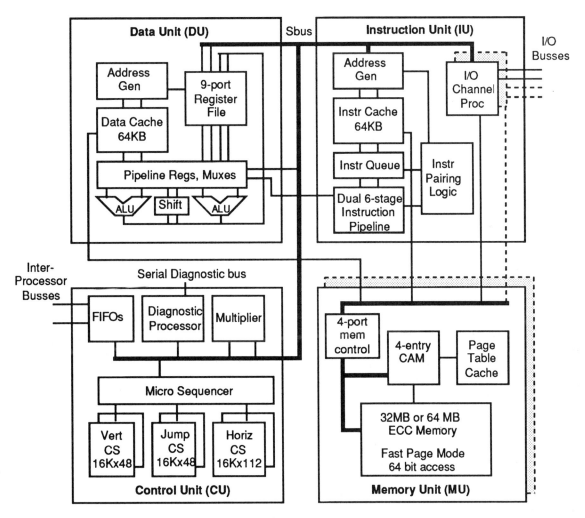

Figure 5. NonStop Cyclone Block Diagram. The processor is partitioned into four 18"x18" boards plus optional boards to add memory and I/O channels.

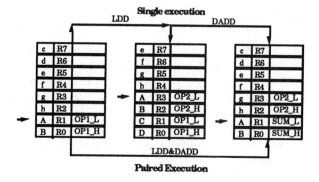

Figure 6. Register stack transition for Load-Double & Double-Add. Each stack shows the register name, the physical register number, and the contents.

limited access to base registers for the address generation logic. Bypass paths are provided to allow families to access registers modified by previous families without stalling the processor.

The block diagram of Figure 5 includes a high-level view of the main data path logic. The execution of a simple LOAD instruction, which comprises a single line of microcode, fetches data from cache while in rank 3 of the pipeline and stores to the register file logic in rank 4. Address generation can come either from a decoding of the rank-2 instruction for short instructions, or from the ALU(s) under microcode control during long algorithms.

This provision of four operand registers and dual ALUs allowed a paired implementation of a double-word load (LDD) with double-precision integer add (DADD). Figure 6 shows schematically the register stack transitions involved. If issued as single instructions, they would require two execution cycles. Data from cache would be loaded to R2 and R3 in the first cycle and then added to R0 and R1 in the second. Issued as a pair, however, LDD&DADD takes only a single execution cycle. In that cycle, data from cache can be simultaneously written to R2 and R3 while the sums of R0+R2 and R1+R3 are computed and stored to R0 and R1. This single-cycle family uses both ALUs, all four of the register file write ports, two of the read ports, and both of

the selector paths. It also takes advantage of the double-word cache access.

Some candidate instruction pairs would have required even more data path resources, but their frequency of occurrence did not warrant the inclusion of these resources. An example is a double-add followed by a load-immediate (DADD&LDI), which is not executable as a pair. Implementation of this pair would have required a fifth operand pipeline register (four for the DADD operands and one for the immediate value). On the other hand, the reverse sequence, LDI&DADD, can be executed as a pair; the immediate value is one of the DADD operands, and only four operand registers are required. Fortunately, due to the frequency of computing 32-bit address offsets, LDI&DADD occurs over 10 times more frequently than DADD&LDI.

6. Cache and Memory

Data gathered by the hardware performance monitor was critical for the design of the caches. The frequency of unaligned doubleword references was higher than the frequency of pairs with two memory references. Therefore, we concentrated on efficient support for unaligned accesses rather than support for two arbitrary memory references per cycle.

The unaligned cache design is shown in Figure 7. The data storage is partitioned into halves that store the data from even and odd addresses. The tag store is duplicated because an unaligned data access could cross cache block boundaries, requiring two different tags to be accessed. For aligned accesses, the same doubleword address is applied to both even and odd caches, and the first word is read from the even cache and the second is read from the odd cache. For an unaligned access, the doubleword address of the first word is applied to the odd cache, and that address is incremented and sent to the even cache. For unaligned accesses, the first data word comes from the odd cache, and the second comes from the even cache. Doubleword cache accesses require only one cache cycle as long as both words reside in the same page.

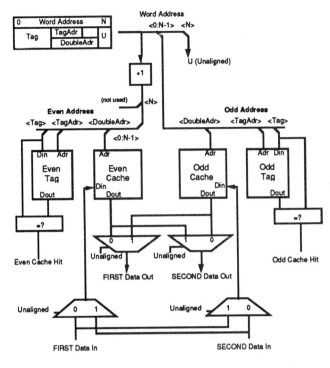

Figure 7. Block diagram of cache for unaligned access.

The unaligned cache design is also used in the instruction cache to allow pairs of arbitrarily-aligned instructions to be fetched each clock. Both the instruction and data cache are direct-mapped 64 Kbyte caches with address hashing, 16-byte blocks, and support for unaligned access.

The even-odd structure is maintained all the way to main memory. The data cache is a store-through design. All cache writes are sent to main memory through a one-entry write buffer. The memory can accept an average of one aligned or unaligned doubleword write every two cycles. Most memory reads are aligned, because full cache blocks are returned. After initial latency, the memory can supply one doubleword per cycle to either of the two caches or to an I/O subsystem.

In Tandem processors, all memory references are mapped to a single virtual address space shared by all processes. This allows the caches to use virtual addressing without the problems of invalidating cache entries on process switches or requiring a reverse translation table to handle synonyms. In the Cyclone processor, the virtual addresses are sent directly to the main memory. A four-entry content-addressable memory (CAM) compares each access to the row address that previously addressed a bank of dynamic RAM. When the addresses match, the dynamic RAM column address is generated by a few bits from the CAM plus the address offset. Translation from virtual to physical address is performed only on a CAM miss. Because the translation is performed infrequently, it was possible to implement the Page Table Cache (translation lookaside buffer) in relatively slow CMOS static RAMS.

7. Performance

The performance gains from issuing multiple instructions per cycle are quite program-specific. Programs that execute only RISC-like instructions show much more benefit from pairing than programs that spend large amounts of time in long instructions (such as block move and scan instructions). The programs using long instructions benefit from many of the data path and memory enhancements made to support pairing, but do not gain much performance from multiple instruction issue because the instruction issue rate is relatively low.

No experiments have yet been run to determine the effects of pairing on large transaction processing benchmarks. However, modeling has shown that the ET1 debit-credit benchmark should run with half of the families issued as instruction pairs. This means that approximately 2/3 of the instructions are issued in pairs. In typical transaction processing tasks, the Cyclone processor averages about 1.5-2 clocks per native instruction (CPI), including all overhead for cache misses and the effects of averaging many short paired instructions with a few very long instructions.

Some simple benchmarks have been analyzed in detail on the microcode simulator. For instance, the inner loop of the simple Sieve benchmark has nine short instructions--a memory load, two register-to-register moves, an integer add, two immediates, an indirect store (3 clocks), and two branches. Without pairing, this loop takes 11 cycles. With pairing enabled, the nine instructions are issued in five families and require seven clocks, for a rate of 0.78 CPI. Running the Sieve benchmark on a real machine shows a performance improvement of 37% when pairing is enabled. Other benchmarks show less improvement with pairing, varying from 12% to 37%. Benchmarks showing smaller improvements with pairing generally make heavy use of block move instructions. If these had been coded instead with simple load and store instructions, the apparent benefit of pairing would increase, but the overall benchmark speed would generally decrease.

8. Conclusions

We have described many of the innovations in the architecture of the NonStop Cyclone processor. New superscalar techniques were developed and applied in the design of an object-code compatible, fault-tolerant mainframe.

While some of the techniques may be peculiar to Tandem's instruction set, most could be applied to either RISC or CISC architectures. The smaller instruction set of a RISC architecture would greatly reduce the number of instruction pairs and simplify the instruction decoding. The new microsequencer ideas and methods of attaining object-code compatibility are especially applicable to CISC designs. Finally, many commercial machines could benefit from new cache designs that allow rapid access to unaligned data.

9. Acknowledgements

The authors wish to thank the outstanding engineers and programmers who contributed their ideas and energy to the design of the NonStop Cyclone system.

References

[1] Acosta, "An Instruction Issuing Approach to Enhancing Performance in Multiple Functional Unit Processors," *IEEE Trans Computers*, vol. C-35, no. 9, pp. 815-828, September 1986.

[2] R. P. Colwell, R. P. Nix, J. J. O'Donnell, D. P. Papworth, P. K. Rodman, "A VLIW Architecture for a Trace Scheduling Compiler," in *proc. Second International Conference on Architectural Support for Programming Languages and Operating Systems*, Boston, MA, pp. 180-192, October 1987.

[3] N. P. Jouppi, D. W. Wall, "Available Instruction-Level Parallelism for Superscalar and Superpipelined Machines," in *proc. Third International Conference on Architectural Support for Programming Languages and Operating Systems*, Boston, MA, 1989.

[4] J. E. Smith, "A Study of Branch Prediction Strategies," in *proc. 8th Annual Symposium on Computer Architecture*, pp. 135-148, May 1981.

[5] R. W. Horst, "Reliable Design of High-speed Cache and Control Store Memories," in *proc. Nineteenth International Symposium on Fault Tolerant Computing*, Chicago, IL, pp. 259-266, June 1989.

Tandem, NonStop, Cyclone, Dynabus, Dynabus+, CLX and VLX are trademarks of Tandem Computers Incorporated.

Session 4B: Applications

Performance of an OLTP Application on Symmetry Multiprocessor System

Shreekant S. Thakkar
Mark Sweiger

Sequent Computer Systems
Beaverton, Oregon 97006

ABSTRACT

Sequent's Symmetry Series is a bus-based shared-memory multiprocessor. System performance in an OLTP relational database application was investigated using the TP1 benchmark. System performance was tested with fully-cached benchmarks and with scaled benchmarks. In fully-cached tests, the entire database fits inside main memory. In scaled tests, the database is larger than available memory. In the fully-cached benchmark, performance was initially limited by bus saturation. The cause was the transfer of process context from processor to processor. This was eliminated by assigning each process to a processor. Processor affinity was combined with reductions in message-passing within the database. Throughput was dramatically improved. The scaled tests were I/O bound. This bottleneck can be eliminated by connecting more disk drives, or by increasing the main memory size.

1. INTRODUCTION

Symmetry systems are bus-based cache-coherent shared memory multiprocessors running a UNIX-based symmetric operating system. Such systems allow multi-user/multi-stream applications to be ported almost transparently from a similar uniprocessor environment.

However, porting does not guarantee that applications will achieve the optimal throughput that the architecture offers. Both system and applications may have to be tuned with appropriate parameters to achieve optimal performance. This paper describes the effect of some of these parameters on system performance when running the TP1 benchmark. We do not know of any other work which describes an evaluation of internal system behavior with this application.

System bus and processor cache mechanisms were major targets of this investigation. The goal was to discover the cause of an unexpected roll-off in database performance as more CPUs were added to the system.

The background and results of the investigation are presented in the following sections:

On-line Transaction Processing - A brief discussion of the application area and the benchmarks used to study performance.

Relational Database Architecture - An overview of the architecture of the database software used in the study.

Symmetry System Hardware Architecture - A discussion of the hardware architecture of the system, and of the bus and cache mechanisms that were investigated.

Performance Evaluation - A presentation of the goals, methods, and results of the performance investigation.

Conclusions

2. ON-LINE TRANSACTION PROCESSING

Characteristics Of OLTP Systems

On-Line Transaction Processing (OLTP) applications demand rapid, interactive processing for large numbers of relatively simple transactions. They are typically supported by very large databases. Automated teller machines and airline reservations systems are familiar examples of OLTP.

OLTP is among the fastest growing segments of database applications. OLTP systems are becoming very important strategically to many businesses because they can give a competitive edge in providing service. Prominent vendors besides Sequent in the OLTP market include Digital Equipment Corporation, IBM, Stratus and Tandem Corporations.

CH2887-8/90/0000/0228$01.00 © 1990 IEEE

OLTP Performance characterization

The TP1 Benchmark

The test used to benchmark OLTP database performance on Symmetry systems was the TP1 benchmark. Originally proposed in 1985 (Anon, 1985), this benchmark has become the de facto standard for gauging relational database performance.

The TP1 test simulates a banking system workload. The benchmark debits or credits a bank customer's account and updates related teller and branch accounts. The purpose of the benchmark is to do as many of these simultaneous debit/credit transactions as possible. Throughput is measured in Transactions Per Second (TPS). The TP1 benchmark is closely related to the Debit Credit benchmark. The chief differentiator is that the TP1 test does not require terminal emulation and support.

TP1 Test Architecture

When written in SQL, the TP1 transaction consists of three UPDATES and one INSERT. The UPDATES are for the customer's bank account balance, the corresponding teller's drawer balance, and the corresponding bank branch balance. The INSERT appends to the history table the audit trail record for that transaction.

In addition to the basic TP1 database transaction, the TP1 test suite performs the following functions:

o   Generates a random branch number.
o   Generates a random teller number at the selected branch.
o   Generates a random account number at the selected branch for 85% of the transactions and at a different branch for 15% of the transactions.

TP1 Database Scaling

Bank accounts are actually updated rather infrequently. It takes a very large account base to generate a sustained high TPS load. For example, in the real world any banking system requiring sustained throughput of 100 transactions per second probably has millions of accounts. The I/O necessary to page such a large database in and out of memory is a significant drain on system throughput.

For this reason the standard TP1 benchmark has strict rules for sizing the branch, teller, and account tables. As TPS ratings increase, the database tables used must grow larger. This insures that audited TP1 benchmarks include a realistic amount of disk I/O, and prevents unrealistic throughput claims based on small tables that can be made memory resident and thus subject to very fast update.

The fully-cached TP1 tests presented in this paper used tables smaller than those required by the TP1 standard. This was done specifically to eliminate disk I/O operations. Early testing revealed that bus saturation occurred even with few I/O operations. Since the purpose of the initial test series was to find the cause of the bus saturation, the database tables used were sized to fit completely into system memory.

Following the fully-cached tests, a second series of TP1 tests used scaled database tables that required large amounts of disk I/O. Some of the scaled TP1 test results presented in this paper come close to the standard TP1 scaling criteria and would provide auditable test results with more tuning. As mentioned earlier the purpose here was to study the performance of the architecture for such an application rather than get an auditable TP1 number. For correct scaling of TP1 a larger database would be required which was not possible to create because of limitation of hardware resources available during this experiment.

3. RELATIONAL DATABASE ARCHITECTURE

Two-Process Architecture

The relational database system used in this investigation utilizes a client-server architecture consisting of a front-end application program and a back end database engine. The front-end handles user interfaces and compiles user input into messages containing SQL statements which are sent to the back end. The back end executes the SQL statements and returns results to the front-end, handles disk I/O, and maintains database integrity.

Because it uses two separate address spaces, the two-process architecture isolates and protects the database engine from problems in the front-end application code. It also simplifies applications development because a standard database engine can serve a wide variety of different front-end applications.

In the TP1 benchmark, the front-end process is a relatively light-weight process. This effectively emulates the client-server architecture, where the front-end process may run on personal computer or workstation and the back end on a database server.

Single-Process Architecture Tests

For comparison purposes, some tests were also run on an earlier version of the database that did not use the two-process architecture (single-process model).

4. SYMMETRY SYSTEM HARDWARE ARCHITECTURE

Sequent Symmetry Hardware

Sequent's Symmetry Series is a bus-based shared-memory multiprocessor (Lovett and Thakkar, 1988). A diagram is shown in Figure 1. A machine can contain from two to thirty CPUs with a peak performance of around 120 MIPS. Each processor subsystem contains a 32-bit microprocessor, a floating point unit, optional floating point accelerator, and a private cache.

The system features a 56 MB/sec pipelined system bus, up to 240 MB of main memory, and a diagnostic and console processor. Symmetry systems can support five dual-channel disk controllers (DCCs), with up to 8 disks per channel. Each channel can transfer at 1.8 MB/sec.

The DYNIX operating system is a parallel version of UNIX, designed and implemented by Sequent for their Balance and Symmetry machines. It provides all services of ATT System V UNIX as well as Berkeley 4.2 BSD UNIX.

Symmetry Architecture

Since system bus and processor cache mechanisms were a major target of this investigation, a brief overview of bus and cache architectural issues is provided below:

Caches In Uniprocessor Systems

To sustain peak performance a uniprocessor system has to be able to access instructions and data rapidly. Main memory speeds are usually much slower than those required to support the desired access rates. Thus a cache memory that can be rapidly accessed and is transparent to software is used to sustain the processor's peak performance. The cache lies close to the processor and is a part of the memory hierarchy in the system.

Both the temporal and spatial locality of program access behavior allows a relatively small cache to satisfy a majority of processor's request. Because of this, large caches show diminishing returns in uniprocessor systems. They are relatively expensive and may not significantly increase system throughput.

Caches In Bus-Based Shared Memory Multiprocessors

In the bus-based shared memory multiprocessor cache memory is used to sustain peak processor performance in a manner similar to uniprocessor systems. More importantly though, caches are used to keep the processor's memory accesses off the bus.

The bus is the most critical resource in a multiprocessor system, and bus utilization in these systems is directly proportional to the cache-miss rate. For example, in a 30 CPU system if the miss-rate for individual processors goes up by 1/4%, this increase, when multiplied by 30 processors, amounts to 7 1/2% for the system. Thus bus utilization increases by 7 1/2%.

If an application exhibits a miss-rate exceeding a critical percentage, the system bus will be saturated by main memory accesses. Increases in miss-rates may be generated by legitimate application behavior or by applications operating in a non-optimal manner for the architecture. Thus there is potential to increase the performance of these later applications by realizing this behavior and fixing it.

In bus-based shared-memory multiprocessor systems, larger caches are generally worth the cost because they eliminate potential bus traffic due to cache misses.

Symmetry Cache Coherency Protocol

The Symmetry multiprocessor system supports an efficient copyback cache coherency protocol. This protocol enables Symmetry to scale to a larger number of processor for parallel and multi-user workloads (Thakkar, 1989). The scaling enabled by this protocol compares well with the protocols simulated by Archibald (Archibald and Baer, 1986).

The protocol allows a dirty copy of a data block to exist in one of the caches in the system. The dirty block gets copied back to memory implicitly when another cache makes a non-exclusive read access to that the block. Alternatively, it gets copied back to memory explicitly when that line in the cache is replaced to make room for another block.

The Symmetry copyback cache coherency protocol (Lovett and Thakkar, 1988) supports four cache states: *invalid*, *private*, *shared* and *modified*. Both *private* and *modified* are exclusive states. The *private* state is a read exclusive state and *modified* state is a write exclusive state. The coherence protocol is similar to Illinois protocol (Papmarcos and Patel, 1984). The differences are described in (Lovett and Thakkar, 1988).

The cache coherency protocol is based on the concept of ownership. That is, to perform a write operation on a block (assuming a cache miss), a cache has to first perform an exclusive read operation on the bus to gain ownership of the block. Only then can the block be updated in the cache.

If another cache is holding the block in *modified* state, it has to respond to the read exclusive request and invalidate its copy. The responding cache asserts the owned line on the bus, indicating that memory should not respond to that request.

For a non-exclusive read request on the bus, all caches that hold the block in *shared* state will assert the *shared* line on the bus. The memory responds and the block is loaded into the requesting cache as *shared*.

Synchronization Mechanism

The synchronization mechanism on the Symmetry model uses cache-based locks. The locks are also ownership based. That is, the cache controller treats a locked read from a processor like a write operation.

Assuming a cache miss, the cache controller performs an exclusive read operation on the bus to gain ownership of the block. The atomic lock operation is then completed in the cache. These locks are optimized for multi-user systems where locks are lightly contested and the critical sections are short. They do not work well in some parallel applications where a lock is heavily contested. Several other software synchronization schemes can be used to reduce contention for the locks in the hardware (Archibald and Baer, 1986, Graunke and Thakkar, 1990).

Response latency

In general, caches in multiprocessor systems serve two masters, the processor and the bus. A cache has to respond to bus requests when it owns a dirty block, and also to processor requests. The memory only responds to a single processor access at a time, hence it can respond much faster. On Symmetry, the Sequent System Bus can be thought of as a pipe to memory. The pipe depth is optimized for memory latency. The caches have an asynchronous interface to the bus and have to support processor accesses. Thus a cache-to-cache transfer is slower than a memory-to-cache transfer in such a system.

The Sequent System Bus is an unpended (split-transaction) bus. A fixed number of requests are allowed on the bus, and responses to requests are strictly ordered. Responses to earlier requests have to come back before responses to later requests can be allowed on the bus.

The number of requests allowed on the bus is optimized for the number of cycles required by a memory response, because memory responds to the majority of bus requests. Cache responses, having longer latency, require more bus cycles than memory responses. The additional bus cycles spent waiting for non-optimal, slower-than-memory responses are wasteful of bus bandwidth because they prevent further requests from being put on the bus. These additional cycles can be classified as "hold" cycles. Thus if a cache responds to a bus request, potentially useful bus cycles are wasted as hold cycles.

Process Migration Effect On Shared-Memory Bus Traffic

In a multi-user environment, a process is scheduled to run on a processor until it gets context switched as a result of operating system scheduling (i.e., time-slicing) or when it blocks on a resource. This is known as involuntary context switch.

At present, DYNIX makes little effort to schedule a process to be allocated to the same processor after it has been context switched. Thus, a process may start on a different processor when DYNIX schedules it to run again. This is called *process migration*, since a process migrates from one processor to another.

The potential problem is that the process's context may still be in its previous processor's cache. The context then has to be moved from the previous cache to the current cache. (This only applies to dirty blocks.) This cache-to-cache traffic is totally unnecessary, and has a detrimental effect on bus and processor performance, because cache-to-cache traffic adds hold cycles on the bus.

In Symmetry Model B systems, caches are relatively small (64K bytes), and the process migration caused by involuntary context switches is not normally a significant problem. Contexts, in general, stay in the cache for a longer time in multiprocessor systems than in uniprocessor machines, and in a small cache they almost certainly wipe out previous context. Since multiprocessors provide more individual processor resources, the competing processes do not interfere as much on a per processor basis. As caches grow larger though, a bigger percentage of previous contexts may stay in the cache. Then process migration will cause cache-to-cache bus traffic. Thus, process migration can be a performance limiter in multiprocessor systems with large caches.

5. PERFORMANCE EVALUATION

Goal and methods

The goal of this investigation was to analyze the behavior of the shared-memory architecture for OLTP applications. First, fully-cached databases were used to determine the upper bound on performance of this application on Symmetry Model B hardware and software. Next, tests requiring I/O operations were used, but these tests were not fully scaled according to strict TP1 criteria because the application features that were studied did not require it.

System Configuration

A Symmetry Model B system with 16 MHz Intel 80386/80387 and Weitek 1167 processor subsystems and 64-KB local caches was used for the experiments. A system with faster processors and larger caches was also used for some experiments. 96 MB of physical memory were available in the system. About 15% of the physical memory is used by the operating system for code, internal tables, and file system I/O buffer space.

The experimental system was equipped with 12 CPU boards (24 CPUs) 3 DCCs, and 12 disks, 2 disks on each channel. Two of the disks were used for DYNIX file systems, In order to measure only comparable numbers, we used only the other four DCCs for the experiments reported here. These 10 disks were opened in raw mode, i.e., DYNIX did not provide buffering, read-ahead, or write-behind for these disks.

The number of database front-end/back end process pairs used was always equal to one less than the number of processors. One processor has to be left free in the DYNIX environment to handle operating system functions.

Results Summary

Analysis shows that processor migration can be detrimental to performance of OLTP applications because of the amount of bus traffic generated by this activity. Disabling process migration with the processor affinity function gives a significant throughput improvement for this application.

When bus traffic is reduced to allow maximum performance, the system potentially can become I/O bound. The number of I/O accesses per second is the limiting factor.

Increasing the size of system memory improved performance because caching more of the database in main memory reduced the number of I/O requests.

Early Approaches

Larger Cache Sizing Was Tried

When we first encountered the performance roll-off, we suspected that processor cache size was the problem. If processor caches were too small, the processor might be going to memory frequently to fetch data. These requests could saturate the bus. The observed cache miss rate was high, providing possible evidence of a cache that was too small. This led to testing of a processor subsystem with a cache twice the size of the Model B. This processor subsystem also ran at a 25% faster clock rate.

The larger cache did reduce bus utilization. However, system performance only improved by about 20%. As in the Model B tests, the system bus became saturated and throughput was flat after 16 CPUs, despite the bigger cache. The relatively uniform 20% performance increase seen was slightly less than the increase in clock rate.

High-Contention Locks Were Suspected

It was then obvious that the high bus traffic was caused by some other activity in the system. Bus measurements showed that a significant portion of bus cycles were being wasted as hold cycles.

The type of bus traffic that has the most potential to generate hold cycles is cache-to-cache traffic. High contention locking activity can generate large amounts of cache-to-cache traffic involving lock data structures (Graunke and Thakkar, 1990).

A particular database-related lock was suspected, and a test was run with a modified synchronization lock algorithm, designed to reduce contention. The new algorithm had no effect.

Process Migration Was Identified

Next, the Sequent Database and System Performance personnel tried to reduce the high cache miss-rate and identify the source of the high bus utilization. It turned out that the process migration problem feared in large cache systems had materialized here.

One of characteristics observed during this test was that the context switching rate for the application was too high. It was significantly higher than that observed for other multi-user environments. The majority of context switches were voluntary context switches. This rate was proportional to the message passing between front-end and back end processes in the database.

High context-switch activity generated high cache-to-cache traffic because, since the processes had voluntarily context switched to pass messages, the contexts of the switched processes were still warm in the cache.

This context then gets moved from one cache to another as the operating system schedules the processes on other processors. The cumulative system activity resulting from these moves causes the performance degradation. The degradation manifests itself as bus saturation when a significant percentage of the bus is consumed by the cache-to-cache traffic and its side effects.

Affinity Was Used To Reduce Context Switching

The way to increase performance transparently to the application is to eliminate the cache-to-cache traffic. This traffic can be eliminated by restricting the movement of processes when they are context switched. Thus we needed to override the existing process scheduling algorithm actions.

The solution was to assign a process to a processor using the DYNIX processor affinity function. The affinity function allows a process to stay on the same processor forever. Thus after a context switch the process gets restarted on the same processor. Since the cache is still warm with respect to that process, the strategy maintains processor access rate and reduces bus utilization.

This affinity function is not an ideal environment for multi-user system since this disturbs the load-balancing. Ideally we would like to use a time heuristic affinity function which does not allow a process to resume on the same processor if a certain amount of time has elapsed. However, for the purpose of this experiment the use of the available function was sufficient since we were running experiments to determine effects of using the processor affinity versus not using it. The amount of users was held constant per processor. The tests were conducted on an isolated machine thus no other load was present on the system.

Message-Passing Overhead Was Reduced

At the same time, the database developer took the initiative to develop a version of the database that passed fewer messages between the front-end and back end processes, to reduce the high context-switch rate.

This is a technique that is used in decoupled front-end/back end environments, where the application front-end and the database back end run on different machines. In such applications, network overhead caused by interprocess communication between the front-end and back end is quite significant. This overhead can be reduced by batching adjacent back end database requests into a single message from the front-end to the back end.

For example, the TP1 transaction consists of four adjacent SQL statements, three UPDATES and an INSERT. Normally this would result in four send/receive message pairs. But if the requests are batched, only one send/receive message is required for the four commands.

This same batching facility also helps performance in a co-resident environment like the one created for the Symmetry TP1 tests. The batching technique reduced message traffic between the front-end and the back end, which reduced the context switch rate. Reduced context switching, in turn, reduces much of the bus overhead caused by process migration. It also reduces CPU-related message processing overhead caused by loading and unloading data into message buffers, verifying it, etc.

An interesting point to note is that with a fully cached database reduction of message passing between the front-end and back end achieved 91% of the throughput that was achieved by using the affinity function. This is with the number of processes being twice the number of processors.

So, the high context switch rate caused by high message passing activity did contribute significantly to the performance degradation. However, the best performance numbers are achieved by both reducing the number of messages (i.e., the number of voluntary context switches), and by stopping process migration (i.e., eliminating unnecessary cache traffic).

Performance Analysis

Observations On Two-Process Model versus Single-Process Model

When tests were run on a version of the database that did not use the two-process architecture (single-process model), some interesting comparisons could be seen. These tests led to discovering the process migration problem.

In the two-process model the context switch rate was directly proportional to the message passing rate. Because of the volume of messages passing between the front-end and back end processes, the context switch rate with the two-process model was nearly 10x the context switch rate of the single task model. Further, the two-process model generated more bus hold cycles than the single-process model.

The high context switch rate with the two-process model caused a high cache miss-rate. However, the context switch rate did not go up when processors were added. It remained constant. And, as processors were added, the miss-rate came

down. This effect can be seen in the performance graphs that follow.

Results From Processor Subsystem With 2x Larger Cache And 25% Faster Clock

Tests were also run on a processor subsystem with a 2x larger cache and 25% faster clock rate, to investigate the effects of larger cache size.

The context switch rate with the larger cache/faster processor was slightly higher than for the Model B subsystem. However, fewer hold cycles were generated than with Model B, and bus utilization was better. Some bus bandwidth was still available.

Single-process tests were also run on the larger cache/faster processor subsystem.

Throughput increases with the larger cache/faster processor were lower for the two-process model than for the single-process model. Increases with the two-process model varied from 35% with 12 processors to 20% with 24 processors. This compares with improvements of 42% with 12 processors to 50% with 24 processors the for single task model. These results show that using more processors is not resulting in a throughput increase for the two-process model of the database over the single-process model. The study described in this paper was conducted because we did not see a this gain in throughput.

The larger cache/faster processor reduced the cache miss-rate, but the reductions were greater with the single-process model. For the two-process model, the larger cache/faster processor showed a miss-rate decrease of 19%. For the single-process model the decrease was 45%.

Results of performance tuning on Model B

The rest of the report describes the process of effectively tuning the database, using the two-process model, to run efficiently on Symmetry multiprocessor system.

In the attached performance graphs, Figures 2 - 5 show total TPS numbers, cache miss rate, and bus utilization for fully-cached tests on Symmetry Model B system.

Figures 6 - 9 show the same parameters with scaled database tests, which required I/O operations in addition to log writes.

Figures 10 - 11 show the effect of affinity on the demand for I/O operations, and the effect of page cache size on performance.

Fully Cached Tests

Figure 2. Model B - TPS rate (affinity vs. non-affinity)

The non-affinity test shows little increase in TPS rate as the number of processors is increased. The affinity test shows over 40% increase in TPS rate as processors are doubled.

Figure 3. Model B - Miss rate (affinity vs. non-affinity)

In the non-affinity case the miss-rate drops steadily as processors are added. This is because the total cache space in the system is increased, and the work done is spread across the entire system. The affinity case shows a negligible decline in the miss-rate as processors are added. This is because a fixed amount of work is assigned to each processor.

Figure 4. Model B - Bus Utilization (affinity vs. non-affinity)

The bus utilization in the non-affinity case starts to drop as a result of lower miss-rate. However, the bus utilization rises steadily in the affinity case because the miss-rate per processor is constant as processors are added.

Figure 5. Model B - Hold Cycles (affinity vs. non-affinity)

The hold cycles in the affinity case are half that of the non-affinity case. The decrease in the hold cycles for the affinity case is entirely due to stopping the process migration and decreasing message passing between the front and back ends of the database application.

I/O Based Scaled Tests

Figure 6. Model B - TPS (affinity vs. non-affinity)

In tests requiring significant disk I/O activity, the flattening of the TPS rate as processors are added is more dramatic for the affinity based test than for the non-affinity test. This flattening is entirely due to the I/O limitation of this particular configuration. The non-affinity test shows less degradation because the major limitation in this case is the hold cycles caused by process migration.

Figure 7. Model B - Miss Rate (affinity vs. non-affinity)

The miss-rate for the affinity test with I/O follows the miss-rate for the fully cached affinity tests. It decreases gently as more processors are added. It is much lower than in fully-cached affinity test because much the I/O limitation allows less work to be done. The miss-rate for the non-affinity test is missing because of an error in recording the results. However it is little different from the non-affinity fully-cached test.

Figure 8. Model B - Bus Utilization (affinity vs non-affinity)

The bus utilization for the affinity case follows the miss-rate trend. The bus utilization with affinity is much lower than for the non-affinity case. This is really because the affinity test is more I/O bound.

Figure 9. Model B - Hold Cycles (affinity vs. non-affinity)

The affinity case shows less than 3% hold cycles. Once again, this indicates that the test is I/O bound. The hold cycles in the non-affinity case with I/O are marginally lower than the fully-cached non-affinity case. This indicates that the non-affinity case is only marginally I/O bound. (Note that the bus utilization and cache miss-rate are similar indications for the non-affinity case.)

Figure 10. Model B - I/O Performance (affinity vs non-affinity)

Six of the 10 disks were accessed heavily during the tests. This partitioning was done in accordance with TP1 benchmark specifications. The other four disks were lightly accessed.

The peak rate for accessing 2K bytes blocks randomly from each of the heavily-loaded disks is around 36 I/O's per second. This gives an aggregate rate of 210 I/O's per second for those disks. The graphs show that Model B with affinity approaches this number with 207 I/O's per second, indicating that the application is now I/O bound.

Figure 11. Throughput With I/O vs Page Cache Size (affinity vs non-affinity)

The affinity test results indicate that as the page cache size (M bytes) is increased the performance of the test approaches that of the fully cached affinity test. The test results shown are for 24 processors.

6. CONCLUSIONS

The TP1 testing revealed a hierarchy of performance bottlenecks which show the limitations of the current hardware and software. Each type of test highlighted a different type of limitation. These limitations were overcome by tuning the application to utilize the shared memory architecture more effectively. The hardware monitoring tools showed the effects the initial effects of process migration on the hardware and was later to effectively as tuning aid.

The fully-cached testing was only limited initially by bus bandwidth. After the addition of affinity and message batching, the fully-cached tests showed linear increases in performance throughout the processor range, with no bottlenecks at all in the tested range.

The scaled testing revealed a bottleneck caused by disk I/O. These tests show that limiting factor for the OLTP application is I/O throughput and not processor speed. The I/O throughput can be improved by adding more disks to the system or by having large memory sub-system that can cache the large portions of database.

Process migration was shown to cause significant performance degradation for this application. A simple recommendation for an operating system process scheduler would be to use a time-base scheduling heuristic algorithm. This would resolve the problem caused by process migration. A process would be scheduled to stay on a processor and would be reinvoked on the same processor if the time duration from the last context switch was less than some number.

Shared memory architectures have been shown to be suitable for relational database OLTP operations, and can deliver very high performance when the system and application are properly tuned. There is a need for an I/O solution that will match the performance of the next generation of microprocessors, which will operate in the 100-plus MIPS range. This I/O need is even higher for multiprocessor system,

which will incorporate several of these microprocessors.

Acknowledgements

We would like to thank Prof. Dan Siewiorek and other reviewers for improving the readability of the paper. We would also like to thank Betty Fuller for assistance in putting this paper together. Finally, though not the least, we would like to thank Joe Turner for editorial assistance.

References

Anon. "A Measure of Transaction Processing Power", Datamation, April 1985.

Archibald, J, and J. L. Baer. "Cache Coherence Protocols: Evaluation Using a Multiprocessor Simulation Model", TOCS 4, November 1986.

Graunke, G., and S. S Thakkar. "An Analysis of Synchronization Algorithms for Shared-Memory Multiprocessors", IEEE Computer, June 1990.

Lovett, T, and S. S Thakkar, "The Symmetry Multiprocessor System", Proceedings of Proceedings of ICPP, Penn State University, 1988.

Papmarcos, M, and J Patel, "A low overhead coherence solution for multiprocessors with private cache memories", Proceedings of 11th International Symposium on Computer Architecture, 1984.

Thakkar, S. S., "Performance of Symmetry Multiprocessor System", Proceedings of Cache and Interconnect Workshop, Eilat, Israel: Kluwer, 1989.

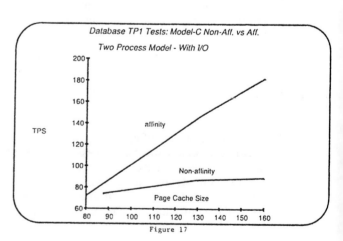

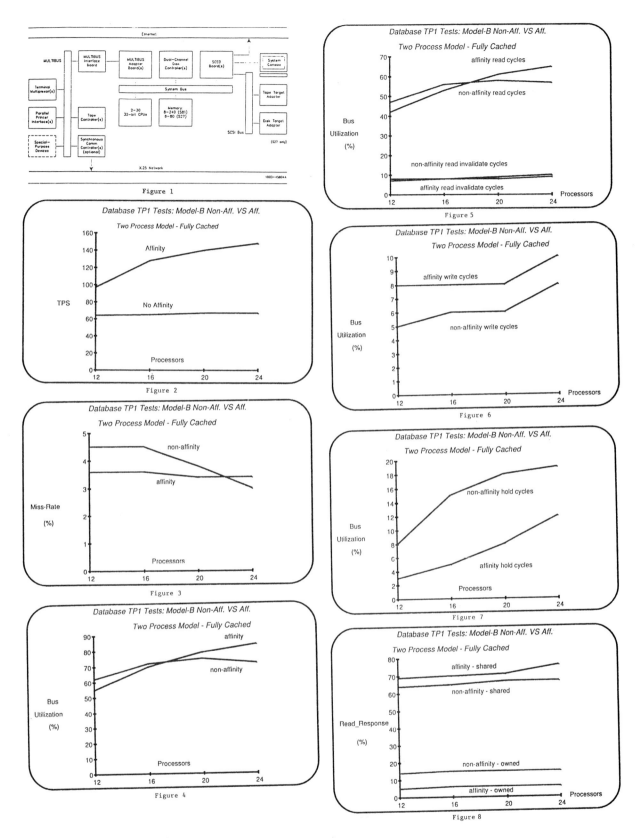

Figure 1

Database TP1 Tests: Model-B Non-Aff. VS Aff.

Two Process Model - Fully Cached

Figure 2

Database TP1 Tests: Model-B Non-Aff. VS Aff.

Two Process Model - Fully Cached

Figure 3

Database TP1 Tests: Model-B Non-Aff. VS Aff.

Two Process Model - Fully Cached

Figure 4

Database TP1 Tests: Model-B Non-Aff. VS Aff.

Two Process Model - Fully Cached

Figure 5

Database TP1 Tests: Model-B Non-Aff. VS Aff.

Two Process Model - Fully Cached

Figure 6

Database TP1 Tests: Model-B Non-Aff. VS Aff.

Two Process Model - Fully Cached

Figure 7

Database TP1 Tests: Model-B Non-Aff. VS Aff.

Two Process Model - Fully Cached

Figure 8

237

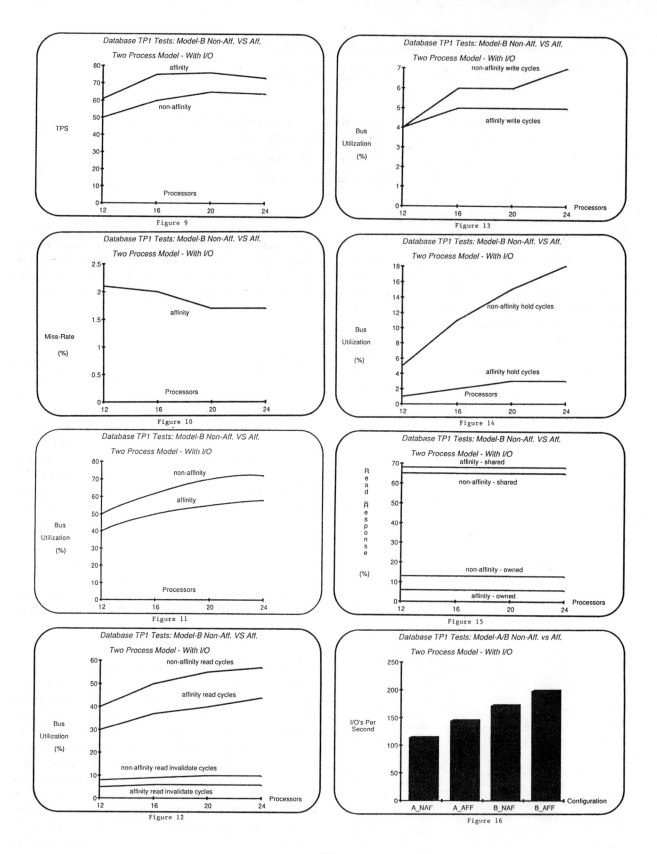

Figure 9

Figure 10

Figure 11

Figure 12

Figure 13

Figure 14

Figure 15

Figure 16

238

The Impact of Synchronization and Granularity on Parallel Systems

Ding-Kai Chen, Hong-Men Su, and Pen-Chung Yew
Center for Supercomputing Research and Development
University of Illinois at Urbana-Champaign
Urbana, Illinois, 61820

Abstract

In this paper, we study the impact of synchronization and granularity on the performance of parallel systems using an execution-driven simulation technique. We find that even though there can be a lot of parallelism at the fine grain level, synchronization and scheduling strategies determine the ultimate performance of the system. Loop-iteration level parallelism seems to be a more appropriate level when those factors are considered. We also study barrier synchronization and data synchronization at the loop-iteration level and found both schemes are needed for a better performance.

1 Introduction

As hardware components become more powerful and less expensive, parallel processing has become an indispensable means for achieving higher performance. From the well-known Amdahl's law [3], software issues are very critical in such parallel systems. Due to the added complexity in multiple system components, the interaction between software and hardware becomes more complicated. For example, it is no longer enough just to manage register sets, to reduce operation strength, and to pass parameters between procedures effectively. We are faced with more complicated issues, such as determining (1) the level of granularity to exploit; (2) the synchronization schemes needed in exploiting such parallelism; (3) the effects of synchronization overhead on overall system performance; and (4) scheduling strategies on resources.

These issues are critical not only from the software

point of view; they are also essential in system architecture design. The kind of architectural support needed in exploiting a particular level of granularity and its synchronization and scheduling requirements can be determined only through studying those issues.

People have been exploiting all possible levels of granularity, from fine grain to coarse grain. VLIW machines [9] and superscalar machines [12, 22] exploit operation level parallelism across basic blocks using either software or hardware techniques to schedule low level operations. Dataflow machines [4] exploit lowest operation level parallelism with drastically different processor architecture and language support. In machines like Cedar [13], RP3 [19], Ultracomputer [11], and Alliant FX/80, loop-iteration level parallelism is exploited. These systems all have different architecture and system requirements.

There have been some studies of parallelism for different granularities and constraints. Some of them need optimizing compilers for specific target machines [4, 14], and others consider only unlimited resources or small kernels [16, 17].

In this paper we discuss some of those issues using real application programs. We concentrate primarily on numerical applications. A simulator called MaxPar is used to collect the necessary statistics for those programs. The techniques used in MaxPar are described in section 2. These techniques allow us to study parallel systems without using a parallelizing compiler to detect and extract parallelism from programs. In section 3, we explore the amount of "inherent" parallelism in those programs at different granularity levels and scheduling strategies. In section 4, we describe the effects of synchronization overhead on system performance. We present our conclusions in section 5.

*This work is supported in part by the National Science Foundation under Grant No. US NSF MIP 8410110 and NSF MIP F8-07775, the U.S. Department of Energy under Grant No. US DOE DE-FG02-85ER25001, NASA NCC 2-559, Digital Equipment Corporation and IBM Corporation.

239

CH2887-8/90/0000/0239$01.00 © 1990 IEEE

2 MaxPar Simulator: Features and Techniques

A conventional simulator usually contains instructions that simulate and collect statistics of a target system using benchmark application programs as its input. Such techniques require parallel application programs or parallel traces obtained from those programs as input. It may also require a parallelizing compiler to extract and detect parallelism in application programs. However, parallel programs are very difficult to come by, and in most of today's parallel systems, parallelizing compilers are used primarily to obtain parallel programs. The problem with this approach is that we need a "super-intelligent" parallelizing compiler which can target toward different granularities and machine organizations to be studied. Many of those parallelizing techniques are still at the research stage and are not available for use.

To avoid these problems, we use a technique similar to [16] and [10] in MaxPar [5]. Instead of writing a simulator for a target system, simulation instructions are actually instrumented into application programs. The instrumented application programs are then executed with the simulation instructions to simulate and collect statistics for the target parallel system. This technique can detect the maximum inherent parallelism in a particular application program, and hence can actually be used to measure the effectiveness of a parallelizing compiler. It can also produce real results from the application program to verify the correctness of a simulation.

The basic idea is to associate each data element with several timing stamps and some accounting information, called "shadows" in [16]. One of the timing stamps is to record when a data element was last fetched; another is to record when the data element was last updated (see Figure 1).

The earliest time "$C = A$ op B" can be executed is determined by finding the maximum of (1) twA, twB – the time each of its operands A and B was last updated (for satisfying read-after-write data dependences); (2) twC – the time C was last updated (for satisfying write-after-write data dependences); (3) trC – the time C was last fetched (for satisfying write-after-read data dependences); (4) $tCOND$ – the time when the condition determining the execution of the current operation was resolved (for satisfying control dependences); and some other constraints such as the cpu available time described later in this section. Note that branch prediction is not currently implemented in MaxPar since MaxPar observes control dependence. On the other hand, MaxPar does exploit some parallelism which can be realized by

$$twC = Compute\_Time(op) + $$
$$max(twC, trC, twA, twB, tCOND, cpu\_avail)$$

$$twA = max(twC, twA)$$
$$twB = max(twC, twB)$$
where

- twC, twA , and twB are the write timing stamps for A, B, and C.

- trC is the read timing stamp for C.

- $tCOND$ is the time when the condition determining this operation is resolved.

- max returns the maximum of its arguments.

Figure 1: Equation for computing timing for $C= A$ op B

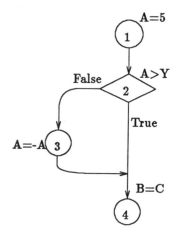

Figure 2: Example of program with conditional branching statement

techniques such as trace scheduling [9]. For example, in Figure 2 statement 3 can be executed after the condition in statement 2 is resolved. But if the true branch is taken, MaxPar will allow statement 4 to be executed before statement 2 because there is no data dependence from statement 3 to statement 4 (for more details, refer to [16] and [5]).

Without loss of generality, MaxPar assumes 1 time unit for each operation. All other timing parameters (e.g., synchronization overhead) use that time as the base time unit.

Once we know the earliest time in which each operation can be executed, we can create an execution profile indicating the amount of parallelism available, or the number of operations that can be executed in parallel at any instance of time. We can also obtain the parallel execution time of the program assuming that all this parallelism can be exploited by the target system. Because we actually execute the program to obtain this information, we often obtain a better result than we could with a parallelizing compiler because a lot of information is unknown or is hard to estimate at the compile time. We can also instrument a program after it is restructured by a compiler and compare the effectiveness of various parallelizing techniques.

2.1 Granularity

Generally speaking, a program can be viewed as a collection of subroutines or procedures. Each subroutine consists of several nested loop blocks. Each loop block consists of a certain number of statements, and each statement consists of a few elementary operations. Hence, roughly four different levels of granularity, namely, operation, statement, loop-iteration, and sub-program levels, can be identified and exploited in a parallel execution model.

The granularity determines the unit of work (called a "task" from now on) to be scheduled on a compute resource in the system. To simplify our system model, we assume a compute resource is a processor. The scheduling of a processor occurs only when a task becomes available for execution. All of the work in a task is performed sequentially on the same processor. With this model, parallelism with different grain sizes can be measured. Because only the necessary data dependences, control dependences, and the resource limitation need to be considered for a correct parallel execution of a program, operations from different tasks can be executed concurrently if they do not have those constraints. The maximum inherent parallelism can thus be measured for a program with different grain sizes. We can also add delays into the timing computation to account for possible scheduling overhead [5].

When an unlimited number of processors are assumed, the obtained parallelism is the performance upper bound for that particular program assuming its maximum inherent parallelism can be fully exploited without considering scheduling strategies. However, in reality, there will only be a limited number of processors in a system, and we have to consider scheduling.

The scheduling of processors needs two kinds of information. One is the partial ordering of the tasks from their control and data dependences. The second is the status or the available time of the processors. An optimal scheduling can be obtained if we have such information. The partial ordering among the tasks is not easy to obtain. In MaxPar, we don't try to locate where the critical path is in the partial ordering. To preserve the dependences in the original program, an instrumented program is executed sequentially, following the control flow in the original program. In this case, scheduling becomes more difficult, and only a near-optimal scheduling can be obtained. This is one drawback of this approach. However, the results obtained are still quite useful because, in reality, even with a partial ordering known, the optimal scheduling often requires a lot of overhead and is quite difficult to achieve. Therefore, we use some *near-optimal* scheduling methods with the limited information available. The basic idea is to keep all processors as fully utilized as possible. The less frequently the processors are left idle, the better the scheduling strategy is. This strategy is particularly effective in the dynamic processor self-scheduling on parallel loops [8, 20].

MaxPar determines the earliest possible starting time for a task as follows:

- An operation can be started after all its data and control dependences are satisfied.

- The earliest possible starting time of the first operation of a Fortran statement is the earliest possible starting time of that statement.

- A loop iteration can be started after the lower bound, the upper bound, and the stride of its index increment are available.

- A sub-program can be started after the control dependence imposed upon the subroutine call or the function call is satisfied.

Since MaxPar keeps track of the available time for each processor, it can find a processor with the available time *closest* to, and earlier than (if possible), the time at which a task can be executed. We call this scheme the near-optimal scheme. However, we cannot estimate how much off it is from the optimal scheduling strategy using such a scheme, because finding an optimal scheduling with a limited number of processors and a partial ordering on tasks is an NP-complete problem. We tried several other scheduling methods to see the effect of scheduling. One is called the *earliest-available* scheme. It is similar to the near-optimal scheme, except that we use the earliest available processor for the task to be scheduled. Its available time may not be the *closest* to the task scheduling time as in the near-optimal scheme. Hence, the processor may have to wait longer for tasks to become available for scheduling. Another scheme is called the *random* scheme: A randomly chosen processor is scheduled to a task ready for execution. This scheme requires minimal scheduling overhead because no information needs to be kept or processed before selecting a processor. The fourth scheme is called the *circular* scheme: All processors form a circular queue. A pointer indicates the next processor to be scheduled regardless of its available time. This scheme should have a better performance than the random scheme because the processor just scheduled will most likely be unavailable for further scheduling. The relative performance of these scheduling methods are discussed in section 3.3.

A variable, *cpu_avail*, is associated with each processor to record the available time of the processor (see Figure 1). The earliest time an operation can be executed will be determined not just by the timing stamps of its operands, but also by the available time of the chosen processor with a preassigned scheduling overhead. The next available time for the assigned processor is, of course, the time the task is completed. In the case of an unlimited number of processors, each processor needs to be scheduled just once and its available time can simply be set to zero; i.e., all of the processors are available at time 0.

2.2 Synchronization Overhead

Data dependences need to be enforced if they occur across task boundaries. Because we assume tasks are our scheduling units and they can be assigned to different processors, if a data element is updated in one task and fetched in another, some kind of synchronization scheme is needed to enforce such an order. It is called data synchronization in [23]. If the granularity is at the operation level, every single data dependence needs to be explicitly enforced, possibly with a lot of synchronization overhead. But in the loop-iteration level parallelism, data dependences within the same iteration can be satisfied automatically because they are executed in the same processor sequentially. Only data dependences across loop-iterations need to be explicitly enforced.

To account for such synchronization overhead, two *scheduling* variables are used in addition to the two *timing* stamps described earlier for each data element. One for data fetches and the other for data updates. A counter, *task_id*, is incremented to provide a new task number each time a new task is assigned to a processor. This task number is compared with the *scheduling* variables of the operation's operands and then these *scheduling* variables are updated with this new task number. If the task numbers differ (i.e., data dependences occur across task boundary), some delay may need to be added to account for the synchronization overhead.

Synchronization overhead for control dependences should also be considered. However, they only need to be accounted for at the time the task is first scheduled. No further overhead is needed within the task

for the control dependences.

2.3 Barrier Synchronization

Another way to enforce data dependences is to use barrier synchronization. Barrier synchronization is quite effective in loop-iteration level parallelism. It has been attempted in statement level parallelism as well [7]. Some optimizing compilers [1, 2] can generate barrier synchronization for parallel programs. A carefully placed barrier can eliminate a lot of inter-task data synchronization and its overhead.

To simulate the effect of barrier synchronization, the MaxPar uses a variable *barrier_time* to record the completion time of the last operation (among all tasks) in the portion of the code being enforced by the barrier. The available time for all of the processors are then set to *barrier_time* at the barrier. No tasks after the barrier can be scheduled before *barrier_time* even if they are available for execution; i.e., no processors can pass the barrier until all of the processors reached the barrier. A variable, *barrier_task_id*, is used to record the last task number in the parallel code enforced by the barrier. All dependences whose sources reside in the tasks with task numbers smaller than *barrier_task_id* and whose sinks reside in the tasks with task numbers larger than *barrier_task_id* will be satisfied by the barrier and need no more data synchronization. The effect of synchronization overhead and the effectiveness of barriers are discussed in section 3.2 and section 4.

3 Exploiting Different Granularities

3.1 How Much Parallelism Is There?

We use seven application programs in our study. Four of them (QCD, FLO52Q, TRACK, and MDG) are from PERFECT CLUB benchmarks [18] which are used to measure the performance of supercomputers. The problem sizes of these programs are carefully chosen so that we can obtain the simulation results in a shorter time without losing important program characteristics. Those programs are listed in Table 1. The parallelisms measured with different levels of granularity assuming an unlimited number of processors without anti- and output- dependences are shown in Figure 3. All of the programs exhibit similar trends in the amount of parallelism available at different granularity levels. That is, the amount of parallelism at the statement level is fairly close to that at operation level, and there is only a small amount of parallelism at the sub-program level (all

Benchmark	Lines	Application (problem size)	No. of Subroutines
SIMPLE	2121	Hydrodynamics and heat flow (32x32)	14
PIC	378	Particle in cell (256)	2
LINPACK	609	Linear system software (10x10)	9
QCD	2326	Quantum chromodynamics (2x2x2x2)	34
FLO52Q	2250	Computational fluid dynamics (NX=40, NY=8)	27
TRACK	3784	Signal processing (10 sites, 480 boosters)	31
MDG	1231	Liquid water simulation (40 molecules)	15

Table 1: Characteristics of the Benchmarks

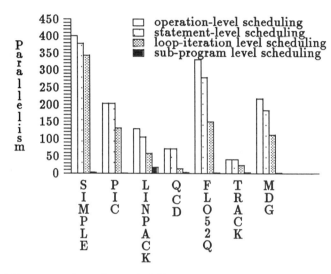

Figure 3: Speedup of different granularities and benchmarks

less than 4 except LINPACK). As the granularity becomes smaller, more parallelism can be exploited in a program [4]. These results confirm that we should move away from coarse grain parallelism to a finer grain parallelism. For example, Cray has moved away from macrotasking to support microtasking for better performance.

However, we did not consider synchronization overhead here. It is obvious that synchronization overhead will increase as the granularity becomes smaller and the parallelism increases. The amount of parallelism alone cannot determine the best granularity level to exploit. We should also consider synchronization overhead and other factors, such as scheduling, to determine the best level.

3.2 The Effect of Synchronization Overhead

Because the sub-program level has very little parallelism, and the characteristics of the operation level and the statement level are very similar (perhaps be-

cause the operations within a statement are often executed sequentially at the operation level due to dependences), we discuss only the statement level and the loop-iteration level parallelism in this section. Several codes: SIMPLE, Particle-In-Cell (PIC), and TRACK are simulated further with different synchronization overhead. The results are shown in Figures 4, 5, and 6.

From these results, it is quite clear that as long as there is synchronization overhead, the performance at the loop-iteration level becomes very close to the statement level. In many cases, when there is only a moderate amount of synchronization overhead, the loop-iteration level actually outperforms the statement level.

Notice that these results show only the effect of the synchronization overhead. We assume there is an unlimited number of processors in the system. The effect of scheduling with a limited number of processors is considered in the next section.

3.3 Scheduling

Scheduling can affect system performance quite significantly. Figure 7 compares the performance of the four scheduling methods described in section 2.1 using 100 processors. The most important characteristic is that, without the near-optimal scheme, performance at the operation level and at the statement level is actually worse than at the loop-iteration level. In reality, the near-optimal scheme is very difficult to implement because it requires the scheduler to know the completion time of each processor at every instance of time. However, the results indicate that unless we have a very sophisticated scheduling strategy, exploiting very fine grain parallelism with only a limited amount of resources can yield poorer results than we have anticipated, because, in finer grain parallelism, tasks usually have a more complicated partial ordering. It is much more difficult to schedule tasks close to the critical path of the partial ordering unless a more sophisticated scheduling

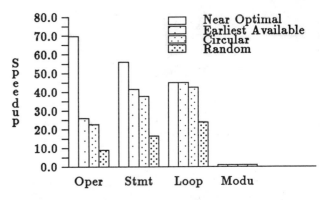

Figure 7: Comparison of different scheduling strategies for 100 processors using the PIC benchmark.

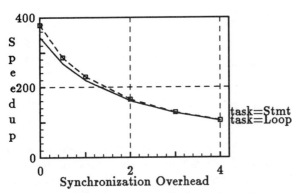

Figure 4: Performance of SIMPLE with unlimited number of processors and different amounts of synchronization overhead.

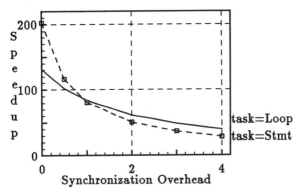

Figure 5: Performance of PIC with unlimited number of processors and different amounts of synchronization overhead.

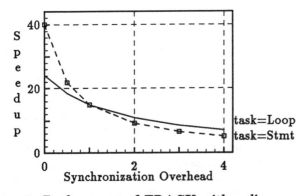

Figure 6: Performance of TRACK with unlimited number of processors and different amounts of synchronization overhead.

scheme is used. Unfortunately, because of the small grain size of each task, finer grain parallelism cannot afford the runtime overhead of sophisticated scheduling schemes,

With a limited number of processors, loop-iteration level parallelism seems to perform better and is less sensitive to a scheduling strategy because loops have a very regular structure which makes them easier to schedule. Of course, if we have a large number of processors (e.g., close to unlimited) where scheduling becomes very trivial, then finer grain parallelism becomes much better.

4 Data Synchronization vs. Barriers

In this section, we focus on loop-iteration level parallelism. We try to compare the effectiveness of data synchronization vs. barriers. Barriers are quite effective in enforcing data dependences **between** different loops if they are used properly. However, they are not for enforcing data dependences between iterations **within** the same loop. With efficient low-level data synchronization supports such as that used in Cedar [25], HEP [21], and Horizon [15], data dependences can be enforced explicitly, which allows a loop with cross iteration data dependences (a so-called **Doacross loop** [6]), to execute its iterations in parallel with some degree of overlap. It also allows iterations from different loops to be executed in parallel to achieve even higher performance. Such a technique is called **high-level spreading** [24], or task pipelining. An example is shown in Figure 8, where high-level spreading allows Loop-i and Loop-j to be partially overlapped.

In the following experiments, we execute programs

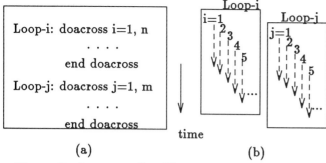

Loop-i: doacross i=1, n

    . . . .

    end doacross

Loop-j: doacross j=1, m

    . . . .

    end doacross

(a)

time

(b)

Figure 8: An example of Doacross and high-level spreading execution: (a) Two adjacent Doacross loops. (b) Execution of the loops with high-level spreading.

Strategies	Meanings
0	Data sync only
1	Data sync + barrier sync after each computation phase
2	*Strategy 1* with outermost parallel/inner serial
3	*Strategy 1* without high-level spreading
4	*Strategy 1* without Doacross execution

Figure 9: Meanings of different strategies

using several different strategies:[1]

- **Strategy 0.** Execute a program using only data synchronization, i.e., without using barriers. High level spreading is used whenever possible. This strategy exploits all possible parallelism in a program.

- **Strategy 1.** Same as *strategy 0* except that a barrier is added after each "main computation phase," which roughly corresponds to each major subroutine. Each barrier is simulated as an ideal one, i.e. it is completed as soon as all processors have arrived.

- **Strategy 2.** It restricts *strategy 1* by serializing some inner loops which do not have "enough" parallelism, i.e., loop bounds are small, or the overlap between loop iterations is insignificant. The outer loops are still executed in parallel. In all the programs simulated, all those outer loops have cross iteration data dependences, i.e., they are all Doacross loops.

- **Strategy 3.** It restricts *strategy 1* by disallowing high-level spreading. A barrier is inserted between every two loops if they have data dependences.

- **Strategy 4.** It restricts *strategy 1* by disallowing Doacross loops, i.e., a loop is serialized if cross iteration dependences exist.

Strategy 0 corresponds to unconstrained parallelism. *Strategy 1* allows just a few barriers in a program. *Strategy 2* demonstrates that constrained parallelism can have significantly better performance than unconstrained parallelism. We should not exploit parallelism indiscriminately in a parallel pro-

---
[1] Inserting barriers and forcing some loops to execute sequentially is done manually.

gram. We need to select the right portion of the parallel code to exploit parallelism and to give up some "insignificant" parallelism to achieve a better performance. *Strategy 3* and *Strategy 4* are to show the impact of high-level spreading and Doacross execution, respectively. The main features in these strategies are summarized in Figure 9. The simulation results are analyzed in the next section. From the discussion in section 2, the earliest-available scheme is a practical scheduling scheme; hence, it is used in all of those simulations.

4.1 The Effect of Using Barriers

As shown in Figure 10 for the program SIMPLE, *strategy 0* outperforms *strategy 1* (with 8 barriers added to the program) when there is no overhead in explicit data synchronization. This finding is obvious because when barriers are added, the length of the critical path increases and so does the total execution time. However, as data synchronization overhead increases, there is a crossover at the point where data sync overhead is 0.5. This can be explained by the number of data syncs executed: there are about 970,000 data syncs using *strategy 0*, and about 660,000 data syncs using *strategy 1*. One third of the data syncs are eliminated by simply adding eight barriers.

In practice, most data accessed in one phase of computation should have been completed before the next phase starts. Hence, many data syncs in *strategy 0* could be redundant, even though we don't know which ones are redundant and all of them need to be enforced to guarantee the correctness. A barrier can ensure all theses dependences with less overhead. This is why as data sync overhead increases, the speedup of *strategy 0* degrades faster than that of *strategy 1*.

Barriers should not be used without discretion. Figure 10 shows that when sync overhead is less than 2.5, *strategy 3* does not perform as well as *strategy 1*, even though *strategy 3* has less data synchronization.

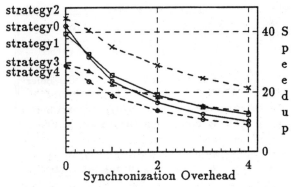

Figure 10: SIMPLE code with sync overhead and 100 processors

Its performance is constrained by the use of too many barriers.

Often, two adjacent loops can be executed with some overlapping if there are a large number of processors. When the first loop has only a few iterations left, the remaining processors can start executing the next loop, even though some data synchronization may be needed.

Using *strategy 1* to add 8 barriers after some loops, we can reduce one third of the data synchronizations; however, adding a barrier after every parallel loop, such as in *strategy 3* (which results in adding 73 more barriers) only eliminates another one third of data synchronizations (to about 430,000). The reduction in parallelism due to increasing barriers more than offsets the gain in reducing the number of data synchronizations.

Thus, too many barriers hurt performance. But, where should we place barriers to get the anticipated performance? Figures 11-13 show, for programs SIMPLE, PIC, and MDG, the speedup with different numbers of processors, P, assuming sync overhead is 1. *Strategy 3* performs better than all other strategies except *strategy 2* when P is less than 40 in SIMPLE code. Beyond this point, too many barriers begin to hurt performance. It offsets the gain from reducing data synchronization overhead. Apparently, data syncs should be used at this point to allow more processors to exploit high-level spreading.

It is very difficult to determine when we should use high-level spreading instead of barriers. The decision depends on such factors as the overhead of each data synchronization, the amount of time synchronization is overlapped with other computation, and the time to perform a barrier synchronization. We give a very rough guideline as follows.

Consider two loops, A and B. Loop A has N iterations and loop B has M iterations. Iteration i of loop A must precede iteration i of loop B. After each iteration of loop A is completed, a signal is sent. Each

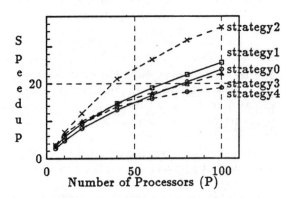

Figure 11: SIMPLE code with different numbers of processors

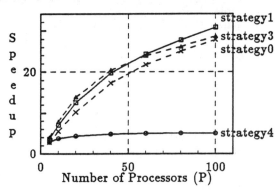

Figure 12: PIC code with different numbers of processors

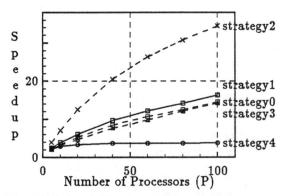

Figure 13: MDG code with different numbers of processors

iteration of loop B must check the signal before it can start. We have

- Execution time using data sync$= (T1 + so) * N/P + (so + T2) * M/P$

- Execution time using barriers$= T1 * N/P + Barr_P + T2 * M/P$

$T1$ and $T2$ are the average execution times of an iteration of loop A and loop B respectively; P is the total number of processors; $Barr_P$ is the average barrier synchronization overhead for P processors. We also assume P can divide N and M (this assumption favors barrier synchronization.) Data synchronization overhead so is defined to be the average time between sending a signal from a source to the receipt of the signal by its sink. Thus, the difference between the execution times of these two schemes is

$data\_sync - barrier\_sync = so * (N/P + M/P) - Barr_P$

From this equation we can observe the followings:

- When P is fixed, larger problem size (i.e., larger N and M) makes barrier synchronization more competitive;

- If the workload for each processor ($N/P + M/P$) is fixed, the overhead of barrier syncs becomes larger when we have a larger P;

- If the problem size (N and M) is fixed, larger P makes high-level spreading more attractive than barriers;

- The smaller the overhead for data sync (so), the more attractive it becomes.

The above parameters can help a compiler to determine which strategy to use if their values can be known at the compile time. However, data sync overhead so and $Barr_P$ are not easy to estimate because some of the overhead can be overlapped with other computation. In this case, user assertions may be needed to help a compiler to determine the appropriate strategy.

4.2 Discussion

From the above simulation results, it is clear that Doacross loops have a very significant impact on performance. Serializing Doacross loops (i.e., comparing *strategy 4* to *strategy 1*) can degrade performance very severely, sometimes by as much as 6 times (see Figure 12). Data synchronization is the only means to enforce data dependences across iterations within a loop. For some programs (such as SIMPLE and MDG) it is also very important to select loops to be executed as Doacross loops. Limiting inefficient

parallelism in some loops, as in *strategy 2*, and allowing outer loops to be executed as Doacross loops, can further improve the performance (Figure 11 and Figure 13).

The simulation results also show the performance improvement achieved by adopting high-level spreading (comparing *strategy 3* to *strategy 1*). Although the improvement is not as significant as that from Doacross loops, high-level spreading becomes more important as the number of processors increases. A barrier can reduce the amount of data synchronization between two loops, but only at the expense of limiting the parallelism between the loops. If we can hide the data synchronization overhead between two loops, then high-level spreading can also be attractive in small systems.

5 Conclusions

Using an execution-driven simulation technique, we have studied the impact of granularity and synchronization schemes on parallel systems. This technique allows us to ignore the limitation imposed by a parallelizing compiler and to study directly the "inherent" characteristics of a program.

We study four granularity levels: operation level, statement level, loop-iteration level, and subprogram level. From the simulations, we confirm the findings of other studies [4, 16, 17] that as the granularity becomes smaller, more parallelism can be found in a program. However, our studied also shows that the performance cannot be determined by the amount of parallelism alone. It also depends on the synchronization overhead and the scheduling strategies required to support such parallelism. When all these factors are considered, loop-iteration level parallelism seems to be a more appropriate level to exploit.

We also study two synchronization strategies used at the loop-iteration level: barriers and data synchronization. We found both schemes should be used together for better performance. Compiler techniques are also needed to determine the best mixes of these two schemes.

References

[1] R. Allen, D. Gallahan, and K. Kennedy. Automatic decomposition of scientific programs for parallel execution. *ACM Symp. on Principles of Programming Languages*, 63–76, Jan. 1987.

[2] Alliant. *FX/Series Architecture Manual*. Alliant Computer Systems Corp., Jan. 1986.

[3] G. Amdahl. Validity of the single-processor approach to achieving large-scale computer capabilities. *AFIPS Conf.*, 483–485, 1967.

[4] Arvind, D. Culler, and G. Maa. Assessing the benefits of fine-grain parallelism in dataflow programs. *Supercomputing*, 60–69, Nov. 1988.

[5] D.-K. Chen. *MaxPar: An Execution Driven Simulator for Studying Parallel Systems*. CSRD TR-917, Center for Supercomputing Research and Development, Univ. of Illinois at Urbana-Champaign, Sep. 1989.

[6] R. Cytron. Doacross: beyond vectorization for multiprocessors. *1986 Int. Conf. on Parallel Processing*, 836–845, Aug. 1986.

[7] H. Dietz, T. Schwederski, M. O'keefe, and A. Zaafrani. Static synchronization beyond VLIW. *Supercomputing*, 416–425, Nov. 1989.

[8] Z. Fang, P. Yew, P. Tang, and C. Zhu. Dynamic processor self-scheduling for general parallel nested loops. *1987 Int. Conf. Parallel Processing*, 1–10, Aug. 1987.

[9] J. Fisher. Very long word instruction architecture and the ELI-512. *Int. Sym. Computer Architecture*, 140–150, June 1983.

[10] M. Flynn, C. Mitchell, and J. Mulder. And now a case for more complex instruction sets. *IEEE Computer*, 71–83, Sep. 1987.

[11] A. Gottlieb, R. Grishman, C. Kruskal, K. McAuliffe, L. Rudolph, and M. Snir. The NYU Ultracomputer – designing an MIMD shared memory parallel computer. *IEEE Trans. Comput.*, 175–189, Feb. 1983.

[12] N. Jouppi and D. Wall. Available instruction-level parallelism for superscalar and superpipelined machines. *Int. Conf. Architectural Support for Programming Languages and Operating Systems*, 272–282, Apr. 1989.

[13] D. Kuck, E. Davidson, D. Lawrie, and A. Sameh. Parallel supercomputing today and the Cedar approach. *Science*, 231:967–974, Feb. 1986.

[14] D. Kuck, A. Sameh, R. Cytron, A. Veidenbaum, C. Polychronopoulos, G. Lee, T. McDaniel, B. Leasure, C. Beckman, J. Davies, and C. Kruskal. The effects of program restructuring, algorithm change, and architecture choice on program performance. *1984 Int. Conf. on Parallel Processing*, Aug. 1984.

[15] J. Kuehn and B. Smith. The Horizon supercomputing system: architecture and software. *Supercomputing*, 28–34, Nov. 1988.

[16] M. Kumar. Effect of storage allocation/reclamation methods on parallelism and storage requirements. *Int. Symp. on Computer Architecture*, 197–205, June 1987.

[17] A. Nicolau and J. Fisher. Using an oracle to measure potential parallelism in single instruction stream programs. *Annual Microprogramming Workshop*, 171–182, 1981.

[18] The Perfect Club, et al. The Perfect Club benchmarks: effective performance evaluation of supercomputers *Int. J. of Supercomputer Applications*, 5-40, Fall 1989.

[19] G. Pfister, W. Brantley, D. George, S. Harvey, W. Kleinfelder, K. McAuliffe, E. Melton, V. Norton, and J. Weiss. The IBM research parallel processor prototype (RP3): introduction and architecture. *1985 Int. Conf. on Parallel Processing*, 764–771, Aug. 1985.

[20] C. Polychronopoulos and D. Kuck. Guided self-scheduling: a practical scheduling scheme for parallel supercomputers. *IEEE Trans. Computer*, 1425–1439, Dec. 1987.

[21] B. J. Smith. A pipelined, shared resource mimd computer. *1978 Int. Conf. on Parallel Processing*, 6–8, Aug. 1978.

[22] M. Smith, M. Johnson, and M. Horowitz. Limits on Multiple Instruction Issue. *Int. Conf. Architectural Support for Programming Languages and Operating Systems*, 290–302, Apr. 1989.

[23] H. Su and P. Yew. On data synchronization for multiprocessors. *Int. Sym. Computer Architecture*, 416–423, May 1989.

[24] A. Veidenbaum. *Compiler Optimizations and Architecture Design Issues for Multiprocessors*. Ph.D. Thesis, Dept. of Computer Science, Univ. of Illinois at Urbana-Champaign, Champaign, May 1985.

[25] C. Zhu and P. Yew. A scheme to enforce data dependence on large multiprocessor systems. *IEEE Trans. Software Eng.*, 726–739, June 1987.

Session 5A: Memory Traces and Simulation

TRACE-DRIVEN SIMULATIONS FOR A TWO-LEVEL CACHE DESIGN IN OPEN BUS SYSTEMS

Håkon O. Bugge, Ernst H. Kristiansen, and Bjørn O. Bakka

Dolphin Server Technology A.S, Oslo , NORWAY

Two-level cache hierarchies will be a design issue in future high-performance CPUs. In this paper we evaluate various metrics for data cache[*] designs. We discuss both one- and two-level cache hierarchies. Our target is a new 100+ *mips* CPU, but the methods are applicable to any cache design. The basis of our work is a new trace-driven, multiprocess cache simulator. The simulator incorporates a simple priority-based scheduler which controls the execution of the processes. The scheduler blocks a process when a system call is executed. A workload consists of a total of 60 processes, distributed among seven unique programs with about nine instances each. We discuss two open bus systems supporting a coherent memory model, Futurebus+ and SCI, as the interconnect system for main memory.

1 INTRODUCTION

We at Dolphin Server Technology are currently developing a Super Scalar Machine [Jouppi89] using ECL technology. The instruction set is that of a Motorola M88000, licensed in an agreement with Motorola Inc. Our implementation will be able to issue up to eight instructions every 8 ns cycle. In order to satisfy the extremely high bandwidth requirement of the instruction dispatch unit, we have decided to use a special cache organization for the instruction part. To achieve the required load/store bandwidth, we are implementing a dual data cache organization. This effectively doubles the bandwidth towards data memory. The CPU micro-architecture will be the topic of a later paper.

The size of each data cache will be 128K bytes. The cache cycle time is 8 ns, whereas load latency is 16 ns. We expected serious deficiencies in the memory hierarchy if the data caches were directly coupled to standard DRAM. Our solution is to implement a two-level cache. By studying the available literature we found that no other work described a cache organization with the performance requirements we were demanding. This is the background for the work described in this paper.

In the following section, we will briefly discuss our memory hierarchy and compare it to others described in the literature. Section 3 contains a description of the methods applied in this work. The different interconnect systems we have studied are discussed in section 4. Through a first-level cache study in section 5, we will argue that our workload seems realistic compared to other work. The same workload will then be used to study two-level caches in section 6. Both sections 5 and 6 focus on the data accesses of a full Harvard cache organization. Hereafter, we will use the phrase *primary cache* for the first-level cache. Misses in the primary cache will be accesses into the second-level cache, the *secondary cache*.

2 OVERVIEW AND REFERENCES TO PREVIOUS WORK

There are many issues to consider when it comes to cache design. Today, single-level cache implementations are dominating, but many are considering expanding to two-level caches. Determining cache sizes is very important, with sizes ranging from a few bytes to many megabytes. Cache line size has been investigated thoroughly [Smith87], and is a critical issue. The degree of associativity affects both performance and complexity. Further, caches may be either virtually- or physically-addressed. The coherence issue, with a wide range of possibilities, is taken seriously. These are the main topics of papers describing caches today.

When cache size exceeds page size multiplied by the degree of associativity, virtually-addressed caches have an advantage compared to physically-addressed caches. It is necessary for a physically-addressed cache exceeding this limit to perform a virtual-to-physical address translation before the cache can be accessed [Hill88]. A virtually-addressed cache avoids the translation, and thereby achieves shorter load latency.

In the literature, virtually-addressed caches are viewed with some skepticism. The main problem areas are recognition of synonyms and maintenance of unique address spaces for different processes. The synonym recognition can be done in three major ways. The SPUR machine [Wood89] does it by software convention. A combination of software and hardware method as in the Sun-3 architecture [Sun85] is another possibility. We prefer to do synonym recognition by a pure hardware scheme. Goodman and Wang *et al.* have published similar hardware coherence schemes [Goodman87], [Wang89].

---

[*] By data cache we mean the cache for the data part of a Harvard architecture.

CH2887-8/90/0000/0250$01.00 © 1990 IEEE

There are typically two ways to maintain unique address spaces. The brute force method is to invalidate the whole cache at context switch points. A more elegant method is to maintain unique process identifiers as part of the virtual address [Mips88]. We implement the latter method. Since the TLB in essence is a virtually-addressed cache, we easily extend this method to cover the TLB as well. [Agarwal89] has shown that process identifiers improve multiprocess cache performance. According to his book, this improvement holds especially true for large caches.

By studying various primary cache implementations, we resolved a number of arguments. We feel that the write-through/write-back primary cache organization is a performance/robustness tradeoff. A write-back cache is part of the memory image. To be fault tolerant, the entire memory image requires error correction logic. Introducing error correction logic on a write-back primary cache would both increase cycle time (i.e. reduce performance) and increase complexity. We stick with a write-through primary cache algorithm in combination with a clever write buffer algorithm.

A pure write-through primary cache needs high write-bandwidth. We feel that a write buffer able to concatenate adjacent memory writes is a good solution for reducing the bandwidth requirements. A write instruction accesses the cache twice, first with hit checking and then with the actual write. A clever write buffer may exploit idle cache cycles to perform the actual writes. For coherence purposes, we prefer the inclusion property described in [Wang89]. The inclusion property implies that the write buffer contains a subset of the primary cache, which contains a subset of the secondary cache. The secondary cache effectively shields the primary cache and write buffer from unnecessary coherence traffic interference.

We feel a write-back policy is the correct choice for a secondary cache. It shields the system bus from excess memory traffic. Error correction logic on the secondary cache is easier to justify. Also, there is a problem with virtually-addressed caches at the nth-level of an n-level cache hierarchy. Bus addresses are physical. For the cache to participate in cache coherence protocols, a physical-to-virtual address translation is necessary. Since we are considering a physically-addressed secondary cache, we avoid the problem. For a more detailed discussion of this topic, see [Wang89].

Three recently published papers ([Przybylski89], [Short88] and [Wang89]) investigate multi-level cache hierarchies. [Przybylski89] studies a two-level cache hierarchy where both the primary and secondary caches are virtually-addressed. The primary cache is a split 4K or 32K (half each I and D). It is a direct-mapped organization with a 16-byte line employing the write-back algorithm. The secondary cache is also direct-mapped, with a 32-byte line employing a write-back algorithm. The effects of

secondary cache size, set size and latency are investigated in his paper.

[Przybylski89] uses both trace-driven simulations and analytical methods. The workload for the simulations consists of eight multiprocess traces. The findings are based on a geometric mean of the simulation results from the eight traces. His paper describes a particular method for avoiding cold start uncertainties for the primary cache. We believe he did not use this method to avoid similar problems in the secondary cache.

[Short88] has kept cache line at 4 bytes during his two-level cache study. Both the primary and secondary cache are direct-mapped, unified, and physically-addressed. Cache sizes ranging from 8K to 512K (primary) and 32K to 512K (secondary) are targeted. The effect of write-through and write-back algorithms is investigated. We feel 4 bytes is a small cache line when we see most real systems increase their cache line size significantly above this figure. We also feel the workload is too small to produce reliable results for large secondary caches. We discuss this topic further in section 3.

[Wang89] investigates a two-level cache hierarchy specifically studied for multiprocessor applications. The primary cache is a virtually-addressed cache with an assumed line size of 16 bytes (not stated in his paper!) and applying a write-back algorithm. The secondary cache is a physically-addressed cache, also applying a write-back algorithm. The secondary cache ranges from 64K to 256K, with the primary cache 1/4 or 1/128 (half each I and D) of this size. The workload is restricted to three multiprocessor applications. We feel that the workloads may not be adequate for a high-performance scalar CPU.

Our conclusion from this literature study was that we had to conduct further research to be able to design a high-performance cache system for our new series of Super Scalar Machines.

3 METHODS

For any application, we can separate the execution time into two parts: CPU time and I/O wait. A high-performance Super Scalar Machine is expected to give a radical CPU time reduction, while the I/O wait time is assumed to be approximately the same as today. This implies low CPU utilization for a single process when executing on an extremely fast CPU. Our simulations indicate that the applications from which we have captured our traces will each utilize only about 2% of a CPU, executing the instruction stream at a rate of 100 million instructions per second. We would, therefore, like to introduce a new rule of thumb for trace-driven cache simulation:

The workload used in a trace-driven cache simulation should have a realistic utilization of the CPU for which the caches are targeted.

The basic tool we have used to investigate the effects of different cache design metrics is a trace-driven, multiprocess cache simulator. A trace is a collection of instruction/data accesses of an application. The applications are all ND-500 hosted [nd500], running SINTRAN III [ndsIII], and the capture was performed using the Single-Instruction-Trap feature on the ND-500 series of computers [Bakken86]. Due to the demand for large traces, disk space was a problem. Therefore, a compression algorithm was applied to the trace data.

Since the target of this study is a machine in the 100+ *mips* range, it was not sufficient to use single applications as workloads. Therefore, a model capable of simulating multiple processes was developed. The model incorporates a simple priority-based, preemptive scheduler, and the processes are blocked when they execute a system call. The amount of time a process is blocked depends on the system call in question: a random value between 0.8 and 2 milliseconds if the system call doesn't involve any disk accesses, otherwise a random value between 20 and 40 milliseconds. The reason for introducing randomness is to avoid having two instances of the same application follow in each other's footsteps. When a process is terminated (reached the end of the trace file), the process is restarted using the same process identifier.

In order to get a time perspective into the model, a CPU speed of 100 million ND-500 instructions per second was selected (One million ND-500 instructions per second is equivalent to 2.28 VUP). A time slice of 10 milliseconds restricts any process from running more than 1 million instructions before it is preempted.

A workload was composed of traces from seven different applications, which are described in Table 1. The total number of instructions (I), data-read (Rd) and data-write (Wr) accesses, the number of unique word (32-bit) accesses (IWd/DWd), the number of unique page (4K) accesses (IPg/DPg) and number of system calls are presented.

The workload is simulated on a CPU model which executes one instruction per cycle, independent of memory accesses. The memory accesses generate stimuli to the primary caches we want to simulate. The primary caches are all direct-mapped, write-through, virtually-addressed and they incorporate a process identifier field in the tag, which removes any demand for cache clearing at context switch points. An allocation-on-write (also called fetch-on-write) strategy is used because it simplifies the problem of maintaining coherence between the two-levels of caches. Allocation-on-write means that a write miss in the cache produces a request to the line in question from the next level of storage, and the primary cache is updated before the write is performed, i.e. the write miss is turned into a read miss. The effect of write contention is not considered, since we are assuming a write buffer which handles writes to both the primary and the secondary cache. A coherence scheme between the virtually-addressed primary cache and the physically-addressed secondary cache, as described in section 2, is assumed but not simulated. This means that no transactions generated for maintaining coherence are taken into account, and that no cache clearing whatsoever is needed. An overview of the simulation system is given in Figure 1.

The primary caches are parameterized by their size and line size in bytes. The size is the number of lines multiplied by the number of bytes per line. A line, also called a block, is the amount of data associated with each tag.

One of the most common pitfalls in cache studies is the cold start of the cache in the simulated environment, that is, the effect of transient misses [Stone]. Let us assume that we want to study a direct-mapped cache with 8K entries, and to use a workload which produces 1M accesses to the cache. We will get up to 8K transient misses due to the cold start of the simulated cache, which we may not observe in a real environment. If the cache hit ratio is 99%, the workload will produce 10K misses, but up to 8K of these are due to the cold start of the cache in the simulated environment.

Name	Description	Total I/Rd/Wr	Unique IWd/IPg	Unique DWd/Dpg	#sys calls
ftn	FORTRAN-77 compiler generating object file with debug info & listing	20.3M/11.9M/6.1M	18.3K/52	9.1K/33	350
led	language-sensitive editor	19.3M/10.6M/7.0M	12.3K/34	62.9K/90	703
sib2a	CODASYL database server written in F77, single-thread version	13.4M/7.7M/6.1M	5.5K/21	61.5K/130	3.9K
linpack	all FORTRAN LINPACK 64-bit	10.3M/10.3M/4.7M	2.7K/9	42.6K/91	151
sibrp	CODASYL database server written in F77, multi-thread version	11.9M/7.6M/6.5M	5.4K/31	127.7K/408	3.9K
cobol	COBOL-85 compiling many small files, generating object files with debug info & listing	18.1M/11.7M/7.2M	18.3K/45	11.0K/25	1.5K
nll	loader, loading the above COBOL system	21.0M/11.4M/5.7M	6.2K/25	62.3K/93	1.2K

Table 1: A description of the various applications from which the workload is composed

One solution to this problem is to have traces large enough so that the number of transient misses is small compared to the total number of misses generated. If this effect is reduced to 5%, it means the 8K transient misses will be less than 5% of the total misses, i.e. the trace must be large enough to produce 160K misses. A hit ratio of 99% implies that the trace must contain 16M accesses.

The effect mentioned above will increase for several reasons if two-level caches are used. First, the accesses to the secondary cache are misses in the primary cache. A primary hit ratio of 95% reduces the accesses into the secondary cache by a factor of 20. Second, it is common to use a much larger secondary cache. A secondary cache with eight times as many lines as the primary one produces up to eight times as many transient misses. If we assume a 90% hit ratio in the second-level cache, the number of misses is further reduced by a factor of 10. This means that you need 80 times as many accesses into the primary cache to simulate the secondary cache with the same accuracy as the primary cache, with respect to transient misses.

Keeping this in mind, we examined how this problem was attacked in [Przybylski89], [Short88] and [Wang89]. The first paper treats this issue elegantly with respect to first-level caches. They have split their traces into two parts, where the initialization part establishes a steady-state footprint in the (primary) caches, before the last part of the trace starts. This method reduces the size of the traces, without loosing accuracy due to transient misses. However, we were not able to verify whether this method was applied to the secondary cache. There might, therefore, be some noise in their figures for large secondary caches. Let us examine their biggest trace (rd2n7 in [Przybylski88]) and do some back-of-the-envelope calculations. The number of references to the primary caches (32K altogether) is 1.6M. A primary miss ratio of 0.04 produces 67K misses, which refer to the secondary cache. The 512K secondary cache contains 16K lines, and has a miss ratio of 0.2. This implies that the number of misses in the secondary cache is about 13K, i.e. every one of the misses in the secondary cache might be caused by transient

misses. The primary cache (128K) simulated in [Short88] has a miss ratio of 0.03. They simulate 6.8M references in their 128K byte primary cache. This produces about 204K references to the secondary cache. The miss ratio of the secondary cache is 0.68, producing about 139K secondary cache misses. The cache contains 131K lines, which implies that out of the 139K misses, 94% of them could be caused by transient misses. Similar numbers from [Wang89] range from 25% to 29%, with a 16K primary cache followed by a 256K secondary cache, assuming a virtual-real organization. We have here assumed a line size equal to 16 for the secondary cache.

At the time, it was impractical for the authors to create a sufficiently large trace for the secondary cache to avoid the effect of transients. We therefore looked at another solution. We kept track of the different kinds of misses, transient misses and real misses. Transient misses can easily be detected by keeping track of initial invalid states in the cache, while real misses are detected by either an address/PID mismatch or a non-initial invalid state. The miss ratio was then calculated under the following circumstances:

1) We ignored the effect of the transient misses, i.e. the transient misses were considered to be real misses. This is a *worst case* miss ratio. This miss ratio is correct if transient misses were also misses in the real environment.

2) We turned the transient misses into hits. This is a *best case* miss ratio. This miss ratio is correct if all the lines in the simulated cache which generated transient misses had generated hits in the real environment.

3) We estimated the miss ratio by first calculating the miss ratio based on accesses excluding those which produced transient misses. We then assumed that the accesses which produced transient misses would have the same miss ratio as the other group. The *estimated* miss ratio was then calculated. This miss ratio is correct if one assumes that the references producing transient misses behave statistically equal to the other references with respect to hits/misses. It is worthwhile pointing out that the estimated miss ratio is close to the best miss ratio if the miss ratio is low.

When the simulation terminates, the miss ratios for the different caches are captured. The cache miss ratios are used to calculate the cache miss cost factor, or CMC. The CMC for a given cache indicates the increase in mean cache cycle time. We would like to argue that the CMC is a good measurement for evaluating cache performance, because it is independent of both technology and CPU architecture. We think it is of great importance to isolate the cache design from the CPU design as much as possible. The CMC is calculated in the following way:

$$CMC = (1-MR) + MR*(1+D+(LS/TS)*TR) - 1$$

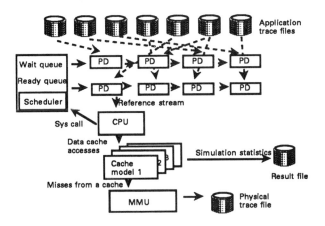

Figure 1: Simulation system overview

MR is the cache miss ratio. D is the delay (latency) between a request being sent from the cache to the next level of storage (secondary cache or memory) and the first response returns. LS is the line size of the cache. TS is the number of bytes transferred between the next level of storage and the cache-per-transfer cycle. TR is the ratio between the transfer cycle time and the cache-hit cycle time, e.g. if cache-hit cycle time is 20 ns and transfer cycle time is 40 ns, TR has the value 2. An example of a miss in a cache is given in Figure 2.

The simulation captures misses generated by the workload when the cache is 128K bytes, with a 16-byte line size. A virtual-to-physical address translation is performed, and a unique physical page is assigned to each unique virtual page in the simulated system. Main memory is considered to be "big enough" to avoid paging. The physical addresses of the misses are collected and used to make a new trace, which in turn is used for the simulation of the secondary caches. A description of the composite workload which was used for capturing the trace for the second-level cache, and of the trace itself, is given in Table 2. The number of instructions (I), data-read (Rd), data-write accesses (Wr) and the number of context switches (Cntx) are given for the workload, together with the total number of read/write accesses and the number of unique word/page accesses to the second-level cache.

Capture				Second-level trace			
Tot			Cntx	Total		Unique	
I	Rd	Wr		Rd	Wr	DWd	Dpg
433M	320M	176M	52K	6.3M	7.6M	768K	5.9K

Table 2: Description of the trace for the second-level cache and the workload used to capture it

The second-level cache simulations exploit different degrees of set associativity and different line sizes. Write-

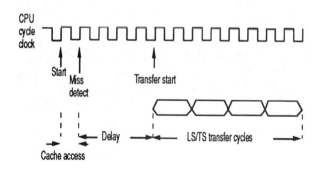

Figure 2: Miss in a cache

back strategy is used, with allocation on write miss. The replacement policy is Least Recently Used (LRU). The tag field is assumed to contain various data for maintaining cache coherence between the different nodes in the interconnect system and between the virtually-addressed primary cache and the physically-addressed secondary cache. Transactions for maintaining coherence are not simulated. Due to the coherence scheme, no cache clear is necessary.

4 OPEN BUS SYSTEMS

For the interconnect system between the main memory and CPU (with cache), we have looked at several possibilities, from designing a proprietary high-speed bus system to adopting an open bus standard. In the future it will be important that processor designs support open bus systems. Our models, in order to support a multiprocessor design, exploit cache coherence which is addressed by only two open bus systems: Futurebus+ [Hahn89] [FB+] and Scalable Coherent Interface [SCI]. These two proposed standards are now under development in working groups of the IEEE Computer Society.

Futurebus+ is an extension of the IEEE 896.1 (1987) with the MESI model defined for cache coherence. The implementation will be a backplane bus with different options for the width of the bus (32, 64, 128 or 256 bits wide), and also different transfer modes. The bus bandwidth will be close to what can be achieved on a backplane bus. For Futurebus+, both 32-bit and 64-bit transfers, called F32 and F64, are considered. We are using the compelled mode of operation. These choices will not give the maximum bus bandwidth, but the latency to first data will be the same, and the implementation will be possible in the 1990/91 time frame.

The Scalable Coherent Interface (IEEE P1596) will establish an interface standard for very high-performance multiprocessors, supporting a coherent memory model scalable to systems with up to 64K nodes. This Scalable Coherent Interface (SCI) will supply a peak bandwidth of 1 gigabyte/second per node. We have considered what can be implemented for SCI in the 1990/91 time frame, and have decided to limit the packet size to 64 bytes.

Interconnect system	Delay (ns)	D	Transfer Size (TS) (bytes)	Transfer Cycle Time (ns)	TR
F32 compelled	250	25	4	40	4
F64 compelled	250	25	8	40	4
SCI	240	24	2	2	0.2

Table 3: Data for delay (latency), transfer size and transfer speed used in the CMC calculations for Futurebus+ and SCI

For both bus systems, we have assumed idle bus arbitration and a main memory access time of 120 ns on the memory module itself. The parameters of the open bus systems under consideration are summarized in the table 3.

5 PRIMARY CACHES

Twenty-five different primary caches have been simulated. Cache size varies from 16K to 256K, while line size varies from 8 to 128 bytes. The workload, consisting of 60 processes, executed 100M instructions, with 17K context switches, and 73M read and 41M write accesses were generated. CPU utilization of the simulated CPU was 57%. The contribution from cold start misses in the simulated caches was less than 0.5% of the total misses. An overview of the simulation system for the primary caches is given in Figure 3.

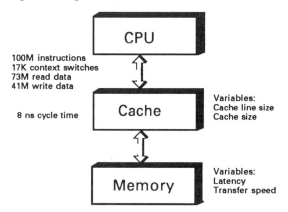

Figure 3: Primary-cache simulation overview

The cache miss ratios (MR) of the various caches are plotted in Figure 4, together with similar numbers from the Design Target Miss Ratios [Smith87] and hit ratios from Trace 1 and Trace 2 [Alexander86]. We would like to make three observations about Figure 4. First, we can see that Smith's numbers are worse than ours, and that the ones from Alexander et al. are better. The fact that Smith's miss ratios might be somewhat too pessimistic has also been reported in [Przybylski88]. Furthermore, we are pleased that the slopes of the curves correlate well. That means the ratio of ratios with respect to line size are similar for the different workloads simulated. The third point we see is that our curves are flattening out when the line size reaches 64 bytes, contrary to those of Smith. We explain this by the difference in associativity: Smith uses a fully-associative cache, while ours is direct-mapped. As the line size is increased, our cache will suffer more from intrinsic interference than Smith's.

Figure 5 shows the clear tendency that the miss ratio curve flattens out when the caches become larger than 64K bytes. This is consistent with other research.

The environment for the caches is described in section 4. We have assumed an 8 ns primary-cache cycle time The CMCs of the caches in the three environments are presented in Figure 6.

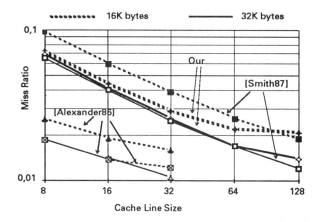

Figure 4: Cache miss ratios compared with results from Alexander et al. and Smith

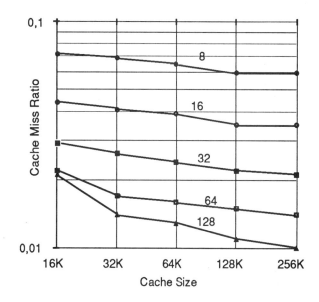

Figure 5: Primary cache miss ratios

An SCI environment with a line size less than 64 bytes is hypothetical, but is included as a study of the 64 byte coherence line size chosen by the SCI standardization group [SCI]. The CMC varies from 2.36 to 0.336, indicating that the mean cache access time varies from 3.36 to 1.336 cycles. The best line size in the F32 environment is clearly 32 bytes, and 32 or 64 bytes for the F64 environment, depending on the cache size. The optimum line size in the SCI environment is 64 or 128 bytes, depending on the cache size. The authors would like to stress that reasons other than cache performance have also influenced the SCI standardization group's choice of a 64-byte coherence line.

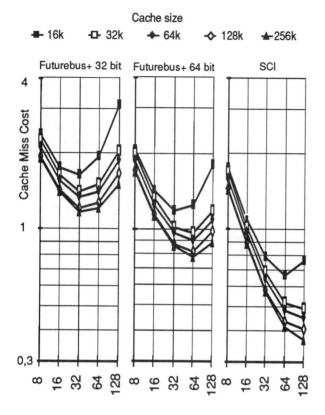

Figure 6: Cache miss cost in a single-level cache environment as a function of cache line size.

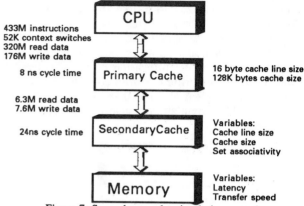

Figure 7: Secondary cache simulation overview

There is a significant deficiency in the above environment. Let us examine the 128Kx16 cache in an F32 environment. The CMC is 1.43. If we assume a Super Scalar Machine performing one memory access per cycle, the performance of the CPU is reduced by 60% due to the data cache miss penalty alone.

6 SECONDARY CACHES

In section 5 we showed serious deficiencies in an environment for a Super Scalar CPU based on one of the highest-performance interconnect systems that has been defined. We do not see any way to reduce the primary cache miss ratio. If we look at the contribution of the initial delay and the data transfer phase to the cache miss cost, we see that it is dominated by the delay. This indicates that any improvement must come from reducing the D term. The traditional approach to this problem is another cache, the "secondary cache". For other reasons for introducing a two-level cache hierarchy, see [Przybylski88] and [Short88].

Since the accesses to the secondary cache are misses in the primary, the locality of the accesses will be reduced. This indicates that a set-associative cache might be preferable to a direct-mapped one. Different secondary caches have been simulated. Set associativity, line size and total size are parameterized. The cache miss ratios are given in Table 4. The worst, estimated and best hit ratios are presented for each secondary cache.

From Table 4, we can see that the cache miss ratio decreases significantly as either line size, set associativity or cache size increases. Note the ratio of miss ratios of a cache to the "next" cache on either axis, starting from a 1Mx32 direct-mapped cache. The two-way, set-associative 1Mx32 produces 0.75 times the number of misses. A 1Mx64 cache, direct-mapped, produces 0.64 times the number of misses. If we double the cache size, i.e. 2Mx32, we get 0.61 times the number of misses. This indicates that the cache size is the most important factor, but we must keep in mind that doubling the cache size at least doubles the cost of the implementation. We need twice the number of memory packages, and the cache cycle time might increase. A doubling of the degree of associativity will increase the cost, but not as dramatically as doubling the cache size.

To consider the influence of line size, we must calculate the CMC of the secondary caches. The results for the three environments are given in Figure 8 for a 2M cache. The secondary-cache cycle time is 24 ns in all cases. The parameters for Futurebus+ and SCI are as in Table 3. The Figure is based on the estimated cache miss ratios. The maximum uncertainty, expressed as the difference in the average cache cycle time, is less than 5.0, 3.8, 3.2, 2.3 and 2.2% for the line sizes 16-256.

In the F32/F64 environment, a 64-byte line size is a good choice if single-CPU performance is to be maximized. However, the improved cache performance when going from a 32-byte line to a 64-byte line does not seem to be significant. This indicates that if bus bandwidth consumption is to be minimized, a 32-byte line could be preferable. The SCI environment benefits more from a larger line size than F32/F64, due to the higher transfer speed. In fact, a 128 byte line seems reasonable, but the benefit of increasing the line size from 64 to 128 bytes must be compared to the increased bandwidth requirement and implementation cost.

Set Associativity	Cache Line Size	Cache Size in Megabytes											
		1			2			4			8		
		W	E	B	W	E	B	W	E	B	W	E	B
Dir.Map.	16	.295	.292	.291	.190	.183	.181	.107	.091	.089	----	----	----
	32	.176	.174	.174	.111	.107	.107	.061	.052	.052	.040	.026	.026
	64	.113	.112	.112	.070	.067	.067	.036	.032	.032	.023	.016	.016
	128	.081	.081	.081	.048	.047	.047	.024	.021	.021	.014	.010	.010
	256	----	----	----	.038	.037	.037	.017	.016	.016	.010	.008	.008
2-Way	16	.226	.222	.221	.116	.107	.106	.073	.056	.055	.050	.020	.019
	32	.134	.132	.131	.066	.062	.062	.04	.031	.031	.027	.011	.011
	64	.085	.084	.084	.041	.039	.038	.023	.019	.019	.015	.007	.007
	128	----	----	----	.028	.027	.027	.015	.013	.012	.009	.004	.004
	256	----	----	----	----	----	----	.011	.009	.009	.005	.003	.003
4-Way	16	.186	.182	.181	.090	.081	.080	.060	.042	.042	.046	.013	.013
	32	.109	.107	.107	.050	.046	.045	.032	.023	.023	.024	.008	.008
	64	----	----	----	.030	.028	.028	.018	.014	.013	.014	.005	.005
	128	----	----	----	----	----	----	.011	.008	.008	.008	.003	.003
	256	----	----	----	----	----	----	----	----	----	.005	.002	.002
8-Way	16	.164	.160	.159	.080	.071	.070	.059	.040	.040	.044	.010	.010
	32	----	----	----	.044	.039	.039	.031	.022	.022	.024	.006	.006
	64	----	----	----	----	----	----	.017	.013	.013	.013	.004	.004
	128	----	----	----	----	----	----	----	----	----	.008	.003	.003

Table 4: Worst (W), Estimated (E) and Best (B) cache miss ratio in a secondary cache as a function of set associativity, cache size and cache line size

The different cache-miss cost factors for secondary caches of different sizes are plotted in Figure 9. The line size is 64 bytes for all three environments. The maximum possible deviation in cache cycle time due to the problem of transient misses is less than 0.9,3.2 and 6.8% for cache sizes 1-4M. For the 8M cache, the maximum possible deviation is less than 23.6% for the Futurebus+ environment, while it is 9.3% for the SCI environment. One conclusion that can be drawn from Figure 9 is that the CMC reduction of increased secondary caches is roughly of the same ratio, independent of the organization and interconnect system. Just as in Figure 8, it can be seen that cache organization seems more important than bus size in a Futurebus+ environment. The F32 two-way line crosses the F64 direct-mapped one when going from 1 to 2M bytes. The F64 two-way also crosses the SCI direct-mapped line when going from 4 to 8M bytes. However, due to the uncertainty tied to the 8M byte cache figures, no certain conclusion should be drawn[*].

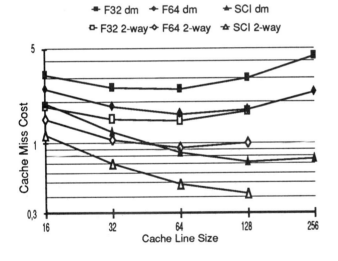

Figure 8: CMC for a 2M secondary cache as a function of line size

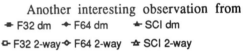
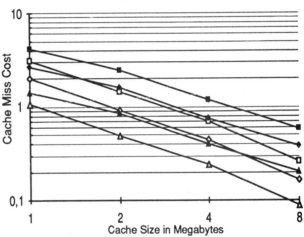

Figure 9: CMC for a 64-byte line secondary cache as a function of cache size

An interesting observation from Figure 8 is that the secondary cache organization is more important than the databus width for a Futurebus+ system. The two-way set-associative secondary cache in an F32 environment performs better than a direct-mapped one in an F64 environment. This does not hold true for F64 and SCI. A direct-mapped secondary cache in an SCI environment performs better than a two-way set-associative cache connected through F64, when 64- or 128-byte lines are considered.

Figure 9 is the great impact the cache design has on the CMC. If, for example, we go from 1Mx64 direct-mapped to 2Mx64 two-way set-associative, the CMC is reduced

---

[*] The 8Mx64 two-way set-associative cache has a worst case miss ratio of 0.015, producing 208K misses. Of those, a maximum of 128K might be caused by transient misses.

from 4.153 to 1.446 (F32), 2.660 to 0.926 (F64) and from 1.419 to 0.494 (SCI).

With the numbers from Table 4, the effective CMC (as seen from the CPU) can be calculated. The line size is 64 bytes (since this is the actual coherence size of the interconnect systems in question). The overall impact of secondary-cache cycle time has been studied. We have calculated the effective CMC with secondary-cycle times of 24, 32 and 40 ns. The primary-cache cycle time is fixed at 8 ns, the transfer ratio between primary and secondary cache (TR) is 1 and the number of bytes transferred between the two caches on a primary miss is 8. The primary cache is 128Kx16, with a miss ratio of 0.035. The findings are presented in Table 5. The maximum deviation (expressed as the difference in effective primary-cache cycle time) due to transient noise is 2.9%(F32), 1.9%(F64) and 1.0%(SCI).

secondary caches, and it has a negative impact on the larger secondary caches.

In Table 5, we can see that within each environment the overall secondary-cache size is the most important parameter. If we change the size of a 24 ns direct-mapped secondary cache from 1 to 8M, the mean effective primary-cache cycle will be reduced significantly for all three environments: 23.2% (F32), 16.4%(F64) and 10.7%(SCI).

The impact of the different environments on the effective primary-cache cycle time is also significant for the smaller secondary-cache sizes, but differences decrease as secondary cache size increases. Another way to interpret this is to say that as secondary-cache miss ratio increases, the importance of the interconnect system will increase.

If the numbers in Table 5 are compared to those of Figure 6, we see that the effective cache cycle time as seen from the CPU is dramatically improved. The 128Kx16 primary cache coupled directly to a 32-bit wide Futurebus+ has an effective CMC of 1.43. If a 4Mx64 24 ns two-way set-associative cache is inserted between the primary cache and the F32 system, the effective CMC is reduced to 0.249. This is a cycle time reduction of 48.5% or, in other words, a doubling of the CPU's performance.

Environment	2nd size	24 ns set-associativity			32 ns set-associativity			40 ns set-associativity		
		dm	2	4	dm	2	4	dm	2	4
F32	1M	0.611	0.502	----	0.646	0.537	----	0.681	0.572	----
	2M	0.436	0.327	0.284	0.471	0.362	0.319	0.506	0.397	0.354
	4M	0.300	0.249	0.230	0.335	0.284	0.265	0.370	0.319	0.300
	8M	0.237	0.202	0.194	0.272	0.237	0.229	0.307	0.272	0.264
F64	1M	0.454	0.384	----	0.489	0.419	----	0.524	0.454	----
	2M	0.342	0.272	0.245	0.377	0.307	0.280	0.412	0.342	0.315
	4M	0.255	0.222	0.210	0.290	0.257	0.245	0.325	0.292	0.280
	8M	0.215	0.192	0.187	0.250	0.227	0.222	0.285	0.262	0.257
SCI	1M	0.324	0.287	----	0.359	0.322	----	0.394	0.357	----
	2M	0.264	0.227	0.212	0.299	0.262	0.247	0.334	0.297	0.282
	4M	0.218	0.200	0.194	0.253	0.235	0.229	0.288	0.270	0.264
	8M	0.196	0.184	0.182	0.231	0.219	0.217	0.266	0.254	0.252

Table 5: CMCs seen from the CPU. The primary cache is a 128K direct-mapped, write-through cache

The major finding from Table 5 is the surprisingly small influence of secondary-cache cycle time on the overall cache performance. Examine the 24 ns, 1M byte direct-mapped secondary cache in the F32 environment. The effective mean primary-cache cycle time is 1.611 cycles. If the cycle time of the secondary cache is increased by 66% to 40 ns, the effective mean cycle time of the primary cache will be 1.681, i.e. an increase of only 4.3%. However, the influence of the secondary-cache cycle time will increase slightly as the overall performance improves. If a 4M-byte four-way set-associative secondary cache in a SCI environment has its cycle time increased from 24 to 40 ns, the effective cache cycle time of the system will be increased from 1.194 to 1.264 cycles, i.e. 5.8%.

Due to the small influence of secondary-cache cycle time, it is interesting to see how increased set-associativity performs on the expense of cycle time. If we compare a direct-mapped secondary cache with a two-way set-associative of the same size, but with cycle time increased by 8 ns, we see that this is marginally beneficial for the two Futurebus+ environments in regard to the three smallest secondary caches. For the SCI environment, it does not seem to be significant for 1- and 2M-byte

7 CONCLUSION

In this paper we have developed a measurement for CPU cache performance comparisons, the CMC. The CMC is based on miss ratios and timing information relative to the cache cycle time. We have further developed a trace-driven, multiprocess cache simulator. It is able to synthesize a workload which seems adequate for the performance range of machines for which this work has been conducted. In our secondary-cache simulations, we have limited the maximum noise caused by transient misses in our figures by estimating the correct miss ratio. The deviation between the effective cycle times based upon estimated and worst case ratios has been calculated.

By comparing our primary-cache results with those of others ([Alexander86] and [Smith87]), we have shown that the workload used seems representative of a multiprocess, timesharing environment. In our study of a two-level cache system, we have shown that the secondary cache organization is more important than the choice of a 32- or 64-bit bus width in a Futurebus+ system. The importance of the interconnect system has been documented: <u>An SCI environment performs significantly better than the two Futurebus+ environments</u> when the secondary cache miss ratio is 0.1 or worse. However, the most important factor in the memory hierarchy design is the size of the secondary cache. The speed of the secondary cache does not seem that important.

We have compared a single-level cache implementation with a two-level implementation for a CPU executing several hundred *mips*. <u>A CPU with a two-level cache system performs twice as fast</u>, when data cache misses are taken into account. We find this result promising. It is possible to build a high-performance scalar processor, even though the access latency of the main memory system is as long as 250 ns.

We have further verified that a coherence line size of 64 bytes for an environment based on Futurebus+ seems reasonable, but it does not perform significantly better that the 32-byte line. This implies that if bus traffic is to be minimized, a 64-byte line for Futurebus+ might be too large.

A 64- or 128-byte line seems to be the best choice for SCI. Due to the lack of coherence transactions in our simulation (which statistically increases with increased line size, due to the probability of false sharing) and that we see great difficulties in implementing SCI nodes with line sizes longer than 64 bytes, we conclude that a 64-byte coherence line size is a good choice for SCI.

ACKNOWLEDGMENTS

The authors would like to thank James R. Goodman for his encouragement and fruitful comments. We would also like to thank project leader Einar Rustad at Dolphin Server Technology for his patience. During some periods we spent more time preparing this paper than on the design of the CPU which will use the memory hierarchy described.

REFERENCES

[Agarwal89] Anant Agarwal, "Analysis of Cache Performance for Operating Systems and Multiprogramming", Kluwer Academic Publishers, 1989

[Alexander86] C. Alexander, W. Keshlear, F. Cooper and F. Briggs, "Cache Memory Performance in a UNIX Environment", Computer Architecture News, 14, 3, 1986

[Bakken86] Pål Bakken, "Cache Memory for ND-500", University of Trondheim, Norway, 1986

[FB+] Futurebus+, Logical Layer Specifications, Draft 8.02, P896.1/D8.02, IEEE Computer Society Working Group, September, 1989

[Goodman87] J. Goodman, "Coherency for Multiprocessor Virtual Address Caches", ASPLOS-II, IEEE, October 1987

[Hahn89] E. Hahn, "Performance Considerations in Futurebus+", Buscon East 1989.

[Hill88] M. Hill, "A Case for Direct-Mapped Caches", Computer, December 1988

[Jouppi89] N. Jouppi and D. Wall, "Available Instruction-Level Parallelism for Superscalar and Superpipelined Machines", 1989, ASPLOS-III Proceedings, ACM Sigplan Notices Vol 24, May 1989

[Mips88] Gerry Kane, "Mips RISC Architecture", Prentice-Hall Inc., 1988

[nd500] ND-500 Reference Manual, ND-05.009.4 EN, Norsk Data A.S, P.O. Box 25, Bogerud, N-0621 Oslo 6, Norway

[ndsIII] SINTRAN Reference Manual, ND-60.128.04 EN, Norsk Data A.S, P.O. Box 25, Bogerud, N-0621 Oslo 6, Norway

[Przybylski88] S. Przybylski, M. Horowitz and J. Hennessy, "Performance Tradeoffs in Cache Design", Proc. 15th Ann. Int'l Symp., Computer Architecture, No.861, Computer Society Press, Los Alamitos, Calif., 1988

[Przybylski89] S. Przybylski, M. Horowitz and J. Hennessy, "Characteristics of Performance-Optimal Multi-Level Cache Hierarchies", Proc. 16th Ann. Int'l Symp., Computer Architecture, No. 948, Computer Society Press, Los Alamitos, Calif., 1989

[SCI] SCI (Scalable Coherent Interface), Draft 0.48 P1596, IEEE Computer Society Working Group, March, 1990

[Short88] R. Short and M. Levy, "A Simulation Study of Two-Level Caches", Proc.15th Ann. Int'l Symp. Computer Architecture, No. 861, Computer Society Press, Los Alamitos, Calif., 1988

[Smith87] A. J. Smith, "Line (Block) Size Choice for CPU Caches", IEEE Trans. Computers Vol. C-36, No. 9, Sept. 1987

[Stone] H. Stone, "High-Performance Computer Architecture", Addison-Wesley Publishing Company, 1987

[Sun85] Sun Microsystems Inc., Sun-3 Architecture Manual, 1985

[Wang89] W-H. Wang, J-L. Baer and H. Levy, "Organization and Performance of a two-Level Virtual-Real Cache Hierarchy", Proc. 16th Ann. Int'l Symp. Computer Architecture, No. 1948, Computer Society Press, Los Alamitos, Calif., 1989

[Wood89] D. Wood, R. Katz, "Supporting Reference and Dirty Bits in SPUR's Virtual Address Cache", Proc. 16th Ann.Int'l Symp. Computer Architecture, No. 1948, Computer Society Press, Los Alamitos, Calif., 1989

Performance Measurement and Trace Driven Simulation of
Parallel CAD and Numeric Applications on a Hypercube Multicomputer [*]

Jiun-Ming Hsu and *Prithviraj Banerjee*

Center for Reliable and High-Performance Computing
Coordinated Science Laboratory
University of Illinois at Urbana-Champaign
Urbana, IL 61801

ABSTRACT

This paper presents the performance evaluation, workload characterization and trace driven simulation of a hypercube multicomputer running realistic workloads. Six representative parallel applications were selected as benchmarks. Software monitoring techniques were then used to collect execution traces. Based on the measurement results, we investigated both the computation and communication behavior of these parallel programs, including CPU utilization, computation task granularity, message interarrival distribution, the distribution of waiting times in receiving messages, and message length and destination distributions. The localities in communication were also studied. A trace driven simulation environment was developed to study the behavior of the communication hardware under real workload. Simulation results on DMA and link utilizations are reported.

1. INTRODUCTION

Hypercube multicomputers have recently offered a cost-effective and feasible approach to supercomputing by connecting a large number of low-cost processors with direct links [1]. Each processor has its own local memory. Processes running on these processors communicate via message passing. This type of architecture is more readily scaled up to large numbers of processors than multiprocessor designs based on globally shared memory. Implementations of the hypercube architecture range from experimental prototype systems [2], to commercially available systems from Intel [3], Ametek, and NCUBE.

The evaluation of performance of parallel machines such as hypercubes is extremely important for exploring parallel program characteristics and parallel architecture behavior. One of the goals of our research was to implement a general performance evaluation environment for hypercubes based on software monitoring. In order to do an accurate evaluation, we decided to do some measurements of several realistic parallel applications (four in VLSI CAD and two in numerical domain) written for hypercubes. We used an Intel iPSC/2 hypercube as a testbed for our study.

On the basis of the measurements, we studied issues in both computational and communication behavior of realistic parallel programs on hypercubes. The computational characteristics that we measured were the statistics on CPU utilization, relative system time, user application time, idle time of various CPUs in the parallel system, statistics on task granularity between message generation, etc. The communication characteristics that we measured included the distribution of interarrival times of messages, the distribution of waiting times in receiving messages, and message length and destination distributions.

The motivation behind these measurements was to validate the assumptions typically made by researchers in the parallel computer systems modeling area. The application of queueing network models to computer network performance analysis typically assume some kind of message arrival interval, length, and destination distributions. The most common assumptions are Poisson message arrival, exponentially distributed message lengths, and evenly distributed message destinations [4]. Researchers in the load balancing area make various assumptions about task granularity and intertask dependencies in computational task graphs that are mapped on to processors [5]. We wanted to verify if indeed the above assumptions are valid, and if not, what distributions more accurately model the real world applications on hypercubes.

In experimental studies of hypercube performance [6,7], simulations have been performed using various synthetic communication benchmarks, which assume different kinds of message interval, length and destination distributions. Again, based on the results of the measurement, we can verify whether these synthetic benchmarks are close to real applications by modeling the empirical data using statistical distributions [8,9]. The resulting model will also help us in designing more realistic synthetic benchmarks.

The communication patterns of the parallel programs can critically affect the performance of the message passing machines, hence we were also interested in the localities of message destination and length. Models for both the spatial and temporal localities of message destinations have been proposed before in [10]. In this study we propose a model for the locality of message size based on the LRU stack model [11]. The accuracy of this model was verified by measurement results.

In distributed-memory multicomputers like hypercubes, synchronization and data sharing are achieved by explicit message passing. Hence, the speed and efficiency of communication are very important in the overall performance of such machines. In this study, we also investigate the performance of the communication channels in detail. The behavior of the communication hardware components (DMA channels and communication links) is not easily observable via software monitoring. Therefore a

---
[*] This research was supported in part by the National Science Foundation Presidential Young Investigator Award under Grant NSF MIP 86-57563 PYI, and in part by an equipment grant NSF CCR 87-05240.

CH2887-8/90/0000/0260$01.00 © 1990 IEEE

simulation environment was developed to model the hardware and software components of typical hypercube nodes. Experiments were then run using communication traces (message transmission patterns) collected from the earlier part of this work. We were therefore able to obtain reasonably accurate performance information of the communication channels.

The benchmarks used in the measurement are briefly described in Section 2. Section 3 gives an overview of the measurement facilities. Section 4 reports the results of the measurement and the characteristics of the communication workload. In Section 5, we present the trace driven simulation methodology and results.

2. BENCHMARKS

Six hypercube applications are used as benchmarks, which solve real-life VLSI CAD and numerical problems. Different data partitioning schemes are employed in these applications, and the communication patterns vary from ring, nearest neighbors, distance-two, to broadcast communication. The communication workload ranges from very light to very heavy. Together, these applications represent a typical workload of hypercube multicomputers. Four parallel VLSI CAD programs are used, which are: a standard cell placement program, a channel routing program, a VLSI circuit extractor, and a test pattern generator. In addition, two numeric applications, QR factorization and Fast Fourier Transformation, are also used.

The parallel standard cell placement program [12] is based on simulated annealing technique whose objective is to minimize the total estimated wirelength in a standard cell layout. Processors pair up to perform parallel moves, and synchronize with each other using a ring-based broadcast mechanism. The parallel channel routing program [13] is also based on simulated annealing and uses similar communication patterns to minimize the number of horizontal tracks in a channel. The parallel test pattern generator [14] is based on a parallel branch and bound algorithm. The scheduling and control of the parallel search is done by one processor, while other nodes do the searches in parallel. The parallel circuit extraction program [15] consists of two phases. The first phase, dominated by communication, is the distribution of data from the host to the node processors in a tree fashion. The second phase is the circuit extraction phase which is computationally intensive.

The parallel QR factorization algorithm [16] maps the matrix onto a ring of processors and eliminates matrix elements in parallel. The parallel Fast Fourier Transform (FFT) program [17] involves an even distribution of the input points among the processor nodes initially. The nodes subsequently perform the iterative sequential FFT algorithm on the points in parallel. At the end of each step, messages are exchanged across nodes to set up the points for the next iteration.

In each of the above applications, with the exception of the circuit extractor, only the main execution part is measured. The downloading of the data and the uploading of the results are not included. For the extractor, both the downloading of the data and the execution part are traced.

3. MEASUREMENT FACILITIES

The system on which we performed the measurement is a 16 node Intel iPSC/2 hypercube [3], where the application programs access the message passing capabilities through two sets of systems calls: 1) blocking message calls, *csend*() and *crecv*(), and 2) non-blocking message calls, *isend*() and *irecv*(). Messages of 100 bytes or less (short messages) are unsolicited. Long messages must request the receiving buffer from the destination node first before sending the message, so they follow a three-trip protocol — request, acknowledge, send.

We have implemented a software monitoring tool in the iPSC/2 processor nodes. The monitoring facility can be used to tune the software for better performance, to investigate resource utilization, and to determine the characteristics of computation and communication workload. The measurement methodology basically followed the same approach as [18], which is software monitoring in the operating system level. The user program need not be modified except that two commands, *monitor_init*() and *monitor_end*(), are added to the node program to initiate and terminate the software monitoring facilities.

The instrumentation is done by inserting *probe points* at various places in the node operating system. An event is triggered during the execution of the application program when any of the probe points is hit. The monitoring facilities record each event onto a trace buffer in the memory together with the time-stamp and an optional number of parameters of the particular event. At the end of the monitoring, when the *monitor_end*() command is executed, the trace buffer is sent to a background process in the host which stores the trace in the file system. One trace file is generate by each of the processor nodes.

The places where we insert probe points are:

(1)   entry and exit points of system calls (message and non-message),

(2)   entry and exit points of interrupt service routines (message and non-message),

(3)   points where the CPU enters and leaves idle state,

(4)   points where the operating system performs message related activities, like start sending a message, set up receiving for a message, and

(5)   entry and exit points of buffer operations, e.g. buffer allocation and buffer copying.

The first three types of probe points enable us to observe the CPU state and the specific operating system routine executed. The fourth one provides the information about communication activities, and the last type of probe points help us determine the cost of various buffer operations.

Software monitoring slows down the execution of the benchmarks by 0.2 to 35 percent, as shown in Table 1. It also shows the input data used in the measurement, average number of messages sent and received, average message size, size of trace file, and number of trace events, of each node. Since the emphasis of the monitor is on communication and system activities, the percentage of the overhead is directly proportional to the rate of message and

Application Program	Input Data	Monitoring Statistics (Average/Per Node)				Running Time		
		Messages Sent & Recv'd	Average Msg. Size (Bytes)	Trace File Size (Bytes)	No. of Events	Monitor Off (Sec)	Monitor On (Sec)	Overhead (%)
Placement	286 cells	12316	153.72	1036K	154K	89.84	93.82	4.4
Routing	229 nets	18780	17.1	1212K	159K	11.91	16.08	35.0
Test Gen.	3540 nets	872	113.4	801K	158K	15.32	19.81	29.3
Extraction	66K rectangles	791	8519.0	122K	21K	181.76	182.14	0.2
QR	128×128 matrix	4128	1206	518K	71K	12.58	14.41	14.6
FFT	2^{12} points	600	4096	102K	16K	28.29	28.69	1.4

Table 1. Monitoring Statistics (on an 8 Node Hypercube).

Application Program	System Time (%)			User Time (%)			Idle Time (%)		
	Min.	Max.	Avg.	Min.	Max.	Avg.	Min.	Max.	Avg.
Placement	4.80	4.88	4.82	50.40	78.44	61.86	16.68	44.79	33.32
Routing	30.42	31.86	30.93	37.01	60.85	44.66	8.73	31.78	24.41
Test Gen.	3.36	8.63	5.91	1.55	61.07	45.01	30.70	91.26	49.08
Extraction	0.31	0.46	0.39	51.61	55.86	53.84	43.68	48.07	45.77
QR	13.30	14.72	13.95	54.40	59.95	57.11	25.33	32.31	28.94
FFT	1.97	2.02	2.00	96.49	96.59	96.54	1.39	1.51	1.46

Table 2. CPU Utilization (on an 8 Node Hypercube).

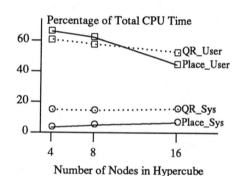

Figure 1. CPU Utilization as a Function of Hypercube Size.

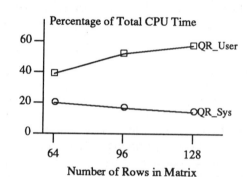

Figure 2. CPU Utilization as a Function of Data Size for QR Program on 8 Processors.

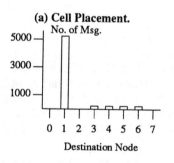
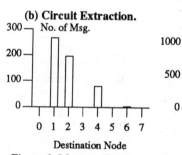
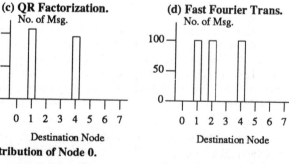

Figure 3. Message Destination Distribution of Node 0.

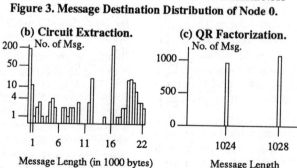
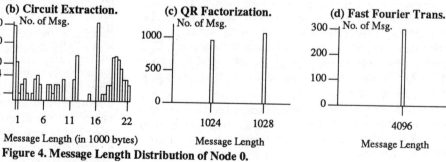

Figure 4. Message Length Distribution of Node 0.

system calls. The channel routing program has a high message transmission rate and the test pattern generation program makes frequent system calls, therefore their overhead percentages are very high.

4. PERFORMANCE MEASUREMENT RESULTS

This section presents the results of the measurement of the six benchmarks running on an eight node hypercube. We show the utilization of the CPU and the characteristics of the computation and communication workload. Models for the locality of message length and the distributions of various time intervals are also proposed.

4.1. CPU Utilization

The utilization of the CPU gives a good indication of the efficiency of the parallel algorithm. Table 2 shows the CPU utilization of the six applications running on a eight node hypercube. The total execution time of the CPU is divided into three parts, which are system, user and idle times. For each of the three parts, the average percentage is shown together with the maximum and minimum among the eight nodes.

The system time includes both the message-related and message-unrelated calls. In the benchmarks, most of the system calls are message-related, hence the system percentage is proportional to the rate of message sending and receiving. The variations in the user time percentages indicate the computation workload distribution of the applications. The CPU idle time occurs mostly in waiting for the completion of message sending and receiving. Lower idle time translates to more efficient use of system resources.

The channel router is a communication intensive program. In the test generation program, the communication and computation workloads are not balanced. This is because processor zero acts as the scheduler of the parallel branch and bound search, hence it has the lowest user time, highest system and idle time percentages. The circuit extraction program, which does explicit load balancing, and the numeric applications, QR and FFT, are well load-balanced. The first phase of the circuit extractor is I/O intensive, and the second phase is computation intensive. Due to its large data size, the FFT program is very computation intensive.

Figure 1 shows the CPU utilizations of the cell placement and QR programs when the number of processors increases from 4 to 16. As expected, for both of the programs, the user time percentage goes down and the system time percentage goes up when the size of the hypercube grows. This is because the granularity of the computation task becomes smaller. Note that the user time percentage of the placement program declines faster than that of the QR program because the placement program sends more messages per node when the hypercube size grows. Figure 2 shows the CPU utilizations of the QR program when the data size increases. It again confirms that when the task granularity becomes larger, the user CPU utilization also increases.

4.2. Message Length and Destination

Figures 3 and 4 summarizes the message destination and length distributions of node zero for four of the applications: placement, extraction, QR and FFT. The cell placement program communicates only with distance one and two nodes, with most of the messages going to one distance-one node. The message length varies from 0 to 4K bytes, but most are under 100 bytes. The circuit extractor sends almost all the messages to distance-one nodes, mostly with length less than 100 bytes or around 16K bytes. The nodes in the QR factorization program communicate in a ring fashion, sending 1028 byte messages to their successors and 1024 byte messages to their predecessors. In the FFT program, the nodes send equal amount of messages to all of the distance-one nodes, all with the same length.

Table 3 summarizes the spatial locality of message passing for the six benchmarks on an 8 node hypercube. Except for the test generation program, all the benchmarks send most of the messages to the nearest neighbors. The communication patterns do not change for a 16 node configuration. This indicates that the message destination has spatial locality which favors nearest neighbors. Evenly distributed message destination is often assumed in both experimental [7] and analytical [4] approaches of computer network performance analysis. This assumption is not true in most of the applications for hypercubes because the programmers often try to avoid sending long distance and global messages.

In addition to the spatial locality, we were also interested in the temporal locality of the message destination. We model the temporal locality using the *least recently used* (LRU) stack model [11, 10], in which the message destination is treated like memory address. In the LRU stack model of stack size n, each node has a stack which contains the n most recent message destinations. If the destination of the next message is in the stack, it is called an LRU stack hit, otherwise it counts as a miss. In Table 4, we show the average LRU stack hit rate of the six applications when stack size varies from one to four. Four out of the six benchmarks have a high hit rate when the stack size is only one. All programs have a hit rate of 85 percent or more when the stack size is three. In the FFT program, each node alternately sends messages to the three distance-one neighbors and the destinations always hit the third stack location.

If the message length is also treated like a memory address, then the sizes of messages also have spatial and temporal localities. From the distributions of the message length in Figure 4, it is clear that the lengths concentrate around only one or two peaks in every application, which shows that the lengths have high spatial locality. To investigate the temporal locality of the message length we propose a model called the **Most Recent Message Length** (MRML) stack model, which is based on the LRU stack model. In the MRML stack model of stack size m, each node has several stacks each corresponds to one possible message destination and contains the m most recent message sizes send to that node, with the most recent length in the first location. The message is considered a MRML

Application Program	Message Distance (%)		
	1 Hop	2 Hop	3 Hop
Placement	88.5	11.5	0
Routing	91.9	8.1	0
Test Gen.	52.8	37.2	10.0
Extraction	99.4	0.6	0
QR	100	0	0
FFT	100	0	0

Table 3. Average Message Distance Distribution.

Application Program	Destination LRU Stack Hit Rate (%)			
	DSS=1	DSS=2	DSS=3	DSS=4
Placement	83.52	85.52	85.96	86.35
Routing	81.82	90.90	99.96	99.96
Test Gen.	87.68	88.75	90.15	91.27
Extraction	39.51	74.05	98.51	98.78
QR	87.94	99.90	99.90	99.90
FFT	0	0	99.00	99.00

Table 4. Message Destination Hit Rates as a Function of Destination LRU Stack Size.

Application Program	MRML Stack Hit Rate (%)				MRML Stack Hit Rate (%) Min. Msg. Size = 100 Bytes			
	LSS=1	LSS=2	LSS=3	LSS=4	LSS=1	LSS=2	LSS=3	LSS=4
Placement	82.0	87.9	90.6	91.7	89.3	92.2	94.1	94.8
Routing	91.2	94.1	94.6	95.0	99.9	99.9	99.9	99.9
Test Gen.	78.1	86.1	93.7	96.5	88.4	92.2	97.3	98.3
Extraction	48.1	74.1	82.3	85.8	49.1	74.1	82.3	85.8
QR	99.9	99.9	99.9	99.9	99.9	99.9	99.9	99.9
FFT	99.0	99.0	99.0	99.0	99.0	99.0	99.0	99.0

Table 5. Message Length Hit Rates as a Function of MRML Stack Size.

Application Program	Destination and Length Stack Hit Rate (%) Min. Msg. Size = 100 Bytes					
	MRML Stack Size = 1			MRML Stack Size = 2		
	DSS=1	DSS=2	DSS=3	DSS=1	DSS=2	DSS=3
Placement	80.93	82.59	82.77	81.62	83.37	83.62
Routing	81.78	90.85	99.90	81.78	90.85	99.90
Test Gen.	76.50	77.57	78.98	80.26	81.33	82.74
Extraction	15.91	33.00	48.96	28.28	54.11	73.95
QR	87.94	99.90	99.90	87.94	99.90	99.90
FFT	0	0	99.00	0	0	99.00

Table 6. Message Destination and Length Hit Rate.

stack hit if its length is smaller than or equal to the longest of the m last messages send to the same destination, i.e. the largest in the MRML stack. Note that this model is for the upper bound of the message length.

For example, if a node x sends messages to four other nodes, there will be four MRML stacks for node x each corresponds to one destination. Stack $x.y$ contains the sizes of the most recent 3 messages node x sent to y, assuming a stack size of 3. If the current content of $x.y$ is $(6,10,5)$ and the next message is of size 7, then it is a MRML stack hit. The stack distance is two, since 7 is smaller than the second stack location but larger than the first one. The new $x.y$ stack will be $(7,6,10)$. If the next message length is 12, then it counts as a miss.

Table 5 shows the average MRML stack hit rate of the six benchmarks when the stack size increases from one to four. The left hand side of this table reports the pure MRML stack hit rate without any limitation on minimum message length. The hit rates of QR and FFT are almost 100 percent, since, for each destination node, the message length is constant. The placement and routing programs also have high hit rates when the stack size is only one.

In the right hand side of Table 5, following the message transmission protocol of iPSC/2, we assume that the minimum buffer size is 100 bytes, hence messages shorter than 100 bytes will be treated as 100 bytes. The hit rates of

placement, routing and test generation programs improves substantially. The circuit extraction program often sends a short message and then a very long message alternately to each destination node, therefore the hit rate is very low when the stack size is one, and the minimum message size requirement does not make any difference.

We now show the predictability of the communication patterns by combining both of the models for the temporal localities of message destination and length. The message is considered a hit only when its destination is in the LRU stack *and* its length hits the MRML stack. Table 6 shows the average message hit rates of the benchmarks when the MRML stack size increases from one to two, and the destination LRU stack size varies from one to three. We also assume the minimum message size to be 100 bytes. Compared to the pure destination LRU stack hit rates shown in Table 4, the hit rates for the placement and routing programs decline a little bit, while those of the numeric applications stay the same since the length prediction always hits. For the test generator and the circuit extractor, the hit rates drop by a large amount, but recover substantially when the MRML stack size becomes two.

These measurements indicate that message length and destination have high spatial and temporal localities, hence the communication patterns are highly predictable. By utilizing these locality properties, the cost of message communication could be reduced by intelligent routing

264

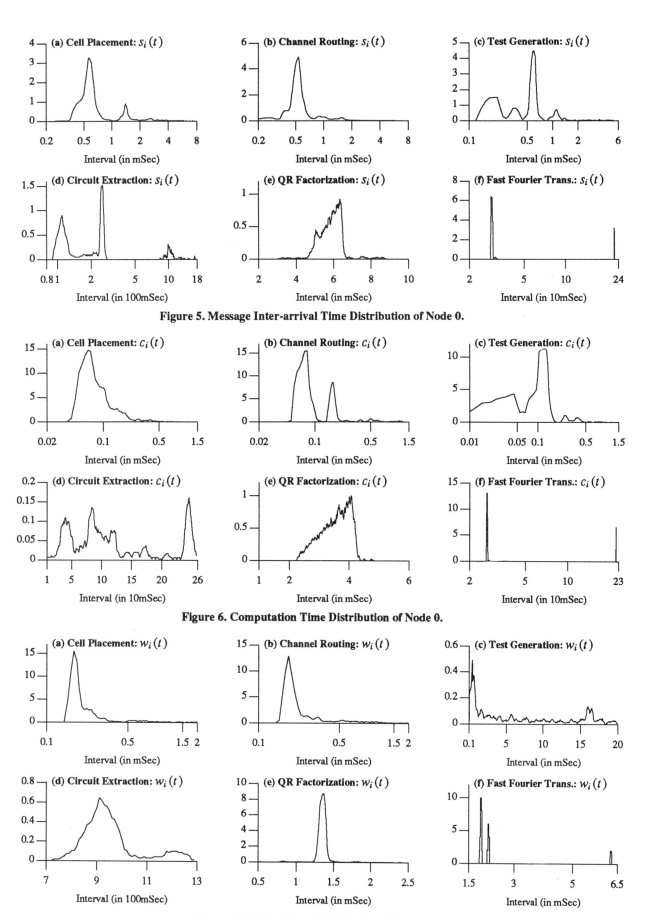

Figure 5. Message Inter-arrival Time Distribution of Node 0.

Figure 6. Computation Time Distribution of Node 0.

Figure 7. Waiting Time Distribution of Node 0.

Number of Stages	Model		
	Normal	Hypoexp.	Gamma
1	63.1	46.6	50.1
2	6.5	11.1	12.6
3	1.7	7.5	4.1

Table 7. SSE of Curve Fitting on Message Interval Dist. of Node 0 of the Cell Placement Program.

Number of Stages	Model		
	Normal	Hypoexp.	Gamma
1	5.3	12.1	6.0
2	1.3	7.5	2.7

Table 8. SSE of Curve Fitting on Message Interval Dist. of Node 0 of the QR Factorization Program.

Appl. Prog.	Distributions	Two-stage Normal pdf Model Parameters					
		a_1	μ_1	σ_1	a_2	μ_2	σ_2
Placement	Msg. Interval	0.49	0.57	0.07	0.51	1.45	1.01
	Computing Time	0.52	0.07	0.02	0.48	0.14	0.07
	Waiting Time	0.54	0.18	0.02	0.46	0.47	0.42
QR	Msg. Interval	0.84	5.77	0.60	0.16	6.23	0.16
	Computing Time	0.71	3.38	0.50	0.29	3.98	0.19
	Waiting Time	1.00	1.35	0.05	-	-	-

Table 9. Two-stage Normal pdf Model Parameters for Placement and QR (Node 0).

controllers and efficient buffer management strategies. In a circuit-switched message routing paradigm, the circuit can be kept connected even after the message is transmitted. If the next message also goes to the same destination, this circuit can again be used, thereby reducing circuit set-up time. Software overhead can also be reduced by predicting the sizes of the incoming messages and pre-allocating buffers for them.

4.3. Communication and Computation Workload

In experimental and analytical studies of computer network performance, different kinds of message interarrival time distributions are often assumed, including exponential [4], normal distribution [7], and constant interval [6]. We wanted to verify these assumptions by analyzing the data collected from the measurements.

Figure 5 shows the distribution of the time interval between message sending of node zero for the six benchmarks. The interarrival time between messages $i-1$ and i, t_i, can be broken down into three parts, which are the computation time, c_i, the waiting time for receiving messages, w_i, and the system time for processing messages, s_i. Hence, $t_i = c_i + w_i + s_i$. Figures 6 and 7 show the distributions of the computation time and waiting time interval of node zero. The system time for processing messages can be approximated by a linear function of the message size, $s_i = f(l)$, hence it is very predictable and will not be discussed here.

The message interarrival distribution of the placement program has two peaks, which correspond to the two types of messages it sends, ring broadcast and cell exchange. The distributions of the placement program are similar to those of the channel router, because they use similar algorithms and have similar message transmission patterns. The circuit extractor sends infrequent messages and, in the first phase, spends most of the time waiting for messages from the host. Its computing time interval is irregular. As expected, the distributions of the numeric algorithms, especially those of the FFT, are very regular. Each of the three distributions of the QR program has a single peak, and those of the FFT have two peaks.

Due to the multiple peaks, the distributions clearly can not be modeled by simple exponential, normal or gamma probability density functions (pdf). Therefore, we model the distributions by multi-stage pdf's [8], defined as:

$$f(t) = \sum_{i=1}^{n} a_i \, g_i(t),$$

where $a_i \le 1$ is the weight for each stage, $\sum_{i=1}^{n} a_i = 1$, and n is the number of stages. The probability density functions $g_i(t)$ can all be chosen from one of the following:

(1) Normal:

$$g_i(t) = \frac{1}{\sigma_i \sqrt{2\pi}} \exp\left[-\frac{1}{2}\left[\frac{t-\mu_i}{\sigma_i}\right]^2\right], \quad t \ge 0,$$

where $\mu_i > 0$, and $\sigma_i > 0$.

(2) Shifted hypoexponential:

$$g_i(t) = \begin{cases} 0, & t \le s_i, \\ \frac{\lambda_{1i}\lambda_{2i}}{\lambda_{1i}-\lambda_{2i}}\left[e^{-\lambda_{1i}(t-s_i)}-e^{-\lambda_{2i}(t-s_i)}\right], & t > s_i, \end{cases}$$

where $\lambda_{1i} \ne \lambda_{2i}$, and $s_i > 0$ is the offset in time.

(3) Shifted gamma:

$$g_i(t) = \begin{cases} 0, & t \le s_i, \\ \frac{\lambda_i^{\alpha_i} (t-s_i)^{\alpha_i-1} e^{-\lambda_i(t-s_i)}}{\Gamma(\alpha_i)}, & t > s_i, \end{cases}$$

where $\alpha_i > 0$, $\lambda_i > 0$ and $s_i > 0$. The gamma function is defined by the integral:

$$\Gamma(\alpha_i) = \int_0^\infty x^{\alpha_i-1} e^{-x} \, dx, \quad \alpha_i > 0.$$

Thus, we have multi-stage normal, multi-stage shifted hypoexponential, and multi-stage shifted gamma pdf's. To determine the best model for the empirical distributions shown in Figures 5 through 7, we applied curve fitting technique (nonlinear regression) [19] to fit the distributions into the above models. Similar studies have been reported by [9] for file usage analysis and [8] for resource utilization. The criterion of the nonlinear regression procedure is

```
Node 0:                                    Node 1:
    Start node 0.                              Start node 1.
    Compute 350 µSec.                          Compute 500 µSec.
    Csend(type 1, length 100, to node 1).      Crecv(type 1, length 100).
    Compute 400 µSec.                          Compute 500 µSec.
    Crecv(type 2, length 500).                 Csend(type 2, length 500, to node 0).
    Compute 450 µSec.                          Compute 400 µSec.
    End.                                       End.
```

Figure 8. HSIM Input for a Two Node Hypercube.

to minimize the sum of square of errors (SSE) when estimating the parameters of a nonlinear model.

Table 7 shows the SSE of curve fitting for the message interval distribution of the placement program (shown in Figure 5.a). The models used are the three types of distributions with 1, 2 and 3 stages. The results indicate that two or three stage normal pdf models this distribution better than the other two types of pdf's. The same experiment repeated for the message interarrival time distribution of QR factorization program, shown in Table 8, also confirms this observation. By performing nonlinear regression on all the empirical distributions including the computation and waiting time intervals, we found that, while not the best model in every case, the multi-stage normal pdf has better overall performance than the other two models. A two-stage normal pdf models the distributions reasonably well, as can be seen from Tables 7 and 8, therefore it was chosen to model the empirical data.

Table 9 shows the two-stage normal pdf parameters for the distributions of cell placement and QR factorization programs. For the placement program, the two model parameters, μ_1 and μ_2, correspond to the two peaks in its message interarrival distribution, as shown in Figure 5.a. The parameters of its computing time and waiting time distributions indicate that the task granularity is small and the waiting times for messages are also not long. The waiting time distribution of the QR program can be modeled by one normal pdf with a small variance. Since $t_i = c_i + w_i + s_i$, as previously stated, and the waiting time w_i and system time s_i are almost constant, the message interval and computing time distributions are very similar except that one is time shifted by about 1.4 mSec from the other, as can be seen from μ_1 and μ_2 of the two distributions.

In this subsection, we have shown that the distributions of message arrival, computation time and waiting time can be modeled reasonably well by the two-stage normal pdf models. The results of such a study can be useful in the generation of realistic synthetic benchmarks and accurate analytical models for the evaluation of hypercube applications and architectures.

We also note that the statistics on the computation time between messages relate to the computation task granularity, and the statistics on message length and destination distributions represent the inter-task dependencies in computation task graphs. Our results will therefore provide realistic models of task graphs for load balancing researchers.

5. TRACE DRIVEN SIMULATION

5.1. Simulation Methodology

A trace driven simulator for hypercube — HSIM has been developed to study the behavior of the communication hardware under real workload. HSIM, written in C++, is based on CSIM [20], which is a process oriented simulation language. The emphasis of HSIM is in communication activities, therefore the message transmission is modeled in detail. The computation time of CPU between message sending and receiving is derived directly from the traces.

The inputs to HSIM are the *communication traces* which are derived from the execution traces of real applications by a post-processing program. Figure 8 shows a sample input to HSIM for a two node hypercube. Here the two processors exchange two messages while performing some computation in between. Since HSIM actually executes *csend*( ) and *crecv*( ) commands, it has to wait for the completion of message transmissions before continuing execution. Hence, it is very realistic in modeling the execution behavior of parallel programs.

HSIM models the architecture and communication protocol of the iPSC/2 [3], which uses circuit-switched message routing scheme. Each communication link consists of two bi-directional, bit-serial channels. Two DMA channels are used to transmit data, one for memory to routing logic transfers (the *outgoing DMA*), the other for transfers in the opposite direction (the *incoming DMA*).

It has been found that the errors are within five percent when comparing the simulation and measurement results on the total execution time and CPU utilization of the application programs. This enables us to justifiably put reliance on the results of the trace driven studies of link and DMA channel behavior.

5.2. Simulation Results

This subsection presents the results of the trace driven simulation on DMA and link utilizations. The inputs to the simulator were converted from the same set of traces that we characterized in Section 4. Table 10 shows the utilizations of the incoming and outgoing DMA channels, each with the minimum, maximum and average utilizations among the eight nodes, and the average service time for each message. Also shown are the overlap between the two channels, the overall DMA utilization and the CPU and DMA overlap percentage. Table 11 shows the link utilization and average bandwidth for each of the

Application Program	Incoming DMA Channel				Outgoing DMA Channel				In/Out Overlap (%)	DMA Util. (%)	Average CPU & DMA Overlap (%)
	Utilization (%)			Service Time Avg. (μSec)	Utilization (%)			Service Time Avg. (μSec)			
	Min.	Max.	Avg.		Min.	Max.	Avg.				
Placement	1.24	1.27	1.25	135.7	1.30	1.34	1.32	143.3	0.15	2.42	0.304
Routing	8.39	8.43	8.41	105.3	8.54	8.63	8.60	107.7	2.11	14.90	1.607
Test Gen.	0.30	3.18	0.72	115.7	0.55	2.61	0.87	172.2	0.04	1.55	0.101
Extraction	1.50	2.74	2.43	1344.6	1.37	4.50	2.48	1331.1	0.01	4.90	1.127
QR	8.19	9.01	8.60	179.3	8.28	9.10	8.67	180.7	0.02	17.26	0.210
FFT	1.71	1.71	1.71	544.6	1.80	1.82	1.81	576.8	0.29	3.22	0.253

Table 10. DMA Utilization (8 Node Hypercube).

Application Program	Node 0						Node 4						Overall	
	Link 0		Link 1		Link 2		Link 0		Link 1		Link 2			
	Util.	BW	Util.	BW	Util.	BW	Util.	BW	Util.	BW	Util.	BW	Util.	BW
Placement	0.38	6.79	0.23	4.71	1.02	15.09	1.02	15.11	0.22	4.33	0.39	7.22	0.55	9.05
Routing	0.98	11.62	0.32	3.80	7.84	94.68	8.18	98.40	0.32	3.83	0.65	7.71	3.06	36.64
Test Gen.	0.55	7.17	1.27	16.31	2.24	28.19	0.60	7.03	1.22	13.45	0.36	4.08	0.48	5.60
Extraction	1.31	35.69	0.20	4.37	0.02	0.24	1.27	35.00	0.26	5.43	1.01	27.68	0.83	22.20
QR	4.57	110.36	0	0	4.09	99.14	4.14	100.79	0	0	4.08	98.83	2.87	69.84
FFT	0.60	15.27	0.60	15.27	0.60	15.27	0.60	15.27	0.60	15.27	0.60	15.27	0.60	15.27

(Utilization in percentage, bandwidth in KBytes/Sec.)
Table 11. Link Utilization (8 Node Hypercube).

Data Size (Cells)	Number of Nodes	CPU			DMA		Link	
		Sys. (%)	User (%)	Idle (%)	In (%)	Out (%)	Util. (%)	BW (KB/Sec)
286	4	2.25	68.99	28.76	0.85	0.90	0.54	9.72
286	8	4.10	62.38	33.52	1.25	1.32	0.55	9.05
286	16	5.10	46.02	48.88	1.50	1.59	0.47	7.18
183	8	10.39	48.31	41.29	2.96	3.18	1.28	17.10

Table 12. Placement Program on Different Number of Nodes and Data Size.

three outgoing links of node zero and four, and the average utilization and bandwidth of all the links.

The DMA utilization table indicates that there is not much overlap between CPU and DMA. Part of the reason is that the DMA utilizations are not high anyway. In addition, most of these benchmarks use blocking communication calls, therefore almost all of the overlap occurs between CPU and the incoming DMA channel. The execution time could be reduced by overlapping communication with computation using non-blocking communication calls.

The channel routing program has high DMA and link utilization, this confirms the measurement result that it is a communication intensive application. Also, both of its CPU/DMA and incoming/outgoing channel overlaps are high. This is not due to explicit non-blocking message calls, but rather, it is caused by the asynchronous communication pattern of the processors where messages arrive when they are doing computation or sending out messages.

QR factorization program is also a communication intensive application, as can be seen from the high DMA and link utilizations. However, in contrast to the channel router, QR has low overlap between CPU/DMA and incoming/outgoing channels. This is because QR has a more regular communication pattern and its computation load is more balanced. It is interesting to note that the channel router has a higher link utilization rate than QR,

but its average link bandwidth is almost half of that of QR. The reason is that most of the messages of the channel router are very short, while QR sends long messages of 1K bytes. Hence the data transmission rate of QR is much higher.

The circuit extraction and FFT programs have longer average DMA service times because their average message sizes are larger than the other programs. Except the FFT program, where every node communicates with all of its distance-one neighbors, there exist high variations among the utilizations of the links of each node.

Table 12 gives the resource utilization summary of the cell placement program running on different hypercube sizes and with different input data. The CPU utilization part of the table again confirms the results of measurement, which were shown in Figure 1. As the cube size grows, the program becomes less computation intensive and more communication intensive. Therefore, the user time percentage goes down and the utilization of DMA increases. However, the average utilization and bandwidth decrease despite the fact that there are more messages. This is because the total number of links increases in a higher rate than that of node number. When data size decreases, the program also becomes less computation intensive.

For all the benchmarks except channel router and QR, the DMA and link utilizations are under 5 and 1 percent respectively, and the average bandwidths are well under the 2.8 Megabytes per second maximum. The low utilization rate indicates that a mesh architecture could probably do as well as the hypercube for these programs. In addition, in the iPSC/2 system, the delays in messages are not due to congestion in the links. With the existing hardware, better performance could be achieved just by reducing software overhead. The low transmission rate of small messages also shows that the system is not suitable for exploring low level parallelism in the applications.

6. CONCLUSION

We have investigated the computation and communication behavior of six parallel programs on a message passing multicomputer. An LRU stack model was used to study the temporal locality of message destinations. We also proposed a model for the temporal locality of message length which is called the *Most Recent Message Length* (MRML) stack model. By using these models, we have demonstrated that both the message destination and length have high temporal and spatial localities. These measurements and models have shown that the communication cost can be reduced by intelligent routing controllers and efficient buffer management strategies.

Multi-stage probability density functions were used to model computation task granularity distribution, message interarrival distribution, and the distribution of waiting times in receiving messages. It has been found, by nonlinear regression technique, that two-stage normal pdf's are most suitable in modeling the above distributions.

We also described a trace driven simulator which was used to study the communication activities in detail. The results of simulation show that the utilizations of DMA and links are very low, which indicates that there are still rooms for improvement even with the existing hardware.

By modeling the computation and communication workloads of realistic parallel programs, this study provided us some very important information that will be useful in both analytical and experimental study of hypercube communication networks. Based on the models for distributions and localities, representative synthetic benchmarks and accurate analytical models can be designed which will hopefully produce more precise results. System designers can also benefit from these information in developing more efficient communication hardware and software.

REFERENCES

[1] C. L. Seitz, "The Cosmic Cube," in *Comm. of the ACM.* pp. 22-33, Jan. 1985.

[2] J. Tuazon, J. Peterson, and M. Pniel, "Mark IIIfp Hypercube Concurrent Processor Architecture," in *Proc. 3rd Conf. on Hypercube Concurrent Computers and Applications*, Pasadena, CA, pp. 71-80, Jan. 1988.

[3] P. Close, "The iPSC/2 Node Architecture," in *Proc. 3rd conf. on Hypercube Concurrent Computers and Applications*, Pasadena, CA, pp. 43-50, Jan. 1988.

[4] P. Kermani and L. Kleinrock, "Virtual Cut-Through: A New Computer Communication Switching Technique," *Computer Networks*, vol. 3, pp. 267-286, Sep. 1979.

[5] S. H. Bokhari, "Partitioning Problems in Parallel, Pipelined and Distributed Computing," *IEEE Trans. on Computers*, vol. C-37, No. 1, pp. 48-57, Jan. 1988.

[6] D. C. Grunwald and D. A. Reed, "Networks for Parallel Processors: Measurements and Prognostications," in *Proc. 3rd Conf. on Hypercube Concurrent Computers and Applications*, Pasadena, CA, pp. 610-619, Jan. 1988.

[7] G. Buzzard and T. Mudge, "High Performance Hypercube Communication," in *Proc. 3rd Conf. on Hypercube Concurrent Computers and Applications*, Pasadena, CA, pp. 600-609, Jan. 1988.

[8] M. C. Hsueh, R. K. Iyer, and K. S. Trivedi, "Performability Modeling Based on Real Data: A Case Study," *IEEE Trans. on Computers*, vol. 37, No. 4, pp. 478-484, April 1988.

[9] M. V.-S. Devarakonda, "File Usage Analysis and Resource Usage Predition: A Measurement-Based Study," Technical Report CSG-79, Coordinated Science Lab., Univ. of Illinois, Urbana, IL, Dec. 1987.

[10] D. A. Reed and R. M. Fujimoto, in *Multicomputer Networks: Message-Based Parallel Processing.* Cambridge, MA: MIT Press, 1987.

[11] R. L. Mattson, J. Gecsei, D. R. Slutz, and I. L. Traiger, "Evaluation Techniques for Storage Hierarchies," *IBM Systems Journal*, vol. 9, 1970.

[12] J. Sargent and P. Banerjee, "A Parallel Row-Based Algorithm for Standard Cell Placement with Integrated Error Control," in *Proc. 26th Design Automation Conf.*, Las Vegas, NV, Jun. 1989.

[13] R. Brouwer and P. Banerjee, "A Parallel Simulated Annealing Algorithm for Channel Routing on a Hypercube Multiprocessor," in *Proc. Int. Conf. on Computer Design*, Rye Brook, NY, pp. 4-7, Oct. 1988.

[14] S. Patil and P. Banerjee, "A Parallel Branch and Bound Approach to Test Generation," in *Proc. 26th Design Automation Conf.*, Las Vegas, NV, Jun. 1989.

[15] K. P. Belkhale and P. Banerjee, "PACE2: An Improved Parallel VLSI Extractor with Parametric Extraction," in *Proc. Int. Conf. Computer-Aided Design*, Santa Clara, CA, Nov. 1989.

[16] A. Pothen, S. Jha, and U. Vemulapati, "Orthogonal Factorization on a Distributed Memory Multiprocessor," *Proc. 2nd SIAM Conf. on Hypercube Computers and Applications*, pp. 587-596, 1987.

[17] G. C. Fox, M. A. Johnson, G. A. Lyzenga, S. W. Otto, J. K. Salmon, and D. W. Walker, in *Solving Problems on Concurrent Processors, Vol. I.* Prentice-Hall, 1988.

[18] D. C. Rudolph, "Performance Instrumentation for the Intel IPSC/2," Technical Report UIUCDCS-R-89-1524, Dept. of Computer Science, Univ. of Illinois, Urbana, IL, July, 1989.

[19] SAS Institute Inc., "SAS User's Guide: Statistics," Version 5, Cary, NC, 1985.

[20] H. Schwetman, *CSIM Reference Manual (Revision 13).* Austin, TX: Microelectronics and Computer Tech. Corp., May, 1988.

Generation and Analysis of Very Long Address Traces

Anita Borg*   R. E. Kessler**,1   David W. Wall*

Western Research Laboratory*
Digital Equipment Corporation
100 Hamilton Avenue
Palo Alto, CA 94301
borg@decwrl.dec.com
wall@decwrl.dec.com
(415) 853-6600

Computer Sciences Department**
University of Wisconsin-Madison
1210 W. Dayton
Madison WI 53706
kessler@cs.wisc.edu
(608) 262-6618

Abstract

Existing methods of generating and analyzing traces suffer from a variety of limitations including complexity, inaccuracy, short length, inflexibility, or applicability only to CISC machines. We use a trace generation mechanism based on link-time code modification which is simple to use, generates accurate long traces of multi-user programs, runs on a RISC machine, and can be flexibly controlled. On-the-fly analysis of the traces allows us to get accurate performance data for large second-level caches. We compare the performance of systems with 512K to 16M second-level caches, and show that for today's large programs, second-level caches of more than 4MB may be unnecessary. We also show that set associativity in second-level caches of more than 1MB does not significantly improve system performance. In addition, our experiments also provide insights into first-level and second-level cache line size.

1. Introduction

1.1. Background

Effective analysis of cache designs is becoming crucial as caches become dramatically faster than main memory and cache misses are an ever more important factor in system performance. For 20 years the primary means of cache analysis has been the use of traces of memory access patterns to drive simulators that evaluate different cache designs [12]. Very long traces are needed to accurately simulate the behavior of the very large caches which are needed to buffer the imbalance in processor and memory speeds. Until recently, the longest available traces contained about 10 million references. These traces are sufficient for the simulation of small caches, but they are too short to simulate multi-megabyte caches.

Previous methods cannot produce long traces and cannot be used on RISC machines. The most common software method involves simulation of program execution to record all instruction and data references. This method is slow and limited. A 1000x or more slowdown makes real-time behavior, including kernel and multiprogrammed execution, impossible to simulate accurately. Hardware methods that spy on address lines to trace execution in real time usually have limited capacity. In ATUM [1], fast trace generation requires microcode modification making it unusable on RISC machines that do not have microcode.

We have developed a method of trace generation that we use to trace multiple processes in different address spaces and has been designed to eventually allow tracing of operating system references as well. We use link-time code modification to generate code that will create a record of data and instruction references with 8 to 12x slowdown. On-the-fly trace analysis, in which trace data is analyzed as it is collected, eliminates the need to store traces and makes the analysis of very long traces feasible. Traces are generated and analyzed on Titans, experimental high performance 32-bit RISC workstations, which were designed and built in our lab. The method is particularly well suited to RISC machines, but should also be implementable on CISC architectures.

---

[1]R. E. Kessler was supported by a summer internship at Digital Equipment Corporation and during the academic year by a University of Wisconsin graduate fellowship and the NSF (graduate fellowship and CCR-8902536)

CH2887-8/90/0000/0270$01.00 © 1990 IEEE

1.2. Goals and Status

Our primary goals have been to implement a set of tools for trace generation on our RISC machines and to use them to analyze large multi-level memory systems. We require that:

- The traces must be complete. They must represent multiple users as they execute on a real machine. The memory references must be interleaved as they are during execution.

- Traces must be accurate. The mechanism used must not slow down execution to the extent that the behavior of the system is no longer realistic.

- Tracing must be flexible. We must be able to choose the processes to be traced and turn tracing on and off at any time.

- The traces must be long enough to make possible the realistic simulation of very large caches.

A new trace generation mechanism can satisfy the first three requirements, but new trace management techniques are required to meet the fourth. Therefore our research extends into methods of managing and analyzing long traces.

This paper describes an ongoing project. The first portion presents the design of the trace generation mechanism and on-the-fly analysis. In the second part of the paper we review experiments tracing single and multiple user processes. The experiments validate our claim that long traces are both useful and necessary to understand the behavior of large multi-level cache systems. They provide insight into the usefulness of associativity and the effects of changing line size and overall cache size.

2. Trace Generation

2.1. Link-time Code Modification

Our trace generation technique involves modifying code at link time to insert tracing code whenever an address reference is to be recorded. When executed, the trace code computes an address and stores it in a *trace buffer*. Insertion of trace code is easy for the linker, since it depends only on the ability to determine basic block boundaries and to relocate addresses modified by the insertion of code. A linker must relocate addresses as part of its job, so it has all the information it needs to allow code insertion as well. By using link-time rather than compile-time techniques [6, 14], we are sure to automatically modify all executed code including that from libraries.

As a true RISC machine, the Titan references memory only during loads, stores and instruction fetches. The linker inserts a branch to trace code at each load and at each store. This trace code inserts into the trace buffer the data address to be referenced and a bit identifying the reference as a load or store.

The linker also inserts a branch to trace code at every basic block. A basic block is a sequence of instructions with a single entry and a single exit. The trace code for basic blocks inserts the first instruction address of the block and the size of the block into the trace buff-

er. An instruction address computed and written into the trace buffer is the address at which the instruction would have been located had the code not been expanded with trace branches. Thus, a trace resulting from the execution of expanded trace-linked code represents an execution of normally linked code. Since all of the instructions in a basic block are executed if the first one is, a single trace entry is sufficient to later simulate the correct sequence of instruction fetches. The current implementation does not record the interleaving of loads and stores with instruction fetches within each basic block. The information is obtainable and may be added later.

For efficiency, the current implementation minimizes memory accesses in the trace code by reserving 5 of the 64 available general purpose registers. The return address from trace code is saved in a reserved register, thereby avoiding a complex call/return mechanism. Registers also hold arguments to the trace routines and a value used to assure proper synchronization if an interrupt occurs during tracing.

2.2. Operating System Support

The trace buffer is shared by all processes and the kernel. User processes running specially linked code insert data into the shared buffer. Another user process is used to extract and analyze data from the buffer. The operating system manages and synchronizes access to the trace buffer.

At boot time, the buffer is allocated from the free page pool. The trace pages are permanently associated with the trace buffer and are not pageable. The current system runs on a Titan with 128 megabytes of memory. We use 32 megabytes for the trace buffer.

From within the operating system, the buffer is referenced directly using its physical addresses. To speed user references to the trace buffer, the buffer is mapped into the high end of every user's virtual address space. This mapping allows the user trace code to write directly to the trace buffer, referencing it by its virtual address. The 1-gigabyte address space is large enough that this does not constrain user programs.

Additional information can be inserted into the trace buffer by explicit calls to the trace code. On every transfer into or out of the kernel, a change mode entry is made in the trace buffer. The entry indicates whether the change is from user to kernel or kernel to user and which user process is involved. Sequences of virtual addresses generated by different processes can be distinguished in this way. Eventually, this will also allow us to distinguish physical addresses generated by the kernel.

The set of programs traced is determined by those that are specially linked. Only those processes that have been linked for tracing modify the trace buffer. They may run with programs that are not traced. Tracing may be turned on and off explicitly at chosen points during execution.

2.3. Process Switch Interval

Decreasing the execution speed of traced processes influences the accuracy of multiple process traces. If the process switch interval is unchanged, the number of original instructions executed between process switches is 8-12 times less than normal. Cache simulation based on such traces will predict erroneously poor cache performance. Since we are interested in simulating machines that are faster than the Titan, we increased the process switch interval 16 times, to 400,000 cycles. The average number of instructions executed between switches for a multiprocess benchmark is 175,000. This is because the Titan executes less than one instruction per cycle and because only compute-bound programs always use their entire time quantum on each switch. The ATUM microcode-based trace generation scheme can slow down timer interrupts to assure correct process switching intervals. We do not know of any other multiprocess trace generation system which attempts to take this into account.

2.4. Extracting the Traces from Memory

The system as described can quickly gather an address trace whose length is the size of the trace buffer. Tracing slows execution by 8 to 12 times. Even with a 32-megabyte trace buffer, the trace represents only about 1 second of untraced execution. While such traces are longer than those commonly available, they are not nearly long enough to analyze the behavior of a very large cache. To obtain longer traces, the data must be repeatedly extracted from the buffer.

Neither extraction nor analysis of the data can be done simultaneously with tracing because either is orders of magnitude slower than trace generation. Thus, all methods of dealing with long traces require that tracing be periodically interrupted for a significant amount of time. The challenge is to assure that the resulting traces are *seamless*, that is, that they reflect address reference patterns that would have occurred had the machine continued tracing without interruption. The interruption may entail extracting the partial trace and writing it, possibly in a compressed form, to some storage medium for later analysis. Alternatively, the partial trace might be analyzed immediately, eliminating the need to save the trace.

While we have implemented a mechanism to extract, compress, and write partial traces to high density tape[2], our preferred method is to analyze the trace data on the machine being traced as it is generated. When the trace buffer becomes full, the operating system turns off tracing and runs a high priority analysis process. Since the trace buffer is mapped into the analysis program's address space, the data can be directly accessed as an array.

Execution of the analysis program is controlled by the use of a variant *read* system call which blocks until the trace buffer becomes full. When the *read* returns, the analysis program may do anything it chooses with the trace data. The operating system guarantees that during the execution of the analysis program, tracing is turned off and traced programs are not scheduled for execution. When all current data in the buffer has been processed, a *read* is once again executed, tracing is turned back on, and traced user programs can execute.

---

[2]Using compression techniques described in [3], we have produced a set of eight Exabyte™ tapes containing 45 billion references from a variety of experiments. These are available from WRL.

2.5. Trace Analysis

Our cache analysis program is flexible and easily modifiable so that cache characteristics can be changed from run to run. It is small so that large user programs can be run without additional paging overhead. Since analysis is the slowest part of the process, taking easily 10 times as long as trace generation, we wanted it to be as fast as possible.

To achieve speed and small size, we sacrificed runtime flexibility and were satisfied with compile-time flexibility. A version of the program is compiled for each cache configuration, thus minimizing space allocated for run-time data structures and eliminating code not executed for that configuration.

The program works well, but remains a candidate for speed optimization. When simulating split instruction and data first-level caches and a direct-mapped second-level cache, trace generation and analysis together take about 100 times as long as untraced execution. For example, tracing and analyzing a run of TV, a timing verification program, extends the run time from 25 minutes to 45 hours.

3. Experiments with Single and Multiple Process User Traces

3.1. Base Architecture

Our assumptions concerning machine and memory design are based on discussions with our hardware engineers and represent some broadly accepted projections for workstations of the future. They define the basic architecture whose cache characteristics were then varied and simulated.

The only assumption related to the form of the traces is that of a RISC architecture in which instruction fetches and explicit data loads and stores are the only forms of memory reference. This makes the simple form of the traces useful though they contain no information about instruction types other than loads and stores.

The remaining characteristics are reflected in specific configurations of the analysis program. We assume a pipelined architecture where, in the absence of cache misses, a new instruction is started on every cycle. Since we do not consider delays other than those caused by cache misses, we count the base cost of an instruction as one cycle. The goal of memory hierarchy design is to add as little to this as possible.

We assume the machine has a 2ns cycle time and so is fast enough to require two levels of cache. The additional cost of going to the second-level cache, in case of a miss in the first-level cache, is assumed to be 12 cycles (24ns). The main memory latency is presumed to be 120 cycles (240ns) with a transfer rate of 8 bytes every 10ns. Thus for a 128 byte line, the retrieval cost of a second-level cache line from memory is 200 cycles (.4us.).

The first-level data cache is presumed to be a write-through cache with an associated 4 entry write buffer. First-level caches are virtually addressed.

The second-level cache is write back. It may be virtually or physically addressed. Since the traces contain virtual user addresses and we choose not to simulate full memory management, the analysis program uses pid hashing, a mapping based on trace addresses and process id, to distribute references in the large second-level cache [1]. This may be viewed as an implementation for a virtually addressed cache or as an approximation of the distribution provided by physical addressing.

3.2. Choice of User Programs

Our choice of benchmark user programs assumes that future machines will have much larger memories and that programs will be written to use that memory. Ideally, the programs should characterize the average workload of a future system, a difficult task at best. Nearly every program we have chosen to trace is real and currently in use on existing large machines. Many are memory hogs by today's standards because the problems they are solving are inherently large.

We have traced many different programs but will focus on the following four examples in this paper.

- **TV** is a timing verifier for VLSI circuits that was written in Pascal and is in regular use at our lab [9]. It generates a linked data structure and then traverses it. The program is traced while analyzing a CPU chip with 180,000 transistors. This run requires 96 Mbytes of memory.

- **SOR** executes a Fortran implementation of the successive overrelaxation algorithm using sparse matrices [4, 10]. It operates on a 800,000 by 200,000 sparse matrix with approximately 4 million (0.0025%) non-zero entries and takes 62 Mbytes.

- **Tree** is a compiled Scheme program [2], which builds a tree data structure and then searches for the largest element in the tree. The implementation of Scheme uses a garbage collection algorithm in which memory space is split into two halves. When no memory is left in one of the halves, data is compacted into the empty half. It uses 64Mbytes of memory.

- **Mult** is a multiprogramming workload consisting of:

  - a Unix *make* run compiling (from C) portions of the *Magic* VLSI editor [11] source code

  - *grr* printed circuit board router [5] routing the DECstation 3100 printed circuit board

  - *Magic* design rule checking the MultiTitan CPU chip

  - *Tree* on a smaller problem given 10Mbytes of working space

  - another *make* run that links the *Magic* code

  - an infinitely looping shell of interactive commands (*cp, cat, ex, rm, ps -aux,* and *ls -l /**)

This set of programs uses approximately 75 Mbytes of memory.

Figure 3-1 contains some characteristics of the example traces. Not surprisingly, the number of instructions as a percent of memory references is higher than in

User Program Trace Information				
	Tree	Tv	Sor	Mult
References (billions)	5.4	17.1	9.6	7.6
Instructions (% of refs)	67.2	72.9	73.2	68.5
Loads (% of instrs)	30.3	26.8	28.1	30.6
Stores (% of instrs)	18.6	10.4	8.2	15.4

Figure 3-1: User trace characteristics

CISC programs. The average percent of references that are instructions is 70.5%, whereas the average value for traces examined in [8] was 53.3%. All of the programs were compiled with all available optimization including global register allocation [15].

3.3. *CPI* as a Measure of Cache Behavior

The most common measure of cache performance is the *miss ratio*, the fraction of requests that are not satisfied by a cache. Miss ratio is a useful measure for comparing individual caches, but it does not give a clear picture of the effect of a cache's performance on the performance of the machine as a whole, or of the relative importance of the performance of each cache in a multi-cache system. For example, one cache may have a much higher miss ratio than another, but be used much less frequently and result in less overall performance degradation than the first.

To get a better picture of performance in a multi-cache system, we compute *CPI*, the average *cycles per instruction*. *CPI* accounts for variations in the number of references to the different caches and differences in the costs of misses to the caches. It can be broken down into the components contributed by each part of the memory hierarchy. We are concerned only with memory delays and ignore all other forms of pipeline stalls. In the absence of memory delays, one instruction is issued per cycle. Therefore, for our base machine the *CPI* over some execution interval is:

$$CPI = 1 + CPI_{data} + CPI_{inst} + CPI_{level2} + CPI_{wtbuf}$$

where $CPI_{cache-type}$ is the contribution of a cache and CPI_{wtbuf} is the contribution of the write buffer. If for each cache,

$m_{cache-type}$ = number of misses during the interval

$c_{cache-type}$ = cost in cycles of a miss

i = the number of instructions in the interval

then

$$CPI_{cache-type} = (m_{cache-type} \times c_{cache-type})/i$$

The goal is to minimize the *CPI*.

CPI is an architecturally dependent measure, but machine designers are interested in the performance of a specific architecture rather than cache performance in a vacuum. *CPI* tells much more about the performance of our base architecture than do the miss ratios of the individual caches.

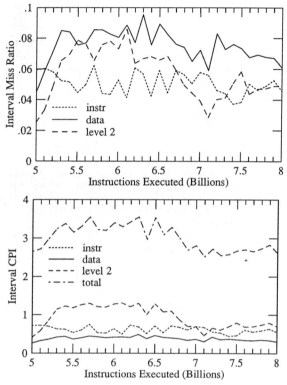

Figure 3-2: Interval miss ratios and interval *CPI*s

The miss ratios (top) and *CPI*s (bottom) were measured at intervals of 100 million instructions during a run of Mult. The instruction and data caches are both 4K bytes with 16 byte lines. The second-level cache is 512K bytes with 128 byte lines.

For example, the top graph in Figure 3-2 shows the miss ratios for the three caches during 3 billion instructions from a run of the Mult set of programs. The bottom graph shows the corresponding *CPI* and the CPI_{cache} for each cache. While the miss ratio for the data cache usually exceeds that of the instruction and second-level caches, its actual contribution to the *CPI* is much smaller than that of the instruction or second-level caches. The *CPI* graph also shows that the second-level cache often contributes nearly twice as much to the overall performance degradation as either the instruction or data cache.

In the rest of this paper, we will present trace results in terms of two different measures of *CPI*, the *interval CPI* and the *cumulative CPI*. The *interval CPI* is measured at regular intervals over the course of a run, and at each point is the average for the previous interval. The *cumulative CPI* is the *CPI* averaged over the entire preceding portion of a run.

3.4. Long Traces are Nice and Necessary

Some of our first simulations showed that we need very long traces to understand the behavior of large caches. A dramatic example is shown in Figure 3-3, which shows 1.5 billion instructions of a run of TV that executed for 12.5 billion instructions. Each point on the graph represents an average *CPI* over the previous 10 million instructions, which is about the entire length of most previously available traces. A technique that examined only 10 million instructions could conclude that the *CPI* was anywhere between 1.7 and 6.8.

The situation is not always this extreme. This part of the execution is processing a large amount of data and the second-level cache is thrashing; the *CPI* for the previous 9 billion instructions was nearly constant. Without the broader context provided by a long trace, however, there is no way to know whether a shorter trace is typical.

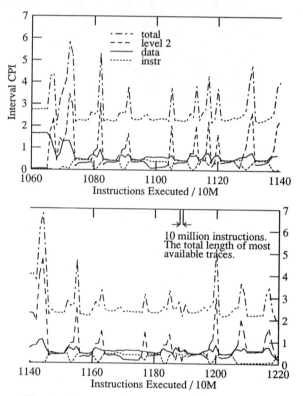

Figure 3-3: Interval *CPI*s for TV in two parts

This example used a 4K byte instruction cache with 64 byte lines, a 4K byte data cache with 32 byte lines, and a 16M byte second-level cache with 256 byte lines.

Other aspects of the program's behavior are revealed by a long trace. The two major phases of TV's computation are the max and min delay analysis, start about 1065 and 1140, respectively. Note the similarity in the graphs of CPI_{inst} for each phase. Eight subphases corresponding to the rising and falling of the four clock phases of the simulated chip are also clearly identifiable. The high points in the graphs of CPI_{data} and CPI_{level2} that match lows in the graph of CPI_{inst} are loops that execute small sections of code and go through large volumes of data. This information can be used to identify candidates for memory use optimization.

We have shown that very long traces give a great deal of information about a program's behavior and that using traces that are too short can lead to erroneous performance estimation. We have not yet dealt with the question of how long a trace must be to get valid performance data. How long is long enough? Unfortunately, that depends on the application or set of applications running. The graphs in Figure 3-4 show the extent of variations in interval CPI over the course of a run and between the different user programs. The cumulative CPI for the same runs, shown in Figure 3-5, shows how the long run average CPI behaves for longer and longer runs.

TV appears to stabilize early but shows extreme behavior only after 10 billion references. SOR begins its cyclic behavior after 1 billion references and the cumulative CPI stabilizes only after 10 billion references. In these two cases, a single number such as long-term CPI cannot adequately reflect the program's memory performance. The cumulative CPIs for Tree and Mult seem to stabilize reasonably well, and even so take at least 1 billion references to do so. It appears that even to have the cache warm up one needs a trace of many hundreds of millions of references!

3.5. Multiple Process Traces

A feature of our system is that we do not need to save traces. To analyze a program with a different cache organization, we need only rerun the program with a differently parameterized analysis program. This works well for single user programs that are deterministic; they generate identical traces on different runs. For multiple processes, however, the pattern of memory references is no longer deterministic, resulting in variations in cache behavior from run to run. The same set of programs can be interleaved differently depending on a variety of external uncontrollable factors. This is not necessarily bad. Differences in the results for the same set of programs represent differences that will occur on a real machine. On the other hand, variations between runs may make it difficult to understand precisely the significance of variations due to cache modifications.

Actually, the variations in the cumulative CPI between same sized runs are quite small, usually less than 1%. So far, we have been interested in comparing models that differ by much more than this. When more detailed distinctions between similar results are needed, we will modify the cache analysis program to simulate multiple caches at the same time.

3.6. Second-Level Cache Size

Next, we present the results of varying only the size of the second-level cache. We did not simulate the case without a second-level cache but can easily argue that its performance would be unacceptable. Let us assume that the first-level caches have miss ratios of 5%, and that the data cache is used 40% as often as the instruction cache. Without a second-level cache, a processor 20 times slower than ours would handle a miss in 10 cycles,

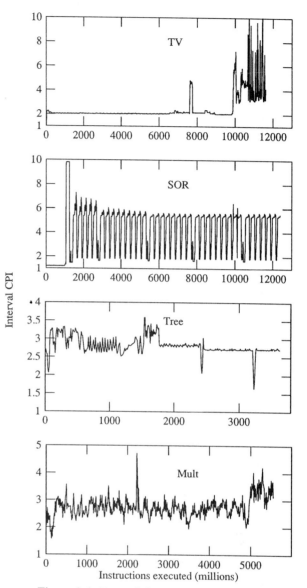

Figure 3-4: Interval CPI for the four examples.

These runs used 4K instruction and data caches with 16 byte lines and a 512K second-level cache with 128 byte lines. The interval size is 10M instructions. Note that scales on both axes vary.

resulting in a CPI of 1.7. In contrast, without a second-level cache, our faster processor would require 200 cycles to handle a miss, resulting in a CPI of 15! The factor of 20 in processor speed would give us a factor of only 2 in system speed.

Figure 3-6 shows the second-level cache behavior for three sizes of the second-level cache: 512K, 4M, and 16M. Except during the early part of the TV run, there is a significant reduction in CPI_{level2} when the cache size is increased to 4M but a considerably smaller improvement resulting from the jump to 16M.

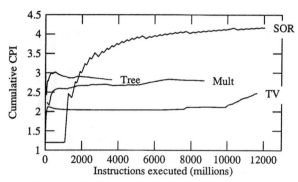

Figure 3-5: Cumulative *CPI* for the four examples.

This graph shows the cumulative *CPI* for the runs shown in Figure 3-4.

The cumulative *CPI*s shown in Figure 3-7 show the effect of cache size increases on long run average performance of the whole system. SOR, with its periodic behavior, is the only program that greatly benefits from an increase to 16M. This is most likely because it actually references a large part of its large address space. We can conclude from these examples that most of the programs we have chosen do not have large working sets. Mult is the most realistic of the examples, but its usefulness may be limited by the relatively small size of each of the individual programs it runs. There is definitely a need to put together much larger multiprocessing workloads.

3.7. Direct-Mapped vs Associative Second-Level Caches

Increasing associativity can decrease the miss ratio of a cache, but it may have a limited or even an adverse effect on system performance [7]. If a direct-mapped cache already has a low miss ratio, then reducing the miss ratio can only have a small effect on overall performance, even if associativity comes with no cost. In such cases, the implementation cost of associativity may outweigh its benefits. Increased associativity decreases the miss ratio but increases the cost of every cache reference.

We simulated direct-mapped and fully associative caches under the optimistic assumption that associativity is free. The improvement seen in the fully associative case should bound the improvement possible from a more realistic degree of set associativity. Figure 3-8 shows the cumulative *CPI* and miss ratios after 2.5 billion instructions for four runs of Mult. It compares the direct-mapped and associative cases for four second-level cache sizes. LRU replacement was used in the associative case. The results show that even in this most optimistic case, associativity is not effective for large caches (4M and 16M) where the *CPI* contribution is already small, but may be useful for 1M or 512K caches.

Cache implementors need to know limits for the cost in additional execution time of associativity. In other words, how much longer can each associative reference take before the *CPI* is worse than it is in the direct-mapped case? Using formulas derived in a longer version of this paper [3], we determined the ratio k of the cost of an associative reference to the cost of a direct-mapped reference at which the *CPI* is the same for both

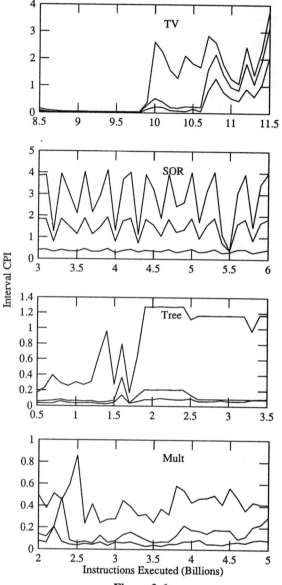

Figure 3-6:

Interval CPI_{level2} for three second-level cache sizes: 512K, 4M, and 16M. In each graph, the top line is for the 512K cache, the middle line is for the 4M cache, and the bottom line is for the 16M cache. The interval size is 100M instructions. Only partial runs are shown. Note the difference in the scale on both axes.

cases. Figure 3-9 shows this as a function of cache size for each of the benchmarks.

SOR is anomalous because in the 4M case, full associativity does worse than direct-mapped. In the graph, this shows up as the single point with k < 1. It is a result of the size of SOR's data structures and the cyclic way they are used. Evidently, the LRU replacement strategy

276

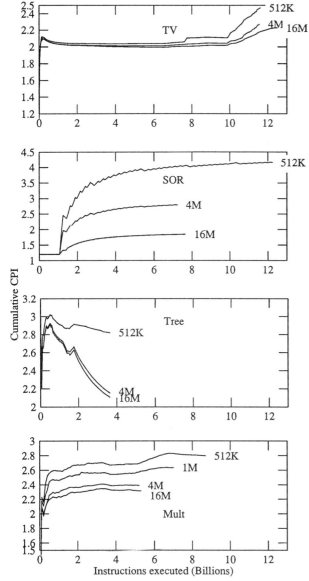

Figure 3-7: System performance with three cache sizes

Cumulative *CPI* for the four example programs with three second-level cache sizes: 512K, 4M, and 16M. Only SOR substantially benefits from an increase in size to 16M. Note the difference in scale on the y axis.

results in the frequent replacement of data items which are about to be used [13].

For the other examples, the graph shows that when the smallest (512KB) second-level cache is used, each associative reference can be 12-28% slower than a direct-mapped reference to perform identically. It must be faster than that to benefit from associativity. For the larger cache sizes, an associative reference must be very nearly as fast a direct-mapped reference for even full

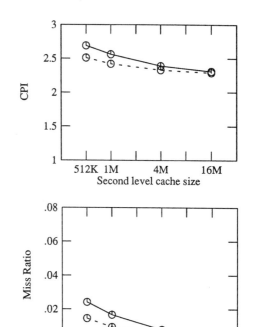

Figure 3-8:

Cumulative *CPI* (top) and miss ratios (bottom) for Mult with direct-mapped (solid) and fully associative (dotted) second-level caches of four sizes. Graphs are log (base 2) on the x axis.

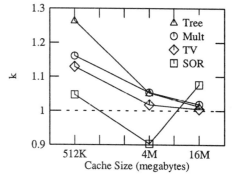

Figure 3-9:

k is the ratio of the cost in execution time of an associative reference to the cost of a direct-mapped reference. The points on the graph represent the value of k at which systems with direct-mapped and associative second-level caches have the same *CPI*. The x-axis is log scale base 2. Values for caches of 512K, 4M and 16M are shown.

associativity to break even. A more realistic degree of associativity is unlikely to pay off.

277

3.8. Line Size in First and Second-Level Caches

Experiments varying the line sizes of the first-level and second-level caches have shown quite clearly the danger of relying solely on miss ratio data for cache design decisions.

Figure 3-10 shows the effects on the *CPI* and miss ratios of doubling and then quadrupling the line size for the first-level caches. A retrieval time of 12 cycles was estimated for a 16 byte line size. An additional 4 cycles per 16 bytes were added to the retrieval cost for the longer line sizes, resulting in 16 and 24 cycle costs for the 32 and 64 byte lines.

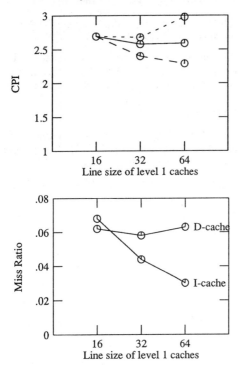

Figure 3-10: Three lines sizes for the first-level caches

Graphs show *CPI* (left) and miss ratios (right) for 16, 32, and 64-byte line sizes in the first-level instruction and data caches. Data is after 2.5 billion instructions of Mult. The first-level caches were 4K bytes each. The second-level cache was 512K bytes.

Not surprisingly, the instruction cache miss ratio decreases rather dramatically as the line size increases, but the data cache miss ratio changes very little. On the other hand, the *CPI* graph shows that miss ratio data is not sufficient to decide on the appropriate cache line size. The dotted line represents the case in which the data and instruction cache line sizes are both increased. This is clearly inadvisable. The solid line represents a constant data cache line size of 16 bytes and an increasing instruction cache line size. Even in this case, when one would expect the most benefit based on the miss ratio data, there is very little decrease in *CPI*.

The dashed line is the *CPI* that would result if the cost of retrieval were a constant 12 cycles for all three line sizes. This is the limit of the benefit to be gained

from line size increases. If it were possible to retrieve a 32-byte line in 12 cycles, the improvement in the *CPI* would be almost identical to that resulting from an 8-fold increase in the size of the second-level cache. This can be seen by comparing the above *CPI* graph to that in Figure 3-8.

Figure 3-11 shows the cumulative *CPI* and the second-level cache miss ratios for four different second-level cache line sizes at two cache sizes. With an assumed memory latency of 240ns (120 cycles) and transfer rate of 8 bytes per 10ns, the cost of a miss for the four line sizes is 140, 160, 200, and 280 cycles.

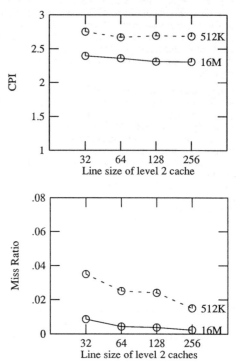

Figure 3-11: Four line sizes for a second-level cache

The graphs show cumulative *CPI* (left) and miss ratios (right) for four second-level cache line sizes. The solid lines represent a 16M cache. The dotted line represents a 512K cache. They are all for runs of Mult measured after 2.5 billion instructions.

For the large 16M second-level cache, the miss ratio and thus the CPI_{level2} are so low that improvements in overall performance resulting from line size increases are barely noticeable. Even for the smaller 512K second-level cache, where miss ratio data indicate that line size increases could improve performance, the *CPI* is nearly flat. The additional cost of retrieving longer lines offsets the lower miss ratio. Longer lines may result in more improvement in the *CPI* if early arriving portions of the long lines can be used before the entire line has been filled. We have yet to simulate that situation.

4. Conclusion

We have presented a new software method for generating extremely long traces of program execution. The system is designed to allow tracing of multiple user processes in different address spaces. On-the-fly analysis solves the storage problem for the billions of bytes generated. On-the-fly data collection allows long traces to be compacted and written to tape if necessary. The system is easy to use, requiring only the relinking of programs to be traced.

We have used the system to generate and analyze traces for a variety of single-user and multi-user programs. Our experiments confirm the need for long traces for the accurate analysis of very large caches. A conservative estimate of the number of references we have traced and analyzed is 500 billion. We have produced tapes of compressed traces containing 45 billion references.

The trace analysis has provided insights into the behavior of systems with large second-level caches. While secondary caches are clearly necessary, our traces do not currently justify sizes over 4M bytes. Only individual programs such as SOR with large working sets rather than just large address spaces benefit from the largest caches. Associativity in large second-level caches is not justified. Our analysis of various cache line sizes in both first-level and second-level caches show that miss ratio comparisons can be deceptive. System performance was surprisingly insensitive to second-level line size.

The project is not complete. In fact, the system was designed from the start to do simultaneous user and operating system tracing. We were recently able to generate long address traces for multiuser programs which include system references. This will be the subject of a future paper. Our future plans include porting the system to a more accessible architecture, probably the MIPS-based DECstation 3100. We hope that the system will make it possible to do detailed performance comparisons of operating systems such as Ultrix, Sprite and Mach.

References

1. Agarwal, A., Sites, R., and Horowitz, M. ATUM: A New Technique for Capturing Address Traces Using Microcode. 13th Annual Symposium on Computer Architecture, June, 1986, pp. 119-127.

2. Bartlett, J. F. SCHEME->C: A Portable Scheme-to-C Compiler. WRL Research Report 89/1, Digital Equipment Western Research Laboratory, 1989.

3. Borg, A., Kessler, R. E., Lazana, G. and Wall, D. Long Address Traces from RISC Machines: Generation and Analysis. Digital Equipment Western Research Laboratory, 1989.

4. De Leone, R. and Mangasarian, O. L. *Lecture Notes in Economics and Mathematical Systems 304*. Volume : Serial and Parallel Solution of Large Scale Linear Programs by Augmented Lagrangian Successive Overrelaxation. In *Optimization, Parallel Processing and Applications*, Kurzhanski, A., Neuman, K., and Pallaschke, D., Eds., , 1988, pp. 103-124.

5. Dion, J. Fast Printed Circuit Board Routing. WRL Research Report 88/1, Digital Equipment Western Research Laboratory, 1988.

6. Eggers, S. J., Keppel, D. R., Koldinger, E. J. and Levy, H. M. Techniques for Efficient Inline Tracing on a Shared-Memory Multiprocessor. SIGMETRICS International Conference on Measurement and Modeling of Computer Systems, May, 1990.

7. Hill, M. D. "A Case for Direct-Mapped Caches". *IEEE Computer 21*, 12 (December 1988), 25=40.

8. Hill, M., and Smith, A. Evaluating Associativity in CPU Caches. Computer Science Technical Report 823, University of Wisconsin, February, 1989. To appear in *IEEE Transactions on Computers* C-38(12),December,1989.

9. Jouppi, N. P. "Timing Analysis and Performance Improvement of MOS VLSI Designs". *IEEE Transactions on Computer Aided Design 6*, 4 (1987), 650-665.

10. Mangasarian, O. L. "Sparsity-Preserving SOR Algorithm for Separable Quadratic and Linear Programming". *Comput. and Ops. Res. 11*, 2 (1982).

11. Ousterhout, J., Hamachi, G., Mayo, R., Scott, W., and Taylor, G.S. "The Magic VLSI Layout System". *IEEE Design and Test of Computers 2*, 1 (February 1985), 19-30.

12. Smith, A. J. "Cache Memories". *ACM Computer Surveys 14*, 3 (September 1982), 473-530.

13. Smith, J. E. and Goodman, J. R. "Instuction Cache Replacement Policies and Organizations". *IEEE Transactions on Computers 34*, 3 (March 1985), 234-241. .

14. Stunkel, C., and Fuchs, W. TRAPEDS: Producing Traces for Multicomputers Via Execution Driven Simulation. International Conference on Measurement and Modeling of Computer Systems, , 1989.

15. Wall, D. W. Global Register Allocation at Linktime. SIGPLAN '86 Symposium on Compiler Construction, 1986, pp. 264-275. Also available as WRL Technical Report 86/3.

Unix is a registered trademark of AT&T.
Ultrix is a trademark of Digital Equipment Corporation.
Exabyte is a trademark of Exabyte Corporation.

Session 5B: Prolog/Potpourri

Fast Prolog with an Extended General Purpose Architecture

Bruce K. Holmer, Barton Sano, Michael Carlton, Peter Van Roy,
Ralph Haygood, William R. Bush, Alvin M. Despain

Computer Science Division
University of California, Berkeley

Joan M. Pendleton

Harvest VLSI Design Center, Inc.

Tep Dobry

Electrical Engineering Department
University of Hawaii, Manoa

ABSTRACT

Most Prolog machines have been based on specialized architectures. Our goal is to start with a general purpose architecture and determine a minimal set of extensions for high performance Prolog execution. We have developed both the architecture and optimizing compiler simultaneously, drawing on results of previous implementations. We find that most Prolog specific operations can be done satisfactorily in software; however, there is a crucial set of features that the architecture must support to achieve the best Prolog performance. The emphasis of this paper is on our architecture and instruction set. The costs and benefits of the special architectural features and instructions are analyzed. Simulated performance results are presented and indicate a peak compiled Prolog performance of 3.68 million logical inferences per second.

1. Introduction

Logic programming in general and Prolog [1] in particular have become popular for rapid software prototyping, natural language translation, and expert system programming. Prolog's use of dynamic typing, backtracking, and unification place heavy computational demands on general purpose computers. In an attempt to achieve ever higher performance, several special purpose architectures have been proposed and built. Early Prolog architectures [2] were microcoded interpreters. Because no compilation was done, performance was disappointing. Higher performance processors [3-6] have since been based on the Warren Abstract Machine (WAM) [7]. Their instruction sets were derived from the WAM to support execution of Prolog programs. These processors are special purpose, microcoded engines which depend on parallel execution of operations within each relatively coarse-grained instruction for high performance. Initial designs implemented only the instructions that supported the WAM and depended on a host processor for non-WAM computations. To support Prolog built-ins (primitive Prolog operations provided by the system) and system I/O, newer designs incorporate general purpose instructions to minimize dependence on a host. Alternatively, the use of a simple, non-WAM instruction set better supports compiler optimization. Several such special purpose reduced instruction set architectures have been proposed for logic programming [8-11]. These architectures include primitives which support the use of tagged data, pointer dereference, and multi-way branches. Our hypothesis is that providing support for both compiler optimization and low-level operations can best be accomplished by extending a simple general purpose architecture to support Prolog without compromising the general purpose performance.

The performance improvements of recent general purpose architectures over older architectures can be traced to research in which both the compiler and architecture were developed together [12-14]. Architectural features that cannot be used by the compiler or which cannot demonstrate performance improvement are not included. Likewise, architectural features are added which support often used primitive operations. We have adopted this approach from the beginning of our project.

It has been conjectured that commercial special purpose symbolic processing architectures are doomed because they are not commodity items, and consequently, economics prevent them from staying on the leading edge of implementation technology. However, if the architectural features necessary to improve symbolic performance are modest and do not interfere with the general purpose architecture, then as more chip area becomes available, future implementations of general purpose processors can deliver high performance symbolic computing in a standard product. We hope that our work is a step towards this result.

This paper presents the design of a processor based on the Berkeley Abstract Machine (BAM) architecture and motivates its design with the results of our preliminary studies. We also present a brief discussion of the optimizing compiler, a cost/benefit analysis of the architectural features, and the simulated performance. Familiarity with the WAM is helpful. Section 2 summarizes the processor architecture and hardware implementation. Section 3 presents the instruction set along with the results of our studies which motivated instruction selection. The compilation of Prolog programs is described in section 4, and in section 5 we present a cost/benefit analysis of the special features and instructions. Section 6 gives the performance results. The final section concludes with a summary of our results.

2. Processor Architecture and Implementation

The BAM processor is a general purpose, single chip, pipelined processor with extensions to support Prolog execution (Figure 1). Both data and instruction words are 32 bits, and most instructions execute in a single cycle. The main features for Prolog are tag manipulation (integrated into arithmetic and the memory system), a double-word data port to memory, special branch on tag support, and several instructions to support our execution model for Prolog.

The architecture is presented in detail along with our motivations in the subsections below. Retaining a core general purpose architecture imposes constraints on the symbolic extensions. For example, the processor should be able to handle tagged data items as single entities, with no special treatment for the tags. We discuss the ramifications of this on the word format and the virtual memory system. Then we present the architecture's register structure and memory interface. Finally, we present some details of the implementation such as the pipeline structure and our mechanism for

CH2887-8/90/0000/0282$01.00 © 1990 IEEE

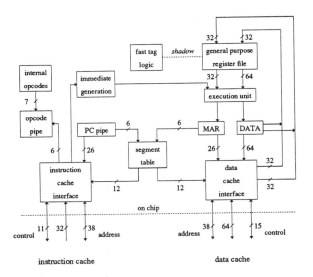

Figure 1
Block Diagram of the BAM Processor

multiple-cycle instructions.

2.1. Word Format

Prolog does not require the user to specify the type of a data item. This requires that run time type checking be implemented by adding a tag to each data item to encode the type of that item. Many Prolog processors handle the tag and value fields separately. This approach does not satisfy our goal of integrating tagging into a general purpose architecture. Instead, we use a standard 32-bit word length and place the tag in the most significant four bits of the word. Arithmetic computations and addresses, however, use the entire 32-bit word, so general purpose computations are not affected by Prolog's use of tags. Tag values fixed by the hardware are those for non-negative integers (0000) and negative integers (1111). This selection of tags for integers is a common technique used by Lisp implementations on general purpose machines [15]. We have also fixed the tag value for variable pointers (tvar = 0001) to increase the number of bits available for branch displacements in several Prolog specific instructions. All other tag values are software defined. Our Prolog implementation uses tags similar to those of the WAM.

2.2. Segmented Virtual Addresses

One consequence of using both the tag and value as an address is that each data type is mapped into its own area of virtual memory. For Prolog's execution model one wishes to place several data types in the same stack or heap. One possible solution is to mask (zero) the tag bits of the address before using it to access memory. This solution is not satisfactory when applied to applications not using tags (for example, C programs). To avoid this difficulty, we have introduced a segment table which maps the most significant six bits of an address to a twelve-bit value (Figure 2). An address before mapping is referred to as a short virtual address (SVA), and the 38-bit address resulting from the mapping is referred to as a long virtual address (LVA). This memory segmentation scheme is similar to the segmentation used in the 801 processor [16]. The 801 uses segmentation to extend the virtual address space; however, our primary motivation for using segmentation is to allow multiple data types to be mapped to the same LVA segment. Mapping two bits in addition to the tag bits allows the use of several memory areas for a given

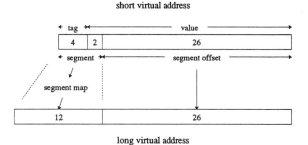

Figure 2
Segmentation of Virtual Address Space

data type, each area using a different mapping. At one extreme all data types can be mapped to the same LVA segment (this is equivalent to masking the most significant six address bits). At the other extreme, all SVA segments can be mapped to distinct LVA segments. In our current implementation of Prolog, variable, list, and structure pointers are mapped to the same LVA segment, whereas the environment/choice point stack, the trail stack, and the symbol table are mapped to separate segments.

Another use of segmentation is for sharing data in a multiprocessor system. In this case the 38-bit LVA is used as the global virtual address and sharing of data by cooperating processes is done at the segment level.

2.3. Memory Interface

The high memory bandwidth requirement of Prolog dictates separate instruction and data buses (Figure 1). In addition, we have expanded the data bus to double-word width. A double-word data bus is motivated by Carlson's study [17] of the architectural requirements of high performance Prolog processors. Carlson compiled Prolog programs into basic register transfer level operations and then compacted them into more complex instructions while enforcing microarchitectural constraints. His results show that the best performance/cost tradeoff occurs when the architecture provides a double-word port to data memory.

A double-word memory port improves the performance of term creation and speeds block transfers to and from environments and choice points. Some previous Prolog processors support fast choice point creation and restoration through the use of specialized buffers or shadow registers [3,9]. Such hardware solutions are costly and do not fit our goal of maintaining a general purpose architecture. Instead, we rely on double-word memory operations and on compiler optimization to minimize shallow backtracking [18].

Our processor design is tightly coupled with the cache design. We decided against on-chip caches since, in our case, it is more appropriate to use processor chip area for architectural features and use fast, dense static RAM chips for large caches. To speed cache accesses, however, protection violation and consistency checks and address tag comparison are done on-chip. More details about the cache interface are given in [19].

2.4. Base Architecture

All programmer visible processor registers are accessed as two sets of 32 registers: the general purpose register set and the special register set. The general purpose registers are used for procedure argument passing, temporary storage, and as stack pointers. The only general purpose register with a preassigned use is the continuation pointer (r31). This register is implicitly set to the return address by the call instruction. All other uses of the general purpose registers are defined by software convention.

The special registers provide access to the processor status word (PSW), program counter (PC), partial product/quotient register (PQ), segment mapping table, cache interface configuration registers, and a set of fifteen extra registers (s0-s14).

2.5. Implementation Details

The execution pipeline consists of five stages (Figure 3). All instructions which modify registers or memory do so in the last pipeline stage. Bypassing forwards available results of calculations to instructions following in the pipeline. Hardware interlocks are provided for both load and store delays. If data from a load instruction is used by the next instruction, then the next instruction is delayed by a cycle. Also, memory instructions immediately following a store are delayed by a cycle.

I	instruction fetch
R	register read
A	ALU
M	memory read
W	register/memory write

Figure 3
BAM Processor Execution Pipeline

All instructions are 32 bits with a 6-bit opcode and fixed source register format. Instruction execution is controlled by an opcode pipeline which operates in parallel with the execution pipeline. Each stage of the opcode pipe decodes the opcode associated with that stage of the execution pipeline. Multi-cycle instructions and conditional instructions are implemented using "internal opcodes" [20]. The internal opcodes of multi-cycle instructions are fetched from a PLA and inserted into the opcode pipeline. When an internal opcode is inserted, no instruction is fetched during that cycle. Thus a single external opcode can invoke a sequence of internal opcodes to provide for often used complex operations (for example, pointer dereferencing). Internal opcode insertion is also used for atomic synchronization operations, for pipeline interlock delays, and for trap and interrupt handling. Conditional execution is implemented by conditionally replacing an opcode in the opcode pipe with an internal opcode. Our design uses 55 external opcodes and 24 internal opcodes; of the internal opcodes, nine are related to traps (*trap*, *rft*), 13 implement multi-cycle instructions (*dref*, *stx*, *std*, *pushd*, *las*, *jmpr*), and two implement conditional operation instructions (*uni*, *pusht*).

"Fast tag logic" is used to implement single-cycle tag-compare-and-branch instructions. The fast tag logic consists of an extra register file which duplicates the tag portion of the general purpose register file and special tag comparison logic which allows quick tag comparison and branch. Previous Prolog processors [3] have also duplicated tag bits to accelerate branching on tag value.

The general purpose register file has two read ports (one single-word and one double-word) and two write ports (both single-word). This port structure provides the bandwidth required by single-cycle double-word memory accesses without greatly increasing the complexity of the register file design.

3. Instruction Set

In this section we present the BAM instruction set. The

instructions are divided into three groups: general purpose, Prolog inspired general purpose, and Prolog specific. The general purpose instructions are those which can be found in typical processors. The Prolog inspired instructions are those which are not often present in general purpose processors, but which can still be used for general computation. The remaining instructions are tailored specifically to the requirements of Prolog execution.

The general purpose instructions are summarized in Table 1. It is important to point out that all arithmetic and logic operations operate on the full 32-bit word. Also, conditional branches consist of separate compare and branch instructions. Compare instructions set or clear the TF (true-false) condition code bit, and the branch instructions take the branch when TF is set. Branches, jumps, and calls are delayed by one instruction. The instruction in a branch delay slot can always be executed (*bt*), annulled (turned into a nop) if the branch is taken (*btat*), or annulled if the branch is not taken (*btan*). Both directions of annulling are included because Prolog often favors annulling when the branch is taken (for example, branching out of straight-line code to the unification failure routine), whereas conditional branches to the top of a loop (common in procedural languages) favor annulling when the branch is not taken

The remainder of this section motivates and presents our extensions to the general purpose instruction set. A major influence on the design of these extensions was the simultaneous development of an optimizing Prolog compiler. The abstract machine used by the compiler was initially designed using a top-down approach [21]. We assumed a set of data structures similar to those used by the WAM. Knowledge of possible compiler optimizations was applied to the semantics of Prolog to decompose Prolog's general operations into their components. These components, the abstract instruction set, are the instructions and addressing modes required to compile Prolog operations into efficient code. Efficient translation of abstract machine instructions into the architectural instruction set was a prime influence in the first pass of the instruction set design.

In addition to our studies of abstract instruction sets, we investigated the microarchitectural requirements for high performance Prolog [17] and gathered execution statistics for the VLSI-PLM [4]. These investigations pointed out those microarchitectural features that would give the greatest performance gains and the Prolog operations that most need instruction set support.

3.1. Prolog Inspired General Purpose Instructions

Prolog inspired general purpose instructions are those instructions which support Prolog and which also may be useful in the implementation of other languages (Table 2). These instructions include load and store of immediates, single-cycle double-word load and store, and push and pop memory operations.

Immediates can be loaded, stored, or used in a comparison (*ldi*, *sti*, *stid*, *cmpi*). The immediates are tagged and are created by sign-extending a 12 or 17-bit immediate and replacing the four most significant bits with an immediate tag. Load immediate (*ldi*) is used for creating integers and atoms. Store immediate (*sti*) is an optimization of a *ldi*, *st* sequence and is used to bind an atom with a variable that is known at compile time to be unbound.

Double-word memory operations (*ldd*, *std*, *stdc*, *pushd*, *pushdc*) are motivated by Prolog's large memory bandwidth requirements. A double-word store or push is single-cycle only if the source registers form a consecutive, even/odd register pair, because only three registers, two of which must be adjacent, can be read per cycle from the register file. Although non-consecutive double store and push (*std*, *pushd*) are two-cycle instructions, this is offset by the

Instruction	Operands	Action	Cycles
ld, ldl	r(i), disp16, r(k)	r(k) ← M[r(i)+disp16] (ldl distinguishable to cache)	1
ldx	r(i), r(j), r(k)	r(k) ← M[r(i)+r(j)]	1
st, stu	r(i), r(k), disp16	M[r(k)+disp16] ← r(i) (stu distinguishable to cache)	1
stx	r(i), r(k), r(l)	M[r(k)+r(l)] ← r(i)	2
las	r(i), disp16, r(k)	r(k) ← M[r(i)+disp16]; M[r(i)+disp16] ← -1	2
add, sub, and, or, xor	r(i), r(j), r(k)	r(k) ← r(i) op r(j)	1
add32, sub32	r(i), r(j), r(k)	r(k) ← r(i) op r(j) (trap on signed 32-bit overflow)	1
addi, andi, ori, xori	r(i), imm16, r(k)	r(k) ← r(i) op imm16	1
sll, sra, srl	r(i), r(j), r(k)	r(k) ← r(i) op r(j)<4:0>	1
slli, srai, srli	r(i), imm5, r(k)	r(k) ← r(i) op imm5<4:0>	1
divs, mpys	r(i), r(j), r(k)	(r(k), PQ, TF) ← op(r(i), r(j), PQ, TF)	1
cmp	cond, r(i), r(j)	TF ← (r(i) cond r(j))	1
bt	addr26	if (TF) PC<25:0> ← addr26	1
btan	addr26	if (TF) PC<25:0> ← addr26; else annul next instruction	1
btat	addr26	if (TF) { PC<25:0> ← addr26; annul next instruction }	1
jmp	addr26	PC<25:0> ← addr26	1
jmpr	r(i), disp16	PC ← r(i) + disp16	2
call	addr26	r(31) ← PC+1; PC<25:0> ← addr26	1
rd	s(i), r(k)	r(k) ← s(i)	1
wr	r(i), s(k)	s(k) ← r(i)	1
trap	imm5	save PCs and PSW; set supervisor bit; PC ← 2*(32+imm5<4:0>)	6
rft		restore saved PSW; fetch at saved PCs	4

Table 1
General Purpose Instructions

Tables 1–3 summarize the BAM processor instruction set, divided into three groups: general purpose, Prolog-inspired general purpose, and Prolog specific. The first two columns give the instruction mnemonic and operands. The third column gives the instruction's register transfer description. R(i) denotes general purpose register i; s(i) denotes special register i; $disp\,n$ is a sign-extended n-bit displacement; $imm\,n$ is a sign-extended n-bit immediate; addr26 is a 26-bit segment offset; off1_8 and off2_8 are zero-extended 8-bit displacements; tag is a four-bit immediate tag value; and cond is one of twenty comparison conditions. M[x] is the memory location at address x. Tag^value specifies the tag insertion operation. Tvar represents the value of the unbound variable tag (0001). Cycle counts assume no pipeline stalls due to load or store delays. All branch and jump instructions are delayed, and the following instruction is executed unless it is annulled. The cycle count of *dref* depends on the number of memory operations (l) performed.

absence of a pipeline stall when they are immediately followed by a memory operation.

Push instructions are included to support compound term creation. Using branch-and-bound search techniques, we determined an optimal set of single-cycle instructions for creation of all possible two and three-word structures. This set of instructions is optimal in the sense that, for our microarchitecture, each structure is created in the smallest number of cycles. The resulting "compound term creation instruction set" favors the idiom of placing two words of data in registers and then moving them to memory using a double-word push. Push operations also allow the fill of the cache line from memory to be skipped if a push incurs a cache miss and also refers to the first word of the cache line [19]. This optimization has been used in a previous Prolog design [5]. The push instructions allow the amount of the increment to be specified, and any general purpose register can be used as a stack pointer.

Prolog requires that variable assignment be undone on backtracking. This unbinding of variables is implemented by recording variable addresses on a "trail" stack. The original WAM model requires several pointer comparisons to determine if trailing is necessary. Our implementation restricts variables to the global stack (which reduces the number of comparisons to one) and uses a compare instruction followed by a conditional push (*pusht*). The *pop* instruction is used during backtracking to retrieve variable addresses from the trail stack. The compiler can reduce the amount of trailing and detrailing through the use of flow analysis to determine when uninitialized variables [22] can be used (our use of uninitialized variables is different from [22] —we use the same tag for both initialized

and uninitialized variables and determine at compile time when destructive assignment is safe).

Unsigned maximum (*umax*) is provided to simplify the management of the environment and choice point stack pointers. Because these stacks are intermixed, allocation occurs at the maximum of the two stack pointer values.

3.2. Prolog Specific Instruction Set Support

Prolog specific instructions are those instructions which are tailored specifically for efficient execution of Prolog (Table 3). These instructions support tagged pointer creation, two and three-way branch on tag, pointer dereferencing, and unification of atoms.

3.2.1. Tagged Data Support

Pointer creation is accomplished by the load effective address (*lea*) instruction which calculates an address and then replaces the most significant four bits with an immediate tag. This instruction is used to create pointers to unbound variables and compound terms (lists and structures).

Type checking built-ins are supported with single-cycle compare-and-branch-on-tag instructions (*btgeq* and *btgne*). These instructions also allow the compiler to replace shallow backtracking with a conditional branch on an argument's tag.

Prolog allows unbound variables to be bound together. The resulting reference chain must be dereferenced before subsequent variable binding. WAM instructions always dereference their operands, often resulting in superfluous dereferencing. However, our

Instruction	Operands	Action	Cycles
ldi	tag, imm17, r(k)	r(k) ← tag^imm17	1
sti	tag, imm17, r(k)	M[r(k)] ← tag^imm17	1
stid	tag, imm12, r(k), disp5	M[r(k)+disp5] ← tag^imm12	1
cmpi	cond, r(i), tag, imm12	TF ← (r(i) cond tag^imm12)	1
ldd	r(i), disp11, r(k), r(l)	r(k) ← M[r(i)+disp11]; *(r(i)+disp11 even)* r(l) ← M[r(i)+disp11+1]	1
std	r(i), r(j), r(k), disp11	M[r(k)+disp11] ← r(i); *(r(k)+disp11 even)* M[r(k)+disp11+1] ← r(j)	2
stdc	r(i), r(k), disp16	M[r(k)+disp16] ← r(i); *(i and r(k)+disp16 even)* M[r(k)+disp16+1] ← r(i+1)	1
push	r(i), r(k), disp16	M[r(k)] ← r(i); r(k) ← r(k) + disp16	1
pusht	r(i), r(k), disp16	if (TF) { M[r(k)] ← r(i); r(k) ← r(k) + disp16 }	1
pushd	r(i), r(j), r(k), disp11	M[r(k)] ← r(i); M[r(k)+1] ← r(j); *(r(k) even)* r(k) ← r(k) + disp11	2
pushdc	r(i), r(k), disp16	M[r(k)] ← r(i); M[r(k)+1] ← r(i+1); *(i and r(k) even)* r(k) ← r(k) + disp16	1
pop	r(i), disp16, r(k)	r(k) ← M[r(i)-disp16]; r(i) ← r(i) - disp16	1
umin, umax	r(i), r(j), r(k)	r(k) ← unsigned_min/max(r(i), r(j))	1

Table 2

Prolog Inspired General Purpose Instructions

Instruction	Operands	Action	Cycles
lea	tag, r(i), disp12, r(k)	r(k) ← tag^(r(i)+disp12)	1
btgeq, btgne	tag, r(i), disp16	if (r(i)<31:28> =/≠ tag) { PC ← PC + disp16; annul next instruction }	1
dref	r(i)	if (r(i)<31:28> = tvar) *(l = number of memory refs)* do { tmp ← r(i); r(i) ← M[r(i)] } until ((r(i)<31:28> ≠ tvar) or (tmp = r(i)))	$l=0$: 1 $l\neq0$: 2+2l
add28, sub28, and28, or28, xor28	r(i), r(j), r(k)	r(k) ← r(i) **op** r(j) *(trap on non-integer tags)*	1
cmp28	cond, r(i), r(j)	TF ← (r(i) cond r(j)) *(trap on non-integer tags)*	1
uni	tag, imm17, r(i)	if (r(i)<31:28> = tvar) { M[r(i)] ← tag^imm17; TF ← 0 } else if (r(i) = tag^imm17) TF ← 0; else TF ← 1	1
swb	r(i), r(j), off1_8, off2_8	if ((r(i)<31:28> = tvar) and (r(j)<31:28> ≠ tvar)) PC ← PC + off1_8; else if ((r(i)<31:28> ≠ tvar) and (r(j)<31:28> = tvar)) { PC ← PC + off2_8; annul next instruction } else annul next instruction	1
swt	r(i), tag1, tag2, off1_8, off2_8	if (r(i)<31:28> = tag1) *(tag1 or tag2 is tvar)* PC ← PC + off1_8; else if (r(i)<31:28> = tag2) { PC ← PC + off2_8; annul next instruction } else annul next instruction	1

Table 3

Prolog Instructions

optimizing compiler keeps track of which variables are dereferenced and generates explicit dereferences only when necessary. Implementing dereference as a single instruction reduces static code size and allows dereference memory reads to be pipelined, resulting in a tighter loop than the equivalent assembly code [9, 10]. We use the same tag value for both unbound variables and reference pointers (unbound variables are self referential). The dereference instruction (*dref*) is implemented as a sequence of internal opcodes.

All of the basic arithmetic and compare instructions (*add*, *sub*, *and*, *or*, *xor*, *cmp*) have a version which traps on 28-bit overflow. These instructions operate on the full 32-bit word, but 28-bit overflow occurs if either of the sources or the result do not have integer tags (0000 or 1111). The trap on 28-bit overflow allows Prolog arithmetic operations to be compiled to fast, safe code which avoids extra instructions for tag overflow checking. If a 28-bit overflow does occur, the trap routine can signal an overflow error or convert the data into an alternative representation.

3.2.2. Unification Support

Unification is one of the primary operations of Prolog; it is used for argument passing, structure creation, structure decomposition, and pattern matching. Although general unification is a complex algorithm, if one is given information about the arguments being unified, the general algorithm can be greatly simplified. This is one of the advantages of the WAM instruction set over an interpreter. Our compiler takes this principle further and propagates information to simplify unification as much as possible.

Analysis of the primitives necessary to support unification of a Prolog variable with an atom [21] motivates the single-cycle unify-immediate instruction (*uni*) which binds the atom to the variable if the variable is unbound, and otherwise tests them for equality.

Unification of a Prolog variable with a compound term also benefits from special support. Analysis of the primitives necessary to support unification of a Prolog variable with a list or structure [21]

286

Program	Argument Type (%)			Cost (cycles)	
get_list	variable	list	other	swt	two-way
prover	18.7	80.5	0.8	1.20	1.40
meta_qsort	42.1	42.0	16.0	1.58	2.32
simple_analyzer	24.4	67.4	8.3	1.33	1.74
chat_parser	8.8	84.8	6.4	1.15	1.37
average	23.5	68.7	7.9	1.32	1.71
get_structure	variable	structure	other	swt	two-way
prover	26.7	73.3	0.0	1.27	1.53
meta_qsort	37.6	62.4	0.0	1.38	1.75
simple_analyzer	13.5	86.5	0.0	1.14	1.27
chat_parser	44.0	52.5	3.5	1.48	1.98
average	30.4	68.7	0.9	1.31	1.64

Table 4
WAM Variable/Compound Term Unification Statistics

This table gives the percent occurrence of the argument type for variable/compound term unification in the WAM (get_list and get_structure instructions). Columns 2–4 give the percent occurrence of variable, list/structure, and other types. The swt column gives the average time to execute the three-way branch assuming that the execution times for the three directions, (variable, list/structure, other), are (2, 1, 2) cycles respectively. Likewise, the two-way column assumes that the three-way branch is simulated using two two-way branches and that the execution times for the three directions are (3, 1, 4). The statistics for tables 4 and 5 were gathered using the VLSI-PLM [4] microarchitecture simulator.

motivates the switch-tag instruction (*swt*), a three-way branch based on the tag of one register. One direction of the branch is taken if the tag is an unbound variable; a second direction is taken if the tag matches a specified immediate tag (usually list or structure); and a third direction is taken for all other tags. The three-way branch could be implemented using two two-way branches, however, WAM execution statistics (Table 4) show that there is a small but significant performance advantage to the three-way branch.

The LOW RISC processor [8] provides a 5-way branch and the Carmel-2 processor [10] provides a 10-way branch based on the tag of a single register. WAM execution statistics show that such generality is unnecessary for unification of a Prolog variable with a compound term.

When the compiler cannot determine any information about the types of the arguments to be unified, then general unification must be used. In this case one can still take advantage of dynamical properties of the argument types. The common cases of general unification should be done quickly in-line and infrequent cases passed to a general unification subroutine. Analysis of WAM execution (Table 5) indicates that about 70% of all general unifications are simple bindings of an unbound variable with a nonvariable. These statistics motivate the switch-bind instruction (*swb*), a three-way branch based on the tags of two registers. The conditions of the three branch directions are: variable/nonvariable, nonvariable/variable, and otherwise (order of the arguments matters). This allows the common cases of variable/nonvariable and nonvariable/variable to be done in-line. A general unification subroutine is called for all other cases. Note that although the quick success and quick failure cases are simple to check for, their execution frequency is low enough that we have chosen not to do these checks in-line.

The Pegasus processor [9] supports general unification with a 16-way branch based on two tag bits from each of two registers. The LIBRA processor [11] has a "partial unify" instruction. This single-cycle instruction performs either a nop, a store, a call, or a branch depending on the tags and comparison of the two arguments. It executes the variable/nonvariable case of general unification in

Program	Argument Type (%)					
	quick success	quick failure	var nonvar	nonvar var	var var	recursive
prover	15.6	15.6	0.0	61.4	0.0	7.5
meta_qsort	0.0	0.0	0.0	50.5	49.5	0.0
simple_analyzer	0.1	2.3	13.3	70.5	11.5	2.1
chat_parser	0.3	11.8	13.6	69.3	2.3	2.5
average	4.0	7.4	6.7	62.9	15.8	3.0

Table 5
WAM General Unification Statistics

This table gives the percent occurrence of various argument types passed to general unification in the WAM (get_value and unify_value instructions). In the quick success column both arguments are identically equal. In the quick failure column both arguments are nonvariable and have unequal tags or both are atomic and are unequal. In the var/nonvar column the first argument is a variable and the second is a nonvariable. Likewise, in the nonvar/var column the first argument is nonvariable and the second is variable. In the var/var column both arguments are variable. The last column contains the remaining cases which must be passed to a recursive unification subroutine.

four cycles (not counting dereferencing of the arguments). Using switch-bind (*swb*), BAM executes this case in five cycles. Although the partial unify instruction of the LIBRA has a slight performance advantage, its complexity does not fit with our goal of minimally extending a general purpose architecture.

4. Compilation of Prolog

A significant aspect of our project was the simultaneous development of an optimizing Prolog compiler [21, 23]. The compiler incorporates techniques for determinism extraction and use of destructive assignment. The compiler accepts standard Prolog and produces code for a simple non-WAM abstract machine. Although the compiler uses stacks and data structures similar to WAM implementations, it does not use the WAM during compilation, but instead directly compiles to its own abstract machine. Automatic mode generation (type inferencing) is implemented using abstract interpretation [24]. It derives ground, uninitialized variable [22], and dereference modes. Optimizations are still being implemented, and we expect our performance numbers to improve compared to the numbers listed in the following sections.

Compilation of Prolog is done in three stages. First, the compiler produces code for its abstract machine. Second, this code is macro-expanded into the BAM instruction set. Finally, the BAM code is optimized by a peephole optimizer and instruction reordering stage that maximizes the use of the double-word bus and minimizes the number of nops and pipeline stalls.

5. Cost/Benefit Analysis of Architectural Features and Instructions

In section 3 we motivated our instruction selection based on several sources of information: work on abstract instruction sets for compilers, bottom-up analysis of microarchitectural requirements for high performance Prolog, and analysis of WAM execution statistics. In this section we give a more rigorous validation of the architectural design and instruction selection by analyzing the cost and performance benefits of each special purpose feature and instruction. There has been some work to determine such results for other designs [9, 10, 15], but no complete analysis has been done.

5.1. Cost of Features

Table 6 shows the implementation cost of those features which

Feature	Active area	Design complexity	Instructions affected
segment mapping	4.8%	~100% compiled	—
tagged-immediate	2.2%	100% compiled	ldi, cmpi, sti, stid, lea, uni
double-word memory port	1.9%	95% compiled; 5% by hand	ldd, std, stdc, pushd, pushdc
fast tag logic	1.6%	~100% compiled	btgeq, btgne, swt, swb, dref, uni
multi-cycle/conditional	0.1%	100% compiled	stx, std, pushd, pusht, dref, uni
tag overflow detect	~0.0%	100% by hand (10 gates)	cmp28, add28, sub28, and28, or28, xor28
total special features	10.6%	99% compiled; 1% by hand	

Table 6
Cost of Special Architectural Features

For each special feature of the BAM processor, this table gives the percentage of active area (transistors and wires) required to implement the feature, the design complexity of the layout, and a list of instructions which depend on the feature. The design complexity is given as a percentage of the layout that was automatically generated (using tilers, routers, etc.) and the percentage that was laid out by hand. ~100% compiled indicates that less than 30 gates were placed by hand. Multi-cycle/conditional is a subset of internal opcodes—the 0.1% active area refers to the entire internal opcode implementation.

extend the BAM beyond a general purpose architecture. Implementation cost is expressed in terms of chip area required to implement the feature and in terms of VLSI design effort required. The chip area is measured in percent of total active area which includes both transistor and wiring area. The chip contains approximately 110,000 transistors, and the total active area is 91 square millimeters using 1.2 μ CMOS. The VLSI layout was done using a symbolic layout editor with custom designed, parameterized cells. The building blocks were assembled into larger units using a datapath compiler, PLA compiler, tiler, and router. The design effort for each feature is given as a percentage of its design that was automatically performed by the design tools. The last column of Table 6 lists those instructions which depend on a given feature. We do not give each feature's effect on the cycle time, since the microarchitecture and logic designs were done carefully to prevent these features from being on the critical path.

Segment mapping requires the greatest area of the special features. This area is primarily due to the 32 by 24-bit register file which contains the segment map. This register file is used to extend the address space as well as perform tag mapping. A smaller register file tailored to tag mapping alone would take less area. The next greatest area consuming feature is the tagged-immediate generation circuitry. This is due in part to the use of three distinct instruction formats for tagged-immediates. The double-word memory port requires extra ports on the general purpose register file to support the increased bandwidth. The area listed is the difference in size between our four/five-port register file and the more usual three-port register file. The extra pads required by the double-word bus are not included in the cost. After the fast tag logic, the remaining features use a very small portion of the total active area.

5.2. Benefits of Features

To determine the performance benefit of each feature, we calculated the cycle count increase caused by omitting the use of all instructions that depend on the feature [25]. For example, if omitting the instructions *ldd, std, stdc, pushd,* and *pushdc* increases execution time from 100 cycles to 111 cycles, then the performance benefit due to the double-word memory port is 11%. An instruction is omitted by replacing it with its macro-expansion into simpler instructions. An effort was made to determine optimal expansions, and after macro-expansion, peephole optimization and instruction reordering are performed. Omission of segment mapping requires that explicit instructions be inserted to mask tag bits before tagged-pointers are used as addresses. A detailed description of the analysis techniques is given in [26].

Table 7 lists the performance benefit of the features given in

Table 6. Fast tag logic, double-word memory port, segment mapping, multi-cycle support, and tagged-immediate support are consistently important features. Tag overflow detection is important only in programs which make heavy use of integer arithmetic. The overall Prolog support column is determined by using only the instructions from Table 1 (and non-tagged versions of *ldi* and *cmpi*), omitting segment mapping and all instructions in Tables 2 and 3.

To summarize, the specialized support added for Prolog does not require unreasonable amounts of chip space or hand layout (11% active area for all Prolog related features), and it provides a performance benefit of 70%.

5.3. Benefits of Individual Instructions

Table 8 provides a similar analysis applied to individual instructions or instruction groups, rather than to architectural features. Significant (greater than one percent) performance benefit is obtained from a majority of the special purpose instructions (*dref, umin/umax, lea, push/d/c, swt,* and *btgeq/ne*). The multi-cycle pointer dereference instruction (*dref*) has an average execution time of 1.6 cycles. Macro-expansion of *dref* into an explicit loop increases the average dereference time to 2.2 cycles. Although the benefit of *dref* per dereference is only 0.6 cycle, the total performance benefit is significant because of its frequent use. Some of the smaller benchmarks, however, show no benefit for *dref* due to the complete elimination of dereferencing by compiler optimization. Unsigned maximum (*umax*) is used during environment and choice point creation. Omission of *umax* causes the time to determine the top of stack to increase from one to three cycles. Tagged-pointer creation (*lea*) is a frequent operation, and its omission adds an extra cycle for tag insertion (using *or*). Elimination of auto-increment addressing (*push, pushd, pushdc*) requires one extra cycle for each block allocation. The three-way branch on tag (*swt*) can be replaced by two *btgeq* instructions, adding an extra cycle to two of the branch directions. Elimination of the two-way branch on tag (*btgeq/ne*) would require a two instruction compare and branch.

The remaining instructions have less than one percent average performance benefit. Because the VLSI-PLM spends about 5% of its time trailing variable addresses, we included special support in the BAM (*pusht*). However, due to the compiler's use of uninitialized variables, which do not have to be trailed, trailing time is reduced to 1.4% in the BAM. Omitting *pusht* causes a slow down of 0.7%, which corresponds to trail time increasing from 2 to 3 cycles. Preliminary analysis using macro-expanded WAM for the chat_parser benchmark indicated that the benefit for *pop* would be 1.5%. Compiler optimization of trailing has reduced this result. Similarly, compiler optimization reduces the number of general unifications,

Benchmark	Feature Performance Benefit (%)						
	fast tag logic	double-word memory port	segment mapping	multi-cycle conditional	tagged-immediate	tag overflow detect	all Prolog support
log10	2.4	8.1	5.3	0.0	9.3	0.0	30.0
ops8	6.6	14.7	4.2	2.6	9.2	0.6	42.6
times10	6.2	14.1	4.0	1.0	12.0	0.0	47.1
divide10	5.6	15.4	3.6	1.7	13.5	0.0	46.9
nreverse	14.0	14.6	22.1	0.7	25.0	0.0	99.8
qsort	11.1	4.1	10.6	1.6	14.0	13.0	75.5
serialise	24.0	18.2	9.4	7.0	5.0	2.3	83.5
query	0.0	3.6	1.7	0.0	2.3	2.7	12.6
mu	36.0	14.5	20.0	15.3	8.0	0.1	95.9
queens_8	6.9	17.0	5.9	0.7	3.0	34.6	105.9
poly_10	18.8	9.8	8.9	3.3	9.7	3.1	71.5
tak	0.0	8.3	4.2	2.8	4.2	28.1	66.6
prover	18.3	20.6	7.4	6.3	9.0	0.0	72.6
meta_qsort	19.6	17.6	12.8	10.7	9.1	0.6	72.3
simple_analyzer	20.5	12.4	12.3	10.6	5.6	5.0	67.6
chat_parser	17.3	17.9	8.8	8.8	7.7	0.0	67.7
average	18.9	17.1	10.3	9.1	7.9	1.4	70.1

Table 7
Performance Benefit of Special Architectural Features

Benchmark	Instruction Performance Benefit (%)										
	dref	umin umax	lea	push pushd/c	swt	btgeq btgne	pusht	swb	uni	sti stid	pop
log10	0.0	0.3	5.3	2.2	0.2	1.9	0.0	0.0	0.0	0.2	0.0
ops8	0.9	3.2	5.0	3.2	0.9	2.5	0.3	0.0	0.0	0.4	0.0
times10	0.0	4.1	5.9	4.2	1.1	2.0	0.0	0.0	0.0	1.1	0.0
divide10	0.0	3.7	7.1	3.8	1.0	1.8	0.0	0.0	0.0	1.0	0.0
nreverse	0.0	1.4	22.8	11.0	11.0	0.0	0.0	0.0	0.0	0.0	0.0
qsort	0.0	1.6	10.6	3.7	4.5	0.0	0.0	0.0	0.0	0.0	0.0
serialise	3.7	6.1	2.8	2.6	2.5	1.1	0.5	1.4	0.0	0.1	0.4
query	0.0	0.1	0.6	0.0	0.0	0.0	0.0	0.0	0.0	1.1	0.0
mu	10.9	1.6	3.4	2.7	4.8	4.4	2.1	0.5	0.7	0.0	0.3
queens_8	0.0	2.6	2.3	3.3	2.9	1.3	0.0	0.0	0.0	0.0	0.0
poly_10	0.9	3.2	5.4	2.8	2.8	0.8	0.4	0.1	0.0	0.0	0.0
tak	0.0	2.8	4.2	0.0	0.0	0.0	0.0	0.0	0.0	0.0	0.0
prover	1.3	3.4	2.3	3.5	2.2	1.2	0.3	0.2	0.7	0.4	0.2
meta_qsort	5.8	5.0	3.2	2.4	2.6	0.8	0.7	0.5	0.1	0.2	0.2
simple_analyzer	7.3	3.3	2.5	1.4	1.6	1.5	0.3	0.2	0.1	0.3	0.0
chat_parser	3.5	3.3	3.0	2.4	1.7	1.6	1.6	1.6	0.7	0.2	0.7
average	4.5	3.8	2.8	2.4	2.0	1.3	0.7	0.6	0.4	0.3	0.3

Table 8
Performance Benefit of Individual Instructions

Tables 7 and 8 give the percent performance benefit for each special feature and instruction of the BAM processor. The last column of Table 7 lists the performance benefit of segment mapping and all instructions given in Tables 2 and 3. Averages are calculated using only the last four benchmarks which are representative of well written, medium sized (100-1000 line) Prolog programs. All benchmarks are compiled with automatic mode generation, and cache effects are not included.

minimizing the benefit of *swb*. Our initial studies also overestimated the benefits of special support for unification of atoms (*uni*, *sti*, *stid*). Although *pusht*, *swb*, *pop*, *uni*, *sti*, and *stid* provide marginal performance benefit, their implementation uses only features already required by other instructions.

An interesting conclusion about the number of directions needed in multi-way branches can be made from these measurements. Multi-way branches are implemented in the BAM with the *swt* and *swb* instructions, which are both single-cycle three-way branches (Table 3). *Swt* is used for unification of compound terms, for which greater than a three-way branch is not needed (Table 4 and [21]). *Swb* is used for unification of terms whose types are unknown at compile time. It takes care of 70% of these cases (Table 5), which gives an 0.6% execution time improvement (Table 8). If some

single-cycle branch took care of 100% of these cases, we calculate the further improvement would be about 0.7%. Given the additional complexity that such a branch implies, we conclude that a multi-way branch with more than three directions is not effective for Prolog.

6. Performance Results

Table 9 compares the performance of the BAM processor to that of other Prolog systems. The results for BAM are simulated assuming a 30 MHz clock and include overhead due to cache misses [19]. The simulated system has 128 KB instruction and data caches. The caches are direct mapped and use a write back policy. They are run in warm start, that is, each benchmark is run twice and the results of the first run are ignored. Cache effects are significant only for the last five programs in Table 9. The cache overhead is greatest for

289

Benchmark	Quintus		VLSI-PLM		KCM		BAM no modes		BAM auto modes	
log10	0.468	(31.5)	0.137	(9.22)	0.039	(2.62)	0.0263	(1.77)	0.0149	(1.00)
ops8	0.767	(40.8)	0.177	(9.41)	0.059	(3.14)	0.0289	(1.54)	0.0188	(1.00)
times10	1.05	(39.4)	0.247	(9.26)	0.082	(3.08)	0.0403	(1.51)	0.0267	(1.00)
divide10	1.27	(42.4)	0.287	(9.58)	0.091	(3.04)	0.0433	(1.44)	0.0300	(1.00)
nreverse	4.87	(36.2)	2.10	(15.6)	0.65	(4.83)	0.308	(2.28)	0.135	(1.00)
qsort	16.9	(86.2)	4.24	(21.6)	1.32	(6.73)	0.371	(1.89)	0.196	(1.00)
serialise	10.8	(23.0)	2.47	(5.27)	1.22	(2.60)	0.516	(1.10)	0.469	(1.00)
query	72.3	(18.9)	–		12.6	(3.30)	5.22	(1.37)	3.82	(1.00)
mu	28.3	(35.0)	5.18	(6.41)	–		1.02	(1.26)	0.808	(1.00)
prover	24.1	(26.2)	6.83	(7.41)	–		1.07	(1.16)	0.921	(1.00)
queens_8	73.7	(65.1)	28.8	(25.4)	–		1.88	(1.66)	1.13	(1.00)
meta_qsort	231	(49.0)	44.5	(9.45)	–		5.25	(1.11)	4.71	(1.00)
simple_analyzer	636	(19.0)	–		–		36.9	(1.10)	33.4	(1.00)
poly_10	1420	(40.0)	307	(8.65)	–		62.5	(1.76)	35.5	(1.00)
tak	3300	(62.8)	940	(17.9)	–		71.1	(1.35)	52.6	(1.00)
chat_parser	3590	(27.0)	781	(5.87)	–		161	(1.21)	133	(1.00)
geometric mean		(36.7)		(10.3)		(3.48)		(1.44)		(1.00)

Table 9

Performance Results

This table compares the performance of BAM with that of several other Prolog implementations for which benchmark results are available—Quintus Prolog, the VLSI-PLM, and the KCM. Each result is presented as a time in milliseconds followed in parentheses by the ratio to the best BAM time. The Quintus Prolog results are for compiled code executing under Quintus Prolog Release 2.0 on a Sun 3/60. The VLSI-PLM [4] results are simulated assuming a cycle time of 100 ns with no cache misses. The KCM results [6] are derived from actual measurements of a system with a cycle time of 80 ns. The BAM results are simulated assuming a 30 MHz clock and 128 KB instruction and data caches [19]. For BAM, the *auto modes* and *no modes* columns give results with and without automatic mode generation. Results are presented for the well-known Warren benchmarks (the first eight in the table), of which query is modified to use integer division in place of the original floating point; for mu, which proves a theorem of Hofstadter's "mu-math"; for prover, a simple theorem prover; for queens_8, which solves the eight queens problem using an incremental generate-and-test strategy; for meta_qsort, a meta-interpreter running Warren's qsort; for simple_analyzer, a flow analyzer analyzing Warren's qsort; for poly_10, which symbolically raises a polynomial to the tenth power; for tak, which executes recursive integer arithmetic; and for chat_parser, which parses a set of English sentences. Further information about the benchmarks may be found in [28]. The benchmarks are available by anonymous ftp from arpa.berkeley.edu.

simple_analyzer, poly_10, and tak; for these programs the overhead ranges from 11% to 38%. For meta_qsort and chat_parser the overhead is less than 3%.

Although programs are usually compiled with automatic mode generation, we have included numbers without modes to show the effect on performance. The average performance improvement due to automatic mode generation is 1.44. The number is higher for some of the smaller benchmarks because mode generation is able to do a better job for them. For example, the qsort and queens_8 benchmarks perform well because the mode information allows the compiler to eliminate most choice point creation and replace variable binding with destructive assignment. The number is lower for the simple_analyzer benchmark because it uses built-in predicates heavily.

The KCM [6], one of the best WAM implementations, has a relatively large amount of specialized hardware to execute a WAM-like instruction set efficiently, whereas the BAM processor uses modest hardware to support an optimizing compiler. We find that the speed advantage of the BAM over the KCM is equal to or greater than the cycle time ratio.

A common measure of Prolog speed is logical inferences per second (LIPS). In general this quantity is ambiguous; however, it is well defined for the naive reverse benchmark. The execution time for naive reverse with automatic modes (Table 9) gives a performance of 3.68 million LIPS.

Table 10 compares the static code sizes of the BAM, the KCM [6], and the SPUR [27] relative to the PLM [3]. Macro expansion of WAM code into SPUR instructions causes the large code size of the SPUR. Static code size for the BAM is surprisingly small, only

slightly larger than that of the KCM. This is due to direct compilation into simple instructions, the success of flow analysis in reducing code size, and the appropriateness of the BAM instruction set for Prolog.

	BAM / PLM	KCM / PLM	SPUR / PLM
bytes	3.1	3.0	14.1
instructions	2.6	1.1	12.0

Table 10

Static code size ratios

This table gives the static code sizes of the BAM, the KCM, and the SPUR relative to the PLM, a micro-coded implementation of the WAM [3]. The BAM code size is calculated from prover, meta_qsort, simple_analyzer, and chat_parser. The KCM code size is from [6]. The SPUR code size is from [27].

7. Conclusions

The primary goal of our research has been to determine a minimal set of extensions to a general purpose architecture necessary for achieving high performance logic programming. At the same time, however, performance of the general purpose architecture has not been compromised. We have identified tagged-immediate support, segment mapping, double-word memory bus, special logic for fast branch on tag, and multi-cycle instruction support as important Prolog specific features. Our measurements justify the utility of push, pointer dereference, and tagged-pointer creation instructions. Our special instructions for trailing and unification of atoms, however, are of marginal benefit. Finally, we conclude that a multi-way branch with more than three directions is not effective for Prolog.

We have demonstrated that one can extend a general purpose architecture to include explicit support for symbolic languages such as Prolog with modest increase in chip area (11%) and yet attain a significant performance benefit (70%).

ACKNOWLEDGEMENT

First and foremost, we would like to thank Charlie Burns of Harvest VLSI for continued CAD tool development as required by the BAM processor and for help with the processor layout. We would also like to thank Dave Chenevert of Sun Microsystems, for key contributions to CAD algorithms and other assistance. And special thanks to Wayne Rosing—VP ESG at Sun Microsystems, for making computers, CAD tools, and other resources available.

Thanks to Jim Testa for encouraging us to start a new Prolog chip design and to Georges Smine for work on cache board design and simulation. Thanks to Vason Srini, Ashok Singhal, and Hervé Touati for comments on earlier drafts of this paper. We also acknowledge the members of the Aquarius project.

We wish to thank Zycad Corporation for the use of their N.2 hardware simulation tools that simplified the task of simulating the microarchitecture. This work is partially funded by the Defense Advance Research Projects Agency (DARPA) and monitored by the Office of Naval Research under contract No. N00014-88-K-0579. Equipment and other support for the project has been provided by SUN, DEC, ESL, and Xenologic.

References

1. L. Sterling and E. Shapiro, *The Art of Prolog*, MIT Press, 1986.

2. M. Yokota, A. Yamamoto, K. Taki, H. Nishikawa, and S. Uchida, "The Design and Implementation of a Personal Sequential Inference Machine: PSI," *New Generation Computing*, pp. 125 - 144, 1983.

3. T. P. Dobry, *A High Performance Architecture for Prolog*, Kluwer Academic Publishers, 1990.

4. V. P. Srini, J. V. Tam, T. M. Nguyen, Y. N. Patt, A. M. Despain, M. Moll, and D. Ellsworth, "A CMOS Chip for Prolog," *Proceedings of the International Conference on Computer Design*, pp. 605 - 610, October 1987.

5. H. Nakashima and K. Nakajima, "Hardware Architecture of the Sequential Inference Machine: PSI-II," *1987 Symposium on Logic Programming*, pp. 104 - 113, August 1987.

6. H. Benker, J. M. Beacco, S. Bescos, M. Dorochevsky, Th. Jeffre, A. Pohimann, J. Noye, B. Poterie, A. Sexton, J. C. Syre, O. Thibault, and G. Watzlawik, "KCM: A Knowledge Crunching Machine," *16th International Symposium on Computer Architecture*, pp. 186 - 194, May 1989.

7. D. H. D. Warren, "An Abstract Prolog Instruction Set," TR 309, SRI International, October 1983.

8. J. W. Mills, "A High-Performance LOW RISC Machine for Logic Programming," *Journal of Logic Programming*, vol. 6, no. 1 & 2, pp. 179 - 212, January/March 1989.

9. K. Seo and T. Yokota, "Design and Fabrication of Pegasus Prolog Processor," in *VLSI 89*, North-Holland.

10. A. Harsat and R. Ginosar, "CARMEL-2: A Second Generation VLSI Architecture for Flat Concurrent Prolog," *Proceedings of the International Conference on Fifth Generation Computer Systems*, pp. 962 - 969, November 1988.

11. J. W. Mills, "LIBRA: A High-Performance Balanced Computer Architecture for Prolog," Ph.D. Thesis, Arizona State University, December 1988.

12. G. Radin, "The 801 Minicomputer," *Symposium on Architectural Support for Programming Languages and Operating Systems (ASPLOS I)*, pp. 39 - 47, March 1982.

13. J. L. Hennessy, N. P. Jouppi, S. Przybylski, C. Rowen, and T. Gross, "Design of a High Performance VLSI Processor," *Third CalTech Conference on Very Large Scale Integration*, pp. 33 - 54, 1983.

14. M. G. H. Katevenis, *Reduced Instruction Set Computer Architectures for VLSI*, MIT Press, 1985.

15. P. Steenkiste and J. Hennessy, "Tags and Type Checking in LISP: Hardware and Software Approaches," *Second International Conference on Architectural Support for Programming Languages and Operating Systems (ASPLOS II)*, pp. 50 - 59, October 1987.

16. A. Chang and M. F. Mergen, "801 Storage: Architecture and Programming," *ACM Transactions on Computer Systems*, vol. 6, no. 1, pp. 28 - 50, February 1988.

17. R. Carlson, "The Bottom-Up Design of a Prolog Architecture," Report No. UCB/CSD 89/536, University of California, Berkeley, May 1989.

18. P. Van Roy, B. Demoen, and Y. D. Willems, "Improving the Execution Speed of Compiled Prolog with Modes, Clause Selection, and Determinism," in *TAPSOFT '87*, Lecture Notes in Computer Science, 250, pp. 111 - 125, March 1987.

19. M. Carlton, B. Sano, J. Pendleton, B. Holmer, and A. Despain, *Cache Innovations in the BAM Microprocessor*, November 1989.

20. J. Pendleton, S. Kong, E. Brown, F. Dunlap, C. Marino, D. Ungar, D. Patterson, and D. Hodges, "A 32-bit Microprocessor for Smalltalk," *IEEE Journal of Solid State Circuits*, vol. SC-21, no. 5, pp. 741 - 749, October 1986.

21. P. Van Roy, "An Intermediate Language to Support Prolog's Unification," in *Proceedings of the North American Conference on Logic Programming*, ed. Lusk & Overbeek, pp. 1148 - 1164, MIT Press, October 1989.

22. J. Beer, "The Occur-Check Problem Revisited," *Journal of Logic Programming*, vol. 5, no. 3, pp. 243 - 261, September 1988.

23. P. Van Roy, "Can Logic Programming Execute as Fast as Imperative Programming?," Ph. D. Thesis (in preparation).

24. S. K. Debray and D. S. Warren, "Automatic Mode Inference for Prolog Programs," *1986 Symposium on Logic Programming*, pp. 78 - 88, September 1986.

25. D. M. Ungar, *The Design and Evaluation of a High Performance Smalltalk System*, MIT Press, 1987.

26. B. Sano, *Performance vs. Cost of the BAM*, December 1989.

27. G. Borriello, A. R. Cherenson, P. B. Danzig, and M. N. Nelson, "RISCs vs. CISCs for Prolog: A Case Study," *Second International Conference on Architectural Support for Programming Languages and Operating Systems (ASPLOS II)*, pp. 136 - 145, October 1987.

28. R. Haygood, "A Prolog Benchmark Suite for Aquarius," Report No. UCB/CSD 89/509, University of California, Berkeley, April 1989.

Architectural Support for the Management of Tightly-Coupled Fine-Grain Goals in Flat Concurrent Prolog

Leon Alkalaj
Jet Propulsion Lab., MS 198-231
Caltech, Pasadena, CA 91109

Tomás Lang and **Miloš Ercegovac**
Computer Science Department
University of California Los Angeles, CA 90024

ABSTRACT

We propose architectural support for goal management as part of a special-purpose processor architecture for the efficient execution of Flat Concurrent Prolog. Goal management operations: halt, spawn, suspend and commit are decoupled from goal reduction, and overlapped in the Goal Management Unit. Their efficient execution is enabled using a Goal Cache. We evaluate the performance of the goal management support using an analytic performance model and program parameters characteristic of the System's Development Workload. Most goal management operations are completely overlapped, resulting in a speedup of 2. Higher speedups are obtained for workloads that exhibit greater goal management complexity.

1 Introduction

Flat Concurrent Prolog (FCP) is a high-level, parallel programming language [10] whose syntax and semantics is characteristic of a group of *flat committed-choice* logic programming languages [5], [7], [16], [11]. The main unit of concurrency in FCP is a goal. An FCP program typically creates numerous concurrent goals that have to *reduce* for the program to successfully terminate. A goal can create new goals, communicate with other goals using shared logical variables as asynchronous communication channels, and terminate execution. The scheduling of goals is non-deterministic, and their synchronization is performed by sending and receiving messages that result in *goal-suspension* and data-driven *goal-activation*.

Preliminary performance evaluation of a distributed implementation of FCP written in Occam and simulated on a system of Transputers [4], as well as performance analysis of FCP execution on a hypercube multiprocessor [13], indicate that the overhead of goal suspensions and the locking of distributed data structures result in performance degradation relative to execution on a single processor [14]. It is suggested that a more efficient single processor implementation is necessary.

To propose an efficient single processor implementation of FCP, a detailed analysis of FCP program execution was performed [2]. The analysis determined algorithmic properties of FCP program execution at the sequential abstract machine level, under a workload that is characteristic for systems development and prototyping. The *System's Development Workload* consists of seven large benchmark programs which include the Logix Operating System, FCP Compiler, FCP Debugger, FCP Program Analyzer and three Simulators.

The analysis reveals the following characteristics of FCP program execution that are relevant to this paper. A goal performs several iterations prior to termination, suspends frequently waiting for data to be communicated by other concurrent goals, and activates goals when the data arrives. A goal may wait for several messages, and several goals may be activated upon the arrival of a single message. An average of 1.3 goal management operations are performed per goal reduction. We characterized a goal as a fine-grain computation tightly coupled with other goals in the program. By *fine-granularity*, we imply that the average goal reduction granularity ranges from 20 to several hundred single-cycle instructions.

In a general-purpose implementation, the relative execution time of software-implemented goal management increases as goal reduction is more efficient. Moreover, an environment that supports goal reduction using special-purpose instructions may further increase the relative execution time of goal management. For the System's Development Workload and a single-cycle instruction execution environment, almost 50% of the execution time is spent performing goal management operations [2]. These results strongly motivate the use of special-purpose architectural support for goal management.

We propose architectural support for goal management as part of a special-purpose processor architecture for the efficient execution of FCP [1]. Goal management

CH2887-8/90/0000/0292$01.00 © 1990 IEEE

operations are decoupled from goal reduction operations and overlapped in the Goal Management Unit. The efficient execution of goal management is performed using a Goal Cache that stores recently spawned goals.

In this paper we evaluate the performance of the Goal Management Unit using an analytic performance model. The program parameters of the model are measured using an instrumented version of the Logix Operating System [12], and executing the System's Development Workload. Using the Goal Management Unit, most goal management operations are completely overlapped with goal reduction, and their execution time is reduced from 50% to less than 3%, resulting in a speedup of 2. We also generalize our results for workloads that have different goal management complexities.

In the following section we describe the behavior of goals in FCP. We then describe the special-purpose FCP processor followed by the Goal Management Unit and Goal Cache. Finally we evaluate the overlapped execution of goal reduction and goal management, and generalize our results.

2 FCP Goals

An FCP program is a set of conditional sentences called guarded clauses [10] that have the following form: $H \leftarrow G \mid B.$, where H denotes the *head* of the clause, '$\leftarrow$' the implication operator, the guard G represents a set of conditional goals, '$\mid$' is the commit operator and B the set of body goals. The declarative reading of a guarded clause implies that goal H can be reduced to a new set of goals B, given that all of the condition goals G are previously satisfied. Consider the actions of goal a that consists of the following clauses:

$$
\begin{array}{llll}
a & \leftarrow & C_1, C_2 & \mid b, c, d. \\
a & \leftarrow & C_3, C_4 & \mid a. \\
a & \leftarrow & C_5 & \mid .
\end{array}
$$

The clauses denote three alternative actions that can take place when goal a executes. Either a reduces to goals b, c and d if conditions C_1 and C_2 are satisfied; or to goal a if conditions C_3 and C_4 are satisfied; or if condition C_5 is satisfied, goal a reduces without creating new goals, that is, terminates execution. Note that the second clause represents the iteration of goal a.

The execution mechanism that distinguishes FCP from non committed-choice logic programming languages is that only one clause may be used to reduce goal a. For example, if all conditions $C_1, ..., C_5$ in the above example are satisfied, any one of the clauses may be used to reduce goal a. However, once execution commits to one clause, the possibility of using alternative clauses to reduce the same goal is not considered. That

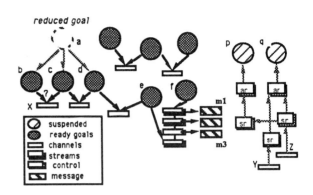

Figure 1: A System of Concurrent Communicating Goals

is, only the forward continuation of applied clauses is permitted in FCP. Other logic programming languages like Prolog support both forward and backward program continuations.

In FCP, user annotation of shared logical variables is used to discriminate between the sender and receiver of a message. Consider two goals b(X?) and c(X) that share the variable X. The read-only annotation of X, denoted as X?, implies that goal b can not send a message via channel X, but only receive. However, goal c that shares the writable version of the channel can send a message. If, due to non-deterministic goal scheduling, goal b attempts to receive a message before goal c sends it, goal b will suspend execution until the message is received. A similar synchronization mechanism to support the parallel execution of tasks is described in [6].

In Figure 1, we show a system of concurrent goals: goal a reduced to goals b, c and d; e sent three messages to goal f; goal p is suspended on variable Z; and goal q is suspended on both variables Y and Z. Goal suspension is implemented using a linked list of *suspension records* (sr) for each suspending variable. Also, *activation records* (ar) are allocated for each suspended goal to prevent the same goal from being activated more than once [8]. This enables a goal to suspend on several variables, and several goals to suspend on a single variable.

Goal suspension occurs as a result of a goal reduction attempt that does not fail or succeed. Therefore, goal suspension must occur only if no clause can be used for immediate goal reduction, but some clause may be applicable in the future, when more data becomes available. If there are several clauses that are applicable to the current goal, suspension occurs only after attempting all of them, and finding that none of them succeeded.

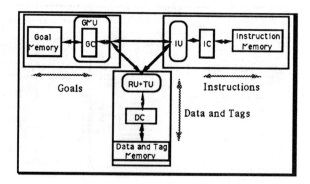

Figure 2: FCP Processor Architecture

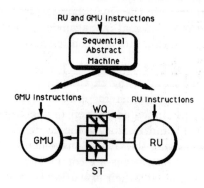

Figure 3: Overlapped RU-GMU Execution

3 FCP Processor Organization

We propose an FCP processor architecture that consists of multiple functional units for the execution of FCP programs [1]. It is characterized by a high-bandwidth memory which enables the concurrent manipulation of three types of objects: goals, tagged-data, and instructions. The hierarchical structure of the processor architecture contains tightly coupled *execution units*, specialized *cache units* and dedicated *memory modules*, as shown in Figure 2.

The Reduction Unit, RU, is the main instruction-set unit in the FCP processor. It executes a RISC instruction set that supports pointer dereferencing, multi-way branching and the allocation of data structures on the heap. RU is tightly coupled with the Tag Unit, TU, which concurrently performs tag decoding, setting and extraction. The goal management system supplies RU with reducible goals, and efficiently executes all goal management operations. It consists of the Goal Management Unit (GMU), Goal Cache (GC) and Goal Memory.

The Instruction Unit, IU, provides the execution units with executable instructions. A single instruction contains separate opcode fields for each functional unit. The functionality of the execution units is partitioned so that RU manipulates program data structures, TU manipulates data tags, GMU manipulates goal structures, and IU manipulates instructions. The processor has dedicated cache units that enable faster access to objects requested by the execution units. Objects are requested from the memory modules only on a *cache miss*.

Memory is also divided into dedicated sections, accessed and managed only by the corresponding execution unit. The Data Memory is used for storing all program data structures such as lists, variables, tuples and constants; Tag Memory is used to store all the data tags; Instruction Memory stores processor instructions and Goal

Memory stores all control structures used for goal creation, suspension, activation and termination.

RU-GMU Overlapped Execution

In an FCP implementation that is based on the sequential abstract machine executing on a general-purpose physical machine, FCP programs are translated to a sequence of goal reduction operations, interleaved with high-level goal management functions. Both goal reduction and goal management operations are thus executed sequentially. In the processor architecture that we propose, goal management operations are decoupled from goal reduction instructions using a Suspension Table (ST) and a Wakeup Queue (WQ) as shown in Figure 3. During a goal reduction, RU stores in ST addresses of those (*read-only*) variables that the current goal may suspend on. At goal suspension, RU switches to an alternate ST, thus allowing GMU to access the old ST and perform overlapped goal suspension. A similar policy applies to the use of WQ: during goal reduction RU stores in WQ pointers to goals that may be activated if the current clause commits, so that, if it does, goal reduction switches to an alternate WQ while GMU activates goals based on the old WQ [3].

GMU executes four high-level goal management instructions: halt, spawn, suspend and commit. Meanwhile, RU continues to execute subsequent instructions, fetched by IU. If, prior to the termination of the current GMU operation, another goal management instruction is fetched, RU blocks until GMU completes its operation.

4 Goal Management System

The purpose of the goal management system is to reduce the contribution of the goal management execution time

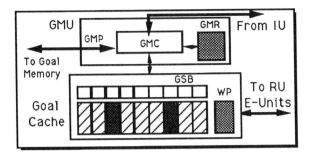

Figure 4: GMU Organization

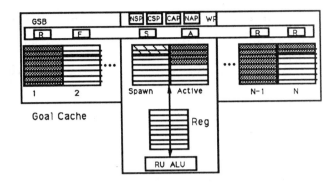

Figure 5: Goal Cache Organization

to the program execution time. This is achieved by using the Goal Management Unit to overlap goal management and goal reduction, and using a Goal Cache to efficiently implement goal management.

4.1 Goal Management Unit

As shown in Figure 4, GMU consists of a Goal Management Controller (GMC), Goal Memory Port (GMP) and Goal Memory Management Registers (GMR). The execution of goal management instructions consists of managing goals stored in the Goal Cache (GC).

GMC uses a *Busy Flag* control signal to synchronize RU and GMU execution. When GMU receives an instruction from IU, the GMU *Busy Flag* is set. Subsequent instructions (fetched by IU) that contain goal management instructions are blocked until the flag is reset. When GMU completes the execution of the current instruction, it resets the flag so that any pending instruction is then resumed. The separate memory port, GMP, enables the transfer of goal control structures between GMU and Goal Memory.

GMU contains five special-purpose registers used for the dynamic management of Goal Memory: the Heap Pointer (HP) is used to allocate structures on top of the heap; the Goal Free List (GFL) and the Suspension Free List (SFL) registers store pointers used for reclaiming discarded control structures; and GQF and GQB registers store pointers to the front and the back of the goal queue in memory.

4.2 Goal Cache

A goal is represented as a record that consists of a program counter and goal argument pointers. For the System's Development Workload, a goal has on the average 4.8 arguments. If we include the program counter and

additional control information, a fixed goal size of 10 words would be sufficient for approximately 95% of all goal record structures [2]. The FCP compiler detects if a goal has more than the maximum number of arguments, and compacts the remaining arguments into a single complex data structure that is dynamically expanded [8]. Having the same size for all goal record structures makes dynamic memory management simpler.

The Goal Cache, shown in Figure 5, consists of N goal windows for storing goals, Goal Status Bits (GSB) that denote the state of the goals, and goal Window Pointers (WP) that point to specific windows. Each window is implemented using (10) words.

The status of a goal window can be one of the following four states. An *active* window contains the currently executing goal, the *spawn* window is used for spawning a new goal, a *ready* window contains a goal that is ready for execution, and a *free* window is empty. During program execution, there is only one *active* and one *spawn* window in the Goal Cache, and they are both addressable by RU. The remaining windows can be *ready* or *free*, and are addressable by GMU.

The four registers CAP, CSP, NAP and NSP, contain pointers to the Current Active, Current Spawn, Next Active and Next Spawn windows respectively. CAP is used by RU to access the currently active goal, and CSP to spawn a new goal. If GC contains several *ready* goals, goal-switching consists of changing CAP to an alternative *ready* window. Similarly, spawning a new goal consists of changing its status from *spawn* to *ready*, while terminating an active goal consists of changing its status from *active* to *free*.

The next goal pointer values NAP and NSP are always set by GMU, while RU reads them. The efficient interpretation of goal management operations, as seen by RU, is performed by managing the four goal pointers. To interpret goal termination or suspension, RU moves NAP to CAP while CSP remains the same. By prefetching an instruction from the next active goal stored in the window pointed to by NAP (and if there is no wait delay due to RU-GMU synchronization), the goal management instruction is completely overlapped, without contributing to the total program execution time. While RU starts to execute the newly scheduled goal, GMU performs the goal management operation and then determines the new value for NAP. For the spawn instruction, NSP is moved to CSP whereas CAP remains the same. The commit instruction, however, does not affect the goal pointer values.

Two exceptional conditions are detected in the Goal Cache. First, *GC-overflow* occurs when the goal cache becomes full and there is no *free* window for spawning. Upon overflow, a goal is moved to the goal queue in Goal Memory. To implement efficient spawning of new goals, overflow is detected before the Goal Cache becomes completely full. That is, there is always one empty goal window available for fast spawning.

The second exceptional condition is *GC-underflow*, which occurs after a sequence of goal terminations depletes the Goal Cache of available goals for scheduling. To implement efficient halting, there is always at least one prefetched goal available in the Goal Cache. This enables a new goal to be scheduled whenever the current goal terminates execution. Otherwise, RU may need to wait until a new goal is fetched from the Goal Memory.

Those goal management instructions that are implemented by manipulating only the Goal Status Bits in the Goal Cache, are considered *cache hits* whereas, all goal management instructions that require access to the Goal Memory are considered *cache misses*.

5 Performance Evaluation

We present a simplified version of the analytic performance model of RU-GMU execution [1]. First we define the performance measures, followed by a description of the system organization and workload, and finally the performance analysis.

5.1 Performance Measures

We define the following two performance measures:

1. The average RU-GMU wait time per executed instruction, $\overline{W}$, is a measure of the time that RU waits for GMU. The wait time directly affects program execution time and the objective is to reduce it.

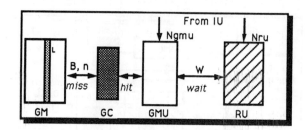

Figure 6: System Organization

2. The GMU (RU) utilization, $U_{gmu}(U_{ru})$, determines the fraction of time spent performing goal management (reduction) relative to the program execution time. Together, the utilization factors are a measure of the workload balance.

5.2 System Organization and Workload

In Figure 6 we show the RU-GMU system organization used to define the performance model. It shows the functional units RU and GMU, the Goal Cache and the Goal Memory. RU executes a RISC instruction set whereas GMU executes goal management instructions. GMU instructions that execute only in the Goal Cache are modeled as cache hits, whereas those instructions that require access to Goal Memory are goal cache misses.

The program parameters used in the performance model are characteristic of the *System's Development Workload*. These parameters are obtained by instrumenting the Logix Operating System at the abstract machine level, and running existing, large applications.

5.3 Performance Model

In this simplified performance model, we make the following assumptions:

1. The average RU instruction execution rate is one per cycle. We do not take into account that the average execution time can be greater than one due to misses in the Data Cache, branches in the processor pipeline, etc. This assumption is reasonable since there are standard techniques that can be used to bring the execution rate close to one instruction per processor cycle (for example delayed branch).

2. The *absolute* execution time of a goal management instruction that results in a cache hit is one cycle, since it only requires changing the goal status bits.

3. All goal management instructions that result in a Goal Cache hit are completely overlapped with goal reduction execution, and do not result in wait time. Therefore, their *effective* execution time is zero.

We define the following performance model program parameters: the total number of GMU and RU instructions is N_{gmu} and N_{ru} respectively; the frequency of GMU instructions is F_{gmu}; the average goal size is S; the average number of variables per goal suspension is N_{var}^s, and the average number of activations per goal commit is N_{act}^c. Implementation dependent parameters include the Goal Memory bandwidth B, and the Goal Memory word size L.

Average RU-GMU Wait Time, $\overline{W}$

The average RU-GMU wait time, $\overline{W}$, is equal to the ratio of the total wait time W and the number of executed instructions N_{ru}. That is,

$$\overline{W} = \frac{W}{N_{ru}} = F_{gmu} \times \overline{W}_{gmu} \qquad (1)$$

where F_{gmu} is the frequency of GMU instructions, and $\overline{W}_{gmu}$ is the average wait time per executed GMU instruction. Since each fetched instruction contains opcode fields for both RU and GMU, the total number of executed instructions is equal to N_{ru}. The frequency of GMU instructions then expressed as $F_{gmu} = \frac{N_{gmu}}{N_{ru}}$.

To determine W, we consider the execution of two consecutive GMU instructions. Let d_i denote the elapsed time between two consecutive GMU instructions gmu_i and gmu_{i+1}, and t_{gmu}^i the time it takes to execute GMU instruction i that results in a Goal Cache miss. If the duration of GMU instruction i is less than the distance d_i, the wait time, w_i, is equal to zero. However, if the duration is greater than the distance, a non-zero wait time is incurred. Thus, we express the wait time for the ith GMU instruction as

$$w_i = \begin{cases} (t_{gmu}^i - d_i) & \text{if } d_i < t_{gmu}^i \\ 0 & \text{otherwise} \end{cases} \qquad (2)$$

The total RU-GMU wait time is then represented as the sum over all executed GMU instructions, that is,

$$W = \sum_{i=1}^{i=N_{gmu}} (w_i) \qquad (3)$$

Note that t_{gmu}^i is the *absolute* execution time of the ith GMU instruction, and the wait time w_i is its *effective* execution. Therefore, the average effective execution time of GMU instructions is also the average wait time per goal management instructions. The *absolute* execution

GMU		Execution Time
$t_{halt/sp}^m$	$=$	$\lceil L \times (S+3)/B \rceil +$ $\lceil L/B \rceil + 1$
t_{susp}^m	$=$	$\lceil L \times (S+2)/B \rceil +$ $2(\lceil (2/B) \rceil) +$ $\lceil N_{var}^s (3 \times \lceil L/B \rceil + \lceil (2/B) \rceil + 2) \rceil$
t_{com}^m	$=$	$\lceil N_{act}^c (3\lceil (2/B) \rceil + \lceil L/B \rceil) \rceil + 4$

Table 1: GMU Instruction Execution Times

time of the goal management instructions that result in a goal cache miss is shown in Table 1, and is determined by inspecting the goal management algorithms.

The halt and spawn instructions move the goal to memory and perform garbage collection or memory allocation. The execution time of suspend is linearly proportional to the number of variables, N_{var}^s, the goal suspends on, and the execution time of commit is linearly proportional to the number of goals activated at commit time, N_{act}^c. The suspend instruction always results in the transfer of the suspended goal to the goal memory, thus effectively behaving as a goal cache miss.

RU and GMU Utilizations, U_{ru}, U_{gmu}

We define the RU utilization U_{ru}, as the ratio of the RU execution time, T_{ru}, and the total program execution time, T. That is,

$$U_{ru} = \frac{T_{ru}}{T} = \frac{1}{1 + \overline{W}} \qquad (4)$$

GMU utilization U_{gmu} is similarly defined as the ratio of the GMU execution time, T_{gmu}, and the total program execution time T. That is,

$$U_{gmu} = \frac{T_{gmu}}{T} = \frac{F_{gmu} \overline{t}_{gmu}}{(1 + \overline{W})} \qquad (5)$$

The average *absolute* GMU instruction execution time $\overline{t}_{gmu}$ is expressed as the sum of the products of the average execution times for the halt, spawn, suspend and commit instructions, and their corresponding frequencies. That is,

$$\overline{t}_{gmu} = F_{halt}\overline{t}_{halt} + F_{sp}\overline{t}_{sp} + F_{susp}\overline{t}_{susp} + F_{com}\overline{t}_{com} \quad (6)$$

If we denote the goal management instruction execution times for a goal cache hit and miss as t_j^h and t_j^m respectively, the average execution time of instruction $j \in (halt, spawn, suspend, commit)$, $\overline{t}_j$, is:

$$\overline{t}_j = F_j^h t_j^h + (1 - F_j^h)t_j^m \qquad (7)$$

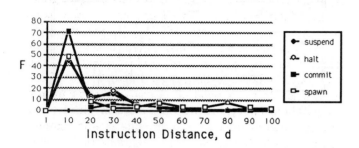

Figure 7: GMU Instruction Distance Distribution

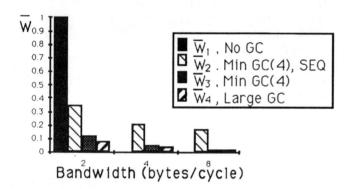

Figure 8: Average Wait Time, $\overline{W}$

5.4 Performance Model Analysis

Average RU-GMU Wait Time, $\overline{W}$

To analytically determine the average RU-GMU wait time under the System's Development Workload, we first determine the distribution of RU instruction distances, d, between two consecutive GMU instructions. In Figure 7 we show these distributions for the goal management instructions: halt, spawn, suspend and commit. Using these distributions and the *absolute* GMU instruction execution times, we determine the RU-Wait time $\overline{W}$, shown in Figure 8, for three different cases of goal memory bandwidth and two cases for the goal cache size.

The goal memory bandwidth considered is 2, 4 and 8 bytes/cycle. The two goal cache sizes are a minimal cache that consists of 4 windows: *active, spawn ready* and *free*, and a goal cache that is *large*. A large goal cache enables all halt and spawn instructions to always execute in the goal cache. We do not correlate the actual goal cache size and the captured locality of halt and spawn, but just examine the two extreme cases.

In the first column of Figure 8 we show the average wait time $\overline{W}_1$ when goal management operations are implemented in software, that is, without GMU and GC. $\overline{W}_2$ represents the average wait time when the goal management operations execute sequentially using the same execution times as if a minimal goal cache is used. The third and fourth column represent the average wait times when goal management operations are overlapped using a minimal cache $\overline{W}_3$ and a large cache size $\overline{W}_4$.

If the goal management operations are implemented in software, using RU instructions, the average wait time is $\overline{W}_1 = 1$ cycle. That is, half the time is spent performing goal management. Using the goal cache and the goal management algorithms, but not overlapping goal management operations reduces the average wait time almost three fold, for a memory bandwidth of 2 bytes/cycle. That is, $\overline{W}_1/\overline{W}_2 = 3$. The reduction in the average wait time further increases with the goal memory bandwidth.

Overlapping goal management execution using the Goal Cache further reduces the average wait time. For the goal memory bandwidth of 2 bytes/cycle, $\overline{W}_2/\overline{W}_3 = 2.75$. Further reductions in the average wait time are obtained by increasing the goal cache size, but these changes are not significant. The total reduction of the average wait time, from software implementation to overlapped execution using a goal cache is 8.1.

The Goal Cache size, however, does not affect the average execution time of the suspend instruction since every goal that suspends is moved to goal memory. Its execution time depends only on the goal memory bandwidth. The goal cache size influences the average execution time of halt and spawn. Most halt and spawn instructions are overlapped even with a minimum goal cache configuration of 4 goal windows. The difference between the minimum goal cache and a large goal cache becomes even less significant as the goal memory bandwidth increases, since the execution times of halt and spawn are further reduced. Consequently, the wait time is mainly caused by the goal suspension instruction. For the goal memory bandwidth of 2 bytes/cycle, the reduction in the average wait time obtained by increasing the goal cache size is $\overline{W}_3/\overline{W}_4 = 1.8$.

Increasing the goal memory bandwidth reduces the time it takes to transfer a goal to goal memory, which reduces the effective execution time of halt and spawn. Moreover, goal suspension also requires the allocation of suspension lists. Increasing goal memory bandwidth reduces the goal suspension time as long as it affects the transfer time to goal memory. Further increases in memory bandwidth have no effect on the goal suspension execution time. From the results shown in Figure 8 a minimum goal cache of 4 goal windows, together with a goal memory bandwidth of 4 bytes/cycle results in a

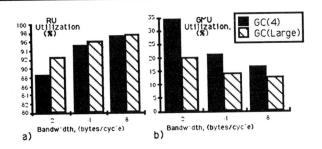

Figure 9: RU and GMU Utilizations, U_{ru} and U_{gmu}

system with an average wait time of less than 4%.

RU and GMU Utilization, U_{ru}, U_{gmu}

In Figure 9a we show RU utilization which is over 88%. As the goal cache size or the goal memory bandwidth increase, U_{ru} increases because the average execution times of the goal management operations are reduced, and thus the RU wait time is reduced. This is not the case for the GMU utilization shown in Figure 9b; as the average execution time of GMU instructions is reduced, so is the GMU utilization. This is because the reduction of goal instruction execution time is more significant than the reduction of the resulting wait time.

For the minimum goal cache size and a goal memory bandwidth of 4 bytes/cycle, the GMU utilization is $U_{gmu} = 20\%$. This implies an imbalance of goal management and goal reduction leading to an underutilized GMU. One way to improve GMU utilization is to allow GMU to perform additional work instead of being idle. These operations should be of lower priority, so that the requests for goal management are not delayed.

6 Goal Mangement Complexity

We showed that, for the System's Development Workload, using GMU and GC can double the performance of FCP program execution relative to a software implementation. We now consider workloads that have different *granularities* of goal reduction and goal management.

Granularity of Goal Reduction

We define the granularity of goal reduction as the average execution time of goal reduction, T_r. For a processor that executes one instruction per cycle, the granularity can be measured as the average number of executed instructions per goal, N_r.

Compared to previously reported measurements, the System's Development Workload exhibits a higher granularity of goal reduction. This is because it mainly consists of list oriented operations that do not explicitly model inter-goal communication and synchronization. In Table 2 we show N_r for each workload program. The high variance of N_r is due to two different types of applications. In the simulators, a goal reduction mainly consists of modifying the processor state for each fetched and executed instruction. This results in a low granularity of 20 to 40 instructions. Programs that exhibit a higher granularity, like the *Debugger* and the *Solver* are *meta-interpreters*. They symbolically interpret FCP programs as data, resulting in high-granularities of 400 to 800 instructions.

Granularity of Goal Management

We define the granularity of goal management as the average execution time of goal management, T_{gm}, or N_{gm} if measured as the number of executed single-cycle instructions. The System's Development Workload exhibits a higher goal suspension and activation rate than previously reported in [15]. The *granularity* of goal management, T_{gm}, is a function of several program parameters. For example, it depends on the average goal size, the number of variables a goal suspends on, etc. In Table 2, we also show the goal management granularities, N_{gm}.

Complexity of Goal Management

The complexity of goal management, $\mathcal{C}$, is the ratio of goal management and goal reduction granularities:

$$\mathcal{C} = \frac{T_{gm}}{T_r} \qquad (8)$$

When we refer to applications with higher complexity of goal management, it means that they have a higher execution time of goal management relative to goal reduction. In Table 2 we show the complexity of goal management for each program in the workload.

	FCP Benchmark Programs						
	Com.	Sim1	Sim2	Deb.	Sol.	Dist.	Log.
N_r	25	43	20	485	728	416	78
N_{gm}	38	139	98	95	56	102	66
$\mathcal{C}$	1.5	3.2	5	0.2	0.1	0.3	0.8

Table 2: Goal Reduction and Management Granularities

6.1 Overlapped Goal Management vs Complexity

The maximum possible speedup due to overlapped execution of goal management, S^{max}, is achieved when goal management operations are completely overlapped using GMU, resulting in zero wait time. That is,

$$S^{max} = 1 + \frac{T_{gm}}{T_r} = 1 + \mathcal{C} \qquad (9)$$

Realistically, a delay of W results from the overlapped execution of GMU. Speedup is then represented as:

$$S^r = \frac{T_r + T_{gm}}{T_r + W} = \frac{1 + \mathcal{C}}{1 + \frac{W}{T_r}} \qquad (10)$$

If we consider granularities greater than 200 as high, and 10-30 instructions as low, we then partition the space of goal management and reduction granularities into the following four regions, as shown in Figure 10.

- **M-domain**: Low goal management and high goal reduction granularities are characteristic of *Meta-Interpreters*, and other applications that perform symbolic interpretation of programs as data.

- **A-domain**: Low goal management and goal reduction granularites are typical of small applications, often used for comparative benchmarking, such as the list *Append* program. These applications perform very little goal management and the reduction granularity is approximately 20 RISC operations.

- **S-domain**: High goal management and goal reduction granularity was observed in the *System's* Development Workload.

- **C-domain**: High goal management and low goal reduction granularity is characteristic of applications that explicitly model the inter-goal communication and synchronization. The set of FCP programming stereotypes used in [13] are of this type.

In Figure 10 we show the average program execution time of the System's Development Workload, T, which consists of the granularities T_r and T_{gm}. When goal management instructions are implemented in software, we showed that $T_r \approx T_{gm}$. Therefore, the complexity of goal management for the S-domain is $\mathcal{C} \approx 1$, and the maximum speedup is $S_S^{max} = 2$. In this case, the goal management operations were considered a bottleneck, which motivated special-purpose support using GMU. We showed that the wait time due to overlapped execution can be made small, less than 4% of T_r. Therefore, S_S^r is close to the maximum possible, since the

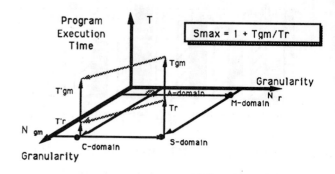

Figure 10: Goal Management Complexity Domains

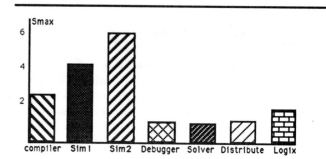

Figure 11: S^{max} for Different Applications

operations are almost completely overlapped. Thus, $S_S^r \approx S_S^{max} \approx 2$.

If we label the goal reduction and goal management times in the C-domain as T_r' and T_{gm}' respectively, where $T_r' < T_r$, then $\mathcal{C}_C > \mathcal{C}_S$. Therefore, the maximum possible speedup due to overlapped goal management using GMU in the C-domain, S_C^{max}, is $S_C^{max} > S_S^{max} = 2$

In Figure 11 we show the maximum speedup due to overlapped and efficient execution of goal management operations for each program in the workload. Programs like the Simulator2 spent more time performing goal management than goal reduction. In addition, we considered simple applications that are used to describe specific distributed algorithms and communication protocols. For example, in the *Lord of the Rings* algorithm that computes the extreme value of nodes connected in a unidirectional circle using $O(N \log N)$ messages [9], a goal reduction consists of executing only a few instructions that check whether the input channel has a message. If it has, a reply message is sent on the output channel, whereas, if the message has not arrived, the goal reduction suspends. The average goal reduction granularity is 30 RU instructions. To compute the goal management granularity, in Table 3 we show the total number of goal management operations and goal reductions for

Lord of the Rings, N = 200				
Create	Terminate	Suspend	Activate	Reduce
7342	7342	6779	6779	22745

Table 3: Goal Management Activity

$N = 200$. If each goal suspension suspends on only one variable, a goal management complexity of $\mathcal{C} \approx 5$ was obtained, resulting in $S^{max} = 6$ and a realistic speedup of 5 due to the wait time.

7 Conclusion

We propose special-purpose architectural support as a way to reduce the goal management execution time in FCP. The architectural support consists of a dedicated Goal Management Unit that executes high-level goal management operations concurrently with goal reduction. Moreover, the efficient execution of goal management is enabled using a Goal Cache that stores recently spawned goals. Operations such as goal-switching, spawning and halting are efficiently performed by changing their status in the Goal Cache. More complex operations such as suspension and activation are decoupled from goal reduction by using two Suspension Tables and Wakeup Queues. For the System's Development Workload, which consists of large FCP programs, we show, using an analytic performance model, that the overhead of software-implemented goal management is 50% of the program execution time. This is reduced to 4% using the Goal Management Unit and Goal Cache, resulting in a speedup of almost 2. We generalize our results for workloads that exhibit different goal management complexities. Programs that explicitly model inter-goal communication and synchronization exhibit higher goal management granularity than goal reduction. For these programs, the speedup due to overlapped and efficient execution of goal management is greater than 2; for a simple distributed algorithm a speedup of 5 was obtained.

References

[1] L. Alkalaj. Architectural Support for Concurrent Logic Programming Languages. Doctoral Dissertation UCLA/CSD 890047, University of California, Los Angeles, June 1989.

[2] L. Alkalaj. Flat Concurrent Prolog Abstract Machine Characteristics. TR CSD-890018, University of California, Los Angeles, April 1989.

[3] L. Alkalaj and E. Shapiro. An Architectural Model for a Flat Concurrent Prolog Processor. In *Proceedings of the 5th Inter. Conference/Symposium on Logic Programming*, Aug 88.

[4] U. Bar-on. A Distributed Implementation of Flat Concurrent Prolog. Master's Thesis CS 86, Weizmann Institute of Science, Applied Mathematics Department, January 1986.

[5] J. Crammond. An Execution Model for Committed-Choice Non-Deterministic Languages. In *1986 Symposium on Logic Programming*, pages 148 – 158, Sept. 1986.

[6] W. J. Dally and D. S. Wills. Universal Mechanisms for Concurrency. Artificial Intelligence Laboratory and Laboratory for Computer Science, MIT, Cambridge, Massachusetts, 1989.

[7] S. Gregory. *Parallel Logic Programming in PARLOG, The Language and its Implementation*. Addison-Wesley, 1987.

[8] A. Houri and E. Shapiro. The Sequential Abstract Machine for Flat Concurrent Prolog. Master's Thesis CS 86-20, Weizmann Institute of Science, Applied Mathematics Department, July 1986.

[9] A. Shafrir and E. Shapiro. Distributed Programming in Concurrent Prolog. TR CS 84-02, Weizmann Institute of Science, Applied Mathematics Department, January 1984.

[10] E. Shapiro. A Subset of Concurrent Prolog and its Interpreter. ICOT, tr-003, Institute of Fifth Generation Computers, January 1983.

[11] E. Shapiro. The Family of Concurrent Logic Programming Languages. TR CS 89-08, Weizmann Institute of Science, Applied Mathematics Department, May 1989.

[12] W. Silverman, M. Hirsch, A. Houri, and E. Shapiro. The Logix System User Manual. TR CS 21, Weizmann Institute of Science, Applied Mathematics Department, Nov. 1988.

[13] S. Taylor. *Parallel Logic Programming Techniques*. Prentice Hall, 1989.

[14] S. Taylor, R. Shapiro, and E. Shapiro. FCP: A Summary of Performance Results. In *The Third Conference on Hypercube Concurrent Computers and Applications*, pages 1364 – 1373, January 1988.

[15] E. Tick. Performance of Parallel Logic Programming Architectures. TR 421-88, ICOT, Japan.

[16] K. Ueda. Guarded Horn Clauses. Doctoral dissertation, University of Tokyo, March 1986.

Balance in Architectural Design

Samuel Ho and Lawrence Snyder*
University of Washington
Seattle, Washington 98195

Abstract

We introduce a performance metric, *normalized time,* which is closely related to such measures as the area-time product of VLSI theory and the price / performance ratio of advertising literature. This metric captures the idea of a piece of hardware "pulling its own weight," i.e. contributing as much to performance as it costs in resources. We then prove general theorems for stating when the size of a given part is in balance with its utilization, and give specific formulas for commonly found linear and quadratic devices. We also apply these formulas to an analysis of a specific processor element, and discuss the implications for bit-serial *vs* word-parallel, RISC *vs* CISC, and VLIW designs.

1 Introduction

Architectural design – in buildings – demands both art and engineering from the architect. Architectural design of computers also requires art and engineering, but, to date, the rationale for computer designs seems not to be founded on either a clear artistic basis, a matter which we do *not* consider further, nor a clear engineering basis, a matter which we will.

Specifically, we will conceptualize a computer as a collection of its components, e.g. a datapath, ALU, register file, etc., capable of running programs. New components, added to this base architecture, will carry a cost and, presumably, deliver a performance improvement. Using this point of view, a mathematical formulation of principles of computer design can be developed. One such principle emerges stating that optimal designs must be balanced.

> **Balance:** The cost of a given part relative to the cost of the entire system must be equal to the time on the critical path spent by that part, relative to the total running time.

The principle that computer parts have to "pull their own weight" clearly makes sense. However, by

giving it mathematical precision, we are able to quantify many aspects of computer design. Thus, qualitative statements such as "CISC machines have too much control," which have been bandied about in connection with the RISC / CISC controversy, can be made quantitatively precise to "four decimal places."

The basis for our mathematical formulation is a concept of *normalized time* which we developed from a concept of *normalized analysis* [4] developed by Holman in his doctoral dissertation [3].

In his thesis Holman analyzed parallel computer processor elements. He had to measure both cost and performance improvement. To expose the performance improvement due to a component, such as a floating point coprocessor, he compared machines whose PE's had the component with machines whose PE's did not. A difference in performance could then be ascribed to this component. To keep the machines on the same cost basis, he allowed the parallel machine without the feature to have more PE's until the total amount of hardware was the same in both machines. Comparing the two machines on benchmarks showed either a performance improvement for the enhanced PE's, suggesting it to be a worthwhile addition to a parallel machine, or a performance loss, showing it to be worthless. Thus, Holman's normalized analysis [4] compared PE enhancements with the "no action" alternative of added parallel PE's.

There were two problems with normalized analysis. First, it applied only to parallel computer processor elements, since it is necessary to equalize the costs of the two machines by adding additional parallel processors to the one without the enhancement. Second, normalized analysis applied to computer components on a "take it or leave it" basis, i.e. a PE either has a multiplier or not; considering, say, the benefit of a smaller multiplier couldn't be done, except by tedious independent analyses. But the idea of downsized components makes sense from a cost performance point of view. Holman observed: *Reducing the width of a shifter by half reduces its area by a factor of four, but cuts performance by only a factor of two* [3].

The first problem, the limitation to parallel PE's,

*Supported in part by DARPA under ONR contract N00014-88-K-0453 and ONR contract N00014-89-J-1368

CH2887-8/90/0000/0302$01.00 © 1990 IEEE   302

was solved [5] by introducing the concept of *normalized time*. (See next section.) The solution of the second problem, scaling components, is a contribution of this paper. We introduce *parameterized enhancements*.

We develop a theory of parameterized enhancements and prove two fundamental theorems about normalized time for computer components: One applies to components whose cost grows linearly, such as adders, buses, register files, etc. and the second applies to quadratically growing components such as multipliers, shifters, etc. We also show how to evaluate waiting time in evaluating a design for parallel machines. Another contribution of this paper is to illustrate the theory by applying it to a specific set of components designed in $3\mu m$ CMOS. Though the examples are necessarily sensitive to the VLSI implementation, they show how the theory is applied, and suggest trends that might be more general. As an example, our numbers show that the optimal size of a VLIW machine is about 7 instructions wide, the width of the (small) Multiflow machine [9].

The paper begins with a definition of normalized time, an analysis of waiting time, and a derivation of the Balance principle. There follows a mathematical development for linear and quadratic components. The theorems are then illustrated in an extensive applications section that is interspersed with discussion about the relationship of the results to matters such as bit serial *vs* word parallel, RISC *vs* CISC, and optimal VLIW.

2 Normalized Model

The first order of business is to fix the environment for the analysis. All analyses will be conducted with respect to some target computation, which is fixed in advance. A standard benchmark does well in this application, but all the usual warnings about the applicability of measurements taken from a benchmark apply. Clearly, some designs are more suited to some problems than others.

We make all of our comparisons relative to a reference design known as the *base architecture*. As such, the units specified for the time T and cost C are irrelevant, since they will cancel when making any comparisons. The units of cost deserve more detailed mention. We interpret cost to be more general than merely the suggested retail price. Instead, cost is whatever factor limits the total amount of hardware available. For instance, in this papers we will use a cost measure suited to VLSI design, chip area. Other possible costs include weight, volume, and heat dissipation, as well as price. For convenience, we set the time T_0 and cost C_0 of

the base architecture on the target computation to be unity.

The *normalized time* of a program running on a specific machine is the product of its time and cost, TC, when running on that machine. Normalized time allows trading time for cost, and vice versa. So, for example, a parallel machine whose processor elements are half as fast, but cost half as much as another machine's PE's can compensate by having twice as many. Or, replacing an ALU with one that costs twice as much but runs twice as fast won't change the normalized time of a program.

In each case, there is an assumption that the change in hardware can be used: Adding processor elements assumes there is sufficient parallelism in the program; accelerating the ALU assumes operations get done faster and are not inhibited by other factors. Such assumptions are often reasonable, at least over small ranges. As with any theory, however, the extent to which the assumptions are realized must be assessed when interpreting the results. Of course, the price-performance points of personal computers and supercomputers differ. We can take this into consideration by suitably scaling the cost or performance to reflect the desired price-performance level. This scaling does not affect the analysis, so we will not mention it further.

To the base architecture we will add an enhancement, such as a multiplier, floating point unit, or the like. By analogy to Amdahl's law [1], we assume that some fraction f of the total computation time is affected by the enhancement, and the rest is left undisturbed. This fraction would be the fraction of time spent multiplying for multipliers, and so forth. We also assume that the affected part of the computation speeds up by a constant factor S, and that the improvement carries a cost c.

Definition 1 *An enhancement affecting a fraction f with speedup S and cost c results in time*

$$T = 1 - f + \frac{f}{S}$$

and cost

$$C = 1 + c.$$

At this point, we generalize from a single enhancement to a range of enhancements. This is the simple expedient of adding a parameter u which parameterizes the value of the speedup $S(u)$ and cost $c(u)$. We assume that the affected fraction f remains constant, since the family of enhancements should be closely enough related that they affect the same operations.

For many types of enhancements, the family of potential enhancements is discrete, but still large. An example is the varying widths of multiplier or shifter elements. In these cases, we may approximate the discrete parameter by a continuous one, bearing in mind the possibility of intermediate results which lie between values of the discrete parameter.

In addition to this categorization of the total time into the parts affected or unaffected by the enhancement, there is another important effect, especially for parallel systems. In a parallel computer, a processing element may often find itself without anything to process, because it is waiting for something to happen.

Let us assume that the base architecture spends a fraction W_0 of its time waiting. We also denote the waiting time in the modified architecture by W. Then, the modified running time is given by

$$T = 1 - W_0 - f + W + \frac{f}{S}.$$

The waiting time can, in principle be an arbitrarily complicated function. However, a linear function is a reasonable approximation. Such a function contains two major terms. The constant term ω_0 represents waiting that does not depend on the speed of the rest of the computation, such as communication delay. The linear term ωT is proportional to the speed of the computation, and encapsulates waiting associated with acquiring results from other subcomputations. This results in waiting time

$$W = \omega_0 + \omega T.$$

Substituting this into our original formula gives

$$T = 1 - \omega_0 - \omega - f + \omega_0 + \omega T + \frac{f}{S}.$$

From this, bringing terms dependent on T to the left yields

$$(1 - \omega)T = 1 - \omega - f - \frac{f}{S},$$

which is

$$T = 1 - \frac{f}{1 - \omega} + \frac{f}{(1 - \omega)S}.$$

This is equal to

$$T = 1 - f' + \frac{f'}{S}$$

if we define an adjusted fraction

$$f' = \frac{f}{1 - \omega}.$$

Thus, the constant term of waiting is indistinguishable from computation that is not affected by the enhancement, and the linear term is equivalent to an adjustment in the fraction affected by the enhancement. In the remainder of the discussion, we make no further mention of waiting time, but include it implicitly, by the adjustments described above.

3 A General Principle

Now, let us recall that we have described the time and cost of an enhancement by using a parameter. The first theorem expresses the conditions for which the normalized time is at a local minimum. This occurs when the fraction of cost added by a further step is equal to the fraction of time removed by that step. At this point, small changes in the size of the enhancement exactly balance small changes in its cost. In general, though, there may be many such points, which may be maxima, minima, or points of inflection. Furthermore, if the range of the parameter is restricted, the absolute minimum may lie at an end point, instead of a local minimum.

Theorem 1 *Given the cost $C(u)$ and time $T(u)$, parameterized by u, the normalized time is minimized at a point where*

$$\frac{C'(u)}{C(u)} = -\frac{T'(u)}{T(u)}.$$

The minimum occurs when the first derivative of the normalized time is zero, or the equation

$$0 = \frac{d}{du}(TC) = T'(u)C(u) + T(u)C'(u).$$

Rearranging this equation provides the desired result. $\square$

This theorem provides a mathematical justification, and a quantitative test, for the concept of a machine component pulling its own weight. Therefore, we can state a general principle for choosing the size of an enhancement.

> **General Principle of Design:** To be cost-effective, the additional cost of an enhancement, relative to the cost of the whole, must be outweighed by the reduction in computation time resulting from the enhancement, relative to the total time.

4 Common Solutions

Substituting several common functions for the time and cost functions permits solving for the optimum size of enhancement.

4.1 Linear Speedup

Linear scalability characterizes a large number of circuits. In such circuits, a circuit of twice the size performs a given operation in half the time. Any design limited by register transfers or communication will be linearly scalable. For instance, an k-bit wide adder will require n/k cycles to perform an n-bit addition. A bus of k wires requires n/k cycles to transmit an n-bit number.

Definition 2 *A linear speedup has time given by $T(u) = 1 - f + f/u$ and cost given by $C(u) = 1 - \alpha + \alpha u$, where α and f are constants between 0 and 1.*

The constants α and f represent the fraction of the cost and time, respectively, associated with the enhancement. The remainder of the cost and time is not affected by the enhancement.

Theorem 2 *The width at which the normalized time of a linear speedup is optimal is given by the formula*

$$u = \sqrt{\frac{f(1-\alpha)}{\alpha(1-f)}}.$$

For a linear speedup, the normalized time is

$$C(u)T(u) = 1 - \alpha + \alpha u - f + \frac{f}{u} + 2\alpha f - \alpha f u - \frac{\alpha f}{u}.$$

Setting the first derivative to zero results in the equation

$$0 = \frac{d}{du}(CT) = \alpha - \frac{f}{u^2} - \alpha f + \frac{\alpha f}{u^2}$$

This produces the quadratic equation

$$\alpha(1-f)u^2 - f(1-\alpha) = 0$$

which has the solution

$$u = \sqrt{\frac{f(1-\alpha)}{\alpha(1-f)}}$$

as in the theorem.

Verification that this is indeed a minimum comes from examining the sign of the second derivative, which is

$$\frac{d^2}{du^2}(CT) = \frac{2f}{u^3} - \frac{2\alpha f}{u^3} = \frac{2f(1-\alpha)}{u^3} > 0. \ \square$$

A corollary to this theorem is that the processor is already balanced with respect to a linear enhancement when the time and cost fractions are equal. If these fractions are equal, a small change to the size of the enhancement has no effect, so there is no need for any departure from the base architecture. Furthermore, since linear enhancements have normalized time concave upward, there is no other lower minimum.

Corollary 3 *For a linear enhancement, the base architecture is already optimal in the case when $\alpha = f$.*

Substituting $\alpha = f$ means that the optimal value is at $u = 1$, or the original architecture. $\square$

4.2 Quadratic Growth

A second major class of enhancements is that of the quadratic circuits. The transitive functions, including multiplication, cyclic shifting, and other operations, exhibit an area-time tradeoff of the form AT^2 in the VLSI model [11, 12]. We shall adapt that argument to find the size which optimizes the normalized time.

The original argument considers the minimum bisection width w. In any transitive function, there exists some input such that $\Omega(n^2)$ bits must cross this bisection, which requires time $\Omega(n^2/w)$. On the other hand, since any bisection cuts at least w wires, the total wire area is $\Omega(w^2)$. This results in the requirement of $AT^2 = \Omega(n^2)$.

We use w directly, to parameterize the various circuits. We assume that for each w, there is a corresponding circuit for the function requiring time $O(n^2/w)$ and area $O(w^2)$. We also have, as usual, a fraction f of transitive function computation in the circuit, and a fraction α of the total cost charged to the transitive function circuit. The factor of n^2 may be absorbed into these constants, as well.

A transitive function computation obeys the conditions

$$T(w) = 1 - f + \frac{f}{w}$$
$$C(w) = 1 - \alpha + \alpha w^2$$

with the restrictions $0 < f < 1$, $0 < \alpha < 1$, and $w > 0$, to avoid singularities.

To find the minimum, we set the derivative to zero, producing the equation

$$0 = \frac{\partial}{\partial w}TC = \frac{1}{w^2}\left(2\alpha(1-f)w^3 + \alpha f w^2 - f(1-\alpha)\right).$$

Since both α and f are between 0 and 1, this derivative is negative near $w = 0$, and positive at large w. Therefore, there exists at least one point where it is zero, since the derivative is continuous.

In order to obtain a numerical solution, we multiply the derivative by w^2, to get the cubic equation

$$2\alpha(1-f)w^3 + \alpha f w^2 - f(1-\alpha) = 0.$$

The final numerical value may be obtained from the cubic equation formula for equations $w^3 + pw^2 + r$ by setting the values

$$p = \frac{f}{2(1-f)}$$
$$r = -\frac{f(1-\alpha)}{2\alpha(1-f)}$$
$$a = -\frac{1}{12}\left(\frac{f}{1-f}\right)^2$$

$$b = \frac{1}{108}\left(\frac{f}{1-f}\right)^3 - \frac{f(1-\alpha)}{2\alpha(1-f)}$$

$$A = \sqrt[3]{-\frac{b}{2} + \sqrt{\frac{b^2}{4} + \frac{a^3}{27}}}$$

$$B = \sqrt[3]{-\frac{b}{2} - \sqrt{\frac{b^2}{4} + \frac{a^3}{27}}}$$

$$x = A + B$$

$$w = x - \frac{p}{3}. \quad \square$$

5 Applications of the Analysis

We now turn to several examples of normalized analysis. The first example is setting up the equations for the quadratic functions of shifting and multiplication. Then, we consider concrete values for scaling a 32-bit processor, first downward to smaller word sizes, then upward to a VLIW structure. We can also combine these last two into a single, piecewise linear analysis, covering an entire span of datapath sizes.

5.1 Quadratic Functions

Here, we make a more careful study of shifters and multipliers. The AT^2 results provide only a lower bound, not a tight bound. Furthermore, even if the AT^2 tradeoff holds, the lower order terms neglected in the computation can be larger than the highest order term at the moderate widths seen in actual design.

For instance, we can take the shifter from the Quarter Horse processor [HJKSTY85], depicted in Figure 1. This is a 32-bit crossbar shifter, of approximately two million square microns, in the $3\mu m$ CMOS process. If we examine the actual design, though, we see that the crossbar array is only 42 percent of the width of the shifter. The remaining 58 percent consists of the input latches, the array input and output cells, and the output drivers. In the vertical dimension, the 32 bit-slices make up 90 percent of the shifter height, with 10 percent devoted to decoders and control logic. Thus, if we set w to be the width, relative to the 32-bit base architecture, we have cost $(0.58 + 0.42w)(0.1 + 0.9w)$. Thus, the cost is $0.38w^2 + 0.56w + 0.06$. With this cost, the linear term is larger than the quadratic term until the shifter reaches at least 47 bits. This means that to test Holman's observations concerning narrow shifters, the linear model is most accurate for 32 bit words.

This cost function, though is highly sensitive to the VLSI implementation. The shifter from the RISC II microprocessor [7] is quite similar, but is designed in a $4\mu m$ nMOS process. This shifter, though, has a

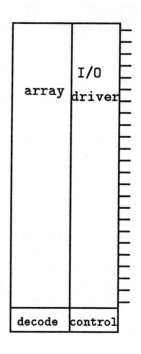

Figure 1: The Quarter Horse shifter

total area of $640,700\lambda^2$. This area is divided into $417,200\lambda^2$ for the crossbar array, and $223,500\lambda^2$ for the input latches, drivers, and decoders. The cost function, omitting the relatively small control area, is then $0.65w^2 + 0.35w$. The balance of the linear and quadratic terms has been reversed, compared with the Quarter Horse shifter. In fact, the quadratic term outweighs the linear term for any size larger than 17 bits.

Another case is that of the multiplier. Here, while the AT^2 results require a lower bound of n^2/w for the running time, given a width w, the straightforward method of accumulating partial products on w bits of the operands produces a running time of n^2/w^2. If we change our function for the running time accordingly, to $1 - f + f/w^2$, the equation becomes identical to that for a linear enhancement, except that w has been replaced by w^2. As a result, the optimal width is now given by

$$w = \sqrt[4]{\frac{f(1-\alpha)}{\alpha(1-f)}}.$$

Both of these cases show how we can adjust the theoretical results given previously to account in a more detailed way for the actual behavior of a datapath element. The modified functions can be directly substituted, and solving these revised equations will provide a better estimate of the optimal size.

306

Component	Area
Register File (16)	445,603 λ^2
ALU	404,954 λ^2
Shifter	424,844 λ^2
Control	466,041 λ^2
Communication (8)	1,458,000 λ^2
Total	3,199,442 λ^2

Table 1: Processor element area estimates.

Program	f	W	f'	w
Bitonic Sort	.75	.17	.90	162
Matrix Product	.94	.03	.97	307
LU Decomposition	.76	.17	.92	183
Cholesky Decomp.	.25	.73	.89	154
Jacobi Method	.91	.04	.95	235
SOR Method	.96	.02	.98	377
SIMPLE	.71	.27	.97	307

Table 2: Fraction of time affected by data path width.

5.2 Datapath Width – Smaller Processors

Next, we can consider changing the width of the entire datapath, taken as a whole. The extremes of this experiment are the bit-serial and word-parallel processors, but there are several intermediate widths, also. Clearly, the parameter must be the width, in bits, of the datapath.

Once we make this choice, we must now divide the time and area of a processor and program into the affected and unaffected categories. For this example, we provide some concrete values for the parameters. The analysis below is based on estimates [4] of sizes of elements taken from the Quarter Horse [6] and Mosaic [8] processor elements, scaled to a $3\mu m$ process, for a hypothetical processor element. See Table 1.

The category of area that is not affected by a change in the datapath width can be described, loosely, as control and storage. This category includes the actual control, in the form of random logic, microcode, and the like, as well as support structures, such as the program counter. Storage is also unaffected, since changing the storage capacity is a separate question. (We may also study this question, with structures such as the register windows found in the Berkeley RISC [10]. Here, though, the parameter would be the number of registers, and not the width of the datapath.)

The parts that are affected by the width include the ALU, as well as any shifter or multiplier that may be present. Also, many other, less prominent, parts are also affected. For instance, drivers and latches for bus interfaces and register bit lines are affected by datapath width. Though these buffers are smaller than ALU-sized parts, there is typically one bus driver and one latch for each datapath element, so their cumulative effect is significant.

Next, we determine the sizes for a specific processor. As we have postulated above, the registers, control, and communication are unaffected by changes to the datapath width. Furthermore, we postulate that the ALU and shifter are affected linearly. While one might expect the shifter array to be quadratic, its buffers and bus drivers are linear, and, as we noted earlier, the buffers of our shifter are actually larger than the array. This effect becomes even more pronounced as we move to smaller sizes. This results in a total unaffected area of $2,369,644\ \lambda^2$, and a total linearly affected area of $829,798\ \lambda^2$. The ratios are then 0.74 unaffected to 0.26 affected. If we specify the cost in the standard form of $1 - \alpha + \alpha w$, we have $\alpha = 0.26$, and w defined as the datapath width divided by 32.

Next the value for f is obtained for several benchmarks [4]. Since the original values are for f and W, we must adjust for the waiting time to give an effective fraction f'. These are shown in Table 2.

We can then use the formula from the linear analysis to find the best data path width. This is given by

$$32\sqrt{\frac{f(1-\alpha)}{\alpha(1-f)}}.$$

The results are also given in Table 2.

The datapath widths shown in Table 2 are enormous, and require some careful examination. First, even before considering the numbers, observe that enormous numbers are to be expected based on the values of $\alpha = 0.26$ and the f' values of about 0.9 given in Table 2. An architecture is in balance when $\alpha = f'$, so one fully expects the equations to mandate a dramatic increase in width when the gap between α and f' is so large.

Second, as explained earlier (Section 5.1), the linear formulation of the shifter is accurate only to about 47 bits; after that, a quadratic formulation is needed. Beyond that, the nature of the computation changes after 32 or 64 bits. Discussion of datapath width concerns operations on values within an instruction. Most programs have little need for integers suitable for representing the number of electrons in the universe. When the widths get as large as those shown in Table 2, we have moved into a VLIW situation – separate instructions operating on subfields of the datapath. (See Section 5.3 below.) This is simply a different case, with different growth. The best way to interpret this analysis is that *normalized time for a datapath diminishes throughout the range of applicability*. This confirms Holman's [3] analysis (in the range 1 to 32, a datapath of 32 is best) conjectured on the basis of independent tests of a few widths in this range.

Third, even with an interest in BIGNUMs and a proper mathematical model, the data are not quite precise enough to make an exact prediction of datapath speedup. The values for f in Table 2 are the fraction of all instructions using the datapath, but what we really need is the fraction of the time the datapath is in use. These two numbers would be the same if all instructions took the same amount of time and all overhead (fetching, decoding, etc.) were hidden, say in a pipeline. Even so, the we can conclude something from the value of w, as found in Table 2. The proper interpretation is that these values are so large, that in the range of 1 to 32 bit datapaths, the larger datapath is strongly favored. In other words, the datapath should be at least 32 bits wide.

We now turn to the more general question of bit-serial and word-parallel computers. Given the high fraction of computation affected by datapath width, the analysis essentially states that unless it directly leads to an improvement in datapath utilization, control logic is dead weight. As such, it should be amortized over as large a number of datapath bits as possible. Using a word-parallel processor meets this requirement. On the other hand, a bit-serial processor seems to be the worst possible arrangement, with only one bit of data path per unit of control.

Using SIMD design for bit serial processors solves this problem, of course. A large part of the fixed cost logic, that dealing with instruction fetch, decoding, and control flow, is amortized over not one, but 65,536 bits of datapath, in the Connection Machine, for example. Effectively, these parts are now scaled by neither datapath width nor number of processors, so they disappear from both sides of the equation. Thus, an SIMD architecture can help greatly in restoring balance in a highly parallel processor.

We can also consider this problem from the viewpoint of instruction set complexity. The RISC *vs* CISC controversy is not as closely related to the results of this analysis, but we can describe some of the principal arguments as attempts to solve the problem of datapath balance.

On the RISC side of the coin, we have seen how most processors have, relatively, too much control for a given amount of data path. The RISC advocates address this by reducing the amount of control. This reduces the unaffected cost term in the normalized time analysis. (Using the extra space for another part, such as the register windows of the Berkeley RISC [10] is actually two separate changes, •first deleting the extra control, then adding the register windows, which should be analyzed separately.)

On the CISC side, the argument is that the problem is not so much an excess of control, but an inability to use a larger data path. Thus, the solution is to add some more control, and larger instructions, so that there is more chance to exploit parallelism within an instruction. Having several words in process simultaneously then effectively allows for a wider data path.

5.3   Wider Processors – VLIW

Even among word-parallel designs, the desired data path widths are still much larger than the average word size. The VLIW design addresses this concern. By putting several operations into one instruction word, the effective word size is larger, allowing use of wider data paths. Meanwhile, the amount of control is increased by only a small amount.

In a VLIW design, though, it is often the case that, because of data or control dependencies, the extra calculations possible are wasted. Our model can take this into account, by repeating the analysis, but with a value of f reflecting, now, the fraction of time that two or more operations are simultaneously ready to execute. In fact, we can generalize f to a piecewise linear function, and still carry out the analysis. The data of how many instructions are ready to be issued at each time step are not exactly known, but the data of Table 2 are for a 64-way parallel computation, so generally, there would be a substantial number.

In our analysis of VLIW processors, we will use the same processor as the last analysis. We will make a large number of simplifying assumptions, but the results should still provide at least a general guideline. We assume that the register file now grows linearly, since each ALU segment needs its own temporary storage. The ALU, of course, still grows linearly. The shifter is now a linear, and not quadratic, part, since there is no need to shift data all the way across the processor, but only within one set of operands. As a result, the width is fixed at 32 columns, but the height grows with the number of bits of datapath. We assume that the control and communication sections are affected to only a negligible degree by the changes needed for the VLIW structure.

These assumptions result in an affected area of $1,275,401\lambda^2$, and an unaffected area of $1,924,041\lambda^2$. When normalized into the form $1 - \alpha + \alpha w$, this is a value of $\alpha = 0.40$. The parameter w is taken as the size, in words, of the datapath.

We next assume, in the absence of data to the con-

Program	w
Bitonic Sort	3.67
Matrix Product	6.96
LU Decomposition	4.15
Cholesky Decomp.	3.48
Jacobi Method	5.33
SOR Method	8.57
SIMPLE	6.96

Table 3: Optimal width of VLIW datapath (in words.)

trary, that the fraction of computation f affected by the extra ALU capacity is equal to the fraction of computation affected by reducing the datapath. In defense of this assumption, note that the benchmarks are already designed for highly parallel systems, and so using a VLIW structure is akin to increasing the parallelism. We should note though, that especially for the larger word sizes, we will need to adjust the analysis again, to take into account the reduced utilization of highly parallel systems.

To solve for the optimal number of ALU's in the system, we use our familiar equation

$$w = \sqrt{\frac{f(1-\alpha)}{\alpha(1-f)}}.$$

The results appear in Table 3. Note that the values for the width are of the same order of magnitude as the number of datapaths, 7, in the Multiflow [9], a commercial VLIW machine. While the Multiflow architecture differs from the sample architecture evaluated above, this correspondence suggests that the predictions from the model are reasonably consistent with real-world designs.

6 Conclusion

Using the model of *normalized time*, we have created a combined value that describes both the time and the cost of a processor. In this way, we can evaluate whether a particular enhancement is cost-effective. By parameterizing a set of possible enhancements, we can evaluate a range of designs in a single analysis.

Even for the most general case, we show that an enhancement is optimized when it is "doing its fair share." We can also state quantitatively the meaning of that intuitive concept.

For more specific cases, we can provide a formula for the optimal size of a part. After supplying some experimentally determined constants, an optimal value

emerges. The principal impediment to further investigation is the lack of empirical data. In one sense, this paper is a call to the experimentalists to gather more data, and apply the formulae.

In the long-standing RISC *vs* CISC and bit-serial *vs* word-parallel controversies, the model quantifies the reasoning behind the arguments for each case, and allows isolation of the aspects of a given processor or problem responsible for observed performance.

References

[1] G. M. Amdahl, "Validity of the single processor approach to achieving large-scale computing capabilities," in *Proc AFIPS Vol. 30*, pp. 483-465, 1967.

[2] W. D. Hillis, *The Connection Machine*, PhD Thesis, MIT 1985.

[3] T. J. Holman, *Processor Element Architecture for Non-shared Memory Parallel Computers*, PhD Thesis, University of Washington, 1988.

[4] T. J. Holman and L. Snyder, "Architectural Tradeoffs in Parallel Computer Design," in *Decennial Caltech Conference on VLSI*, 1989.

[5] S. Ho, T. Holman, L. Snyder, "Normalized Time and Its Use in Architectural Design," in *27th Allerton Conferences on Communication, Control and Computing*, pp 712-713, 1989.

[6] S. Ho, B. Jinks, T. Knight, J. Schaad, L. Snyder, A. Tyagi, C. Yang, "The Quarter Horse: A Case Study in Rapid Prototyping of a 32-bit Microprocessor Chip," in *Proceedings IEEE International Conference on Computer Design: VLSI in Computers*, pp. 261-266. IEEE, October 1985.

[7] M. Katevenis, R. Sherburne Jr., D. Patterson, Carlo Séquin, "The RISC II Micro-Architecture," in *VLSI '83*, F. Anceau and E. J. Aas (eds.) Elsevier Science Publishers B. V. (North-Holland), 1983.

[8] C. Lutz, S. Rabin, C. Seitz, D. Speck. "Design of the Mosaic Element," in *Conference on Advanced Research in VLSI*, Artech Books, 1984.

[9] Multiflow, *Technical Summary*, Multiflow Computer Incorporated, 1987.

[10] D. A. Patterson and C. H. Sequin, "A VLSI RISC," *Computer*, 15(9):8-21, 1982.

[11] C. D. Thompson, "Area-Time Complexity for VLSI," in *11th annual ACM Symposium on Theory of Computing,* pp. 81-88, 1979.

[12] J. Vuillemin, "A Combinatorial Limit to the Computing Power of VLSI circuits," in *21st IEEE Symposium on Foundations of Computer Science,* 1980.

A STUDY OF I/O BEHAVIOR OF PERFECT BENCHMARKS ON A MULTIPROCESSOR

A. L. Narasimha Reddy
Prithviraj Banerjee

Center for Reliable and High Performance Computing
University of Illinois
1101, W.Springfield Ave.
Urbana, IL 61801.

ABSTRACT

The I/O behavior of some scientific applications, a subset of Perfect bechmarks, executing on a multiprocessor is studied. The aim of this study is to explore the various patterns of I/O access of large scientific applications and to understand the impact of this observed behavior on the I/O subsystem architecture. I/O behavior of the program is characterized by the demands it imposes on the I/O subsystem. It is observed that implicit I/O or paging is not a major problem for the applications considered and the I/O problem is mainly manifest in the explicit I/O done in the program. Various characteristics of I/O accesses are studied and their impact on architecture design is discussed.

1. INTRODUCTION

The performance of processors has been growing steadily, and with multiprocessor organizations, the processing power of a computer system has been increasing at a rapid pace. However, the I/O performance has not kept pace with the gains in processing power. Currently, there exists a huge disparity between the I/O subsystem's performance and the processing power. With such differences in processing and I/O capacities, eventually the problem solving speed will be determined by how fast the I/O can be done. To avoid the I/O bottleneck, it is essential that some kind of improvements be made in I/O performance. The importance of balancing the I/O bandwidth and the computational power has been pointed out by Kung [1], where it is shown that for some of the applications, the I/O problem cannot be alleviated by adding more memory at the processors. For such applications, it is essential that the I/O power grows as fast as the processing power of the system. Hence, to improve the overall performance of a system, it is essential that the I/O subsystem performance also has to be improved. Examples of I/O limited applications include graphics and other real-time visualization applications [2].

Recently, there have been many proposals into improving the I/O response time of disk systems. Most of these proposals are based on improving the read-time either by interleaving the data block-wise across many disks [3], or byte-wise across many disks [4]. Some of the existing commercial systems employ these techniques [5, 6, 7] and experimental projects are currently being carried out [8, 9]. Some performance evaluations of the parallel disk systems have been carried out [10, 11, 12, 13]. Most of these studies have been based on simulated workloads or very simplistic models of workloads. The aim of this paper is to study the I/O behavior of scientific applications to guide further evaluation of these I/O systems. Some studies on I/O behavior of file systems in a multi-user environment are reported in [14, 15].

I/O is categorized as implicit I/O and explicit I/O. Implicit I/O refers to the disk service due to paging in a virtual memory system. Explicit I/O is the disk access explicitly initiated by a program through READ, WRITE commands. We wish to answer the following questions. What is the observed I/O traffic at the I/O subsystem when an application runs on a parallel machine? What impact does the observed I/O behavior have on the I/O architecture? Should the I/O subsystem be connected to the global memory in a shared-memory multiprocessor or should it be connected to the local memories of individual processors? Which is the dominant factor in I/O, implicit I/O or explicit I/O? How can these I/O times be reduced?

Section 2 describes the applications used for benchmarking. Section 3 looks at the working set sizes of the programs under study. Section 4 deal with the explicit I/O of the same programs. Section 5 summarizes the work reported in this paper and points to future work that needs to be done.

This research was supported in part by an IBM Graduate Fellowship and in part by National Science Foundation Presidential Young Investigator Award under contract no. NSF MIP 86-57563 PYI.

CH2887-8/90/0000/0312$01.00 © 1990 IEEE

2. APPLICATION BENCHMARKS

We used a subset of the Perfect Benchmarks [16] as the test set of applications. Perfect benchmarks are put together as a test suite for supercomputer evaluation and consist of 13 practical applications. Perfect benchmarks as a set do not contain highly I/O intensive applications because of portability constraints. However, by suitably scaling the processor speeds relative to the I/O speeds, we can get an idea of the balance of computation time and the I/O time of these applications. The main reason for using these benchmarks is the availability of the source codes. We chose five applications out of the 13 benchmarks that involve large I/O files, NA, SM, WS, TF, SR. NA is a molecular dynamics package for the simulations of the hydration structure and dynamics of nucleic acids, developed at IBM Kingston. SM is a seismic migration code used to investigate the geological structure of the Earth developed at Tel Aviv University, Israel. WS provides a global spectral model to simulate atmospheric flow, developed at the National Meteorological Center. TF performs an analysis of a transonic inviscid flow past an airfoil by solving the unsteady Euler equations developed at Princeton University. SR is a general-purpose, implicit finite-difference code for analyzing three-dimensional fluid flow problems by solving Euler and Navier-Stokes equations, developed at NASA Ames research center. The details about sizes of different files used for these codes is listed in Table 1. The applications were all written in FORTRAN with no parallel constructs.

3. IMPLICIT I/O

3.1. Methodology

The set of applications mentioned above are parallelized using the Alliant parallelizing and vectorizing compiler for execution on 8 processors. An Alliant emulator was used to emulate the program execution on an 8-processor Alliant. The emulator is used to generate the memory reference traces during the program's execution. The generated memory traces are compacted into page addresses since we are mainly interested in finding the working set characteristics of these programs. The working set of a program is defined as the set of pages referenced by a program within a particular specified time frame [17]. The Alliant emulator gives the following information for each memory address generated: *pid*, id of the processor making this reference; *address*, the byte address of the memory reference; *time*, the time (measured in cycles) at which the reference is made; *nbytes*, the number of bytes accessed by the memory reference; *rwtype*, whether the memory reference is a read or write or a test-and-set type. This information is used for our purposes as explained later. The time (as measured in cycles) is a typical value and the exact time at which a reference is made can vary. The addresses generated during program emulation correspond to physical addresses. The external file memory references are not emulated. Hence, if a write statement of the following form is present in the program, READ(ARRAY, FILE), then only the writes into the array are simulated and the reading of the external file does not generate memory addresses during the program emulation. Hence, the emulator only provides us with a way of measuring the internal memory referencing behavior. Our approach is to use these memory reference traces to generate the necessary I/O behavior of the program.

First, it should be noted that program emulation does not give us any idea of the explicit I/O that may be carried out during the program execution. We will deal with the explicit I/O problem in the next section. The generated memory address is converted into a page address by throwing away the least significant 12 bits of the address, i.e., 4K byte pages are considered. Pages of smaller size are not considered because of performance considerations. Information about larger page sizes can be obtained by suitably merging the 4K pages to form larger pages. It should be pointed out that the emulator assumes that an instruction cache is present and only generates those instruction addresses that do not result in a cache hit. The emulator generates all the data addresses since no data cache is assumed. However, for our purposes, emulating the instruction cache does not pose a problem. Each cache line must result in at least one cache miss when it is brought into cache and that is enough to register the fact that a particular page is referenced. The time given by the emulator does not take into account the time spent in fetching a page from secondary storage. Hence, the time at which a reference is made represents the time a reference may be made if all the pages were in memory. This enables us to hide the effects of the I/O architecture and lets us study the inherent paging behavior of the applications.

We used a working set approach to generate the necessary information about page usage and page faults. A window of 1 million word (4 bytes) references was used. All the page references in this window are collected along with the following information: a time-stamp of when the page is first accessed within this window, a time-stamp of when this page is last accessed, the number of bytes accessed within the page (multiple references to the same word are counted), the ids of the different processors that accessed this page. After a million word references, the set of pages accessed in the current window W_i is compared with the set of pages accessed in the previous window W_j. The new pages in W_i that were not accessed in W_j are printed out to a file. This set of pages in $W_i - W_j$ may be treated as page faults. Actually, these pages could have been brought into memory prior to W_j. So, this process of comparing only the neighboring windows gives us a maximum possible page-fault rate. The process of comparing only neighboring windows is equivalent to assuming that the system has only as many pages as referenced to in a window. Since we used a fairly small window (1 million word references), the generated page faulting pattern can be used to generate page fault rates for any reasonable size memory in the system. Another reason for using this approach was to eliminate any bias in the page-fault patterns due to the replacement policy used. Using our approach, we can impose any replacement policy on top of the generated faults to get modified page fault patterns.

In addition to collecting information about the new pages being faulted in, as explained above, whenever the number of new pages in $W_1 - W_2$ exceeded 25, we printed out all the information about all the pages in W_1. We treated these points as possible transition points in the working set of the program. The results from this study are explained below.

3.2. Results

Table 2 shows the number of references the program has been traced and the number of pages referenced by the program. The table also shows the percentage of pages shared by all the processors in the system. The programs could not be completely traced since the system never stayed up for long enough periods. It is to be noted that all the programs have been traced for at least 300 million word references. As we will see later, the number of references were large enough to get the working set of the programs into the memory. The number of pages referenced by these programs is fairly low, less than 2500 pages, each page of 4K bytes size. Since the working sets of these programs are low, it can be concluded that implicit I/O is not a major concern for these applications on multiprocessors since they have large amounts of memory. The main reason for this seems to be the fact that the perfect benchmarks were chosen to be of such sizes that they can be ported to many different machines, some of them with not considerable amounts of memory. If the programs were written for systems with larger amounts of memory, these numbers could have been considerably different.

One of the questions we wanted to answer following this study was, should the disk system be connected to the main memory of a shared-memory multiprocessor or to the local memories of the processors. Here, the local memory of a processor is assumed to be a private intermediate storage level between the cache at the processor and the shared memory. For this we needed to look at the pattern in which the pages were referenced by different processors in the system. If a higher fraction of pages are referenced individually by different processors, e.g., if page 1 is referenced only by processor 1 and page 2 is only referenced by processor 2, it would be viable to connect the disk system to the local memories of different processors. On the other hand, if a higher fraction of pages are referenced by all the processors in the system, then it would be more efficient to connect the disk system to the global memory or the shared memory of the system. Two or more processors referencing the page does not

necessarily mean they access the same word in the page, but that they access the same page. The fourth column of Table 2 shows the percentages of pages that are referenced by all the processors in the system. As the table shows, the percentages are quite high and on an average about 60% of the pages are shared by all the eight processors in the system. Besides these, some of the pages are shared by fewer than eight processors. From Table 2, we see that 85% of the pages are shared by two or more processors. This indicates that it would be more efficient to connect the disk system to the shared memory of the system. The main reason for such a high percentage of page sharing is array access within loops. When loops are parallelized, the arrays within the loop are referenced by all the processors and normally the granularity of these parallelized loops is such that each page is referenced by all the processors. This result is somewhat biased by the fact that we used applications written for serial machines and parallelized them to run them on a parallel machine. If the user was allowed to use parallel constructs, it is possible that the user could have specified parallel constructs at a larger granularity and thus lowering the percentage of pages referenced by all the processors. It is also to be noted that distributed memory machines such as hypercubes will have a very different accessing pattern.

The page faulting pattern of different programs as a function of the number of memory references made is shown in Fig. 1. All the applications show that most of the pages are brought into memory in a very short period of time and at the start of the program. This shows that most of the I/O requests occur in a burst. It also shows that these programs do not have drastically different working sets during different phases of the program execution. It should be noted that if different data are written into an array through explicit I/O commands at different times they are only counted as page faults the first time when the array is written into. Subsequent writes to that array through explicit I/O do not count as page faults. The subsequent disk accesses will be counted in the explicit I/O measurements.

Our next study is targeted to evaluate the advantages of prefetching pages into the main memory of a multiprocessor system. Fig. 2 shows the sequentiality in accessing data and code pages. A sequential page fault run of length L is defined to be the event of L page faults occurring on L consecutive pages. A similar measure is used for indicating sequentiality of access by [18]. The figure shows the fraction of the page faults occurring at different run lengths. Here, the sequential runs refer to the actual page accesses resulting in faults. The main reason for concentrating on the initial accesses is that they result in I/O. If L pages are brought into memory randomly, but used sequentially later, we do not treat the later accesses as a run of length L since these later accesses may not result in page faults if sufficient memory is available. As seen from figure, the code pages have far less sequentiality than the data pages. The ordinate axis in the figures represent the total fraction of pages that are brought in each run and not the number of runs themselves. The data pages of all the programs show substantial amount of sequentiality. Some of the programs have runs of substantial length. The total number of code pages in all these programs is fairly small, of the order of 60 pages, that all the code pages could be brought into memory in a single I/O operation. Since data pages show substantial sequentiality, performance benefits can be obtained by prefetching them into memory.

3.3. Impact on I/O performance

From the observed behavior of these applications, it can be concluded that implicit I/O is not a major concern for these applications. As explained above, this trend may not be generalized to other applications. It was observed that most of the pages are brought into memory in a short interval. This poses non-uniform demands on the I/O system. One possible way to reduce some of the peak demand rates is to prefetch pages. Our study also showed that most of the pages are accessed sequentially and hence prefetching could be beneficial. The observed properties such as sequentiality of access, advantages of prefetching, burst I/O demands are similar to the observed behavior of file systems in a multi-user environment.

4. EXPLICIT I/O

4.1. Methodology

In this section, we study several aspects of the explicit I/O behavior of the programs. To study the explicit I/O behavior, the READ and WRITE commands were modified to print out the related information to a file. The relevant information collected was, the time the I/O was initiated, the time the I/O was completed, the file from which the I/O was done, whether it was a read or a write, how many data items were written out, and a unique identifier for each READ and WRITE operation. The identifier gives us information about the data being read or written, whether a scalar variable, one dimensional vector, two dimensional matrix or a three dimensional matrix. Rewind operations (or fseeks to beginning of the file) are also traced with the same information. The program is executed at normal pace and the above information is collected for the full program execution. This study gives us an indication of the amount of time spent in performing the I/O operations during a program execution, what is the distribution of the data elements being read or written. The data will give an indication of the granularity of the I/O operations and hence an idea about possible speedups in using a parallel I/O system.

4.2. Results

Table 1 shows the total sizes of the different files used in explicit I/O. The amount of time spent in doing explicit I/O as a fraction of the total computation is given in Table 3. It is observed that the time spent doing I/O is not a considerable part of the problem solving time with the considered system. However, as the computing speeds improve because of parallelization or improvements in processor speeds, if the I/O rates stay constant, the fraction of time spent doing I/O will increase. The last column in the table indicates the effects of increasing the computing speeds by a factor of 10. As noticed from the table, most applications under this projection already are I/O bound. If we considered more than 8 processors in the system, the fractions of I/O time would be more significant. This clearly shows the need for improving the I/O performance in future computer systems. To avoid such future bottlenecks, parallel I/O organizations need to be considered and that is the main reason for this study. One of the reasons for such low fractions of I/O time is that a large number of subroutines were not parallelized owing to the compiler's inability to do inter-procedural analysis. Had these subroutines been parallelized, the corresponding fractions of I/O would have been much higher. In addition to doing I/O reads/writes in parallel, parallel formatting can also be carried out as suggested by [19].

The I/O times shown in Table 3 correspond to doing buffered I/O. Hence, most of the times are lower than actual values. The read times are timed correctly. But the write times are affected due to doing buffered I/O. When a write statement is executed, the write is considered complete when the data are transferred to the buffer since the actual transfer to the disk takes place later. However, read operation is considered complete only when the data are read into memory and hence the timing of read statements includes the time spent reading the data from the disk. These times are what are observed by the program and indicate the extent to which I/O delays the program completion.

Figure 3 shows histograms of the various data granularities in an explicit I/O operation. Different programs have quite different data granularities. Data granularity is defined here to be the number of data elements that are read or written using a single READ/WRITE statement. Different data elements may have different sizes in bytes depending on whether they are integers or floating point numbers and the format that may be used.

We observed two trends in doing explicit I/O, one is to read/write a large array of elements and the second one is to read/write different elements from a table. Reading/writing arrays results in large granularity of data transfer. Reading/writing different data elements in the form of a table results in smaller granularity of data transfer per I/O statement. However, these I/O transfers can also benefit from parallel I/O systems by appropriately transferring different portions of the table in parallel. Besides the parallelism available in each I/O statement, there is potential parallelism across different I/O statements. Input files typically consist of many data arrays that can potentially be read in parallel. Similarly, the output files consist of several different data arrays. The current practice of piecing together disparate data arrays into large files seems to have arisen out of the need to minimize the times for file opening and closing. Parallel file systems (with block-wise interleaving) can exploit this parallelism in reading/writing different pieces of the same file that are currently read/written sequentially.

Figure 4 shows the pattern of computation times between two different I/O calls in a program. The time between an I/O statement completion and the next I/O initiation is considered to be the computation time. The computation time between two I/O calls is plotted as function of the I/O call index. I/O call index is equal to the number of I/O statements executed till that point. Different programs have different profiles. The figure shows that in most cases, the computation time between two I/O calls is fairly low. Only the SM program shows a consistent profile with large computation time between two successive I/O calls. The SR program shows a very uniform computation profile with very small computation time between two I/O calls. Low computation time between two I/O calls is due to doing I/O within a loop. Table 4 shows some statistics about the computation time between two different I/O calls and the I/O time per I/O call. As seen from the table, the standard deviations are quite high indicating that the behavior is quite random.

Table 5 shows the fractions of explicit I/O transfers by different datatypes. The table lists the % of I/O calls made by each datatype and % of total data elements transferred by each datatype. The column that shows % data shows percentage of data elements transferred and not the percentage of actual bytes transferred. The 'scalars' column contains all the data that can not be classified as matrices of any dimension. This column mostly contains scalar values, headers and comments. It is seen from the table that most of the transfers take place either as scalars or vectors or two-dimensional matrices. Very few transfers are three dimensional matrices and no higher order matrices were noticed. Also, it is noticed that the % of I/O calls do not always correlate to the % data elements transferred. This is due to the fact of varying data granularities in I/O operations.

Though the I/O operations consist of different data types, the I/O operations always constituted sequential accesses. We did not observe any random access of files in these applications. Though the SM application uses a large temporary file of 94 Mbytes that was declared 'direct' access, all the records were accessed in serial order. Again, it is to be stressed that the observed sequential accesses may be a direct result of user's awareness of the performance implications of random accesses to an external file.

Table 6 shows the rereference count of files in each application. The rereference count of an application is the sum of the rereference counts of its files. The rereference count of a file is the number of times the file is rereferenced. The rereferencing count gives an idea of the advantages of using a disk cache. As seen from the table, the file rereference counts are not very high. The number of files used in that particular application are also shown for comparison. But two applications WS, SM show considerable rereferencing that they could benefit from a disk cache. The low rereference counts indicate that it is not necessary to cache all the files. This shows that the observed behavior of file systems in multi-user environments [14, 15] do not accurately represent the I/O behavior of large scientific applications. This also points to the advantages of using a compiler to give hints on rereferencing of files to aid the functioning of disk cache.

4.3. Impact on I/O performance

The observed granularity in I/O varied among the different applications. Larger granularity leads to more efficient I/O transfer. Buffered I/O considerably improves the granularity of actual transfer to secondary storage and the data collected shows the need for such a mechanism. If parallel disk systems are used, different blocks of data can be transferred in parallel. Hence, we would need to provide for more buffer storage in such systems to exploit the available parallelism in the I/O system. It was observed that the external files are not rereferenced that often for a disk cache to be very effective. This also points to the need for compiler support to efficiently utilize the disk cache.

In the previous section, it was observed that implicit I/O is not a concern for the applications considered. In this section, it was found that with increasing computing speeds, explicit I/O will become a bottleneck in the near future. Loop blocking techniques can reduce the implicit I/O rates and increase the explicit I/O rates. I/O also affects compilation of programs for parallel execution. Some of the I/O compilation issues are being currently investigated [20].

CONCLUSIONS

In this paper, we presented results from studying the I/O behavior of large scientific applications on a multiprocessor. It was observed that the I/O accesses are very sequential. It was argued that this may be partly due to the knowledge of the programmer about the sequential file system. It was shown that parallel file systems can exploit the available parallelism in I/O transfers. The observed I/O behavior of these applications is quite similar to the observed behavior of file systems in multi-user environments except for a few differences. One of the noted differences was that the files are not rereferenced that often in these applications. It was shown that pages are shared extensively in a shared memory multiprocessor machine that the I/O system should be connected to the global memory. More applications need to be studied for getting a more comprehensive idea of the I/O requirements of different applications.

ACKNOWLEDGEMENTS

The authors wish to acknowledge the generous support of CSRD, Center for Supercomputing Research and Development, University of Illinois in providing various facilities during this research. The referees' and Prof. Dave Patterson's comments have improved the presentation of the paper. We also like to acknowledge the help given by Lyle Kipp and John Fu during this work.

References

[1] H.T.Kung, "Memory Requirements for Balanced Computer Architectures," *Proc. of 13th Ann. Int. Symposium on Computer Architecture*, pp. 49-54, 1986.

[2] "Scientific Visualizaion," *IEEE Computer magazine*, vol. 22, no.8, Aug. 1989.

[3] K.Salem and H.Garcia-Molina, "Disk Striping," *Int. Conf. on Data Engineering*, pp. 336-342, 1986.

[4] M.Y.Kim, "Synchronized Disk Interleaving," *IEEE Trans. on Computers*, vol. C-35, no.11, pp. 978-988, Nov. 1986.

[5] "Connection Machine Model CM-2 Technical Summary," *Tech. Rep. HA87-4*, vol. Thinking Machine Co., April 1987.

[6] Cray Research, "Cray X-MP and Cray-1 Computer Systems: Disk Systems Hardware Reference Manual," vol. HR-0077, 1440 Northland Drive, Mendota Heights, Minnesota 55120, 1985.

[7] Fujitsu America, "M2360A Parallel Transfer Disk Engineering Specifications," vol. B03P-4905-0001A, 3055 Orchard Drive, San Jose, CA 95134-2017, 1986.

[8] D.A.Patterson, G.Gibson, and R.H.Katz, "A Case for Redundant Arrays of Inexpensive Disks (RAID)," *ACM SIGMOD Conference*, June 1988.

[9] "Special Issue: Input/Output Architecture," *Computer Arch. News, ACM magazine*, Sept. 1989.

[10] M. Livny, S.Khoshafian, and H.Boral, "Multi-Disk Management Algorithms," *Proc. of ACM SIGMETRICS*, pp. 69-77, May 1987.

[11] A.L.Narasimha Reddy and P. Banerjee, "An Evaluation of Multiple-Disk I/O Systems," *to appear in IEEE Trans. on Computers*, Dec. 1989.

[12] A. L. Narasimha Reddy and P. Banerjee, "Design, Analysis and Simulation of I/O Architectures for Hypercube Multiprocessors," *to appear in IEEE Trans. on Parallel and Distributed Systems*.

[13] P. M. Chen, "An Evaluation of Redundant Arrays of Disks using an Amdahl 5890," *Tech. Rep. UCB/CSD 89/506*, vol. University of California, Berkeley, May 1989.

[14] J.K.Ousterhout et al, "A Trace-Driven Analysis of the UNIX 4.2 BSD File System," *Proc. of 10th Symp. on Operating System Principles*, pp. 15-24, Dec. 1985.

[15] Murthy V.S.Devarakonda, "File Usage Analysis and Resource Usage Prediction: A Measurement-Based Study," in *Tech. Report: CSG-79*, Univ. of Illinois, Urbana-Champaign, Dec. 1987.

[16] "The Perfect Club Benchmarks: Effective Performance Evaluation of Supercomputers," *CSRD Tech. Rep. no. 827, CSRD, University of Illinois, Urbana*, May 1989.

[17] P. J. Denning, "Virtual Memory," *ACM Computing Surveys*, vol. 2, no.3, pp. 62-97, Sept. 1970.

[18] J. P. Kearns and S. DeFazio, "Diversity in Database Reference Behavior," *Proc. of SIGMETRICS Conf.*, pp. 11-19, May 1989.

[19] W. Abu-Sufah, H. E. Husmann, and D. J. Kuck, "On Input/Output Speedup in Tightly Coupled Multiprocessors," *IEEE Trans. on Computers*, vol. C-35, no.6, pp. 520-530, June 1986.

[20] A. L. Narasimha Reddy and P. Banerjee, "Software Support for Parallel I/O," *under preparation*.

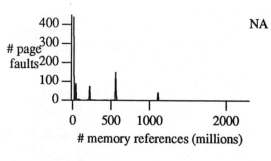

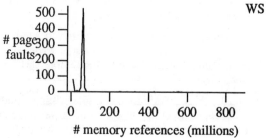

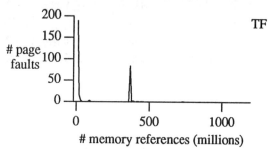

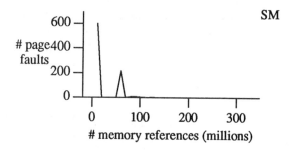

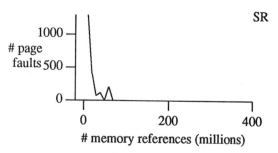

Fig. 1. Page faulting patterns.

Table 1. File sizes for the test suite.

Application	Files I(input) O(output)	Size bytes
NA	Executable	270k
	NAI10	247
	NAI11	46k
	NAI12	42k
	NAI13	2976
	NAI14	5376
	NAI5	346
	NAI9	2398k
	NAO20	602k
	NAO6	640
	NAO66	10k
	NAO8	823k
WS	Executable	155k
	WSD	8138
	WSI16	1249k
	WSI17	2407k
	WSI18	1139k
	WSI5	59
	WSO14	1139k
	WSO15	1235k
	WSO19	1139k
	WSO6	8969
TF	Executable	147k
	TFI5	2013
	TFO6	1198k
SM	Executable	143k
	SMI41	76k
	SMO6	1925
	Temp 1	94M
	Temp 2	240k
SR	Executable	205k
	SRI5	184
	SRO11	411k
	SRO4	823k
	SRO6	20k

Table 2. Page reference characteristics of programs.

Application	# of word refs. traced Millions	# of pages used 4k bytes	shared by all procs. # of pages	%	shared by 2 or more # of pages	%
NA	2226	755	549	72.72	577	76.42
WS	801	683	532	77.89	568	83.16
TF	1121	313	258	82.43	282	90.10
SM	321	836	396	47.37	710	84.93
SR	382	2115	387	18.30	1993	94.23

Table 3. I/O time as a fraction of total time.

App.	Total time Secs.	I/O time Secs.	% I/O time	% proj. I/O
NA	125.61	23.78	18.93	65.44
WS	989.04	101.64	10.28	50.68
TF	88.63	1.67	1.88	15.86
SM	8086.97	110.78	1.37	12.05
SR	223.78	9.89	4.42	30.65

Table 4. Statistics of I/O and Computation times.

App.	Comp. time Avg.(sec)	St. Dev.	I/O time Avg.(ms)	St.Dev.
NA	0.99	4.36	230	200.21
WS	1.61	7.54	184.5	109.34
TF	0.44	0.46	8.4	39.00
SM	15.95	20.17	221.6	55.98
SR	1.98	0.55	91.6	884.8

Table 5. Frequency of explicit I/O by datatypes.

Application	Datatype Scalars %data	% I/O	1-dim matrices %data	%I/O	2-dim matrices %data	%I/O	3-dim matrices %data	%I/O
NA	0.05	16.35	99.94	79.24	0.01	4.40	0.00	0.00
WS	0.02	6.31	3.13	37.01	96.85	56.67	0.00	0.00
TF	79.58	81.86	8.34	12.83	6.04	2.65	6.04	2.65
SM	0.00	0.60	100.00	99.40	0.00	0.00	0.00	0.00
SR	0.74	96.49	0.00	0.00	33.17	2.63	66.09	0.88

Table 6. Rereference count of applications.

Application	rereference count rereference/ # of files
NA	1/11
WS	3/8
TF	0/2
SM	2/4
SR	0/4

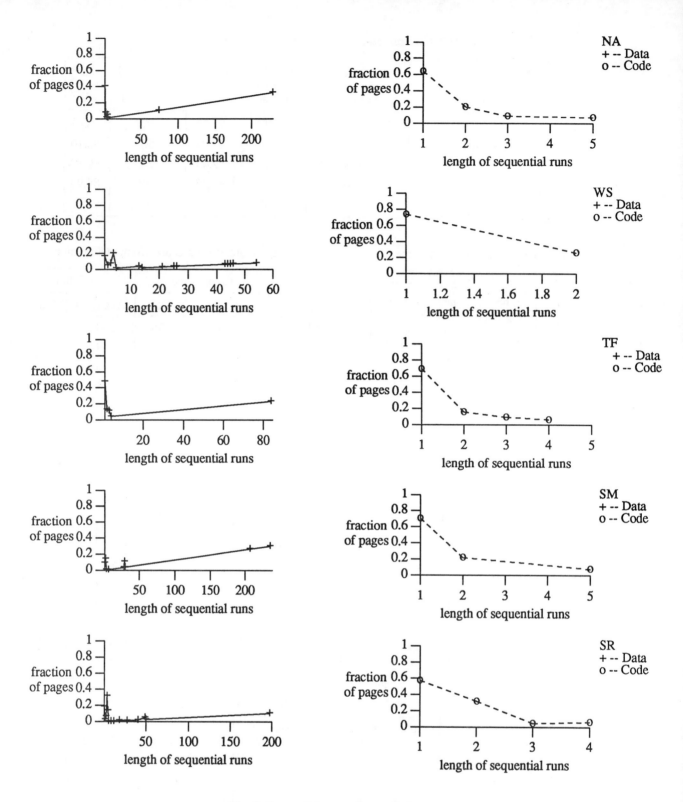

Fig. 2. Sequential runs of page faults.

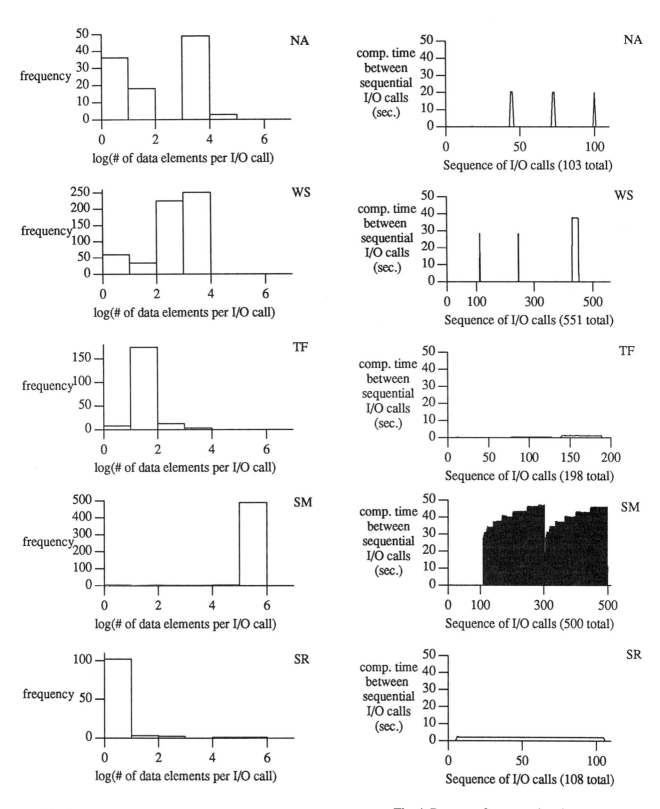

Fig. 3. Data granularity in I/O operations.

Fig. 4. Patterns of computation time between two I/O calls.

Maximizing Performance in a Striped Disk Array

Peter M. Chen   David A. Patterson

Computer Science Division, University of California, Berkeley

Abstract. *Improvements in disk speeds have not kept up with improvements in processor and memory speeds. One way to correct the resulting speed mismatch is to stripe data across many disks. In this paper, we address how to stripe data to get maximum performance from the disks. Specifically, we examine how to choose the striping unit, i.e. the amount of logically contiguous data on each disk. We synthesize rules for determining the best striping unit for a given range of workloads.*

We show how the choice of striping unit depends on only two parameters: 1) the number of outstanding requests in the disk system at any given time, and 2) the average positioning time × data transfer rate of the disks. We derive an equation for the optimal striping unit as a function of these two parameters; we also show how to choose the striping unit without prior knowledge about the workload.

1. Introduction

In recent years, computer technology has advanced at an astonishing rate: processor speed, memory speed, and memory size have grown exponentially over the past few years [Bell84, Joy85, Moore75, Myers86]. However, disk speeds have improved at a far slower rate. As a result, many applications are now limited by the speed of their disks rather than the power of their CPUs [Agrawal84, Johnson84]. As improvements in processor and memory speeds continue to outstrip improvements in disk speeds, more and more applications will become I/O limited.

One way to increase the data rate (bytes transferred per second) and the I/O rate (I/O requests per second) from a file system is by distributing, or striping, the file system over multiple disks. In this paper, we examine how to choose the striping unit, i.e. the amount of logically contiguous data to store on each disk. If this choice is made incorrectly, 80% or more of the potential disk throughput can be lost. Our goal is to synthesize rules for determining the optimal striping unit under a variety of loads, request sizes, and disk hardware parameters.

We show how the choice of striping unit depends on only two parameters: 1) the number of outstanding requests in the disk system at any given time, and 2) the average positioning time × data transfer rate of the disks. We derive an equation for the optimal striping unit as a function of these two parameters; we also show how to choose the striping unit without prior knowledge about the workload.

2. Definitions

We define the *striping unit* as the maximum amount of logically contiguous data that is stored on a single disk (see Figure 1). A large striping unit will tend to keep a file clustered together on a few disks (possibly one); a small striping unit tends to spread each file across many disks. Unlike [Patterson88, Chen90], we do not include any redundant data into our data striping scheme; data from each file is simply distributed round-robin over the disks.

We use parallelism to describe the number of disks that service a user request for data. A higher degree of parallelism increases the transfer rate that each request sees. However, as more disks cooperate in servicing each request, fewer independent requests can be serviced simultaneously. We define the degree of *concurrency* of a workload as the average number of outstanding user requests in the system at one time. A small striping unit causes higher parallelism but supports less concurrency in the workload; a large striping unit causes little parallelism but supports more concurrency in the workload.

3. Previous Work

Disk striping is not a new concept—Cray Research has been striping files over multiple disks for many years to increase data rate [Johnson84]. However, with the proliferation of smaller diameter disk drives, striping over many disk drives could provide order of magnitude benefits in performance/cost, capacity/cost, power, and volume [Patterson88]. As a result, disk striping research has increased dramatically over the past few years.

Kim [Kim86] proposes a striping unit of one byte (byte-interleaving). Using queuing models, she finds that, under light loads, byte-interleaving yields higher throughput than a collection of non-cooperating disks

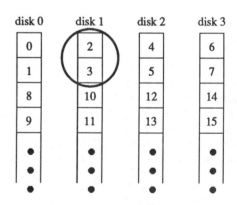

Figure 1: Definition of a Striping Unit. This figure shows the mapping of logical data to the disks for a striping unit of two sectors. The numbers in the figure are logical sectors; the circled two sectors constitute one stripe unit.

CH2887-8/90/0000/0322$01.00 © 1990 IEEE   322

Default Disk Parameters	
bytes/sector	512
sectors/track	60
tracks/cylinder	15
cylinders/disk	885
average seek	14.7 ms
full rotation	16.7 ms
average rotational latency	8.35 ms
rotationally synchronized	yes
number of disks	16

Table 1: Specifications of Default Disk System.

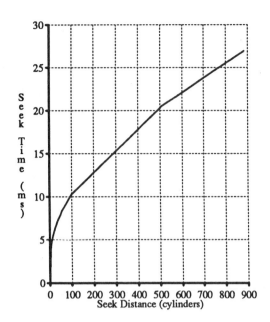

Figure 2: Seek Time Model. Graphed above is seek time in ms as a function of seek distance in cylinders [Thisquen88]. We model this as

$$seektime(x) = \begin{cases} 0 & \text{if } x=0 \\ 1.9-x/50+\sqrt{x} & \text{if } 0<x\leq50 \\ 8.1+.044*(x-50) & \text{if } 50<x\leq100 \\ 10.3+.025*(x-100) & \text{if } 100<x\leq500 \\ 20.4+.017*(x-500) & \text{if } 500<x\leq885 \end{cases}$$

(disks with an infinitely large striping unit). She also notes that byte-interleaved disks reach saturation under much lighter loads than non-cooperating disks.

Livny, et al. [Livny87] propose a scheme called declustering where the striping unit is 1 track (26 KB in their study) and compare its performance to a scheme with an infinitely large striping unit, called clustering. They conclude that declustering consistently yields higher throughput than clustering. They attribute this difference to two factors: 1) declustering allows increased parallelism, and 2) declustering load-balances the disks by spreading each file across multiple disks.

Patterson, et al. [Patterson88] investigate five ways to introduce redundancy into disk arrays to increase data availability. One of the redundancy schemes, RAID Level 3, has a striping unit of one byte. Two of the redundancy schemes, RAID Levels 4 and 5, have a striping unit of one block (block-interleaving), where a block remains unspecified.

Chen [Chen90] conducts hardware experiments on an Amdahl mainframe to further investigate two of the redundancy schemes in [Patterson88]. As part of his evaluation, he compares disk arrays with a striping unit of

one sector (4 KB) and one track (40 KB). The workloads that we use in this experiment are essentially the same as in [Chen90].

Reddy, et al. [Reddy 89] evaluate a range of disk striping schemes ranging from byte-interleaving to block-interleaving, with a typical block size of 4 KB. In his evaluation, Reddy, et al. assume that byte-interleaved disks are rotationally synchronized with each other, but that block-interleaved disks are not synchronized. Reddy, et al. also propose several hybrid striping schemes where blocks are interleaved across units which are themselves made of several byte-interleaved disks.

4. Experimental Introduction

4.1. Simulator

Using a disk simulator, we evaluate the performance of disk arrays with various striping units and disk parameters under several workloads. Because we are primarily interested in the performance of the disk subsystem, we that assume the CPU and the data path to memory are infinitely fast. Our system is thus completely disk limited.

At the start of a run with workload concurrency N, N user requests for data are issued. Depending on the striping unit, each user request is mapped into one or more disk requests. When one user request finishes, another user request is generated, maintaining a degree of concurrency of N. This process continues until 1000-N requests have been issued, after which the last N user requests are allowed to complete. Thus, a total of 1000 user requests are issued per run. This number of user requests was found to be sufficient to render the start-up and ending overhead of each run insignificant. Five independent runs are averaged together in order to produce a tight confidence interval. Each data value in this paper has a 90% confidence interval whose width is less than 5% of that data value (typically 1%-3%).

4.2. Disk Parameters

Several types of disks were modeled. The default disks, approximately the same as an Amdahl 6380A [Thisquen88], are characterized by parameters given in Table 1 and Figure 2. Note that the disks are rotationally synchronized, where we define rotational synchronization as rotating in unison. I.e., disks that are synchronized rotate at the same rate and have sector 0 on each track pass underneath the read/write head at the same time. When multiple disks cooperate on a single user request, the user must wait until all disks have transferred their data. In a rotationally unsynchronized disk system, the rotational latency which a multi-disk request sees is approximately a full rotation; in a rotationally synchronized disk system, this rotational latency is one-half of a full rotation. In past research, disk arrays with a striping unit of byte are usually synchronized [Kim86, Reddy89], whereas disk arrays with a striping unit larger than one byte are not [Reddy89, Livny87]. This practice stems from the common assumption that 1) a group of byte-interleaved disks is viewed as a single unit and can only service one request at a time and 2) block-interleaved disks allow independent requests but do not cooperate together on one request. However, synchronizing block-interleaved disks does not inherently prevent them from operating independently and servicing different requests to different addresses. And, synchronized block-interleaved disks still benefit from synchronization when cooperating on a single request. Throughout this paper, we use rotationally synchronized disks.

For all disks modeled, we assume sector gaps are zero-length and head switch time is instantaneous. We do, however, model the cylinder switch time and skew the sector layout of consecutive cylinders to maximize the performance of sequential requests.

To explore how the striping unit affects performance for a variety of disk parameters, we experiment with several modifications on the above default disks. Variations explored were: disks that seeked twice as quickly (all seek times were halved), disks that rotated twice as quickly, and disks that had twice as many sectors per track. We also simulate Imprimis Sabre disks (8" diameter) [Imprimis89].

4.3. Workload

The workload supplied to the disks is characterized by three parameters: degree of concurrency, request size,

and request starting location. The degree of concurrency is varied between 1 and 20. At a concurrency of 1, each newly issued request sees an idle system; by concurrency 20, the 16-disk system is saturated.

Four distributions of request sizes were used:

(1) *exp4k*: An exponential distribution with a mean of 4 KB.

(2) *exp16k*: An exponential distribution with a mean of 16 KB.

(3) *norm400k*: A normal distribution with a mean of 400 KB and a standard deviation of 400 KB.

(4) *norm1.5m*: A normal distribution with a mean of 1.5 MB and a standard deviation of 1.5 MB.

The starting location for each request consists of two components: starting disk and starting sector on that disk. The starting disk is chosen uniformly out of all the disks in the system; the starting sector on the disk is chosen uniformly out of all sectors on that disk. This location distribution does not favor any disk over any other; i.e. over time, independent of the striping unit and request size distribution, each disk will see approximately the same number of requests. Some past research (for example, [Chen90]), assumed the presence of *hot* disks, i.e. disks that received more accesses than the others. However, we believe that hot disks are becoming less of a problem for two reasons: first, the increasing file cache size of today's systems will buffer hot data from small files. Second, a striped disk system will spread large files (files much larger than the striping unit) across all disks in a round-robin fashion. This round-robin distribution will result in each disk containing file data which is separated by N striping units. So, unless a user accesses striping units 0, N, 2N, etc. of a file more frequently than 1, N+1, 2N+1, etc., there is no reason to expect any disk to see more accesses to that file than any other disk.

5. Metrics

Common disk system performance metrics are throughput and response time. With a fixed level of concurrency, higher throughput generally leads to faster response time. In this paper, we use throughput as the main performance metric. Most throughput values will be given as a percentage of the maximum throughput over all striping units. For example, if the maximum throughput over all striping units for a particular workload is 10 megabytes per second, and a striping unit S, yields a throughput of 3 megabytes per second, then the throughput for striping unit S will be given as 30% of maximum throughput.

6. General Performance Trends

Fundamentally, disk striping impacts the amount of data that each disk transfers before re-positioning (seeking and rotating to the next request). This amount of data has a drastic influence on disk throughput. For our default disks, if a disk transfers one sector per request, throughput will be .02 MB/s; if it transfers one track per request, throughput will be .8 MB/s; if it transfers one cylinder per request, throughput will be 1.6 MB/s. In choosing the

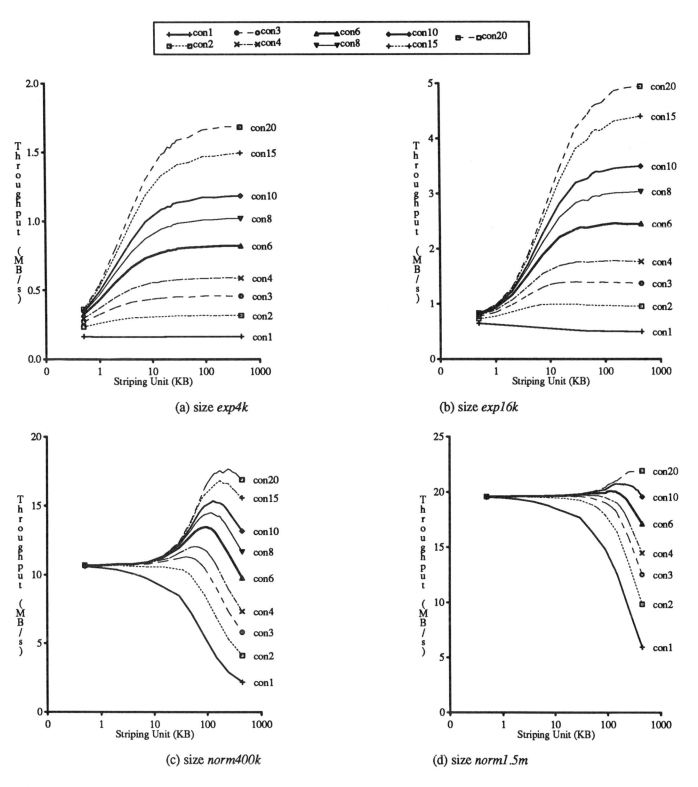

Figure 3: Throughput for a Range of Sizes and Concurrencies. Throughput is shown as a function of striping unit. The throughput increases with larger request sizes and higher degrees of concurrency, as expected.

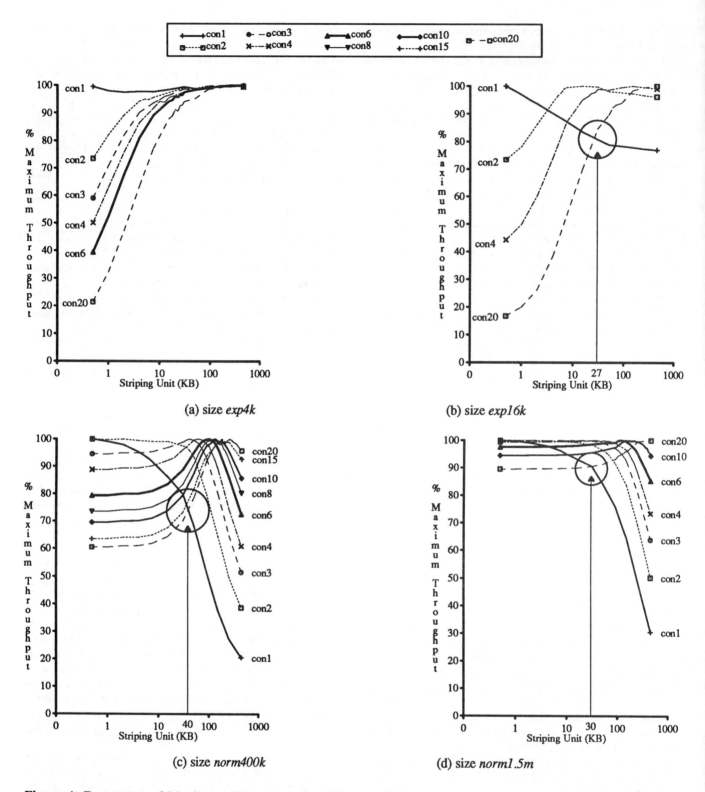

Figure 4: Percentage of Maximum Throughput for a Range of Sizes and Concurrencies. Percentage of maximum throughput is shown as a function of striping unit. The circled point on each graph indicates the striping unit which guarantees the highest percentage of maximum throughput to all workloads shown on that graph.

striping unit, we strive to maximize the amount of useful data each disk transfers per request and still make use of all disks. Large striping units maximize the amount of data a disk transfers per access but require higher concurrency in the workload to make use of all disks. Small striping units can make use of all disks even with low workload concurrency, but cause the disks to transfer less data per access.

Figure 3 shows the throughput versus the striping unit for a range of sizes and concurrencies. We vary the striping unit from .5 KB (1 sector) to 450 KB (1 cylinder). At any fixed striping unit, the throughput increases with larger request sizes and higher degrees of concurrency. Increasing request sizes result in each disk accessing more data per request; higher degrees of concurrency are able to make use of more disks. In order to compare trends from different workloads more easily, we scale the throughput of each workload, expressing it as a percentage of the maximum throughput (Figure 4).

In Figure 4, there are three categories of workloads: workloads whose maximum throughput is at the smallest striping unit (e.g. Figure 4b concurrency 1), workloads whose maximum throughput is at the largest striping unit (e.g. Figure 4b concurrency 20), and workloads whose maximum throughput is between the smallest and largest striping unit (e.g. Figure 4c concurrency 6).

When the maximum throughput of a workload is at the smallest possible striping unit, the workload has low enough concurrency that it makes best use of the disks by having the maximum possible parallelism. In particular, at a concurrency of one, the striping unit which yields the highest throughput is 1 sector (.5 KB)—all other striping units at a concurrency of 1 will yield far less throughput. An exception is the *exp4k* request size distribution. Because striping over multiple disks decreases only the data transfer time, the response time of 4 KB requests can at most be decreased by 2 ms,[1] which is less than 10% of the total response time. In addition, even in an idle system, involving multiple disks in a request can sometimes lead to worse performance. For example, when disks take different amounts of time to position, the request must wait for the slowest-positioning disk to transfer its data. When disks are rotationally synchronized, the rotational latency among multiple disks is usually equal. However, even with rotationally synchronized disks, if the involved disks do not start at the same cylinder, the positioning time will vary, causing slower response time. For large request sizes, the advantage gained in decreased data transfer time far offsets this small penalty in positioning synchronization. For *exp4k*, however, the amount of time saved in data transfer is approximately equal to the amount of time lost to positioning synchronization.

When the maximum throughput of a workload is at the largest possible striping unit (450 KB), the workload has enough concurrency that we should maximize the amount of data each disk transfers per request—the workload concurrency will inherently use all the disks. For example, for a concurrency of 20, each disk can service a different user request, and throughput is maximized by having each request access one disk.

When the maximum throughput of a workload is between the smallest and largest striping units, the workload has enough concurrency that each request should not occupy all the disks. However, concurrency in these workloads is low enough that having each request access only one disk would not use all the disks.

7. Choosing the Striping Unit

If one knows the parameters of a workload, i.e. the request size distribution and the concurrency, one can use Figure 4 to choose the striping unit which maximizes throughput. However, in most systems, the exact workload is not known. One of, or possibly both, the request size and the concurrency will be unspecified. Thus, it is desirable to be able to choose a good striping unit with as little knowledge about the workload as possible. In this paper, we will strive to maximize the *minimum percentage throughput over a range of considered workloads*. In other words, we wish to guarantee the highest percentage of maximum throughput to all workloads in consideration. For example, if the request size is known to be *norm400k* but the concurrency is unknown, we can use Figure 4c to choose a striping unit. In Figure 4c, over the range of concurrencies between 1 and 20, the striping unit which maximizes the minimum percentage throughput is 40 KB. At that striping unit, all workloads considered yield at least 74% of their maximum possible throughput. Note that when the request size distribution is known, only the maximum and minimum concurrency workloads need to be graphed to calculate the desired striping unit.

Figure 5 graphs the percentage of maximum throughput for systems where the workload concurrency is known, but the request size distribution is unknown. Using the same "maximize the minimum percentage throughput" criterion as above, we can choose a desirable striping unit for a range of request sizes. Note that even if only the concurrency is known, *it is possible to choose a striping unit which yields over 95% of the maximum throughput for all request sizes*. On the other hand, if only the request size is known, then the best striping unit choice can guarantee only 70%-90% of the maximum throughput for all workload concurrencies (Figure 4). Thus, *concurrency is the important workload parameter in choosing the striping unit*.

To further examine how concurrency affects the choice of a striping unit when the average request size is unknown, we graph a range of possible striping unit choices at each concurrency (Figure 6). We display the range of striping units at each degree of concurrency which guarantees at least 95% of maximum throughput for all

---

[1] 4 KB is 8 sectors (.133 of track) and takes .133 * 16.7 ms to transfer.

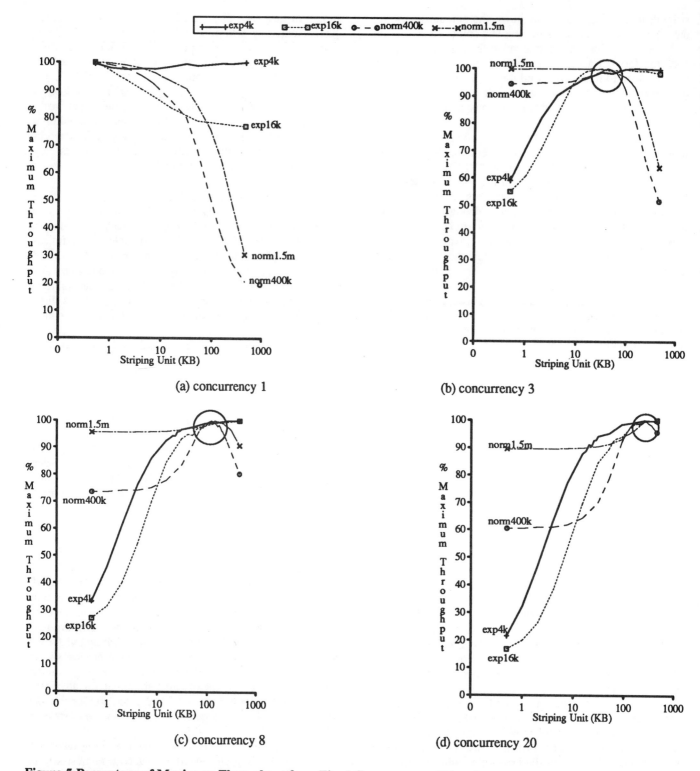

Figure 5:Percentage of Maximum Throughput for a Fixed Concurrency. When the concurrency is known, it is possible to choose a striping unit which yields over 95% of maximum throughput for all request sizes. The circled area on each graph is the range of striping units that guarantees 95% of maximum throughput for all workloads.

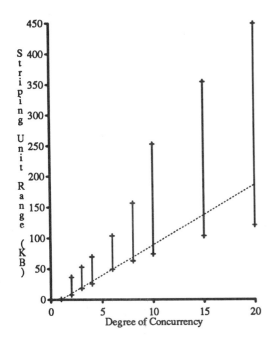

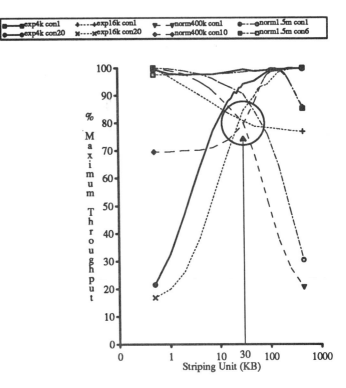

Figure 6: Striping Unit Chosen versus Concurrency— Default Disks. Shown here is the range of striping units which yield at least 95% of the maximum throughput for all request sizes (*exp4k, exp16k, norm400k, norm1.5m*). Also shown is the line with smallest slope which lies entirely in the striping unit range. The largest striping unit simulated was 450 KB.

Figure 7: Percentage of Maximum Throughput for a Wide Range of Workloads. Shown here is the percentage of maximum throughput for a wide range of concurrencies and request sizes. The striping unit which guarantees the highest percentage of maximum throughput to each workload is 30 KB.

request sizes (*exp4k, exp16k, norm400k, norm1.5m*). We can express our choice of striping unit as a linear function of workload concurrency by 1) fixing the striping unit choice for a concurrency of one at 1 sector (.5 KB), and 2) measuring the minimum slope of any striping unit vs. concurrency line that lies entirely in the displayed range. Our choice of striping unit in Figure 6 can then be expressed as

(1) Striping Unit in KB =
        9.8 KB × (Degree of Concurrency - 1) + .5 KB

The slope of this line is 9.8 KB/Degree of Concurrency. This means that for every additional simultaneously outstanding request in the system, the striping unit should be increased by 9.8 KB. We shall see later how to express this slope in terms of disk parameters.

If little or no workload information is given, we can choose a good compromise striping unit by graphing the maximum and minimum concurrency for a range of request sizes (Figure 7). In Figure 7 we consider a lower range of concurrencies for workloads with higher average request sizes. This was done because systems with users who issue large requests (such as supercomputers) typically have

fewer simultaneous users than systems with users who issue small requests (such as networks of workstations).

The striping unit which guarantees the highest percentage of maximum throughput to all workloads in Figure 7 is 30 KB. At this striping unit, all workloads considered yield at least 80% of maximum throughput. In guessing *a priori* the best compromise striping unit, one which suits a wide range of request sizes and concurrencies, consider the benefit and cost which arise from striping data across multiple disks. The benefit is the decreased transfer time of a single request, which saves approximately the transfer time of a stripe unit. The cost is the increased disk utilization which arises from an additional disk positioning itself to access the data. Without any workload information, it seems reasonable to balance the benefit, which is approximately the striping unit divided by the transfer rate of a disk, and the cost, which is an average positioning time (an average seek plus an average rotation). Or, stated slightly differently,

(2) Compromise Striping Unit in KB =
        Z × average positioning time × data transfer rate

disk type	(1) average positioning time	(2) data transfer rate	(1)x(2)	concurrency-slope coefficient	zero-knowledge coefficient
Amdahl 6380 (14")	23.1	1.8	41.4	.24	.72
2X fast seek	15.7	1.8	28.2	.22	.67
2X fast rotate	18.9	3.59	67.8	.23	.65
2X KB/track	23.1	3.59	82.8	.23	.63
Imprimis 97209 Sabre (8")	23.9	2.40	57.1	.26	.70

Table 2: Concurrency-Slope and Zero-Knowledge Coefficients Over a Range of Disk Types. Over a wide range of hypothetical and real disks, with an average positioning time × data transfer rate ranging from 28 to 83, both the concurrency-slope and the zero-knowledge coefficients stay relatively constant. This verifies our model in which both the slope of the striping unit versus concurrency line and the striping unit choice made with minimal workload information are proportional to the disks' average positioning time × data transfer rate.

---

where we expect Z, the data transfer time for the best compromise striping unit over the positioning time, to be in the neighborhood of one. We call Z the *zero-knowledge coefficient*, since it applies when no workload information is given. For the default disk, the best compromise striping unit is 30 KB. A request which accesses exactly one 30 KB striping unit would, on average, see a 23 ms positioning delay (14.7 ms seek plus 8.35 ms rotation), and a 16.7 ms data transfer. Thus Z in this case is .72.

Similarly, we wish to express the slope of the striping unit vs. concurrency line (Equation 1) in terms of disk parameters. As in Equation 2, we hypothesize that this slope will be proportional to the average positioning time multiplied by the data transfer rate.

(3) slope =
   $S \times$ *average positioning time × data transfer rate*

For the default disk parameters, S, which we call the *concurrency-slope coefficient*, is .24. Substituting into Equation 1, we can express our striping unit choice at each concurrency *con* as

(4) Striping Unit =
   $S \times$ *average positioning time × data transfer rate × (con - 1)*
   + .5 KB

To verify these hypotheses, we repeat the simulation study above with different disk parameters. The disk parameters that we vary are seek speed, rotational speed, and sectors per track. These parameters all impact the average positioning time × data transfer rate factor in Equations 2 and 4. We also simulate an Imprimis Sabre disk drive (8" diameter) [Imprimis89].

For each disk technology, we also calculate S, the *concurrency-slope coefficient*, as for the default disks. First, at each concurrency, we measure throughput for a range of request sizes and determine the range of striping units which guarantee 95% of the maximum throughput to all request sizes. We then plot the line with the minimum slope which lies entirely in the striping unit range for all concurrencies. Lastly, we solve

slope = S ×average positioning time ×data transfer rate

for S.

For each disk technology, we calculate Z, the *zero-knowledge coefficient*, by 1) graphing the percentage of maximum throughput for the same range of workloads as in Figure 7, 2) determining the best compromise striping unit by the "maximizing the minimum percentage throughput" criterion, and 3) dividing the transfer time of the best compromise striping unit by the average positioning time.

Over a technology range where the average positioning time × data transfer rate varies by a factor of 3, from 28.2 to 82.8, both S and Z vary by only a small amount. This verifies our model in which both the slope of the striping unit versus concurrency line and the striping unit choice made with minimal workload information are proportional to the disks' average positioning time × data transfer rate.

8. Conclusions

We have seen that the striping unit choice is primarily dependent on the concurrency of the applied workload and is relatively insensitive to the request size distribution of the workload. Knowing the concurrency of the applied workload allows one to choose a striping unit which yields close to optimal performance for all request sizes. This choice can be expressed as

Striping Unit =
   $S \times$ *average positioning time × data transfer rate × (con - 1)*
   + .5 KB

where S, the concurrency-slope coefficient, is approximately ¼. This relationship, and the specific value of S, was shown to hold over a wide range of disk technologies.

Also, without knowing the concurrency of the workload, the best compromise striping unit for a wide range of workloads and concurrencies can be chosen by
Compromise Striping Unit in KB =
   $Z \times$ *average positioning time × data transfer rate*

where Z is roughly $\frac{2}{3}$.

Both the slope of the striping unit vs. concurrency line and the best compromise striping unit are dependent on only one disk parameter: the average positioning time $\times$ data transfer rate.

9. Future research

We are continuing to evaluate disk striping, with and without redundancy. Issues include varying the number of disks, the redundancy scheme used, the effects of disk synchronization, and the possible use of zero-latency disk accesses for single track transfers.

At Berkeley, we are in the process of designing and building RAID II, a disk array capable of utilizing hundreds of disks to act as a supercomputer file server. Design issues that we are exploring include the maximum number of disks to stripe over, the redundancy scheme used, the optimal striping unit for each redundancy scheme, and the amount and placement of buffers along the path between the disks and the application.

10. Acknowledgements

The starting idea which motivated this paper was provided by Garth Gibson. He and Edward Lee provided great feedback throughout the process of research and writing.

This research was supported in part by National Science Foundation grant #MIP-8715235. Peter Chen is supported in part by an Office of Naval Research (ONR) Fellowship.

11. References

[Agrawal84] R. Agrawal, D.J. DeWitt, *"Whither hundreds of processors in a database machine?,"* Proceedings of the International Workshop on High-Level Architectures, 1984.

[Bell84] C.G. Bell, *"The Mini and Micro Industries,"* IEEE Computer, Vol. 17, No. 10 (October 1984), pp. 14-30.

[Chen90] P. M. Chen, *"An Evaluation of Redundant Arrays of Disks Using an Amdahl 5890,"* to appear in Proceedings of the 1990 ACM SIGMETRICS Conference on Measurement and Modeling of Computer Systems, May 1990.

[Imprimis89] *"Imprimis Product Specification—97209 Sabre Disk Drive, IPI-2 Interface,"* Document Number 64402302, revision F, May 1989.

[Johnson84] O.G. Johnson, *"Three-dimensional wave equation computations on vector computers,"* Proc. IEEE, vol. 72, January 1984.

[Joy85] B. Joy, presentation at ISSCC 1985 panel session, Feb. 1985.

[Kim86] M.Y. Kim, *"Synchronized Disk Interleaving,"* IEEE Transactions on Computers, Vol. C-35, No. 11, November 1986, pp. 978-988.

[Lineback85] J.R. Lineback, *"New features tune unix for high-end machines,"* Electronics, August 1985.

[Livny87] M. Livny, S. Khoshafian, H. Boral, *"Multi-Disk Management Algorithms,"* Proceedings of the 1987 ACM SIGMETRICS Conference on Measurement and Modeling of Computer Systems, pp. 69-77.

[Moore75] G. Moore, *"Progress in Digital Integrated Electronics,"* Proc. IEEE Digital Integrated Electronic Device Meeting, 1975, p. 11.

[Myers86] W. Myers, *"The Competitiveness of the United States Disk Industry,"* IEEE Computer, Vol. 19, No. 11, January 1986, pp. 85-90.

[Patterson88] D. Patterson, G. Gibson, R. Katz, *"A Case for Redundant Arrays of Inexpensive Disks (RAID),"* Proceedings of the 1988 ACM SIGMOD Conference on the Management of Data, pp. 109-116.

[Reddy89] A.L.N. Reddy, P. Banerjee, *"Performance Evaluation of Multiple-Disk I/O Systems,"* to appear in IEEE Transactions on Computers, December 1989.

[Salem86] K. Salem, H. Garcia-Molina, *"Disk Striping,"* Proceedings of the Second Data Engineering Conference, 1986, pp. 336-342.

[Thisquen88] J. Thisquen, *"Seek Time Measurements"*, Amdahl Peripheral Products Division Technical Report, May 9, 1988.

A DISTRIBUTED I/O ARCHITECTURE FOR HARTS

Kang G. Shin and Greg Dykema

Real-Time Computing Laboratory
Department of Electrical Engineering and Computer Science
The University of Michigan
Ann Arbor, Michigan 48109–2122

Abstract

The issue of I/O device access in HARTS — a distributed real-time computer system under construction at the Real-Time Computing Laboratory (RTCL), The University of Michigan — is explicitly addressed. Several candidate solutions are introduced, explored, and evaluated according to cost and complexity, reliability, and performance: (1) "node-direct" distribution with the intra-node bus and a local I/O bus, (2) use of dedicated I/O nodes which are placed in the hexagonal mesh as regular applications nodes but which provide I/O services rather than computing services, and (3) use of a separate I/O network which has led to the proposal of an "interlaced" I/O network. The interlaced I/O network is intended to provide both high performance without burdening node processors with I/O overhead as well as a high degree of reliability. Both static and dynamic multi-ownership protocols are developed for managing I/O device access in this I/O network. The relative merits of the two protocols are explored and the performance and accessibility which each provide are simulated.

1 Introduction

To date, work on distributed computing systems — by which we mean loosely-coupled networks of processing elements — has centered on interconnection networks, programming and communications paradigms, algorithms, and task decomposition. However, little has been said specifically about the I/O subsystem in a distributed environment, despite its obvious importance. Work which has been done has focused primarily on the hypercube and has not addressed the accessibility of I/O devices in case of failures in the system [9, 11], and research which looks at fault-tolerance has not considered the multi-accessibility required by a distributed environment [7]. Clearly, a computer can process

data no faster than it can acquire the data; this has been the rationale behind the attention paid to memory subsystems and increasing the accessibility and access speed of memories. But one cannot assume that data somehow appear in memory for the computer to use and process. We must look realistically at the accessibility and capability of I/O devices, especially as more powerful computing systems place more and more demands on all of their subsystems.

Distributed computing systems are being used for demanding applications, such as binary hypercubes for scientific processing, and a variety of systems, such as HARTS (Hexagonal Architecture for Real-Time Systems [1, 3, 4, 8]), for real-time processing. The demands of a real-time computing system include both high performance and reliability [10]. In the case of a distributed I/O subsystem, this also means accessibility.

The focus of this paper is on developing an I/O subsystem for HARTS, an experimental system for research in distributed real-time computing under construction at the RTCL. HARTS uses a wrapped hexagonal mesh as its interconnection topology. The wrapped hexagonal topology is known to be quite attractive due mainly to its hardware constructibility, fine scalability, and fault–tolerance. (See [1, 2] for a detailed account of the advantages of this topology and its comparison with other topologies.) We will begin with a brief discussion of the architecture of HARTS. Following this we will examine a variety of ways of implementing the I/O subsystem in this distributed environment. Although much of what will be said will apply to many other distributed computer system topologies, we will look specifically at I/O device placement and management in HARTS. Each proposal for the design of an I/O subsystem will be analyzed with regard to cost and complexity, accessibility, and performance.

CH2887-8/90/0000/0332$01.00 © 1990 IEEE

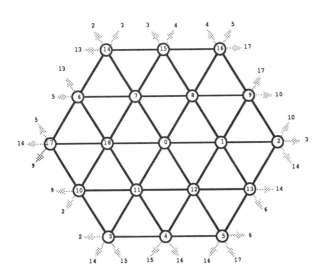

Figure 1: A hexagonal mesh of dimension 3.

2 Description of HARTS

The interconnection topology used in HARTS is a C-wrapped[1] hexagonal mesh (H–mesh). Each node in an H–mesh is connected to six neighboring nodes. As the solid lines of Fig. 1 shows, however, the peripheral nodes of a non-wrapped H–mesh are connected to only three or four neighbors rather than six. The C-wrapping used in HARTS is a means of connecting every node to six other nodes to create a homogeneous network [1]. Any node can thus be viewed as the "center" of the network. Moreover, a transparent addressing scheme can be developed for any size H–mesh such that the shortest paths between any two nodes can be computed with a $\Theta(1)$ algorithm given the addresses of the two nodes [1]. This addressing scheme also makes possible a simple message routing algorithm that can be efficiently implemented in hardware [3].

The *dimension* of an H–mesh is defined as the number of nodes on its peripheral edge. Fig. 1 shows a C-wrapped H–mesh of dimension three, with gray arrows indicating the extra connections between the peripheral nodes. A C-wrapped H–mesh of dimension n is comprised of $p = 3n^2 - 3n + 1$ nodes, labeled 0 to $3n^2 - 3n$, where each node s has six neighbors labeled $[s+1]_p$, $[s+3n-1]_p$, $[s+3n-2]_p$, $[s+3n(n-1)]_p$, $[s+3n^2-6n+2]_p$, and $[s+3n^2-6n+3]_p$, where $p = 3n^2 - 3n + 1$ and $[a]_b$ denotes $a \bmod b$ [1].

One can better visualize what is happening in the C-wrapping by first partitioning the nodes of a non-wrapped

H–mesh into rows in three different directions. The mesh can be viewed as composed of $2n-1$ horizontal rows, $2n-1$ rows in the 60-degree counter-clockwise direction, or $2n-1$ rows in the 120-degree counter-clockwise direction. In each of these partitions we label from the top the rows R_0 through R_{2n-2}. The C-wrapping is then performed by connecting the last node in R_i to the first node in $R_{[i+n+1]_{2n-1}}$ for each i in each of the three partitions [1].

The version of HARTS presently under construction at the RTCL is of dimension three and composed of 19 nodes. Each node of HARTS consists of from one to three applications processors (AP's) (thus permitting multiprocessor nodes) and a custom–designed network processor (NP) for handling inter-process communications. The nodes currently used in HARTS are VME-bus systems with 68020-based AP's. The NP's front-end is a custom VLSI routing controller designed to manage the six pairs of half–duplex communications links and route messages between nodes. The routing controller provides support for routing based on packet switching, circuit switching, and *virtual circuit cut-through* [6], where messages are not buffered at intermediate nodes if a circuit to the next node in the message route can be established. The design of the routing controller is detailed in [3]. Also part of the NP will be a buffer management unit to buffer messages and a general-purpose processor to perform various functions of HARTOS, an operating system being developed for HARTS [5].

HARTOS is built on top of a real-time kernel called pSOS (by Software Components Group. Inc.), which implements a multi-tasking environment with message exchanges and events for communications. HARTOS extends the uniprocessor pSOS to provide similar communication facilities over the network.

3 Critiques of Candidate Solutions

Before proposing a viable solution, it is important to explore and evaluate other candidate solutions to see what problems are presented in trying to develop a distributed I/O subsystem with high accessibility and performance together with low cost and complexity. These alternate solutions represent the evolution by which we shall arrive at our solution, showing the rationale for our decisions and why we did not choose certain more obvious solutions. We shall touch on some of these points in the discussion of the proposed multi-ownership solution and explore them in more detail.

---

[1] 'C' stands for the word 'continuous'.

3.1 "Node-Direct" Distribution of I/O

Since centralizing I/O results in performance and accessibility bottlenecks, I/O devices must be physically distributed. One way of doing this is to connect sets of I/O devices directly to computation nodes. In a system such as HARTS which uses a dedicated processor to handle inter-process communications (IPC), there are two principal methods for connecting the I/O devices to the node: via the intra-node bus or a separate I/O bus connected to either an AP or the NP.

A. Intra–Node Bus

If I/O devices are connected to the intra-node bus via a suitable I/O controller (IOC), there remains the question of which node will control and administer the devices. Logically, if the NP is the "node master" (as is the case in HARTS, since it manages all communication, both intra-node in the case of a multiprocessor node and inter-node communication in all cases), then it would also administer the I/O devices. It would then be natural for all AP's, whether residing in the given node or not, to use the existing IPC methods for communicating with I/O devices. However, if the NP is not powerful enough to take on administration of the I/O devices, then an AP can also perform such tasks. An AP used as the I/O administrator can be dedicated to this task or may perform these functions in addition to its other duties.

This is one of simplest designs for the I/O subsystem since all that is required is a suitable interface card for the intra-node bus used (VME in the case of HARTS). This gives all processors in the home node easy access to the I/O devices, although access will probably be controlled by a single I/O master—the NP or an AP. The accessibility of the I/O devices depends on the correct operation of the I/O master. If an AP serves as I/O master in addition to acting as a general AP, it would be possible for another AP in the (multiprocessor) node to take over should it fail.

The two major disadvantages of this method are obvious: poor accessibility and potentially poor performance. If other nodes need to access the I/O devices belonging to a given node, the I/O transactions must pass through the NP at the home node. Should this NP fail, all access to the I/O devices would be lost. It may be possible to replicate the I/O devices in question, but this would increase the total network and intra-node overhead (now for more than one node) required to access the device. Even without the overhead introduced by replication, I/O traffic, regardless of its destination, will always pass over the home node's intra-node bus, possibly penalizing the home node even for remote I/O transactions.

Regardless of whether or not the consumption of VME-bus bandwidth by I/O is acceptable, it is certainly not in keeping with the philosophy of HARTS communications, in which traffic not bound for a node should not penalize the performance of a node and in fact, need not even be buffered there temporarily, i.e., virtual cut–through.

B. Local I/O Bus

Connecting I/O devices to the intra-node bus increases the traffic on this bus, perhaps beyond its bandwidth. Another solution is to use a separate, perhaps simpler, I/O bus, connected to either the NP at the node or an AP. This time it makes more sense to connect the I/O bus to the NP; otherwise, I/O traffic bound for other nodes or AP's must still travel through the intra-node bus, thus defeating our purpose.

Assuming the NP can handle the I/O service and control overhead in addition to its primary functions, this method is approximately as complex and cost-effective as the former. The dedicated I/O bus need not be as versatile as the intra-node bus, so the interfacing requirements may in fact be simpler.

The advantage of this method is clearly that the only I/O traffic which must travel over the local intra-bus is traffic destined for a processor at the node itself. In a sense we are just trading processor bandwidth for bus bandwidth, but this is a justifiable tradeoff in that the job of the NP is likely to be better specified than that of the rest of the node. We will always have the problem of characterizing the NP traffic and workload regardless of whether it handles only I/O communications or I/O communications and rudimentary administration. This method allows us to eliminate the variable of non-local I/O traffic from the intra-node bus.

Finally, this solution opens up the possibility of connecting these I/O buses together to form a separate I/O network, allowing direct access to non-local I/O devices without having to use the regular IPC channels, a prospect we will be looking at in Section 3.3.

3.2 I/O Nodes

A typical node in a distributed computing system may be thought of as a computation node if its processors perform strictly computational tasks as opposed to I/O tasks, e.g., I/O device drivers. Similarly, a node which serves only to connect I/O devices to the computation nodes in the network would be referred to as an *I/O node*. Thus in the given topology of the node interconnection network, some nodes can be made to provide strictly I/O services while others provide computational services. All I/O traffic uses the IPC

334

channels provided by the network.

The I/O devices at a given I/O node can be interfaced to the intra-node bus and serviced by the NP. If sufficiently powerful processors were used as I/O controllers, the operating system interface between the NP and the I/O controllers could be the same as that between an NP and the AP's in an ordinary node (e.g., send and reply mailboxes) [5]. I/O–process communication (IOPC) could be handled exactly like inter-computation-process communication (ICPC), making the operation of the specialized I/O node and I/O controllers completely transparent to the rest of the network.

However, this is one of the most complex and expensive solutions because an NP, including routing controller and associated hardware, must be dedicated to a group of I/O devices. Decreasing the cost per I/O device by increasing the number of I/O devices per I/O node begins to defeat the purpose of distributing the I/O access in the first place. Also, *all* access to I/O devices must use the same network/protocol as ICPC, which may or may not be a good idea depending on the nature of IOPC traffic vs. ICPC traffic. Special care may have to be taken to ensure adequate bandwidth for I/O bursts as well as the timely delivery of critical inter-process messages. If both IOPC and ICPC traffic are heavy, it may not be economical to build enough bandwidth into the one network to handle both traffic streams.

Access to the I/O devices at the I/O node depends on the correct operation of the NP, a device which may well be more complex than the average AP. However, the node-direct designs also suffer from this vulnerability, assuming that access to the I/O device(s) connected to a node is required outside the node (if this is never the case then the flexibility offered by the I/O node design is probably not needed).

All IOPC with the devices connected to a given I/O node must take place over the H–mesh interconnection network; however, no AP is saddled with service/control overhead for the I/O devices and the same processor which controls and services peripherals can also format data, handle the results of multiple sensors, and so on.

This approach also requires that load distribution algorithms be part of any application running on such a system and that the application be flexible enough not to depend on a particular number of AP's. The effect is similar to that of a network in which several applications processors have failed, where the I/O nodes can be visualized as the "holes" in the computation network. Applications which are intended to survive node failures will have to take this effect into account anyway, so this is not a drawback for serious fault-tolerant applications.

3.3 I/O Network

All of the alternate methods presented thus far require the use of the standard IPC channels to send I/O information to processors on remote nodes. Furthermore, they are also dependent on the correct operation of the NP at the node administering a given I/O device. If the NP should fail, access to the devices administered at the node in question would be impossible. Thus to increase the accessibility of the I/O devices and the reliability of the system as a whole, we could give the I/O devices (relatively) simple control processors which are in turn connected via a separate I/O network to each other and to the nodes. This method is likely to be the most expensive since it requires a completely separate network and I/O control processors in addition to the applications and network processors already in place. However, it has potentially the highest accessibility and performance because it can support multiple I/O transactions in parallel as well as providing more than one way of accessing given devices.

The issue of what network topology to use for this separate I/O network is somewhat problematic. If we want to provide direct contact between each of the computation nodes and the I/O network, then we need some way of mapping the I/O network onto the H–mesh. An important problem is the fact that while most interconnection topologies which have been explored involve an even number of nodes or a number of nodes which is a power of two, an H–mesh will always have an odd number of nodes, and for small-diameter meshes it tends to have a prime number of nodes.

One obvious choice is to use a completely separate H–mesh mesh for the I/O network. One way to do this would be to give each computation node two NP's, one for the computation network and one for the I/O network. Although this solves the mapping problem, it is an expensive solution because it would require an additional p NP's to manage the communication in the I/O network where p is the total number of nodes in the H–mesh. Moreover, access to I/O devices still depends on the correct operation of a complex device, the NP. There are some interesting advantages to having essentially two complete H–meshes. IOPC and ICPC could be completely separated, possibly simplifying bandwidth and message scheduling and delivery issues. Taking a different approach, it would also be possible to "borrow" one network to deliver messages for the other. Thus if a computation–NP decided that it could not send an inter-process message in time, it could ask the I/O–NP if it could send the message before its deadline on the I/O network, possibly allowing a greater number of messages to be delivered on time. The same applies to delivering messages at all—if one NP ascertained that its messages to a particular node were not getting through, it could forward them to the other NP to see if it could successfully deliver the messages on its network.

Despite the advantages of a separate I/O network, we have not adopted it due mainly to the mapping problem on the one hand and the expense of a completely separate mesh on the other.

4 Non-Distributed I/O

Obviously, I/O does not have to be distributed in a distributed computer system; nodes can simply be connected to some central I/O handling facility. This may involve using a single node as an I/O center, with I/O traffic using the standard IPC channels or some single entity acting as the I/O center with connections to all of the computation nodes (e.g., the original NCUBE design and other early hypercubes). Although this may be the simplest way of handling I/O distribution, accessibility and performance problems will make it unusable in all but a few circumstances. The rationale for using a distributed computer system for a particular application is to obtain a desired level of performance and/or accessibility which could not be obtained (at least not as cost-effectively) with a uniprocessor or multiprocessor architecture. Thus by centralizing I/O access, performance suffers because the I/O center becomes a bottleneck, and accessibility suffers because the system is susceptible to single-point failures.

We will next present our proposed I/O subsystem design which we believe to provide the best accessibility and performance at the lowest cost and complexity.

5 Multi-Owner I/O Devices

To avoid the accessibility problems of non-distributed I/O, we would like I/O devices to be managed or "owned" by relatively simple, and reliable, controllers. Moreover, to improve both accessibility and performance, we want multiple access paths to these I/O devices.

The desire for simple I/O controllers presents a problem in HARTS, because the natural tendency would be to have I/O devices belong to individual nodes or network processors, both relatively complex and expensive devices, and use the given IPC channels in HARTS to handle the I/O traffic. We can still use the given IPC channels, but instead of permanently tying down a given I/O device to one node, we will allow several nodes to communicate with each I/O

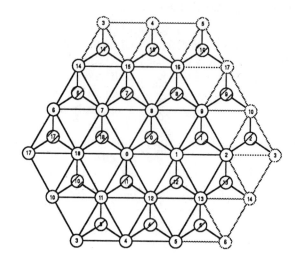

Figure 2: I/O controller placement.

device. There are at least two fundamentally different protocols for managing this communication, but we will explain the architectural considerations first and then discuss the protocols.

5.1 Interconnection Architecture

We will cluster I/O devices together and give them a controller to manage access to the devices. However, the controller can be made simple because we will be using simple data links to the HARTS nodes (presumably serial since the standard inter-node links in HARTS are serial, but this is not required). The I/O controller need only be able to handle sending and receiving simple messages via a set of full-duplex links, not providing virtual cut-through capabilities and other features of a full-blown NP. To keep the number of I/O controllers and the number of I/O links down to a reasonable number, we will restrict the number of I/O controllers (IOC's) to be no greater than the number of computation nodes in the mesh, p. This will have certain benefits for one of the management protocols explained later.

Now that we have established the potential number of I/O stations, we need to decide how many nodes each IOC will be connected to. If we assume the maximum number of IOC's in an H_3, for example, then Fig. 2 suggests a logical connection scheme. Each IOC can be thought of as being in the center of one of the upward-pointing triangles created by this representation of the hexagonal mesh interconnections and the IOC is then connected to each of the nodes which make up this triangle. This gives three possible avenues of access to each IOC. Note that if the maximum number of IOC's are used, the number of I/O links required will be equal to the number of standard communication links, or $9n^2 - 9n + 3$ for an H_n. There is no particular reason that one could not similarly place IOC's at the (logical) center of the downward-pointing triangles as well, allowing for up to $2p$ IOC's, but this will double the maximum possible number of I/O links required and will disturb certain homogeneous effects of limiting the number of IOC's to the number of nodes, as we will see shortly.

5.2 Management Protocol

The first management protocol we will look at assigns one node to each IOC as its owner, but with the important provision that the owner can be changed if the original owner becomes faulty. In this protocol one of the IOC links is defined to be the primary or active link and the rest remain inactive as spares. The second protocol allows the IOC owner to be defined dynamically, allowing for greater accessibility in some cases and fewer average hops required to reach the IOC owner. In this protocol the IOC decides which link will be active at any given time.

Let us call the three nodes to which an IOC is connected its "I/O partners." We will number these nodes 0, 1, and 2, where 0 is the "left partner," 1 is the "upper partner," and 2 is the "right partner" (see Fig. 3). For the purpose of our discussion, we will label each IOC with the node number of its left partner. This only a notational convenience for explaining the ownership protocols; IOC's themselves have no real identity as far as the system in general is concerned. The relevant labels are those of the I/O partners (for routing the I/O messages within the network) and those of the I/O devices themselves (so that they can be located in the network and their I/O partners identified).

5.2.1 Static Ownership

Under this protocol each IOC is initially assigned an owner node through which all I/O traffic will pass until such a time as the the owner fails or becomes unreachable. In this case a new owner is chosen, which then retains ownership until it fails or can longer reach the IOC. To access a particular I/O device, a process broadcasts an I/O inquiry on the network, similar to the process for finding a message exchange in HARTOS [5]. This inquiry contains the system name of the desired I/O device. The owner of the IOC which controls the I/O device will find the device name in its I/O name server and respond to the I/O inquiry. The process desiring

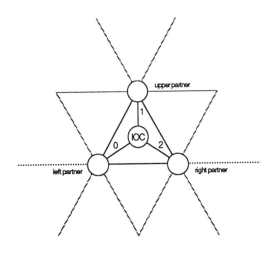

Figure 3: I/O controller partners.

I/O service will then send its requests to that particular node.

Upon boot-up, each IOC sends a message to its default owner node, partner 0, to notify the node that it owns the IOC. This message contains information regarding the I/O devices this controller has at its disposal, their system names, boot-up status, etc. During its operation, the IOC periodically sends a test message to its owner to ascertain the owner's status. If it fails to obtain a satisfactory response from its owner node (e.g., time-out), the IOC will attempt to find itself a new owner. When a suitable partner has been found, the IOC will declare this partner its new owner and send the I/O device information to it.

The owner and the IOC also agree in advance on the frequency at which the IOC will send the test message to the owner. The owner can then use this information to detect missing test messages and attempt to communicate with the IOC to see if the link is still operational. If it cannot establish a satisfactory dialogue with the IOC, it will resign as owner and go about its regular business. It is then up to the IOC to recognize the situation on its end as just explained (which it will, assuming it is operating correctly) and find itself a new owner. Furthermore, each time the owner receives a test message from the IOC or its watchdog timer wakes it up to check the IOC, the owner will evaluate the status of its mesh links. If it finds that none of its mesh links are functioning, it will send a resignation message to the IOC informing it that it is resigning as the IOC owner and that it should choose a new owner. If it cannot communicate this information, then the IOC will have already detected the unreachability of the owner and will choose a new owner on its own. In either case the owner resigns.

Both of these schemes are required to handle the ownership issue correctly. If only the first method were used, where the IOC assumes all the responsibility of checking the link, then we could have the new owner send a message to the old owner to inform it that it is no longer the owner. If it could not send this message, it means only that the old owner is not reachable by the new owner. The old owner could still be reachable by other nodes requesting I/O service and there would be no way to prevent the old owner from responding to these requests and trying to service them. If only the second method were used, then an owner which found itself unable to communicate successfully with its IOC could try to inform the I/O partners that a new owner needed to be chosen, but it may be unable to communicate with them due to mesh link failures. Thus the IOC is given the task of finding itself a new owner if the old owner becomes unreachable since only if the IOC itself fails or all three partners have failed is it impossible to find a new owner. The owner is given the responsibility of revoking its ownership status if it finds itself unable to reach its IOC.

If a process requesting I/O service does not obtain a response to its inquiry, then either there is no owner for the IOC (which can be because the IOC itself is faulty, because all links between the IOC and its partner nodes have failed, or because all of its partners are faulty) or the owner of the IOC is unreachable. In either case, the I/O device in question is unreachable and the situation should be handled in the same manner regardless of the cause—no node will reply to the I/O service inquiry and the process must execute whatever contingency plan it has. (An obvious plan is to retry one or more times before bringing in more expensive recovery methods.)

We still need a method of finding a new owner for the IOC when it determines that its old owner is no longer reachable. The IOC can maintain the status of its three links/partners (the IOC has no way of distinguishing between a link failure and a partner node failure). When looking for a new owner, it polls each of the remaining intact partners, asking them how many other IOC's they each own and how many of their mesh links are still intact, information which a computation node can and should maintain. It will then choose the partner with the greatest number of functional links, to increase the chances of other nodes reaching the owner, and if each of two remaining partners have the same number of operating links, it will choose the partner which owns the fewest IOC's. If no distinction can be made on this basis, it will choose a new owner at random.

This management protocol is desirable for a number of reasons. First, it is simple to implement and efficient because the only overhead involved with establishing a partner's right to access to the IOC occurs when a new owner is being chosen. Second, for certain I/O devices it is desirable to perform some level of the I/O device management in some predetermined node. For a disk, for example, this might involve maintaining some level of the file system on the owner node. Otherwise, the IOC might have to be made more complex to handle this function. But under this management protocol it is possible for the owner of an IOC to be unreachable to a particular process desiring I/O service while there is another partner of the IOC which is reachable by that process. Thus if this other partner were the owner instead of the current owner, the process in question would be able to obtain I/O service. In Fig. 4 we have an example where a process in node 13 wants service from IOC 18, but since node 18 is the owner and is not reachable from 13, it cannot obtain service. If node 0 were the owner instead of 18, it could obtain service. Also one IOC partner may be closer to the node requesting service than the current owner. If ownership could be determined per request instead of remaining in effect until the owner is forced to resign due to failures, we could provide faster average service. These two factors make up the rationale for the next management protocol using dynamic ownership.

5.2.2 Dynamic Ownership

Under this protocol the owner of an IOC is determined on a per-request basis. A process desiring I/O service will send its request to the nearest partner of the IOC it wants to access. This partner will then petition the IOC for access, which the IOC will grant as soon as it is free. To access a particular I/O device, a process broadcasts an I/O inquiry on the network. This inquiry contains the system name of the desired I/O device. Each partner of the IOC which controls the I/O device in question will find the device name in its I/O name server and respond to the I/O inquiry. The process desiring I/O service will then collect the responses to its inquiry and after a certain time-out period it will compute the closest partner and sends its I/O request to this node. The time-out period is necessary because the process requesting service has no way of knowing how many partners are operational or can currently reach the IOC. This may result in a request being to a node which is not the closest if the closest node does not respond within the time-out period.

Upon boot-up, each IOC will send a message to each of its partner nodes. This message contains information regarding the I/O devices this controller has at its disposal,

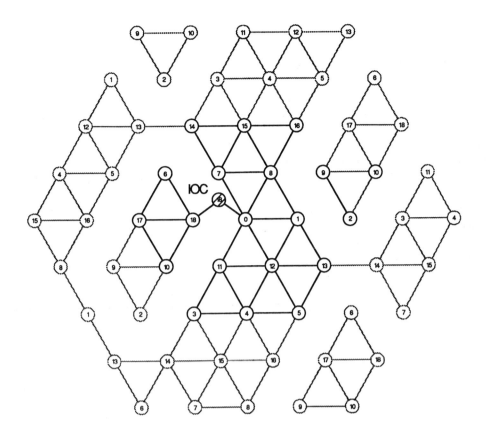

Figure 4: Unreachable static owner.

their system names, boot-up status, etc. During operation each IOC will monitor its links for access requests coming from its partners. When it receives a valid request, it will declare the sending partner to be the current "owner" and allow it to send an I/O request. While it is servicing the request it will send back deferment messages to any other partners requesting access and place these requests on its deferred queue. Upon receipt of a deferment message, a partner requesting I/O access will refrain from sending any more requests and wait until it has been granted access. When it has finished servicing the current request, the IOC will grant access to the next partner on its deferred queue.

In addition to leaving IOC's accessible where static ownership would make them inaccessible, this protocol also takes into account the fact that one partner may be closer to a node requesting service than the other partner. Since this protocol chooses the closest of the partners that respond, the I/O traffic may have fewer hops to travel. However, its disadvantages are that it is more difficult to implement, it involves arbitration overhead after each I/O request has

been serviced, and it may be undesirable because there is no single node through which all I/O requests will travel and which could perform some I/O management tasks.

5.3 Simulation of Static vs. Dynamic Ownership

In order to determine how much of an advantage dynamic ownership offers over static ownership, a simulator was written to evaluate the average accessibility of IOC's and the average number of hops required to reach the owner of an IOC from each node in an H_3. This simulator is similar in function to the one used in [8] for evaluating a fault-tolerant message routing algorithm for HARTS. It tests the effects of link failures alone and the combined effect of link and node failures on accessibility and shortest-path distance to IOC owners.

Mesh links (links between nodes) and IOC links (links from IOC's to their partners) are assumed to fail with equal probability. This is a reasonable assumption since the physical implementation of these two types of links is likely to be similar. Moreover, the failure of a link of either type is assumed to be as likely as the failure of any other link of that type. In the simulations that we ran, we also assumed that nodes are always more likely to fail than links of any type, because processors are more complex than links. The ratio of the probability of node failure to the probability of link failure is a parameter in the simulation.

The simulator works by selecting a random set of IOC links, node links, and processor nodes to declare faulty and then testing to see if a path exists between each node and each IOC owner, if one exists. Note that in the case of the dynamic ownership protocol, an IOC owner is a partner with an intact IOC link. If a path does exist, this fact and the length of the path (measured in "hops," the number of links which must be traversed) are noted. This process is repeated a sufficient number of times to assure consistent results (between 0.7 and 1.2 million) for each total number of failures in the system.

Initially, only the effect of link failures was simulated. Here, numbers of faulty links between 0 and 85 were simulated for both static and dynamic ownership. The simulator computes the average number of hops a message must travel from source to destination (IOC owner, not the IOC itself) and the number and percentage of messages which were and were not deliverable.

The effects of combined node and link failures are then simulated. Again, the total number of failures is varied, this time between five and 85 in increments of five, and the relative probability of node vs. link failures is used to declare this number of components faulty. The same statistics are measured as for the case where only link failures were tested.

Although the dynamic ownership can indeed improve the reachability of I/O devices, the improvement is not significant—no more than 3% better than static ownership in the best case. Naturally, with relatively few link failures, the difference is negligible. Thus dynamic ownership may not be worth implementing for this reason, especially if I/O management can be simplified by using static ownership instead. Moreover, dynamic ownership both places greater demands on the IOC and results in somewhat higher protocol (arbitration) overhead.

When both node and link failures are taken into account, the average improvement in reachability achieved by dynamic ownership is even less. However, it should be noted that when considering the combined effect of node and link failures, the net effect on the system of a 50% component failure rate is much more deleterious than in the case where only link failures are considered, so the apparent loss of im-

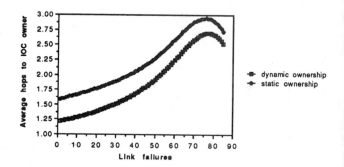

Figure 5: Average hops to reach IOC owner vs. link faults.

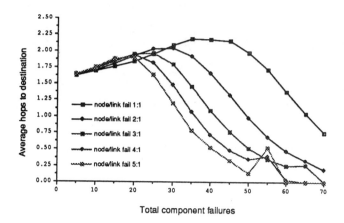

Figure 6: Static ownership: Average hops to reach IOC owner vs. system faults.

provement in the dynamic case may make little difference in practice because so much of the system's processing power has been lost.

However, Fig. 5 shows that in all cases we can substantially reduce the average shortest-path length by using dynamic ownership rather than static. With as many as 50% of the links faulty, the improvement is still at least 0.35 hops shorter average path length. If I/O traffic is expected to be high, especially with large transfers, then dynamic ownership may well be worthwhile in order to improve I/O performance, with the additional benefit of a slight improvement in I/O accessibility.

From Figs. 6 and 7 we can see that although dynamic ownership always results in a shorter average path length, the difference grows less and less as the probability of node failure increases, as mentioned above for deliverability.

These are the relative differences in performance between the two protocols; the simulations also show that even with half of the links faulty, 85% of I/O traffic can still be routed.

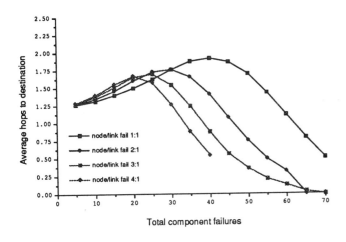

Figure 7: Dynamic ownership: Average hops to reach IOC owner vs. system faults.

In the case where both node and link failures are considered, this number drops dramatically as the ratio of node to link failures increases, again due to the very serious effects of so many processor failures.

This is, of course, assuming a routing algorithm which can always find the shortest path, even in a faulty mesh. The simple algorithm proposed in [8] is not perfect, but even under 50% link failures, it fails to deliver only less than 10% of actually deliverable messages.

5.4 IOC Architecture

We have assumed that the connection between the IOC's and their partner nodes is the same as that used to connect the processor nodes themselves. In HARTS this implies the use of high-speed full-duplex serial lines. Other mechanisms are certainly possible, but given that there may well be good reasons for physically isolating IOC's from the processor nodes, serial links will offer the most flexibility.

An IOC must therefore provide three serial links as its interface to the partner nodes as well as some interface to whatever I/O devices it actually services. This could be SCSI or ESDI in the case of mass-storage devices, IEEE-488 or RS-232/422 in the case of instrumentation, or custom/proprietary interfaces or buses as needed.

Two problems must be addressed in an effective IOC design: general applicability of the IOC and the communication protocol used on the I/O links to the partner nodes. One way to address both of these concerns without necessarily limiting the actual I/O device interface would be to implement a time-division multiplexed (TDM) serial protocol and allow several I/O processors to use the I/O links in

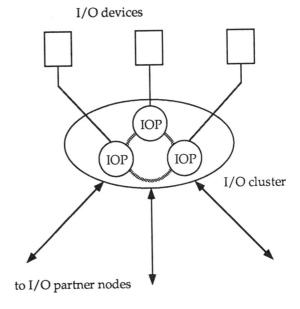

Figure 8: I/O cluster architecture.

turn. This provides greater flexibility because the only standard to which an I/O processor need conform is that of the TDM protocol—it is free to use whatever interface is most appropriate for the I/O devices for which it is responsible. It may also offer an arbitrary level of services as well, ranging from simple one-way data transmission in the case of a sensor interface, to file-system support in the case of a disk interface. It also permits a wide variety of I/O processors to be used.

Today's high-speed microprocessors are more than capable of implementing this style of IOC design with sustained transfer rates well in excess of 5 megabits/second. Keeping in mind that the total bandwidth of the I/O links is shared among some number of I/O processors residing at a cluster, this should be adequate. If a high-performance device requires greater bandwidth, it would be possible for it to be allocated more than one time-slot in the TDM protocol, provided the I/O processor could keep up.

This approach has the effect of turning an "I/O controller" into an "I/O cluster" consisting of one to n processors, where n is determined by the exact nature of the TDM protocol used. Fig. 8 illustrates this design. This in turn offers a degree of scalability to the IOC concept. Instead of forcing all I/O traffic at the level of a given IOC to pass through a single processor, multiple I/O processors can easily be used to support devices which require more processor attention. Moreover, this further increases the reliability of the I/O cluster. If one I/O processor should fail, there would simply be a wasted time-slot in the transport protocol (assuming that the processor had not failed in such a manner as to disrupt the protocol). Other processors would be able to continue operation.

Thus not only is there flexibility in the number of IOC's used in a particular system, there is flexibility in the number of the I/O processors in a given I/O cluster. This flexibility and the multiple connectivity of the IOC's permit an I/O system with a high degree of performance, accessibility, and scalability.

6   Conclusion

We have examined a variety of solutions for implementing a distributed I/O subsystem for HARTS: node-direct connection, where nodes own sets of I/O devices, dedicated I/O nodes, separate I/O network, and multi-owner I/O controllers. The multi-owner method is judged to be the best solution in terms of cost and complexity, accessibility, and performance. It is scalable with the hexagonal mesh itself and allows simultaneous access to I/O controllers. It has many of the accessibility benefits of the separate I/O network while using a simple, less expensive interconnection scheme. We have developed two different management protocols, static ownership and dynamic ownership, which offer different advantages and options. Static ownership is simpler and allows certain I/O device management processes to reside on an owner node. Dynamic ownership makes nodes accessible in instances where they would not be accessible under static ownership, and can also reduce the distance which I/O traffic must travel.

Acknowledgement

The work reported in this paper was supported in part by the Office of Naval Research (ONR) under Contract No. N00014–85–0122. Any opinions, findings, and conclusions or recommendations expressed in this paper are those of the authors and do not necessarily reflect the views of the ONR.

The authors would like to thank Alan Olson and Jim Dolter of the Real-Time Computing Laboratory, The University of Michigan for the preparation of figures in this paper, and Andre van Tilborg and Gary Koob of the Office of Naval Research for financial support of the work reported in this paper.

References

[1] M.–S. Chen, K. G. Shin, and D. D. Kandlur, "Addressing, routing, and broadcasting in hexagonal mesh multiprocessors," *IEEE Trans. Comput.*, vol. C–39, no. 1, pp. 10–18, Jan. 1990.

[2] A. Davis, R. Hodgson, B. Schediwy, and K. Stevens, "Mayfly system hardware," Technical Report, HPL–SAL–89–23, Hewlett–Packard Corp., Apr. 1989.

[3] J. W. Dolter, P. Ramanathan, and K. G. Shin, "Microprogrammable VLSI routing controller for HARTS," *Proc. ICCD'89*, pp. 160–163.

[4] J. W. Dolter, P. Ramanathan, and K. G. Shin, "Performance analysis of message passing in HARTS: A hexagonal mesh multicomputer," *IEEE Trans. on Comput.* (in press).

[5] D. D. Kandlur, D. L. Kiskis, and K. G. Shin, "HARTOS: A distributed real-time operating system," *ACM Operating Systems Review*, vol. 23, no. 3, pp. 72–89, Jul. 1989.

[6] P. Kermani and L. Kleinrock, "Virtual cut–through: A new computer communication technique," *Computer Networks*, vol. 3, pp. 267–286, 1979.

[7] J. H. Lala, A. Ray, R. Harper, and D. B. Mulcare, "A Fault and Damage Tolerant Network for an Advanced Transport Aircraft," *Proc. of American Automatic Control Conf.*, pp. 1138–1142, June 1984.

[8] A. Olson and K. G. Shin, "Message routing in HARTS with faulty components," *Digest of Papers, FTCS-19*, pp. 331-338, Jun. 1989.

[9] J. Salmon, "Cubix: An I/O system for the hypercube," Caltech Concurrent Computation Project, Technical Report 293, Jul. 1986.

[10] K. G. Shin, C. M. Krishna, and Y.–H. Lee, "A unified method for evaluating real-time computer controllers and its application," *IEEE Trans. on Automatic Control*, vol. AC–30, no. 4, pp. 357–366, Apr. 1985.

[11] A. Witkowski, K. Chandrakumar, and G. Macchio, "Concurrent I/O system for the hypercube multiprocessor," *Proc. Third Conference on Hypercube Concurrent Computers and Applications*, pp. 1398–1407, Jan. 1988.

Session 6B: High-End Design

Boosting Beyond Static Scheduling in a Superscalar Processor

Michael D. Smith, Monica S. Lam, and Mark A. Horowitz
Computer Systems Laboratory
Stanford University, Stanford CA 94305-4070

Abstract

This paper describes a superscalar processor that combines the best qualities of static and dynamic instruction scheduling to increase the performance of non-numerical applications. The architecture performs all instruction scheduling statically to take advantage of the compiler's ability to efficiently schedule operations across many basic blocks. Since the conditional branches in non-numerical code are highly data dependent, the architecture introduces the concept of *boosted* instructions, instructions that are committed conditionally upon the result of later branch instructions. Boosting effectively removes the dependences caused by branches and makes the scheduling of side-effect instructions as simple as those that are side-effect free. For efficiency, boosting is supported in the hardware by *shadow structures* that temporarily hold the side effects of boosted instructions until the conditional branches that the boosted instructions depend upon are executed. When the branch condition is determined, the buffered side effects are either committed or squashed. The limited static scheduler in our evaluation system shows that a 1.6-times speedup over scalar code is achievable by boosting instructions above only a single conditional branch. This performance is similar to the performance of a pure dynamic scheduler.

1 Introduction

Superscalar processors are uniprocessor organizations capable of increasing machine performance by executing multiple scalar instructions in parallel. Since the amount of instruction-level parallelism within a basic block is small, superscalar processors must look across basic block boundaries to increase performance. In numerical code, the do-loop branches, which are a large percentage of the total branches executed, can be resolved early to expose the parallelism between many iterations. Unfortunately, many of the branches in non-numerical code are data dependent and cannot be resolved early. Thus, speculative execution, the execution of operations before previous branches, is an important source of parallelism in this type of code.

Instruction-level parallelism can be extracted statically (at compile-time) or dynamically (at run-time). Statically-scheduled superscalar processors and Very Long Instruction Word (VLIW) machines exploit instruction-level parallelism with a modest amount of hardware by exposing the machine's parallel architecture in the instruction set. For numerical applications, where branches can be determined early, compilers harness the parallelism across basic blocks by techniques such as software pipelining [11] or trace scheduling [7]. However, the overhead and complexity of speculative computation in compilers has prevented efficient parallelization of non-numerical code.

Dynamically-scheduled superscalar processors, on the other hand, effectively support speculative execution in hardware. By using simple buffers, these processors can efficiently commit or discard the side effects of speculative computations. Unfortunately, the additional hardware necessary to look far ahead in the dynamic instruction stream, find independent operations, and schedule these independent operations out of order is costly and complex.

We are interested in using superscalar techniques to increase the performance of non-numerical code at a reasonable cost. To accomplish this goal, we propose a superscalar architecture, which we call *TORCH*, that combines the strengths of static and dynamic instruction scheduling. The strength of static scheduling is the compiler's ability to efficiently schedule operations across many basic blocks; consequently, TORCH performs all instruction scheduling in the compiler. The strength of dynamic scheduling is in its ability to efficiently support speculative execution; consequently, TORCH provides hardware that allows the compiler to schedule any instruction before preceding branches, an operation we term *boosting*. Boosted instructions are conditionally committed upon the result of later branch instructions. Boosting, therefore, removes the scheduling constraints that result from the dependences caused by conditional branches and makes aggressive instruction scheduling in the compiler simple.

To make the conditional evaluation of boosted instructions efficient at run-time, the TORCH hardware includes two shadow structures: the *shadow register file* and *shadow store buffer*. These structures buffer the side effects of a boosted instruction until its dependent branch conditions are determined. On a correctly predicted branch, the hardware commits the appropriate values in the shadow structures. On a mispredicted branch, the hardware guarantees correct program operation by squashing all

CH2887-8/90/0000/0344$01.00 © 1990 IEEE

shadow values.

In this paper, we overview the TORCH architecture, describe the TORCH hardware to support boosting, and present the results of a simple static scheduler which performed limited instruction boosting and no load/store reorganization. The simple scheduler and our evaluation system allow us to quickly assess the viability of boosting on non-numerical programs. The results of this evaluation are supportive and indicate that TORCH, with only a subset of its full functionality, can approach the performance level of a dynamically-scheduled superscalar processor. As a result, we are proceeding to implement a compiler and a full simulator for TORCH.

The next section covers in more detail how different schedulers handle the issues involved in scheduling across conditional branches. Section 3 overviews the organization and operation of TORCH. Section 4 presents the specifics of the evaluation system, the limitations on the instruction schedulers, and the details of the dynamically-scheduled superscalar machine used in our evaluations. Section 5 reports on the results of the experiments, and the final section presents the conclusions of the study.

2 Scheduling Across Branches

Instruction-level parallelism within a basic block or extended basic block can be easily exploited by providing an adequate number of functional units and by limiting the effects of storage conflicts[1] in the code. However, the amount of instruction-level parallelism within a basic block is limited. An effective superscalar machine must move instructions across basic block boundaries to find larger amounts of concurrency.

2.1 Dynamic Scheduling

Dynamically-scheduled superscalar processors support code motion across basic block boundaries by looking ahead in the instruction stream, by buffering the internal state, and by executing instructions conditionally and out of order. These techniques were first utilized in the IBM Stretch [2] and IBM 360/91 [22]. These machines attempted to increase processor performance by hiding memory latency and decoupling instruction fetch from instruction execution. They provided internal buffering for issued but unexecuted instructions and extra state to keep track of the out-of-order results. Though these machines only fetched and decoded a single instruction per cycle, later machines incorporated multiple-instruction fetch and decode to further enhance machine performance (Johnson provides a good overview of these machines [9]). These investigations culminate in today's dynamically-scheduled superscalar designs which try to isolate instruction fetch/decode from instruction issue/execute to allow each to run at its own pace [8, 14, 16, 20].

Multiple instruction execution occurs when the hardware is-

[1]Storage conflicts are anti- and output data dependences caused by the reuse of registers or memory locations.

sues independent instructions from a window of dynamic instructions. To maintain scalar code compatibility, all instruction scheduling is done from this window by the hardware. Out-of-order execution and branch prediction provide these machines with the ability to simultaneously execute instructions from multiple basic blocks. Buffering within the processor supports the conditional evaluation of instructions that are executed before previously fetched branches, increasing the opportunities for the hardware to find instructions to issue in parallel.

Unfortunately, dynamic scheduling has many shortcomings. All of these shortcomings result from the detection of parallelism and the scheduling of independent operations at run time. First of all, the detection and scheduling of independent operations by the hardware increases its complexity, possibly lengthening the cycle time of the machine and reducing the actual speedup over the scalar processor. Another effect of using hardware to detect instruction-level parallelism is that the hardware can only analyze a small window of dynamic instructions during each cycle, thus limiting the possible candidates for parallel issue. Finally, *instruction fetch efficiency*, defined in Smith et al. [21] as the average number of useful instructions fetched per cycle, is reduced when executing from scalar object code. As a result of the large number of branches during the execution of non-numerical code, dynamic schedulers suffer a significant performance penalty due to branch point misalignment in a fetch block.

2.2 Static Scheduling

Statically-scheduled machines overcome the run-time scheduling problems of dynamically-scheduled machines by making the parallelism explicit in the instruction set architecture and depending upon the compiler to identify and schedule all instruction-level parallelism in a program. The compiler explicitly specifies which instructions are issued and executed in parallel. There is no overhead during run-time to schedule instructions, and the hardware is simple. The compiler essentially has a infinite instruction window and uses global program knowledge, program semantics (dependences), and resource constraints in constructing each instruction schedule. Finally, instruction alignment is not an issue in static scheduling since the compiler schedules instructions in fetch blocks.

The basis for statically-scheduled superscalar processors comes from the field of horizontally-microcoded machines and Very Long Instruction Word (VLIW) architectures. Early on, VLIW machines were similar to horizontally-coded microcode in that each instruction word had a field for each independent functional unit [3]. More recent VLIW machines [5] remove this restriction by providing dynamic NOPs for idle functional units. In fact, the distinction between statically-scheduled superscalar processors and VLIW machines is blurry. Both machines rely on the compiler to explicitly specify the instruction-level parallelism and manage the hardware resources. The difference between statically scheduled superscalar processors and VLIW machines is basically one of terminology. VLIW machines refer to operations within a singly-fetched instruction, while statically-scheduled superscalar processors refer to instructions within a single fetch block. A VLIW operation is equivalent to a superscalar instruction since both control a single functional unit. Many statically-scheduled machines have been announced either as superscalar processors [1, 17] or as VLIW processors [4].

Unfortunately, all these machines encounter difficulties when scheduling across conditional branches even though software branch prediction can be as accurate as hardware branch prediction [13]. Delay-branch schedulers are able to perform some limited movement of instructions across basic block boundaries. The compiler either moves instructions down from within a basic block to fill the branch delay slot; the branch must not depend upon these instructions so that it does not matter whether the machine executes them before or after the branch. The other way to fill branch delay slots is to lift an instruction up from the fall-through or target basic block. These instructions must not have any side effects so that their execution does not affect the machine state if the branch goes the other direction. Though these schemes are able to effectively fill a single branch slot, the effectiveness of these motions drops off significantly as the number of branch slots increases. For instance, a compiler can fill approximately 70% of single branch slots, but only 25% of double branch slots [13]. As we can see from the percentages of multiple branch slots filled, these reorganizing schemes are very limited in their ability to move instructions across conditional branches.

Trace scheduling [7] is a compiler technique that was designed to increase the compiler's ability to move instructions across basic block boundaries. It utilizes branch predictions to create a single long block of code out of individual basic blocks without hardware support. A greater level of concurrency is achieved by scheduling this long block instead of the individual basic blocks, but at the expense of fix-up code at the entry and exit points of the trace. The difficulty and overhead of saving and restoring state for instructions with side effects and of finding a few major traces in non-numerical code with its large number of run-time branches makes trace scheduling an unattractive choice.

Other statically-scheduled machines reduce the effects of conditional branches by scheduling both paths of a conditional branch in parallel [18]. This scheme requires hardware support to NOP the instructions along the non-taken branch path. Though this technique allows for some overlap between the schedules of the basic blocks before and after the conditional statement with the combined branches of the conditional statement, the compiler's ability to move instructions with side-effects is not improved.

2.3 Scheduling in TORCH

Boosting combines into one architecture the best aspects of static and dynamic scheduling to overcome the difficulties of scheduling instructions across conditional branches. Boosting relies on the compiler's knowledge of the program semantics and ability to explore many schedules to find the best instruction schedule. Boosting simplifies scheduling by assigning the hardware the responsibility of handling side effects. To the scheduler, all boosted instructions appear free from side effects.

The hardware efficiently handles boosting by providing extra buffering in the register file and store buffer. The shadow structures hold the results of boosted instructions until they are committed or squashed. Efficiency is guaranteed by performing the commit and squash operations without any performance penalty. For further efficiency, the hardware postpones all exception processing on boosted instructions until the hardware tries to commit the boosted instructions. Exceptions are precise and easy to identify.

3 TORCH

Before expanding on the implementation and operation of boosting in TORCH, we briefly overview the relevant aspects of the TORCH architecture. First of all, our current implementation of TORCH is based upon the MIPS R2000 RISC architecture[2]. We use the R2000 processor because the implementation of superscalar techniques is simpler on a load/store machine with fixed length instructions than on a memory-to-memory machine with variable length instructions.

Like the R2000, TORCH uses delayed branches to eliminate the delay between executing the branch and fetching the first instruction of the target branch. Furthermore, like other scalar processors that contain squashing branches, TORCH encodes static branch prediction information into each condition branch instruction. The branch prediction used in TORCH is based on branch profile statistics, since the accuracy of the branch prediction directly impacts the performance gain. Profiling indicates the most-likely branch path, and TORCH boosts instructions from this path to overlap instructions from different basic blocks.

Storage conflicts and memory disambiguation also constrain instruction scheduling and boosting. TORCH minimizes the effects of storage conflicts by considering register allocation during instruction scheduling. Run-time register renaming is not needed since TORCH issues instructions in order.

Successful memory disambiguation removes constraints on instruction scheduling by permitting the reordering of load and store operations. Compilers can disambiguate some memory references, but not to the extent of the hardware during run-time. Though not discussed further in this paper, the boosting mechanism in TORCH provides a framework for the TORCH compiler to perform speculative reordering of load and store instructions that cannot be completely disambiguated. This reordering by the compiler is supported by similar buffering and checking hardware as is found in dynamically-scheduled superscalar processors.

---

[2]R2000 is a Trademark of MIPS Computer Systems, Inc.

3.1 An ISA for Boosting

TORCH instructions are basically identical in function to the scalar instructions. The TORCH instructions are encoded differently, however, to include bits that specify boosting information. With a single level of boosting, one bit in a TORCH instruction encodes whether or not the instruction is boosted. If the bit is set, the instruction depends upon the outcome of the next conditional branch. The prediction is encoded in the branch instruction itself. With multiple levels of boosting, multiple bits are needed to indicate the level of boosting, i.e. the number of later branches upon which this instruction depends. The following discussion only describes the architecture and hardware necessary to support boosting through a single conditional branch since this produces the largest incremental gain in performance.

TORCH machine instructions are able to address all the locations in both the sequential and shadow register files. Each sequential register location has a dual location in the shadow register file. A single shadow register file is sufficient to buffer all side effects, since we only boost through one conditional branch. For instance, if we boost an instruction that writes into register r3, the boosted instruction would specify shadow register r3 as its destination. If the conditional branch that this boosted instruction depends upon is correctly predicted, the value in shadow register r3 is written into sequential register r3, maintaining sequential semantics. An incorrect prediction would cause shadow register r3 to be invalidated.

As mentioned above, TORCH supports precise exceptions in a clean and efficient manner. Exceptions on sequential instructions are handled immediately, while exceptions on boosted instructions are postponed until the boosted instruction attempts to commit. In this way, exceptions on boosted instructions that never commit do not alter the semantics of the program or degrade machine performance. When TORCH executes a conditional branch that tries to commit an outstanding exception on a boosted instruction, it invalidates the shadow structures and reexecutes all the boosted instructions that depend upon this branch. Since the branch that these "boosted" instructions depend upon is now resolved, the instructions are now sequential, and a sequential interrupt occurs at the precise time.

3.2 Small Example

Figures 1, 2, and 3 show a small piece of C code with its MIPS R2000[3] and TORCH machine code equivalents. Both the R2000 and TORCH have a single load delay slot, and this particular implementation of TORCH issues a maximum of two instructions per cycle. Boosted instructions are indicated by a .b suffix on the opcode, and accesses to registers in shadow register file are indicated by a .s suffix on the particular register specifier. (We use symbolic names instead of register identifiers simply for clarity.) A predicted-taken branch is indicated by a .t suffix and a not-taken prediction is indicated by a .n suffix.

---

[3]This code was generated with the maximum optimization level.

```
register int cnt = 0;
while (ptr) {
    if (ptr->data > 1000) cnt++;
    ptr = ptr->next;
}
```

Figure 1: Example in C

```
(1)             beq      ptr,0,lab1
(2)             move     cnt,0
(3)    lab3:    lw       data,0(ptr)
(4)             nop
(5)             slti     temp1,data,1001
(6)             bne      temp1,0,lab2
(7)             nop
(8)             addiu    cnt,cnt,1
(9)    lab2:    lw       ptr,4(ptr)
(10)            nop
(11)            bne      ptr,0,lab3
(12)            nop
(13)   lab1:
```

Figure 2: MIPS R2000 Machine Code for C Example

The example code simply walks a linked list, updating a count variable depending upon the value of the data at each element. The code contains four basic blocks with nearly no intra-basic-block parallelism. If we assume that the conditional branch at line 6 of Figure 2 is taken 50% of the time and we ignore the while loop startup, the MIPS R2000 code requires 9.5 cycles on average to execute the loop. With boosting, we can completely hide the update of variable cnt and overlap the critical paths of the two inner loop basic blocks. Thus, the while loop only takes an average of 5 cycles to execute on TORCH, just over half the time of the MIPS R2000.

3.3 Hardware Organization

Figure 4 illustrates the overall structure of TORCH. TORCH consists of two operational units, one for integer or logical operations and one for floating-point operations. Within each of these operational units, there exists a variety of independent functional units, register files, and other support hardware. The degree of parallelism in the machine dictates the number of component interconnections. For instance, the TORCH implementation in the previous example supports a degree of parallelism of two, and thus, two buses would connect the functional units with the register file for the transport of results.

The TORCH hardware differentiates itself from other statically-scheduled superscalar processors by including two shadow structures: the shadow register file and the shadow store buffer. The register file contains both a sequential register file and a shadow register file; similarly, the store buffer contains both a sequential store buffer and a shadow store buffer. There

```
(1)                 beq.n   ptr,0,lab1          ; lw.b      data.s,0(ptr)
(2)                 move    cnt,0               ; nop
(3)                 slti    temp1,data,1001     ; nop
(4)       lab3':    bne.n   temp1,0,lab2'       ; addiu.b cnt.s,cnt,1
(5)                 lw      ptr,4(ptr)          ; nop
(6)       lab2':    nop                         ; lw.b      data.s,0(ptr)
(7)                 bne.t   ptr,0,lab3'         ; nop
(8)                 slti.b  temp1.s,data.s,1001 ; nop
(9)       lab1:
```

Figure 3: TORCH Machine code for C Example

is one sequential/shadow register file for the integer unit and one sequential/shadow register file for the floating-point unit. There is only a single sequential/shadow store buffer for the entire processor. The sequential structures contain the sequential state of the machine; they do not contain the results of any instructions executed speculatively. These results are kept in the shadow structures.

The purpose of the shadow structures then is to hold the results of boosted instructions until the conditional branch upon which these boosted instructions depend are resolved. If a conditional branch that a set of boosted results depend upon is executed and found to be predicted correctly, this set of results is copied in mass from the shadow structures to the sequential structures. When a conditional branch executes differently from its prediction, all values in the shadow structures are thrown away since they were boosted assuming the branch would go the way of its prediction.

Similarly, boosted instructions that are in the pipeline when the condition of a branch is determined are also updated. On a correct prediction, the destinations of the boosted instructions in the pipeline are changed from the shadow structures to the sequential structures. On an incorrect prediction, all boosted instructions in the pipeline are squashed.

4 Evaluation Methodology

To measure the effectiveness of boosting and ultimately the viability of the TORCH architecture, we compare its performance against that of an aggressive dynamic scheduler on non-numerical programs.

4.1 MATCH

This section briefly overviews the organization and operation of a dynamically-scheduled superscalar processor that we used for our comparisons. We obtained the dynamically-scheduled model directly from a study by Johnson [9]. Though the simulator for his study allows for many different dynamically-scheduled superscalar organizations, we limit ourselves to using

the basic processor model. This model, which we call MATCH[4], is ambitious in its attempts to exploit instruction-level parallelism at the expense of complex and costly hardware. MATCH is able to execute scalar object code and thus makes no changes to the instruction set architecture.

Figure 5 illustrates the overall structure of MATCH. At first glance, the structure is very similar to TORCH; MATCH still contains two operational units, each with independent functional units. MATCH does not contain shadow structures, but as explained below, its reorder buffer performs a similar function. Since MATCH performs all instruction scheduling in hardware, most of the complexity of the hardware is in the control logic and is not shown in the figure.

In front of each functional unit is a reservation station [22]. The reservation stations are instruction buffers that disassociate the actual instruction fetch rate from the instruction execution rate. With this buffering, MATCH only needs enough hardware in the decoder, register file ports, and buses to support the average instruction-execution rate. These reservation stations also allow the processor to execute instructions out of order even though the instructions are fetched and decoded in program order. Therefore, it is these reservations stations and their control logic that perform the dynamic scheduling of instructions in MATCH.

To provide more opportunities for parallel issue, MATCH allows concurrent issue of a load and a store instruction. The load and store functional units are simply buffers for the memory instructions. The buffers also contain logic to perform memory disambiguation at run-time, thereby allowing loads and stores to bypass each other when advantageous.

Storage conflicts in the original code are eliminated at run-time by performing register renaming in the hardware [10]. Register renaming is implemented by using a reorder buffer [19] associated with each register file. The reorder buffer provides the additional storage necessary to implement register renaming. For example, when an instruction is decoded, MATCH dynamically allocates a location in the reorder buffer for this instruction's result and the instruction's destination-register number is associated with this new location. The next instruction that tries

---

[4]Though Johnson did not name his models, we call one of his models MATCH because TORCH attempts to "match" its performance and because the ideas for TORCH grew out of our work on MATCH.

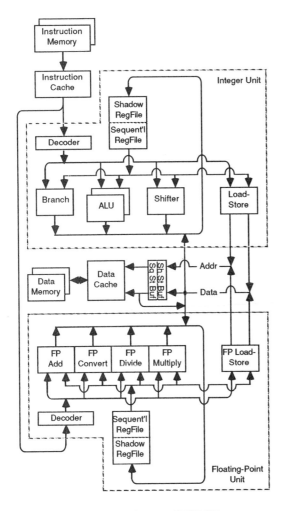

Figure 4: Block Diagram of TORCH

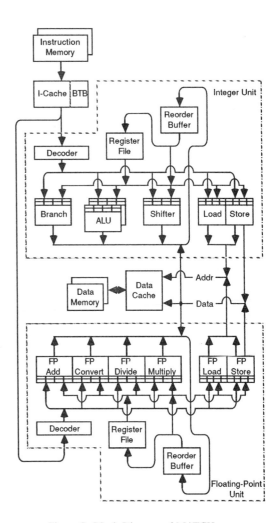

Figure 5: Block Diagram of MATCH

to fetch this register number as an operand will receive the value in the reorder buffer since this location contains the latest value. In effect, the register is renamed.

Furthermore, the reorder buffer allows MATCH to execute instructions across outstanding conditional branches by providing storage for the uncommitted results. MATCH allocates and deallocates locations in the reorder buffer as a FIFO queue. When the instruction at the head of the queue completes and writes its result into the reorder buffer, MATCH proceeds to write that value back to the register file. Since MATCH decodes instructions and allocates locations in the reorder buffer in program order, MATCH maintains updates to the register file in program order. Thus, when a conditional branch instruction reaches the head of the reorder buffer queue, the only values committed to the register file are those that had no dependence upon the conditional branch since they were fetched and decoded before the branch. If a branch is mispredicted, MATCH simply invalidates all locations in the reorder buffer from the

point of the branch backwards, and then starts executing instructions from the correct branch target. As a result, the reorder buffer provides an easy mechanism to eliminate storage conflicts and bypass conditional branches.

To provide conditional branch prediction, MATCH relies on a Branch Target Buffer (BTB) [12] which is incorporated into the instruction cache design. This structure improves the instruction fetch efficiency by removing the need to wait for a branch condition determination. Unfortunately, MATCH cannot eliminate the penalty to fetch efficiency due to instruction misalignment. Even the addition of alignment hardware in the fetch does little to reduce this penalty since the fetcher cannot stay far enough ahead of the decoder [9].

4.2 Evaluation Tools

Using the *pixie* [15] trace facility on the MIPS machines to generate a dynamic instruction trace for a particular program, Johnson's simulator for MATCH analyzes each dynamic instruction in turn. It keeps track of the functional requirements and result latencies of each dynamic instruction to determine the cycle count of this particular program on MATCH. A more indepth description of Johnson's simulator can be found in [9].

To quickly evaluate the viability of boosting, we built a simple scheduler that implements only a small subset of the functionality of the TORCH compiler. Furthermore, this simple scheduler works on optimized object code and therefore does not have access to higher-level program information. Since the disambiguation of memory instructions is extremely difficult at the object code level, the simple scheduler maintains the order of stores with respect to other memory operations. A full-blown implementation of a statically-scheduling superscalar compiler could disambiguate some of these memory references.

It is interesting to note that MATCH uses the buffering in its reservation stations to effectively move instructions both up and down in the execution sequence to try and smooth out the resource utilization. For instance, if an instruction in a basic block does not affect the condition of the branch instruction at the end of the basic block, this instruction can be executed after the branch instruction. The dynamic scheduler effectively moves this instruction down. A TORCH compiler could perform this same movement, but it is not done in the current simple scheduler. The simple scheduler only boosts instructions up through a single conditional branch and *reorganizes* instructions up through a single unconditional branch.

The simple scheduler compacts static basic blocks only individually or in pairs. Each basic block is list scheduled [6] given the current hardware constraints (the number of functional units and the number of instructions in a fetch block, for instance) and the program semantics. The scheduling between basic block pairs is accomplished by first list scheduling the dynamically-preceding basic block and then list scheduling the following basic block into the first schedule as if the two basic blocks were a single large basic block. The combination of the lengths of the individual basic block schedules minus the length of this new schedule is the number of cycles saved by boosting or reorganization. Reorganization always reduces the execution by these cycles; boosting reduces the execution only when the condition branch goes the way of the boost.

The evaluation process begins by running the limited scheduler over the object code for a program. The scheduler calculates the new basic block lengths of a program for a TORCH machine with a specified hardware configuration, a single boosting level, and no memory disambiguation. This data is combined with the basic block execution counts and the profile data for conditional branches to determine the final program cycle count. This calculation is correct since the simple scheduler does not change the number of basic blocks or reorder the conditional branches.

Both evaluation systems use the same machine configuration file. This file contains information on the number of functional units and the issue/result latencies of each functional unit. The evaluation systems, in addition to determining the performance of the superscalar processor, also determine the performance of a scalar processor that has functional units with the same latencies. Thus, we calculate the speedup of each superscalar processor over the scalar processor, and we ensure proper comparison between superscalar processors by requiring that both scalar simulations execute the same number of instructions in the same number of clock cycles.

4.3 Evaluation Specifics

To simplify the experiments, we restricted the scope of our evaluation systems to deal with only those effects we thought would have the greatest impact on the relative performances. We ran both the TORCH and MATCH evaluations using ideal caches, perfect register renaming, and a small number of functional units. We assumed ideal caches to simplify and speedup our runs. Though real caches will have a definite effect on the relative performances, we believe that caches should affect both machines in similar ways.

We also assumed perfect register renaming to reduce the complexity of the scheduling algorithms. With perfect register renaming, the instruction scheduler only considers true dependences when calculating data dependence constraints. We believe that this is a valid assumption given enough reorder buffer space in MATCH and enough general-purpose registers in TORCH.

Finally, we assumed a small number of functional units since the fetch efficiency and not the number of functional units is the limiting factor when exploiting instruction-level parallelism in non-numerical applications [21]. As a result, we maximize the functional unit cost/performance tradeoff by making the load/store pipe, our most expensive functional unit to duplicate, the most frequently used resource. With one of each functional unit, the integer ALU is the most frequently used functional unit. By adding an extra ALU, the load/store unit becomes the most frequently used functional unit, as desired. Thus, our superscalar machines have two integer ALUs and one of every other type of functional unit.

The functional unit characteristics are listed in Table 1, and they are quite similar to those found in the R2000 processor and its associated floating-point coprocessor. All floating-point result latencies are specified for double-precision operands. The FP Convert unit converts floating-point numbers to integer format and vice-versa. The buffering of each store allows the store issue latency in Table 1 to be a single cycle.

We configured the dynamically-scheduled simulation with enough hardware and buffering in MATCH to guarantee that the dynamic scheduler could effectively use all the functional units. In other words, the effectiveness of the scheduler, the size of the instruction fetch, and the available instruction-level parallelism in the program are the only limitations on the performance of the dynamic scheduler. These three parameters are all basic limitations in the statically-scheduled model too. Thus, we are comparing the ability of the TORCH scheduler against the ability of a dynamic scheduler to execute instructions speculatively before branches.

350

Functional Unit	Issue Latency (cycles)	Result Latency (cycles)
Integer ALU	1	1
Barrel Shifter	1	1
Load Pipe	1	2
Store Pipe	1	-
Branch Unit	1	2
FP Adder	1	2
FP Multiplier	1	5
FP Divider	1	19
FP Convert	1	2

Table 1: Functional Units with Issue and Result Latencies

Table 2 lists our benchmark suite of programs, all of which are written in C. Each of these programs ran to completion on a fairly large input data set, as indicated by the size of the dynamic instruction count in Table 2. None of these programs are floating-point intensive, and each exhibits a high frequency of branches during execution. Finally, all of these programs are highly-optimized since we are interested in the true advantage of a superscalar architecture and not in the advantages of executing redundant code in parallel.

Program Name	Static Instrs	Dynamic Instrs	Description
awk	26.9K	60.7M	pattern scanning/processing
ccom	58.1K	19.4M	front-end of a C compiler
espresso	43.6K	340.5M	logic minization
irsim	89.4K	54.3M	simulator for VLSI layouts
latex	53.2K	100.6M	document preparation system

Table 2: Program Descriptions

5 Results

All results in this section report speedups over the base scalar processor. The speedups are reported for each benchmark program along with the harmonic mean of the five benchmark speedups. Of course, we are mostly interested in the relative performance of the TORCH and MATCH processors, but absolute speedups of each superscalar processor over the scalar processor are also interesting. To have a reference point for the absolute speedups, we first present some numbers indicating the amount of exploitable instruction-level parallelism in our benchmark programs given only a few physical constraints.

Performance is always achieved at some cost. For our investigations, we believe that data memory interface is our most expensive resource, and as such we limit our machines to a single load/store pipe. Table 3 presents the maximum theoretical speedups for our benchmark programs if this single load/store pipe is the only constraint on instruction scheduling. These

speedups are simply the ratio of the total serial clock cycles divided by the number of dynamic load and store instructions in the program. In other words, executing one load or store operation every cycle increases performance by a factor two to four over the scalar processor.

awk	ccom	espresso	irsim	latex	hm
3.91	3.03	4.19	2.84	2.88	3.28

Table 3: Maximum Theoretical Speedups Based on Load/Store Frequency

Since the scalar processor executes approximately 0.9 instructions per cycle on average due to pipeline stalls, a speedup of 4 corresponds to executing less than 4 instructions per cycle in the superscalar machine. A balanced machine design requires an average fetch rate of four instructions per cycle to keep this execution unit busy in steady state. Of course, this execution rate is a theoretical maximum and the real execution rates will be less; consequently, we limit the TORCH and MATCH superscalar machines to fetching either two or four instructions per cycle.

5.1 Justifying Boosting

Boosting in a statically-scheduled superscalar processor allows the compiler to schedule instructions up through previous conditional branches. Boosting is not necessary if the compiler can find adequate instruction-level parallelism within the basic block. To determine the speedup from scheduling only within a basic block, we ran four different types of experiments on our TORCH machine, all of which did not use TORCH's ability to boost instructions. Table 4 presents these results.

	awk	cccom	espresso	irsim	latex	hm
Fetch 2	1.17	1.11	1.22	1.11	1.19	1.16
Fetch 4	1.17	1.11	1.22	1.12	1.21	1.16
one IPC	1.19	1.23	1.08	1.27	1.13	1.18
Infinite	1.24	1.32	1.35	1.24	1.41	1.31

Table 4: Speedups on TORCH When Scheduling Only Within a Basic Block

The first two experiments limited TORCH to fetching two and four instructions per cycle respectively. These speedups indicate that our non-numerical programs do not contain a large degree of concurrency within the basic block. Since the amount of instruction-level parallelism in a basic block is so low, fetching and executing two instructions concurrently finds the vast majority of parallelism, and increasing the fetch size to four instructions is not advantageous. In fact, the third line of Table 4, which reports the speedups of a machine executing one instruction per cycle, shows that intra-basic-block scheduling corresponds to executing approximately one instruction per cycle.

351

The final line of Table 4 shows the maximum possible speedups for an infinite, statically-scheduled superscalar machine. This machine has an infinite number of functional units and an infinitely large instruction fetch; its performance is only limited by true data dependences and basic block boundaries. This small amount of instruction-level parallelism, even in an ideal machine, makes a strong argument for boosting and other methods for exploiting the parallelism between basic blocks.

5.2 TORCH Results

In our next experiment, we compared the performance of static scheduling with boosting in TORCH against the performance of dynamic scheduling in MATCH. To isolate the scheduling effects, we made the superscalar models equal in their instruction-fetch size, their handling of branch prediction, and their ability to reorganize load and store operations. For Table 5, both TORCH and MATCH fetch either two or four instructions per cycle, and for this table, both processors predict that all branches are taken. TORCH, in our simple scheduler, is not able to disambiguate memory addresses since we have not implemented a full compiler system. Consequently, for the results in Table 5, we disabled the hardware in MATCH which supports movement of load and store instructions past each other.

	awk	cccom	espresso	irsim	latex	hm
Fetch 2						
TORCH	1.42	1.37	1.61	1.45	1.44	1.45
MATCH	1.34	1.28	1.45	1.31	1.34	1.34
Fetch 4						
TORCH	1.45	1.41	1.69	1.53	1.49	1.51
MATCH	1.40	1.37	1.58	1.43	1.40	1.43

Table 5: Speedups When Predicting Branches Are Taken and No Load/Store Reorganization Is Done

When fetching two instructions per cycle in Table 5, static scheduling with boosting outperforms dynamic scheduling. This advantage comes from the compiler's ability to align instructions in memory to eliminate the instruction misalignment effects that are especially detrimental to MATCH with such a small fetch block. The small fetch block also limits the size of the window of instructions from which the dynamic scheduler tries to find concurrent instructions. Though a four-instruction fetch reduces both of these effects as shown by the smaller performance difference in the bottom half of Table 5, TORCH is still faster.

The TORCH results are a lower bound on the performance of this type of scheduling since the current TORCH scheduler is limited to boosting only through a single branch and reorganizing between dynamically-adjacent basic blocks. As we improve the compiler's ability to boost and reorganize, TORCH could better utilize the two and four instruction fetch, at least up to the limits of the parallelism in the machine or program. For these experiments though, static scheduling with boosting can

already outperform dynamic scheduling because static scheduling is able to align instructions in fetch blocks and analyze larger amounts of code.

If we then allow each scheduler to use its best branch prediction technique, the TORCH scheduler outperforms the dynamic scheduler by an even larger amount as seen in Table 6. Table 7 helps explain this result. The experiment in Table 5 assumed that the superscalar machine predicted all branches are taken. Table 7 shows that this results in a 73.2% accuracy rate for all branches, conditional and unconditional. Using branch profiling statistics to statically predict branches in TORCH though, we can increase the accuracy rate to 90.6% for our benchmark programs; and by using a 4-way set associative, 2048-entry branch target buffer in MATCH, we can increase its accuracy rate to 83.4%. Since the accuracy rate in TORCH is higher than the accuracy rate in MATCH, the TORCH scheduler performs even better than the MATCH scheduler.

	awk	cccom	espresso	irsim	latex	hm
Fetch 2						
TORCH	1.49	1.52	1.70	1.55	1.55	1.56
MATCH	1.41	1.41	1.51	1.40	1.42	1.43
Fetch 4						
TORCH	1.52	1.57	1.79	1.64	1.63	1.63
MATCH	1.48	1.50	1.66	1.53	1.49	1.53

Table 6: Speedups When Using Improved Branch Prediction Techniques and No Load/Store Reorganization

	awk	cccom	espresso	irsim	latex	hm
Predict Take	79.3	68.5	77.6	75.6	66.8	73.2
BTB	87.1	80.8	80.0	88.1	81.5	83.4
Profiling	91.0	92.6	86.9	92.1	90.6	90.6

Table 7: Branch Prediction Accuracies (as percentages)

5.3 Future Expectations

To see how reorganizing load and store instructions with respect to each other affects performance, we reran the MATCH simulations from Tables 5 and 6 with the memory disambiguation hardware in MATCH enabled. These results are reported in Tables 8 and 9 respectively. The TORCH numbers in the new tables are identical to the numbers in the original tables since the simple scheduler for TORCH cannot perform memory disambiguation.

With memory disambiguation, MATCH is able to outperform our limited TORCH scheduler, especially when fetching four instructions. Memory disambiguation, then, is important since it provides more opportunities for parallel issue. By providing static memory disambiguation in the compiler and hardware to

	awk	cccom	espresso	irsim	latex	hm
Fetch 2						
TORCH	1.42	1.37	1.61	1.45	1.44	1.45
MATCH	1.54	1.46	1.58	1.51	1.48	1.51
Fetch 4						
TORCH	1.45	1.41	1.69	1.53	1.49	1.51
MATCH	1.73	1.71	1.88	1.73	1.70	1.75

Table 8: Speedups When Predicting Branches Are Taken and Allowing Load/Store Reorganization in MATCH Only

	awk	cccom	espresso	irsim	latex	hm
Fetch 2						
TORCH	1.49	1.52	1.70	1.55	1.55	1.56
MATCH	1.63	1.59	1.62	1.63	1.61	1.62
Fetch 4						
TORCH	1.52	1.57	1.79	1.64	1.63	1.63
MATCH	1.86	1.97	1.97	1.94	1.95	1.94

Table 9: Speedups When Using Improved Branch Prediction Techniques and Allowing Load/Store Reorganization in MATCH Only

support the speculative reorganization of the other memory operations, we expect to see similar increases in the performance of TORCH. Till then, we feel that the 1.6-times speedup for TORCH is surprisingly good considering our simple TORCH scheduler, and is impressive given TORCH's relatively inexpensive hardware design.

6 Conclusions

This paper introduces a cost-effective way of boosting the performance of statically-scheduled superscalar processors on non-numerical programs. We change the instruction set architecture of a statically-scheduled machine to include boosted instructions, a mechanism that provides the compiler with an efficient method of expressing speculative evaluation.

Boosting removes the dependences caused by conditional branches and makes the reorganization of side-effect instructions as simple as those without side effects. To support boosting in the hardware, we describe relatively inexpensive shadow structures, the shadow register file and shadow store buffer, that hold the side effects of boosted instructions until the conditional branch that the boosted instructions depend upon is executed. When the conditional branch is executed, its prediction is compared to the actual decision and the boosted instructions are either committed or squashed without run-time overhead.

Our experiments on non-numerical code show that adding a single level of boosting to a statically-scheduled superscalar processor yields a 1.6-times speedup over scalar code. This performance is comparable to the performance of an aggressive,

dynamically-scheduled superscalar processor. Consequently, we are working on a compiler and a simulator for the full functionality of TORCH. This system will experiment with the boosting of instructions above multiple conditional branches, the reorganizing of instructions both up and down across multiple basic block boundaries, and the advantages of memory disambiguation.

7 Acknowledgements

Mike Smith was supported in part through Digital Equipment Corporation's contributions to the Center for Integrated Systems at Stanford University. This research was supported in part by DARPA, under contract number N00014-87-K-0828.

We are indebted to Mike Johnson of Advanced Micro Devices, Inc. for the use of his simulator, and to Neil Wilhelm of DEC for his help in the design of the TORCH architecture.

References

[1] Apollo Computer Inc. Marketing Brochure, *The Series 10000 Personal Supercomputer*. Chelmsford, MA, 1988.

[2] W. Buchholz(Editor), *Planning a Computer System: Project Stretch*. McGraw-Hill, 1962.

[3] A.E. Charlesworth, "An Approach to Scientific Array Processing: The Architectural Design of the AP-120B/FPS-164 Family". *Computer* (September 1981), pp. 18-57.

[4] R. Cohn, T. Gross, M. Lam, and P.S. Tseng, "Architecture and Compiler Tradeoffs for a Long Instruction Word Microprocessor." *Proceedings of the Third International Conference on Architectural Support for Programming Languages and Operating Systems* (April 1989), pp. 2-14.

[5] R.P. Colwell et al., "A VLIW Architecture for a Trace Scheduling Compiler." *IEEE Transactions on Computers* (August 1988), pp. 967-979.

[6] S. Davidson, D. Landskov, B. Shriver, and P.W. Mallett, "Some Experiments in Local Microcode Compaction for Horizontal Machines". *IEEE Transactions on Computers* Vol. C-30 (July 1981), pp. 460-477.

[7] J.A. Fisher, "Trace Scheduling: A Technique for Global Microcode Compaction". *IEEE Transactions on Computers* Vol. C-30 (July 1981), pp. 478-490.

[8] R.D. Groves and R. Oehler, "An IBM Second Generation RISC Processor Architecture." *Proceedings 1989 IEEE International Conference on Computer Design: VLSI in Computers and Processors* (October 1989), pp. 134-137.

[9] M. Johnson, "Super-Scalar Processor Design." Technical Report No. CSL-TR-89-383, Stanford University (June 1989).

[10] R.M. Keller, "Look-Ahead Processors." *Computing Surveys* (December 1975), pp. 177-195.

[11] M. Lam, "Software Pipelining: An Effective Scheduling Technique for VLIW Machines." *Proceedings of ACM SIGPLAN '88 Conference on Programming Language Design and Implementation* (June 1988), pp. 318-328.

[12] J.K.F. Lee and A.J. Smith, "Branch Prediction Strategies and Branch Target Buffer Design." *IEEE Computer* (January 1984), pp. 6-22.

[13] S. McFarling and J. Hennessy, "Reducing the Cost of Branches". *Proc. 13th Annual Symposium on Computer Architecture* (June 1986), pp. 396-404.

[14] "Metaflow Targets SPARC and 386 with Parallel Architecture." *Microprocessor Report* (December 1988), pp. 6-9.

[15] MIPS Computer Systems, Inc., *MIPS Language Programmer's Guide* (1986).

[16] K. Murakami, N. Irie, M. Kuga, and S. Tomita, "SIMP (Single Instruction stream / Multiple instruction Pipelining): A novel High-Speed Single-Processor Architecture." *Proceedings of the 16th Annual International Symposium on Computer Architecture* (May 1989), pp. 78-85.

[17] T.S. Perry, "Intel's Secret Is Out." *IEEE Spectrum* (April 1989), pp. 22-28.

[18] B.R. Rau, D.W.L. Yen, W. Yen, and R.A. Towle, "The Cydra 5 Departmental Supercomputer." *IEEE Computer* (January 1989), pp. 12-35.

[19] J.E. Smith and A.R. Pleszkun, "Implementation of Precise Interrupts in Pipelined Processors." *Proceedings of the 12th Annual International Symposium on Computer Architecture* (June 1985), pp. 36-44.

[20] J.E. Smith, "Dynamic Instruction Scheduling and the Astronautics ZS-1." *IEEE Computer* (July 1989), pp. 21-35.

[21] M.D. Smith, M. Johnson, M.A. Horowitz, "Limits on Multiple Instruction Issue." *Proceedings of the Third International Conference on Architectural Support for Programming Languages and Operating Systems* (April 1989), pp. 290-302.

[22] R.M. Tomasulo, "An Efficient Hardware Algorithm for Exploiting Multiple Arithmetic Units." *IBM Journal* (January 1967), pp. 25-33.

The TLB Slice -- A Low-Cost High-Speed Address Translation Mechanism

George Taylor, Peter Davies and Michael Farmwald

MIPS Computer Systems
930 Arques Avenue
Sunnyvale CA 94086

Abstract

The MIPS R6000 microprocessor relies on a new type of translation lookaside buffer – called a *TLB slice* -- which is less than one-tenth the size of a conventional TLB and as fast as one multiplexer delay, yet has a high enough hit rate to be practical. The fast translation makes it possible to use a physical cache without adding a translation stage to the processor's pipeline. The small size makes it possible to include address translation on-chip, even in a technology with a limited number of devices.

The key idea behind the TLB slice is to have both a virtual tag and a physical tag on a physically-indexed cache. Because of the virtual tag, the TLB slice needs to hold only enough physical page number bits -- typically 4 to 8 -- to complete the physical cache index, in contrast with a conventional TLB, which needs to hold both a virtual page number and a physical page number. The virtual page number is unnecessary because the TLB slice needs to provide only a hint for the translated physical address rather than a guarantee. The full physical page number is unnecessary because the cache hit logic is based on the virtual tag. Furthermore, if the cache is multi-level and references to the TLB slice are "shielded" by hits in a virtually indexed primary cache, the slice can get by with very few entries, once again lowering its cost and increasing its speed. With this mechanism, the simplicity of a physical cache can been combined with the speed of a virtual cache.

1. Introduction

Most computer systems use high-speed caches to boost CPU performance [Smith82] and virtual memory to provide protection, large address spaces and convenient allocation of physical memory [Denning70]. Because of the virtual memory, addresses must be translated at some point between the processor and main memory. While most aspects of cache design are unrelated to virtual memory, one that is highly visible to the memory management software is whether address translation occurs before or after the cache access [Cheng87]. If fast cache access were the only considera-

tion, a virtual cache would be attractive because it could be accessed without waiting for the translation. But there are a number of reasons why physical cache systems are simpler to build. Two of the most important are virtual address synonyms and the desire to build cache coherent multiprocessors [Wang89]. Certain architectures have eliminated the synonym problem by definition [Hill86, Lee89], but a constraint in many architectures (including ours [Kane87]) is that synonyms are allowed both within a single address space and between multiple address spaces.

Virtual memory is usually implemented by means of page tables, which translate every virtual page number into the appropriate physical page number. Because the page tables are large and their organization is complicated, common practice is to copy information from the page tables into a translation-lookaside buffer that the hardware can reference [Lee60]. The TLB is just a special cache for the page tables. Almost all previous TLB's have been single level, but one example of a two-level TLB is the MicroVAX [Beck84]. The first level of the MicroVAX TLB is still a traditional cache, however, because it has a virtual tag and its own hit/miss logic, whereas the TLB slice described in this paper has neither a tag nor a hit/miss line.

The TLB slice came about because the R6000 microprocessor [Roberts90] needed to have a physically-indexed cache, but did not have the space or the time for a conventional TLB. In order to attain a high hit rate, on-chip conventional TLB's typically have 32 to 128 entries and a high degree of associativity, which is implemented with a large number of comparators. The time for this comparison plus the time to select the appropriate entry after it is chosen amount to a large fraction of the cycle time. The TLB slice substantially reduces both the time and the space by eliminating the comparison.

The design of the TLB slice was based on three observations:

1) that a physical cache index requires only a few bits of the physical page number, since the remaining bits come from the byte offset within the page,

CH2887-8/90/0000/0355$01.00 © 1990 IEEE

2) that if the cache tag were virtual, the physical page number would not be required for tag comparison[1], and

3) that a TLB would be fast if it were direct-mapped and had only a few entries, although it would be effective only if its hit rate were high and its refill cost were low.

The questions of hit rate and refill cost will be examined in sections 6-9 below. But first we will show how the TLB slice works and compare a TLB slice entry with a conventional TLB entry.

2. How the TLB slice works

Figure 1 shows how TLB slice address translation would be carried out in a system with a 32-bit virtual address, an 8-bit process-ID, a 16K byte page size and a cache with 256K bytes per bank. In this example, the three low order bits of the virtual page number select one of eight TLB slice entries. The entry supplies four low order bits of the physical page number, which are concatenated with the 14-bit page offset to form an 18-

---

[1]Of course, the cache must have a physical tag in addition to the virtual tag, else it would not be a physical cache. Dual cache tags have been suggested before as a part of a solution to the multiprocessor cache coherency problem [Goodman87], although in that design the index for the data portion of the cache was virtual rather than physical.

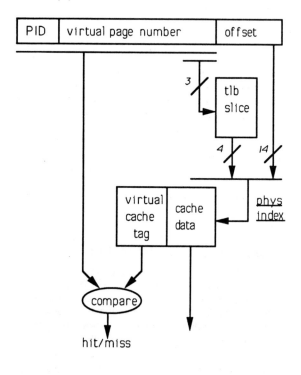

Figure 1. -- A physically indexed cache with a virtual tag.

bit physical cache index. The cache hit logic compares the virtual tag with the process-ID and the given virtual page number. Note that the entire virtual page number is compared with the cache tag; the low order bits that were used to index the TLB slice cannot be left out of the tag comparison.

Figure 2 contrasts the three components of a conventional TLB entry with the single component of a TLB slice entry. The widths of the fields are based on the same assumptions as in Figure 1, plus a 36-bit physical address space. When a conventional TLB is employed, a given virtual address is compared against the process-ID and the virtual page number of each entry in the TLB. If both fields match, the physical page number is extracted and sent to the cache tag comparator. In our example, the widths of the process-ID, virtual page number and physical page number fields add up to 48 bits. For the TLB slice, in contrast, the only information necessary to index the cache is the low order part of the physical page number. In our example, this would be four bits wide because one bank one bank of the cache is 16 times larger than the page size.

PID	virtual page number	physical page number
8	18	22

full TLB entry

TLB slice entry

4

Figure 2. -- A full TLB entry compared with a TLB slice entry.

Besides making the TLB slice very narrow, we also want it to contain as few entries as possible, consistent with a hit high rate. For a given number of entries, the hit rate can be increased three ways:

1) by increasing the page size (because more space is mapped);

2) by using separate TLB slices for instructions and data (see section 9), or

3) by placing a virtually-indexed primary cache in front of a physically-indexed secondary cache so that references to the TLB slice are shielded by hits in the primary cache.

Simulations show that shielding is crucial because a TLB slice with only a few entries works poorly against a complete memory reference stream. However, it works much better (in terms of total misses per program) against the stream of references that missed in a virtual primary cache.

The refill cost for the TLB slice is kept low by backing it with a larger secondary TLB. The R6000 maintains its secondary TLB off-chip and has a refill cost of 8 cycles. The secondary TLB would have been necessary in any case, since access control information has to be available to the hardware. Access control bits could be stored in the TLB slice, but to keep the slice as small as possible, the R6000 stores access information in its off-chip primary and secondary cache tags.

Table 1 contrasts the characteristics of a TLB slice with those of a conventional TLB, such as the one in the MIPS R3000 [Riordan89]. The TLB slice is by necessity direct mapped, since it does not provide any means to determine whether there is a hit. With 96 bits of RAM, the TLB slice's performance cost is about 0.04 cycles per instruction, as demonstrated by the simulation results in sections 7 and 8.

	TLB slice (MIPS R6000)	conventional TLB (MIPS R3000)
depth	16 entries	64 entries
width	4 bits	46 bits
total size	64 bits	2944 bits
associativity	direct mapped	fully associative
page size	16K	4K
cost of TLB misses (cycles per instruction)	.04	.03

Table 1. -- Characteristics of a TLB slice compared with those of a conventional TLB. This example assumes 8 TLB slice entries for instructions and 16 for data. The model for the conventional TLB is the MIPS R3000 microprocessor, whose on-chip TLB contains 64 entries times 46 bits per entry (equals 2944 bits). The miss cost is based on a 4K byte page size, eight cycles to refill the TLB slice (by hardware from a secondary TLB, as in the R6000), and 13 cycles to refill the conventional TLB (by software from the page tables, as in the R3000).

	physical tag	virtual tag
physical index	DEC VAX 11/780 IBM 3033 MIPS R3000	MIPS R6000
virtual index	ELXSI 6400 HP Precision [Lee89]	Berkeley SPUR [Wood86] Sun 3/200 [Cheng87]

Table 2. -- Four combinations of virtual and physical indexes and tags.

3. The design space for virtual and physical caches

Caches need not be completely virtual or completely physical. As shown in Table 2, there are actually four possible combinations of tags and indexes, three of which have been implemented in previous processors. The majority of computers have used physical indexes and physical tags because this is the simplest scheme with respect to synonyms, sharing and cache coherency. A small number of virtual index machines have also been introduced. The most straightforward case (Sun, SPUR) avoids address translation altogether by using virtual tags. The other variant (ELXSI, HP) accesses the TLB and the physical cache tag in parallel, and then compares the two resulting physical addresses to test for a hit. The R6000 implements the fourth alternative, which combines a physical index with a virtual tag.

4. Full translation only after a cache miss

As we have seen, the primary advantages of the TLB slice and virtual cache tag are the low cost and high speed of the on-chip translation hardware. A third advantage is that a full-width translation is necessary only after cache miss, instead of on every cache access. This in turn makes it possible to store the full-width TLB in an inexpensive way, such as within the cache itself. A previous example of this technique was the in-cache TLB used by the Berkeley SPUR microprocessor [Wood86]. SPUR's starting point was a virtually indexed cache rather than a physically indexed one, but in either case, storing the TLB in the cache saves at least one bank of high-speed RAM and allows the TLB to have a large number of entries. The R6000 reserves a portion of its off-chip secondary cache to hold 4096 entries of a two-way set associative main TLB, far more entries than would have been possible in an on-chip TLB.

As we will see in the cache access sequence described in the next section, the physical cache tag is referenced just as infrequently as the full TLB. For this reason, the physical tag could also be stored in a reserved section of the physical cache if there were no other reason to allocate a dedicated bank of RAM for it (a snooping cache coherency protocol might be such a reason).

5. Cache access sequence

The TLB slice does have a cost – a more complicated cache miss sequence. One reason is that slice misses masquerade as cache misses. A second reason is that a physical tag hit can occur despite a virtual tag miss, so both tags must be checked before a true cache miss is detected.

The cache access sequence goes through the following ten steps, which are diagrammed in Figure 4. The specific bit field limits are based on the same assumptions that we used in Figures 1 and 2. The virtual page number consists of bits <31..14>, while the physical cache index bits are numbered <17..0>.

1) Index into the TLB slice with virtual address bits <16..14>. The selected TLB slice entry contains physical address bits <17..14>. Combine these with page offset bits <13..0> to form the complete physical index <17..0>.

2) Use physical index bits <17..0> to read the cache tag and data arrays.

3) The cache tag contains the process-ID and virtual address bits <31..14> for the corresponding cache data line. If the process-ID matches the current process and the virtual address matches the given virtual address, then there is a cache hit.

4) If the virtual tags do not match, then there was either a TLB slice miss or a cache miss (or both). To distinguish them, read the full TLB entry.

5) If there is a miss when reading the full TLB, then trap to software and refill the full TLB from the page table.

6) If physical index bits <17..14> from the full TLB do not match physical index bits <17..14> from the TLB slice, then there was a TLB slice miss in step 1. Otherwise, there was a cache miss in step 3.

7) If there was a TLB slice miss, then copy physical index bits <17..14> from the full TLB into the appropriate TLB slice entry and repeat the process starting with step 1.

8) If there was a cache miss, then read the physical tag for the cache line from wherever it is stored.

9) Compare physical address bits <35..14> from the full TLB entry with physical tag bits <35..14>. If there is a match, then two virtual addresses are mapped to a single physical address and there was in fact a cache hit. To cause a virtual cache hit on the next reference to this cache line, copy the new PID and virtual address bits <31..14> into the virtual cache tag.

10) If the physical tags do not match, then refill the cache line from main memory. If the cache line is dirty, then write it back to the memory address contained in the physical tag. Read the new line from memory using the physical address from the full TLB.

The remainder of the paper is divided into two parts. The first shows simulation results for TLB slice miss rates in the context of a single-level cache. The second part examines TLB slice miss rates in the context of a two-level cache, since in that case the slice works much better than might have been expected. Multi-level caches have been explored in more general terms in [Przybylski89], [Short88] and [Wang89].

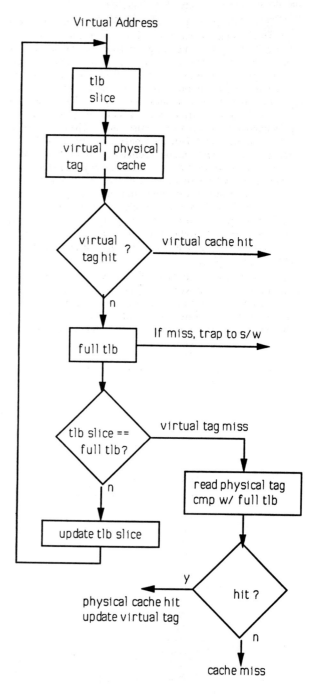

Figure 4. -- Cache access sequence in the presence of a TLB slice.

6. TLB slice miss rates for a single level cache

The simplest way to use a TLB slice is in a processor with a single level physical cache (Figure 1 above). Table 3 shows the miss rate for four to sixteen entries and a 16K byte page size on a suite of fourteen substantial programs. The instruction TLB slice has acceptable behavior when the product of the page size times the number of entries is at least 64K bytes (the same product with more entries and a smaller page size would presumably have no worse miss rate). However, even with 16 entries and 16K byte pages, the data TLB slice causes a large performance penalty. For this reason, it is not surprising that a TLB slice has never appeared in a processor with a single level cache. However, such a possibility should not be ruled out, especially if the refill cost were less than the 8 cycles assumed here. The TLB slice appears to suffer from a granularity problem, since a 256K byte data cache containing far more than 16 lines would have a miss rate per instruction much lower than 0.7%.

The miss rates in Table 3 were gathered by simulating the TLB as if it were a standard cache with the usual hit/miss logic. Actual TLB slice miss rates could be lower for two reasons – (1) random chance, given that the TLB slice is so narrow, and (2) because different virtual page numbers with the same low order bits may map to physical addresses with the same low order bits. These two effects are difficult to simulate because they depend on a particular operating system's page assignment routines and on the state of a processor in a multi-tasking environment. The second effect is discussed in more detail in section 10 below.

7. Shielding by a virtual primary cache

Now suppose that a processor has a two level cache, such as the one shown in Figure 5. This time the primary caches have virtual indexes, but the secondary cache has a physical index (and the virtual and physical tags described above). Memory references that hit in the primary cache are never sent to secondary cache or to the TLB slice. Table 4 shows that when this shielding is taken into account the TLB slice works extremely well for instruction fetches. Even with only two entries and a 4K byte page size, the average miss rate is less than 0.1% and the performance cost is less than .01 cycles per instruction. The data reference stream is significantly more difficult to handle than the instruction reference stream, but with eight entries the cost per instruction can be held to between .02 and .04 cycles, depending on the page size. The primary virtual caches have solved the problem of low granularity in the TLB slices.

	instruction TLB-slice miss rate per instruction (%)			data TLB-slice miss rate per instruction (%)		
	no shielding			no shielding		
number of entries	4	8	16	4	8	16
page size	16K	16K	16K	16K	16K	16K
timberwolf	.01%	.00%	.00%	7.12%	2.59%	.72%
uopt	.54	.08	.00	6.33	3.55	1.57
compress	.00	.00	.00	6.44	3.81	2.26
spice2g6	.09	.00	.00	2.95	1.24	.87
espresso	.19	.16	.00	3.56	1.47	.18
nroff	.00	.00	.00	5.45	.05	.00
tex	.52	.35	.00	8.01	6.09	.46
as1	.25	.12	.00	3.77	2.38	.52
5diff	.00	.00	.00	3.61	1.28	.76
ccom	.88	.50	.00	2.91	1.52	.68
doducd	.16	.14	.00	1.95	.45	.37
gnuchess	.00	.00	.00	.16	.00	.00
yacc	.00	.00	.00	1.66	.52	.00
terse	.52	.00	.00	5.29	1.93	1.10
average	.22%	.10%	.00%	4.2%	1.9%	0.7%
cycles per instruction (@ 8 cycles per miss)	.02	.01	.00	.34	.15	.06

Table 3. -- TLB slice miss rates for single level instruction and data caches.

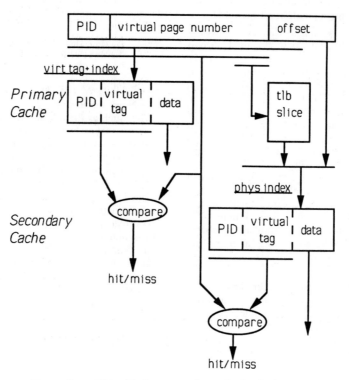

Figure 5. -- Virtual primary cache and physical secondary cache.

number of entries	instruction TLB-slice miss rate per instruction (%) shielded by 16K byte virtual cache			data TLB-slice miss rate per instruction (%) shielded by 16K byte virtual cache		
number of entries	2	4	8	8	16	8
page size	4K	4K	4K	4K	4K	16K
timberwolf	.09%	.08%	.04%	1.16%	.60%	.63%
uopt	.13	.12	.08	.50	.32	.23
compress	.00	.00	.00	2.29	2.07	1.86
spice2g6	.23	.22	.08	.70	.18	.09
espresso	.06	.06	.03	.09	.04	.06
nroff	.23	.20	.04	.15	.10	.00
tex	.41	.37	.22	.25	.15	.11
as1	.73	.63	.36	.23	.13	.13
5diff	.00	.00	.00	.53	.26	.24
ccom	1.02	.89	.78	.44	.25	.18
doducd	.06	.05	.03	.42	.14	.06
gnuchess	.07	.07	.00	.02	.00	.00
yacc	.00	.00	.00	.15	.12	.02
terse	.30	.28	.19	.59	.36	.36
average	.24%	.21%	.13%	.54%	.34%	.29%
cycles per instruction (@ 8 cycles per miss)	.02	.02	.01	.04	.03	.02

Table 4. -- TLB slice miss rates with references shielded by virtually-indexed primary caches. The primary instruction and data cache line sizes are 32 bytes and 8 bytes, respectively. Both are direct-mapped.

	instruction TLB-slice miss rate per instruction (%) shielded by 64K byte virtual cache			instruction TLB-slice miss rate per instruction (%) shielded by 16K byte virtual cache		
number of entries	2	4	8	2	4	8
page size	4K	4K	4K	4K	4K	4K
timberwolf	.00%	.00%	.00%	.09%	.08%	.04%
uopt	.05	.05	.04	.13	.12	.08
compress	.00	.00	.00	.00	.00	.00
spice2g6	.01	.01	.01	.23	.22	.08
espresso	.02	.02	.02	.06	.06	.03
nroff	.00	.00	.00	.23	.20	.04
tex	.14	.13	.12	.41	.37	.22
as1	.13	.12	.11	.73	.63	.36
5diff	.00	.00	.00	.00	.00	.00
ccom	.30	.25	.20	1.02	.89	.78
doducd	.01	.00	.00	.06	.05	.03
gnuchess	.00	.00	.00	.07	.07	.00
yacc	.00	.00	.00	.00	.00	.00
terse	.07	.07	.07	.30	.28	.19
average	.05%	.05%	.04%	.24%	.21%	.13%
cycles per instruction (@ 8 cycles per miss)	.00	.00	.00	.02	.01	.01

Table 5. -- TLB slice miss rates for references shielded by hits in two sizes of virtual primary cache.

	separate i & d TLB slices miss rate per instruction (%) shielded by 16K byte virtual caches			combined TLB slice miss rate per instruction (%) shielded by 16K byte virtual caches		
number of entries	4 each	8 each	16 each	8 total	16 total	32 total
page size	4K	4K	4K	4K	4K	4K
timberwolf	1.57%	1.37%	.60%	1.19%	.81%	.30%
uopt	.81	.58	.37	.66	.44	.26
compress	2.39	2.29	2.07	2.29	2.07	1.68
spice2g6	1.64	.78	.19	.99	.33	.11
espresso	.22	.12	.06	.14	.08	.05
nroff	.43	.19	.10	.28	.19	.10
tex	.71	.47	.30	.61	.43	.24
as1	.95	.59	.27	.84	.50	.29
5diff	.80	.53	.26	.53	.26	.08
ccom	1.56	1.22	.66	1.66	1.19	.85
doducd	.72	.45	.14	.65	.33	.20
gnuchess	.11	.02	.00	.06	.03	.03
yacc	.21	.15	.12	.15	.12	.00
terse	1.03	.78	.43	.90	.58	.36
average	1.0%	.68%	.40%	.78%	.53%	.33%
cycles per instruction (@ 8 cycles per miss)	.08	.05	.03	.06	.04	.03

Table 6. -- Miss rates for separate instruction and data TLB slices vs. a combined TLB slice. All entries reflect shielding by 16K byte virtually-indexed primary instruction and data caches with 32 byte and 8 byte line sizes, respectively. Both caches are direct-mapped.

8. How primary cache size affects shielding

The size and granularity of a virtual primary cache determine how effectively it shields references to a TLB slice. To illustrate this effect, Table 5 compares a 64K byte primary instruction cache with a 16K byte instruction cache having one-fourth as many lines (the line size is 32 bytes in both cases). There is a non-trivial difference in the TLB slice's effect on performance because of the higher hit rate of the 64K byte cache.

9. A combined TLB slice for instructions and data

Table 6 compares the miss rate of a combined instruction and data TLB slice with the miss rates for separate TLB slices, each of which has half as many entries as the combined slice. The bulk of the miss rate for the separate slices comes from the data slice.

For a given number of entries, the combined slice has about a 20% lower miss rate. However, a division more heavily weighted toward data than instructions could perform as well or better than a single combined slice. One of the issues to consider would be worst case performance versus average performance. A slight loss in average performance might be worthwhile due to lower variability.

10. Page coloring

Since the TLB slice is so narrow, there is a non-trivial probability that it will contain the correct value by chance. For instance, a four-bit wide slice tends to be correct 1/16 of the time. This probability can be increased if the operating system's page mapping routine attempts to match the low order bits of the virtual page number (VPN) with the low order bits of the physical page number (PPN), a process referred to as "page coloring".[1] In effect, main memory is treated as an n-way set associative cache rather than as a traditional fully associative cache. In the most extreme case, the mapping routine could achieve perfect coloring, in which n low order bits of the VPN always matched n low order bits of the PPN. In that case, an n-bit wide TLB slice with 2^n entries would become an identity and all references would hit. Of course, thinking about it another way, perfect coloring would also eliminate the need for the TLB slice in the first place. But the point is that partial coloring can reduce the TLB slice miss

rate from what it would have been otherwise. So the operating system has a degree of freedom. If it manages to color perfectly, then the TLB slice will disappear. If it cannot, the slice's miss rate per instruction will be no worse than it would have been in a direct-mapped conventional TLB with the same number of entries.

Page coloring actually works for any fixed mapping between the low order bits of the virtual page number and the physical page number. The mapping need not be direct or even one-to-one, as long as it remains fixed for a given process. However, reducing the TLB slice miss rate is not the only criterion for mapping virtual pages into physical memory. In the most extreme case, all virtual pages could be mapped to a single physical page. This would cause the TLB slice to hit every time, but the page fault rate would explode!

11. Summary

The R6000 combines a virtual cache tag with a physical cache index. Such a cache can be thought of as a physically-indexed, physically-tagged cache that also has a virtual tag in order to allow a shortcut on a cache hit. The address translation mechanism can be thought of as a full TLB that also has a TLB slice in order to allow a shortcut on a combined slice hit and cache hit.

The primary benefits of the TLB slice are that address translation is fast and the hardware mechanism is small. The fast translation makes it possible to use a physical cache index without adding an address translation stage to the processor's pipeline. The small size makes it possible to put address translation on the same chip as the processor even in a technology with a limited number of devices.

The TLB slice hit rate is high enough and the refill cost is low enough to make the scheme practical. The hit rate depends on the page size, the number of entries in the TLB slice and the degree of address space partitioning, but the most important effect is the shielding provided by a multi-level cache. The TLB slice will work even for a single-level cache, but shielding by a virtually indexed primary cache substantially lowers the TLB slice miss rate for a physically indexed secondary cache.

12. Acknowledgements

The authors thank John Hennessy, Mark Hill, Earl Killian, John Mashey, Guri Sohi and the referees for their careful reading and suggestions.

13. References

[Beck84]   John Beck et. al., "A 32b Microprocessor with On-Chip Virtual Memory Management," *1984 IEEE International Solid State Circuits Conference*, pp. 178-179.

---

[1] Page coloring was included in the MIPS operating system some years ago for a completely different purpose than ease of address translation. The problem at that time was a large variance in program runtimes due to changes in the cache miss rate caused by the arbitrary mapping of virtual pages to physical page frames in main memory (the caches were physical). The solution was to search the free list for a certain distance in order to find a page frame whose low order bits matched the low order bits of the virtual page number. The preferred relationship was not a direct match, but rather a constant offset between the VPN and PPN which differed for each region (text, data and stack). The result was a slight reduction in mean runtime and a substantial reduction in variance.

[Cheng87] Ray Cheng, "Virtual Address Cache in UNIX," *Proceedings of Summer 1987 USENIX Conference*, pp. 217-224.

[Denning70] Peter J. Denning, "Virtual Memory," *Computing Surveys*, vol. 2, no. 3, September 1970.

[Goodman87] James R. Goodman, "Coherency for Multiprocessor Virtual Address Caches," *Proc. Second International Conference on Architectural Support for Programming Languages and Operating Systems*, October 1987, pp. 72-81.

[Hill86] Mark Hill et. al., "Design Decisions in SPUR," *Computer,*, vol. 19, no. 11, November 1986, pp. 8-22.

[Kane87] Gerry Kane, *MIPS RISC Architecture*, Prentice-Hall, 1987.

[Lee60] F. F. Lee, "Study of 'Look Aside' Memory," *IEEE Transactions on Computers*, vol. 18, no. 11, November 1960, pp. 1062-1064.

[Lee89] Ruby Lee, "Precision Architecture," *Computer*, vol. 22, no. 1, January 1989, pp. 78-91.

[Przybylski89] Steven Przybylski, Mark Horowitz and John Hennessy, "Characteristics of Performance-Optimal Multi-Level Cache Hierarchies," *Proc. Sixteenth IEEE/ACM International Symposium on Computer Architecture*, June 1989, pp. 114-121.

[Riordan89] Tom Riordan, G.P. Grewel, Simon Hsu, John Kinsel, Jeff Libby, Roger March, Marvin Mills, Paul Ries and Randy Scofield, "System Design Using the MIPS R3000/3010 RISC Chipset," *Digest of Papers Spring 1989 IEEE Compcon*, pp. 494-498.

[Roberts90] David Roberts, Tim Layman and George Taylor, "An ECL Microprocessor Designed for Two-Level Cache," *Digest of Papers Spring 1990 IEEE Compcon*, pp. 228-231.

[Short88] Robert Short and Henry Levy, "A Simulation Study of Two-Level Caches," *Proc. Fifteenth IEEE/ACM International Symposium on Computer Architecture*, June 1988, pp. 81-88.

[Smith82] Alan J. Smith, "Cache Memories," *Computing Surveys*, vol. 14, no. 3, September 1982, pp. 473-530.

[Wang89] Wen-Hann Wang, Jean-Loup Baer and Henry Levy, "Organization and Performance of a Two-Level Virtual-Real Cache Hierarchy," *Proc. Sixteenth IEEE/ACM International Symposium on Computer Architecture*, June 1989, pp. 140-148.

[Wood86] David Wood et. al., "An In-Cache Address Translation Mechanism," *Proc. Thirteenth IEEE/ACM International Symposium on Computer Architecture*, June 1986, pp. 358-365.

Improving Direct-Mapped Cache Performance by the Addition of a Small Fully-Associative Cache and Prefetch Buffers

Norman P. Jouppi

Digital Equipment Corporation Western Research Lab

100 Hamilton Ave., Palo Alto, CA 94301

Abstract

Projections of computer technology forecast processors with peak performance of 1,000 MIPS in the relatively near future. These processors could easily lose half or more of their performance in the memory hierarchy if the hierarchy design is based on conventional caching techniques. This paper presents hardware techniques to improve the performance of caches.

Miss caching places a small fully-associative cache between a cache and its refill path. Misses in the cache that hit in the miss cache have only a one cycle miss penalty, as opposed to a many cycle miss penalty without the miss cache. Small miss caches of 2 to 5 entries are shown to be very effective in removing mapping conflict misses in first-level direct-mapped caches.

Victim caching is an improvement to miss caching that loads the small fully-associative cache with the victim of a miss and not the requested line. Small victim caches of 1 to 5 entries are even more effective at removing conflict misses than miss caching.

Stream buffers prefetch cache lines starting at a cache miss address. The prefetched data is placed in the buffer and not in the cache. Stream buffers are useful in removing capacity and compulsory cache misses, as well as some instruction cache conflict misses. Stream buffers are more effective than previously investigated prefetch techniques at using the next slower level in the memory hierarchy when it is pipelined. An extension to the basic stream buffer, called *multi-way stream buffers*, is introduced. Multi-way stream buffers are useful for prefetching along multiple intertwined data reference streams.

Together, victim caches and stream buffers reduce the miss rate of the first level in the cache hierarchy by a factor of two to three on a set of six large benchmarks.

1. Introduction

Cache performance is becoming increasingly important since it has a dramatic effect on the performance of advanced processors. Table 1-1 lists some cache miss times and the effect of a miss on machine performance. Over the last decade, cycle time has been decreasing much faster than main memory access time. The average number of machine cycles per instruction has also been decreasing dramatically, especially when the transition from CISC machines to RISC machines is included. These two effects are multiplicative and result in tremendous increases in miss cost. For example, a cache miss on a VAX 11/780 only costs 60% of the average instruction execution. Thus even if every instruction had a cache miss, the machine performance would slow down by only 60%! However, if a RISC machine like the WRL Titan [10] has a miss, the cost is almost ten instruction times. Moreover, these trends seem to be continuing, especially the increasing ratio of memory access time to machine cycle time. In the future a cache miss all the way to main memory on a superscalar machine executing two instructions per cycle could cost well over 100 instruction times! Even with careful application of well-known cache design techniques, machines with main memory latencies of over 100 instruction times can easily lose over half of their potential performance to the memory hierarchy. This makes both hardware and software research on advanced memory hierarchies increasingly important.

Machine	cycles per instr	cycle time (ns)	mem time (ns)	miss cost (cycles)	miss cost (instr)
VAX11/780	10.0	200	1200	6	.6
WRL Titan	1.4	45	540	12	8.6
?	0.5	4	280	70	140.0

Table 1-1: The increasing cost of cache misses

This paper investigates new hardware techniques for increasing the performance of the memory hierarchy. Section 2 describes a baseline design using conventional caching techniques. The large performance loss due to the memory hierarchy is a detailed motivation for the techniques discussed in the remainder of the paper. Techniques for reducing misses due to mapping conflicts (i.e., lack of associativity) are presented in Section 3. An extension to prefetch techniques called stream buffering is evaluated in Section 4. Section 5 summarizes this work and evaluates promising directions for future work.

2. Baseline Design

Figure 2-1 shows the range of configurations of interest in this study. The CPU, floating-point unit, memory management unit (e.g., TLB), and first level instruction and data caches are on the same chip or on a single high-speed module built with an advanced packaging technology. (We will refer to the central processor as a single chip in the remainder of the paper, but chip or

CH2887-8/90/0000/0364$01.00 © 1990 IEEE

module is implied.) The cycle time off this chip is 3 to 8 times longer than the instruction issue rate (i.e., 3 to 8 instructions can issue in one off-chip clock cycle). This is obtained either by having a very fast on-chip clock (e.g., superpipelining [8]), by issuing many instructions per cycle (e.g., superscalar or VLIW), and/or by using higher speed technologies for the processor chip than for the rest of the system (e.g., GaAs vs. BiCMOS).

The expected size of the on-chip caches varies with the implementation technology for the processor, but higher-speed technologies generally result in smaller on-chip caches. For example, quite large on-chip caches should be feasible in CMOS but only small caches are feasible in the near term for GaAs or bipolar processors. Thus, although GaAs and bipolar are faster, the higher miss rate from their smaller caches tends to decrease the actual system performance ratio between GaAs or bipolar machines and dense CMOS machines to less than the ratio between their gate speeds. In all cases the first-level caches are assumed to be direct-mapped, since this results in the fastest effective access time [7]. Line sizes in the on-chip caches are most likely in the range of 16B to 32B. The data cache may be either write-through or write-back, but this paper does not examine those tradeoffs.

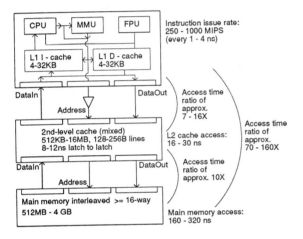

Figure 2-1: Baseline design

The second-level cache is assumed to range from 512KB to 16MB, and to be built from very high speed static RAMs. It is assumed to be direct-mapped for the same reasons as the first-level caches. For caches of this size access times of 16 to 30ns are likely. This yields an access time for the cache of 4 to 30 instruction times. The relative speed of the processor as compared to the access time of the cache implies that the second-level cache must be pipelined in order for it to provide sufficient bandwidth. For example, consider the case where the first-level cache is a write-through cache. Since stores typically occur at an average rate of 1 in every 6 or 7 instructions, an unpipelined external cache would not have even enough bandwidth to handle the store traffic for access times greater than seven instruction times. Caches have been pipelined in mainframes for a number of years [12], but this is a recent development for workstations. Recently cache chips with ECL I/O's and registers or latches on their inputs and outputs have appeared; these are ideal for pipelined caches. The number

of pipeline stages in a second-level cache access could be 2 or 3 depending on whether the pipestage going from the processor chip to the cache chips and the pipestage returning from the cache chips to the processor are full or half pipestages.

In order to provide sufficient memory for a processor of this speed (e.g., several megabytes per MIP), main memory should be in the range of 512MB to 4GB. This means that even if 16Mb DRAMs are used that it will contain roughly a thousand DRAMs. The main memory system probably will take about ten times longer for an access than the second-level cache. This access time is easily dominated by the time required to fan out address and data signals among a thousand DRAMs spread over many cards. Thus even with the advent of faster DRAMs, the access time for main memory may stay roughly the same. The relatively large access time for main memory in turn requires that second-level cache line sizes of 128 or 256B are needed. As a counter example, consider the case where only 16B are returned after 320ns. This is a bus bandwidth of 50MB/sec. Since a 10 MIP processor with this bus bandwidth would be bus-bandwidth limited in copying from one memory location to another [11], little extra performance would be obtained by the use of a 100 to 1,000 MIP processor. This is an important consideration in the system performance of a processor.

Several observations are in order on the baseline system. First, the memory hierarchy of the system is actually quite similar to that of a machine like the VAX 11/780 [3, 4], only each level in the hierarchy has moved one step closer to the CPU. For example, the 8KB board-level cache in the 780 has moved on-chip. The 512KB to 16MB main memory on early VAX models has become the board-level cache. Just as in the 780's main memory, the incoming transfer size is large (128-256B here vs. 512B pages in the VAX). The main memory in this system is of similar size to the disk subsystems of the early 780's and performs similar functions such as paging and file system caching.

The actual parameters assumed for our baseline system are 1,000 MIPS peak instruction issue rate, separate 4KB first-level instruction and data caches with 16B lines, and a 1MB second-level cache with 128B lines. The miss penalties are assumed to be 24 instruction times for the first level and 320 instruction times for the second level. The characteristics of the test programs used in this study are given in Table 2-1. These benchmarks are reasonably long in comparison with most traces in use today, however the effects of multiprocessing have not been modeled in this work. The first-level cache miss rates of these programs running on the baseline system configuration are given in Table 2-2.

program name	dynamic instr.	data refs.	total refs.	program type
ccom	31.5M	14.0M	45.5M	C compiler
grr	134.2M	59.2M	193.4M	PC board CAD
yacc	51.0M	16.7M	67.7M	Unix utility
met	99.4M	50.3M	149.7M	PC board CAD
linpack	144.8M	40.7M	185.5M	100x100 numeric
liver	23.6M	7.4M	31.0M	LFK (numeric)
total	484.5M	188.3M	672.8M	

Table 2-1: Test program characteristics

The effects of these miss rates are given graphically in Figure 2-2. The region below the solid line gives the net performance of the system, while the region above the solid line gives the performance lost in the memory hierarchy. For example, the difference between the top dotted line and the bottom dotted line gives the performance lost due to first-level data cache misses. As can be seen in Figure 2-2, most benchmarks lose over half of their potential performance in first level cache misses. Only relatively small amounts of performance are lost to second-level cache misses. This is primarily due to the large second-level cache size in comparison to the size of the programs executed. Longer traces [2] of larger programs exhibit significant numbers of second-level cache misses. Since the test suite used in this paper is too small for significant second-level cache activity, second-level cache misses will not be investigated in detail, but will be left to future work.

program name	baseline miss rate instr.	data
ccom	0.096	0.120
grr	0.061	0.062
yacc	0.028	0.040
met	0.017	0.039
linpack	0.000	0.144
liver	0.000	0.273

Table 2-2: Baseline system first-level cache miss rates

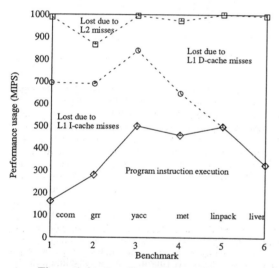

Figure 2-2: Baseline design performance

Since the exact parameters assumed are at the extreme end of the ranges described (maximum performance processor with minimum size caches), other configurations would lose proportionally less performance in their memory hierarchy. Nevertheless, any configuration in the range of interest will lose a substantial proportion of its potential performance in the memory hierarchy. This means that the greatest leverage on system performance will be obtained by improving the memory hierarchy performance, and not by attempting to further increase the performance of the CPU (e.g., by more aggressive parallel issuing of instructions). Techniques for improving the performance of the baseline memory

hierarchy at low cost are the subject of the remainder of this paper. Finally, in order to avoid compromising the performance of the CPU core (comprising of the CPU, FPU, MMU, and first level caches), any additional hardware required by the techniques to be investigated should reside outside the CPU core (i.e., below the first level caches). By doing this the additional hardware will only be involved during cache misses, and therefore will not be in the critical path for normal instruction execution.

3. Reducing Conflict Misses: Miss Caching and Victim Caching

Misses in caches can be classified into four categories: conflict, compulsory, capacity [7], and coherence. Conflict misses are misses that would not occur if the cache was fully-associative and had LRU replacement. Compulsory misses are misses required in any cache organization because they are the first references to an instruction or piece of data. Capacity misses occur when the cache size is not sufficient to hold data between references. Coherence misses are misses that occur as a result of invalidation to preserve multiprocessor cache consistency.

Even though direct-mapped caches have more conflict misses due to their lack of associativity, their performance is still better than set-associative caches when the access time costs for hits are considered. In fact, the direct-mapped cache is the only cache configuration where the critical path is merely the time required to access a RAM [9]. Conflict misses typically account for between 20% and 40% of all direct-mapped cache misses [7]. Figure 3-1 details the percentage of misses due to conflicts for our test suite. On average 39% of the first-level data cache misses are due to conflicts, and 29% of the first-level instruction cache misses are due to conflicts. Since these are significant percentages, it would be nice to "have our cake and eat it too" by somehow providing additional associativity without adding to the critical access path for a direct-mapped cache.

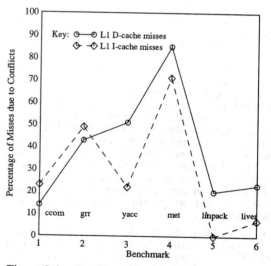

Figure 3-1: Conflict misses, 4KB I and D, 16B lines

3.1. Miss Caching

We can add associativity to a direct-mapped cache by placing a small *miss cache* on-chip between a first-level cache and the access port to the second-level cache (Figure 3-2). A miss cache is a small fully-associative cache containing on the order of two to five cache lines of data. When a miss occurs, data is returned not only to the direct-mapped cache, but also to the miss cache under it, where it replaces the least recently used item. Each time the upper cache is probed, the miss cache is probed as well. If a miss occurs in the upper cache but the address hits in the miss cache, then the direct-mapped cache can be reloaded in the next cycle from the miss cache. This replaces a long off-chip miss penalty with a short one-cycle on-chip miss. This arrangement satisfies the requirement that the critical path is not worsened, since the miss cache itself is not in the normal critical path of processor execution.

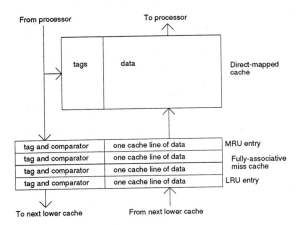

Figure 3-2: Miss cache organization

The success of different miss cache organizations at removing conflict misses is shown in Figure 3-3. The first observation to be made is that many more data conflict misses are removed by the miss cache than instruction conflict misses. This can be explained as follows. Instruction conflicts tend to be widely spaced because the instructions within one procedure will not conflict with each other as long as the procedure size is less than the cache size, which is almost always the case. Instruction conflict misses are most likely when another procedure is called. The target procedure may map anywhere with respect to the calling procedure, possibly resulting in a large overlap. Assuming at least 60 different instructions are executed in each procedure, the conflict misses would span more than the 15 lines in the maximum size miss cache tested. In other words, a small miss cache could not contain the entire overlap and so would be reloaded repeatedly before it could be used. This type of reference pattern exhibits the worst miss cache performance.

Data conflicts, on the other hand, can be quite closely spaced. Consider the case where two character strings are being compared. If the points of comparison of the two strings happen to map to the same line, alternating references to different strings will always miss in the cache. In this case a miss cache of only two entries

would remove all of the conflict misses. Obviously this is another extreme of performance and the results in Figure 3-3 show a range of performance based on the program involved. Nevertheless, for 4KB data caches a miss cache of only 2 entries can remove 25% percent of the data cache conflict misses on average,[1] or 13% of the data cache misses overall. If the miss cache is increased to 4 entries, 36% percent of the conflict misses can be removed, or 18% of the data cache misses overall. After four entries the improvement from additional miss cache entries is minor, only increasing to a 25% overall reduction in data cache misses if 15 entries are provided.

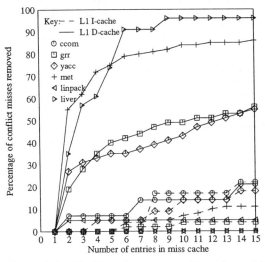

Figure 3-3: Conflict misses removed by miss caching

Since doubling the data cache size results in a 32% reduction in misses (over this set of benchmarks when increasing data cache size from 4K to 8K), each additional line in the first level cache reduces the number of misses by approximately 0.13%. Although the miss cache requires more area per bit of storage than lines in the data cache, each line in a two line miss cache effects a 50 times larger marginal improvement in the miss rate, so this should more than cover any differences in layout size.

Comparing Figure 3-3 and Figure 3-1, we see that the higher the percentage of misses due to conflicts, the more effective the miss cache is at eliminating them. For example, in Figure 3-1 *met* has by far the highest ratio of conflict misses to total data cache misses. Similarly, *grr* and *yacc* also have greater than average percentages of conflict misses, and the miss cache helps these programs significantly as well. *linpack* and *ccom* have the lowest

---

[1] Throughout this paper the average reduction in miss rates is used as a metric. This is computed by calculating the percent reduction in miss rate for each benchmark, and then taking the average of these percentages. This has the advantage that it is independent of the number of memory references made by each program. Furthermore, if two programs have widely different miss rates, the average percent reduction in miss rate gives equal weighting to each benchmark. This is in contrast with the percent reduction in average miss rate, which weights the program with the highest miss rate most heavily.

percentage of conflict misses, and the miss cache removes the lowest percentage of conflict misses from these programs. This results from the fact that if a program has a large percentage of data conflict misses then they must be clustered to some extent because of their overall density. This does not prevent programs with a small number of conflict misses such as *liver* from benefiting from a miss cache, but it seems that as the percentage of conflict misses increases, the percentage of these misses removable by a miss cache increases.

3.2. Victim Caching

Consider a system with a direct-mapped cache and a miss cache. When a miss occurs, data is loaded into both the miss cache and the direct-mapped cache. In a sense, this duplication of data wastes storage space in the miss cache. The number of duplicate items in the miss cache can range from one (in the case where all items in the miss cache map to the same line in the direct-mapped cache) to all of the entries (in the case where a series of misses occur which do not hit in the miss cache).

To make better use of the miss cache we can use a different replacement algorithm for the small fully-associative cache [5]. Instead of loading the requested data into the miss cache on a miss, we can load the fully-associative cache with the victim line from the direct-mapped cache instead. We call this *victim caching* (see Figure 3-4). With victim caching, no data line appears both in the direct-mapped cache and the victim cache. This follows from the fact that the victim cache is loaded only with items thrown out from the direct-mapped cache. In the case of a miss in the direct-mapped cache that hits in the victim cache, the contents of the direct-mapped cache line and the matching victim cache line are swapped.

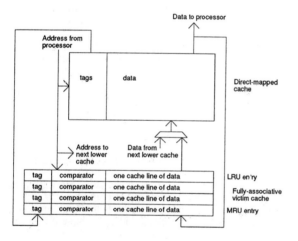

Figure 3-4: Victim cache organization

Depending on the reference stream, victim caching can either be a small or significant improvement over miss caching. The magnitude of this benefit depends on the amount of duplication in the miss cache. Victim caching is always an improvement over miss caching.

As an example, consider an instruction reference stream that calls a small procedure in its inner loop that conflicts with the loop body. If the total number of con-

flicting lines between the procedure and loop body were larger than the miss cache, the miss cache would be of no value since misses at the beginning of the loop would be flushed out by later misses before execution returned to the beginning of the loop. If a victim cache is used instead, however, the number of conflicts in the loop that can be captured is doubled compared to that stored by a miss cache. This is because one set of conflicting instructions lives in the direct-mapped cache, while the other lives in the victim cache. As execution proceeds around the loop and through the procedure call these items trade places.

The percentage of conflict misses removed by victim caching is given in Figure 3-5. Note that victim caches consisting of just one line are useful, in contrast to miss caches which must have two lines to be useful. All of the benchmarks have improved performance in comparison to miss caches, but instruction cache performance and the data cache performance of benchmarks that have conflicting long sequential reference streams (e.g., *ccom* and *linpack*) improve the most.

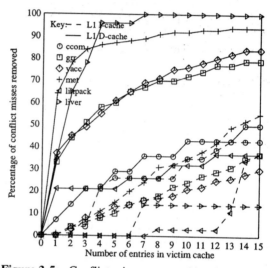

Figure 3-5: Conflict misses removed by victim caching

3.3. The Effect of Direct-Mapped Cache Size on Victim Cache Performance

Figure 3-6 shows the performance of 1, 2, 4, and 15 entry victim caches when backing up direct-mapped data caches of varying sizes. In general smaller direct-mapped caches benefit the most from the addition of a victim cache. Also shown for reference is the total percentage of conflict misses for each cache size. There are two factors to victim cache performance versus direct-mapped cache size. First, as the direct-mapped cache increases in size, the relative size of the victim cache becomes smaller. Since the direct-mapped cache gets larger but keeps the same line size (16B), the likelihood of a tight mapping conflict which would be easily removed by victim caching is reduced. Second, the percentage of conflict misses decreases slightly from 1KB to 32KB. As we have seen previously, as the percentage of conflict misses decreases, the percentage of these misses removed by the victim cache decreases. The first effect dominates, however, since as the percentage of conflict misses increases with very large caches (as in [7]), the victim cache performance only improves slightly.

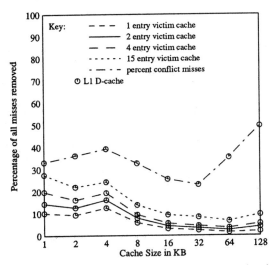

Figure 3-6: Victim cache: vary direct-map cache size

3.4. The Effect of Line Size on Victim Cache Performance

Figure 3-7 shows the performance of victim caches for 4KB direct-mapped data caches of varying line sizes. As one would expect, as the line size at this level increases, the number of conflict misses also increases.

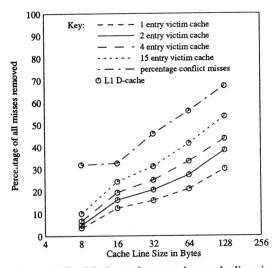

Figure 3-7: Victim cache: vary data cache line size

The increasing percentage of conflict misses results in an increasing percentage of these misses being removed by the victim cache. Systems with victim caches can benefit from longer line sizes more than systems without victim caches, since the victim caches help remove misses caused by conflicts that result from longer cache lines. Note that even if the area used for data storage in the victim cache is held constant (i.e., the number of entries is cut in half when the line size doubles) the performance of the victim cache still improves or at least breaks even when line sizes increase.

3.5. Victim Caches and Second-Level Caches

As the size of a cache increases, a larger percentage of its misses are due to conflict and compulsory misses and fewer are due to capacity misses. (Unless of course the cache is larger than the entire program, in which case only compulsory misses remain.) Thus victim caches might be expected to be useful for second-level caches as well. Since the number of conflict misses increases with increasing line sizes, the large line sizes of second-level caches would also tend to increase the potential usefulness of victim caches.

One interesting aspect of victim caches is that they violate inclusion properties [1] in cache hierarchies. However, the line size of the second level cache in the baseline design is 8 to 16 times larger than the first-level cache line sizes, so this violates inclusion as well.

Note that a first-level victim cache can contain many lines that conflict not only at the first level but also at the second level. Thus, using a first-level victim cache can also reduce the number of conflict misses at the second level. In investigating victim caches for second-level caches, both configurations with and without first-level victim caches will need to be considered.

A thorough investigation of victim caches for megabyte second-level caches requires traces of billions of instructions. At this time we only have victim cache performance for our smaller test suite, and work on obtaining victim cache performance for multi-megabyte second-level caches is underway.

4. Reducing Capacity and Compulsory Misses

Compulsory misses are misses required in any cache organization because they are the first references to a piece of data. Capacity misses occur when the cache size is not sufficient to hold data between references. One way of reducing the number of capacity and compulsory misses is to use prefetch techniques such as longer cache line sizes or prefetching methods [13, 6]. However, line sizes can not be made arbitrarily large without increasing the miss rate and greatly increasing the amount of data to be transferred. In this section we investigate techniques to reduce capacity and compulsory misses while mitigating traditional problems with long lines and excessive prefetching.

A detailed analysis of three prefetch algorithms has appeared in [13]. *Prefetch always* prefetches after every reference. Needless to say this is impractical in our base system since many level-one cache accesses can take place in the time required to initiate a single level-two cache reference. This is especially true in machines that fetch multiple instructions per cycle from an instruction cache and can concurrently perform a load or store per cycle to a data cache. *Prefetch on miss* and *tagged prefetch* are more promising techniques. On a miss *prefetch on miss* always fetches the next line as well. It can cut the number of misses for a purely sequential reference stream in half. *Tagged prefetch* can do even better. In this technique each block has a tag bit associated with it. When a block is prefetched, its tag bit is set to zero. Each time a block is used its tag bit is set to one. When a block undergoes a zero to one transition its successor block is prefetched. This can reduce the number of misses in a purely sequential reference stream to zero, if fetching is fast enough. Unfortunately the large latencies in the base system can make this impossible. Consider Figure 4-1, which gives the amount of time (in instruction issues) until a prefetched line is required during the execution of *ccom*. Not surprisingly, since the line size is four instructions, prefetched lines must be received within four instruction-times to keep up with the machine on uncached straight-line code. Because the base system second-level cache takes many cycles to access, and the machine may actually issue many instructions per cycle, tagged prefetch may only have a one-cycle-out-of-many head start on providing the required instructions.

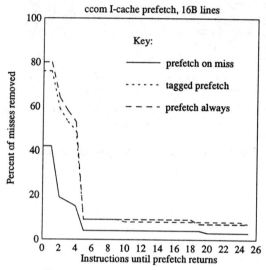

Figure 4-1: Limited time for prefetch

4.1. Stream Buffers

What we really need to do is to start the prefetch before a tag transition can take place. We can do this with a mechanism called a *stream buffer* (Figure 4-2). A stream buffer consists of a series of entries, each consisting of a tag, an available bit, and a data line.

When a miss occurs, the stream buffer begins prefetching successive lines starting at the miss target. As each prefetch request is sent out, the tag for the address is entered into the stream buffer, and the available bit is set to false. When the prefetch data returns it is placed in the entry with its tag and the available bit is set to true. Note that lines after the line requested on the miss are placed in the buffer and not in the cache. This avoids polluting the cache with data that may never be needed.

Subsequent accesses to the cache also compare their address against the first item stored in the buffer. If a reference misses in the cache but hits in the buffer the cache can be reloaded in a single cycle from the stream buffer. This is much faster than the off-chip miss penalty. The stream buffers considered in this section are simple FIFO queues, where only the head of the queue has a tag comparator and elements removed from the buffer must be removed strictly in sequence without

skipping any lines. In this simple model non-sequential line misses will cause a stream buffer to be flushed and restarted at the miss address even if the requested line is already present further down in the queue.

When a line is moved from a stream buffer to the cache, the entries in the stream buffer can shift up by one and a new successive address is fetched. The pipelined interface to the second level allows the buffer to be filled at the maximum bandwidth of the second level cache, and many cache lines can be in the process of being fetched simultaneously. For example, assume the latency to refill a 16B line on a instruction cache miss is 12 cycles. Consider a memory interface that is pipelined and can accept a new line request every 4 cycles. A four-entry stream buffer can provide 4B instructions at a rate of one per cycle by having three requests outstanding at all times. Thus during sequential instruction execution long latency cache misses will not occur. This is in contrast to the performance of tagged prefetch on purely sequential reference streams where only one line is being prefetched at a time. In that case sequential instructions will only be supplied at a bandwidth equal to one instruction every three cycles (i.e., 12 cycle latency / 4 instructions per line).

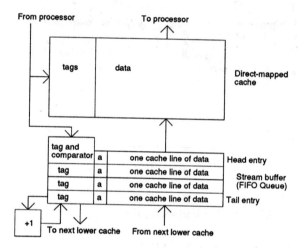

Figure 4-2: Sequential stream buffer design

Figure 4-3 shows the performance of a four-entry instruction stream buffer backing a 4KB instruction cache and a data stream buffer backing a 4KB data cache, each with 16B lines. The graph gives the cumulative number of misses removed based on the number of lines that the buffer is allowed to prefetch after the original miss. (In practice the stream buffer would probably be allowed to fetch until the end of a virtual memory page or a second-level cache line. The major reason for plotting stream buffer performance as a function of prefetch length is to get a better idea of how far streams continue on average.) Most instruction references break the purely sequential access pattern by the time the 6th successive line is fetched, while many data reference patterns end even sooner. The exceptions to this appear to be instruction references for *liver* and data references for *linpack*. *liver* is probably an anomaly since the 14 loops of the program are executed sequentially, and the first 14 loops do not generally call other procedures or do excessive branching, which would cause the sequential miss pattern to break. The data reference pattern of *linpack* can be understood as follows. Remember that the stream buffer is only responsible for providing lines that the cache misses on. The inner loop of *linpack* (i.e., saxpy) performs an inner product between one row and the other rows of a matrix. The first use of the one row loads it into the cache. After that subsequent misses in the cache (except for mapping conflicts with the first row) consist of subsequent lines of the matrix. Since the matrix is too large to fit in the on-chip cache, the whole matrix is passed through the cache on each iteration. The stream buffer can do this at the maximum bandwidth provided by the second-level cache. Of course one prerequisite for this is that the reference stream is unit-stride or at most skips to every other or every third word. If an array is accessed in the non-unit-stride direction (and the other dimensions have non-trivial extents) then a stream buffer as presented here will be of little benefit.

experience the greatest improvement (it changes from 7% to 60% reduction), all of the programs benefit to some extent.

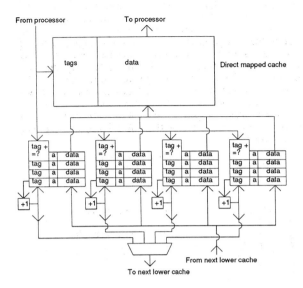

Figure 4-4: Four-way stream buffer design

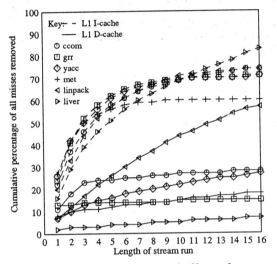

Figure 4-3: Sequential stream buffer performance

4.2. Multi-Way Stream Buffers

Overall, the stream buffer presented in the previous section could remove 72% of the instruction cache misses, but it could only remove 25% of the data cache misses. One reason for this is that data references tend to consist of interleaved streams of data from different sources. In order to improve the performance of stream buffers for data references, a multi-way stream buffer was simulated (Figure 4-4). It consists of four stream buffers in parallel. When a miss occurs in the data cache that does not hit in any stream buffer, the stream buffer hit least recently is cleared (i.e., LRU replacement) and it is started fetching at the miss address.

Figure 4-5 shows the performance of the multi-way stream buffer on our benchmark set. As expected, the performance on the instruction stream remains virtually unchanged. This means that the simpler single stream buffer will suffice for instruction streams. The multi-way stream buffer does significantly improve the performance on the data side, however. Overall, the multi-way stream buffer can remove 43% of the misses for the six programs, almost twice the performance of the single stream buffer. Although the matrix operations of *liver*

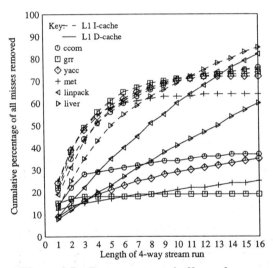

Figure 4-5: Four-way stream buffer performance

4.3. Stream Buffer Performance vs. Cache Size

Figure 4-6 gives the performance of single and 4-way stream buffers with 16B lines as a function of cache size. The instruction stream buffers have remarkably constant performance over a wide range of cache sizes. The data stream buffer performance generally improves as the cache size increases. This is especially true for the single stream buffer, whose performance increases from a 15% reduction in misses for a data cache size of 1KB to a 35% reduction in misses for a data cache size of 128KB. This is probably because as the cache size increases, it can contain data for reference patterns that access several sets of data, or at least all but one of the sets. What misses that remain are more likely to consist of very long single sequential streams. For example, as the cache size increases the percentage of compulsory misses increase, and these are more likely to be sequential in nature than data conflict or capacity misses.

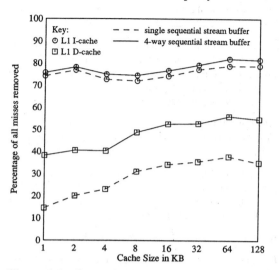

Figure 4-6: Stream buffer performance vs. cache size

4.4. Stream Buffer Performance vs. Line Size

Figure 4-7 gives the performance of single and 4-way stream buffers as a function of the line size in the stream buffer and 4KB cache. The reduction in misses provided by a single data stream buffer falls by a factor of 6.8 going from a line size of 8B to a line size of 128B, while a 4-way stream buffer's contribution falls by a factor of 4.5. This is not too surprising since data references are often fairly widely distributed. In other words if a piece of data is accessed, the odds that another piece of data 128B away will be needed soon are fairly low. The single data stream buffer performance is especially hard hit compared to the multi-way stream buffer because of the increase in conflict misses at large line sizes.

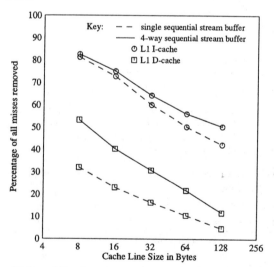

Figure 4-7: Stream buffer performance vs. line size

The instruction stream buffers perform well even out to 128B line sizes. Both the 4-way and the single stream buffer still remove at least 40% of the misses at 128B line sizes, coming down from an 80% reduction with 8B lines. This is probably due to the large granularity of conflicting instruction reference streams, and the fact that many procedures are more than 128B long.

5. Conclusions

Small miss caches (e.g., 2 to 5 entries) have been shown to be effective in reducing data cache conflict misses for direct-mapped caches in range of 1K to 8K bytes. They effectively remove tight conflicts where misses alternate between several addresses that map to the same line in the cache. Miss caches are increasingly beneficial as line sizes increase and the percentage of conflict misses increases. In general it appears that as the percentage of conflict misses increases, the percent of these misses removable by a miss cache also increases, resulting in an even steeper slope for the performance improvement possible by using miss caches.

Victim caches are an improvement to miss caching that saves the victim of the cache miss instead of the target in a small associative cache. Victim caches are even more effective at removing conflict misses than miss caches.

Stream buffers prefetch cache lines after a missed cache line. They store the line until it is requested by a cache miss (if ever) to avoid unnecessary pollution of the cache. They are particularly useful at reducing the number of capacity and compulsory misses. They can take full advantage of the memory bandwidth available in pipelined memory systems for sequential references, unlike previously discussed prefetch techniques such as tagged prefetch or prefetch on miss. Stream buffers can also tolerate longer memory system latencies since they prefetch data much in advance of other prefetch techniques (even prefetch always). Stream buffers can also compensate for instruction conflict misses, since these tend to be relatively sequential in nature as well.

Multi-way stream buffers are a set of stream buffers that can prefetch down several streams concurrently. Multi-way stream buffers are useful for data references that contain interleaved accesses to several different large data structures, such as in array operations. However, since the prefetching is of sequential lines, only unit stride or near unit stride (2 or 3) access patterns benefit.

The performance improvements due to victim caches and due to stream buffers are relatively orthogonal for data references. Victim caches work well where references alternate between two locations that map to the same line in the cache. They do not prefetch data but only do a better job of keeping data fetched available for use. Stream buffers, however, achieve performance improvements by prefetching data. They do not remove conflict misses unless the conflicts are widely spaced in time, and the cache miss reference stream consists of many sequential accesses. These are precisely the conflict misses not handled well by a victim cache due to its relatively small capacity. Over the set of six benchmarks, on average only 2.5% of 4KB direct-mapped data cache misses that hit in a four-entry victim cache also hit in a four-way stream buffer for *ccom, met, yacc, grr,* and *liver.* In contrast, *linpack,* due to its sequential data access patterns, has 50% of the hits in the victim cache also hit in a four-way stream buffer. However only 4% of *linpack*'s cache misses hit in the victim cache (it benefits least from victim caching among the six benchmarks), so this is still not a significant amount of overlap between stream buffers and victim caching.

Figure 5-1 shows the performance of the base system with the addition of a four entry data victim cache, a instruction stream buffer, and a four-way data stream buffer. (The base system has on-chip 4KB instruction and 4KB data caches with 24 cycle miss penalties and 16B lines to a three-stage pipelined second-level 1MB cache with 128B lines and 320 cycle miss penalty.) The lower solid line in Figure 5-1 gives the performance of the original base system without the victim caches or buffers while the upper solid line gives the performance with buffers and victim caches. The combination of these techniques reduces the first-level miss rate to less than half of that of the baseline system, resulting in an average of 143% improvement in system performance for the six benchmarks. These results show that the addition of a small amount of hardware can dramatically reduce cache miss rates and improve system performance.

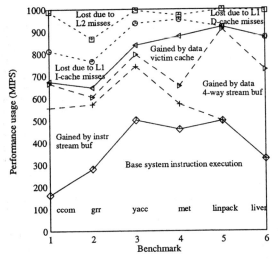

Figure 5-1: Improved system performance

This study has concentrated on applying victim caches and stream buffers to first-level caches. An interesting area for future work is the application of these techniques to second-level caches. Also, the numeric programs used in this study used unit stride access patterns. Numeric programs with non-unit stride and mixed stride access patterns also need to be simulated. Finally, the performance of victim caching and stream buffers needs to be investigated for operating system execution and for multiprogramming workloads.

Acknowledgements

Mary Jo Doherty, John Ousterhout, Jeremy Dion, Anita Borg, Richard Swan, and the anonymous referees provided many helpful comments on an early draft of this paper. Alan Eustace suggested victim caching as an improvement to miss caching.

References

1. Baer, Jean-Loup, and Wang, Wenn-Hann. On the Inclusion Properties for Multi-Level Cache Hierarchies. The 15th Annual Symposium on Computer Architecture, IEEE Computer Society Press, June, 1988, pp. 73-80.

2. Borg, Anita, Kessler, Rick E., Lazana, Georgia, and Wall, David W. Long Address Traces from RISC Machines: Generation and Analysis. Tech. Rept. 89/14, Digital Equipment Corporation Western Research Laboratory, September, 1989.

3. Digital Equipment Corporation, Inc. *VAX Hardware Handbook, volume 1 - 1984.* Maynard, Massachusetts, 1984.

4. Emer, Joel S., and Clark, Douglas W. A Characterization of Processor Performance in the VAX-11/780. The 11th Annual Symposium on Computer Architecture, IEEE Computer Society Press, June, 1984, pp. 301-310.

5. Eustace, Alan. Private communication.

6. Farrens, Matthew K., and Pleszkun, Andrew R. Improving Performance of Small On-Chip Instruction Caches . The 16th Annual Symposium on Computer Architecture, IEEE Computer Society Press, May, 1989, pp. 234-241.

7. Hill, Mark D. *Aspects of Cache Memory and Instruction Buffer Performance.* Ph.D. Th., University of California, Berkeley, 1987.

8. Jouppi, Norman P., and Wall, David W. Available Instruction-Level Parallelism For Superpipelined and Superscalar Machines. Third International Conference on Architectural Support for Programming Languages and Operating Systems, IEEE Computer Society Press, April, 1989, pp. 272-282.

9. Jouppi, Norman P. Architectural and Organizational Tradeoffs in the Design of the MultiTitan CPU. The 16th Annual Symposium on Computer Architecture, IEEE Computer Society Press, May, 1989, pp. 281-289.

10. Nielsen, Michael J. K. Titan System Manual. Tech. Rept. 86/1, Digital Equipment Corporation Western Research Laboratory, September, 1986.

11. Ousterhout, John. Why Aren't Operating Systems Getting Faster As Fast As Hardware? Tech. Rept. Technote 11, Digital Equipment Corporation Western Research Laboratory, October, 1989.

12. Smith, Alan J. ''Sequential program prefetching in memory hierarchies.'' *IEEE Computer 11*, 12 (December 1978), 7-21.

13. Smith, Alan J. ''Cache Memories.'' *Computing Surveys* (September 1982), 473-530.

Panel Session II

PANEL

BETTER THAN ONE OPERATION PER CLOCK: VECTORS, VLIW, AND SUPERSCALAR

Organized by

Edward S. Davidson, *University of Michigan*
Gurindar S. Sohi, *University of Wisconsin*

Panel Members

Joseph A. Fisher, *Multiflow Computer, Inc.*
Greg Grohoski, *IBM Corporation*
Yale Patt, *University of Michigan*
J. E. Smith, *Cray Research, Inc.*
David R. Stiles, *Nexgen Microsystems*

In the 1980s, considerable advances were made in both software and hardware technology, and CPUs that can issue no more than one operation per clock cycle are rapidly approaching this barrier. Further improvements to uniprocessor performance can be obtained by enhancing the architecture of the CPU to allow multiple operations to be issued in a single clock cycle. The focus of this panel is to discuss three architectural approaches to issuing multiple operations per cycle: (i) vector instructions, (ii) very long instruction words (VLIW), and (iii) superscalar execution. We have asked the panelists to address several issues from the vantage point of their preferred architectural approach. These include:

(1) What operation set parallelism are you trying to exploit (as distinct from instruction set parallelism)?

(2) How does mapping from your operation set to your instruction set enhance or restrict the ability to support this parallelism?

(3) What are the performance optimization responsibilities of the compiler?

(4) How well does your architecture tolerate possible run time uncertainties (cache miss, resource conflicts, dependencies, ...) in the context of uniprocessor or multiprocessor systems?

(5) What are the inherent advantages/disadvantages of your architectural approach over the others?

(6) What further enhancements do you envision in the future? How will these affect the choice of architectural approach?

Author Index